BENJAMIN'S SALE OF GOODS

VOLUMES IN THE COMMON LAW LIBRARY

Arlidge, Eady & Smith on Contempt
Benjamin's Sale of Goods
Bowstead & Reynolds on Agency
Bullen & Leake & Jacob's Precedents of Pleadings
Charlesworth & Percy on Negligence
Chitty on Contracts
Clerk & Lindsell on Torts
Gatley on Libel and Slander
Goff & Jones, The Law of Restitution
Jackson & Powell on Professional Negligence
McGregor on Damages
Phipson on Evidence

COMMON LAW LIBRARY

BENJAMIN'S SALE OF GOODS

SECOND CUMULATIVE SUPPLEMENT TO THE
TENTH EDITION

SWEET & MAXWELL

THOMSON REUTERS

Published in 2019 by Thomson Reuters, trading as Sweet & Maxwell.
Thomson Reuters is registered in England & Wales, Company No.1679046.
Registered Office and address for service: 5 Canada Square, Canary Wharf,
London, E14 5AQ.

For further information on our products and services, visit *http://
www.sweetandmaxwell.co.uk.*

Computerset by Sweet & Maxwell.
Printed and bound by CPI Group (UK) Ltd, Croydon, CR0 4YY.
No natural forests were destroyed to make this product: only farmed timber
was used and replanted.
A CIP catalogue record for this book is available from the British Library.

ISBN: 978-0-414-07216-9

Thomson Reuters, the Thomson Reuters Logo and Sweet & Maxwell ® are
trademarks of Thomson Reuters.

BENJAMIN'S TREATISE ON THE LAW OF SALE OF PERSONAL PROPERTY WITH REFERENCES TO THE FRENCH CODE AND CIVIL LAW

First edition	(1868)	Judah Philip Benjamin
Second edition	(1873)	Judah Philip Benjamin
Third Edition	(1883)	A. B. Pearson and H. F. Boyd
Fourth Edition	(1888)	A. B. Pearson-Gee and H. F. Boyd
Fifth Edition	(1906)	W. C. A. Ker and A. R. Butterworth
Sixth Edition	(1920)	W. C. A. Ker
Seventh Edition	(1931)	His Hon. Judge A. R. Kennedy, KC
Eighth Edition	(1950)	The Hon. Sir Donald Leslie Finnemore and Arthur E. James

BENJAMIN'S SALE OF GOODS

First edition	(1974)	General Editor A. G. Guest
Second Edition	(1981)	General Editor A. G. Guest
Third Edition	(1987)	General Editor A. G. Guest
Fourth Edition	(1992)	General Editor A. G. Guest
Fifth Edition	(1997)	General Editor A. G. Guest
Sixth Edition	(2002)	General Editor A. G. Guest
Seventh Edition	(2006)	General Editor A. G. Guest
Eighth Edition	(2010)	General Editor M. Bridge
Ninth Edition	(2014)	General Editor M. Bridge
Tenth Edition	(2017)	General Editor M. Bridge

PREFACE

This cumulative preface combines material from the first preface, published in 2018, and new material concerning subsequent developments. On the legislative side, account is taken of the European Union (Withdrawal) Act (Exit Day) Regulations 2019 and of the Law Applicable to Contractual Obligations and Non-Contractual Obligations (Amendment etc.) (EU Exit) Regulations 2019. Mention is also made of the Directive (EU) 2019/771 on certain aspects concerning contracts for the sale of goods, which modifies Directive 1999/44 on the same subject and is due to come into force in 2022. Given the present uncertainty surrounding Brexit, it is not yet known whether and how account will have to be taken of it.

A substantial feature of this Supplement is the extended treatment of Uniform Rules for Collections (URC 522) Supplement for Electronic Presentation ('eURC'). Account is also taken of the updated version of the Uniform Customs and Practice for Documentary Credits (UCP 600) Supplement for Electronic Presentation (eUCP Version 2.0).

Case law developments have been steady in number. This is not the place to recount them all but particular mention may be made of the following:

> *Classic Maritime Inc v Limbungan Makmur Sdn Bhd*: This important decision deals with a force majeure clause in a multi-trip contract of affreightment. It underlines the distinction between a frustration (or cancellation) clause and an exceptions clause, important because the latter type of the clause has been interpreted in the past as not requiring the party invoking it to show that it was ready and willing to perform at the time of the force majeure event. It also deals with the important question of the measure of damages due to the other party.
>
> *Uttam Galva Steels Ltd v Gunvor Singapore Pte Ltd*: This case concerns the question whether an arbitration clause in a contract of sale dealing with disputes arising out of or connected to the contract including claims brought by the seller on negotiable instruments.
>
> *Ark Shipping Co v Silverburn Shipping (IOM) Ltd*: This is the latest development in the continuing expansion of innominate terms at the expense of promissory conditions. A contractual provision is likely to be construed as an innominate term in long-term contracts where the consequences of breach are not demonstrably very serious. Commercial certainty is of limited assistance in numerous cases in advancing the argument that a term is a promissory condition.
>
> *Bates v Post Office Ltd*: The significance of the lengthy judgment in this case, for present purposes, lies in the extent to which account should be taken of the existence of a *contra proferentem* rule of interpretation of exclusion and similar clauses. At this stage, it is not clear whether it is the rule itself that is being gradually abandoned or the more extreme cases of its application in commercial cases that have been seen in the past.
>
> *Ukraine v Law Debenture Trust Corp Plc*: This case delineates the difference in the conflict of laws between the capacity of a company under its constitution and governing law and the capacity of a sovereign State. In respect of the latter, the following quotation is illuminating: "English law imposes no restrictions on the capacity of those who have legal personality under English law, so as to render any act by them ultra vires and void, save

as imposed by or pursuant to statute. There is no prerogative or statutory authority for limiting the capacity and powers enjoyed by a foreign state, which has legal personality in English law by virtue of its recognition as such by HMG."

Professor M. G. Bridge
London

HOW TO USE THIS SUPPLEMENT

This is the Second Cumulative Supplement to the Tenth Edition of *Benjamin Sale of Goods* and has been compiled according to the structure of the main volume.

At the beginning of each chapter of this Supplement, a mini table of contents of the sections in the main volume has been included. Where a heading in this table of contents has been marked with a square pointer, this indicates that there is relevant information in this Supplement to which the reader should refer. Material that is new to the Cumulative Supplement is indicated by the symbol ■. Material that has been included from the previous supplement is indicated by the symbol □.

Within each chapter, updating information is referenced to the relevant paragraph in the main volume.

TABLE OF CONTENTS

CONTENTS

TABLE OF CASES

TABLE OF STATUTES

TABLE OF STATUTORY INSTRUMENTS

TABLE OF EUROPEAN LEGISLATION

TABLE OF INTERNATIONAL CONVENTIONS

TABLE OF FOREIGN LEGISLATION

THE CONTRACT OF SALE OF GOODS

1. THE SALE OF GOODS ACTS

The Sale of Goods Act 1979

Replace footnote 11 with:

[11] Ervine, Woodroffe and Thomas, *Encyclopedia of Consumer Law* (1980). On the impact on EU law within the UK of the planned withdrawal from the European Union see the European Union (Withdrawal) Act 2018 under which EU-derived domestic legislation (such as EU directives incorporated into UK law under the European Communities Act 1972, s.2(2)) "as it has effect in domestic law immediately before exit day, continues to have effect in domestic law on and after exit day" (s.2(1) 2018 Act), and direct EU legislation (such as EU regulations) "so far as operative immediately before exit day, forms part of domestic law on and after exit day" (s.3(1) 2018 Act). (These provisions are not yet in force: s.25(4).)

1-001

Replace footnote 15 with:

[15] cf. *Koubi v Mazda Canada Inc* [2012] BCCA 311 at [72].

Replace title footnote 18 with:

Construction of codifying statute[18]

[18] See generally Halsbury, *Laws of England* (2018), Vol.96 paras 239, 735.

1-002

Replace footnote 19 with:

[19] Halsbury, *Laws of England* (2018), Vol.96 para.239. This is to be contrasted with a consolidation Act, which only "presents the whole body of the statute law": Halsbury, *Laws of England* (2018), Vol.96 para.238. Other codifying Acts are the Bills of Exchange Act 1882, Partnership Act 1890 and Marine Insurance Act 1906: Rodger, 106 L.Q.R. 570 (1992). The experiment of codifying a substantial body of commercial law, which occurred between 1882 and 1906, has not been repeated.

Construction of consolidating statute

Replace paragraph with:

   The object of the Sale of Goods Act 1979, in contrast with that of 1893, was to consolidate the existing statutory law:

1-004

"... the general object of such Acts is to present the whole body of statutory law on the subject in a complete form, repealing the former statutes."[27]

A consolidating Act should, like any other statute, be construed according to its natural meaning,[28] but there is a strong presumption that no alteration of the previous law was intended, so that it is legitimate to have regard to judicial decisions on the superseded statutes in order to determine the meaning of the consolidating measure.[29] The presumption applies even if the language of the two provisions is not identical, but this view must yield to plain words to the contrary.[30]

[27] *Conservators of the River Thames v Smeed, Dean & Co* [1897] 2 Q.B. 334 at 346 per Chitty LJ. See generally *Craies on Legislation*, 11th edn, paras 29.1.6–29.1.10.

[28] *Edwards (Inspector of Taxes) v Clinch* [1981] Ch. 1 at 5.

[29] *Stevenson v Rogers* [1999] Q.B. 1028 at 1040. See also, *Gilbert v Gilbert and Boucher* [1928] P. 1 at 7–8; *Maunsell v Olins* [1975] A.C. 373 at 382; *Farrell v Alexander* [1977] A.C. 59 at 73–74.

[30] *MacConnell v E Prill & Co* [1916] 2 Ch. 57 at 63; *Gilbert v Gilbert and Boucher* [1928] P. 1 at 7–8; *Grey v Inland Revenue Commrs* [1960] A.C. 1 at 13; *Beswick v Beswick* [1968] A.C. 58 at 79; *MacDonald v Pollock: The Monaco* [2012] CSIH 12; 2013 S.C. 22.

General scope of the Act

Replace the first paragraph with:

1-006   The Sale of Goods Act 1979, like its predecessor of 1893, applies to contracts for the sale of all types of goods. In so far as special rules exist governing particular categories of goods, they are to be found in other enactments.[37] With one or two exceptions (e.g. s.57, dealing with sales by auction), most provisions of the original legislation of 1893 were made to apply generally to every kind of contract, regardless of the circumstances in which it might have been formed and of the standing of the parties. It was a feature (and, perhaps, a fault) of this legislation that virtually no distinctions were made between commercial sales and private sales,[38] between merchants' sales and retail sales, or between sales of new and of second-hand goods. Yet, later legislation, which was consolidated or expressly saved by the Act of 1979, introduced important changes,[39] so that it is no longer possible to regard the Sale of Goods Act as a single code of rules that in principle applies to all contracts of sale. Factors such as that one of the parties is acting in the course of a business[40] or through an agent who is so acting,[41] or that the transaction has an international element[42] may alter the rules that are applied. The circumstances of the parties and the nature or description of the goods may also have a bearing on the question whether a contractual term satisfies the "requirement of reasonableness" imposed by some sections of the Unfair Contract Terms Act 1977[43] or whether a term is "unfair" under the Consumer Rights Act 2015[44]; and similar considerations may be relevant to the question whether the goods supplied under a contract of sale are of satisfactory quality for the purposes of the Sale of Goods Act 1979 ss.14(2)-(2C) and 15(2)(C), or the Consumer Rights Act 2015 s.9.[45]

[37] cf. the special rules as to the transfer of title to motor vehicles in the Hire-Purchase Act 1964 ss.27–29 (below, paras 7-087 et seq.), and the statutory warranties implied by law in the sale of certain classes of goods (below, paras 14-098 et seq.). In addition, the sale of many types of goods is regulated by legislation for which the sanctions are primarily penal: see below, paras 14-112 et seq.

[38] The most notable exception was that a term as to fitness for purpose would be implied only where (inter alia) the goods were of a description which it was in the course of the seller's business to supply (1979 Act s.14(1)), and a term as to merchantable quality only where goods were bought by description from a seller who dealt in goods of that description (s.14(2)). The corresponding provisions of the 1979 Act are more broadly worded, even so they only apply to a sale in the course of business (s.14(2), (3)) of the 1979 Act, below, paras 11-025 et seq.

[39] Supply of Goods (Implied Terms) Act 1973; Unfair Contract Terms Act 1977 (see Sale of Goods Act s.55(1)).

[40] Unfair Contract Terms Act 1977 s.1(3) (but see s.6(4)), below, paras 13-063 et seq.; Sale of Goods Act s.14(2), (3), below, paras 11-026 et seq. The Consumer Rights Act 2015 applies to contracts for the supply of goods by a trader to a consumer (s.1(1)).

[41] Sale of Goods Act s.14(3), (5), below, para.11-029.

[42] Unfair Contract Terms Act s.26, below, paras 13-088 et seq.

[43] Unfair Contract Terms Act s.11 and Sch.2, below, paras 13-075 et seq.

[44] Consumer Rights Act 2015 s.63 and Sch.2 Pt.1, see below paras 14-150 et seq.

[45] See below, paras 11-025 et seq.

Replace title footnote 47 with:

Saving of common law rules and the law merchant[47]

[47] Burrows, 128 L.Q.R. 232 (2012); W. Swain, *The Law of Contract 1670-1870* (2015).

1-007

2. RELATED STATUTES

Bills of Sale Acts

Replace footnote 100 with:

[100] *Report of the Committee on Consumer Credit* (the "Crowther Report"), Cmnd.4596 (1971), paras 4.2.11, 5.3.4, 6.2.60, recommended their repeal, observing, "it is difficult to imagine any legislation possessing more technical pitfalls", but no provision to this effect was made by the Consumer Credit Act 1974. A similar recommendation is contained in Professor Diamond's report, *A Review of Security Interests in Property* (HMSO, 1989). On the other hand, after noting an increase in loans secured by bills of sale in recent years (generally, consumer loans secured over cars), the Law Commission recommended the replacement of the current legislation with a modern system of registration of security over consumer goods, although no firm recommendation was made as to the shape of such a scheme: the Law Commission, *Company Security Interests*, Law Com. No.296, Cmnd.6654 (2004), p.xiv, paras 1.52, 1.53. See also Dillon L.J.'s criticism of the Acts in *Welsh Development Agency v Export Finance Co Ltd* [1992] B.C.C. 270 at 286. In December 2009, the Department of Business, Investment and Skills initiated a consultation on, inter alia, whether the Bills of Sale Acts 1878 and 1882 should be repealed. Eventually, while acknowledging criticism of loans secured against bills of sale was increasing (e.g. *Welcome Financial Services Ltd v Nine Regions Ltd (t/a Log Book Loans)* [2010] 2 Lloyd's Rep. 426), government decided against regulation and instead placed its faith in a voluntary code of practice: BIS, *Government Response to the Consultation on Proposals to Ban the Use of Bills of Sale for Consumer Lending* (2011); Consumer Credit Trade Association, *Code of Practice: Bills of Sale for Lending Regulated under the Consumer Credit Act: A Commitment to Responsible Lending* (2011); Sheehan, 126 L.Q.R. 356 (2010); McBain, 5 J.B.L. 475 (2011). The Law Commission conducted another inquiry in 2015–16 which criticised the Bills of Sales Acts as unduly complex, since compliance is difficult and the registration regime archaic, and as offering little protection to borrowers and none at all to innocent purchasers. The Law Commission drafted the Goods Mortgages Bill (Law Commission, *Bills of Sale*, Law Com. No.369 (2016)); *From Bills of Sale to Goods Mortgages*, HC 495 (2017); but, although the Government announced its intention to introduce the bill, this decision was reversed following further consultation. See Swaby, Kelly and Richards, 81 M.L.R. 308 (2018); HM Treasury, *Goods Mortgages Bill: Response to the Consultation* (May 2018)); Stephen Lewis, Law Commissioner, at *https://www.lawcom.gov.uk/government-shelves-goods-mortgages-bill/*.

1-016

Replace footnote 114 with:

[114] Bills of Sale Act 1878 s.17; *Online Catering Ltd v Acton* [2010] EWCA Civ 58; [2011] Q.B. 204. "Company" has been restrictively interpreted so as to exclude (e.g.) a society incorporated under the Industrial and Provident Societies Acts: *Great Northern Railway Co v Coal Co-operative Soc* [1896] 1 Ch. 187. For the present position regarding such societies, however, see Co-operative and Community Benefit Societies Act 2014 s.59(2).

Replace heading footnote 134 with:

The Hire-Purchase Acts and the Consumer Credit Acts[134]

1-019   [134] See Lomnicka and Bowden, *Encyclopedia of Consumer Credit Law* (looseleaf); and below, paras 14-167 et seq.

Scope of the Consumer Credit Acts

Replace footnote 146 with:

1-021   [146] Defined (Consumer Credit Act s.189(1)) as including a partnership or other unincorporated body of persons not consisting entirely of bodies corporate. The term clearly excludes a corporation and, under s.1 of the 2006 Act, a partnership of more than three members; but it includes a sole trader. For other definitions of consumer, see below, paras 14-001, 14-023 et seq. The financial limit on a consumer credit transaction has been removed by s.2 of the 2006 Act, so that all consumer credit agreements are regulated by the 1974 Act, unless specifically exempted: see below, para.1-022. There are also provisions regarding "unfair relationships": ss.140A, 140B of the 1974 Act (inserted by ss.19, 20 of the 2006 Act). The Financial Conduct Authority has reported on the Consumer Credit Act (as required by the Financial Services and Markets Act 2000 (Regulated Activities) (Amendment) Order 2014 (SI 2014/366) Pt 5), with recommendations for changes to the Act: FCA, *Review of retained provisions of the Consumer Credit Act: final report* (2019).

The meaning of "credit"

Replace paragraph with:

1-022   The word "credit" in the Consumer Credit Act 1974 is defined in wide terms[150] which are capable of embracing all contracts for the supply of goods where payment of the price is deferred so as to be paid either in one amount or in instalments. Certain agreements are, however, exempted from the operation of the Act.[151] These include credit agreements relating to regulated mortgages, or to the purchase of land where the lender is a local authority; a secured loan for the purchase of buying land used or intended for use in connection with a dwelling where the lender is a housing authority; a credit agreement where the lender is an investment firm or credit institution and the agreement is to allow the borrower to enter into a transaction relating to financial instruments; a borrower-lender-supplier agreement involving fixed-sum credit and limited repayments and repayment period; a borrower-lender agreement that has a credit charge or interest rate below a stipulated figure and the lender is a credit union or the loan is not offered to the general public; and an agreement where the borrower consents to forgo the protections available for regulated credit agreements and the agreement is secured on land or is for credit exceeding a stipulated amount. The Act has only limited application to other types of agreement including a small agreement, which is a consumer credit agreement (other than a hire purchase or conditional sale agreement) below a stipulated amount; a debtor-creditor agreement enabling the debtor to overdraw a current account; and a small debtor-creditor-supplier agreement for restricted-use credit.[152] In addition to the provisions in the Consumer Credit Act, the regulator, which is the Financial Conduct Authority, has issued conduct of business standards for consumer credit firms.[153]

[150] Consumer Credit Act 1974 s.9(1): "'credit' includes a cash loan, and any other form of financial accommodation".

[151] The Financial Services and Markets Act 2000 (Regulated Activities) Order 2001 (SI 2001/544) arts 60C–60HA, as inserted by the Financial Services and Markets Act 2000 (Regulated Activities) (Amendment) (No.2) Order 2013 (SI 2013/1881) Ch.14A and Pt 5 art.20(5), (6), the Financial Services and Markets Act 2000 (Regulated Activities) (Amendment) Order 2014 (SI 2014/366) art.2(24)–(28) (with amendments), and the Mortgage Credit Directive Order 2015 (SI 2015/910) Sch.1(2), para.4(19). These provisions replaced the Consumer Credit Act 1974 ss.16 and 16A. Under the Consumer Credit Act 1974 s.8(3) (as amended by the order of 2013 art.20(3)) a consumer credit agreement is a regulated agreement if it is "a regulated credit agreement for the purposes of Chapter 14A of Part 2 of the Regulated Activities Order".

[152] Consumer Credit Act 1974 ss.17 and 74 (as amended by the Consumer Credit (EU Directive) Regulations 2010 (SI 2010/1010) Pts 2 and 5, and the Financial Services and Markets Act 2000 (Regulated Activities) (Amendment) (No.2) Order 2013 (SI 2013/1881) art.20(26)).

[153] Financial Conduct Authority, *Consumer Credit Sourcebook (CONC)* at *https://www.handbook.fca.org.uk/handbook* [Accessed 26 June 2019].

EU legislation

Replace paragraph with:

The law of sale of goods in the UK has been supplemented, and to some extent **1-023** modified, by legislation emanating from the EU. In particular, a number of directives applicable to the sale of goods have been adopted and implemented into the domestic law of this country by statute or regulation. The most important of these are: (i) the Consumer Protection Act 1987 Pt I,[154] dealing with product liability; (ii) the Enterprise Act 2002,[155] empowering the certain public bodies to obtain injunctions for the protection of consumers' interests; (iii) the Electronic Commerce (EC Directive) Regulations 2002,[156] which are concerned, inter alia, with contracts concluded by email or through the internet; (iv) the Late Payment of Commercial Debts Regulations 2002,[157] designed to combat the practice of paying commercial debts late; (v) the Price Marking Order 2004,[158] dealing with the indication of prices of products offered to consumers; (vi) the Consumer Protection from Unfair Trading Regulations 2008,[159] which implements a directive that sought to harmonise law across the European Community on unfair commercial practices; (vii) the Consumer Contracts (Information, Cancellation and Additional Charges) Regulations 2013,[160] which obliges the supplier to provide the consumer with certain information prior to contract, distinguishing between on-premises, off-premises and distance contracts, and gives the consumer certain rights, including the right of cancellation[161]; and (viii) the Consumer Rights Act 2015 (apart from a few specified exceptions, the act applies to the supply of goods and digital content to consumers generally and not just to contracts for the sale of goods), which defines the rights and remedies of consumers under consumer contracts and restricts the use of terms deemed unfair.[162] In addition there are many European Community measures dealing with the sale of particular categories of goods, e.g. medicinal and tobacco products. In the event that the UK withdraws from the EU, the European Union (Withdrawal) Act 2018 provides that EU-derived domestic legislation (such as EU directives incorporated into UK law under the European Communities Act 1972 s.2(2)) "as it has effect in domestic law immediately before exit day, continues to have effect in domestic law on and after exit day" (s.2(1) 2018 Act), and direct EU legislation (such as EU regulations) "so far as operative immediately before exit day, forms part of domestic law on and after exit day" (s.3(1) 2018 Act). (These provisions are not yet in force: s.25(4).)

[154] Implementing Directive 1985/374 [1988] O.J. L307/54, as amended by 1999/34 [1999] O.J. L141/20; below, para.14-222 et seq.

[155] Pt 8 (implementing Directive 1998/27 [1998] O.J. L166/51). Amended by the Enterprise and Regulatory Reform Act 2013 Pt 3, Sch.4, which replaced the Office of Fair Trading with the Competition and Markets Authority.

[156] Electronic Commerce (EC Directive) Regulations 2002 (SI 2002/2013) (implementing Directive 2000/31 [2000] O.J. L178/1); below, para.14-209.

[157] Late Payment of Commercial Debts Regulations 2002 (SI 2002/1674) (implementing Directive 2000/35 [2000] O.J. L200/35). Note also the Late Payment of Commercial Debts (Interest) Act 1998 and the Late Payment of Commercial Debts (Rate of Interest) (No.3) Order 2002 (SI 2002/1675), below, para.16-010.

[158] Price Marking Order 2004 (SI 2004/102) (replacing SI 1999/3042) (which implemented Directive 1998/6 [1998] O.J. L190/86), below, para.14-259.

[159] Consumer Protection from Unfair Trading Regulations 2008 (SI 2008/1277) (which came into effect on 26 May 2008), implementing Directive 2005/99 [2005] O.J. L149/22; paras 14-261 et seq. Amended by the Consumer Protection (Amendment) Regulations 2014 (SI 2014/870) with effect from 1 October 2014, which seeks to address criticism of the failure by Member States to provide consumers with redress. See also, the Law Commission's report, *Consumer Remedies for Faulty Goods* (Law Com. No.317, Cm.7725, 2009); Devenney (2018) 6 J.B.L. 485.

[160] Consumer Contracts (Information, Cancellation and Additional Charges) Regulations 2013 (SI 2013/3134). This implements the Directive on Consumer Rights (2011/83/EU), which replaces or amends directives on distance contracts (97/7/EC), contracts negotiated away from business premises (85/577/EEC), unfair terms (93/13/EEC) and consumer sales and guarantees (1999/44/EC).

[161] It replaced the Consumer Protection (Distance Selling) Regulations 2000 (SI 2000/2334) (as amended by SI 2005/689) (implementing Directive 1997/7 [1997] O.J. L144/19); below, paras 14-201 et seq.

[162] Further amendments will follow from the Directive on certain aspects concerning the supply of digital content and digital services (2019/770/EU) and the Directive on certain aspects concerning contracts for the sale of goods (2019/771/EU), which must be brought into force by 1 January 2022. The EU Commission proposed the Common European Sales Law (COM(2011) 635 final), which would exist alongside national sales laws and apply if both parties to a cross-border contract (whether business-business or consumer-business) adopted it and one of the parties were established in the EU. Although approved by the European Parliament in February 2014, it was criticised (by, among others, the UK Government) and withdrawn in 2015. But the idea has not been abandoned. The Commission has promised a "Modified proposal in order to fully unleash the potential of e-commerce in the Digital Single Market": Communication from the Commission to the European Parliament, the Council, the European Economic and Social Committee and the Committee of the Regions: Commission Work Programme 2015: A New Start (COM/2014) 910 final, p.12). See Hesselink, 20 E.R.P.L. 195 (2012); McMeel, 27 B.J.I.B. & F.L. 3 (2012); Monaghan, 33 Comp. Law 111 (2012); C.M.L. Rev. (special issue) (2013); Dannemann and Vogenauer (eds), *The Common European Sales Law in Context* (2013, OUP); Lehmann (ed.), *Common European Sales Law Meets Reality* (2015, SELP).

The Uniform Laws on International Sales, and the Vienna Convention on Contracts for the International Sale of Goods

Replace footnote 164 with:

1-024   [164] There is a growing literature on the Convention. See, e.g. Schlechtriem and Schwenzer, *Commentary on the UN Convention on the International Sale of Goods* (CISG), 4th edn. For a list of contracting states:*https://www.cisg.law.pace.edu/cisg/countries/notables.html* (Accessed 26 June 2019).

Replace footnote 165 with:

[165] For a discussion of the UK position, see the DTI's consultation document, United Nations Convention on Contract for the International Sale of the Goods (The Vienna Sales Convention), URN 97/875 (1987); Hayward, Zeller and Anderson (2018) 67 I.C.L.Q. 607. Other major trading countries that have not ratified the Convention are India, South Africa and Taiwan.

Replace the fourth paragraph with:

Mention should also be made of another international agreement concluded under the aegis of UNCITRAL, the Model Law on Electronic Commerce (1996), which sets out provisions designed to ensure that contracts concluded by electronic means are legally recognised.[168] The Model Law has no force of its own, but depends upon the enactment by individual States of domestic legislation which incorporates its terms. The UK's Electronic Communications Act 2000,and the Electronic Identification and Trust Services for Electronic Transactions Regulations 2016[169] cover some of this ground (e.g. in relation to the recognition of electronic signatures), but do not directly address other contractual issues dealt with by the Model Law.

168 See, *http://www.uncitral.org/uncitral/en/uncitral_texts/electronic_commerce/1996Model.html* (Accessed 26 June 2019); Faria, "Legal Certainty for Electronic Transactions: The Role of the UNCITRAL Model Law on Electronic Commerce" in Schulz (ed), *Legal Aspects of an E-Commerce Transaction* (2006); Law Commission, *Electronic Commerce; Formal Requirements in Commercial Transactions* (2001).

169 SI 2016/696, implementing Regulation (EU) No.910/2014 (the eIDAS Regulation).

3. THE CONTRACT OF SALE

(a) Sale and Agreement to Sell

The contract of sale: statutory definitions

Replace footnote 170 with:

170 Williston, *Sales*, 3rd edn, para.6, suggested that a present agreement that the property in goods shall pass at some time in the future, without any further act on the part of the seller, might fall into an intermediate category. However, by s.2(5) of the Act, these are declared to be agreements to sell in English law, and under the Consumer Rights Act 2015 ss.3, 5 they are "sale contracts" and, therefore, contracts to supply goods.

1-025

Agreement to sell

Replace footnote 174 with:

174 Sale of Goods Act s.2(5). An agreement to sell is a "sales contract" and, therefore, "a contract to supply goods" under the Consumer Rights Act 2015 ss.3, 5.

1-026

Sale

Replace the second paragraph with:

The word "sale" is sometimes used purely in the sense of conveyance, so as to refer to that aspect of the transaction which concerns the transfer of the property, divorced from all contractual considerations. Benjamin, writing before the Act of 1893, defined a sale as "a transfer of the absolute or general property in a thing for a price in money",[181] and similarly in the US the Uniform Commercial Code provides that a sale "consists in the passing of title from the seller to the buyer for a price".[182] A sale in this sense may be accomplished on the making of the contract of sale (in which case it is conveniently termed, as in the US, "a present sale"),[183] or by the performance of an agreement to sell. The expressions executed sale and actual sale are used as equivalent to sale, mainly to emphasise the distinction between that term and agreement to sell. By s.61(1) of the Act, sale includes a bargain and sale as well as a sale and delivery. These expressions are explained in a later paragraph.[184] The interpretation of terms such as sale, sell and purchase as used in other statutory provisions is not always consistent with the definitions given by this Act, but it has been said that the Act "may be regarded as reflecting the terminology generally employed in the common law in relation to sale."[185]

1-027

181 *Sale of Personal Property*, 2nd edn (1873), p.1.

182 Uniform Commercial Code Art.2-106; but note that the price need not be in money (Art.2-304(1)): below, paras 1-034, 2-044.

183 Uniform Commercial Code Art.2-106.

184 See below, para.1-029.

185 *Wm Morrisons Supermarkets Plc v Reading BC* [2012] EWHC 1358 (Admin); [2012] 2 Cr. App. R. 16 at [17] per Lloyd Jones J (case on Children and Young Persons Act 1933 s.7(1)(a) involving tobacco sale to a minor). The court did not follow the logic of the Sale of Goods Act, concluding there had been a "sale" within the Act of 1933, even if property had not passed to the minor. See Munday, 72 C.L.J. 50 (2013). See also decisions concerning the sale of liquor in clubs, below, para.1-121; the defini-

tions of "purchase" and "sale" in the Law of Property Act 1925 s.205(1)(xxi)(xxiv); and "conveyance on sale" in the Stamp Act 1891 ss.54 (since repealed), 55, explained in *Coats v IRC* [1897] 2 Q.B. 423; *IRC v Maple & Co (Paris) Ltd* [1908] A.C. 22. Other expressions judicially considered have included: "make a sale" (*Milner v Staffs Congregational Union (Inc)* [1956] Ch. 275); "sale by way of wholesale dealing" (*Oxford v Sangers Ltd* [1965] 1 Q.B. 491); "offer for sale" (*Fisher v Bell* [1961] 1 Q.B. 394; cf. *Newman v Lipman* [1951] 1 K.B. 333; *Partridge v Crittenden* [1968] 1 W.L.R. 1204); "offer to sell" (*British Car Auctions Ltd v Wright* [1972] 1 W.L.R. 1519; *CA Norgren Co v Technomarketing, The Times* March 3, 1983); "sell" (*Mischeff v Springett* [1942] 2 K.B. 331; *Watts v Seymour* [1967] 2 Q.B. 647); "agreement ... for the sale purchase or exchange of any property" (*Doyle v East* [1972] 1 W.L.R. 108); "exposing goods for supply" (*Haringey LBC v Piro Shoes Ltd* [1976] Crim. L.R. 462); "are to be sold" (*Re Westminster Property Group Plc* [1985] 1 W.L.R. 676); "disposition as sale" in the Hire Purchase Act 1964 (*VFS Financial Services Ltd v JF Plant Tyres Ltd* [2013] EWHC 346 (QB); [2013] 1 W.L.R. 2987). cf. *Hughes v Australian Competition & Consumer Commission* [2004] FCAFC 319.

Bargain and sale, and sale and delivery

After "By s.61(1),", replace "'sale'" with:

1-029   "'sale'

(b)   Contract of Sale Distinguished from Other Transactions

Contract of sale distinguished from other transactions

Replace footnote 199 with:

1-030   [199] *PST Energy 7 Shipping LLC v OW Bunker Malta Ltd: The Res Cogitans* [2016] UKSC 23 at [35]; [2016] A.C. 1034; see paras 4-001 et seq. below for a fuller discussion. Lord Mance (at [35]) questioned the classification as sales of the contracts in *Borden (UK) Ltd v Scottish Timber Products Ltd* [1981] Ch. 25 and *Armour v Thyssen Edelstahlwerke AG* [1991] 2 A.C. 339. See *Wood v TUI Travel Plc (t/a First Choice)* [2017] EWCA Civ 11; [2018] 2 W.L.R. 1051 (supply of food to hotel guests came within the Supply of Goods and Services Act 1982): "The conclusion reached by the Supreme Court [in The Res Cogitans] depended upon the relationship between the retention of title clause and the liberty nonetheless to consume fuel in which property had not already passed" (at [25]).

Common law and statutory rules governing transactions analogous to sales

Replace footnote 217 with:

1-031   [217] Unfair Contract Terms Act 1977 s.7; and see 1982 Act s.11(1).

Sale distinguished from gift

Replace footnote 224 with:

1-032   [224] *Cochrane v Moore* (1890) 25 Q.B.D. 57. For the rules regarding delivery, see Crossley Vaines, *Personal Property*, 5th edn, pp.305 et seq.

"Free offers" under promotional schemes

Replace footnote 228 with:

1-033   [228] *Esso Petroleum Co Ltd v Customs and Excise Commissioners* [1976] 1 W.L.R. 1; cf. *GUS Merchandise Corp Ltd v Customs & Excise Commrs* [1981] 1 W.L.R. 1309 (liability to value added tax on gifts to mail-order representatives); *Ford Motor Co Ltd v Revenue and Customs Commissioners* [2007] EWCA Civ 1370; [2008] B.T.C. 5029 (liability to VAT on free insurance and breakdown cover supplied with motor cars); and *AH Gen v L D Nathan & Co Ltd* [1990] 1 N.Z.L.R. 129, where the *Esso Petroleum* case [1976] 1 W.L.R. 1 was not followed.

Sale distinguished from barter or exchange

Replace the first paragraph with:

1-034   To constitute a sale it is necessary that the consideration for the transfer of the property in the goods should be in money.[233] This may be either paid or promised (i.e. the sale may be for cash or on credit), but if the consideration is something other than money[234] the contract is not, strictly speaking, one of sale in English law.[235] The Consumer Rights Act 2015, however, defines a "sales contract" more broadly, requiring only that "the consumer pays or agrees to pay the price".[236] Under that act, there is "a contract for transfer of goods" where the trader transfers or agrees to transfer ownership of goods to the consumer, who provides or agrees to provide "consideration other than by paying a price".[237] Where goods are supplied or promised in exchange for goods, the transaction is a barter or exchange. Similarly, goods may be exchanged for work done,[238] for the making of another contract,[239] for rent, or for board and lodging,[240] or in return for the extinction of a right[241] or the abandonment of a claim, or any other valuable non-money consideration.[242] None of these bargains is a sale within the Act. The same is true, it is submitted, where the owner of waste materials or other unwanted goods pays someone to take them away since the transfer of property by the owner is not made in exchange for payment by the person who removes the materials.[243]

[233] Sale of Goods Act s.2(1); cf. *Re Westminster Property Group Plc* [1985] 1 W.L.R. 676 (shares). A price payable in a foreign currency will normally be regarded as money for this purpose: see *Daewoo Australia Pty Ltd v Suncorp-Metway Ltd* (2000) 33 A.C.S.R. 481; and cf. below, para.1-084. Where the parties agree to treat fungible goods as money, the transaction is virtually a sale, though semble not a sale within the statutory definition. cf. *Barbe v Parker* (1789) 1 H.Bl. 283 (gold case valued as cash); *South Australian Insurance Co v Randell* (1869) L.R. 3 P.C. 101 (wheat), discussed below, paras 1-057, 1-062. A bill of exchange or other negotiable instrument will be regarded as money only if it is given and accepted as conditional payment of a money price (see below, paras 9-030 et seq.), and not if it is exchanged as such: *Read v Hutchinson* (1813) 3 Camp. 352. A trading check or similar voucher may be treated as a consideration in money: see *Davies v Customs and Excise Commissioners* [1975] 1 W.L.R. 204 (VAT). Similarly, payment using "money" issued by local communities or traders, such as the Brixton Pound in London, may constitute money for the purposes of a sale contract where the scheme gives holders of the notes the right to exchange them for legal tender and in so far as a holder of such a note uses it to pay for goods. On this basis, bitcoins (a peer-to-peer system which does not involve either governments or banks) do not constitute "money" because, although they may be sold for legal tender, they give no right to such an exchange. On virtual currencies, see Financial Markets Law Committee, *Issues of Legal Uncertainty Arising in the Context of Virtual Currencies* (2016) at *http://www.fmlc.org* [Accessed 11 July 2018]. As regards payment by credit card, see below, para.1-034 n.242 and below, para.9-032. In *Skatteverket v Hedqvist* (C-264/14) EU:C:2015:78; [2016] S.T.C. 372, bitcoins were held to be currency for the purposes of VAT, and in *Coinstar Ltd v Revenue and Customs Commissioners* [2017] UKUT 256; [2017] S.T.C. 1519, a voucher, produced by a coin counting machine and only usable in the supermarket where the machine was located, was money and exempt from VAT.

[234] Foreign currency may, depending on the circumstances, be treated as a medium of exchange (i.e. money) or as a commodity (i.e. goods): see below, para.1-084; and *Daewoo Australia Pty Ltd v Suncorp-Metway Ltd* (2000) 33 A.C.S.R. 481. A contract to exchange a sum in one foreign currency for a sum in another could well be regarded as a species of barter.

[235] The distinction is not made in the uniform legislation in the US, where the price may be payable in money or otherwise; if it is payable in whole or in part in goods, each party is a seller of the goods which each is to transfer: Uniform Commercial Code Art.2-304(1); Uniform Sales Act s.9(2). A similar provision was proposed by Chalmers in his original draft Bill: see Chalmers, *The Sale of Goods*, 1st edn (1890), p.87.

[236] s.5(1(b). A bitcoin sale would, therefore, seem to be a "sales contract" under the act.

[237] Consumer Rights Act 2015 s.8.

[238] *Garey v Pyke* (1839) 10 Ad. & El. 512; cf. *Doyle v East* [1972] 1 W.L.R. 1080 (agreement to convey land in return for building work).

[239] *Esso Petroleum Co Ltd v Customs and Excise Commissioners* [1976] 1 W.L.R. 1 at 5, 7, 11.

[240] *Keys v Harwood* (1846) 2 C.B. 905.

[241] In *Simpson v Connolly* [1953] 2 All E.R. 474, a contract under which a debtor to transfer land to a creditor in exchange for the creditor excusing the debt was held to be an agreement, not to pay money in return for land, but to extinguish the debt if land were transferred. It is suggested that this decision is to be preferred over *Sands v Norman* (1903) 4 S.R.N.S.W. 234, where the opposite conclusion was reached on facts not materially distinguishable. See also *Robshaw Bros Ltd v Mayer* [1957] Ch. 125.

[242] *Read v Hutchinson* (1813) 3 Camp. 352 (bill of third party, without recourse); cf. *Robshaw Bros Ltd v Mayer* [1957] Ch. 125 (assumption of tenant's obligations). Where a seller of goods agrees to accept payment by credit card, without recourse to the buyer in the event of non-payment by the credit-card company, it appears that the transaction is a sale: see below, para.9-032. But where payment is effected by use of a credit system such as Bartercard it will not be a sale: members of the scheme receive a line of credit on joining, which is increased by sales to, and reduced by purchases from, other members, but, although the balance of an account is expressed in the local currency, members do not acquire a right to payment in money: see *Michael v Ogun* [2009] NSWDC 52. The passage in the text was cited in *VFS Financial Services Ltd v JF Plant Tyres Ltd* [2013] EWHC 346 (QB); [2013] 1 W.L.R. 2987 at [12], [14].

[243] See Sale of Goods Act s.2(1). Such a transaction has been held to be a sale under the wider definition adopted in the US; *HS Crocker Co v McFaddin*, 148 Cal. App. 2d 639 (1957).

Sale distinguished from contract for work and materials

Replace the first paragraph with:

1-041   It is sometimes extremely difficult to decide whether a particular agreement is more properly described as a contract of sale of goods, or a contract for the performance of work or services to which the supply of materials or some other goods[266] is incidental[267]: for example, when an order is given to a tailor to make a suit or to an artist to paint a portrait, or when a meal is supplied in a restaurant.[268] The cases provide no general principles that might clarify the distinction. Since both the old forms of pleading and the provisions of the Statute of Frauds formerly made a distinction between the two types of contract, the success or failure of an action could frequently turn on the drawing of an artificial line of demarcation. In modern law the distinction is, however, much less important. Although the Sale of Goods Act cannot apply to a contract for work and materials,[269] the courts have shown little hesitation in applying analogous common law rules, such as warranties as to fitness for purpose.[270] The Supply of Goods and Services Act 1982 now implies similar terms by statute.[271] It is possible that different rules may govern the passing of property and risk, or the consequences of a frustrating event,[272] or the remedies of the parties in the event of a breach[273] in the two classes of contract, but otherwise the distinction now appears to be of little significance,[274] except in relation to those statutory provisions which apply only to a sale or a contract of sale. Many of the transactions with which we are concerned may, if the parties choose, be expressed either as a contract of sale or a contract for work; their legal relationship will then be different during the performance of the work, but the same ultimate result will be achieved. For instance, we may take the case posed by Roman lawyers of a bystander who agrees with a fisher to pay an agreed sum for what is yielded by the next cast of his net.[275] This may be expressed indifferently as an agreement by the fisher to sell the catch, or to catch fish for reward. Again, chickens may be bailed to a grower for rearing until maturity on behalf of the bailor, whose property they are to remain throughout, or they may be sold to the grower with an agreement to repurchase them when reared. In either case it is possible to make any desired provisions for the remuneration of the grower and for the allocation of cost and risk.

[266] Where the product supplied falls outside the statutory definition of "goods", the contract may be construed as being neither for the sale of goods nor for the supply of services, but sui generis: see *St Albans City and DC v International Computers Ltd* [1996] 4 All E.R. 481; *Beta Computers (Europe) Ltd v Adobe Systems (Europe) Ltd* 1996 S.L.T. 604 (computer software), below, para.1-086. Some consumer protection laws have sought to remove the distinctions between these contracts, such as the Consumer Contracts (Information, Cancellation and Additional Charges) Regulations 2013 (SI 2013/3134), but even these regulations, which apply to the supply of goods or services by a trader to a consumer, distinguish between a "sales contract" and a "service contract" (e.g. regs 5, 11(1)(a) and 30); and a contract for works and materials falls within the meaning of a sales contract for the purposes of

the regulations, except where the contract involves the supply of water, gas or electricity other than in a limited volume or a set quantity or the supply of district heating (reg.5).

[267] In *Hyundai Shipbuilding & Heavy Industries Co Ltd v Papadopoulos* [1980] 1 W.L.R. 1129 at 134, 1148; and *Stoczina Gdanska SA v Latvian Shipping Co* [1996] 2 Lloyd's Rep. 132 at 138 it was held that a contract to build a ship, though a contract of sale of goods, had also some of the characteristics of a building contract.

[268] The Consumer Rights Act 2015 definition of "a sales contract" seems broader than in the 1982 Act or the Sale of Goods Act 1979, since it refers to "goods that are to be manufactured or produced" (s.5(2)). See below, paras 1-046-47.

[269] In *Jones v Gallagher* [2004] EWCA Civ 10; [2005] 1 Lloyd's Rep. 377, the court, having held that the contract to supply and install kitchen fittings came within the Supply of Goods and Services Act 1982 s.3(2) and was thus not a contract of sale of goods, nevertheless assumed that the Sale of Goods Act s.35 governed the question of the transferees' right to reject. See Bradgate, (2004) 120 L.Q.R. 558.

[270] See, e.g. *Harmer v Cornelius* (1858) 5 C.B.(N.S.) 236; *Myers & Co v Brent Cross Service Co* [1934] 1 K.B. 46; *Watson v Buckley, Osborne, Garrett & Co Ltd* [1940] 1 All E.R. 174; *Samuels v Davis* [1943] 1 K.B. 526; *Stewart v Reavell's Garage* [1952] 2 Q.B. 545; *Ingham v Emes* [1955] 2 Q.B. 366; *Young & Marten Ltd v McManus Childs Ltd* [1969] 1 A.C. 454; *North East Equity Pty Ltd v Proud Nominees Pty Ltd (No.2)* [2008] FCA 1189 at [64]-[65]; contrast *Helicopter Sales (Australia) Pty Ltd v Rotor-Work Pty Ltd* (1974) 132 C.L.R. 1 (no warranty when manufacturer's spare part fitted); and cf. *St Albans City and DC v International Computers Ltd* [1996] 4 All E.R. 481, below, para.1-086 (contract for supply of computer software).

[271] See above, para.1-031; *Alliott v Cheeld* [2013] EWCA Civ 508 at [19]. The Consumer Contracts (Information, Cancellation and Additional Charges) Regulations 2013 (SI 2013/3134), which relate to distance and off-premises contracts entered into on or after 13 June 2104, apply to both sales of goods and sales of services; but the distinction between these types of contract remains for certain purposes (e.g. regs 6(1)(b), 11(1), 27(1), 28, 29(1), 30(1), 36, 38, 40(3)).

[272] cf. Law Reform (Frustrated Contracts) Act 1943 s.2(5)(c), below, para.6-052.

[273] *Hyundai Shipbuilding & Heavy Industries Co Ltd v Papadopoulos* [1980] 1 W.L.R. 1129 (seller's right to payment of instalments of price following termination of contract): see below, para.16-044.

[274] Note, however, the different provisions regarding exemption clauses contained in ss.6 and 7 of the Unfair Contract Terms Act 1977, both as regards the implied terms as to title (ss.6(1), 7(4)) and in the restriction of the scope of s.7 to "business liability".

[275] Dig.18.1.8. This was the illustration given of emptio spei, or the sale of an expectation dependent upon a chance. Benjamin thought the contract was one of work and labour: *Sale of Personal Property*, 2nd edn (1873), pp.66-67. In *Salo v Anglo-British Columbia Packing Co* [1929] 1 D.L.R. 874, a contract by fishermen to catch fish for a cannery was held to be a contract of sale, even though the sellers submitted to a measure of control by the buyer. On the other hand, for the purposes of VAT, the purchase of a ticket giving the right to fish (whether that right extends to keeping fish caught or returning them to the water) without any promise that fish will be caught is not a sale but the purchase of a chance of catching fish: *Stocks Fly Fishery v The Commissioners for HM Revenue & Customs* [2016] UKFIT 0281 (TC).

Replace footnote 276 with:

[276] *Robinson v Graves* [1935] 1 K.B. 579. See, *Ter Neuzen v Korn* 1995 CanLII 72 (SCC); [1995] 3 S.C.R. 674 at [67]; *Andersen v Deibert* 2007 SKQB 178. **1-042**

Services independent of creation or furnishing of product

Replace footnote 304 with:

[304] *Wood v TUI Travel Plc (t/a First Choice)* [2017] EWCA Civ 11; [2018] 2 W.L.R. 1051. See, however, *Horgan v Driscoll* (1908) 42 I.L.T. 238. **1-046**

Sale distinguished from contract of agency

Replace footnote 319 with:

[319] In this case, the relationship between the parties may be governed by the Commercial Agency Regulations 1993 (SI 1993/3053, implementing EC Directive 1986/653 [1986] O.J. L382/17); *Bowstead and Reynolds on Agency*, 21st edn, Ch.11. **1-048**

Option distinguished from conditional right or obligation

Replace footnote 351 with:

1-051   [351] *Thoresen & Co (Bangkok) Ltd v Fathom Marine Co Ltd* [2004] 1 Lloyd's Rep. 622 ("sub. details", i.e. "subject to details"). See below, para.2-007.

Conditional sale agreements

Replace the first paragraph with:

1-052   It may be a term of a contract of sale that the transfer of the property in the goods is subject to some condition to be fulfilled after the making of the contract. In particular, it may be agreed that the property shall not pass to the buyer until the price has been paid in full, and the expression "conditional sale" (and its variant "conditional purchase") is regularly used to describe such a contract,[360] at least in the common case where the price is payable by instalments. Such contracts are now in part governed by the Consumer Credit Act 1974, which employs the following definition[361]:

> "... 'conditional sale agreement' means an agreement for the sale of goods or land under which the purchase price or part of it is payable by instalments, and the property in the goods or land is to remain in the seller (notwithstanding that the buyer is to be in possession of the goods or land) until such conditions as to the payment of instalments or otherwise as may be specified in the agreement are fulfilled."

It was held in *Lee v Butler*[362] that a person who was in possession of goods under a conditional sale agreement had agreed to buy within the terms of the Factors Act 1889 s.9, so that this buyer could pass a good title to a third party under that provision.[363] The conditional sale agreement was therefore not fully effective as a security to the seller for the unpaid purchase price,[364] and it was to overcome this difficulty that the hire-purchase agreement was devised.

[360] See, however, *Re Bond Worth Ltd* [1980] Ch. 228 at 245, where Slade J. said that contracts containing a retention of title clause (below, paras 1-060, 5-143) were "absolute contracts for the sale of goods within the meaning of section 1(2) of the Sale of Goods Act 1893, though this is not to say that they did not comprise other features in addition". But where the contract contains a retention clause and the "buyer" is permitted to consume or resell the goods before payment falls due and property has not passed, the contract will not be a conditional sale but a sui generis supply contract, comprising a bailment with a licence to consume: *PST Energy 7 Shipping LLC v OW Bunker Malta Ltd: The Res Cogitans* [2016] UKSC 23; [2016] A.C. 1034; see para.1-030 above and paras 4-001 et seq. below for a fuller discussion.

[361] Consumer Credit Act 1974 s.189(1). The definition in the Hire-Purchase Act 1965 s.1(1), was the same, except that the words "or land" were omitted throughout. (The definitions discussed in this and the paragraphs following are not affected by the Consumer Credit Act 2006.)

[362] *Lee v Butler* [1893] 2 Q.B. 318.

[363] On this section, and the similar provision in the Sale of Goods Act s.25(1), see below, paras 7-069 et seq.

[364] See the Hire-Purchase Act 1965 s.54 and the Sale of Goods Act s.25(2), discussed below and para.7-070.

At the end of the last paragraph, after "or otherwise are", replace "met." with:
met, irrespective of whether the consumer possesses the goods.

Financing of hire-purchase agreements

Replace footnote 387 with:

[387] But if the customer signs an agreement containing blank spaces, leaving it to be completed by the dealer, the customer will be bound by what the dealer writes: *United Dominions Trust Ltd v Western* [1976] 1 Q.B. 513.

1-054

Credit-sale agreements

Replace footnote 393 with:

[393] For the definition of a regulated consumer credit agreement, see the 1974 Act s.8(2) and above, para.1-022.

1-055

Sale distinguished from bailment

Replace footnote 410 with:

[410] See, e.g. Uniform Commercial Code Art.7-207(2), replacing Uniform Warehouse Receipts Act s.23; Canada Grain Act R.S.C. 1985 c.G-10.

1-057

Sale distinguished from pledge

Replace paragraph with:

A pledge[438] is "a security intermediate between a lien and a mortgage".[439] It is a bailment—that is, a delivery of possession—of goods, or of documents of title to goods, in order to secure a debt. The creation of a charge over goods or documents of title or the proceeds of goods, without any delivery of possession (which is sometimes called a hypothecation[440]) is operative in equity only. A pledge differs from other bailments and from possessory liens in that the pledgee has a common law right, in the event of default in payment of the debt of the pledgor, to sell the goods without first obtaining the authority of the court. For this reason, the pledgee is sometimes said to have a special property in the goods,[441] and a pledge is then defined as a transfer by the owner of this special property in the goods, in contrast with a sale, where the absolute property is transferred.[442] By the Sale of Goods Act 1979 s.2, a sale is defined as a transfer of the property in goods—that is, "the general property in goods, and not merely a special property".[443] It follows that neither the pledge itself, nor an assignment of the pledgee's interest to a third party, can be a sale of goods. The pledgor retains the general property and may transfer it to a third party, subject to the rights of the pledgee. This is not merely the assignment of a chose in action; it is a sale of the goods.[444]

1-063

[438] See *Chitty on Contracts*, 33rd edn, Vol.2 paras 33-121 et seq.; Palmer and Hudson in Palmer and McKendrick, *Interests in Goods*, 2nd edn, Ch.24.

[439] *Halliday v Holgate* (1868) L.R. 3 Ex. 299 at 302.

[440] *Ryall v Rowles* (1749) 9 Bli.(N.S.) 377; *Ex p. North Western Bank* (1872) L.R. 15 Eq. 69.

[441] *The Odessa* [1916] 1 A.C. 145 at 158–159; cf. *Harper v Godsell* (1870) L.R. 5 Q.B. 422 at 426. The term "special property" (or "a" property as distinct from "the" property) is also used to refer to the interest of a bailee, or other person having an immediate right to possession, which entitles that person to sue for conversion or other wrongful interference with the goods: see *Nyberg v Handelaar* [1892] 2 Q.B. 202. cf. also *Giles v Grover* (1832) 6 Bli. N.S. 277 at 292–293 (sheriff's interest in goods seized).

[442] *Sewell v Burdick* (1884) 10 App. Cas. 74 at p.93; cf. the view of Bowen LJ in the court below, (1884) 13 Q.B.D. 159 at 175. The use of the term "special property" has been criticised and the expression "special interest" suggested as more appropriate: *The Odessa* [1916] 1 A.C. 145 at 158–159. "The exact nature of the pledgee's interest in the pledged goods is not settled": *Bassano v Toft* [2014] EWHC 377 (QB) at [49]; [2014] E.C.C. 14.

[443] See *Revenue and Customs Commissioners v Apollo Fuels Ltd* [2016] EWCA Civ 157; [2016] 4 W.L.R. 96 at [30], The Act does not define special property. See Sale of Goods Act s.61(1) for the meaning of the term property: Battersby and Preston, (1972) 35 M.L.R. 268; Battersby, [2001] J.B.L. 1; Tan Yock Lin, [2011] J.B.L. 749; Rostill, (2018) 134 L.Q.R. 407. The use of the term prevents a contract for the creation or assignment of, e.g. a life interest in goods from being a contract of sale: Battersby and Preston at 271. Similarly, the Consumer Rights Act 2015 s.4(1)).

[444] *Franklin v Neate* (1844) 13 M. & W. 481.

Supply of goods under a public duty

Replace footnote 485 with:

1-071 [485] *Read v Croydon Corp* [1938] 4 All E.R. 631. Alternatively, the buyer may bring an action for breach of statutory duty under the Consumer Protection Act 1987. Redress may also be available under Consumers, Estate Agents and Redress Act 2007; or the Gas and Electricity (Consumer Complaints Handling Standards) Regulations 2008 (SI 2008/1898).

Satisfaction of judgment in tort

Replace footnote 488 with:

1-072 [488] *Marston v Phillips* (1863) 9 L.T. 289 (trover); *Brinsmead v Harrison* (1871) L.R. 6 C.P. 584; affirmed (1872) L.R. 7 C.P. 547 (trover); *Ex p. Drake* (1877) 5 Ch. D. 866 (detinue); *Re Scarth* (1874) 10 Ch. App. 234 (detinue); *Ellis v John Stenning & Son* [1932] 2 Ch. 81 (conversion); *Tanks and Vessels Ltd v Devon Cider Co Ltd* [2009] EWHC 1360 (Ch) (conversion); *Blue Sky One Ltd v Mahan Air* [2009] EWHC 3314 (Comm) (wrongful interference with property). If, in an action for wrongful interference, the claimant recovers the property itself, an alternative judgment for its value becomes inoperative: *Ellis v John Stenning & Son* [1932] 2 Ch. 81 at 90.

Transactions involving persons subject to incapacity

Replace footnote 505 with:

1-076 [505] See *Chitty on Contracts*, 33rd edn, Vol.1 para.9-014, Vol.2 para.44-033; Goff and Jones, *The Law of Unjust Enrichment*, 9th edn, Chs 24, 34. Note that under the Minors' Contracts Act 1987 s.3(1), if a contract is unenforceable because the person with whom it was made was at the time a minor, the court may, if it is just and equitable to do so, require the defendant to transfer the property, which passed under the contract, or any property representing it, to the claimant.

4.   SUBJECT-MATTER OF THE CONTRACT

(a)   Goods

Meaning of "goods"

Replace footnote 510 with:

1-078 [510] The words "and includes an undivided share in goods" were added to the definition by the Sale of Goods (Amendment) Act 1995 s.2(c), otherwise the definition in s.62(1) of the Act of 1893 was in similar terms.

Undivided interest in goods

Replace footnote 539 with:

1-081 [539] On a literal construction, the subsection does not cover the case where a sole owner or part-owner contracts to transfer part of an interest to another so as to create a tenancy in common between them. *Goode on Commercial Law*, 5th edn, p.219 n.82 takes the view that this would not be a contract of sale within the Act, but the two first cases cited in the preceding note held the contrary at common law.

Ships and aircraft

Replace footnote 556 with:

556 Air Navigation Order 2016 (SI 2016/765) Pt.3; cf. *Cadogan Finance Ltd v Lavery* [1982] Com. L.R. **1-082**
248, below, para.7-015. On the registration of interests in aviation assets, see Aircraft Equipment (Cape
Town Convention) Regulations 2015 (SI 2015/912).

Electricity and other forms of energy

Replace footnote 575 with:

575 The supply of electricity is treated as a product for the purposes of the Consumer Protection Act 1987 **1-085**
Pt I (s.1(2)). The abstraction of electricity is now a special statutory offence: Theft Act 1968 s.13. cf.
Low v Blease (1975) 119 Sol. Jo. 695.

Replace title footnote 583 with:

Computer software583

583 Adams, [2009] J.B.L. 396; Clark, [2017] C.T.L.R. 16; Green and Saidov, [2007] J.B.L. 161; **1-086**
Macdonald, (1995) 58 M.L.R. 585; Moon, (2009) 31 E.I.P.R. 396; Napier [1992] C.L.J. 46, 55 et seq.;
Moon, (2009) 31 E.I.P.R. 396; Niranjan, [2009] J.B.L. 799; Hayward, [2016] Syd. L.R. 20.

Replace footnote 586 with:

586 Consumer Rights Act 2015 s.2(9), and Ch.3 of the act. Under s.16, in sales contracts, goods ("tangible
moveable items": s.2(8)) do not conform to the contract where the digital content does not conform. See
Computer Associates UK Ltd v Software Incubator Ltd [2018] EWCA Civ 518; [2019] Bus. L.R. 522
at [63]–[67].

Replace the second paragraph with:

At its core the debate over whether software constitutes goods for the purposes
of the Sale of Goods Act 1979 recognises that for there to be a category of things
that are goods there must be things that are not goods, and that this distinction tends
to rest on the issue of tangibility and the idea that "all personal things are either in
possession or in action".587 Sir Iain Glidewell's discussion of the issue in the Court
of Appeal in *St Albans City and DC v International Computers Ltd*,588 although
obiter, has been treated as authoritative. The question in that case was whether a
contract for the supply of software was subject to any implied term as to quality or
fitness for purpose. In his Lordship's view a computer disk was clearly within the
definition of goods for the purpose of the Sale of Goods Act 1979 and the Supply
of Goods and Services Act 1982,589 while equally clearly a program, "being instructions or commands telling the computer hardware what to do", of itself was not.590
If a disk carrying a program591 was transferred by way of sale or hire and the
program was defective, the seller or hirer of the disk would be in breach of the terms
as to quality and fitness implied by these Acts.592 However, in the *St Albans City*
case the defective program was not sold or hired, it had simply been transferred
from a disk on to the claimants' computer without delivery of the disk; the property
in the program remained in the supplier, and under the contract the claimants were
licensed to use it. The program was not goods and so there was no statutory implication of any term as the quality or fitness for purpose. However, his Lordship went
on to hold that, in the absence of any express term, such a contract would be subject
to an implied term at common law that the program would be reasonably fit for (i.e.
capable of achieving) its intended purpose.593 This conclusion has been criticised
and it has been pointed out that where computer software performs a task previously undertaken by a person, such as running an accounts system, there seems no
reason why by this substitution liability, which would have been based on

negligence, is turned into strict liability.[594] It has been said, "there is no logic in making the status of software as goods (or not) turn on the medium by which they were delivered or installed" but this view was rejected by the Court of Appeal.[595]

[587] *Colonial Bank v Whinney* (1885) L.R. 30 Ch. D. 261 at 285 per Fry LJ.

[588] *St Albans City and DC v International Computers Ltd* [1996] 4 All E.R. 481.

[589] Also, *Southwark LBC v IBM UK Ltd* [2011] EWHC 549 (TCC); 135 Con. L.R. 136 at [97]; *Fern Computer Consultancy Ltd v Intergraph Cadworx & Analysis Solutions Inc.* [2014] EWHC 2908 (Ch) at [86]; [2014] Bus. L.R. 1397 at 1418.

[590] See similarly, *Erris Promotions Ltd v Commissioner of Inland Revenue* [2004] 1 N.Z.L.R. 811 (whether software assets constituted depreciable property for tax purposes); *Gammasonics Institute for Medical Research Pty Ltd v Comrad Medical Systems Pty Ltd* [2010] NSWSC 267 (downloaded software not goods). Glidewell, L.J.'s views have not gone unchallenged in the literature: see Niranjan, [2009] J.B.L. 799. Chissick and Kelman, *Electronic Commerce Law and Practice*, 3rd edn, paras 3.08–3.09 consider that the distinction made by Sir Iain Glidewell between a program supplied in the form of a disk and one transmitted directly via the internet or over the telecommunications system (the former being regarded as a sale of goods and the latter not) is illogical, because different results could follow where identical digital products were sold, merely because a different medium was used. The learned authors submit that digitised services should be treated as "a dematerialised form of goods", and draw support from the judgment in *Advent Systems Ltd v Unisys Corp*, 925 F. 2d. 670 (1991), but this view has attracted no support from the English courts, which have adopted Glidewell LJ's view: cf. *Thunder Air Ltd v Hilmarsson* [2008] EWHC 355 (Ch) (no conversion of electronic information); *Your Response Ltd v Datateam Business Media Ltd* [2014] EWCA Civ 281; [2015] Q.B. 41 (no common law lien over electronic database); *Computer Associates UK Ltd v Software Incubator Ltd* [2018] EWCA Civ 518; [2019] Bus. L.R. 522 (software not "goods" within the Commercial Agents (Council Directive) Regulations 1993). A distinction is drawn between digital content in a tangible and non-tangible form with regard to contracts entered into on or after 13 June 2014 by the Consumer Contracts (Information, Cancellation and Additional Charges) Regulations 2013 (SI 2013/3134) regs 12(5), 16(3), 30(2)(b) and 37, Sch.3.

[591] Or a whole computer system, including hardware and software: *Toby Constructions Products Pty Ltd v Computer Bar (Sales) Pty Ltd* [1983] 2 N.S.W.L.R. 48.

[592] *Brocket v DGS Retail Ltd* [2004] C.L. Jan. 332.

[593] cf. *Saphena Computing Ltd v Allied Collection Agencies Ltd* [1995] F.S.R. 616 at 643.

[594] Bridge, *The Sale of Goods*, 3rd edn, pp.45–46. See *Khuu and Lee Pty Ltd v Micropos Pty Ltd* [2010] SADC 14.

[595] *Software Incubator Ltd v Computer Associates UK Ltd* [2016] EWHC 1587 (QB); [2017] Bus. L.R. 245. The view at first instance that the Commercial Agents (Council Directive) Regulations 1993 reg.2(1) "goods" included intangibles was overturned by the Court of Appeal: [2018] EWCA Civ 518; [2019] Bus. L.R. 522 at [51] (approving *St Albans City and District Council v International Computers Ltd* [1996] 4 All E.R. 481). See also *Accentuate Ltd v Asigra Inc.* [2009] EWHC 2655 (QB); [2010] 2 All E.R. (Comm.) 738.

Water, oil, gases

Replace footnote 598 with:

1-087 [598] While certain rights attach to riparian ownership, flowing water is not the subject of property, but water abstracted from the general flow can be the property of the person who abstracts it during the period it is in that person's possession: *Mason v Hill* (1833) 5 B & Ad 1; generally Halsbury, *Laws of England* (2018), Vol.100, paras 110 et seq. Water, which was supplied, was held to be goods within the Sale of Goods Act 1908 (NZ) in *Hamilton v Papakura DC* [2000] 1 N.Z.L.R. 265, and to be included in the term "goods, wares, or merchandise" in *West Middlesex Water-Works Co v Suwerkrop* (1829) 4 Car. & P. 87. Water in pipes was held to be larcenable in *Ferens v O'Brien* (1883) 11 Q.B.D. 21. It was an "article" in *Longhurst v Guildford Godalming & District Water Board* [1963] A.C. 265; cf. *Walker v Weedair (NZ) Ltd* [1959] N.Z.L.R. 777. cf. *Re Social Services Act* (1970) 74 W.W.R. 246 (steam).

Replace title footnote 608:

Human remains and parts of the body[608]

1-089 [608] Conway, *The Law and the Dead* (2016), Ch.6; Lee, "Yearworth v North Bristol NHS Trust [2009]: Instrumentalism and Fictions in Property Law" in Waring, Douglas and Hickey, *Landmark Cases in Property Law*, Ch.2; Quigley 32 O.J.L.S. 659 (2012); Hawes 73 M.L.R. 130 (2010); Hardcastle, *Law* and the Human Body: Property Rights, Ownership and Control (2007); Magnusson, "Property Rights in Human Tissue" in Palmer and McKendrick, Interests in Goods, 2nd edn, Ch.2; Meyers, The Human Body and the Law, 3rd edn; Lang and McHale, Medical Law, 4th edn; Skegg, 44 Anglo-Am.L.R. 412 (1974); Smith [1976] Crim. L.R. 622; Dickens, 27 U. of Tor. L.J. 142 (1977); Matthews, 36 C.L.P. 193 (1983); Harris, 16 O.J.L.S. 55 (1996); Mason and Laurie, 64 M.L.R. 710 (2001); Nwabueze, 16 Med. L. Rev. 201 (2008); Harmon and Laurie, 69 C.L.J. 476 (2010). See also the Report of the Committee of Inquiry into Human Fertilization and Embryology (Warnock Report), Cmnd.9314, 1984.

Replace the first paragraph with:

It is been said that, "the one person who is least likely to have property rights in body parts is the person from whom these parts were taken".[609] In general, the law recognises no right of property in a dead body or any part thereof,[610] and for this reason human remains cannot ordinarily be considered goods capable of being bought and sold.[611] But there is probably no universal rule to this effect: human hair has been bought and sold for wig-making for centuries, and body parts are capable of being stolen.[612] The law relating to human tissue, organs (e.g. kidneys used for transplants[613]), bodily products (e.g. hair, blood, urine) and genetic materials (e.g. ova, sperm[614] and embryos[615]) has developed rapidly in recent years, and there is now a growing literature on the subject.

[609] Mason and Laurie, 64 M.L.R. 710, 719 (2001).

[610] Williams v Williams (1882) 20 Ch. D. 659 at 664–665; Dobson v North Tyneside Health Authority [1997] 1 W.L.R. 596; L v Human Fertilisation and Embryology Authority [2008] EWHC 2149 (Fam); (2008) 104 B.M.L.R. 200; Yearworth v North Bristol NHS Trust [2009] EWCA Civ 37; [2009] 3 W.L.R. 118.

[611] cf. Bourne (Inspector of Taxes) v Norwich Crematorium Ltd [1967] 1 W.L.R. 691 (cremation not "subjection of goods or materials to any process").

[612] R. v Welsh [1974] R.T.R. 478 (urine); R. v Rothery [1976] R.T.R. 550 (blood); R. v Herbert (1960) 25 Jo.Cr.L. 163 (hair). See further Smith, [1976] Crim. L.R. 622.

[613] In R. v Kelly and Lindsay [1999] Q.B. 621, it was suggested, obiter, that it might be possible to bring a prosecution for the theft of a transplantable organ.

[614] cf. ter Neuzen v Korn (1993) 103 D.L.R. (4th) 473 (artificial insemination using HIV infected semen: held (by jury on direction of judge) not a sale of goods: affirmed, [1995] 3 S.C.R. 674; 1995 CanLII 72 (SCC)). See Clark v Macourt [2013] HCA 56 (sale of semen as part of sale of business); Winterton 38(3) Melb. U.L.R. 27 (2014).

[615] Davis v Davis, 842 SW 2d 588 (Tenn. Sup. Ct., 1992) classified preserved embryos as an interim category between people and property "because of their potential for life". See Pieper 23 Creighton L.R. 807 (1990).

Replace the second paragraph with:

In *Dobson v North Tyneside Health Authority*,[616] it was accepted that once a person has, by the lawful exercise of work or skill, so dealt with a human body or part of a human body that it acquired some attributes distinguishing it from a mere corpse (or part thereof) awaiting burial, it could be the subject of property in the ordinary way, and of a right to retain possession. While it was held in the case that fixing the brain in paraffin for use by the coroner did not turn it into property,[617] the court thought a body or body part might constitute property where there had been a process involving, for example, stuffing or embalming a corpse or preserving an anatomical or pathological specimen for a scientific collection, or preserving a body or body parts, such as a double-headed foetus,[618] that have some value for educational or even merely exhibition purposes. It would follow that such items may be the subject of a contract of sale. This use of the application of skill test derives from the Australian case of *Doodeward v Spence*[619] and was again relied on in *A v Leeds Teaching Hospital NHS Trust*.[620] Similarly, in *R. v Kelly and Lindsay*,[621] it was held that body parts are property for the purposes of the Theft Act 1968 s.4,[622] if they have acquired different attributes through the application of skill, such as dissection or preservation techniques, for exhibition or teaching. The court went on to suggest that body parts may be property, without the acquisition of different attributes, if intended for organ transplant, the extraction of DNA, or as evidence in a trial.

[616] *Dobson v North Tyneside Health Authority* [1997] 1 W.L.R. 596.

[617] The principle was drawn from the judgment of Griffith CJ in *Doodeward v Spence* (1908) 6 C.L.R. 406 at 414. See *A v Leeds Teaching Hospital NHS Trust: Re Organ Retention Group Litigation* [2004] EWHC 644 (QB); [2005] Q.B. 506 at [128] (possession of child's body). In Scotland, the removal and retention of organs for non-diagnostic purposes, or where the diagnostic purpose has been fulfilled and the retention is not for research, is a legal wrong for which damages by way of solatium can be claimed, and the Human Tissues Act 1961 (now the Human Tissue (Scotland) Act 2006) does not affect this position where the procedure has not been authorised: *Stevens v Yorkhill NHS Trust*, 2006 S.L.T. 889.

[618] As in *Doodeward v Spence* (1908) 6 C.L.R. 406.

[619] *Doodeward v Spence* (1908) 6 C.L.R. 406. cf. *Re Cresswell* [2018] QSC 142 (Sup. Ct. (Qld)).

[620] *A v Leeds Teaching Hospital NHS Trust: Re Organ Retention Group Litigation* [2004] EWHC 644 (QB); [2005] Q.B. 506.

[621] *R. v Kelly and Lindsay* [1999] Q.B. 621.

[622] Under this provision "property" is much broader than the definition of "goods" in the Sale of Goods Act 1979 and includes "money and all other property, real or personal, including things in action and other intangible property".

Replace title footnote 669 with:

Fixtures[669]

1-095   [669] Bennett, "Attachment of Chattels to Land" in Palmer and McKendrick, *Interests in Goods*, 2nd edn, Ch.11; Megarry and Wade, *The Law of Real Property*, 8th edn, paras 22-001 et seq.

Replace footnote 676 with:

[676] Megarry and Wade, *The Law of Real Property*, 8th edn, paras 22-011 et seq.

(b)   Classes of Goods

Existing and future goods

Replace paragraph with:

1-102   Section 5(1) of the Act provides that:

"... the goods which form the subject of a contract of sale may be either existing goods, owned or possessed[719] by the seller, or goods to be manufactured or acquired by him after the making of the contract of sale, in this Act called future goods."[720]

It is clear that goods, which the seller neither owns nor possesses, may be existing in an everyday sense since they are in existence and yet they are future goods for the purposes of the Act. In *Varley v Whipp*[721] the contract was for the sale of a reaping machine, which at the time was owned by, and in the possession of, a third party.[722] The statutory definition of "future goods" refers simply to goods to be manufactured or acquired by the seller. In *Kulkarni v Manor Credit (Davenham) Ltd*,[723] Rix LJ remarked:

"That reflects a completely standard way of the world. Sellers and buyers are forever agreeing to sell and buy what sellers at the time of agreement do not then own, for the goods in question have to be fabricated or sourced and acquired before the time when property is to pass."[724]

A more elaborate classification may be made as follows: (a) goods to be manufactured by the seller, whether from materials which are now in existence or not; (b) goods which are to become, or may become, the property[725] of the seller, whether by purchase, gift, succession, occupation[726] or otherwise[727]; (c) goods expected to come into existence as the property of the seller in the ordinary course of nature, e.g. the young to be born of livestock, or the milk to be produced by cows; (d) things attached to or forming part of land (whether belonging to the seller or another) which are to be severed in the future, e.g. minerals to be won, timber to be cut, fixtures to be detached[728]; and (e) crops in the category *fructus industriales* to be grown by the seller in the future.[729]

[719] See below, para.1-106.

[720] The definition of future goods is repeated in the 1979 Act s.61(1).

[721] *Varley v Whipp* [1900] 1 Q.B. 513.

[722] See also, *Arla Foods UK Plc v Barnes* [2008] EWHC 2851; [2009] 1 B.C.L.C. 699 at [46]. It is clear that a contract for future goods may be either specific or unascertained: see below, paras 1-113 to 1-114.

[723] *Kulkarni v Manor Credit (Davenham) Ltd* [2010] EWCA Civ 69; [2010] 2 All E.R. (Comm) 101.

[724] *Kulkarni v Manor Credit (Davenham) Ltd* [2010] EWCA Civ 69; [2010] 2 All E.R. (Comm) 101 at [9].

[725] Or, possibly, to come into the seller's possession: see the wording of the 1979 Act s.5(1).

[726] e.g. wild creatures: see above, para.1-088.

[727] *Hughes v Pendragon Sabre Ltd (t/a Porsche Centre Bolton)* [2016] EWCA Civ 18; [2016] Lloyd's Rep. 311 (agreement by dealer to sell a car to a customer in the event of it being allocated to the dealer by the manufacturer).

[728] Goods in classes (c) and (d) may in some cases be said to have a "potential existence": see below, para.1-106.

[729] Such crops, if already growing, and things in class (d) which are agreed to be severed before sale or under the contract of sale are by the 1979 Act s.61(1) goods and, it seems, existing goods within the statutory definition, but see above, para.1-100.

Obligation of both parties conditional

Replace footnote 759 with:

[759] "There may be a contract for the sale of goods the acquisition of which by the seller depends on a contingency which may or may not happen." On whether there is a conditional sale contract under s.5(2), severable from a broader service contract, see *Stocks Fly Fishery v Commissioners for Her Majesty's Revenue and Customs* [2016] UK FTT 0218 (TC) (charge for use of fishery dependent upon whether angler elected to keep the catch).

1-111

Specific goods

Replace footnote 767 with:

[767] This sentence was cited in *AerCap Partners 1 Ltd v Aviva Asset Management AB* [2010] EWHC 2431 (Comm); [2010] 2 C.L.C. 578 at [56].

1-114

(c)   Part Interests in Goods

Part owners

Replace the first paragraph with:
     The Sale of Goods Act 1979 s.2(2) states that there may be a contract of sale between one part owner and another. It is arguable that this provision is wide enough to include the transfer by a tenant in common of the whole of that tenant's interest or of a portion only of it (so that, in consequence, the proportions in which

1-121

the part owners hold their shares are altered).[801] The subsection does not refer expressly to certain other transactions which appear analogous, for example, the transfer by the owner of a part interest in goods of the whole of that interest to a third party, or the transfer by the owner of goods of one or more part interests in them so as to make the transferee or transferees and the original owner co-owners.[802] There was some doubt prior to 1995 whether these transactions were all sales of goods within the Act, but the Sale of Goods (Amendment) Act 1995 has amended the definition of goods in s.61(1) by adding the words "and includes an undivided share in goods",[803] so it would now seem clear that this is the case. A person who has agreed to buy goods is in no sense the owner of such goods, and therefore cannot make another a part owner of them. All that can be done is assign in part, or charge, the owner's rights under the contract.

[801] *Goode on Commercial Law*, 5th edn, p.219, n.82 expresses the view that there cannot be a contract of sale unless the transferor intends to part with the whole of their interest.

[802] In *Goode on Commercial Law*, 5th edn, p.219, n.82 it is argued that the latter of these transactions would be outside the statutory definition of a contract of sale—even, it would appear, after the 1995 amendments. The Law Commissions, however, took a contrary view, stating that the new definition "would .... make it clear not only that there can be a sale of an undivided share in goods, whether by a sole owner or by someone who is already a part owner, but also that such a sale is a sale of goods for the purposes of the Act" (*Sale of Goods forming Part of a Bulk* (Law Com. No.215, 1993, para.5.3). If, as is submitted, this latter view is correct, it would follow that a part-owner may also make a sale of a portion only of an interest since that interest is now defined in the Act as goods.

[803] See above, para.1-081.

(d)   Non-existent Goods

Alternative construction: seller absolutely liable

Replace footnote 848 with:

1-132   [848] *McRae v Commonwealth Disposals Commission* (1950) 84 C.L.R. 377. See Slade, (1954) 70 L.Q.R. 389, 396-397; Shatwell, (1955) 33 Can. Bar. Rev.164; Gava, (2009) 9 O.U.C.L.J. 141.

CHAPTER 2

FORMATION OF THE CONTRACT

1. AGREEMENT

Application of general contractual principles

Replace footnote 3 with:

³ e.g. *Chitty on Contracts*, 33rd edn, Vol.1 Ch.2.   **2-001**

Offer distinguished from invitation to treat

Replace the first paragraph with:

An offer, which is intended to be binding on the person making it and capable   **2-002**
of acceptance without further negotiation, must be distinguished from an invitation to treat, which is a statement or conduct inviting the making of an offer.⁷ The
use of a word such as "offer" in an advertisement is not necessarily determinative
of its legal nature.⁸ In the law of sale of goods, it is well settled that the display of
goods in a shop or shop-window is ordinarily⁹ nothing more than an invitation to
treat.¹⁰ The shopkeeper does not make an offer to sell; it is the customer who makes
an offer to buy, which the shopkeeper is free to accept or reject. There is therefore
no sale or agreement to sell, even in a self-service shop or supermarket,¹¹ until the
seller assents, and the latter is not bound to sell at the price which has been
advertised or displayed.¹² On the other hand, where goods are exhibited for sale on
an unattended stall¹³ or in an automatic vending machine,¹⁴ the display may itself
be construed as an offer capable of acceptance by the act of the customer.¹⁵ A similar
construction may be appropriate in the case of a contract made in response to a webpage advertisement, where the buyer is required to give consent to purchase by
technological means, e.g. by clicking on an icon on a computer screen,¹⁶ but in others most contracts made online or by email the normal rule is likely to apply.¹⁷

---

⁷ *Chitty on Contracts*, 33rd edn, Vol.1 para.2-007.

⁸ *Datec Electronic Holdings Ltd v United Parcels Ltd* [2007] UKHL 23; [2007] 1 W.L.R. 1325. See also,
Bigg v Boyd Gibbins Ltd [1971] 1 W.L.R. 913 ("acceptance" construed as offer).

⁹ But circumstances may show that the seller does intend the display to be an offer: cf. *R. v Warwickshire
CC Ex p. Johnson* [1993] 2 W.L.R. 1 (statement "We will beat any TV HiFi and Video price by £20 on
the spot" held to be a "continuing offer" to sell at such a price), distinguished in *DSG Retail Ltd v
Oxfordshire CC* [2001] 1 W.L.R. 1765.

¹⁰ *Timothy v Simpson* (1834) 6 Car. & P. 499 at 500; *Pharmaceutical Society of Great Britain v Boots
Cash Chemists (Southern) Ltd* [1952] 2 Q.B. 795 (supermarket); *Fisher v Bell* [1961] 1 Q.B. 394
(window display); *Esso Petroleum Co Ltd v Customs & Excise Commissioners* [1976] 1 W.L.R. 1 at 11
(statement of price of petrol on pumps not an offer to sell; contrast the case of "self-service" pumps,

where it appears that the garage makes an open offer to sell at the stated prices: *Re Charge Card Services Ltd* [1989] Ch. 497 at 510). In penal statutes, the term "offer for sale" has sometimes been construed less strictly, as equivalent to "expose for sale": contrast *Fisher v Bell* [1961] 1 W.L.R. 1, *Wiles v Maddison* [1943] 1 All E.R. 315, *Partridge v Crittenden* [1968] 1 W.L.R. 1204 and *British Car Auctions Ltd v Wright* [1972] 1 W.L.R. 1519 ("offer to sell"); with *Keating v Horwood* (1926) 28 Cox C.C. 198 and *Phillips v Dalziel* [1948] 2 All E.R. 810. The Restriction of Offensive Weapons Act 1959 s.1 (as amended by the Restriction of Offensive Weapons Act 1961 s.1) nullifies the decision in *Fisher v Bell* [1961] 1 W.L.R. 1, by the use of the wider phrase "offers ... or exposes or has in his possession for the purpose of sale". This sort of wording has been widely adopted in regulations designed to control trade in particular goods: e.g. the Pedal Bicycles (Safety) Regulations 2010 (SI 2010/98) r.8. The approach taken in *Fisher v Bell* and *Partridge v Crittenden* of applying a strict contractual analysis rather than giving priority to the mischief the statutes sought to address was questioned in *Wm Morrisons Supermarkets Plc v Reading BC* [2012] EWHC 1358 (Admin); [2012] 2 Cr. App. R. 16 at [25], [30] (sale of tobacco to a person aged under 18 years). But see Munday, (2013) 72 (1) C.L.J. 50.

[11] *Pharmaceutical Society of Great Britain v Boots Cash Chemists (Southern) Ltd* [1952] 2 Q.B. 795. As regards the passing of property when goods are sold in a self-service shop, see *Martin v Puttick* [1968] 2 Q.B. 82; *Lacis v Cashmarts* [1969] 2 Q.B. 400; *Pilgram v Rice-Smith* [1977] Cr. App. R. 142; *Davies v Leighton* [1978] Crim. L.R. 575; *R. v Morris* [1984] A.C. 320 at 332; and below, paras 5-026, 5-082.

[12] There may be an offence committed if the retailer refuses to sell or demands a higher price with the intention of promoting another product ("bait and switch"): Consumer Protection from Unfair Trading Regulations 2008 (SI 2008/1277) reg.3(4)(d) and Sch.1 para.6. See previously, Consumer Protection Act 1987 s.20; *R. v Warwickshire CC Ex p. Johnson* [1993] 2 W.L.R. 1.

[13] cf. *Chapelton v Barry Urban DC* [1940] 1 K.B. 532 (chairs for hire on self-service basis, receipt given by attendant after acceptance).

[14] cf. *Thornton v Shoe Lane Parking Ltd* [1971] 2 Q.B. 163 (car park); *Merton LBC v Sinclair Collis Ltd* [2011] 1 W.L.R. 570 (offence of selling tobacco to a minor does not require face-to-face dealing and can be committed through a vending machine).

[15] A similar inference can be drawn in all situations where the customer's act in selecting the goods is, for practical purposes, irreversible—e.g. where a customer fills the petrol tank of a car from a self-service pump (*Re Charge Card Services Ltd* [1989] Ch. 497), or chooses the items for a meal from a self-service hotplate.

[16] The so-called "click-wrap" contracts. In some cases, contracts of sale may be concluded automatically without human input at the time by either seller or buyer—e.g. where a stock control system is programmed to order replacement of items which fall below a set threshold. Questions such as those discussed in the present paragraph are likely to be resolved by the terms of an electronic data interchange (EDI) agreement between the parties.

[17] *RTS Flexible Systems Ltd v Molkerei Alois Müller GmbH & Co KG* [2010] UKSC 14; [2010] 1 W.L.R. 753. See *M & J Marine Engineering Services Co Ltd v Shipshore Ltd* [2009] EWHC 2031 (Comm) (letters and emails); *Baillie Estates Ltd v Du Pont (UK) Ltd* [2009] CSOH 95 (email); *Vitol SA v Conoil Plc* [2009] EWHC 1144; [2009] 2 Lloyd's Rep. 466 (telephone, email and documents); *Air Studios (Lyndhurst) Ltd v Lombard North Central Plc* [2012] EWHC 3162 (QB); [2013] 1 Lloyd's Rep. 63 (email).

Replace footnote 20 with:

2-002   [20] *Grainger & Sons v Gough* [1896] A.C. 325 at 334; *Esso Petroleum Co Ltd v Customs & Excise Commissioners* [1976] 1 W.L.R. 1 at 11. See, however, *Chitty on Contracts*, 33rd edn, Vol.1 para.2-017.

Sales by auction

Replace the first paragraph with:

2-004   An auction sale is a sale by competitive bidding, normally held in public,[26] at which prospective purchasers are invited to make successively increasing bids for the property, which is then usually sold to the highest bidder.[27] The advertisement of an auction is not an offer to hold it.[28] There are three contracts involved in an auction sale. The first is the contract between the owner of the goods and the highest bidder at the auction. The second is the contract between the owner of the goods and the auctioneer, under which the owner entrusts the goods to the auctioneer, who promises not to part with possession except against payment by the highest bidder and obtains a lien on the proceeds for commission and charges. The third is the contract between the highest bidder and the auctioneer, which allows an auctioneer who does part with the goods before payment to sue the buyer for the price.[29] Only the first of these contracts is a contract of sale of goods. The Sale of Goods Act 1979 s.57 codifies, in regard to sales of goods, some of the special rules governing auction sales.[30]

[26] "Online" or "web" auctions conducted over the internet are now common. In such auctions, there is no act of the auctioneer corresponding to the fall of the hammer; instead, it is usual to set a closing time on the website, by which time all bids must be placed and (unless there is a reserve price which has not been reached) the highest bid is deemed to have been accepted when the auction closes. Unlike ordinary auctions, the terms upon which bidders participate typically restricts the ability to revoke a bid. Online auctions have been held to be auctions within the Sale of Goods Act 1923 s.60 (which closely resembles the Sale of Goods Act 1979 s.57), in New South Wales: *Peter Smythe v Vincent Thomas* [2007] NSWSC 844. Webcast auctions differ from online or web auctions. They are a development from ordinary auctions, which have long permitted absent bidders to place bids by telephone during the auction. In webcast auctions bidders may be present, but most participate by a live internet link. They can ask questions about the lots and bid by telephone or by instant messaging (through the internet). The legal analysis of such auctions is the same as for a traditional auction. Where goods are sold at "public auction" consumer rights under the Consumer Contracts (Information, Cancellation and Additional Charges) Regulations 2013 (SI 2013/3134) are limited; the term goods or services offered by a trader to consumers through "a transparent, competitive bidding procedure run by an auctioneer", the consumers "attend or are given the possibility to attend in person", and "the successful bidder is bound to purchase" (reg.5). The regulations apply to contracts entered into on or after 13 June 2014.

[27] *Harvela Investments Ltd v Royal Trust Co of Canada (CI) Ltd* [1986] A.C. 207; cf. *Frewen v Hays* (1912) 106 L.T. 516 at 518.

[28] *Harris v Nickerson* (1873) L.R. 8 Q.B. 286.

[29] *Chelmsford Auctions Ltd v Poole* [1973] Q.B. 542. Thus, an action for breach of the terms implied by the Sale of Goods Act cannot normally be brought against the auctioneer: *Affinity Auction Group Inc v Manheim Auto Auction*, 2009 BCSC 873; *Thwaytes v Sotheby's* [2015] EWHC 36 (Ch); [2016] 1 W.L.R. 2143. For the liability of the auctioneer: *Tkachuk v Saskatoon Auction Mart Ltd* (2007) 10 W.W.R. 419. An auctioneer to whom goods have been consigned owes a duty of care to the consignor which varies according to the nature of the auction house, so that "a leading international auction house" will owe a more extensive duty than "a provincial auction house": *Luxmore-May v Messenger May Baverstock* [1990] 1 W.L.R. 1009; *Thwaytes v Sotheby's* [2015] EWHC 36 (Ch); [2016] 1 W.L.R. 2143. The auctioneer may be negligent in advising an auction estimate that no reasonable valuer would have placed on the item where that estimate is used to determine the price for private sale *Coleridge v Sotheby's* [2012] EWHC 370 (Ch).

[30] cf. Uniform Commercial Code para.2-328. With limited exceptions therein, the Consumer Rights Act 2015 does not apply to auction sales of second hand goods where the buyer attends in person. It achieves this effect by deeming the buyer not to be a consumer: s.2(5), (6). Auction sales were specifically excluded from the Consumer Protection (Distance Selling) Regulations 2000 (below, para.14-195): see reg.5(1)(f). These regulations have been replaced by Consumer Contracts (Information, Cancellation and Additional Charges) Regulations 2013 for contracts entered into on or after June 13, 2014; reg.28(1)(g) excludes public auction sales from the right to cancel the contract. The Consumer Protection from Unfair Trading Regulations 2008 (SI 2008/1277) apply to auction sales.

Replace footnote 32 with:

[32] *Coys of Kensington Automobiles Ltd v Pugliese* [2011] EWHC 655 (QB); [2011] 2 All E.R. (Comm.) 664 at [15]. This is so even where the auctioneer has accepted a bid in breach of the advertised conditions of sale, and notwithstanding that another bidder was prepared to pay a higher price: *Hordern House Pty Ltd v Arnold* [1989] V.R. 402.

Sales without reserve

Replace footnote 41 with:

[41] *Barry v Davies* [2000] 1 W.L.R. 1962; *Warlow v Harrison* (1858) 1 E. & E. 295; cf. *Harris v Nickerson* (1873) L.R. 8 Q.B. 286 at 288. Consideration would be provided by bidding for the goods in reliance on the auctioneer's advertisement, which is both a detriment to the bidder, since there is the risk of being bound, and a benefit to the auctioneer, as the bidding is driven up: see *Chitty on Contracts*, 33rd edn, Vol.1 para.2-020; and *Barry v Davies* [2000] 1 W.L.R. 1962.

2-005

Revocation of offer

Replace footnote 51 with:

2-010 [51] *Chitty on Contracts*, 33rd edn, Vol.1 para.2-095. There is no exception for revocations sent by post or similar means: cf. below, para.2-015.

Acceptance

Replace paragraph with:

2-011 In order to make a valid contract an offer must be accepted; the acceptance must be unqualified[52]; and, as a general rule, it must be communicated[53] to the offeror.[54] These principles apply to contracts for the sale of goods. In cases where there have been prolonged negotiations or correspondence between the parties, it may be difficult to determine whether (and if so, at what point) agreement has in fact been reached, or whether an agreement once concluded has been effectively varied at a later stage.[55] But acceptance may be inferred from conduct: for example, by sending goods which have been ordered.[56] In these circumstances the normal requirement that acceptance should be communicated may be taken to have been waived by the offeror, but whether the offer can be so construed is a question for the court to determine.[57]

[52] Contrast Vienna Convention on Contracts for the International Sale of Goods Art.19(2): "a reply to an offer which purports to be an acceptance but contains additional or different terms which do not materially alter the terms of the offer constitutes an acceptance unless the offeror, without undue delay, objects orally to the discrepancy or dispatches a notice to that effect. If he does not so object, the terms of the contract are the terms of the offer with the modifications contained in the acceptance". cf. Uniform Commercial Code Art.2-207; and see below, para.2-012.

[53] For the meaning of "communicated", see *Entores Ltd v Miles Far East Corp* [1955] 2 Q.B. 327 at 332; and *Tenax Steamship Co Ltd v The Brimnes (Owners) (The Brimnes)* [1975] Q.B. 929. See Mik, (2011) 19 I.J.L. & I.T. 324.

[54] *Chitty on Contracts*, 33rd edn, Vol.1 paras 2-044 et seq.

[55] *Compagnie de Commerce etc v Parkinson Stove Co* [1953] 2 Lloyd's Rep. 487; *Port Sudan Cotton Co v Govindaswamy Chettiar & Sons* [1977] 1 Lloyd's Rep. 166; *Pagnan SpA v Granaria BV* [1986] 1 Lloyd's Rep. 547; *Pagnan SpA v Feed Products Ltd* [1987] 2 Lloyd's Rep. 601; *Manatee Touring Co v Oceanbulk Maritime SA* [1999] 2 All E.R. (Comm) 306; *Gordon Russell (UK) Ltd v Warwick* [2006] EWCA Civ 1851.

[56] *Chitty on Contracts*, 33rd edn, Vol.1 para.2-029; cf. *Brogden v Metropolitan Ry* (1877) 2 App. Cas. 666; *Carlyle Finance Ltd v Pallas Industrial Finance* [1999] 1 All E.R. (Comm) 659 (delivery of car to customer before formal acceptance of offer); cf. *Greenhouse v Paysafe Financial Services Ltd* [2018] EWHC 3296 (Comm) at [13] (variation through conduct). On "shrink-wrap" contracts (where a buyer of computer software is deemed to have accepted the terms of a licence to use the software by the act of opening the package in which the disk or other medium is contained), see below, para.2-012.

[57] cf. *Rapalli v KL Take Ltd* [1958] 2 Lloyd's Rep. 469; *Boyers & Co v D & R Duke* [1905] 2 I.R. 617.

Replace title footnote 58 with:

Incorporation of standard or printed terms[58]

2-012 [58] See *Chitty on Contracts*, 33rd edn, Vol.1 paras 13-008 et seq.; Lawson, *Exclusion Clauses and Unfair Contract Terms*, 12th edn; and see also below, Ch.13.

Replace the first paragraph with:

A problem, which commonly arises, is whether a party is bound by terms embodied in a notice, ticket, receipt or other standard form document drawn up by the other party and introduced, or allegedly introduced, into the contract at some stage of the negotiations. If the document has been signed, the terms contained in it are incorporated in the contract, whether or not the party signing has read or understood it.[59] If the document is not signed, the terms will not be incorporated unless they were brought to the party's notice before or at the time of the making of the contract. This will be held to be the case if the other party has taken such steps as were reasonably sufficient to draw attention to the existence of the conditions.[60] Where the clauses contained in a document include a particularly onerous or unusual condition, the party seeking to rely on it must show that it was brought fairly and reasonably to the attention of the other party[61]: "the more unusual a clause is, the greater the notice which must be given of it".[62] A party may also be held bound by the other's standard terms if these have habitually been used or referred to in a course of dealing between the parties,[63] but for this purpose consistent dealing to a substantial extent rather than a number of scattered transactions must be shown.[64] Where a contract is made in a commercial setting, it appears that the court will more readily infer that the parties intended to deal on standard terms, particularly where these are well known, or customary in the trade.[65] The express inclusion of some terms only out of a set of standard terms may lead to the inference that the remainder of the set were not intended to apply.[66]

[59] *The Luna* [1920] P. 22 (towage); *L'Estrange v F Graucob Ltd* [1934] 2 K.B. 394; *PS Chellaram & Co Ltd v China Ocean Shipping Co (The "Zhi Jiang Kou")* [1991] 1 Lloyd's Rep. 493 (S.Ct. N.S.W.; carriage of goods; very small print); *Coys of Kensington Automobiles Ltd v Pugliese* [2011] EWHC 655 (QB); [2011] 2 All E.R. (Comm) 664 at [45]; cf. *Gordon v Krieg*, 2013 BCSC 842 at [149]. There is an exception in the case of misrepresentation: *Curtis v Chemical Cleaning & Dyeing Co* [1951] 1 K.B. 805 (cleaning contract).

[60] *Parker v South Eastern Ry Co* (1877) 2 C.P.D. 416 at 421, 423; *Richardson, Spence & Co v Rowntree* [1894] A.C. 217; *Hood v Anchor Line (Henderson Bros) Ltd* [1918] A.C. 837 at 844; *Thompson v LM & S Ry* [1930] 1 K.B. 41 (cases on carriage of passengers); *Burnett v Westminster Bank Ltd* [1966] 1 Q.B. 742 (banking).

[61] *Interfoto Picture Library Ltd v Stiletto Visual Programmes Ltd* [1989] Q.B. 433 (bailment); cf. *Parker v South Eastern Ry Co* (1877) 2 C.P.D. 416 at 428 (carriage of passenger); *J Spurling Ltd v Bradshaw* [1956] 1 W.L.R. 461 at 466 (bailment); *Thornton v Shoe Lane Parking Ltd* [1971] 2 Q.B. 163 at 170, 172–173 (parking); *Hollingworth v Southern Ferries Ltd* [1977] 2 Lloyd's Rep. 70 at 78–79 (carriage of passenger); *Ryanair Ltd v Billigfluege.de GMBH* [2010] IEHC 47 at [21]–[23] (screen scraping: terms brought fairly to attention through hyperlink); cf. *Goodlife Foods Ltd v Hall Fire Protection Ltd* [2018] EWCA Civ 1371; [2018] C.T.L.C. 265 (application of Unfair Contract Terms Act 1977).

[62] *J Spurling Ltd v Bradshaw* [1956] 1 W.L.R. 461 at 466.

[63] *Rapalli v KL Take Ltd* [1958] 2 Lloyd's Rep. 469 at 484; *Henry Kendall & Sons v William Lillico & Sons Ltd* [1969] 2 A.C. 31; *SIAT Di Del Ferro v Tradax Overseas Ltd* [1978] 2 Lloyd's Rep. 470; *McCrone v Boots Farm Sales Ltd*, 1981 S.L.T. 103; *George Mitchell (Chesterhall) Ltd v Finney Lock Seeds Ltd* [1983] Q.B. 284 at 295 (affirmed [1983] 2 A.C. 803); *Johnson Matthey Bankers Ltd v State Trading Corp of India Ltd* [1984] 1 Lloyd's Rep. 427; cf. *J Spurling Ltd v Bradshaw* [1956] 1 W.L.R. 461; *Cockerton v Naviera Aznar SA* [1960] 2 Lloyd's Rep. 450 (carriage of passenger); *Transmotors Ltd v Robertson Buckley & Co Ltd* [1970] 1 Lloyd's Rep. 224; *Eastman Chemical International AG v NMT Trading Ltd* [1972] 2 Lloyd's Rep. 25; *Gillespie Bros & Co Ltd v Roy Bowles Transport Ltd* [1973] Q.B. 400 (cases on carriage of goods); *Lamport & Holt Lines Ltd v Coubro & Scrutton (M & I) Ltd* [1981] 2 Lloyd's Rep. 659 (affirmed [1982] 2 Lloyd's Rep. 42) (contract for services); *Circle Freight International Ltd v Medeast Gulf Exports Ltd* [1988] 2 Lloyd's Rep. 427 (carriage of goods); *Banque Paribas v Cargill International SA* [1992] 1 Lloyd's Rep. 96 at 98; Hoggett, (1970) 33 M.L.R. 518; *SKNL (UK) Ltd v Toll Global Forwarding* [2012] EWHC 4252 (Comm); [2013] 2 Lloyd's Rep. 115 (carriage of goods).

[64] *Chevron International Oil Co Ltd v A/S Sea Team* [1983] 2 Lloyd's Rep. 356; cf. *McCutcheon v David MacBrayne Ltd* [1964] 1 W.L.R. 125 (carriage of goods); *Hollier v Rambler Motors Ltd* [1972] 2 Q.B. 71 (repairs to car); *British Crane Hire Corp Ltd v Ipswich Plant Hire Ltd* [1975] Q.B. 303 (hire of machine); *Salsi v Jet Air Services Ltd* [1977] 2 Lloyd's Rep. 57 (carriage by air); *Lamport & Holt Lines Ltd v Coubro & Scrutton (M & I) Ltd* [1981] 2 Lloyd's Rep. 659; *Neptune Orient Lines Ltd v JVC (UK) Ltd* [1983] 2 Lloyd's Rep. 438 (carriage of goods); *La Rosa v Nudrill Pty Ltd* [2013] W.A.S.C.A. 18 (carriage of goods); *Capes (Hatherden) Ltd v Western Arable Services Ltd* [2009] EWHC 3065 (QB); [2010] 1 Lloyd's Rep. 477 (sale of barley); Transformers and Rectifiers Ltd v Needs Ltd [2015] EWHC 269 (TCC); [2015] B.L.R. 336 (sale of gaskets).

[65] *Chevron International Oil Co Ltd v A/S Sea Team* [1983] 2 Lloyd's Rep. 356; cf. *British Crane Hire Corp Ltd v Ipswich Plant Hire Ltd* [1975] Q.B. 303 (hire of machine).

[66] *Johnson Matthey Bankers Ltd v State Trading Corp of India Ltd* [1984] 1 Lloyd's Rep. 427.

In the third paragraph, after "offered for sale", replace "on" with:
through

In the fifth paragraph replace footnote 74 with:

[74] See *Van Tassell v United Marketing Group LLC* 795 F.Supp.2d 770 (N.D.Ill, 2007). In *Fteja v Facebook, Inc* 841 F.Supp.2d 829 (S.D.N.Y., 2012) there was sufficient notice of terms where a statement immediately above the "sign up" button stated that clicking indicated the person had read and agreed to the terms (also, *Swift v Zynga Game Network Inc* 805 F.Supp.2d 904 (N.D. Cal., 2011); cf. *Nguyen v Barnes & Noble Inc* 763 F.3d 1171 (9th Cir. August 18, 2014)). In *Century 21 Canada LP v Rogers Communications Inc* 2011 BCSC 1196 (Supreme Court, British Columbia), a business-to-business browse-wrap was enforced because of evidence that the buyer had notice of the terms, including use of similar terms on its own website. The New York Circuit Court of Appeals (applying California law) questioned the value of classifying agreements as either click-wrap or browse-wrap and instead determined the issue by looking at whether there was reasonable notice of terms (which might be satisifed by a reasonably conspicuous hyperlink) and unambiguous manifestation of assent to those terms: *Meyer v Kalanick*No. 16-2750 (2d Cir. 17 August 2017).

In the sixth paragraph, replace footnote 77 with:

[77] Note that under the Consumer Protection (Distance Selling) Regulations 2000 (SI 2000/2334) reg.13(d), the right to cancel a contract for the supply of audio or video recordings or computer software may be forfeited if the consumer unseals them; see now Consumer Contracts (Information, Cancellation and Additional Charges) Regulations 2013 (SI 2013/3134) reg.28(3) for contracts entered into on or after 13 June 2014. Under the Consumer Rights Act 2015 Ch.3, in a contract between a trader and a consumer for the supply of digital content, information supplied by the trader in compliance with the obligation under the 2013 Regulations to provide pre-contractual information is treated as a term of the contract (s.36. Also, s.37). That Act's provisions on unfair terms apply to all "consumer notices" (s.62(2)).

Replace title footnote 78 with:

The "battle of forms"[78]

2-013   [78] See *Chitty on Contracts*, 33rd edn, Vol.1 paras 2-033 to 2-037; Adams, [1983] J.B.L. 297.

Replace footnote 79 with:

[79] *A Davies & Co (Shopfitters) Ltd v William Old Ltd* (1969) 67 L.G.R. 395; cf. *British Road Services v AV Crutchley Ltd* [1968] 1 All E.R. 811 at 817 (affirming [1967] 2 All E.R. 785); *Port Sudan Cotton Co v Govindaswamy Chettiar & Sons* [1977] 2 Lloyd's Rep. 5; *Butler Machine Tool Co Ltd v Ex-Cell-O Corp (England) Ltd* [1979] 1 W.L.R. 401; *OTM Ltd v Hydranautics* [1981] 2 Lloyd's Rep. 211; *Zambia Steel & Building Supplies Ltd v James Clark & Eaton Ltd* [1986] 2 Lloyd's Rep. 225; *Chichester Joinery Ltd v John Mowlem & Co Plc* (1987) 42 Build L.R. 100. In the *Butler Machine Tool* case, Lord Denning MR favoured the broader approach of construing all the documents together: see *Sterling Hydraulics Ltd v Dichtomatik Ltd* [2007] EWHC 2004 (QB); [2007] 1 Lloyd's Rep. 8; *J Murphy & Co Ltd v Johnston Precast Ltd* [2008] EWHC 3024 (TCC); but the Court of Appeal, broadly, rejected this approach in *Tekdata Interconnections Ltd v Amphenol Ltd* [2009] EWCA Civ 1209, following the majority in *Butler Machine Tool; GHSP Inc v AB Electronic Ltd* [2010] EWHC 1828 (Comm); [2011] 1 Lloyd's Rep. 432; *Specialist Insulation Ltd v Pro-Duct (Fife) Ltd* [2012] CSOH 79; 2012 S.C.L.R. 641 (construction contract); *Trebor Bassett Holdings Ltd v ADT Fire and Security Plc* [2012] EWCA Civ 1158; [2012] B.L.R. 441; *Transformers and Rectifiers Ltd v Needs Ltd* [2015] EWHC 269 (TCC); [2015] T.C.L.R. 2; *John Graham Construction Ltd v F.K. Lowry Piling Ltd* [2015] NIQB 40. On the determination of which law governs the contract, see *Conductive Inkjet Technology Ltd v Uni-Pexel Displays Inc* [2013] EWHC 2968 (Ch) (non-disclosure agreement relating to exchange of information).

Unsolicited goods

Replace paragraph with:

2-014   At common law a person to whom goods are sent with an express or implied offer to sell them may be deemed to have accepted such an offer and become the buyer by (for instance) using the goods, and perhaps by any conduct which makes it impossible to restore them in integrum to the seller.[82] Acceptance cannot, however, be inferred from mere silence or inactivity, even if the offeror so stipulates.[83] These rules were modified by the Unsolicited Goods and Services Act

1971, which provided by s.1 that in specified circumstances a person who received unsolicited goods could treat the transaction as an unconditional gift of the goods. This provision has now been repealed,[84] and replaced (where the recipient of the goods is a consumer[85]) by the Consumer Protection from Unfair Trading Regulations 2008 (as amended).[86] The regulation applies to "inertia selling": "Demanding immediate or deferred payment for or the return or safekeeping of products supplied by the trade, but not solicited by the consumer, except where the product is a substitute …". In such circumstances, the consumer is "exempted from any obligation to provide consideration". The consumer's consent to payment, or return, or safekeeping of the goods cannot be implied from the absence of a response, and, where the supply of goods is unsolicited, "the consumer may, as between the consumer and the trader, use, deal with or dispose of the goods as if they were an unconditional gift to the consumer".[87] In contrast with s.1 of the 1971 Act, the deemed gift takes effect immediately and is not dependent on the expiration of any period of time or the sending by the recipient of any notice to the supplier. The regulation is also backed by criminal sanctions.

[82] *Chitty on Contracts*, 33rd edn, Vol.1 para.2-005; *Weatherby v Banham* (1832) 5 C. & P. 228.

[83] *Felthouse v Bindley* (1862) 11 C.B.(N.S.) 869; cf. Vienna Convention on the International Sale of Goods, Art.18(1). Exceptionally, it is possible that silence may bind an offeree in some circumstances, e.g. where there has been a course of dealing between the parties in which offers to buy goods have always been accepted as a matter of course by the despatch of the relevant goods; or where the situation gives rise to an estoppel against the offeree; or where the offer is made on a form provided by the offeree which stipulates that silence shall amount to acceptance; although often the circumstances render the silence analogous to conduct: *Rust v Abbey Life Assurance Co Ltd* [1979] 2 Lloyd's Rep. 334 (insurance contract); *Vital SA v Norelf Ltd (The Santa Clara)* [1996] A.C. 800 at 812; *Hotel Aida Opera SARL v Golden Tulip Worldwide BV* [2004] EWHC 1012 (QB) at [92]; Barron, (2009) 7 J.B.L. 633. The question whether an agreement to abandon an arbitration can be inferred from the inactivity of one or both of the parties has been considered in a number of cases: see *Chitty on Contracts*, 33rd edn, paras 2-006, 2-075–2-076; *Austen-Baker*, (2006) 35 C.L.W.R. 247.

[84] See Consumer Protection (Distance Selling) Regulations 2000 reg.22 (which, however, uses the word "omit", rather than words of repeal). It is possible that s.1 is intended to remain in force in regard to contracts other than "distance contracts" (as defined in reg.3(1)), since the Regulations as a whole apply only to such "distance contracts": see reg.4.

[85] Defined (reg.3(1)) as "any natural person who, in contracts to which these Regulations apply, is acting for purposes outside his business".

[86] Consumer Protection from Unfair Trading Regulations 2008 (SI 2008/1277). Amended by Consumer Contracts (Information, Cancellation and Additional Charges) Regulations 2013 (SI 2013/3134) Pt 4 (inertia selling), which applies to contracts entered into on or after 13 June 2014.

[87] Consumer Protection from Unfair Trading Regulations 2008 (SI 2008/1277) reg.27A (as amended by Consumer Contracts (Information, Cancellation and Additional Charges) Regulations 2013 (SI 2013/3134) reg.39) and Sch.1 para.29. Replacing provisions in Consumer Protection (Distance Selling) Regulations 2000 (SI 2000/2334) reg.22 in respect of contracts entered into on or after 13 June 2014.

Replace title footnote 88 with:

Time and place of contract[88]

[88] *Chitty on Contracts*, 33rd edn, Vol.1 Ch.2.

2-015

Replace footnote 90 with:

[90] *Adams v Lindsell* (1818) 1 B. & Ald. 681; *Byrne v van Tienhoven* (1880) 5 C.P.D. 344; *Henthorn v Fraser* [1892] 2 Ch. 27; cf. *Alexander v Steinhardt, Walker & Co* [1903] 2 K.B. 208; *Port Sudan Cotton Co v Govindaswamy Chettiar & Sons* [1977] 1 Lloyd's Rep. 5; contrast *Holwell Securities Ltd v Hughes* [1974] 1 W.L.R. 155 (exercise of option not effective until received). On contracts made by telegram or cable see *Stevenson v McLean* (1880) 5 Q.B.D. 346; *Quenerduaine v Cole* (1883) 32 W.R. 185; *Cowan v O'Connor* (1888) 20 Q.B.D. 640; *Raeburn v Burness* (1895) 1 Com. Cas. 22; *Bruner v Moore* [1904] 1 Ch. 305. As regards the risk of errors in transmission, see *Henkel v Pape* (1870) L.R. 6

Ex. 7; and *Northland Airlines Ltd v Dennis Ferranti Meters Ltd, Times,* 13 February 1970 (reversed on other grounds (1970) 114 S.J. 845). Contrast Vienna Convention on Contracts for the International Sale of Goods Arts 18(2), 24, under which the acceptance becomes effective only when it "reaches" the offeror: in the case of an acceptance sent by post, this means by delivery to the offeror's address. Lord Sumption JSC remarked that, while these "rules provide a perfectly serviceable test for determining whether a contract has been concluded at all... [T]heir deployment for the purpose of determining when or where a contract was made is not at all satisfactory": *Brownlie v Four Seasons Holdings Inc.* [2017] UKSC 80; [2018] 1 W.L.R. 192 at [16].

Replace footnote 91 with:

[91] This analysis is, however, not in accord with the EC Directive on Electronic Commerce (above, para.1-023 and below, para.14-209) which provides (Art.11(1)) that:

"Member States shall ensure, except when otherwise agreed by parties who are not consumers, that in cases where the recipient of the service places his order through technological means, the following principles apply:

— the service provider has to acknowledge the receipt of the recipient's order without undue delay and by electronic means,

— the order and the acknowledgement of receipt are deemed to be received when the parties to whom they are addressed are able to access them."

The latter of these requirements is repeated in virtually identical language in the Electronic Commerce (EC Directive) Regulations 2002 reg.11(2)(a). This could, it is submitted, lead to difficulties if it were held to follow that a message constituting an acceptance of an offer is deemed to be received at the place where the offeror is able to access it, for the service provider could well be situated in a jurisdiction where neither of the parties is based. See further *Chitty on Contracts,* 33rd edn, Vol.1 paras 2-077 to 2-082.

Certainty of terms

Replace footnote 94 with:

2-016 [94] *Chitty on Contracts,* 33rd edn, Vol.1 paras 2-120 et seq.; *Courtney & Fairbairn Ltd v Tolaini Bros (Hotels) Ltd* [1975] 1 W.L.R. 297 (building contract). However, if before a contract is formally concluded one party delivers goods which are accepted by the other, the court may be prepared to hold that this has been done pursuant to a preliminary or informal contract containing terms (e.g. as to the quality of the goods) which are not the subject of the continuing negotiations: *Britvic Soft Drinks Ltd v Messer UK Ltd* [2001] 1 Lloyd's Rep. 20 at [70]; affirmed on other grounds [2002] EWCA Civ 548; [2002] 2 Lloyd's Rep. 368.

Replace footnote 102 with:

[102] *Walford v Miles* [1992] A.C. 128. Also, *Barbudev v Eurocom Cable Management Bulgaria Eood* [2012] EWCA Civ 548; [2012] 2 All E.R. (Comm) 963 (side letter only agreement to agree). Later decisions do not entirely preclude the possibility of negotiating a lock-out agreement: *Global Container Lines Ltd v State Black Sea Shipping Co* [1997] EWCA Civ 3007.

Replace the first paragraph with:

2-017   The courts strive, however, to uphold rather than to destroy bargains which the parties believe themselves to have concluded, and this is especially true in commercial dealings in a trade with which both parties are familiar[103]:

"Business men often record the most important agreements in crude and summary fashion; modes of expression sufficient and clear to them in the course of their business may appear to those unfamiliar with the business far from complete or precise. It is accordingly the duty of the court to construe such documents fairly and broadly, without being too astute or subtle in finding defects; but, on the contrary, the court should seek to apply the old maxim of English law, *verba ita sunt intelligenda ut res magis valeat quam pereat.*"[104]

If the court determines on an objective basis that the parties intended to enter into a contract, it will seek to uphold that contract and:

"... strive to give effect to that intention by construing the words which they have used in a way which does not leave the matter to be agreed in the future incapable of being determined in the absence of future agreement."[105]

In accordance with this approach, the court may import terms from trade custom, or from a previous course of dealing between the parties, and it will endeavour to define what is "usual" or what is "reasonable" where the parties have stipulated for "usual" or "reasonable" terms. In *Hillas & Co Ltd v Arcos Ltd*,[106] the House of Lords decided that an option was enforceable, although expressed in vague terms, because the uncertainty could be resolved by reference to the principal contract of which the option was a part, the parties' previous dealings and the practice in their trade. An agreement will be enforceable even if certain facts on which its operation depends are not ascertained at the time of the agreement, as long as they are ascertainable and are ascertained later without further negotiation.[107]

[103] *G Scammell & Nephew Ltd v HC & JG Ouston* [1941] A.C. 251 at 255; *R & J Dempster Ltd v Motherwell Bridge and Engineering Co Ltd* [1964] S.C. 308 at 332; *Total Gas Marketing Ltd v Arco British Ltd* [1998] 2 Lloyd's Rep. 209 at 223; *Pua Hor Ong v Wu You Yang Pty Ltd* [2008] SASC 365 at [45] (sale of land); *Dicker v Scammell* [2005] EWCA Civ 405; [2005] All E.R. 838 (agreement to settle dispute); *Hodgson and Hodgson v Lipson* [2009] EWHC 3111(QB) at [12]; *GE Commercial Corp (Australia) Pty Ltd v Mell Associates Pty Ltd* [2009] NSWSC 787 at [29]; *Durham Tees Valley Airport Ltd v bmibaby Ltd* [2010] EWCA Civ 485; [2011] 1 Lloyd's Rep. 68 (contract to use airport); *Jet2.com Ltd v Blackpool Airport Ltd* [2012] EWCA Civ 417 (contract to permit use of airport requiring "best endeavours"); [2011] 2 All E.R. (Comm) 988; *Astor Management AG v Atalaya Mining Plc* [2017] EWHC 680 (Comm); [2017] 1 C.L.C. 724 at [3] (use of "all reasonable endeavours" in purchase of mining interest); Fridman, (1960) 76 L.Q.R. 521.

[104] *Hillas & Co Ltd v Arcos Ltd* (1932) 147 L.T. 503 at 514; *Mamidoil-Jetoil Greek Petroleum Co SA v Okta Crude Oil Refinery AD* [2001] EWCA Civ 406; [2001] 2 Lloyd's Rep. 76 (oil refining); *iSOFT Group Plc v Misys Holdings Ltd* [2002] EWHC 2094 (Ch) at [75] (affirmed [2003] EWCA Civ 229); cf. Uniform Commercial Code Art.2–204. "It would be a strong thing to declare unenforceable a clause into which the parties have deliberately and expressly entered": *Petromec Inc v Petroleo Brasileiro SA Petrobas (No.3)* [2005] EWCA Civ 891; [2006] 1 Lloyd's Rep. 121 at 153 per Longmore LJ.

[105] *Mamidoil-Jetoil Greek Petroleum Co SA v Okta Crude Oil Refinery AD* [2001] EWCA Civ 406; [2001] 2 Lloyd's Rep. 76 at 89. See also, *G Scammell & Nephew Ltd v HC & JG Ouston* [1941] A.C. 251 at 268; *Baillie Estates Ltd v Du Pont (UK) Ltd* [2009] CSOH 95 at [26]; *Novus Aviation Ltd v Alubaf Arab International Bank BSC* [2016] EWHC 1575 (Comm) (agreement to enter into finance transaction); *Wells v Devani* [2019] UKSC 4; [2019] 2 W.L.R. 617 at [18].

[106] *Hillas & Co Ltd v Arcos Ltd* (1932) 147 L.T. 503.

[107] *Chitty on Contracts*, 33rd edn, Vol.1 paras 2–141; *Welsh Development Agency v Export Finance Ltd* [1992] B.C.C. 270 at 278 (exporter acting as seller or agent); *R & D Construction Ltd v Hallam Land Management Ltd* [2009] CSOH 128 (price).

Replace the second paragraph with:

It has been held,[108] that in a commercial agreement the further the parties have gone on with their alleged agreement (and a fortiori when it has been fully executed on the part of the claimant[109]), the more ready the courts will be to infer that there was an intention to enter into a contract and to resolve uncertainties rather than holding that there was no binding agreement. Accordingly, an agreement to buy such quantities "as may be agreed between the parties hereto" (during the second year of a contract intended to last for at least five years) has been construed as an agreement to take a reasonable quantity.[110] In *Foley v Classique Coaches Ltd*,[111] a contract which had been in other respects performed provided that the defendants would buy all their requirements of petrol "at a price to be agreed by the parties in writing and from time to time": the Court of Appeal held that the contract was sufficiently certain to be binding and that in default of further agreement the obligation was to pay a reasonable price. On the other hand, in *May & Butcher Ltd v The King*,[112] the price and other details were left to be agreed and the contract was held void for uncertainty. It is perhaps significant that the transaction was wholly executory, and that the contract was not merely silent on the points in question, but expressly stated that further agreement was required. In contrast, it was no doubt an important factor in the cases earlier referred to that the contract contained some machinery or formula (e.g. an arbitration clause) which, if liberally construed, was wide enough to provide a method alternative to agreement by which the uncertainty could be resolved. In these circumstances, the apparent lack of certainty can be cured in the first instance by recourse to this machinery, and if the agreed procedure has for some reason broken down, the court is less inhibited in imposing its own criteria to resolve the issue, unless there is nothing on which the court can base its conclusion as to the intention of the parties.[113]

[108] *F & G Sykes (Wessex) Ltd v Fine Fare Ltd* [1967] 1 Lloyd's Rep. 53 at 57; *Port Sudan Cotton Co v Govindaswamy Chettiar & Sons* [1977] 1 Lloyd's Rep. 5 at 13.

[109] *British Bank for Foreign Trade Ltd v Novinex Ltd* [1949] 1 K.B. 623; cf. *G Percy Trentham Ltd v Archital Luxfer Ltd* [1993] 1 Lloyd's Rep. 25 (construction sub-contract).

[110] *F & G Sykes (Wessex) Ltd v Fine Fare Ltd* [1967] 1 Lloyd's Rep. 53.

[111] *Foley v Classique Coaches Ltd* [1934] 2 K.B. 1.

[112] *May & Butcher Ltd v The King* [1934] 2 K.B. 17 HL.

[113] See further *R & J Dempster Ltd v Motherwell Bridge & Engineering Co Ltd* 1964 S.L.T. 353 (agreement to sub-contract manufacturing work; prices by custom settled after delivery to customers); *Upper Hunter County DC v Australian Chilling and Freezing Co Ltd* (1968) 118 C.L.R. 429 (power to vary price if "costs shall vary in other respects than as has been hereinbefore provided"); *Courtney & Fairbairn Ltd v Tolaini Bros (Hotels) Ltd* [1975] 1 W.L.R. 297 (building contract; agreement to negotiate price); *Vosper Thorneycroft Ltd v Ministry of Defence* [1976] 1 Lloyd's Rep. 58 (shipbuilding: entitlement to additional payment); *Tropwood AG of Zug v Jade Enterprises Ltd (The "Tropwood")* [1982] 1 Lloyd's Rep. 232 (charterparty; payment "for such length of time as owners and charterers may agree upon"); *Sudbrook Trading Estate Ltd v Eggleton* [1983] 1 A.C. 444 (option to purchase "at such price as may be agreed upon" by parties' valuers: fair value payable); *Cedar Trading Co Ltd v Transworld Oil Ltd (The "Gudermes")* [1985] 2 Lloyd's Rep. 623 (agreement to settle dispute "at a price acceptable to the defendants" not enforceable); *Nile Co for the Export of Agricultural Crops v H & JM Bennett (Commodities) Ltd* [1986] 1 Lloyd's Rep. 555 (contract to reach a settlement of dispute by agreement unenforceable); *Pagnan SpA v Granaria BV* [1986] 1 Lloyd's Rep. 547 (prices and other terms never finally agreed: contract void); *Pagnan SpA v Feed Products Ltd* [1987] 2 Lloyd's Rep. 601 (contract binding although certain subsidiary and inessential terms left to be settled later); *Voest Alpine Intertrading GmbH v Chevron International Oil Co Ltd* [1987] 2 Lloyd's Rep. 546 (book-out procedure in circular string contract; base price "to be agreed": upheld); *Queensland Electricity Generating Board v New Hope Collieries Pty Ltd* [1989] 1 Lloyd's Rep. 205 (agreement to extend coal supply contract beyond initial period; arbitration clause held sufficiently comprehensive to enable fair and reasonable revised price structure to be achieved); *CPC Consolidated Pool Carriers GmbH v CTM Cia Transmediterranea SA (The "CPC Gallia")* [1994] 1 Lloyd's Rep. 68 ("subject to details/logical amendments"—no binding contract); *Metal Scrap Trade Corp v Kate Shipping Co Ltd (The "Gladys") (No.2)* [1994] 2 Lloyd's Rep. 402 (contract for sale of ship not binding: blank spaces in standard form still to be completed); *Global Container Lines Ltd v State Black Sea Shipping Co* [1999] 1 Lloyd's Rep. 127 (agreement enforceable in spite of the words "to be finalised"); *Stabilad Ltd v Stephens & Carter Ltd (No.2)* [1999] 2 All E.R. (Comm) 651 (royalties: discretion of one party to decide whether precondition satisfied: void for uncertainty); *Gillatt v Sky Television Ltd* [2000] 1 All E.R. (Comm) 461 (shares: dispute resolution provided for by contract: court not free to substitute own opinion); *Baird Textile Holdings Ltd v Marks and Spencer Plc* [2001] EWCA Civ 274; [2002] 1 All E.R. (Comm) 737 (terms too vague to enforce); *Northern Foods Ltd v Focal Foods Ltd* [2001] EWCA Civ 1262 ("framework contract" not enforceable because no agreement on price, but a contract did come into existence because of subsequent correspondence); *Thoresen Co (Bangkok) Ltd v Fathom Marine Co Ltd* [2004] EWHC 167 (Comm); [2004] 1 All E.R. (Comm) 935 (sale of ship "subject to details": no binding contract); *Willis Management (Isle of Man) Ltd v Cable & Wireless Ltd* [2005] EWCA Civ 806; [2005] 2 Lloyd's Rep. 597 (no agreement on essential term); *Jackson v Thakrar* [2007] EWHC 271 (TCC); [2007] B.P.I.R. 367 (negotiations had not turned into agreement); *Trade Electronix Ltd v Best Buy Today (Wholesale) Ltd (In Administration)* [2009] EWCA Civ 828 (inter alia, no certainty as to the goods that were to be sold); *Pua Hor Ong v Wu You Yang Pty Ltd* [2008] SASC 365 ("[fine] details" to be confirmed, held enforceable); *Whittle Movers v Hollywood Express* [2009] EWCA Civ 1189; [2009] 2 C.L.C. 771 (letter of intent expressed as subject to contract; parties still negotiating terms and such performance as occurred did not indicate existence of contract); *Barbudev v Eurocom Cable Management Bulgaria Eood* [2012] EWCA Civ 548; [2012] 2 All E.R. (Comm) 963 (side letter only agreement to agree); *RTS Flexible*

Systems Ltd v Molkerei Alois Müller GmbH & Co KG [2010] UKSC 14; [2010] 1 W.L.R. 753 (letter of intent to supply and install machinery binding where parties waived subject to contract clause); *Air Studios (Lyndhurst) Ltd v Lombard North Central Plc* [2012] EWHC 3162 (QB); [2013] 1 Lloyd's Rep. 63 (subject to contract requirement withdrawn); *MRI Trading AG v Erdenet Mining Corp LLC* [2013] EWCA Civ 156; [2013] 1 Lloyd's Rep. 638 (charges and shipping schedule implied by reference to other contracts). In *Malago Pty Ltd v A.W. Ellis Engineering Pty Ltd* [2012] NSWCA 227, the court ordered specific performance of a document containing "Heads of Agreement" for the sale of a business. *MRI Trading AG v Erdenet Mining Corporation LLC* [2013] EWCA Civ 156; [2013] 1 Lloyd's Rep. 638 (sale not uncertain where part of broader contractual relationship); *Proton Energy Group SA v Orlen Lietuva* [2013] EWHC 2872; [2014] 1 All E.R. (Comm) 972 ("a classic spot deal where the speed of the market requires that the parties agree the main terms and leave the details, some of which may be important, to be discussed and agreed later" at [39]); *Dany Lions Ltd v Bristol Cars Ltd* [2014] EWHC 817 (QB); [2014] 2 All E.R. (Comm) 403 (agreement to use reasonable or best endeavours not enforceable because objective and criteria unclear); *Hughes v Pendragon Sabre Ltd t/a Porsche Centre Bolton* [2016] EWCA Civ 18; [2016] Lloyd's Rep. 311 (sale contract even though the acquisition of goods by the seller depended on a contingency that might never be fulfilled); cf. *Mushroom Composters Pty Ltd v IS & DE Robertson Pty Ltd* [2015] NSWCA 1 (no contract because no agreement on price); *Stellard Pty Ltd v North Queensland Fuel Pty Ltd* [2015] QSC 119 (binding contract for sale of business even though emails were "subject to contract" where intention was to be bound although there was also an intention that the initial contract would be replaced by a documented agreement); *Baldwin v Icon Energy Ltd* [2015] QSC 12 (agreement to use reasonable endeavours and good faith in negotiating sale unenforceable where no previous contractual framework or relationship). In *Emirates Trading Agency LLC v Prime Mineral Experts Private Ltd* [2014] EWHC 2104 (Comm); [2015] 1 W.L.R. 1145 (term in sale contract requiring resolution of any dispute by "friendly discussion" was enforceable and akin to acting in good faith); *Teekay Tankers Ltd v STX Offshore and Shipbuilding Co Ltd* [2017] EWHC 253 (Comm); [2017] 1 Lloyd's Rep 387 (option to purchase ship merely an agreement to agree). See generally Fridman, 76 L.Q.R. 521 (1960); Samek, 47 Can. Bar Rev. 203 (1970).

Goods supplied without contract

Replace footnote 114 with:

[114] *British Steel Corp v Cleveland Bridge & Engineering Co Ltd* [1984] 1 All E.R. 504; *Whittle Movers v Hollywood Express* [2009] EWCA Civ 1189; [2009] 2 C.L.C. 2804; cf. *Peter Lind & Co Ltd v Mersey Docks & Harbour Board* [1977] 2 Lloyd's Rep. 234 (construction contract); *RTS Flexible Systems Ltd v Molkerei Alois Müller GmbH & Co KG* [2010] UKSC 14; [2010] 1 W.L.R. 753 (supply and install machinery; terms "subject to contract", but work begun and, therefore, agreement on those terms). See further Jones, 18 U.W. Ont.L.Rev. 44 (1980).

2-018

Intention to establish contractual relationship

Replace footnote 116 with:

[116] *Chitty on Contracts*, 33rd edn, Vol.1 paras 2-168 et seq.; *Baird Textile Holdings Ltd v Marks & Spencer Plc* [2001] EWCA Civ 274; [2002] 1 All E.R. (Comm) 737. Yet, even if there is an oral agreement, the courts will look for a clear intention to create legal relations by considering the degree of formality and the environment within which the discussion took place: *RTS Flexible Systems Ltd v Molkerei Alois Müller GmbH & Co KG* [2010] UKSC 14; [2010] 1 W.L.R. 753; *MacInnes v Gross* [2017] EWHC 46 (QB) (alleged consultancy agreement made during dinner). In *Blue v Ashley* [2017] EWHC 1928 (Comm) (alleged consultancy fee "agreed" in a public house) Leggatt J said factors tending to show there was no such intention were, "the fact that it [the agreement] was made in a social context, the fact that it was expressed in vague language and the fact that the promissory statement was made in anger or jest" (at [56]).

2-019

Replace section title footnote 125 with:

2.   FORMALITIES[125]

[125] cf. Vienna Convention on Contracts for the International Sale of Goods Arts 12, 96. On electronic signatures, see the Electronic Communications Act 2000 s.7; and *Standard Bank London Ltd v Bank of Tokyo Ltd* [1995] 2 Lloyd's Rep. 169; and on formal requirements in e-commerce transactions, the Law Commission's *Electronic Commerce: Formal Requirements in Commercial Transactions* (2001); *Chitty on Contracts*, 33rd edn, Vol.1 Ch.5; Saxby, *Encyclopedia of Information Technology Law* (looseleaf), paras 3.312 et seq.; Mason, *Electronic Signatures in Law*, 4th edn. On the EC Directive on Electronic Signatures, the Electronic Communications Act 2000 and the Electronic Commerce (EC Directive) Regulations 2002 (SI 2002/2013), see Saxby, *Encyclopedia of Information Technology Law*, paras 3.239 et seq. Following the issue in 2016 by The Law Society Company Law Committee and The City of

2-021

London Society Company Law and Financial Law Committees of a note on the execution of documents using electronic signatures (*https://www.lawsociety.org.uk/support-services/advice/practice-notes/ execution-of-a-document-using-an-electronic-signature/* [Accessed 2 July 2019]), the Law Commission started a project on this subject in 2018: https://www.lawcom.gov.uk/project/electronic-execution-of-documents/ [Accessed 17 July 2018].

Formal requirements under other statutes

Replace paragraph with:

2-023   Under the Merchant Shipping Act 1995, a registered ship or share therein must be transferred by a bill of sale satisfying the prescribed requirements, and registered.[134] Those supplying certain goods and services to public authorities must observe various procedures during the tendering process, and there are rules about the form and content of the contracts.[135] Formalities apply to certain wholesale business-to-business sales contracts in the grocery trade.[136] The formalities required for the making of hire-purchase, credit-sale and conditional sale agreements[137] are prescribed by the Consumer Credit Act 1974 ss.60–64,[138] and regulations made thereunder,[139] so far as concerns "regulated agreements" as defined by that Act.[140] A regulated agreement which is not properly executed is enforceable against a debtor or hirer on an order of the court only,[141] except with consent of the debtor or hirer given at the time,[142] and any security given is similarly not enforceable without an order of the court.[143] These statutes (and others, such as the Bills of Sale Acts[144]) require the use of a written document and a signature, and possibly also that the signature be witnessed. The application of such provisions to contracts concluded by electronic means is uncertain.[145] The question of electronic bills of lading and other documents of title is discussed in a later chapter.[146]

---

[134]   Merchant Shipping Act 1995 Sch.1 para.2(1); above, para.1-082. This rule does not apply where the transfer will result in the ship ceasing to have a British connection.

[135]   e.g. the Public Contract Regulations 2015 (SI 2015/102), which refer to "supply" of goods or services and so apply not only to sale contracts within the Sale of Goods Act but also contracts for the supply of goods that do not fall within that Act (e.g. *PST Energy 7 Shipping LLC v OW Bunker Malta Ltd: The Res Cogitans* [2016] UKSC 23; [2016] A.C. 1034; see para.1-030 above and paras 4-001 et seq. below for a fuller discussion).

[136]   Groceries (Supply Chain Market Practices) Market Investigation Order 2009, which came into force on 4 February 2010. Schedule 1 established the Groceries Supply Code of Practice, which applies only to sales involving certain types of goods and the buyer is a large retailer. The Groceries Code Adjudicator Act 2013, which came into force in June 2013, established an ombudsman to deal with disputes. See also EU Directive on unfair trading practices in business-to-business relationships in the agricultural and food supply chain (EU) 2019/633 (strengthening position of SME food producers in relationships with large buyers).

[137]   Defined above, paras 1-052 to 1-055.

[138]   For the previous law, see Hire-Purchase Act 1965 s.5, and Hire-Purchase (Documents) (Legibility and Statutory Statements) Regulations 1965 (SI 1965/1646).

[139]   See Consumer Credit (Agreements) Regulations 1983 (SI 1433/1553, as amended) by SIs 1984/1600, 1985/666, 1988/2047 1999/3177, 2001/3649, 2004/1881, 2004/1482, 2010/1014) and Consumer Credit Act 2006.

[140]   For the meaning of "regulated agreement", see above, para.1-022.

[141]   Consumer Credit Act 1974 s.65. Section 127(3), which precluded the court from making an enforcement order if no document containing the prescribed terms (whether or not in the prescribed form and complying with the regulations) has been signed by the debtor, was declared incompatible with the Human Rights Convention: *Wilson v First County Trust Ltd (No.2)* [2001] EWCA Civ 633; [2002] Q.B. 74. The sub-section was repealed with effect from April 6, 2007 by Consumer Credit Act 2006 ss.15, 70, 71(2) and Sch.4 (with Sch.3 para.11); SI 2007/123 art.3(2), Sch.2.

[142]   Consumer Credit Act 1974 s.173(3).

[143] Consumer Credit Act 1974 s.113(2). For the powers of the court, see s.127; and for the power of the Financial Conduct Authority to waive or modify the statutory requirements in a particular case, see s.60(3), (4) (as amended by the Financial Services Act 2012 (Consumer Credit) Order 2013 (SI 2013/1882) reg.7(3)).

[144] Above, para.1-016.

[145] See the authorities referred to at n.125, above, where it is noted that the term "signature" is capable of various meanings and that the legislative definitions vary. It should be noted also that the legislation on electronic signatures referred to in that note is primarily concerned with systems for the authentication of such signatures, rather than the factual question whether a person has "signed" a document. cf. *J Pereira Fernandes SA v Metha* [2006] EWHC 813 (Ch); [2006] 1 W.L.R. 1543, where it was held that the automatic insertion of an email address is not a signature for the purposes of the Statute of Frauds 1677 s.4; but (in relation to a similar requirement in the Statute of Frauds Amendment Act 1828 s.6) it will be sufficient if the email has a written indication of who is sending the email, such as an electronic signature or "concluding words such as 'regards' accompanied by the typed name of the sender": *Lindsay v O'Loughnane* [2010] EWHC 529 (QB); [2012] B.C.C. 153; and (Statute of Frauds 1677 s.4) signing an email with first name may be sufficient: *Golden Ocean Group Ltd v Salgaocar Mining Industries Pvt Ltd* [2012] EWCA Civ 265; [2012] 1 W.L.R. 3674 at [21] and [24]; cf. *Kavia Holdings Pty Ltd v Suntrack Holdings Pty Ltd* [2011] NSWSC 716 (requirements that notice be in writing, served on party and signed satisfied by use of email). A regulated agreement under the Consumer Credit Act 1974 can be concluded by electronic signature: *Bassano v Toft* [2014] EWHC 377 (QB) (Consumer Credit (Agreements) Regulations 2010 (SI 2010/1014) reg.4).

[146] Below, para.18-247.

Written contracts of sale

Replace paragraph with:

Although it is not necessary to make a contract of sale in writing, if the parties choose to do so their contract will be governed by the ordinary rules of evidence which affect written contracts. In particular, under the parole evidence rule, where a document is intended by the parties to express the entire agreement between them, extrinsic evidence generally cannot be used to add to, vary, subtract from or contradict the terms of the written instrument.[147] But this rule is subject to many exceptions.[148] A contract may include an entire agreement clause, which purports to prevent promises not contained in the relevant document from affecting the terms of the contract, although whether it achieves this effect depends on the wording of the clause.[149]

2-024

[147] Extrinsic evidence intended to show that the party named in a written contract was not the true contracting party was rejected in *Shogun Finance Ltd v Hudson* [2003] UKHL 62; [2004] 1 A.C. 919. See on this issue McLauchlan, (2005) 121 L.Q.R. 9. Since these are general principles of contract law, they will apply to a sui generis supply contract which does not fall within the Sale of Goods Act: *PST Energy 7 Shipping LLC v OW Bunker Malta Ltd: The Res Cogitans* [2016] UKSC 23; [2016] A.C. 1034; see para.1-030 above and paras 4-001 et seq below for a fuller discussion.

[148] For a full discussion, see *Phipson on Evidence*, 19th edn, Ch.42; *Chitty on Contracts*, 33rd edn, Vol.1 paras 13-109 et seq. See also the Law Commission's Report, *The Parol Evidence Rule* (L. Com. No.154, Cmnd.9700, 1986), where the view is expressed that the supposed rule is not as far-reaching as has previously been thought.

[149] *Deepak Fertilisers and Petrochemicals v ICI Chemicals & Polymers Ltd* [1999] 1 Lloyd's Rep. 387 at 395; *The Inntrepreneur Pub Company (GL) v East Crown Ltd* [2000] 2 Lloyd's Rep. 611 at 613; *Ryanair Ltd v SR Technics Ireland Ltd* [2007] EWHC 3089 (QB) at [137]–[143]; *AXA Sun Life Services Plc v Campbell Martin Ltd* [2012] EWCA Civ 133; [2011] 2 Lloyd's Rep. 1; Barber, (2012) 6 J.B.L. 486. Such a clause does not necessarily preclude an action or defence based on misrepresentation or estoppel: *Mears Ltd v Shoreline Housing Partnership Ltd* [2013] EWCA Civ 639; [2013] C.P. Rep. 39 (contract for building repair work); *NF Football Investments Ltd v NFFC Group Holdings Ltd* [2018] EWHC 2884 (Ch) (share purchase). A contractual term prohibiting oral variation renders any such purported variation invalid (estoppel remains a possibility): *Rock Advertising Ltd v MWB Business Exchange Centres Ltd* [2018] UKSC 24; [2019] A.C. 119.

3. Parties

Capacity of parties

Replace paragraph with:

2-028   Section 3 of the Act declares that "capacity to buy and sell is regulated by the general law concerning capacity to contract and to transfer and acquire property". There are in general no limitations on the capacity of any person to acquire goods in English law.[163] The capacity of a person to dispose of goods is not necessarily co-extensive with the capacity to contract to do so.[164] In the context of the law of sale, a question not based on contractual capacity will arise where a person under a disability, who has purportedly sold goods, brings an action to have the transfer avoided and the property revested. There is authority for the view that even in those cases where the contract is said to be void, property once transferred is irrecoverable,[165] or at least not recoverable unless there has been a total failure of consideration.[166] The particular category of incapacity may make a difference.[167] In any event, a claim for the return of goods sold under a contract of sale which is voidable on the grounds of incapacity[168] is liable to be defeated by the rights of third parties or other equitable bars to such claims.[169]

[163] *Chitty on Contracts*, 33rd edn, Vol.1 Pt.3. The same principle applies to a sui generis supply contract: *PST Energy 7 Shipping LLC v OW Bunker Malta Ltd: The Res Cogitans* [2016] UKSC 23; [2016] A.C. 1034; see para.1-030 above and paras 4-001 et seq. below for a fuller discussion

[164] *Chitty on Contracts*, 33rd edn, Vol.1 paras 9-072–9-074; *Chaplin v Leslie Frewin (Publishers) Ltd* [1966] Ch. 71 (copyright).

[165] *Stocks v Wilson* [1913] 2 K.B. 235 at 246; *Chaplin v Leslie Frewin (Publishers) Ltd* [1966] Ch. 71 (cases concerning minors). But see now, as regards restitution of such property by the minor, Minors' Contracts Act 1987 s.3, below, para.2-038.

[166] *Pearce v Brain* [1929] 2 K.B. 310 (barter). The proper question should perhaps be whether restitutio in integrum can be made: see Treitel, (1957) 73 L.Q.R. 194, 202–205. But see Goff and Jones, *The Law of Unjust Enrichment*, 9th edn, para.24-23. This may be an issue where the parties to the agreement contemplate the consumption of goods before payment and they are consumed: *PST Energy 7 Shipping LLC v OW Bunker Malta Ltd: The Res Cogitans* [2016] UKSC 23; [2016] A.C. 1034; see para.1-030 above and paras 4-001 et seq. below for a fuller discussion.

[167] *Bell Houses Ltd v City Wall Properties Ltd* [1966] 1 Q.B. 207 at 221 (reversed on other grounds [1966] 2 Q.B. 656); *Cabaret Holdings Ltd v Meeanee Sports & Rodeo Club Inc* [1982] 1 N.Z.L.R. 673 (ultra vires contracts of company held unenforceable); contrast *Re KL Tractors Ltd (In Liquidation)* (1961) 106 C.L.R. 318 (action allowed for price of goods sold ultra vires); and cf. *Hazell v Hammersmith & Fulham LBC* [1992] 2 A.C. 1 at 36: "The consequences of any ultra vires transaction may depend on the facts of each case".

[168] e.g. on the grounds of mental incapacity or drunkenness: below, para.2-041.

[169] See below, paras 12-005 et seq.

Replace title footnote 170 with:

Contractual capacity of minors[170]

2-029   [170] See *Chitty on Contracts*, 33rd edn, Vol.1 paras 9-005 et seq.

Replace paragraph with:

A natural person under full age is known as a minor or infant. By the Family Law Reform Act 1969, the age of majority was reduced from 21 to 18,[171] but this Act did not alter the substantive legal rules governing minors' contracts.[172] Such contracts continued to be governed by the common law as altered by the Infants Relief Act 1874 and as codified in part by the Sale of Goods Act 1979 s.3. However, by the Minors' Contracts Act 1987,[173] the Act of 1874 ceased to apply to any contract made by a minor after June 9, 1987, so that the common law position has been restored.[174] The general rule at common law[175] is that a contract made by a minor is voidable: it is enforceable by the minor, but not binding upon that person unless the minor ratifies it on coming of full age.[176] But contracts for "necessaries"[177] and beneficial contracts of service are binding.[178] So far as concerns the sale of goods, a minor's contracts fall into three categories: (a) contracts for the purchase of necessaries; (b) contracts for the purchase of non-necessaries; and (c) contracts to sell.[179]

[171] Family Law Reform Act 1969 s.1. The Act came into force on 1 January 1970, and all persons then aged 18 or over, but under 21, attained their majority on that date. A person attains the age of 18 at the commencement of the 18th anniversary of birth: s.9.

[172] Recommendations for reform of these rules were made by the *Latey Committee on the Age of Majority* (Cmnd.3342, 1967), whose report led to the passing of the Act of 1969, but these recommendations have not so far been implemented. See also the Law Commission's *Report on Minors' Contracts* (L. Com. No.134, 1984), which led to the passing of the Minors' Contracts Act 1987 (below).

[173] This Act applies only in England and Wales. For the position in Scotland, see the Age of Legal Capacity (Scotland) Act 1991.

[174] In some respects, however, the common law has been modified by the Act of 1987, e.g. as regards restitution of property: see below, para.2-038.

[175] A very young child may lack the capacity to make a contract at all—or at least a contract of any but the most simple kind: *R. v Oldham Metropolitan BC Ex p. Garlick* [1993] 1 F.L.R. 645 (5-year-old held incapable of contracting for the occupation of residential premises).

[176] The term "voidable" is used in more than one sense, meaning at times "not binding unless ratified" and at other times "binding unless repudiated": see *Chitty on Contracts*, 33rd edn, Vol.1 paras 9-007.

[177] Below, para.2-030.

[178] See *Chitty on Contracts*, 33rd edn, Vol.1 para.9-008.

[179] Various statutes provide that the sale of particular categories of goods (e.g. liquor, fireworks) to minors, or to minors under a specified age, is unlawful. The same principles will apply to a sui generis supply contract: *PST Energy 7 Shipping LLC v OW Bunker Malta Ltd: The Res Cogitans* [2016] UKSC 23; [2016] A.C. 1034; see para.1-030 above and paras 4-001 et seq. below for a fuller discussion.

Replace title footnote 180:

Necessaries[180]

[180] The term "necessaries" may include services as well as goods, e.g. lodging and legal advice: see *Chitty on Contracts*, 33rd edn, Vol.1 paras 9-010 et seq, but only the cases concerned with goods are discussed here. The same principle applies whether the agreement is a sale contract, which falls within the Sale of Goods Act, or a sui generis supply contract: *PST Energy 7 Shipping LLC v OW Bunker Malta Ltd: The Res Cogitans* [2016] UKSC 23; [2016] A.C. 1034; see para.1-030 above and paras 4-001 et seq. below for a fuller discussion.

2-030

Replace title footnote 227:

Liability of minor to make restitution[227]

[227] *Chitty on Contracts*, 33rd edn, Vol.1 para.9-055 et seq.

2-038

Liability of minor in tort

Replace footnote 236 with:

[236] *Chitty on Contracts*, 33rd edn, Vol.1 paras 9-053 et seq. A third party cannot be liable in tort for inducing a minor to breach a contract that is voidable: *Proform Sports Management Ltd v Proactive Sports Management Ltd* [2006] EWHC 2903 (Ch); [2007] Bus. L.R. 93.

2-040

Drunkenness and mental incapacity

Replace paragraph with:

2-041   By virtue of the Sale of Goods Act 1979 s.3(2),[239] a person who by reason of drunkenness is incompetent to contract is liable to pay a reasonable price for necessaries sold and delivered to that person[240] in the same way as a minor.[241] The Mental Capacity Act 2005 s.7,[242] which deals with mental incapacity, is expressed in similar terms, except that it refers to services as well as goods and uses the word "supplied" instead of "sale and delivery". In all other respects, the capacity of such persons is governed by the general law concerning capacity to contract, for which reference should be made to standard works.[243] The basic rule is that such a contract is binding, except that it will be voidable by a party able to show that the incapacity prevented an understanding of the nature of the action, and that the other party was aware of this incapacity: where the other party was unaware of the incapacity, the contract is to be treated as entered into by a person with full capacity and cannot be rescinded merely because the bargain is unfair, unless it can be shown that there was some unconscionable conduct by the other party.[244]

[239] As amended by the Mental Capacity Act 2005 Sch.6, para.24.

[240] Or to the person's dependants: *Read v Legard* (1851) 6 Exch. 636.

[241] *Re Rhodes* (1890) 44 Ch. D. 94.

[242] This came into force on 1 October 2007. The Act's definition of "necessary" (s.7) "precisely mirrors the common law rule": *Aster Healthcare Ltd v Shafi* [2014] EWCA Civ 1350; [2016] 2 All E.R. 316 at [31] per Andrews J. The obligation to pay for necessaries under s.7 does not arise where goods are supplied on the understanding that payment is to come from someone other than the person lacking capacity: *Aster Healthcare Ltd v Shafi* [2014] EWCA Civ 1350; [2016] 2 All E.R. 316. This was the position at common law: *Re Rhodes* (1890) 44 Ch. D. 94.

[243] *Chitty on Contracts*, 33rd edn, Vol.1 paras 9-075 et seq.

[244] *Hart v O'Connor* [1985] A.C. 1000. Known as "the rule in *Imperial Loan Co. Ltd v Stone* [1892] 1 Q.B. 599": *Dunhill v Burgin* [2014] UKSC 18; [2014] 1 W.L.R. 933 at [1].

Corporate bodies

Replace footnote 249 with:

2-043   [249] *Chitty on Contracts*, 33rd edn, Vol.1 paras 10-001 et seq.

4. THE PRICE

Price must be in money

Replace footnote 266 with:

2-044   [266] See s.2(1) of the Act, which does not stipulate that the buyer must be the source of the money consideration. This sentence and the next cited in *Haines v Herd* [2019] NZHC 342 at [103]–[104].

Replace footnote 268 with:

[268] *Miliangos v George Frank (Textiles) Ltd* [1976] A.C. 443; *Daewoo Australia Pty Ltd v Suncorp-Metway Ltd* (2000) 33 A.C.S.R. 481; *Haines v Herd* [2019] NZHC 342 (sale of vessel for cash and land not sale of goods).

Reasonable price where none fixed

Replace footnote 284 with:

2-047   [284] *Acebal v Levy* (1834) 10 Bing. 376; *Valpy v Gibson* (1847) 4 C.B. 837 (but see the doubts expressed in *Hall v Busst* (1960) 104 C.L.R. 206 at 234). An analogous rule applies in the case of a contract to supply a service: Supply of Goods and Services Act 1982 s.15. See *Mastercigars Direct LLP v Withers*

LLP [2007] EWHC 2733 (Ch); [2008] 3 All E.R. 417; *BSF Consulting Engineers Ltd v MacDonald Crosbie* [2008] All E.R. (D) 171 (Apr); *MRI Trading AG v Erdenet Mining Corp LLC* [2013] EWCA Civ 156; [2013] 1 Lloyd's Rep. 638. cf. Vienna Convention on Contracts for the International Sale of Goods Art.55, which provides that where the contract does not expressly or implicitly fix or make provision for determining the price, the parties are prima facie considered to have impliedly made reference to the current trade price.

Replace footnote 288 with:

288   *Chitty on Contracts*, 33rd edn, Vol.1 para.29-070 et seq..

Agreement to sell at valuation of third party

Replace paragraph with:

The parties to a contract of sale may agree that the price shall be fixed by one or more independent persons appointed by them. In such circumstances, the parties are bound by their bargain, and the price when so determined is as much part of the contract as if they had originally fixed it themselves. In the case of an agreement to sell goods, the Sale of Goods Act 1979 s.9 makes special provision as follows:

2-049

"(1) Where there is an agreement to sell goods on the terms that the price is to be fixed by the valuation of a third party, and he cannot or does not make the valuation, the agreement is avoided; but if the goods or any part of them have been delivered to and appropriated by the buyer he must pay a reasonable price for them. (2) Where the third party is prevented from making the valuation by the fault of the seller or buyer, the party not at fault may maintain an action for damages against the party at fault."

The assessment of the price by the valuer is in such circumstances a condition precedent to the operation of the parties' obligations respectively to buy and to sell. It is in accordance with general contractual principles both that the failure of the condition should nullify the agreement[296] and that a party, whose act or default has prevented the fulfilment of the condition, should be liable for breach of an implied undertaking.[297] The terms of s.9 confirm decisions under the common law prior to the Act.[298]

296   See *Chitty on Contracts*, 33rd edn, Vol.1 para.13-028.; and cf. *Pym v Campbell* (1856) 6 E. & B.370, where it was understood that there was to be no agreement unless and until approval was given by a third person.

297   *Chitty on Contracts*, 33rd edn, Vol.1 para.14-024.

298   *Thurnell v Balbirnie* (1837) 2 M. & W. 786; *Vickers v Vickers* (1867) L.R. 4 Eq. 527; *Cooper v Shuttleworth* (1856) 25 L.J. Exch. 114; *Clarke v Westrope* (1856) 18 C.B. 765; cf. *Smith v Peters* (1875) L.R. 20 Eq. 511 (party ordered by mandatory injunction not to prevent valuation).

Position of valuer

Replace footnote 308 with:

308   *Re Carus-Wilson and Greene* (1886) 18 Q.B.D. 7; *Re Hammond and Waterton* (1890) 62 L.T. 808; *Palacath v Flanagan* [1985] 2 All E.R. 161; *North-Eastern Co-op Soc v Newcastle-upon-Tyne CC* (1987) 282 E.G. 1409; see further *Russell on Arbitration*, 24th edn.

2-052

CHAPTER 3

APPLICATION OF GENERAL CONTRACTUAL PRINCIPLES

TABLE OF CONTENTS

Introductory

Replace footnote 2 with:

[2] e.g. implied terms as to quality (Sale of Goods Act s.14) applied also at common law in contracts for   **3-001**
the supply of goods generally, and have now been similarly codified, as regards such contracts, by the
Supply of Goods and Services Act 1982 ss.4, 9: see above, para.1-031; also the Consumer Rights Act
2015 ss.9-11. For a general discussion, see the report of the Law Commission on *Implied Terms in
Contracts for the Supply of Goods* (Law Com. No.95, HMSO, 1979).

Replace section title footnote 3 with:

1. AGENCY[3]

[3] See generally *Chitty on Contracts*, 33rd edn, Vol.2 Ch.31; *Bowstead and Reynolds on Agency*, 21st   **3-002**
edn.

Particular types of agent

Replace the first paragraph with:

A mercantile agent is one[6] having in the customary course of business as such   **3-004**
agent authority either to sell goods, or to consign goods for the purpose of sale, or
to buy goods, or to raise money on the security of goods.[7] A factor, as traditionally
defined, is a species of mercantile agent who is normally entrusted by a seller of
goods with the possession either of the goods or of the documents of title representing them. The contract may be made in the factor's own name, and the factor may
receive payment of moneys due from the buyer.[8] A broker, in contrast, usually acts
as an agent for a buyer or seller without having such possession; the contract cannot be made in the broker's own name, and the broker cannot make or receive
payment.[9] (This distinction between factors and brokers was, however, more
important in 19th century commerce than it is today, and the term factor in this sense
is now little used.) An auctioneer sells at an open sale, either with or without having possession of the goods, to the bidder who offers the best price. The auctioneer
has no implied authority to give warranties as to the goods.[10] A *del credere* agent
is one who, usually for an extra commission, undertakes to indemnify the seller
against the non-payment by the buyer of the price or other sums for which the buyer
may be liable under the contract.[11] A person may act as a principal in some respects

and as an agent in others: thus, a confirming house (or "commission agent"), which provides agency services for an overseas buyer, may stand as principal (i.e. as the buyer of the goods) in relation to the seller, and at the same time be in the position of an agent vis-à-vis that overseas buyer.[12]

[6] The statutory definitions in fact here repeat the term "mercantile agent", confirming decisions given under earlier, repealed, Factors Acts that the employment should come within some known category of commercial agency: Chalmers, *Sale of Goods Act* 1979, 18th edn, p.291.

[7] Factors Act 1889 s.1(1); Sale of Goods Act s.26. For the special provisions of the Factors Act as regards dispositions of goods and documents of title by mercantile agents, see below, paras 7-032 et seq.

[8] *Chitty on Contracts*, 33rd edn, Vol.2 para.31-009.

[9] *Chitty on Contracts*, 33rd edn, Vol.2 para.31-009.

[10] *Chitty on Contracts*, 33rd edn, Vol.2 para.31-011. For the provisions of the Act governing sales by auction, see above, para.2-004 and below, para.3-009. See also *Chelmsford Auctions Ltd v Poole* [1973] Q.B. 542 (action for price by auctioneer in own name).

[11] *Chitty on Contracts*, 33rd edn, Vol.2 para.31-010.

[12] *Ireland v Livingston* (1872) L.R. 5 H.L. 395 at 409; *Sobell Industries Ltd v Cory Bros & Co* [1955] 2 Lloyd's Rep. 82 at 90–91; *Anglo-African Shipping Co of New York Inc v J Mortner Ltd* [1962] 1 Lloyd's Rep. 610 at 616–617. cf. *Aluminium Industrie Vaassen BV v Romalpa Aluminium Ltd* [1976] 1 W.L.R. 676, below, para.5-143.

Replace the second paragraph with:

Civil law systems recognise a special category of commercial agent. Although such a distinct category of agency relationships has not traditionally been the subject of separate treatment by the common law, it has now become necessary to identify them because they are governed by an EC Directive,[13] which has been implemented in this country by domestic legislation.[14] A commercial agent is defined as:

"… a self-employed intermediary who has continuing authority to negotiate the sale or purchase of goods on behalf of another person (the 'principal'), or to negotiate and conclude the sale and purchase of goods on behalf of and in the name of that principal."[15]

The legislation provides, inter alia, for the payment of compensation by the principal on termination of the agency relationship.[16]

[13] Directive 1986/653 [1986] O.J. L382/17.

[14] Commercial Agents (Council Directive) Regulations (SI 1993/3053, as amended by SI 1993/3173 and SI 1998/2868).

[15] SI 1993/3053 reg.2(1).

[16] For a more detailed account, see *Bowstead and Reynolds on Agency*, 21st edn, Ch.11.

Replace title footnote 17 with:

Dealers as agents in instalment credit transactions[17]

3-005 [17] *Chitty on Contracts*, 33rd edn, Vol.2 para.31-016.

Replace title footnote 30 with:

Agency of necessity[30]

3-006 [30] *Chitty on Contracts*, 33rd edn, Vol.2 paras 31-035 et seq.; *Bowstead and Reynolds on Agency*, 21st edn, Ch.4; and see *China Pacific SA v Food Corp of India* [1982] A.C. 939; *ENE 1 Kos Ltd v Petroleo Brasileiro SA Petrobas (The Kos)* [2012] UKSC 12; [2012] 2 A.C. 164; *Tongue v Royal Society for the Prevention of Cruelty to Animals* [2017] EWHC 2508 (Ch); [2018] B.P.I.R. 229.

Agency of a married woman

Replace footnote 34 with:

34 *Chitty on Contracts*, 33rd edn, Vol.2 para.31-052; *Bowstead and Reynolds on Agency*, 21st edn, paras 3–041 to 3-044 Note that a wife's former power to bind her husband as his agent of necessity has been abolished: Matrimonial Proceedings and Property Act 1970 s.41(1).

3-007

2. FRAUD AND MISREPRESENTATION

Application of common law principles

Replace footnote 38 with:

38 e.g. *Chitty on Contracts*, 33rd edn, Vol.1 Ch.7.

3-008

3. DURESS AND UNDUE INFLUENCE

Duress and undue influence

Replace paragraph with:

The common law principles of duress (including economic duress[45]), and the wider equitable doctrine of undue influence, appear to apply without any special qualification to contracts for the sale of goods.[46]

3-010

45 *North Ocean Shipping Co Ltd v Hyundai Construction Co Ltd (The "Atlantic Baron")* [1979] Q.B. 705; *Atlas Express Ltd v Kafco (Importers & Distributors) Ltd* [1989] Q.B. 833; *CTN Cash & Carry Ltd v Gallagher Ltd* [1994] 4 All E.R. 714; *Times Travel (UK) Ltd v Pakistan International Airlines Corp* [2019] EWCA Civ 828; [2019] 2 Lloyd's Rep. 89 (agency agreement).

46 Sale of Goods Act s.62(2). For these topics, see *Chitty on Contracts*, 33rd edn, Vol.1 Ch.8; Enonchong, *Duress, Undue Influence and Unconscionable Dealing*, 3rd edn.

Replace section title footnote 47 with:

4. MISTAKE[47]

47 See generally *Chitty on Contracts*, 33rd edn, Vol.1 Ch.6; Macmillan, *Mistakes in Contract Law* (2010).

3-011

Application of common law rules

Replace footnote 49 with:

49 See, e.g. Slade, 70 L.Q.R. 385; and cf. below, para.3-021. Lord Walker pointed out that a mistake is not mere ignorance, inadvertence or failure accurately to predict the future; it involves an incorrect belief or incorrect assumption as to an existing fact or law: *Pitt v Holt* [2013] UKSC 26; [2013] 2 A.C. 108 at [108]-[109] (voluntary settlement).

Replace title footnote 50:

Mistake of identity[50]

50 See *Chitty on Contracts*, 33rd edn, Vol.1 paras 3–036 et seq.

3-012

Replace footnote 53 with:

53 *Chitty on Contracts*, 33rd edn, Vol.1 para.3–036; *Dennant v Skinner and Collom* [1948] 2 K.B. 164.

Mistake as to terms offered

Replace footnote 82 with:

82 *Hartog v Colin & Shields* [1939] 3 All E.R. 566. Similarly, in *McMaster University v Wilchar Construction Ltd* (1971) 22 D.L.R. (3d) 9 (must have been aware of mistake in omission of wage escala-

3-016

tor clause from contract); *Chwee Kin Keong v Digilandmall.com Pte Ltd* [2005] 1 S.L.R. 502 (must have been aware of mistake in quoted price); cf. *Ulster Bank Ltd v Lambe* [2012] NIQB 31 (must have been aware of mistake over currency of settlement offer).

Other fundamental assumptions

Replace paragraph with:

3-022   In *Bell v Lever Bros Ltd*[113] it was accepted as a general proposition that:

"... whenever it is to be inferred from the terms of a contract or its surrounding circumstances that the consensus has been reached on the basis of a particular contractual assumption, and that assumption is not true, the contract is avoided"

provided that the assumption was "fundamental to the continued validity of the contract", or "a foundation essential to its existence". Although it is not easy to reconcile the acceptance of this proposition with the decision in *Bell v Lever Bros Ltd* itself or with subsequent cases,[114] it is apparent that, if the principle so stated is correct, a contract for the sale of goods could be avoided on the grounds of a false and fundamental assumption as to something other than the existence or quality of the goods.[115] The proposition was applied in *Sheikh Bros Ltd v Ochsner*,[116] where a contract granting the respondent a licence to enter and cut sisal on the appellant's land contained a provision that the respondent would deliver to the appellant a minimum of 50 tonnes of processed sisal per month. In fact, the land was, unknown to either party, incapable of producing this amount of sisal, and the Privy Council held that the contract was void.

[113] *Bell v Lever Bros Ltd* [1932] A.C. 161 at 225–226, 235–236.

[114] Above, paras 3-018, 3-020.

[115] The discussion of common mistake in *Associated Japanese Bank (International) Ltd v Crédit du Nord SA* [1989] 1 W.L.R. 255 (above, para.3-021) is confined to mistake as to the "subject-matter" of the contract. Mistake was not pleaded in *Naughton v O'Callaghan* [1990] 3 All E.R. 191 (misrepresentation as to true pedigree of racehorse). It was unsuccessfully argued that there was common mistake concerning a shared assumption as to the existence of state consents in *Triple Seven MSN 27251 Ltd v Azman Air Services Ltd* [2018] EWHC 1348 (Comm); [2018] 4 W.L.R. 97 (aircraft leases).

[116] *Sheikh Bros Ltd v Ochsner* [1957] A.C. 136; the decision was based primarily on the wording of the Indian Contract Act 1872 s.20, but the English cases on the law of mistake were also relied on. cf. *Clifford v Watts* (1870) L.R. 5 C.P. 577 (licence to dig clay). See also *Scott v Coulson* [1903] 2 Ch. 249 (life policy not known to have matured); *Griffith v Brymer* (1903) 19 T.L.R. 434 (room to view procession which had been cancelled); *Galloway v Galloway* (1914) 30 T.L.R. 531 (deed of separation between parties in fact unmarried); *Magee v Pennine Insurance Co Ltd* [1969] 2 Q.B. 507 at 517 per Fenton Atkinson L.J. (insurance policy wrongly believed valid); *Associated Japanese Bank (International) Ltd v Crédit du Nord SA* [1989] 1 W.L.R. 255 (guarantee of lease of fictitious machines); *Apvodedo NV v Collins* [2008] EWHC 775 (Ch) (application for summary judgment: agreement for loan to buy Ritz Hotel based on mistaken belief that seller had title); *British Red Cross v Werry* [2017] EWHC 875 (Ch) (agreement based on mistaken belief that deceased died intestate); and contrast *Amalgamated Investment & Property Co Ltd v John Walker & Sons Ltd* [1977] 1 W.L.R. 164 (purchase of building believed available for redevelopment: no mistake because building not listed at time of contract); *Kyle Bay Ltd (t/a Astons Nightclub) v Underwriters Subscribing under Policy No.019057/08/01* [2007] EWCA Civ 57; [2007] 1 C.L.C. 164 (settlement of claim based on incorrect belief as to terms of insurance policy). See Morgan, (2018) 77 C.L.J. 559.

Documents mistakenly signed, and rectification of written contracts

Replace footnote 120 with:

3-024   [120] See, e.g. as regards non est factum, *Chitty on Contracts*, 33rd edn, Vol.1 paras 3–049 et seq.; *Saunders v Anglia Building Society* [1971] A.C. 1004; and Stone, (1972) 88 L.Q.R. 190.

Replace section title footnote 125 with:

5. ILLEGALITY[125]

[125] See generally *Chitty on Contracts*, 33rd edn, Vol.1 Ch.16; Hamson, (1949) 10 C.L.J. 249; Grodecki, (1955) 71 L.Q.R. 254; Higgins, (1962) 25 M.L.R. 149; Furmston, (1966) 16 Univ. of Toronto L.J. 267; Coote, (1972) 35 M.L.R. 38; Shand [1972A] C.L.J. 144; Law Commission, *The Illegality Defence: A Consultative Report*, C.P. 189 (2009); Strauss, (2016) 132 L.Q.R. 236.

3-027

Illegal contracts generally

Replace paragraph with:

A contract is illegal if it involves the commission of a legal wrong or is contrary to public policy, and there is "an element of moral turpitude".[128] The illegality may be in the terms of the contract itself, or in the purpose for which the contract is made, or in the manner of its performance.[129] The nature of the illegality may vary from the commission of a crime at one extreme to a covenant in unreasonable restraint of trade at the other, and its formal source may be found in statute[130] or in the common law (including the rules of public policy). The Supreme Court has, however, moved from a rule-based approach, where the contract is rendered illegal because its formation or performance depends on illegal conduct, such as the commission of a crime, and instead has adopted the approach set out by Lord Toulson:

3-028

> "one cannot judge whether allowing a claim which is in some way tainted by illegality would be contrary to the public interest, because it would be harmful to the integrity of the legal system, without a) considering the underlying purpose of the prohibition which has been transgressed, b) considering conversely any other relevant public policies which may be rendered ineffective or less effective by denial of the claim, and c) keeping in mind the possibility of overkill unless the law is applied with a due sense of proportionality. We are, after all, in the area of public policy."[130a]

It is not necessary in a work on the sale of goods to discuss the subject at length, but certain topics call for some special mention. These are, first, the effect of illegality (as described above) on the contract itself and related transactions; secondly, its effect on the passing of property in the goods which are the subject of a contract of sale; thirdly, its effect as regards restitutionary remedies; and, finally, the application of the doctrine of restraint of trade and the allied questions (now regulated by statute) of monopolies, restrictive practices and resale price maintenance. These matters will be dealt with in the present chapter. The Consumer Protection Act 1987, the Trade Descriptions Act 1968, and other statutes which prohibit or regulate certain specific types of sale are discussed in Ch.14, below.

[128] *Safeways Stores Ltd v Twigger* [2010] EWHC 11 (Comm); [2010] All E.R. 577 at [26]. See *Gray v Thames Trains Ltd* [2009] UKHL 33; [2009] 1 A.C. 1339; *Les Laboratoires Servier v Apotex Inc.* [2014] UKSC 55; [2015] 1 A.C. 430.

[129] See, however, *Euro-Diam Ltd v Bathurst* [1990] Q.B. 1 (offence under foreign law committed only incidentally in course of performance held irrelevant to claim) (but see *Les Laboratoires Servier v Apotex Inc.* [2014] UKSC 55; [2015] 1 A.C. 430).

[130] A contract may be invalid at common law by reason of illegality which has its formal source in a statute on the same principles as apply in the case of other types of illegality; but in addition, one or both of the parties may be deprived of their remedies under a contract because of a prohibition expressed or implied in the statute itself. For this purpose a statute may: (a) prohibit the making or enforcement of a contract absolutely: *Re Mahmoud and Ispahani* [1921] 2 K.B. 716 (cf. *Yin v Sam* [1962] A.C. 304); *Bedford Insce Co Ltd v Instituto de Resseguros do Brasil* [1985] Q.B. 966; *Stewart v Oriental Fire & Marine Insce Co Ltd* [1985] Q.B. 988; *Phoenix General Insce Co of Greece SA v Halvanon Insce Co Ltd* [1988] Q.B. 216; *Re Cavalier Insce Co Ltd* [1989] 2 Lloyd's Rep. 430 (insurance; but see now Financial Services and Markets Act 2000 ss.26–28); *Mohamed v Alaga & Co* [1998] 2 All E.R. 720 (introduction fee); or (b) prohibit the performance of a contract in a particular way: *Anderson Ltd v*

Daniel [1924] 1 K.B. 138; *Marles v Philip Trant & Sons Ltd* [1954] 1 Q.B. 29; or (c) prohibit certain acts in the course of the performance of a contract without affecting the enforceability of the contract itself: *Smith v Mawhood* (1845) 14 M. & W. 452; cf. *St John Shipping Corp v Joseph Rank Ltd* [1957] 1 Q.B. 267; *Archbolds (Freightage) Ltd v S Spanglett Ltd* [1961] 1 Q.B. 374 (carriage); *Shaw v Groom* [1970] 2 Q.B. 504 (tenancy); *Crédit Lyonnais v PT Barnard & Associates Ltd* [1976] 1 Lloyd's Rep. 557; and *SA Ancien Maison Marcel Bauche v Woodhouse Drake & Carey (Sugar) Ltd* [1982] 2 Lloyd's Rep. 516 (cases on exchange control). For the special rules and problems involved in the construction of statutes for this purpose, see *Chitty on Contracts*, 33rd edn, Vol.1 paras 16-181 et seq.; Buckley, (1975) 38 M.L.R. 535.

[130a] *Patel v Mirza* [2016] UKSC 42; [2017] A.C. 467 at [101].

Effect of illegality on contract

Replace paragraph with:

3-029   The change of approach to illegality mentioned in the previous paragraph does not mean earlier decisions would now be decided differently. Nevertheless, the following review of those cases must be treated with some caution, since they follow the rule-based approach. A contract which is affected by illegality cannot be enforced by a party who was aware of or privy to the illegality.[131] If both parties are in this position, it cannot be enforced by either of them.[132] A party who is innocent of the illegality is not deprived of a remedy: the innocent party cannot compel performance of the illegal promise, but is entitled[133] (and, indeed, bound) to desist from further performance, to sue for a price,[134] or to claim on a quantum meruit in respect of performance rendered,[135] and to sue for damages for breach of the contract.[136] For this purpose, someone is an innocent party if unaware of the facts making the contract illegal or of the illegal purpose which the other party had in mind, and also if the other party intended to perform (or has in fact performed) the contract in an illegal manner without the innocent party's knowledge.[137] An innocent party may also, at least in some cases,[138] sue for breach of a collateral warranty or collateral contract—for instance, an assurance given by the other party that the licence necessary for the lawful performance of the principal contract had been or would be obtained.[139]

[131] *Langton v Hughes* (1813) 1 M. & S. 593; *Anderson Ltd v Daniel* [1924] 1 K.B. 138; *Marles v Philip Trant & Sons Ltd* [1954] 1 Q.B. 29; cf. *Bostel Bros Ltd v Hurlock* [1949] 1 K.B. 74 (building contract); *Ashmore, Benson, Pease & Co Ltd v AV Dawson Ltd* [1973] 1 W.L.R. 828 (carriage). cf. *21st Century Logistic Solutions Ltd v Madysen Ltd* [2004] EWHC 231 (QB); [2004] 2 Lloyd's Rep. 92 (intention to defraud too remote to affect contract).

[132] *Pearce v Brooks* (1866) L.R. 1 Ex. 213; *JM Allan (Merchandising) Ltd v Cloke* [1963] 2 Q.B. 340 (contracts of hire). The court will refuse to enforce a contract tainted by illegality even where it has not been pleaded by either party: *Birkett v Acorn Business Machines Ltd* [1999] 2 All E.R. (Comm) 429. Exceptionally, and only in certain cases (e.g. a promise in restraint of trade), the illegal part of a contract may be severed and the balance enforced: see *Chitty on Contracts*, 33rd edn, Vol.1 paras 16-236 et seq.

[133] *Curragh Investments Ltd v Cook* [1974] 1 W.L.R. 1559.

[134] cf. *Pearce v Brooks* (1866) L.R. 1 Ex. 213 at 219, 221; *Mason v Clarke* [1955] A.C. 778 at 793, 805 (profit à prendre).

[135] cf. *Clay v Yates* (1856) 1 H. & N. 73 (contract to print book).

[136] *Bloxsome v Williams* (1824) 3 B. & C. 232; *Marles v Philip Trant & Sons Ltd* [1954] 1 Q.B. 29; cf. *Shaw v Shaw* [1954] 2 Q.B. 429 (contract to marry). If an innocent party has been compelled to observe an illegal contract and suffers loss through its performance, there is some support for the view that this per se would establish a claim to damages: *Shell UK Ltd v Lostock Garages Ltd* [1977] 1 W.L.R. 1187 at 1200.

[137] See the cases cited in para.3-029, nn.136 to 139, above.

[138] This may not be the case where a contract is absolutely prohibited by statute (*Re Mahmoud and Ispahani* [1921] 2 K.B. 716): cf. Treitel, *The Law of Contract*, 14th edn, pp.603–609.

[139] cf. *Strongman (1945) Ltd v Sincock* [1955] 2 Q.B. 525 (building contract). Alternatively, a remedy may lie in deceit: *Burrows v Rhodes* [1899] 1 Q.B. 816; *Shelley v Paddock* [1980] Q.B. 348.

Parties not in pari delicto, and repudiation of executory contract

After "so that recovery", replace "is now allowed, unless it is against public policy." with:

will not be denied merely because the failed consideration was unlawful.　　**3-032**

Replace title footnote 156 with:

Restraint of trade[156]

[156] See *Chitty on Contracts*, 33rd edn, Vol.1 paras 16-106 et seq.; Heydon, *The Restraint of Trade*　**3-033**
Doctrine (2018).

Replace paragraph with:

Covenants and contracts in restraint of trade (although not in themselves unlawful[157]) are prima facie unenforceable[158] at common law, but they may be upheld if they are shown to be reasonable in the interests both of the parties themselves and of the public. Although the concept of restraint of trade is not capable of exhaustive definition,[159] it has been described as follows:

> "A contract in restraint of trade is one in which a party (the covenantor) agrees with any other party (the covenantee) to restrict his liberty in the future to carry on trade with other persons not parties to the contract in such manner as he chooses."[160]

The party seeking to enforce such a covenant must show it was reasonable at the date of the agreement as between the parties and in the public interest. In determining reasonableness, the court will consider, among other things, the relationship between the parties, and will be slow to intervene where they are of equal bargaining power.[161] The question of the validity of these covenants falls to be considered most often in connection with the sale of the goodwill of a business and with contracts of employment and partnership, but it is not confined to these situations. In the context of sales of goods, it may arise in several ways. First, a contract of sale may itself purport to impose restrictions on the use or subsequent disposal of the goods by the buyer. Secondly, two traders may seek by an agreement to regulate their future dealings inter se and, in particular, one of them may undertake to deal exclusively with the other. Thirdly, an arrangement may be made between two or more parties to establish a common policy under which each of them will deal with the world at large—for instance, by price-fixing, control of production or distribution, or adoption of standard terms of trading. These agreements may all be affected by the common law doctrine of restraint of trade, but it is necessary also to consider the relevant provisions of the competition legislation, both the domestic law of the UK and that of the EU.[162]

[157] *Boddington v Lawton* [1994] I.C.R. 478.

[158] It is sometimes possible to sever the unreasonable part of the covenant and to enforce the remainder, or to enforce the contract without the covenant where the latter is not substantially the whole consideration: see *Chitty on Contracts*, 33rd edn, Vol.1 paras 16-241 et seq.

[159] *Esso Petroleum Co Ltd v Harper's Garage (Stourport) Ltd* [1968] A.C. 269 at 298–299, 332; *Petrofina (Great Britain) Ltd v Martin* [1966] Ch. 146 at 180; accepted as "helpful" in the *Esso case* [1968] A.C. 269 at 307, 317.

[160] *Esso Petroleum Co Ltd v Harper's Garage (Stourport) Ltd* [1968] A.C. 269 at 298–299, 332.

[161] *Cavendish Square Holdings BV v Makdessi* [2012] EWHC 3582 (Comm); [2012] 1 All E.R. (Comm) 787 at [15] (reversed on other grounds); *Merlin Financial Consultants Ltd v Cooper* [2014] EWHC 1196 (QB); [2014] I.R.L.R. 610 at [61]; *Visage Ltd v Mehan* [2017] EWHC 2734 (QB) at [35].

[162] See paras 3-040 et seq. In the event that the UK withdraws from the EU, the European Union (Withdrawal) Act 2018 provides that EU-derived domestic legislation (such as EU directives incorporated into UK law under the European Communities Act 1972, s.2(2)) "as it has effect in domestic law immediately before exit day, continues to have effect in domestic law on and after exit day" (s.2(1) 2018 Act), and direct EU legislation (such as EU regulations) so far as operative immediately before exit day, forms part of domestic law on and after exit day (s.3(1) 2018 Act). (These provisions are not yet in force: s.25(4).)

Restraints affecting goods sold

Replace footnote 169 with:

3-035   [169] See *Chitty on Contracts*, 33rd edn, Vol.1 paras 16-154 et seq.; *Esso Petroleum Co Ltd v Harper's Garage (Stourport) Ltd* [1968] A.C. 269 at 298, 309, 325; *Cleveland Petroleum Co Ltd v Dartstone* [1969] 1 W.L.R. 116; *Robinson v Golden Chips (Wholesale) Ltd* [1971] N.Z.L.R. 257; *Amoco Australia Pty Ltd v Rocca Bros Motor Engineering Pty Ltd* [1975] A.C. 561.

Exclusive dealing agreements

Replace footnote 182 with:

3-037   [182] Above, para.3-033; but the remainder of the contract may be enforceable (para.3-033, n.158, above). Sole agency cases have also now passed into general commercial acceptance (see the *Esso* case [1968] A.C. 269 at 311, 320, 328; and cf. *WT Lamb v Goring Brick Co Ltd* [1932] 1 K.B. 710; *Foley v Classique Coaches Ltd* [1934] 2 K.B. 1; *One Money Mail Ltd v RIA Financial Services* [2015] EWCA Civ 1084), except where the restraint is unusually severe (*Att-Gen for Australia v Adelaide SS Co Ltd* [1913] A.C. 781).

Replace title footnote 186 with:

Legislative control of restrictive trading agreements[186]

3-039   [186] *Chitty on Contracts*, 33rd edn, Vol.2 Ch.43; Whish and Bailey, *Competition Law*, 9th edn. In the event that the UK withdraws from the EU, the European Union (Withdrawal) Act 2018 provides that EU-derived domestic legislation (such as EU directives incorporated into UK law under the European Communities Act 1972, s.2(2)) "as it has effect in domestic law immediately before exit day, continues to have effect in domestic law on and after exit day" (s.2(1) 2018 Act), and direct EU legislation (such as EU regulations) so far as operative immediately before exit day, forms part of domestic law on and after exit day" (s.3(1) 2018 Act). (These provisions are not yet in force: s.25(4).)

Replace footnote 190 with:

[190] Competition Act 1998 s.2(1). For the statutory exemptions, see s.3 and Schs 1–4. The Secretary of State also has power to exclude agreements in certain circumstances (s.3(6)). Sections 6 et seq. make provision for block exemptions.

Replace title footnote 195 with:

EU competition law[195]

3-040   [195] See *Chitty on Contracts*, 33rd edn, Vol.2 paras 43-004 et seq.; Whish and Bailey, *Competition Law*, 8th edn.In the event that the UK withdraws from the EU, the European Union (Withdrawal) Act 2018 provides that EU-derived domestic legislation (such as EU directives incorporated into UK law under the European Communities Act 1972, s.2(2)) "as it has effect in domestic law immediately before exit day, continues to have effect in domestic law on and after exit day" (s.2(1) 2018 Act), and direct EU legislation (such as EU regulations) so far as operative immediately before exit day, forms part of domestic law on and after exit day" (s.3(1) 2018 Act). (These provisions are not yet in force: s.25(4).)

Replace the third paragraph with:

The article has been interpreted so as to include not only agreements which prevent, restrict or distort competition as between the parties to the agreement, but also those that affect the competitive position of one of the parties vis-à-vis others (e.g. an exclusive distributorship agreement between G, a German manufacturer and C, a French distributor, which restricted the ability of other firms to distribute G's products in France in competition with C[202]). The Article is not contravened where the effect of the agreement on the market as a whole is insignificant.[203]Article 101(1) does not apply to pure agency agreements[204] or to agreements which operate exclusively outside the EU.[205] But an agreement between undertakings outside the Community may fall within Art.105(1) if it affects competition within the EU.[206]

[202] *Consten SA and Grundig-Verkaufs GmbH v Commission of the European Communities* [1966] C.M.L.R. 418.

[203] *Volk v Vervaecke* [1969] C.M.L.R. 273; *Metro-SB-Grossmärkte GmbH & KG v Commission of the European Communities* [1978] 2 C.M.L.R. 1; *Miller International Schallplatten GmbH v Commission of the European Communities* [1978] E.C.R. 131; *Delimitis v Henniger Bräu* [1991] I E.C.R. 935; and see the Commission's Notice on Agreements of Minor Importance of August 30 [2014] O.J. C291/01 (defining what Commission considers agreement of minor importance).

[204] See the Commission's Guidelines [2010] O.J. C130/01, paras 12–21; *Société Générale Sucrière v Commission of the European Communities* [1975] E.C.R. 1663.

[205] *Re Grosspillex* [1964] 2 C.M.L.R. 237; *Re Riekermann* [1968] C.M.L.R. D78; cf. *Tepea BV v Commission of the European Communities* [1978] 3 C.M.L.R. 392 (agreement affecting trade only within one Member State and between that Member State and the outside world).

[206] *Re Wood Pulp Cartel* [1988] 4 C.M.L.R. 901.

Replace title footnote 210 with:

Free movement of goods[210]

[210] Oliver, *Free Movement of Goods in the European Union*, 5th edn. In the event that the UK withdraws from the EU, the European Union (Withdrawal) Act 2018 provides that EU-derived domestic legislation (such as EU directives incorporated into UK law under the European Communities Act 1972, s.2(2)) "as it has effect in domestic law immediately before exit day, continues to have effect in domestic law on and after exit day" (s.2(1) 2018 Act), and direct EU legislation (such as EU regulations) so far as operative immediately before exit day, forms part of domestic law on and after exit day" (s.3(1) 2018 Act). (These provisions are not yet in force: s.25(4).)

3-041

6.   ASSIGNMENT

Assignment of rights under contract of sale

Replace paragraph with:

The rights of either party under a contract of sale may in general[215] be assigned in accordance with the normal rules governing the assignment of choses in action.[216] Thus a claim for the price of goods sold may be assigned by the seller to a third party, and the right to receive a price which is not due, though not immediately assignable, may be the subject of an agreement to assign. In the same way, a buyer's right to have delivery of the goods may be transferred to another party, provided that no additional obligation is sought to be imposed on the seller (e.g. to make delivery in a different way). As a general rule,[217] obligations of a party to a contract cannot be assigned, except by a novation with the consent of all parties. It, therefore, follows that where the right of a party (A) is conditional upon the performance by A of an obligation, that right cannot be assigned (except with the consent of the other party (B)) in any way which discharges the duty to perform the obligation. It is, of course, possible to arrange with the intended assignee (C) that C will perform the contract, and in many cases B will be bound to accept that performance,[218] but B will be entitled to hold A liable for any breach that may be committed, and is not bound to look for satisfaction to C.[219]

3-042

[215] On the effectiveness of a stipulation in the contract that a right shall be incapable of assignment, see *Linden Gardens Trust Ltd v Lenesta Sludge Disposals Ltd* [1994] 1 A.C. 85. But see *First Abu Dhabi Bank PJSC v BP Oil International Ltd* [2018] EWCA Civ 14 at [27]–[30]. Restrictions on assignments of receivables are regulated by the Business Contract Terms (Assignment of Receivables) Regulations 2018 (SI 2018/1254) (subject to wide-ranging exemptions: regs 3, 4).

²¹⁶ For a full discussion see *Chitty on Contracts*, 33rd edn, Vol.1 Ch.19; Smith and Leslie, *The Law of Assignment: The Creation and Transfer of Choses in Action*, 3rd edn. An assignment by a buyer of rights under a contract for the sale of goods must be distinguished from a sub-sale, and in particular a sub-sale effected or performed by a transfer of the documents of title to goods: as to this, see below, paras 7-067 et seq., 15-092 et seq. The statutory power of an agent or consignee, who has paid the price or is directly responsible for it (Sale of Goods Act s.38(2), below, paras 15-013 et seq.), may be regarded as a form of assignment.

²¹⁷ Exceptionally, the circumstances may be such as to show that the assignee, in accepting the benefits of the contract, agreed also to accept the associated burdens: see *Tito v Waddell (No.2)* [1977] Ch. 106 at 290–307.

²¹⁸ cf. *British Waggon Co v Lea* (1880) 5 Q.B.D. 149.

²¹⁹ *Tolhurst v Associated Portland Cement Manufacturers (1900) Ltd* [1903] A.C. 414; cf. *Sorrentino Fratelli v Buerger* [1915] 1 K.B. 307 at 312–313 (affirmed [1915] 3 K.B. 367).

7.   BANKRUPTCY, INSOLVENCY AND DEATH

Application of bankruptcy rules

Replace footnote 227 with:

3-044   ²²⁷ See on this topic *Chitty on Contracts*, 33rd edn, Vol.1 paras 20–015 et seq.

Effect of bankruptcy and insolvency on contract of sale

Replace footnote 230 with:

3-045   ²³⁰ Excluding rights of a personal nature: *Chitty on Contracts*, 33rd edn, Vol.1 para.20-034.

Replace title footnote 244 with:

Death of party²⁴⁴

3-049   ²⁴⁴ See generally *Chitty on Contracts*, 33rd edn, Vol.1 paras 20-001 et seq

Replace footnote 246 with:

²⁴⁶ *Chitty on Contracts*, 33rd edn, Vol.1 paras 20-006, 23-037.

CHAPTER 4

THE TITLE OF THE SELLER

TABLE OF CONTENTS

In general

After the first paragraph, add new paragraph:

Although the Act does not say so explicitly, the transfer by the seller of a co-ownership interest should be regarded as a sale. Where the goods, for example a ship or a racehorse, are not to be physically partitioned, this conclusion follows from the Act's inclusion, albeit in an incomplete fashion, of contracts for the sale of shares in goods.[3a] A contract of sale necessarily must result in a sale if it is to be performed in full. Furthermore, it is submitted, the transfer of a co-ownership interest in bulk goods, as an intermediate stage occurring before the agreed quantity is separated from the bulk, should also be regarded as a sale.[3b] The seller's property interest in the contract goods is recharacterised, rather than exhausted, when that later stage of separation occurs.

4-001

[3a] Sale of Goods Act 1979 s.2(2): "There may be a contract of sale between one part owner and another." This does not capture the case of a co-owner selling its interest to someone who is not already a co-owner, and also is expressed in contractual and not proprietary terms. The Act also provides that "specific goods" include an undivided share in goods that have been agreed and identified: s.61(1). A sale of the share would therefore presumptively arise at the time of conclusion of the contract of sale: s.18 r.1. Below, para.5-017.

[3b] The seller of a share will therefore be contractually bound at the time of the transfer of the co-ownership interest to have a right to sell that interest: s.12(1). Below, para.4-002. On the treatment of an undivided interest as property for the purposes of risk and frustration, see below, paras 6-006 et seq and 6-030.

Replace footnote 4 with:

[4] *PST Energy Shipping LLC v OW Bunker Malta Ltd (The Res Cogitans)* [2016] UKSC 23; [2016] A.C. 1034, followed in *Newocean Petroleum Co Ltd v OW Bunker China Ltd* [2016] HKCA 739. The court unanimously upheld the decision of the Court of Appeal ([2015] EWCA Civ 1058; [2016] A.C. 1034), which had unanimously upheld the first instance judge, Males J ([2015] EWHC 2022 (Comm); [2015] 2 Lloyd's Rep. 563), who had upheld a unanimous arbitral award. The "legal entitlement to give such permission" to consume the goods emanates from a single prior seller or from "the chain of contracts by virtue of which [the supplier] obtained the [goods]": [2016] UKSC 23; [2016] A.C. 1034 at [39]. See above, paras 1-027 to 1-028, for the role of property in defining a contract as one of sale of goods. For a compelling criticism of the Court of Appeal judgment, arguing (a) that the property might pass at the point of consumption because the reservation of title clause would cease to be effective at that point, and (b) that the supplier could still be regarded as having agreed to pass the property in the goods conditionally on payment being made, see A. Tettenborn, [2016] L.M.C.L.Q. 24. In the Court of Appeal, Moore-Bick LJ saw no reason why this contract might not "in commercial terms" be regarded as a contract for the sale of goods ([2015] EWCA Civ 1058; [2016] A.C. 1034 at [33]), though it is not clear what legal consequences would be generated by such a commercial approach. See also Bridge, [2017] Singapore Journal of Legal Studies 345; Low and Loi [2018] J.B.L. 229. In a case concerning the assignment by way of security, by a supplier of bunkers to a third party bank, of receivables "relat-

ing to the sale of oil products", the court as a matter of construction and notwithstanding *The Res Cogitans* concluded that the assignment included receivables arising from the supply of bunkers under sui generis supply contracts. This was because assignor and assignee "assumed that [the] supply contracts were contracts of sale and intended that the security provisions of the contract applied to them": *Cockett Marine Oil DMCC v ING Bank NV* [2019] EWHC 1533 (Comm) at [63]–[65].

Replace the fourth paragraph with:

Provided the seller transfers or agrees to transfer the property in the goods, there can therefore be a sale of goods even though, for example, the goods have been stolen from their true owner. The seller will be able to transfer his entire property interest in the goods,[16] even if he is unable to transfer a title that will override the title of the true owner.[17] As far as the contractual aspect of the matter is concerned, an agreement for the sale of the property of another is not null and void.[18] If the seller agrees to divest himself of the general or absolute property in the goods in favour of the buyer, there is a contract of sale notwithstanding that he is not the owner of the goods and has no right to sell them.[19] Moreover, at common law, it did not necessarily follow from the very act of selling the goods that the seller warranted his title or right to sell.[20] There was an implied undertaking on his part that he did not *know* that he had no right to sell; but otherwise, in the absence of such fraud or knowledge, the seller of specific goods was not liable in damages for bad title unless there was an express warranty, or the equivalent to it, by declaration or conduct.[21] Usage of trade might be sufficient to raise such a warranty; and in ordinary sales, e.g. from an open shop or warehouse, the seller was considered to warrant that the buyer would have a good title to keep the goods purchased.[22] However, the circumstances surrounding the transaction might create no such inference, and the sale would then be subject to the principle of caveat emptor.[23]

[16] But for the view, in the case of software, that a sale occurs when a seller transfers a perpetual licence to use it, see *Software Incubator Ltd v Computer Associates UK Ltd* [2016] EWHC 1587 (QB); [2017] Bus. L.R. 245 at [62], reversed in part on other grounds [2018] EWCA Civ 518; [2018] 1 Lloyd's Rep. 613.

[17] See *Kulkarni v Manor Credit (Davenham) Ltd* [2010] EWCA Civ 69; [2010] 2 All E.R. (Comm) 101 at [43]: "I should not be thought of as saying (despite the great authority of anything falling from Atkin L.J.) that a seller cannot complete a sale if he lacks full rights of ownership in the goods". This view, it is submitted, is to be preferred to Atkin LJ's view, expressed with reference to the scope of s.11(4), that "there can be no sale at all of goods which the seller has no right to sell" (*Rowland v Divall* [1923] 2 K.B. 500, 506) and to the view expressed in *Revenue and Customs Commissioners v Apollo Fuels Ltd* [2016] EWCA 157; [2016] 4 W.L.R. 96 at [30] that property "means the absolute ownership interest in the goods" (referring to a work in which that proposition is substantially qualified). Atkin LJ's statement was, however, referred to without disapproval in *Dana Gas PJSC v Dana Gas Sukuk Ltd* [2018] EWHC 278 (Comm) at [13].

[18] *National Employers' Mutual General Insurance Assn Ltd v Jones* [1990] 1 A.C. 24 at 50; cf. at 39–40, 42 CA (this point did not arise on appeal to the House of Lords). cf. also *Rowland v Divall* [1923] 2 K.B. 500 at 506; *Customs and Excise Commissioners v Oliver* [1980] 1 All E.R. 353 at 355. The concept of property is discussed by Kiralfy, (1949) 12 M.L.R. 424; and by Battersby and Preston (1972) 35 M.L.R. 268, 272–275 who suggested that "property" in the Act meant "a title to the absolute legal interest in the goods sold": below, para.5-001 n.1. cf. Battersby [2001] J.B.L. 1.

[19] But if both the seller and buyer know the goods have been stolen or otherwise unlawfully acquired the contract may be unenforceable on the ground of illegality: see Theft Act 1968 ss.22, 24. cf. below, para.4-031 .

[20] *Noy's Maxims* (1641) (c.42).

[21] *Furnis v Leicester* (1619) Cro. Jac. 474; *Crosse v Gardner* (1688) Carth. 90; *Medina v Stoughton* (1699) 1 Salk. 210; *Peto v Blades* (1814) 5 Taunt. 657; *Early v Garrett* (1829) 9 B. & C. 928 at 932; *Morley v Attenborough* (1849) 3 Exch. 500 at 513; *Sims v Marryat* (1851) 17 Q.B. 281. "Warranty" is used here in the sense of guarantee.

[22] *Morley v Attenborough* (1849) 3 Exch. 500 at 512; *Eichholz v Bannister* (1864) 17 C.B.(N.S.) 708.

[23] See, e.g. *Peto v Blades* (1814) 5 Taunt. 657; *Morley v Attenborough* (1849) 3 Exch. 500; *Chapman v Speller* (1850) 14 Q.B. 621; *Page v Cowasjee Eduljee* (1866) L.R. 1 P.C. 127 at 144; *Bagueley v*

Hawley (1867) L.R. 2 C.P. 625; *Re Rogers* (1874) L.R. 9 Ch. App. 432 at 437; *Wood v Baxter* (1883) 49 L.T. 45; and below, para.4-031. By 1893, the exceptions could be stated to have become the rule: *Rowland v Divall* [1923] 2 K.B. 500 at 505.

1. THE SELLER'S RIGHT TO SELL THE GOODS

Right to sell the goods

Replace the first paragraph with:

The Sale of Goods Act 1979 s.12(1)[24] provides that in a contract of sale, other than one to which subs.(3) of s.12 applies,[25] there is an implied term on the part of the seller[26] that in the case of a sale he has a right to sell the goods, and in the case of an agreement to sell he will have such a right at the time when the property is to pass.[27] In those cases where the seller transfers a co-ownership interest to the buyer, whether in accordance with s.20A of the Sale of Goods Act 1979 or otherwise, a breach of the term in s.12(1) will be committed if the seller does not have a right to sell at that time. The liability thus imposed is a strict liability, and does not depend upon the fault or knowledge of the seller. Nor does it depend upon any disturbance of the buyer's possession of the goods by the true owner.[28] It has been stated that the corresponding provision in the 1893 Act re-enacted the rule of common law,[29] but it seems that it both clarified the rule and extended the protection afforded to the buyer.[30]

4-002

[24] This subsection, along with the remainder of s.12, no longer applies to consumer sales: Consumer Rights Act 2015 Sch.1 para.11. The relevant provision now is s.17(1)(b) of the 2015 Act (see below, para.14-089), which applies to both sale and other supply contracts but otherwise leaves the treatment of sale unchanged. The right to "sell" becomes in that Act the right to "transfer" (undefined) because the 2015 Act deals with sale, hire, hire purchase and other transfer contracts together, under the general description of "supply": see s.3(2) of the 2015 Act. On the 2015 Act in general, see Ch.14.

[25] See below, para.4-031.

[26] It may in some complex arrangements not be easy to identify the parties to the contract of sale. In *J D Cleverly Ltd v Family Finance Ltd* [2010] EWCA Civ 1477; [2011] R.T.R. 22, a rogue (Webb, trading as Gwent) placed an order with a dealer (Cleverly, trading as Cardiff Audi) for a new car. At the rogue's request, the dealer delivered the car to T, who had contracted to purchase it from the rogue and who paid the rogue in full. The dealer invoiced the rogue for the car in the expectation that the invoice would be forwarded to the rogue's chosen finance company, and the rogue passed the invoice on to the finance company in the present case (Family Finance). The finance company then paid the dealer and entered into a hire purchase contract with the rogue in contemplation of a sub-lease between the rogue and an unnamed sub-lessee that never materialised. When the rogue defaulted on his hire purchase payments, the finance company brought a claim against the dealer under s.12(1), on the assumption that T had obtained good title to the car, whether under the Factors Act s.2(1) or the Sale of Goods Act s.25. The claim against the dealer failed because, on the facts, the dealer, even though expecting the invoice to be passed on to a finance company, had contracted to sell the car to the rogue and not to the finance company.

[27] Compare the corresponding provisions in the Vienna Convention on Contracts for the International Sale of Goods Arts 30, 41–44 (see above, para.1-024). For consumer "sales contracts" governed by the Consumer Rights Act 2015, equivalent provisions to those contained in s.12 of the 1979 Act are to be found in s.17 of the 2015 Act: below, paras 14-087 to 14-089 and 14-091 to 14-092.

[28] As in the case of Sale of Goods Act 1979 s.12(2)(b); below, para.4-024.

[29] *Rowland v Divall* [1923] 2 K.B. 500 at 505 ("but as a condition, not a warranty").

[30] *Niblett v Confectioners' Materials Ltd* [1921] 3 K.B. 387 at 402; see above, para.4-001.

In the second paragraph after "shipowners consuming the", replace "fuels," with:
bunkers,

Time at which the right to sell must exist

Replace the first paragraph with:

4-005   Where the contract of sale purports to effect a present transfer of the property in the goods from the seller to the buyer, the seller must have a right to sell the goods at the time of the contract. But where the contract of sale is merely an agreement to sell,[48] the obligation on the seller under the statute is to have a right to sell the goods at the time when the property is to pass.[49] Since it is common for contracts of sale to be concluded before the seller becomes the owner of the goods, this has been said to represent "a completely standard way of the world".[50] So, for example, in the case of a conditional sale agreement under which the purchase price is payable by instalments and the property in the goods is not to pass to the buyer until all the instalments are paid notwithstanding that the buyer is to have possession of the goods in the meantime, it is sufficient under s.12(1) that the seller have a right to sell the goods only at the time when the property is to pass. If, therefore, before that time it emerges that the seller has no title to the goods agreed to be sold, the buyer will be unable to treat the contract as repudiated and recover the instalments paid unless he proves that it will be impossible for the seller to pass a good title when the payments are completed[51] or that the situation is such as to lead a reasonable person to conclude that the seller does not intend, or will not then be able, to do so.[52] The conditional buyer, who has taken delivery but whose possession has not yet been disturbed, is therefore in a precarious position. Nevertheless, it may be an express term of such an agreement that the seller is the owner of the goods at the time the agreement is entered into. It was conceded in *Barber v NWS Bank Plc*[53] that a clause providing that "the property in the Goods shall pass to the Customer" upon payment meant that the seller was the owner of the goods at the time the contract was concluded.[54] Although it amounted to a very generous interpretation of the clause in favour of the buyer, this concession was approved as being "both correct and unavoidable".[55] Alternatively, it may be a necessary inference from the terms of the agreement and the surrounding circumstances that the seller must be the owner of the goods at the time of their delivery to the buyer and remain their owner until the time when the property is to pass.[56] The absence of a statutory provision to this effect in s.12(1) means that such a term may not routinely be implied, notwithstanding the gap in the buyer's protection.

[48] See above, para.1-026.

[49] Sale of Goods Act 1979 s.12(1).

[50] *Kulkarni v Manor Credit (Davenham) Ltd* [2010] EWCA Civ 69; [2010] 2 Lloyd's Rep. 431 at [9].

[51] *Chitty on Contracts*, 33rd edn, Vol.1 para.24-031.

[52] *Chitty on Contracts*, 33rd edn, Vol.1 para.24-018.

[53] *Barber v NWS Bank Plc* [1996] 1 W.L.R. 641; below, para.4-020. See Bridge, *The Sale of Goods*, 3rd edn, para.5.03.

[54] The link between the quoted clause and the concession is not as clear as it might be in the report.

[55] *Barber v NWS Bank Plc* [1996] 1 W.L.R. 641 at 646. cf. *Odyssey Aviation Ltd v GFG 737 Ltd* [2019] EWHC 1927 (Comm) at [52]–[58] (express term that seller "holds and is free to convey" full title applied not at the date of the contract but at the date when the property was to pass).

[56] See *Karflex Ltd v Poole* [1933] 2 K.B. 251, as interpreted in *Mercantile Union Guarantee Corp Ltd v Wheatley* [1938] 1 K.B. 490; and *Warman v Southern Counties Car Finance Corp Ltd* [1949] 2 K.B. 576 (hire-purchase).

Improvements

After "the improved value.", add:

If the true owner demands the goods and the buyer surrenders them, nothing in **4-007**
s.6 would prevent the buyer from recovering the price in full from an improving
seller. As well as having no means of resisting the buyer's claim for the return in
full of the price after rescinding the contract, the seller would also have no means
of claiming an allowance from the true owner. The buyer's conjectural right to claim
an allowance against the true owner if sued to judgment should not preclude a
failure of consideration claim as against the seller.

Change of position

Replace paragraph with:

If the buyer claims to recover the purchase price on the ground of failure of **4-008**
consideration, this is a claim in restitution. In principle, therefore, it would be open
to the seller to raise the defence of change of position, which was recognised by the
House of Lords in *Lipkin Gorman v Karpnale Ltd*[80] as a general defence to a
personal restitutionary claim. The defence was there stated to be "available to a
person whose position has so changed that it would be inequitable in all the
circumstances to require him to make restitution or alternatively to make restitution in full".[81] In *Barber v NWS Bank Plc*,[82] the seller was in breach of an express
term as to title and the buyer sued to recover the purchase price. The seller raised
the defence of change of position. The Court of Appeal considered the defence very
briefly and found it not to have been made out on the facts of the case.[83] The seller
was therefore required to refund the purchase price in full. The court did not,
however, specifically reject the defence. A question of some difficulty is whether
the defence should be available to a seller who, innocently, has in breach of an
express or implied term of the contract failed to convey a good title to the goods
which he purported to sell. The same issue could also arise where the supplier of
goods under a sui generis contract for their lawful consumption innocently failed
to obtain permission from the true owner.[84] In *Lipkin Gorman v Karpnale Ltd*,[85]
Lord Goff said that "it is commonly accepted that the defence should not be open
to a wrongdoer". On one view, "wrongdoing" can include a breach of contract by
the payee from whom recovery is sought where it is that breach of contract which
provides the basis for the restitutionary claim. If this were so, it would not be
inequitable to disregard any change of position by the seller as a result of the payment and to require him to make full restitution of the money which he has obtained
in return for an undertaking which he has, in breach of contract, failed to fulfil. It
is submitted, however, in view of Lord Goff's references to good faith, bad faith
and innocent donees, that for present purposes a seller who is not personally at fault
should not be regarded as a "wrongdoer". The defendant's entitlement to the change
of position defence should rest on the equitability of his conduct[86] and upon whether
he acted in good faith,[86a] which will call for the development of the change of position defence on a case by case basis.[86b]

[80] *Lipkin Gorman v Karpnale Ltd* [1991] 2 A.C. 548 at 558, 562, 567–568, 577.

[81] *Lipkin Gorman v Karpnale Ltd* [1991] 2 A.C. 548 at 580. See Goff and Jones, *The Law of Unjust Enrichment*, 9th edn, Ch.27.

[82] *Barber v NWS Bank Plc* [1996] 1 W.L.R. 641.

[83] *Barber v NWS Bank Plc* [1996] 1 W.L.R. 641 at 648.

84 *PST Energy Shipping LLC v OW Bunker Malta Ltd (The Res Cogitans)* [2016] UKSC 23; [2016] A.C. 1034.

85 *Lipkin Gorman v Karpnale Ltd* [1991] 2 A.C. 548 at 579.

86 Goff and Jones, *The Law of Unjust Enrichment*, 9th edn, paras 27-40 et seq.; *Niru Battery Manufacturing Co v Milestone Trading Ltd (No.1)* [2003] EWCA Civ 1446; [2004] Q.B. 985 at [162] and [192].

86a *Lipkin Gorman v Karpnale Ltd* [1991] 2 A.C. 548.

86b *Lipkin Gorman v Karpnale Ltd* [1991] 2 A.C. 548 at 580 (Lord Goff).

Acceptance of the goods

Replace paragraph with:

4-009   By the Sale of Goods Act 1979 s.11(4)[87] the acceptance of the goods by the buyer will normally take away his right to treat the contract as repudiated for breach of condition, and he will be compelled to sue for damages for breach of warranty only.[88] In *Rowland v Divall*,[89] it was argued for the seller that the case fell within this provision, but Atkin LJ held[90] that this subsection had no application to the breach of s.12(1) of the Act in that case as a result of an implied term in the contract to that effect.[91] This approach does not sit well with the restraint shown in modern times toward the recognition of terms implied in fact in a contract.[91a] A separate approach is based upon a claim for the recovery of money on a total failure of consideration, which is not a claim that depends upon the treatment of a contract as having been repudiated. Hence, it should not be limited by s.11(4). Section 11(4) does not apply to sui generis contracts for the lawful consumption of goods.[92] If the common law equivalent of s.12(1) in the case of such contracts were to be treated in a similar way,[93] the loss of the recipient's right to treat the contract as repudiated would depend upon whether there was a failure of consideration arising from the supplier's failure to provide permission from the true owner to consume or dispose of the goods.

87 Previously s.11(1)(c) of the 1893 Act, as amended by the Misrepresentation Act 1967 s.4(1). cf. the Supply of Goods (Implied Terms) Act 1973 s.14 (conditional sales).

88 See below, para.12-038.

89 *Rowland v Divall* [1923] 2 K.B. 500.

90 *Rowland v Divall* [1923] 2 K.B. 500 at 506–507. Even if the goods have been accepted, the buyer's damages may amount to the sum paid, according to the hire purchase case of *Warman v Southern Counties Car Finance Corp* [1949] 2 K.B. 576, where a hirer suing for damages on the ex post facto implied warranty of title was able to recover the sum of instalments paid.

91 *Rowland v Divall* [1923] 2 K.B. 500 at 507. cf. Ellinger, (1969) 5 Victoria Univ. of Wellington L.R. 168. It is arguable that s.11(4) should apply to the claim to reject under s.12(1), even if it does not apply to the claim to recover the purchase price for total failure of consideration. Quaere whether s.11(4) would apply if the buyer knows of the seller's lack of title. (See Atiyah, *The Sale of Goods*, 13th edn, p.93 n.66.)

91a *Marks & Spencer Plc v BNP Paribas Securities Services Trust Co (Jersey) Ltd* [2015] UKSC 72; [2016] A.C. 742; *Bou-Simon v BGC Brokers LP* [2018] EWCA Civ 1525; [2019] 1 All E.R. (Comm) 955.

92 *PST Energy Shipping LLC v OW Bunker Malta Ltd (The Res Cogitans)* [2016] UKSC 23; [2016] A.C. 1034.

93 See para.4-006.

Chain transactions

Replace paragraph with:

4-014   Goods may be sold many times over in breach of s.12(1) before they are ultimately traced by the true owner. A thief, for example, may sell the goods which he has stolen to A, who sells to B, who sells to C. Each party in this chain transaction will be liable for conversion of the goods, for each sale and delivery of the goods, albeit innocent, constitutes an act inconsistent with the true owner's title to the goods.[125] In practice, however, the true owner will seek to recover possession of the goods or their value[126] from the buyer who is actually in possession of them, i.e. from C, and it is against C that an action for wrongful interference will be brought. C will then claim against B as a Pt 20 defendant, and, in turn, B will claim against A as a Pt 20 defendant (2nd claim). Since the thief will normally be insolvent or will have disappeared when the day of reckoning arrives, the person who will have to bear the loss is A, the first innocent purchaser in the chain. But if any buyer in the centre of the chain is insolvent, the person who purchased the goods from him will have to bear the loss. Such a purchaser cannot sue the previous sellers in the chain for between him and them there is no privity of contract, and sales of goods do not, in English law, effect an assignment by the seller to the buyer of the seller's rights under a previous contract of sale. Nor, it is submitted, can any buyer who is sued in conversion claim contribution from previous sellers under the Civil Liability (Contribution) Act 1978.[127] They are not liable "in respect of the same damage"[128] since each successive sale is a separate and distinct conversion of the goods.

[125] As to whether these various tortfeasors commit the "same damage" for the purpose of apportionment under the Civil Liability (Contribution) Act 1978 s.1(1), see Bridge, Gullifer, Low and McMeel, *The Law of Personal Property*, 2nd edn, para.16-048.

[126] cf. *Wickham Holdings Ltd v Brooke House Motors Ltd* [1967] 1 W.L.R. 295; above, para.4-013.

[127] But see the Torts (Interference with Goods) Act 1977 s.9.

[128] Civil Liability (Contribution) Act 1978 s.1.

Fraud or misrepresentation by seller

Replace footnote 163 with:

[163] *Pearson (S) & Son Ltd v Dublin Corp* [1907] A.C. 351; *Boyd & Forrest v Glasgow & SW Ry*, 1915 S.C.(H.L.) 21 at 36; *HIH Casualty and General Insurance Ltd v Chase Manhattan Bank* [2003] UKHL 6; [2003] 2 Lloyd's Rep. 61 at [154]. See also Misrepresentation Act 1967 s.3 (as amended by the Unfair Contract Terms Act 1977 s.8). But this principle does not necessarily apply to cases of mere non-disclosure, as opposed to a positive representation. It may however be possible with suitable language to exclude liability for the fraud of an agent: *Candy v Holyoake* [2017] EWCA Civ 92; [2018] Ch. 297 at [95] ("clear and specific wording is required to exclude remedies arising from dishonesty or fraud, on the assumption that it is, in principle, possible to do so"); *HIH Casualty and General Insurance Ltd v Chase Manhattan Bank* at [16] and [68].

4-021

Replace footnote 164 with:

[164] As a statement of private rights, as distinct from the general law, it is treated as a misrepresentation of fact. This is less important now that misrepresentations of law, so far as they are not opinion statements, are actionable: see *Chitty on Contracts*, 33rd edn, Vol.1 para.7-017.

2. FREEDOM FROM ENCUMBRANCES AND QUIET POSSESSION

Freedom from encumbrances

Replace footnote 174 with:

[174] See Conveyancing Act 1881 s.7; Law of Property Act 1925 s.76 and Sch.2 Pt I (now repealed); Law of Property (Miscellaneous Provisions) Act 1994 s.3; Megarry and Wade, *The Law of Real Property*, 9th edn (Cooke, Bridge and Dixon), para.14-081.

4-022

Quiet possession

Replace footnote 203 with:

4-025   203   *Jones v Lavington* [1903] 1 K.B. 253; *Markham v Paget* [1908] 1 Ch. 697; Megarry and Wade, *The Law of Real Property*, 9th edn (Cooke, Bridge and Dixon), para.18-014 (landlord and tenant).

3.   SALE OF A LIMITED TITLE

Limited title

Replace footnote 245 with:

4-031   245   *Chapman v Speller* (1850) 14 Q.B. 621 at 624. It would seem that this might be the proper construction of the contract if the buyer knew of the seller's defective title: *Clark v England* (1916) 29 D.L.R. 374 at 376; *Northwest Co Ltd v Merland Oil Co of Canada and Gas and Oil Products Ltd* [1936] 4 D.L.R. 248 (but see above, para.4-001). See also the Law Commission's *First Report on Exemption Clauses in Contracts (Amendments to the Sale of Goods Act 1893)* (1969), Law Com. No.24; US Uniform Commercial Code Art.2–312(2).

CHAPTER 5

PASSING OF PROPERTY

In general

Replace footnote 9 with:

[9] It is possible that the property in goods will pass at the point of payment under sui generis supply contracts of the sort considered in *PST Energy Shipping LLC v OW Bunker Malta Ltd (The Res Cogitans)* [2016] UKSC 23; [2016] A.C. 1034. Payment might be made at a time when some or all of the goods remain the hands of the recipient. It is submitted that, by analogy with sale of goods contracts, the passing of property rules in the Sale of Goods Act should be applied as a matter of common law. This is preferable to treating the recipient as having a mere immunity when dealing with the goods as it would permit the recipient to deal with the goods outside the terms of the bailment licence.

5-001

1.   EFFECTS OF THE PASSING OF PROPERTY

Title of the buyer

Replace footnote 19 with:

[19] Despite the title of the statute, there is no action for wrongful interference as such, but actions for trespass, conversion and damage done to a reversionary interest, as well as for negligence: see Bridge, Gullifer, Low and McMeel, *The Law of Personal Property*, 2nd edn, Ch.32.

5-003

Insolvency

In the first paragraph, after "the goods have", add:
been

5-005

Replace footnote 39 with:

[39] i.e. small companies, excluding companies such as banks, insurance companies, and companies involved in the performance of market contracts. There is a pending Government proposal to extend the moratorium to all companies (with some exceptions) meeting "certain eligibility criteria and qualify-

ing conditions": Department for Business, Energy & Industrial Strategy, *Insolvency and Corporate Governance* (26 August 2018), paras 5.5 et seq.

Title to sue

Replace the fourth paragraph with:

5-009   However, in the case of goods carried internationally by rail,[64] road[65] and air,[66] the relevant international convention normally[67] states who is entitled to claim against the carrier, and the rights of action conferred by the convention do not ordinarily depend upon ownership of the goods.

[64] COTIF Convention (as amended): CIM Rules Art.54, see below, paras 21-067 to 21-073.

[65] CMR Convention Art.13. See below, paras 21-059 to 21-065; and *Chitty on Contracts*, 33rd edn, Vol.2 paras 36-118 et seq.

[66] Warsaw Convention (as amended) Arts 13, 14, 24. See below, paras 21-052 to 21-058; and *Chitty on Contracts*, 33rd edn, Vol.2 para.35-077. But see *Western Digital Corp v British Airways Plc* [2001] Q.B. 733 (owner can sue though not named as consignor or consignee).

[67] The CMR Convention is not comprehensive on this point, see *Chitty on Contracts*, 33rd edn, Vol.2 para.36-135.

Replace title footnote 81 with:

Insurance[81]

5-012   [81] See *Chitty on Contracts*, 33rd edn, Vol.2 paras 42-003 to 42-008; Palmer and McKendrick, *Interests in Goods*, 2nd edn (Birds), Ch.4.

2.   Specific Goods

(a)   Specific Goods in a Deliverable State

Conditional contract

Replace footnote 128 with:

5-021   [128] See also Sale of Goods Act 1979 s.43(2); below, paras 15-006, 15-059. cf. Torts (Interference with Goods) Act 1977 s.5(1) (conversion claimant's title extinguished only on actual payment of damages by defendant).

Replace footnote 131 with:

[131] Consumer Credit Act 1974 ss.8(1), 189(1) (as amended by the Consumer Credit Act 2006). The financial limit of £5,000 in the 1974 Act was raised at later dates before being removed by the 2006 Act.

Specific goods

At the end of the second paragraph, after "sale is made.", add new footnote 136a:

5-022   [136a] But note that an undivided share may be regarded as a chose in action for purposes outside the Sale of Goods Act: *Re Sugar Properties (Derisley Wood) Ltd* (1987) 3 B.C.C. 88 (Bills of Sale Acts). See above paras 1-081 and 1-116.

Deliverable state

Replace paragraph with:

5-025   A contract for the sale of an undivided share, specified as a fraction or percentage of goods identified and agreed on at the time of the contract,[146] does not fall within s.18 r.1, if it is the parties' intention that the undivided share is subsequently to be separated from the bulk and delivered to the buyer, since the goods[147] will not be in a deliverable state at the time the contract is made. The deliverable state requirement, however, does not bar the acquisition, by the buyer of a quantity of goods, of an undivided interest in an identified bulk where the conditions required by s.20A for the buyer to acquire that undivided interest have been satisfied.[147a] But if the parties intend that the undivided share is to remain permanently undivided, for example, where a half share in a racehorse is sold to each of A and B, the rule could apply, given that the definition of specific goods now includes an undivided share in goods.[147b] Neither case concerns a contract for the sale of an unascertained quantity in an identified bulk where, in order for an undivided interest to be acquired by the buyer under s.20A, the buyer would have to pay an amount commensurate to that interest.[148]

[146] i.e. "specific goods" within the extended definition in the Sale of Goods Act 1979 s.61(1); see above, paras 1-116, 5-022.

[147] By the Sale of Goods Act 1979 s.61(1), "goods" include an undivided share in goods.

[147a] Below, para.5-109.

[147b] Above, para.5-022.

[148] See below, paras 5-109 et seq.

Different intention

Replace paragraph with:

The presumption contained in s.18 r.1 will not apply where a different intention appears.[149] The most common situation is where the parties intend that the property in the goods shall not pass to the buyer until the price is paid[150] or a bill of exchange has been accepted,[151] or a cheque has been cleared.[151a] Once the property has passed under s.18 r.1, the parties could no doubt agree that it is to be divested from the buyer and revested in the seller; but convincing evidence is required that the parties so intended by a mere subsequent agreement that the goods are to remain the property of the seller until the price has been paid.[152] It is also necessary to consider whether any arrangement as to payment of the price is intended to suspend the passing of property or relates only to the circumstances in which the seller is prepared to deliver the goods to the buyer.[153] Thus, where specific goods are sold across the counter in a shop, property in the goods may pass under the rule when the contract is made, notwithstanding that the goods have not been paid for or that the method of payment, e.g. cash, or credit, or acceptance of a cheque, has still to be agreed.[154] But it may instead be the intention of the parties that property is to pass only on delivery or payment.[155] In a supermarket, property in the goods taken from the shelf will as a matter of reality and commercial practice pass to the customer only upon payment of the proper amount at the checkpoint.[156]

5-026

[149] This refers back to the Sale of Goods Act 1979 s.17.

[150] *McEntire v Crossley Bros Ltd* [1895] A.C. 457; *Re Shipton* [1915] 3 K.B. 676; *Mooney v Lipka* [1926] 4 D.L.R. 647; *Re Anchor Line (Henderson Bros) Ltd* [1937] Ch. 1; *Ward (RV) Ltd v Bignall* [1967] 1 Q.B. 534. See also the Sale of Goods Act 1979 s.19(1); below, para.5-133.

[151] *Saks v Tilley* (1915) 32 T.L.R. 148. But see *Leigh & Sillavan Ltd v Aliakmon Shipping Co Ltd (The Aliakmon)* [1986] A.C. 785. See also s.19(3); below, para.5-140.

[151a] *Dobson v General Accident Fire and Life Assurance Corp Plc* [1990] 1 Q.B. 274 at 280 ("valid building society cheque").

[152] *Dennant v Skinner and Collom* [1948] 2 K.B. 164 at 172. See also *Sirius Shipping Corp v The Ship Sunrise* [2006] NSWSC 398.

[153] *Dennant v Skinner and Collom* [1948] 2 K.B. 164 at 172. See also *Phillips v Brooks* [1919] 2 K.B. 243, as subsequently interpreted in *Lake v Simmons* [1927] A.C. 487 at 501.

[154] This point may be of importance where the contract is entered into under a mistake as to the person; see *Phillips v Brooks* [1919] 2 K.B. 243; *Lake v Simmons* [1927] A.C. 487. cf. *Ingram v Little* [1961] 1 Q.B. 31 at 49; above, para.3-012. But cases on mistake should not be carried over into the criminal law: *R. v Morris* [1984] A.C. 320.

[155] *Mooney v Lipka* [1926] 4 D.L.R. 647; see also *Lambert v G & C Finance Corp* (1963) 107 S.J. 666 (retention of car log-book); *Cheetham & Co v Thornham Spinning Co* [1964] 2 Lloyd's Rep. 17 (retention of shipping document).

[156] *Lacis v Cashmarts* [1969] 2 Q.B. 400 at 407; *Davies v Leighton* [1978] Crim. L.R. 575; *R. v Morris* [1984] A.C. 320.

3. Goods Delivered on Approval or on Sale or Return

Approval or on sale or return

Replace footnote 222 with:

5-041   [222] *Harrison v Allen* (1824) 2 Bing. 4; *Johnson v Kirkaldy* (1840) 4 Jur.Rep. 988; *Moss v Sweet* (1851) 16 Q.B. 493 at 495; *Kirkham v Attenborough* [1897] 1 Q.B. 201; *Bryce v Ehrmann* (1904) 7 F. 5, 13; *Bradley & Cohn Ltd v Ramsey & Co* (1912) 107 L.T. 771; *Genn v Winkel* (1912) 107 L.T. 434; *Poole v Smith's Car Sales (Balham) Ltd* [1962] 1 W.L.R. 744. Depending on the terms of the contract, the buyer may be entitled to purchase part of the goods and return the remainder: *Atari Corp (UK) Ltd v Electronics Boutique Stores (UK) Ltd* [1998] Q.B. 539.

Bailment

Replace paragraph with:

5-044   The position of a person who has received goods on approval or on sale or return is that he has the option of becoming the purchaser of them, being free to do so or not as he chooses.[234] One analysis of the transaction is that the seller makes to the buyer an irrevocable offer to sell, which the buyer may accept by signifying his acceptance to the seller or in one of the other ways set out in the rule.[235] Alternatively, the seller may be regarded as having granted to the buyer an option to purchase. The granting of the option imposes no obligation on the buyer and an obligation on the seller which is contingent on the exercise of the option.[236] Whichever analysis is adopted, pending acceptance of the offer or the exercise of the option, the buyer is in lawful possession of the goods[237] and holds them as bailee.[238] In certain situations, it may therefore be difficult to distinguish a contract on sale or return from a bailment for hire[239] or from a simple bailment with an option to purchase,[240] or from a bailment on terms that the bailee is to have the power to sell or dispose of the goods to third parties.[241] If such is the true nature of the transaction, property will not pass to the bailee under s.18 r.4, e.g. simply by the expiration of a reasonable time.

[234] See above, para.5-041.

[235] *Kirkham v Attenborough* [1897] 1 Q.B. 201 at 203; *Atari Corp (UK) Ltd v Electronics Boutique Stores (UK) Ltd* [1998] Q.B. 539.

[236] *Spiro v Glencrown Properties Ltd* [1991] Ch. 537 (land).

[237] *Colwill v Reeves* (1811) 2 Camp. 575.

[238] *Atari Corp (UK) Ltd v Electronics Boutique Stores (UK) Ltd* [1998] Q.B. 539; Bridge, *The Sale of Goods*, 3rd edn, para.3.17. See below, para.5-057.

[239] *General Motors Acceptance Corp (UK) Ltd v IRC* (1986) 59 T.C. 651.

[240] In some respects, this type of transaction is not dissimilar from a hire-purchase agreement, where the hirer has an option to purchase the goods or return them to the owner, and the owner is bound contingently to sell: *Helby v Matthews* [1895] A.C. 471. But a hire-purchase agreement is distinguishable by the presence of a bailment for hire. cf. Consumer Credit Act 1974 s.189(1): "hire-purchase agreement". See above, paras 1-021, 1-053.

[241] *Whitehorn Brothers v Davison* [1911] 1 K.B. 463 at 480. See also *Poole v Smith's Car Sales (Balham) Ltd* [1962] 1 W.L.R. 744.

Agency

Replace footnote 242 with:

[242] See *Bowstead and Reynolds on Agency*, 21st edn, para.1–036; and above, para.1-048.   **5-045**

Notice of rejection

Replace paragraph with:

Property will not pass to the buyer by the expiration of time[284] where he has noti-   **5-052**
fied the seller of his rejection of the goods within the appropriate time.[285] If goods
are sold on approval, then, in the absence of provision to the contrary, the buyer can
reject the goods for reasons other than that the goods are defective or
unsatisfactory.[286] The form of the notice depends upon the terms, express or implied,
of the particular contract. But any intimation to the seller which clearly
demonstrates that the buyer does not wish to exercise his option to purchase will
ordinarily suffice,[287] although it is open to the parties to agree that the buyer shall
be entitled to reject only by returning the goods or in some other specified manner.[288]
In *Atari Corp (UK) Ltd v Electronics Boutique Stores (UK) Ltd,*[289] the Court of Appeal held that, in the absence of a contrary intention, the notice did not have to be
in writing or identify precisely the goods to which it related: it sufficed to identify
the goods generically (e.g. "unsold stock") or in such other way as to enable
individual identification later by some objective means. The Court of Appeal further
held that the goods did not have to be physically capable of collection at the time
the notice was issued.

[284] Notice of rejection must also be given before the property in the goods has passed by acceptance, adoption or approval: above, para.5-047.

[285] Sale of Goods Act 1979 s.18 r.4(b).

[286] *Berry v Star Brush Co* (1915) 31 T.L.R. 603.

[287] *Atari Corp (UK) Ltd v Electronics Boutique Stores (UK) Ltd* [1998] Q.B. 539. See also *Bradley & Cohn Ltd v Ramsey & Co* (1911) 28 T.L.R. 13; (1912) 106 L.T. 771 where it was held at first instance that a refusal to pay the seller's price was a rejection of the goods. Contrast *Ellis v Mortimer* (1805) 1 B. & P.N.R. 257.

[288] *Ornstein v Alexandra Furnishing Co* (1895) 12 T.L.R. 128.

[289] *Atari Corp (UK) Ltd v Electronics Boutique Stores (UK) Ltd* [1998] Q.B. 539.

Effect of notice

Replace footnote 291 with:

[291] *Atari Corp (UK) Ltd v Electronics Boutique Stores (UK) Ltd* [1998] Q.B. 539.   **5-053**

Goods returned in a damaged condition

After "would be liable", add:
as bailee   **5-056**

4. UNASCERTAINED GOODS

Unascertained goods

Replace footnote 320 with:

5-060   [320] *Healy v Howlett & Sons* [1919] 1 K.B. 337; *Re Wait* [1927] 1 Ch. 606; *Thames Sack & Bag Co v Knowles* (1919) 88 L.J.K.B. 585; *The Aramis* [1989] 1 Lloyd's Rep. 213; *AstraZeneca UK Ltd v Albemarle International Corp* [2011] EWHC 1574 (Comm); [2011] 2 C.L.C. 252 at [304]; *SSL International Plc v TTK LIG Ltd* [2011] EWCA Civ 1170; [2012] 1 W.L.R. 1842 at [89]–[92]; *NEC Corp v Steintron International Electronics Ltd* (1985) 59 C.B.R. (N.S.) 91 (Can). In *Re Yukon Zinc Corp* 2015 BCSC 836, goods were held to be ascertained when part of a bulk, the remainder of which had been bought by the same buyer under a contract that was not in issue (at [123]).

Estoppel

Replace footnote 371 with:

5-065   [371] *Maynegrain Pty Ltd v Compafina Bank* [1982] 2 N.S.W.L.R. 141. See *Bowstead and Reynolds on Agency*, 21st edn, paras 8-168 et seq..

(a)   Appropriation with the Assent of the Other Party

Meaning of appropriation

After "to pass it.", add:

5-069   The first meaning is barely distinguishable at all from ascertainment.

After "in this sense", add:

5-070   has to be unconditional and

Unconditional appropriation

After "act is done.", add footnote 401a:

5-072   [401a] cf. *NEC Corp v Steintron International Electronics Ltd* (1985) 59 C.B.R. (N.S.) 91 (Can); *Boroni Foods Ltd v PK Wholesale Supplies Ltd* [2017] NZHC 335 (perishable goods set aside for the buyer, prior to delivery at buyer's premises, where "[t]he goods had been specifically ordered for [the buyer] and there was no other buyer for them" (at [83]).

"Ex works", etc contracts

Replace footnote 473 with:

5-089   [473] *Fisher Reeves & Co v Armour & Co* [1920] 3 K.B. 614 at 620, 622–623, 624. The property was held to pass in an ex works contract containing special carriage terms (above, para.5-072) when the goods left the factory gate in *Sabaf SpA v MFI Furniture Centres* [2002] EWCA Civ 976; [2003] R.P.C. 14 at [61], revd on other grounds [2004] UKHL 45; [2005] R.P.C. 10. See also *Pignataro v Gilroy* [1919] 1 K.B. 459, above, para.5-077.

(b)   Appropriation of Future Goods

Goods to be manufactured and sold

Replace footnote 483 with:

5-091   [483] *Mucklow v Mangles* (1808) 1 Taunt. 318 (above, para.5-080); *Atkinson v Bell* (1828) 8 B. & C. 277. See also *SSL International Plc v TTK LIG Ltd* [2011] EWCA Civ 1170; [2012] 1 W.L.R. 1842 at [89]–[92].

(c) Appropriation by Delivery

Delivery to the buyer

Replace paragraph with:

The property in ascertained goods[518] will, in the absence of a contrary intention,   **5-097**
pass by delivery[519] to the buyer or his agent.[520] A different intention was held to be
absent in *R. (on the application of Valpak) v Environment Agency.*[520a] In that case,
the property in bottles from which publicans poured drinks was held to pass to
customers on appropriation of the bottles, even though it might not be known at that
time whether customers preferred to drink from the glass or from the bottle, and
even though publicans might insist on retaining the bottle in the interest of public
order. Where the goods at the time of sale are in the possession of a third person,
e.g. a warehouseman or wharfinger, delivery will take place when the third person
attorns to the buyer, that is to say, acknowledges to the buyer that he holds the goods
on his behalf,[521] but not before.[522] If a delivery order[523] is merely received without
acknowledgment by the warehouseman or wharfinger, no delivery, and therefore no
transfer of ownership, will occur.[524] Yet if the goods are unascertained, no property
will pass unless they become ascertained by reason of the attornment.[525]

[518] See above, para.5-059, below, para.5-099.

[519] Defined in s.61(1) of the Act as "voluntary transfer of possession from one person to another"; see
below, para.8-002.

[520] *Ogle v Atkinson* (1814) 5 Taunt. 759; *Studdy v Sanders* (1826) 5 B. & C. 628; *Colonial Insurance
Co of New Zealand v Adelaide Marine Insurance Co* (1886) 12 App. Cas. 128; *Denny v Skelton* (1916)
115 L.T. 305; *Caradoc Nurseries Ltd v Marsh* (1959) 19 D.L.R. (2d) 491, Can. At a filling station,
property in the fuel will pass when it is put into the vehicle's fuel tank: *Edwards v Ddin* [1976] 1 W.L.R.
942; *Re Charge Card Services Ltd* [1989] Ch. 497.

[520a] *R. (on the application of Valpak) v Environment Agency* [2002] EWHC 1510 (Admin); [2002] Env.
L.R. 36. Where shipping documents are not ready to be tendered to the buyer, but the goods are neverthe-
less released to the buyer, a different intention is not present merely because the buyer might later reject
the documents for non-compliance, and thus also the goods themselves: *Huyton SA v Peter Cremer
GmbH & Co* [1999] 1 Lloyd's Rep. 620 at 623; *BCL Trading GmbH v Trafigura Beheer BV* [2002]
EWCA Civ 251 at [26]–[28].

[521] *Wardar's (Import and Export) Co Ltd v Norwood & Sons Ltd* [1968] 2 Q.B. 663.

[522] Sale of Goods Act 1979 s.29(4); see below, para.8-012.

[523] But contrast the position where a document of title is issued or transferred: below, para.8-013.

[524] *Laurie & Morewood v Dudin & Sons* [1926] 1 K.B. 223; *Mount (DF) Ltd v Jay and Jay (Provisions) Co Ltd* [1960] 1 Q.B. 159.

[525] *Re London Wine Co (Shippers) Ltd* [1986] P.C.C. 121; above, para.5-065.

(d) Appropriation of Goods forming part of an Identified Bulk

Different intention

Replace paragraph with:

Section 18 r.5 of the 1979 Act as a whole applies only "unless a different inten-   **5-108**
tion appears". In relation to para.(4), there may be situations where the circumstances are such as to show that the parties intend that the remaining goods are to
be divided up and each portion appropriated to a particular contract before the
property in the goods is to pass. And in relation to both paras (3) and (4) the parties may intend that property is to pass only on delivery, or on transfer of the shipping documents against payment or securing of the price.[569-570] The seller may also
have reserved the right of disposal,[571] in which case property will not pass under

these paragraphs until the conditions imposed by the seller (usually payment in full of the price) have been fulfilled.

569-570 See below, para.18-336.

571 Below, para.5-133.

Replace section title footnote 572 with:

5.   Undivided Shares in Goods Forming Part of a Bulk[572]

5-109   572 See Bridge, [2019] L.M.C.L.Q. 57; Burns, (1996) 59 M.L.R. 260; Ulph, [1996] L.M.C.L.Q. 93; Bridge, *The Sale of Goods*, 3rd edn, paras 3.51 et seq.; Bridge, *The International Sale of Goods*, 4th edn, paras 7.16 et seq; Palmer and McKendrick, *Interests in Goods*, 2nd edn (McKendrick), Ch.16; and below, para.18-337.

Section 20A

Replace footnote 573 with:

573 It is possible, though perhaps unlikely, that a bulk may consist of goods supplied to 2 or more recipients under sui generis supply contracts of the sort considered in *PST Energy Shipping LLC v OW Bunker Malta Ltd (The Res Cogitans)* [2016] UKSC 23; [2016] A.C. 1034 and that the bulk has not been exhausted by the time that one or more recipients has paid in full. Section 20A, not declaratory of the common law, cannot apply to such contracts by analogy but it is arguable that a more relaxed inference of a tenancy in common than was displayed in *Laurie & Morewood v Dudin & Sons* [1926] 1 K.B. 223 would be appropriate in such a case. A flexible approach would be needed for those cases where the bulk consists of goods destined for a combination of buyer or buyers under a contract of sale and recipient or recipients under a sui generis contract. But see the refusal to infer a tenancy in common where stock held for buyers was subjected at intervals to a manual override so that there was less stock in hand than the amount due to all the relevant buyers in *Re Far Pavilions Interiors Pty Ltd* [2016] FCA 1602.

Sale of a specified quantity of unascertained goods

After "from its ambit.", add:

5-111   The seller's later election to crystallise the contract amount will then satisfy the specified quantity requirement.

Identified bulk

Replace paragraph with:

5-114   The third requirement is that the bulk must be identified, either in the contract or by subsequent agreement between the parties. It must be certain from which bulk the goods are to come.[603] However, this must be established by agreement between the parties. A unilateral identification of the bulk by either seller or buyer will not suffice, even if communicated to the other party, unless the other party can be taken to have agreed or assented to that identification. Particular problems arise in relation to this requirement in the case of c.i.f. contracts, where the seller gives to the buyer a notice of appropriation, declaration of shipment or notice of nomination identifying the cargo on a named ship, part of which cargo is appropriated (in the contractual sense) to the buyer's contract.[604] It is submitted that a buyer who contracts on terms allowing the seller unilaterally to select the bulk has agreed to that bulk for the purposes of the section. The buyer in such a case is bound to accept a seller's notice if it is timely and compliant with the formal requirements of the contract.[604a]

603 A reference in warehouse receipts to metals "Inwarehouse Singapore" was held to be insufficient to identify the bulk in *RBG Resources Plc v Banque Cantonale Vaudoise* [2004] 3 S.L.R. (R.) 421, Sing, at [68].

604 See below, para.18-343.

[604a] *Waren Import Gesellschaft Krohn & Co v Alfred C Toepfer (The Vladimir Ilich)* [1975] 1 Lloyd's Rep. 322; Bridge, *The International Sale of Goods*, 4th edn, para.4.50.

Undivided share

Replace footnote 608 with:

[608] This may in any case amount to the required agreement. Above, para.5-114 and below, para.18-343.

5-116

Different types of bulk

After "of 5,000 gallons.", add new footnote 614a:

[614a] See *Pars Rams Brothers (Pte) Ltd v Australian & New Zealand Banking Group Ltd* [2018] SGHC 60.

5-119

6.   RESERVATION OF THE RIGHT OF DISPOSAL

Right of disposal

After "in the subsection.", add:

A reservation of the right of disposal is also to be distinguished from a contractual provision, the effect of which is that on a designated event the goods are to be returned to the seller.[680a]

5-133

[680a] *DFS Australia Pty Ltd v Comptroller-General of Customs* [2017] FCA 547 at [72] (failure by traveler to export goods within a stipulated period), citing *McPherson, Thom, Kettle & Co v Dench Bros* [1921] V.L.R. 437.

Documentary bills

Replace footnote 708 with:

[708] See Chalmers and Guest, *Bills of Exchange and Cheques*, 18th edn, (Gleeson) paras 6-043 et seq.; and below, para.18-272.

5-140

Priorities

Replace footnote 868 with:

[868] *Dearle v Hall* (1828) 3 Russ. 1. See *Chitty on Contracts*, 33rd edn, Vol.1 para.19-069.

5-163

Voluntary arrangements

Replace footnote 897 with:

[897] Insolvency Act 1986 Sch.A1 para.2. There is a pending Government proposal to extend the moratorium to all companies (with some exceptions) meeting "certain eligibility criteria and qualifying conditions": Department for Business, Energy & Industrial Strategy, *Insolvency and Corporate Governance* (26 August 2018), paras 5.5 et seq.

5-166

Non-corporate buyer

Replace footnote 907 with:

[907] Bills of Sale Act 1878; Bills of Sale Act 1878 (Amendment) Act 1882. The Law Commission has recommended that the Bills of Sale Acts should be repealed and replaced with modern legislation: *Bills of Sale*, Law Com. No.369 (2016). But the Government announced in May 2018 that it would not bring forward the Goods Mortgages Bill designed to implement this recommendation and would not seek to reform the law in the immediate future.

5-169

Disadvantages of a Romalpa clause

Replace footnote 920 with:

5-172 [920] *Aluminium Industrie Vaassen BV v Romalpa Aluminium Ltd* [1976] 1 W.L.R. 676 at 690; *Re Bond Worth Ltd* [1980] Ch. 228 at 262–263; McCormack, 11 B.L.R. 109 (1990). cf. *FG Wilson (Engineering) Ltd v John Holt & Co (Liverpool) Ltd* [2013] EWCA Civ 1232; [2014] 1 Lloyd's Rep. 180.

CHAPTER 6

RISK AND FRUSTRATION

1.   RISK

(a)   Property and Risk

Identification of the goods

Replace footnote 27 with:

[27] *Stock v Inglis* (1884) 12 Q.B.D. 564; affirmed sub nom. *Inglis v Stock* (1885) 10 App. Cas. 263 (below,   **6-004**
para.6-014). See also *Incoterms* (2010) (f.o.b.), B.5 and below, para.18-348.

Risk in relation to rejected goods

Replace footnote 69 with:

[69] *Hiort v Bott* (1874) L.R. 9 Ex. 86 at 90; *Howard v Harris* (1884) Cab. & El. 253. But contrast *New-*   **6-011**
man v Bourne and Hollingsworth (1915) 31 T.L.R. 209; *Summer v Challenor* (1926) 70 S.J. 760; *Elvin
and Powell Ltd v Plummer Roddis Ltd* (1933) 50 T.L.R. 158; *Houghland v Low (RR) (Luxury Coaches)
Ltd* [1962] 1 Q.B. 694 at 698; *Chitty on Contracts*, 33rd edn, Vol.2 para.33-036.

Insurable interest

Replace paragraph with:

    The question of the allocation of risk is often of importance where a claim is   **6-012**
made on an insurance policy, since the insured must have an insurable interest in
the goods at the time of the loss.[70] It will be sufficient that the goods are at his risk
even though he has no property in them.[71] The topic of insurance is, however,
outside the scope of this work and reference should be made to specialist treatises
on insurance law.

[70] See *Anderson v Morice* (1876) 1 App. Cas. 713; Marine Insurance Act 1906 ss.4–8, and generally
Chitty on Contracts, 33rd edn, Vol.2 paras 42-005 to 42-017. But see also Marine Insurance Act 1906
s.4; and above, para.5-012.

⁷¹ See, e.g. *Inglis v Stock* (1885) 10 App. Cas. 263; *Colonial Insurance Co of New Zealand v Adelaide Marine Insurance Co* (1886) 12 App. Cas. 128. In *Milos Equipment Ltd v Insurance Corp of Ireland* (1990) 47 B.C.L.R. (2d) 296, a dealer with a right to sell a trade-in vehicle, but who had neither possession of nor the property in the vehicle, was held to have an insurable interest in it.

(b)   Carriage of Goods to the Buyer

Seller's responsibilities at point of delivery

After "buyer to frame", add:

6-015   it

(d)   Liability as Bailee

Seller or buyer as bailee

Replace footnote 130 with:

6-021   ¹³⁰ *Houghland v Low (RR) (Luxury Coaches) Ltd* [1962] 1 Q.B. 694 at 698; *Morris v CW Martin & Sons Ltd* [1966] 1 Q.B. 716 at 726, 731. See also *Coggs v Bernard* (1703) 2 Ld. Raym. 909 at 916; *Bullen v Swan Electric Engraving Co* (1907) 23 T.L.R. 258; *Blount v War Office* [1953] 1 W.L.R 736 at 739; *James Buchanan & Co Ltd v Hay's Transport Services Ltd* [1972] 2 Lloyd's Rep. 535 at 543; *Port Swettenham Authority v Wu (TW) & Co (M) Sdn Bhd* [1979] A.C. 580 at 589; *Mitchell v Ealing LBC* [1979] Q.B. 1; *China Pacific SA v Food Corp of India* [1982] A.C. 939 at 960; *Sutcliffe v Chief Constable of West Yorkshire* [1998] R.T.R. 86; *Chitty on Contracts*, 33rd edn, Vol.2 paras 33-032, 33-036.

Remedies

Replace footnote 137 with:

6-023   ¹³⁷ See the definition of "fault" in s.4 of the 1945 Act; and *Sayers v Harlow UDC* [1958] 1 W.L.R. 623; *Quinn v Burch Bros (Builders) Ltd* [1966] 2 Q.B. 370 at 381; *de Meza v Apple* [1974] 1 Lloyd's Rep. 508; [1975] 1 Lloyd's Rep. 498; *Rowe v Turner Hopkins & Partners* [1980] 2 N.Z.L.R. 550; *Basildon DC v JE Lesser Ltd* [1985] Q.B. 839; *AB Marintrans v Comet Shipping Co Ltd* [1985] 1 Lloyd's Rep. 568; *Forsikringsaktieselskabet Vesta v Butcher* [1989] A.C. 852 CA; *Chitty on Contracts*, 33rd edn, Vol.1 para.26-085. See also the Torts (Interference with Goods) Act 1977 s.11(1).

Replace section title footnote 149 with:

2.   FRUSTRATION¹⁴⁹

6-028   ¹⁴⁹ See Treitel, *Frustration and Force Majeure*, 3rd edn; McKendrick (ed), *Force Majeure and Frustration of Contract*, 3rd edn. For the range of circumstances that might be considered, see *Edwinton Commercial Corp v Tsavliris (Worldwide Salvage & Towage) Ltd (The Sea Angel)* [2007] EWCA Civ 547; [2007] 2 Lloyd's Rep. 517.

Generally

Replace paragraph with:

   A contract of sale may be frustrated where, after the contract has been entered into,¹⁵⁰ but before the property in the goods has passed to the buyer,¹⁵¹ without default of either party,¹⁵² the contract has become impossible of legal performance, or incapable of being performed because the circumstances in which performance is called for render it a thing radically different from that which was undertaken by the contract.¹⁵³ The principle of frustration is, of course, not confined to contracts of sale of goods,¹⁵⁴ but the rules of common law relating thereto are applicable to contracts of sale by virtue of the Sale of Goods Act 1979 s.62(2).¹⁵⁵

¹⁵⁰ As contrasted with initial impossibility (above, para.1-122) or initial illegality (above, para.3-027).

¹⁵¹ In most cases, the passing of property will preclude the operation of frustration, but in some circumstances the relevant time will be the passing of the risk, or even the delivery of goods to the buyer

where, e.g. he is an alien enemy (see below, para.6-036). In the case of instalment sales, the property in some of the goods may have passed, but the contract still be frustrated as to the remainder.

[152] See *Bank Line Ltd v Arthur Capel & Co* [1919] A.C. 435 at 452; *Maritime National Fish Ltd v Ocean Trawlers Ltd* [1935] A.C. 524 at 530; *Joseph Constantine SS Line Ltd v Imperial Smelting Corp Ltd* [1942] A.C. 154 at 170–171; *Ocean Tramp Tankers Corp v V/O Sovfracht (The Eugenia)* [1964] 2 Q.B. 226; *Denmark Productions Ltd v Boscobel Productions Ltd* [1969] 1 Q.B. 699; *Paal Wilson & Co A/S v Partenreederi Hannah Blumenthal* [1983] 1 A.C. 854 at 882, 909, *J Lauritzen A/S v Wijsmuller BV (The Super Servant Two)* [1990] 1 Lloyd's Rep. 1 at 8–10;Treitel, *Frustration and Force Majeure*, 3rd edn, Ch.14; *Chitty on Contracts*, 33rd edn, Vol.1 para.23-061 (self-induced frustration).

[153] See below, para.6-035.

[154] See generally *Chitty on Contracts*, 33rd edn, Vol.1 Ch.23.

[155] See also s.11(6).

(a)   Specific Goods which have Perished

Section 7

In the first paragraph, after "of specific goods.", add new footnote 167a:

[167a] But the share may be a chose in action for purposes outside the Sale of Goods Act: above, paras 1-081 and 1-116.

6-030

Howell v Coupland

Replace paragraph with:

It is generally thought that s.7 of the Act was formulated in reliance on the decision of the Court of Appeal in *Howell v Coupland*,[177] where the defendant agreed to sell to the claimant 200 tons of potatoes to be grown on a particular field.[177a] The crop failed, so that the defendant was able to deliver only 80 tons. It was held that he was relieved of liability to deliver the other 120 tons by reason of impossibility of performance.[178] Sir Mackenzie Chalmers was of the opinion that s.7 applied to specifically described goods, whether in existence at the time the contract was made or not.[179] But this interpretation does not accord with the definition of "specific goods" in s.61(1) of the Act.[180] It seems better[181] to regard the situation in *Howell v Coupland* either as an instance of a sale upon a contingency covered by s.5(2) or as a sale subject to a condition implied at common law[181a] as preserved by s.62(2) of the Act. It was not decided in *Howell v Coupland* whether the seller might have refused delivery of the 80 tons which he in fact delivered. This will depend on the presumed intention of the parties.[181b] A condition may be implied that, in such circumstances, the contract is wholly discharged. Alternatively, a condition may be implied that the buyer shall have the option of accepting part delivery.[182] In this type of case, therefore, one or both parties may be relieved, in whole or in part, from further performance of his obligations under the contract. But the contract is not avoided by s.7 of the Act; nor is it otherwise discharged automatically by frustration.

6-032

[177] *Howell v Coupland* (1876) 1 Q.B.D. 258.

[177a] In *JGL Commodities Ltd v Puddell Farms Ltd* 2018 SKQB 345, the seller of durum wheat was a producer but, not being required to supply wheat from its own land, could not claim the protection of s.7 when adverse growing conditions restricted the availability of durum wheat of the contract quality.

[178] *Howell v Coupland* (1876) 1 Q.B.D. 258 at 262. See also the decision at first instance (1874) L.R. 9 Q.B. 462.

[179] Mark (ed), Chalmers' Sale of Goods Act, 1893, 18th edn, p.100. See also *PS International Canada Corp v Palimar Farms Inc* 2016 SKQB 232 at [98].

[180] See Treitel, *Frustration and Force Majeure*, 3rd edn, para.4-052, and above, paras 1-113, 5-022.

[181] *Re Wait* [1927] 1 Ch. 606 at 630–631; *Sainsbury Ltd v Street* [1972] 1 W.L.R. 834.

[181a] *PS International Canada Corp v Palimar Farms Inc* 2016 SKQB 232 at [88] , affirmed 2017 SKCA 78 at [30].

[181b] But see *Islamic Republic of Iran Shipping Lines v Steamship Mutual Underwriting Association (Bermuda) Ltd* [2010] EWHC 2661 (Comm) at [125]; [2010] 2 C.L.C. 534 ("the seller will have an excuse for non-performance of the part of the crop that has failed").

[182] *Sainsbury Ltd v Street* [1972] 1 W.L.R. 834. cf. *Lovatt v Hamilton* (1839) 5 M. & W. 639; *Lipton Ltd v Ford* [1917] 2 K.B. 647.

(b)   Other Instances of Frustration

Unascertained goods

Replace paragraph with:

6-035   Section 7 of the 1979 Act deals only with the particular case of specific goods which have perished, and it is of course possible for a contract for the sale of specific goods to be frustrated by other events, e.g. by the requisitioning of the goods.[192] Where, however, the contract is one for the sale of unascertained generic goods, it is obvious from the very nature of the contract that the circumstances necessary for frustration will only rarely arise. The seller is normally free to obtain supplies from any source he chooses, and *genus numquam perit*. Thus, it has been said:

"… a bare and unqualified contract for the sale of unascertained goods will not (unless most special facts compel an opposite implication) be dissolved by the operation of the principle [of frustration], even though there has been so grave and unforeseen a change of circumstances as to render it impossible for the vendor to fulfil his bargain."[193]

In most cases, therefore, it is no defence for the seller to plead that goods of the description mentioned in the contract are no longer available from the source from which he intended to obtain them: the contract is not frustrated.[194] Only if the parties have contracted expressly or impliedly on the basis of a *common* assumption that the goods are to come from that particular source and no other will frustration occur,[195] as might be so where the seller is a producer. In such a case, where the parties have contracted for a particular grade of goods, the buyer may not demand delivery of a lower grade that happens to be available.[195a] Even if the source contemplated is the sole source from which the goods can be obtained, a mere interruption or reduction of supplies due to commonplace difficulties such as breakdown of machinery or inadequacies of transport will not frustrate the contract: they are "the warp and woof of industrial and commercial aggravation".[196] Nevertheless it must not be supposed that an unqualified contract for the sale of unascertained goods can never be frustrated.[197] Frustration can occur if the contract becomes physically or legally impossible of performance or if:

"… without default of either party the contractual obligation has become incapable of being performed because the circumstances in which performance is called for would render it a thing radically different from that undertaken by the contract."[198]

In *CTI Group Inc v Transclear SA (The Mary Nour)*,[199] a contract for the supply of cement was, to the knowledge of the parties, dependent upon the sellers' ability to procure a cargo despite the opposition of a monopolist in the intended country of importation. The sellers' attempts were unsuccessful but the court at first instance reversed an arbitral finding that the contract had become commercially impossible to perform, though on appeal it was noted that a contract would not necessarily be frustrated because it had become impossible to perform.[200] The sellers were liable for non-delivery because they had assumed the risk of a failure of supply, which they might have guarded against, but had not, either by entering into a binding contract with a supplier or by making their own obligations conditional upon the availability to them of goods for delivery.[201] They had also succumbed to pressure as a matter of choice.[202]

[192] *Re Shipton, Anderson & Co and Harrison Bros & Co* [1915] 3 K.B. 676; see below, para.6-044.

[193] *Blackburn Bobbin Co Ltd v TW Allen & Sons Ltd* [1918] 1 K.B. 540 at 550 (affirmed [1918] 2 K.B. 467). See below, para.19-129.

[194] *King v Parker* (1876) 34 L.T. 886; *Jacobs v Crèdit Lyonnais* (1884) 12 Q.B.D. 589; *Gelling v Crispin* (1917) 23 C.L.R. 443; *Blackburn Bobbin Co Ltd v Allen (TW) & Sons Ltd* [1918] 1 K.B. 540; *Lebeaupin v Crispin & Co* [1920] 2 K.B. 714; *Re Thornett and Fehr and Yuills Ltd* [1921] 1 K.B. 219; *George Wills & Sons Ltd v RS Cunningham, Son & Co Ltd* [1924] 2 K.B. 220; *Twentsche Overseas Trading Co Ltd v Uganda Sugar Factory Ltd* (1944) 113 L.J.P.C. 25; *Monkland v Jack Barclay Ltd* [1951] 2 K.B. 252 at 258; *Beves & Co Ltd v Farkas* [1953] 1 Lloyd's Rep. 103; *Hong Guan & Co Ltd v R Jumabhoy & Sons Ltd* [1960] A.C. 684; *Parrish & Heimbecker Ltd v Gooding Lbr. Ltd* (1968) 67 D.L.R. (2d) 495; *Gold Group Properties Ltd v BDW Trading Ltd* [2010] EWHC 323 (TCC) at [74]; *JGL Commodities Ltd v Puddell Farms Ltd* 2018 SKQB 345. cf. *Lipton v Ford* [1917] 2 K.B. 647; *Brooke Tool Manufacturing Co Ltd v Hydraulic Gears Co Ltd* (1920) 89 L.J.K.B. 263.

[195] *Re Badische Co Ltd* [1921] 2 Ch. 331; *Société Co-operative Suisse des Céreales et Matières Fouragères v La Plata Cereal Co SA* (1947) 80 Ll. L.R. 530; *CTI Group Inc v Transclear SA (The Mary Nour)* [2008] EWCA Civ 856; [2008] 2 Lloyd's Rep. 256 at [23]; *Sanschagrin v Echo Flour Mills Co* (1922) 70 D.L.R. 380. See also *Howell v Coupland* (1876) 1 Q.B.D. 258; above, para.6-032.

[195a] *PS International Canada Corp v Palimar Farms Inc* 2016 SKQB 232 at [81] et seq., affirmed 2017 SKCA 78 at [43] (contract for grade #2 lentils but only grade #3 were available), even though the seller was able to sell the sub-standard goods for a price higher than the contract price for the superior goods (2016 SKQB 232 at [107], affirmed 2017 SKCA at [54]).

[196] *Intertradex SA v Lesieur Tourteaux SARL* [1977] 2 Lloyd's Rep. 146 at 154 (affirmed [1978] 2 Lloyd's Rep. 509). See also *George Eddy Co Ltd v Corey* [1951] 4 D.L.R. 90.

[197] *Re Badische Co Ltd* [1921] 2 Ch. 331 at 381–383. See also *E Hulton Co Ltd v Chadwick and Taylor Ltd* (1918) 34 T.L.R. 230 (all-round embargo on goods in question); and below, paras 18-381 et seq.

[198] *Davis Contractors Ltd v Fareham UDC* [1956] A.C. 696 at 729. See also *Acetylene Co of GB v Canada Carbide Co* (1922) 8 Ll. L.R. 456; *Tsakiroglou & Co Ltd v Noblee Thorl GmbH* [1962] A.C. 93; *National Carriers Ltd v Panalpina (Northern) Ltd* [1981] A.C. 675 at 688, 700, 717; *Pioneer Shipping Ltd v BTP Tioxide Ltd* [1982] A.C. 724 at 744, 745, 751; *Paal Wilson & Co A/S v Partenreederei Hannah Blumenthal* [1983] 1 A.C. 854; *Exportadora de Azucar v Industria Azucarera Nacional SA* [1983] 2 Lloyd's Rep. 171; *Atisa SA v Aztec AG* [1983] 2 Lloyd's Rep. 579.

[199] *CTI Group Inc v Transclear SA (The Mary Nour)* [2007] EWHC 2070 (Comm); [2008] 1 Lloyd's Rep. 179; affirmed [2008] EWCA Civ 856; [2008] 2 Lloyd's Rep. 256.

[200] *CTI Group Inc v Transclear SA (The Mary Nour)* [2008] EWCA Civ 856 at [13]–[14]; [2008] 2 Lloyd's Rep. 256.

[201] The court at first instance also considered an alternative ground for holding the sellers liable, because the fault of their own suppliers could be attributed to them under the contract of sale. This ground was inapplicable on the present facts because the sellers did not have the benefit of a binding contract to supply them with the goods, so there was no supplier fault, to be attributed to them or not, in their capacity of sellers: [2007] EWHC 2070 (Comm); [2008] 1 Lloyd's Rep. 179 at [36].

[202] *CTI Group Inc v Transclear SA (The Mary Nour)* [2008] EWCA Civ 856; [2008] 2 Lloyd's Rep. 256 at [27].

Outbreak of war

Replace the first paragraph with:

By the Trading with the Enemy Act 1939 s.1(1)[203] it is a criminal offence to supply any goods to or for the benefit of an enemy[204] or to obtain any goods from an enemy in time of war. Indeed, both at common law and under this statute, all commercial intercourse between a British subject[205] and an enemy becomes illegal upon the outbreak of war.[206] As a result, any existing contract of sale which involves such

6-036

intercourse by reason of the performance or further performance of the contract is frustrated by the outbreak of war, or upon one of the parties acquiring the status of an enemy.[207] Even if the contract contains a clause which suspends its entire operation during the period of war, it nevertheless becomes illegal and is discharged.[208] It is otherwise, however, if the parties expressly provide that, in the event of war, an illegal method of performance is to be cancelled and a legal method substituted therefor.[209]

[203] For the definition of trading with the enemy, see the Trading with the Enemy Act 1939 s.1(2), (3), as amended by Emergency Laws (Miscellaneous Provisions) Act 1953 s.2 and Sch.2 para.2(1), (2).

[204] Defined in the Trading with the Enemy Act 1939 ss.2(1), 15(3), (5), as amended by Emergency Laws (Miscellaneous Provisions) Act 1953 s.2 and Sch.3 para.3(a), (b).

[205] Or a person owing temporary allegiance to the Crown. See also *Kuenigl v Donnersmarck* [1955] 1 Q.B. 515 at 539.

[206] See generally McNair and Watts, *The Legal Effects of War*, 4th edn; Rogers, *Effect of War on Contracts* (1940); Trotter, *Law of Contract during and after War*, 4th edn; Webber, *Effect of War on Contracts*, 3rd edn; Howard, *Trading with the Enemy* (1943) and Suppt (1945); Treitel, *Frustration and Force Majeure*, 3rd edn, para.8-004.

[207] *Wolf (W) & Sons v Carr, Parker & Co Ltd* (1915) 31 T.L.R. 407; *Zinc Corp Ltd v Hirsch* [1916] 1 K.B. 541; *Distington Hematite Iron Co v Possehl* [1916] 1 K.B. 811; *Veithardt and Hall Ltd v Rylands Bros Ltd* (1917) 116 L.T. 706; *Ertel Bieber & Co v Rio Tinto Co* [1918] A.C. 260; *Naylor Benzon Co Ltd v Krainische Industrie Gesellschaft* [1918] 2 K.B. 486; *Re Continho Caro & Co* [1918] 2 Ch. 384; *Re Badische Co Ltd* [1921] 2 Ch. 331; *Cantiare San Rocco SA v Clyde Shipbuilding and Engineering Co Ltd* [1924] A.C. 226; *Fibrosa Spolka Akcyjna v Fairbairn Lawson Combe Barbour Ltd* [1943] A.C. 32.

[208] *Distington Hematite Iron Co v Possehl* [1916] 1 K.B. 811; *Veithardt and Hall Ltd v Rylands Bros Ltd* (1917) 116 L.T. 706; *Ertel Bieber & Co v Rio Tinto Co* [1918] A.C. 260; *Naylor Benzon & Co Ltd v Krainische Industrie Gesellschaft* [1918] A.C. 260; *Re Badische Co Ltd* [1921] 2 Ch. 331; *Fibrosa Spolka Akcyjna v Fairbairn Lawson Combe Barbour Ltd* [1943] A.C. 32 at 41.

[209] *Smith Coney and Barrett v Becker Gray & Co* [1916] 2 Ch. 86 at 92.

After "vessels. A buyer under", add:

6-037   a

Export and import prohibitions

Replace footnote 229 with:

6-040   [229] *Andrew Millar & Co Ltd v Taylor & Co Ltd* [1916] 1 K.B. 402. cf. *Embiricos v Sydney Reid & Co* [1914] 3 K.B. 45; *Atlantic Maritime Co Inc v Gibbon* [1954] 1 Q.B. 88; *Walton (Grain and Shipping) Ltd v British Italian Trading Co Ltd* [1959] 1 Lloyd's Rep. 223; *Bunge SA v Nidera NV* [2015] UKSC 43; [2015] 2 Lloyd's Rep 469. See below, para.18-384.

Replace footnote 238 with:

6-042   [238] *O'Neil v Armstrong* [1895] 2 Q.B. 418; *Prodexport State Co for Foreign Trade v Man (ED & F) Ltd* [1973] Q.B. 389. But see *Rederiaktiebolaget Amphitrite v The King* [1921] 3 K.B. 500; *Commissioner of Crown Lands v Page* [1960] 2 Q.B. 274 at 291; *Chitty on Contracts*, 33rd edn, Vol.1 paras 11-007 to 11-009; and see below, para.18-390.

Contract becomes unprofitable for seller

Replace paragraph with:

6-048   The fact that a contract of sale has become, because of a rise in prices or costs or by the occurrence of an extraneous event, unprofitable for the seller is insufficient to frustrate the contract.[282] Although it has been suggested[283] that it would be possible for a court to find that "a serious and sudden depreciation of monetary values, could disrupt the intended equivalence of performances on either side" and bring about a radical change in the obligation sufficient to frustrate a contract, the better view is that a devaluation of the currency in which the price is expressed[284] or the effect of inflation on the profitability of a fixed-price contract (even if of long duration)[285] are risks which must be borne by the seller.[286] Frustration alters the bargain between the parties and so should be sparingly invoked and not employed to rewrite contracts with the benefit of hindsight.[286a]

[282] *Instone (S) & Co Ltd v Speeding Marshall & Co Ltd* (1915) 32 T.L.R. 202; *Bolckow Vaughan & Co v Compania Minera de Sierra Minera* (1916) 33 T.L.R. 111; *Tennants (Lancashire) Ltd v Wilson (CS) & Co Ltd* [1917] A.C. 495; *Blackburn Bobbin Co Ltd v Allen (TW) & Sons Ltd* [1918] 2 K.B. 467; *Hulton (E) & Co Ltd v Chadwick & Taylor Co Ltd* (1918) 34 T.L.R. 230; *Beves & Co Ltd v Farkas* [1953] 1 Lloyd's Rep. 103; *Davis Contractors Ltd v Fareham UDC* [1956] A.C. 696 at 729; *Tsakiroglou & Co Ltd v Noblee Thorl GmbH* [1962] A.C. 93; *Exportelisa SA v Rocco Giuseppe & Figli Soc Coll* [1978] 1 Lloyd's Rep. 433; *National Carriers Ltd v Panalpina (Northern) Ltd* [1981] A.C. 675 at 700. cf. *Brauer & Co (GB) Ltd v James Clark (Brush Materials) Ltd* [1952] 2 All E.R. 497 at 500, 501.

[283] *Mann on the Legal Aspect of Money*, 7th edn (Proctor), 9.65.

[284] See Downes, (1985) 101 L.Q.R. 98; and below, para.26-176.

[285] *British Movietonews v London and District Cinemas Ltd* [1952] A.C. 166 at 185; *Wates Ltd v GLC* (1983) 25 Build. L.R. 1 at 34; cf. *Staffordshire AHA v South Staffordshire Water Authority* [1978] 1 W.L.R. 1387 at 1397–1398.

[286] The seller may protect himself by express provisions in the contract of sale whereby the price is to be adjusted, e.g. in the event of a rise in raw material, labour or transport costs, or (in long-term contracts) by a "hardship" clause: see *Superior Overseas Development Corp v British Gas Corp* [1982] 1 Lloyd's Rep. 262; *Wates Ltd v GLC* (1983) 25 Build. L.R. 1.

[286a] *The Flying Music Company Limited v Theater Entertainment SA* [2017] EWHC 3192 (QB) at [18].

(c) Express Clauses

Provisions of contract

Replace paragraph with:

Conversely, in many contracts of sale, clauses are inserted which provide for the **6-051** cancellation, variation, suspension or extension of the contract, or of particular obligations arising thereunder, upon the happening of certain events, even though such events may be insufficient in law to bring about frustration.[297] It is a question of construction whether such a clause is a cancellation clause that may be invoked whether or not the obligor was otherwise ready and willing to perform, or whether it was an exception clause that did not dispense with such prior readiness and willingness, for in the latter case the obligor would have to demonstrate that in fact the event in question prevented performance.[297a] And, in overseas sales,[298] the contract of sale may contain the term "subject to licence" or "subject to licence being granted" or "subject to quota"[299] or some such similar provision. There is then introduced into the contract a condition that the licence must be obtained and that neither party will be liable[300] to perform the duties under the contract unless the licence is obtained.[301]

[297] See below, para.8-074.

[297a] See *Classic Maritime Inc v Limbungan Makmur Sdn Bhd* [2018] EWHC 2389 (Comm); [2019] 1 Lloyd's Rep. 349, affirmed on this point at [2019] EWCA Civ 1102. See also *Bremer Handelsgesellschaft mbH v Vanden-Avenne Izegem PVBA* [1978] 2 Lloyd's Rep. 109; *Continental Grain Export Corp v STM Grain Ltd* [1979] 2 Lloyd's Rep. 460. See below, para.8-074.

[298] See below, para.18-366.

[299] cf. *Partabmull Rameshwar v Sethia (KC) (1944) Ltd* [1951] 1 All E.R. 352n.

[300] But "subject to licence" will itself be subject to the duty on the part of one party to use reasonable endeavours to obtain a licence: *Charles H Windschuegl Ltd v Alexander Pickering & Co Ltd* (1950) 84

Ll. L.R. 89 at 92. See above, para.6-041; below, para.18-362. See also *Kyprianou v Cyprus Textiles Ltd* [1958] 2 Lloyd's Rep. 60 (duty to co-operate).

[301] *Charles H Windschuegl Ltd v Alexander Pickering & Co Ltd* (1950) Ll. L.R. 89 at 92; *Société D'Avances Commerciales (London) Ltd v A Besse & Co (London) Ltd* [1952] 1 T.L.R. 644 at 646; *Brauer & Co (GB) Ltd v James Clark (Brush Materials) Ltd* [1952] 2 All E.R. 497 at 501; *Aaronson Bros Ltd v Maderera del Tropico SA* [1967] 2 Lloyd's Rep. 159 at 160; *Czarnikow (C) Ltd v Central Handlu Zagranicznego Rolimpex* [1979] A.C. 351. cf. *Peter Cassidy Seed Co Ltd v Osuustukkukauppa IL* [1957] 1 W.L.R. 273 ("as soon as export licence granted"). See below, paras 18-371, 18-372.

(d)   Consequences of Frustration

Consequences

Replace footnote 302 with:

6-052   [302] See *Chitty on Contracts*, 33rd edn, Vol.1 para.23-070.

The benefit

Replace footnote 331 with:

6-057   [331] Contrast *Chitty on Contracts*, 33rd edn, Vol.1 para.23-090 (just sum).

CHAPTER 7

TRANSFER OF TITLE BY NON-OWNERS

1. IN GENERAL

Nemo dat quod non habet

After "sections which follow.", add new footnote 9a:

7-001

[9a] For a criticism of the rule and its exceptions taken together as lacking in coherent principle, see Tettenborn [2018] C.L.J. 151.

Remedies of the owner

Replace paragraph with:

7-002

An owner[10] who has an immediate right to possession of goods is entitled to recover possession of them from a person who is wrongfully in possession of the goods. He may either retake them without action[11] or bring an action for delivery up of the goods[12] or for damages for wrongful interference.[13] Damages, though compensatory, will normally be measured by the value of the goods at the date of the conversion.[14] Further, any person who has wrongfully converted the goods either to his own use or to the use of another will be liable to an action for damages for wrongful interference at the suit of the owner[15] provided that, at the time of the conversion, the owner had an immediate right to possession of the goods.[16] Thus, even though the owner has been deprived of his title by the operation of one of the exceptions to the nemo dat rule, he will nevertheless be entitled to institute proceedings in tort for wrongful interference against any person who converted the goods before his title was extinguished.[17] The acquisition by a buyer of a good title under one of the nemo dat exceptions will not confer immunity from tort liability on the seller. Contributory negligence on the part of the owner is no defence in proceedings founded on conversion.[18] The decision of the House of Lords in *OBG v Allan*[19] not to extend the tort of conversion to choses in action means that a buyer not yet in possession and lacking a right to immediate possession of the goods may not sue a purchaser, innocent or not, in conversion for interference with the buyer's contractual right to acquire the goods.[19a]

[10] See below, para.7-002, n.16.

[11] On recaption of chattels, see *Clerk and Lindsell on Torts*, 22nd edn, paras 30-14 to 30-15; *18th Report of the Law Reform Committee* (1971), Cmnd.4774, paras 116-126. Contrast the Consumer Credit Act 1974 s.90 (no recovery of "protected" goods otherwise than by action).

[12] Torts (Interference with Goods) Act 1977 s.3(2)(a), (b). The remedy of specific delivery of goods is, however, discretionary: see s.3(3)(b) of the 1977 Act. See also s.4 and CPR 25.1(1)(e) (interim remedy) and below, para.15-116.

[13] Torts (Interference with Goods) Act 1977 s.3(2)(c). See Bridge, Gullifer, Low and McMeel, *The Law of Personal Property*, Ch.32. Normally the measure of damages will be the value of the goods at the date of conversion if the goods have not been returned, detinue having been abolished by s.2(1): *Solloway v McLaughlin* [1938] A.C. 247 at 257; *BBMB Finance (HK) Ltd v Eda Holdings Ltd* [1990] 1 W.L.R. 409. cf. *IBL Ltd v Coussens* [1991] 2 All E.R. 133. But consequential damages are recoverable if not too remote: see *Clerk and Lindsell on Torts*, 22nd edn, para.17-108; *Sachs v Miklos* [1948] 2 K.B. 22; *Strand Electric Engineering Co Ltd v Brisford Entertainments Ltd* [1952] 2 Q.B. 246; *Sargent (J) (Garages) Ltd v Motor Auctions (West Bromwich) Ltd* [1977] R.T.R. 121; *Hillesden Securities Ltd v Ryjack Ltd* [1983] 1 W.L.R. 959; *Kuwait Airways Corp v Iraq Airways Co (Nos 4 and 5)* [2002] UKHL 19; [2002] 2 A.C. 883; Palmer and McKendrick, *Interests in Goods*, 2nd edn, Chs 32–34 (Tettenborn, Hudson, and Palmer and Hudson). For cases where both claimant and defendant have an interest in the goods, see *Gillard v Brittan* (1841) 8 M. & W. 575; *Brierly v Kendall* (1852) 17 Q.B. 937; *Chinery v Viall* (1860) 5 H. & N. 288; *Massey v Sladen* (1868) L.R. 4 Ex. 13; *Mulliner v Florence* (1878) 3 Q.B.D. 484; *Moore v Shelley* (1883) 8 App. Cas. 285; and (goods let under hire-purchase agreement) *Wickham Holdings Ltd v Brook House Motors Ltd* [1967] 1 W.L.R. 295; *Belvoir Finance Co Ltd v Stapleton* [1971] 1 Q.B. 210; *Chubb Cash Ltd v John Crilley & Son* [1983] 1 W.L.R. 599; below, para.7-105. cf. *Astley Industrial Trust Ltd v Miller* [1968] 2 All E.R. 36.

[14] *Kuwait Airways Corp v Iraqi Airways Corp (Nos 4 and 5)* [2002] UKHL 19 at [67]; [2002] 2 A.C. 883; *Hill v Reglon Pty Ltd* [2007] NSWCA 295; Bridge, Gullifer, Low and McMeel, *The Law of Personal Property*, paras 32-052 to 32-053.

[15] cf. *North West Securities v Alexander Breckon* [1981] R.T.R. 518 (action by non-owner who had entered into binding contract to purchase the goods). An equitable owner has no right to sue in conversion unless he had possession or an immediate right to possession of the converted goods: *MCC Proceeds Inc v Lehman Bros International (Europe)* [1998] 4 All E.R. 675, not following *International Factors Ltd v Rodriguez* [1979] Q.B. 351.

[16] *Union Transport Finance Ltd v British Car Auctions Ltd* unreported, 16 February 1977 (CA Transcript No.87 of 1977); *Willis (RH) & Son v British Car Auctions Ltd* [1978] 1 W.L.R. 438 (auctioneers).

[17] See below, paras 7-105, 7-115.

[18] Torts (Interference with Goods) Act 1977 s.11(1). cf. Tettenborn, [1993] C.L.J. 128. But the award of damages has been reduced by a failure of the claimant to mitigate: *Uzinterimpex JSC v Standard Chartered Bank Plc* [2008] EWCA Civ 819; [2008] 2 C.L.C. 80.

[19] *OBG v Allan* [2007] UKHL 21; [2008] 1 A.C. 1.

[19a] On the inadequacy of a contractual right to ground a right of suit, see *Jarvis v Williams* [1955] 1 W.L.R 71 (detinue) with which cf. *Government of the Islamic Republic of Iran v Barakat Galleries Ltd* [2007] EWCA Civ 374; [2009] Q.B. 22 at [26] and [30]. See also Bridge, Gullifer, Low and McMeel, *The Law of Personal Property*, 2nd edn, para.32-039.

Replace paragraph with:

7-003   Alternatively the owner may "waive the tort"[20] and pursue a restitutionary claim to recover any sum received as a result of the sale or use of the goods by the wrongdoer in an action in restitution for money had and received.[21] Further the proprietary right of the owner is recognised, both at common law and in equity, by allowing him to "trace" or "follow" his property into the proceeds of its sale, so long as these have not been dissipated,[22] or into other identifiable assets which have been purchased with those proceeds.[23] This will be particularly important where the defendant is insolvent and the owner seeks to establish a claim in priority to the defendant's general creditors. At common law, tracing is a limited remedy. It is available only where the proceeds of sale have not been mixed with other moneys, e.g. in a bank account,[24] or (if a claim is made to other assets) where these have been purchased exclusively with the unmixed proceeds.[25] But equity will trace into a mixed fund or into assets purchased with the mixed fund[26] and will follow the moneys into the hands of anyone other than a bona fide purchaser for value without notice,[27] giving the owner a charge over the fund or assets in question.[28] However, tracing in equity requires the owner to establish that the defendant or a third party[29] is in a fiduciary relationship to him,[30] and that he has an equitable proprietary interest in the property claimed.[31]

[20] See *Chitty on Contracts*, 33rd edn, Vol.1 para.29-147; Goff and Jones, *The Law of Restitution*, 7th edn, Ch.36 (subsequent editions do not deal with waiver of tort); Burrows, *The Law of Restitution*, 3rd edn, Ch.24; and above, para.1-073.

[21] See Palmer and McKendrick, *Interests in Goods*, 2nd edn, Chs 32 (Tettenborn), 35 (McKendrick).

[22] *Re Diplock* [1948] Ch. 465 at 521, 546.

[23] *Chitty on Contracts*, 33rd edn, Vol.1 para.29-170; Goff and Jones, *The Law of Unjust Enrichment*, 9th edn, Ch.7. See *Foskett v McKeown* [2001] 1 A.C. 182.

[24] *Taylor v Plumer* (1815) 3 M. & S. 562; *Banque Belge pour l'Etranger v Hambrouck* [1921] 1 K.B. 321 at 329; *Re Diplock* [1948] Ch. 465 at 518; *Agip (Africa) Ltd v Jackson* [1991] 1 Ch. 447; *Lipkin Gorman v Karpnale Ltd* [1991] 2 A.C. 548.

[25] *Re Diplock* [1948] Ch. 465 at 519; *Re Leslie (J) Engineering Co Ltd* [1976] 1 W.L.R. 292 at 297; *Lipkin Gorman v Karpnale Ltd* [1991] 2 A.C. 548 at 573; *Trustee of the Property of Jones (FC) & Sons v Jones* [1997] Ch. 159.

[26] *Re Diplock* [1948] Ch. 465 at 520.

[27] *Re Diplock* [1948] Ch. 465 at 521, 546; *Foskett v McKeown* [2001] 1 A.C. 102 at 129.

[28] See, e.g. *Re Hallett's Estate* (1880) 13 Ch. D. 696; *Re Oatway* [1903] 2 Ch. 356. See also *Clayton's Case* (1816) Mer. 572 (withdrawals from mixed fund); and *Chitty on Contracts*, 33rd edn, Vol.1 para.29-179.

[29] i.e. a third party through whose hands the owner's property has passed.

[30] *Re Diplock* [1948] Ch. 465 at 532; *Buhr v Barclays Bank Plc* [2001] EWCA Civ 1223; [2002] B.P.I.R. 25 at [17]. But if goods or money are stolen or obtained by fraud, equity imposes a constructive trust on the fraudulent recipient: *Westdeutsche Landesbank Girozentrale v Islington LBC* [1996] A.C. 669 at 716.

[31] *Re Diplock* [1948] Ch. 465 at 520, 529; *Westdeutsche Landesbank Girozentrale v Islington LBC* [1996] A.C. 669.

Restitution and seizure orders

Replace footnote 46 with:

7-006

[46] Powers of Criminal Courts (Sentencing) Act 2000 s.148(2)(a). For the other types of order that may be made, see s.148(2)(b), (c), and s.149 (currently the subject of draft amending legislation).

Replace the second paragraph with:

7-007

Numerous other statutes confer a power of seizure.[58] Where there is an obligation to return the property seized,[59] it is to be returned to the person from whom it was seized unless some other person has a "better right" to the property than the person from whom it was seized.[60] Very broad powers are, however, conferred by the Proceeds of Crime Act 2002[61] upon the Crown Court[62] to make confiscation orders[63] in respect of property[64] where it decides that a defendant has benefited from his criminal conduct. In particular the court may make an order in respect of property held by the recipient of a "tainted gift"[65] from the defendant (which includes a transfer at a significant undervalue).[66] It is immaterial that the recipient of a tainted gift received it in good faith.

[58] Criminal Justice and Police Act 2001 ss.50, 51, 52 and Sch.1 amended by the Police Reform Act 2002 s.59 and Sch.4 paras 9, 24; Proceeds of Crime Act 2002 ss.47A–47R (as added by the Policing and Crime Act 2009 as amended) and 352 Sch.11 para.40; Criminal Justice Act 2003 Sch.1 para.19.

[59] Criminal Justice and Police Act 2001 ss.53–57 amended by the Police Reform Act 2002 s.60 and Sch.4 para.2; Proceeds of Crime Act 2002 Sch.11 para.40 Sch.12; Criminal Justice Act 2003 Sch.1 paras 14, 19. Section 56(2) was further repealed in part by the Companies Act 2006 (Consequential Amendments, Transitional Provisions and Savings) Order (SI 2009/1941) Sch.1 para.189(2). Section 57(1) was further repealed in part by the Companies Act 2006 (Consequential Amendments, Transitional Provisions and Savings) Order (SI 2009/1941) Sch.1 para.189(3), and the Finance Act 2007 Sch.27(5)(1) para.1, and amended by the Weights and Measures (Packaged Goods) Regulations (SI 2006/659) Sch.1(2) para.1, the Human Tissue Act 2004 Sch.6 para.5(2), the Human Fertilisation and Embryology Act 2008 Sch.7 para.19, Enterprise Act 2002 (Amendment) Regulations (SI 2006/3363) reg.25, the Animal Welfare Act 2006 Sch.3 para.14(1), the Financial Services Act 2012 Sch.18(2) para.92, the Consumer Rights Act 2015 Sch.6, para.62(b), the Data Protection Act 2018 Sch.19, para.71(b) and the Financial Services and Markets Act 2000 (Market Abuse) Regulations 2016 (SI 2016/680).

[60] Criminal Justice and Police Act 2001 s.58. See also s.59 (application to the appropriate judicial authority) and ss.60, 61 (duty to secure), amended by the Police Reform Act 2002 s.60; Proceeds of Crime Act 2002 Sch.11 para.40 Sch.12.

[61] Proceeds of Crime Act 2002 Pt 2 (ss.6–91).

[62] The power may be extended to magistrates' courts by an order made under the Serious Organised Crime and Police Act 2005 s.97.

[63] Restraint orders may also be made (Proceeds of Crime Act 2002 ss.40–44A and 46–47).

[64] Defined in Proceeds of Crime Act 2002 s.84.

[65] Defined in Proceeds of Crime Act 2002 s.77.

[66] Proceeds of Crime Act 2002 ss.78, 81, 83.

2. ESTOPPEL

Title by estoppel

Replace paragraph with:

7-008   The Sale of Goods Act 1979 s.2(1) provides that the rule *nemo dat quod non habet* is not to apply where "the owner of the goods is by his conduct precluded from denying the seller's authority to sell".[67] It might be supposed that this exception embodies the broad principle enunciated by Ashhurst J in *Lickbarrow v Mason*[68] that:

> "... wherever one of two innocent persons must suffer by the acts of a third, he who has enabled such third person to occasion the loss must sustain it."

But it is clear that this dictum, if too literally construed, is much too wide: it has often been criticised[69] and seldom applied.[70] At the other end of the scale, it might be thought that the language of the exception ("authority to sell") confined its operation to cases of agency by estoppel[71] or apparent (or ostensible) authority.[72] But s.62(2) of the Act expressly preserves the rules of the common law relating to the law of principal and agent,[73] so that there is little doubt that the exception relates to situations other than those in which the seller is the agent of the true owner of the goods or in which the owner holds out the seller to be his agent. The cases in which this provision has been canvassed indicate that it was intended to give statutory effect to a particular principle of estoppel in English law,[74] and that the terminology used may have been intended to render this principle intelligible in Scots law where the specific term "estoppel" is unknown. The true owner of goods can be estopped from denying the apparent ownership of the seller,[75] so that the buyer acquires a good title to the goods by estoppel. Such an estoppel may arise either: (i) by reason of a representation made by the true owner that the seller is the owner of the goods; or (ii) by negligence on the part of the true owner which enables the seller to create an appearance of ownership. For reasons of commercial convenience, however, the effect of its application is to transfer to the buyer a real title and not a metaphorical title by estoppel.[76] The estoppel is thus an unusual one in that it not only binds the true owner personally and those claiming under him, but confers a good title against all the world.

[67] This provision preserves common law estoppel principles: *Kino v Prestige Philately Pty Ltd* [2014] VSC 469 at [55] and [72]. The question whether the section goes beyond the common law has been extensively debated in Australian case law, with the conclusion that it does not: see *Thomas Australia Wholesale Vehicle Trading Co Pty Ltd v Marac Finance Australia Ltd* (1985) 3 NSWLR 452; *Haines Bros Earthmoving Pty Ltd v Rosecell Pty Ltd* [2016] NSWCA 112.

[68] *Lickbarrow v Mason* (1787) 2 T.R. 63 at 70, reversed sub nom. *Mason v Lickbarrow* (1790) 1 Hy. Bl. 357.

[69] *Farquharson Bros & Co v King & Co* [1902] A.C. 325 at 335, 342; *Rimmer v Webster* [1902] 2 Ch. 163 at 169; *London Joint Stock Bank v Macmillan* [1918] A.C. 777 at 836; *Jones Ltd v Waring and Gillow Ltd* [1926] A.C. 670 at 693; *Mercantile Bank of India Ltd v Central Bank of India Ltd* [1938] A.C. 287 at 298-299; *Wilson and Meeson v Pickering* [1946] K.B. 422 at 425; *Jerome v Bentley & Co* [1952] 2 All E.R. 114 at 118; *Central Newbury Car Auctions Ltd v Unity Finance Ltd* [1957] 1 Q.B. 371 at 389, 396.

[70] cf. *Commonwealth Trust v Akotey* [1926] A.C. 72; which was disapproved in *Mercantile Bank of India Ltd v Central Bank of India Ltd* [1938] A.C. 287; *Central Newbury Car Auctions Ltd v Unity Finance Ltd* [1957] 1 Q.B. 371 at 383.

[71] See *Bowstead and Reynolds on Agency*, 21st edn, paras 2-100 and 8-028.

[72] *Bowstead and Reynolds on Agency*, 21st edn, para.8-010.

[73] See also s.21(1), (2) of the Act.

[74] cf. *Eastern Distributors Ltd v Goldring* [1957] 2 Q.B. 600 at 607. See also *Bowstead and Reynolds on Agency*, 21st edn, paras 8-125 and 8-129; *Spiro v Lintern* [1973] 1 W.L.R. 1002 at 1010.

[75] To that extent, the common law goes beyond the wording of s.2(1) since there is a difference between apparent authority and apparent ownership (on which see *Rosecell Pty Ltd v JP Haines Plumbing Pty Ltd v* [2015] NSWSC 1235 at [53]).

[76] *Eastern Distributors Ltd v Goldring* [1957] 2 Q.B. 600; *Mercantile Credit Co Ltd v Hamblin* [1965] 2 Q.B. 242 at 275; *Stoneleigh Finance Ltd v Phillips* [1965] 2 Q.B. 537 at 578; *Moorgate Mercantile Co Ltd v Twitchings* [1977] A.C. 890 at 918.

Estoppel by representation

Replace footnote 80 with:

[80] *Cole v North Western Bank* (1875) L.R. 10 C.P. 354 at 363; *Colonial Bank v Cady* (1890) 15 App. Cas. 267 at 285; *Farquharson Bros & Co v King & Co* [1902] A.C. 325 at 330; *Rimmer v Webster* [1902] 2 Ch. 163 at 173; *People's Bank of Halifax v Estey* (1904) 34 S.C.R. 429. See also *Bowstead and Reynolds on Agency*, 21st edn, para.8-129. An estoppel could also arise if the true owner represents or permits it to be represented that he has no interest in the goods: *Shaw v Commissioner of Metropolitan Police* [1987] 1 W.L.R. 1332 at 1335, 1338. cf. *Moorgate Mercantile Co Ltd v Twitchings* [1977] A.C. 890.   **7-009**

Replace footnote 100 with:

[100] *Amalgamated Investments & Property Co Ltd v Texas Commerce International Bank Ltd* [1982] Q.B. 84. See *Chitty on Contracts*, 33rd edn, Vol.1 para.4-108.   **7-012**

Documents of title

Replace paragraph with:

The mere delivery by the true owner to another person of the possession of documents of title to goods does not, at common law,[101] estop him from asserting his title   **7-013** against one who has purchased[102] the goods from that person.[103] Even though, in one sense, he could be said to have enabled the seller to represent that he was the owner of the goods by investing him with the indicia of title,[104] it is clear that the delivery of possession of documents of title in itself has no greater effect than the delivery of possession of the goods themselves.[105] There must be some further act on the part of the true owner which amounts to a representation by him of the seller's right to sell, as for example, where he executes a document in which he acknowledges that he has been paid in full for the goods by the seller.[106] Most cases in which the true owner has been precluded from recovering the goods from the buyer prove, on examination, to be cases where the true owner's relationship with the seller was that of principal and agent. The true owner may deliver the document of title to the seller and at the same time authorise him to sell or otherwise deal with the goods.[107] Or he may indorse the document of title in blank and transfer it to a broker who, by the nature of his employment, may be taken prima facie to have the right to sell the goods.[108] In such an event, the true owner may be "estopped" from asserting his title to the goods if the agent disregards the terms of his mandate and wrongfully sells the goods to a third party. It has been argued[109] that these cases are anomalous within the law of agency inasmuch as there is no actual or apparent[110] authority. But they would appear to depend on the existence of some initial authority given to the agent rather than on estoppel by a representation of apparent ownership under the provisions of s.21(1) of the Act.

[101] But see Factors Act 1889 s.2; below, para.7-031.

[102] Or receives the goods, e.g. as pledgee.

[103] *Boyson v Coles* (1817) 6 M. & S. 14; *Kingsford v Merry* (1856) 1 H. & N. 502; *Lamb v Attenborough* (1862) 1 B. & S. 830; *Cole v North Western Bank* (1875) L.R. 10 C.P. 354 at 363; *Johnson v Crédit Lyonnais* (1877) 3 C.P.D. 32; *Mercantile Bank of India Ltd v Central Bank of India Ltd* [1938] A.C. 287. cf. *Union Credit Bank Ltd v Mersey Docks and Harbour Board* [1899] 2 Q.B. 205.

[104] *Commonwealth Trust v Akotey* [1926] A.C. 72; *Central Newbury Car Auctions Ltd v Unity Finance Ltd* [1957] 1 Q.B. 371 at 382-386. A car registration document is not a document of title: *Beverley Acceptances Ltd v Oakley* [1982] R.T.R. 417; and see below, para.7-036, n.258.

[105] *Mercantile Bank of India Ltd v Central Bank of India Ltd* [1938] A.C. 287 at 303.

[106] *Rimmer v Webster* [1902] 2 Ch. 163 at 173; *Abigail v Lapin* [1934] A.C. 491.

[107] *Weiner v Gill* [1906] 2 K.B. 574 at 582; *Fry v Smellie* [1912] 3 K.B. 282. See also *Bowstead and Reynolds on Agency*, 21st edn, para.8-134. cf. *Lloyds Bank Ltd v Bank of America National Trust and Savings Assoc* [1938] 2 K.B. 147.

[108] *Colonial Bank v Cady* (1890) 15 App. Cas. 267 at 278, 283; *Fuller v Glyn, Mills, Currie & Co* [1914] 2 K.B. 168, as interpreted in *Mercantile Bank of India Ltd v Central Bank of India Ltd* [1938] A.C. 287 at 302. See also *Pan-Electric Industries Ltd v Overseas Chinese Banking Corp Ltd* [1994] 1 S.L.R. (R.) 185. cf. *Zwinger v Samuda* (1817) 7 Taunt. 265.

[109] *Bowstead and Reynolds on Agency*, 21st edn, para.8-135.

[110] The existence of the principal may not be known to the buyer.

Estoppel by judgment

Replace footnote 150 with:

7-019   [150] *Chitty on Contracts*, 33rd edn, Vol.1 para.25-011; Halsbury, *Laws of England*, 5th edn, Vol.12A para.1591.

3. SALE IN MARKET OVERT

Market overt

After "after that date.", add new footnote 153a:

153a The market overt rule survives in Hong Kong: Sale of Goods Ordinance Cap 26), s.24 ("a shop or market in Hong Kong"). It also survives in Ireland: Sale of Goods Act 1893 s.22(1).   **7-020**

4. SALE UNDER A VOIDABLE TITLE

Seller with a voidable title

Replace paragraph with:
By s.23 of the Sale of Goods Act 1979:   **7-021**

> "When the seller of goods has a voidable title to them, but his title has not been avoided at the time of the sale, the buyer acquires a good title to the goods, provided he buys them in good faith and without notice of the seller's defect of title."[154]

The paradigm case of the operation of this section is where A, the true owner of the goods, is induced by the fraud of B (the seller) to sell goods to B which B then resells to C, an innocent buyer. A fraudulent representation made by B may arise from B's conduct, as where B, paying by cheque, impliedly represents that there are funds in the drawee bank or an available overdraft facility for the cheque to be honoured.[154a] The effect of the fraud is not absolutely to avoid the contract of sale between A and B, but to render it voidable at the option of A. Property in the goods passes to B, although B's title is subject to A's right to avoid it. Provided that A has not effectively exercised this right at the time of the sale of the goods by B to C, then C will acquire an indefeasible title to the goods notwithstanding the fact that B had only a voidable title to them.[155]

154 This provision does not apply to sui generis supply contracts of the sort considered in *PST Energy Shipping LLC v OW Bunker Malta Ltd (The Res Cogitans)* [2016] UKSC 23; [2016] A.C. 1034 but a rule of the common law should apply to the same effect in such cases where the supplier's reservation of title has been lifted, as might occur where the recipient has paid for the goods before they are consumed.

154a *Property Alliance Group Ltd v Royal Bank of Scotland Plc* [2018] EWCA Civ 355; [2018] 1 W.L.R. 3529 at [126].

155 *Wright v Lawes* (1801) 4 Esq. 82; *Load v Green* (1846) 15 M. & W. 216 at 219; *White v Garden* (1851) 10 C.B. 919; *Powell v Hoyland* (1851) 6 Ex. Ch. 67 at 72; *Stevenson v Newnham* (1853) 13 C.B. 285 at 302; *Pease v Gloahec* (1866) L.R. 1 P.C. 219; *Cundy v Lindsay* (1878) 3 App. Cas. 459 at 463-464, 466; *King's Norton Metal Co v Edridge, Merrett & Co* (1897) 14 T.L.R. 98; *Phillips v Brooks Ltd* [1919] 2 K.B. 243; *Nanka Bruce v Commonwealth Trust* [1926] A.C. 77; *Terry v Vancouver Motors U-Drive Ltd* [1942] 4 D.L.R. 399; *Dennant v Skinner and Collom* [1948] 2 K.B. 164; *Robin and Rambler Coaches Ltd v Turner* [1947] 2 All E.R. 284; *Hendrickson v Mid City Motors Ltd* [1951] 3 D.L.R. 276; *Macleod v Kerr* 1965 S.C. 253; *Lewis v Averay* [1972] 1 Q.B. 198; *Young v Dalgleish (DS) & Son (Hawick)* 1994 S.C.L.R. 696 (Sh. Ct.).

Voidable and void

Replace paragraph with:
An innocent buyer will only acquire a good title to goods under s.23 if the title   **7-023**
of the seller is voidable, but not if the seller has no title at all. The title of the seller may be voidable at the option of the true owner, for example, on the ground of fraud at common law[164] or in equity,[165] misrepresentation,[166] non-disclosure,[167] duress[168] or undue influence.[169] In these instances, the true owner is normally entitled to

rescind the contract between himself and the seller, but the contract is not void ab initio. If, however, it is completely void, for example, on the ground of mistake as to identity[170] or because of a lack of coincidence between the terms of the offer and of the acceptance,[171] then no property in the goods will pass to the seller, and the buyer will not acquire a good title under this section even if he purchases the goods in good faith and without notice of the seller's defect of title.[172] For the same reason, the buyer will not acquire a good title under this section as against the true owner of the goods from whom they have been stolen,[173] whether by the seller or some other person.

[164] See *Chitty on Contracts*, 33rd edn, Vol.1 paras 7-048, 7-116.

[165] *Chitty on Contracts*, 33rd edn, Vol.1 para.7-118.

[166] *Chitty on Contracts*, 33rd edn, Vol.1 Ch.7.

[167] *Chitty on Contracts*, 33rd edn, Vol.1 paras 7-158 et seq.

[168] *Chitty on Contracts*, 33rd edn, Vol.1 paras 8-001 et seq.

[169] *Chitty on Contracts*, 33rd edn, Vol.1 paras 8-058 et seq.

[170] *Hardman v Booth* (1862) 32 L.J. Ex. 105; *Cundy v Lindsay* (1878) 3 App. Cas. 459; *Morrisson v Robertson*, 1908 S.C. 332; *Ingram v Little* [1961] 1 Q.B. 31; *Shogun Finance Ltd v Hudson* [2003] UKHL 62; [2004] 1 A.C.69. Contrast *King's Norton Metal Co v Edridge, Merrett & Co* (1897) 14 T.L.R. 98; *Phillips v Brooks Ltd* [1919] 2 K.B. 243; *Hendrickson v Mid-City Motors Ltd* [1951] 3 D.L.R. 276; *Lewis v Averay* [1972] 1 Q.B. 198. See *Chitty on Contracts*, 33rd edn, Vol.1 paras 3-036 to 3-048; above, para.3-012. Whether a contracting party has been incorrectly identified in the contract is to be distinguished from whether a person is a contracting party: *Liberty Mercian Ltd v Cuddy Civil Engineering Ltd* [2013] EWHC 2688 (TCC); [2014] 1 All E.R. (Comm) 761 ("misnomer").

[171] *Morrison v Robertson* 1908 S.C. 332. cf. *R. v Williams* [1980] Crim. L.R. 589. See also *Chitty on Contracts*, 33rd edn, Vol.1 paras 3-022 to 3-028.

[172] cf. *12th Report of the Law Reform Committee* (1966), Cmnd.2958, para.15.

[173] i.e. without the true owner's consent. But the mere fact that the wrongdoer is guilty of the crime of theft is in itself insufficient: see *R. v Lawrence* [1972] A.C. 626; *Dobson v General Accident and Life Assurance Corp Plc* [1990] 1 Q.B. 274. cf. *R. v Harris* [1984] A.C. 327; *R. v Gomez* [1993] A.C. 442.

Avoidance

Replace paragraph with:

7-026   In any event, in order to avoid the seller's voidable title, the true owner must be in a position to rescind the contract made between himself and the seller, that is to say, the remedy of rescission must not for any reason have become barred.[186] In particular, the true owner must not have elected to affirm the contract and so lost his right to rescind.[187]

[186] See below, paras 12-005 to 12-009; and *Chitty on Contracts*, 33rd edn, Vol.1 paras 7-132 to 7-144.

[187] See below, para.12-006; and *Chitty on Contracts*, 33rd edn, Vol.1 para.7-133. See also below, para.12-009 (lapse of time, but this does not extend to cases of fraud).

5.   MERCANTILE AGENTS

Agency

Replace footnote 205 with:

7-031   [205] See *Bowstead and Reynolds on Agency*, 21st edn, paras 3-004 to 3-005, 8-126 et seq.

Replace title footnote 231 with:

Disposition by mercantile agent[231]

7-034   [231] See also *Bowstead and Reynolds on Agency*, 21st edn, para.8-143.

Consent of the owner

Replace footnote 265 with:

[265] *Du Jardin v Beadman Bros* [1952] 2 Q.B. 712 at 718. See *Chitty on Contracts*, 33rd edn, Vol.1 para.3-037; and above, para.3-012.

7-037

Disposition

Replace paragraph with:

Protection is afforded by s.2(1) of the Act to "any sale, pledge, or other disposition of the goods" made by the mercantile agent, or by a clerk or other person authorised in the ordinary course of business[275] to make contracts of sale or pledge on his behalf.[276] Where a mercantile agent deposited with an auctioneer goods entrusted to him for sale, and subsequently obtained an advance from the auctioneer on the proceeds of sale, this was held not to be a pledge or other disposition of the goods.[277] Similarly where a mercantile agent delivered to the purchaser of a car the registration document and a post-dated cheque, it being agreed that the agent could repurchase the car within a limited period of time, it was held on the facts that there was no "sale, pledge or other disposition" of the car, but only a device to enable the agent to obtain temporary financial accommodation.[278] There is no reference to delivery in s.2(1), hence a good title may be obtained prior to delivery under a sale or other disposition, though not a pledge, entered into by the mercantile agent. For sui generis supply contracts[279] it is submitted that the receipt of goods with a licence to use or consume them should be regarded as a disposition.[279a]

7-041

[275] See below, para.7-043.

[276] Factors Act 1889 s.6.

[277] *Waddington & Sons v Neale & Sons* (1907) 96 L.T. 786; *Roache v Australian Mercantile Land and Finance Co Ltd (No.2)* [1966] 1 N.S.W.L.R. 384 at 386. See also *Suttons Motors (Temora) Pty Ltd v Hollywood Motors Pty Ltd* [1971] V.R. 684.

[278] *Joblin v Watkins and Roseveare (Motors) Ltd* [1949] 1 All E.R. 47.

[279] Of the sort considered in *PST Energy Shipping LLC v OW Bunker Malta Ltd (The Res Cogitans)* [2016] UKSC 23; [2016] A.C. 1034.

[279a] See further below, para.7-064.

Ordinary course of business

Replace footnote 299 with:

[299] See Goodhart, (1951) 67 L.Q.R. 3; Powell, *Law of Agency*, 2nd edn, p.228; *Bowstead and Reynolds on Agency*, 21st edn, para.8-153.

7-044

Good faith and notice

Replace paragraph with:

The expression "in good faith" is not defined in the Act of 1889[308] but would appear to mean "honestly", that is to say, not fraudulently or dishonestly.[309] It is submitted that negligence or carelessness is not in itself sufficient evidence of bad faith and the fact that the person dealing with the agent did not behave with the prudence to be expected of a reasonable man does not mean that he acted in bad faith.[310] On the other hand, negligence or carelessness, when considered in connection with the surrounding circumstances, may be evidence of bad faith.[311] But the facts and circumstances should then be such as to lead to the inference that the disponee must have had a suspicion that there was something wrong, and that he

7-046

refrained from asking questions because he thought that further enquiry would reveal an irregularity.[312] Deliberately refraining from making inquiries may be evidence of bad faith,[313] likewise acting out of the ordinary course of business.[314] Proof that the goods were purchased at a much lower price than the ordinary trade price is not absolute proof of bad faith, but it may be evidence of fraudulent knowledge on his part.[315] Also an unusually high rate of interest charged on a pledge may be evidence of bad faith on the part of a pledgee.[316] Although it has been said that the courts view with suspicion any dealing with a second-hand motor vehicle without the registration document,[317] a failure on the part of the buyer to ask for the registration document of a second-hand vehicle does not necessarily show bad faith[318] and may be of little evidentiary value in the case of the sale of a new vehicle.[319]

[308] But see the Sale of Goods Act 1979 s.61(3) and the Bills of Exchange Act 1882 s.90. These provisions codified the common law: see J. W. Jones, *Position and Rights of a Bona Fide Purchaser for Value of Goods Improperly Obtained* (Cambridge: 1921).

[309] *Mogridge v Clapp* [1892] 3 Ch. D. 383 at 392. See also *Barclays Bank Plc v TOSG Trust Fund* [1984] B.C.L.C. 18 ("genuinely and honestly in the circumstances of the case"); *Dodds v Yorkshire Bank Finance* [1992] C.C.L.R. 92 CA; *GE Capital Bank Ltd v Rushton* [2005] EWCA Civ 1556; [2006] 1 W.L.R. 899 (Hire-Purchase Act 1964). For a survey of the various indicia of bad faith in title transfer cases, see *Countinho & Ferrostaal Gmbh v Tracomex Canada Ltd* 2015 BCSC 787 at [161] et seq.

[310] *Re Gomersall* (1875) 1 Ch. D. 137 at 146. See also *Vane v Vane* (1873) 8 Ch. App. 383 at 399; *Jones v Gordon* (1877) 2 App. Cas. 616; *Moody v Pall Mall Deposit and Forwarding Co Ltd* (1917) 33 T.L.R. 306; *Palin v Vetterli* [2013] NSWSC 893 at [66]; Bills of Exchange Act 1882 s.90; Sale of Goods Act 1979 s.61(3).

[311] *Re Gomersall* (1875) 1 Ch. D. 137 at 146. A Canadian court, interpreting the equivalent of s.61(3), which provides that negligence is not inconsistent with honesty, has ruled that gross negligence, recklessness and wilful blindness, unmentioned in that provision, mean that a disponee's behavior is not in good faith: *Alberta Treasury Branches v Cam Holdings LP* 2016 ABQB 33 at [40]–[41]. A preferable approach is to look for evidence of dishonesty in such conduct.

[312] *Jones v Gordon* (1877) 2 App. Cas. 616 at 629; *Whitehorn Bros v Davison* [1911] 1 K.B. 463 at 478; *Patry v General Motors Acceptance Corp of Canada Ltd* (2000) 187 D.L.R. (4th) 99 at 105; *Mercedes-Benz Financial Services Pty Ltd v State of New South Wales* [2011] NSWSC 1458 at [97]–[98] (buyer aware that seller could not prove that it had paid luxury tax on a car and transaction was being promoted at speed when there was no need for haste); cf. *Mercantile Credit Co Ltd v Waugh* (1978) 32 Hire Trading 16.

[313] *Summers v Havard* [2011] EWCA 1164 at [17].

[314] *Summers v Havard* [2011] EWCA 1164 at [16]–[17].

[315] *Re Gomersall* (1875) 1 Ch. D. 137 at 150; *Heap v Motorists' Advisory Agency Ltd* [1923] 1 K.B. 577 at 590; *Davey v Paine Bros (Motors) Ltd* [1954] N.Z.L.R. 1122 at 1130. cf. *GE Capital Bank Ltd v Rushton* [2005] EWCA Civ 1556; [2006] 1 W.L.R. 899 at [43].

[316] *Janesich v Attenborough & Son* (1910) 102 L.T. 605 at 607.

[317] *Pearson v Rose and Young Ltd* [1951] 1 K.B. 275 at 289. See also *Heap v Motorists' Advisory Agency Ltd* [1923] 1 K.B. 577 at 591; *Bishopsgate Motor Finance Corp Ltd v Transport Brakes Ltd* [1949] 1 K.B. 322 at 338. cf. Goodhart, (1951) 67 L.Q.R. 3. But a private purchaser from a vehicle dealer would not ordinarily expect to see the registration document.

[318] *Stadium Finance Ltd v Robbins* [1962] 2 Q.B. 664 at 672, 675.

[319] *Astley Industrial Trust Ltd v Miller* [1968] 2 All E.R. 36.

Effect of sale

Replace footnote 335 with:

7-048   [335] Factors Act 1889 s.12(3). For the right of set-off, see *Bowstead and Reynolds on Agency*, 21st edn, para.8-107. See also para.8-112 (illustration 9).

Rights of owner preserved

Replace footnote 357 with:

357 See *Bowstead and Reynolds on Agency*, 21st edn, paras 8-159 and 8-164.   **7-054**

6. SELLER IN POSSESSION

Possession of seller

Replace paragraph with:
    The seller must also be in possession of the goods sold, or of the documents of   **7-057**
title384 to the goods. By the Factors Act 1889 s.1(2), this is deemed to be the case
where the goods or documents are in the seller's actual custody or control or are
held by any other person subject to his control or for him or on his behalf. The same
interpretation is to be applied to the word "possession" in s.24.385 Thus, if a seller
sells goods which are stored for him by a warehouseman, but subsequently pledges
the goods and causes them to be delivered by the warehouseman to an innocent
third party in return for an advance, the buyer cannot recover the goods from the
third party without paying off the advance.386 Goods which are currently let by the
seller to hirers under hire-purchase agreements are not within this provision.387 A
seller who has constructively delivered the goods to another person remains
nevertheless a seller in possession.388

384 See above, para.7-036.

385 See also Sale of Goods Act 1979 s.25; *Archivent Sales and Developments Ltd v Strathclyde RC*
(1984) 27 Build. L.R. 98; *Forsythe International (UK) Ltd v Silver Shipping Co Ltd* [1993] 2 Lloyd's
Rep. 268 at 275; *Angara Maritime Ltd v Oceanconnect UK Ltd* [2010] EWHC 619 (QB); [2011] 1
Lloyd's Rep. 61; *Bartin Pipe & Piling Supply Ltd v Epscan Industries Ltd* (2004) 236 D.L.R. (4th) 75
at [22]. But see *Michael Gerson (Leasing) Ltd v Wilkinson* [2001] Q.B. 514 at 527.

386 *City Fur Manufacturing Co v Fureenbond* [1937] 1 All E.R. 799. cf. *Nicholson v Harper* [1895] 2
Ch. 415.

387 *Anglo-Irish Asset Finance v DSG Financial Services* [1995] C.L.Y. 4491.

388 *Bartin Pipe & Piling Supply Ltd v Epscan Industries Ltd* (2004) 236 D.L.R. (4th) 75 (seller retained
possession of the goods but armed the first buyer with a document of title); distinguishing *Gamers Motor Centre (Newcastle) Pty Ltd v Natwest Wholesale Australia Pty Ltd* (1987) 163 C.L.R. 236.

Replace paragraph with:
    These decisions were, however, not followed by the Judicial Committee of the   **7-059**
Privy Council in *Pacific Motor Auctions Pty Ltd v Motor Credits (Hire Finance)
Ltd*.392 The Board there held that the words "continues ... in possession" indicated
that s.24 did not contemplate as relevant a change in the legal title under which the
seller was in possession of the goods, for this legal title could not continue. Before
the sale he would be in possession as an owner, whereas after the sale he would be
in possession as bailee holding the goods for the new owner.393 In order to defeat
the operation of s.24, there would have to be a break in the physical possession of
the seller, i.e. by delivering the goods to the buyer394 or to some third person.395 The
section did not cease to apply where the seller simply attorned to the buyer as
bailee.396 Although this decision is strictly only of persuasive authority in England,
it has been followed by the Court of Appeal in *Worcester Works Finance Ltd v
Cooden Engineering Co Ltd*,397 where it was said:

    "It does not matter what private arrangement may be made by the seller with the
    purchaser—such as whether the seller remains bailee or trespasser or whether he is law-

fully in possession or not. It is sufficient if he remains continuously in possession of the goods that he has sold to the purchaser."[398]

It therefore means, for example, that a seller continuing in possession who in breach of contract is either late in delivering the goods to the first buyer, or who repudiates the obligation to do so, has the power to transmit a good title under s.24. A seller, however, not in possession of the goods at the time of the first sale, and who thereafter comes into possession only as a bailee of that first buyer after delivery has been made to that buyer, is not in possession at any time as a seller and therefore cannot pass good title under s.24 to a second buyer.[399]

[392] *Pacific Motor Auctions Pty Ltd v Motor Credits (Hire Finance) Ltd* [1965] A.C. 867. See Merrett [2008] C.L.J. 376.

[393] See *Dore v Dore*, *Times*, 18 March 1953.

[394] *Mitchell v Jones* (1905) 24 N.Z.L.R. 932; *Worcester Works Finance Ltd v Cooden Engineering Co Ltd* [1972] 1 Q.B. 210 at 217–218. In the latter case Lord Denning MR suggested that the break ought to be "substantial".

[395] *Olds Discount Co Ltd v Krett* [1940] 2 K.B. 117.

[396] But in the *Pacific Motor Auctions* case, the Board stated ([1965] A.C. 867 at 889) that the seller had not attorned.

[397] *Worcester Works Finance Ltd v Cooden Engineering Co Ltd* [1972] 1 Q.B. 210. See also *Astley Industrial Trust Ltd v Miller* [1968] 2 All E.R. 36; *Mercantile Credit Ltd v Upton (FC) & Sons Pty Ltd* (1974) 47 A.L.J.R. 301.

[398] *Worcester Works Finance Ltd v Cooden Engineering Co Ltd* [1972] 1 Q.B. 210 at 217.

[399] *Fadallah v Pollak* [2013] EWHC 3159 (QB), following *Mitchell v Jones* (1905) 24 N.Z.L.R. 932.

Disposition

Replace the first paragraph with:

7-064   "Disposition" involves some transfer of an interest in property,[419] and it has been said that it extends "to all acts by which a new interest (legal or equitable) in the property is effectually created".[420] The reference to an equitable interest is, however, problematical; and it further seems unlikely that a purely gratuitous disposition, e.g. a gift, would suffice.[421] In its context, the word "disposition" must also mean something more than a mere transfer of possession.[422] It is a moot point, however, whether a bailment by the seller which creates some sort of proprietary interest in the bailee analogous to the specific instance mentioned of a pledge, would constitute a "disposition" within the meaning of s.24. For example, if a seller in possession wrongfully lets the goods to a hirer under a hire-purchase agreement, there must be some doubt whether the buyer is bound by this hire-purchase agreement,[423] since it can be argued that this only transfers possession of the goods to the hirer[424] and the seller does not sell or dispose of the property in the goods, or agree so to do.[425] Nevertheless, although the hirer's option may not explicitly be recognised as a proprietary right over and above the hirer's possession, in indirect ways a property right is recognised when the damages of a claimant are reduced to take account of the hirer's disbursements in the tort of conversion.[426] If, however, the hirer were subsequently to exercise his option to purchase the goods under the agreement, he might acquire a good title, provided that a constructive delivery of the goods can be spelt out in consequence of this disposition.[427] Where goods sold to a first buyer are subsequently the subject of a bailment with a licence to consume,[427a] this bailment transaction, it is submitted, should be regarded as a disposition under s.24. The bailee in such transactions is at liberty wholly to dispose of the goods before payment. Although the matter is not free from difficulty, it should follow that the bailee's possessory right to retain and consume the goods continues even if a claim is made for any surviving goods by the earlier buyer, or if the bailee is apprised of the seller's defective title before the goods are consumed.

[419] *Worcester Works Finance Ltd v Cooden Engineering Co Ltd* [1972] 1 Q.B. 210 at 218, 219, 220.

[420] *Worcester Works Finance Ltd v Cooden Engineering Co Ltd* [1972] 1 Q.B. 210 at 218; citing *Carter v Carter* [1896] 1 Ch. 62 at 67. For the view that "disposition" is a word of "wide application" and does not need to be a sale or in the nature of a sale, see *P4 Ltd v Unite Integrated Solutions Plc* [2006] B.L.R. 150 at [18]. A bailment with a right to use or consume under a sui generis supply contract of the sort considered in *PST Energy Shipping LLC v OW Bunker Malta Ltd (The Res Cogitans)* [2016] UKSC 23 will therefore be a disposition for present purposes. The effect of a disposition that is not in the nature of a sale, however, is a different matter: see below, para.7-084.

[421] See Bridge, *The Sale of Goods*, 3rd edn, para.5.146. cf. *Kitto v Bilbie, Hobson & Co* (1895) 72 L.T. 266 at 267; *Worcester Works Finance Ltd v Cooden Engineering Co Ltd* [1972] 1 G.B. 210 at 219. See Preston, (1972) 88 L.Q.R. 239. The provisions of the Factors Act 1889 s.5 are not applicable: see above, para.7-055 n.373.

[422] *Worcester Works Finance Ltd v Cooden Engineering Co Ltd* [1972] 1 Q.B. 210 at 219, 220. See also *P4 Ltd v Unite Integrated Solutions (No.2)* [2006] EWHC 2640 (TCC) at [115].

[423] cf. Goode, *Hire-Purchase Law and Practice*, 2nd edn, pp.606, 607.

[424] cf. *Karflex Ltd v Poole* [1933] 2 K.B. 251 at 264–265.

[425] *Helby v Matthews* [1895] A.C. 471 at 477.

[426] *Belsize Motor Supply Co v Cox* [1914] 1 K.B. 244; *Whiteley v Hilt* [1918] 2 K.B. 808; *Wickham Holdings Ltd v Brooke House Holding Ltd* [1967] 1 W.L.R. 295; *Belvoir Finance Co v Stapleton* [1971] 1 Q.B. 210.

[427] See above, para.7-063. But, by that time, the hirer might no longer be without notice.

[427a] *PST Energy Shipping LLC v OW Bunker Malta Ltd (The Res Cogitans)* [2016] UKSC 23; [2016] A.C. 1034.

Effect of delivery or transfer

Replace footnote 431 with:

[431] Factors Act 1889 s.8. If, as submitted above (para.7-064), a bailment with a licence to consume is a disposition when the goods are delivered, it will not be an agreement to make a disposition for present purposes.

7-065

Goods in bulk

Replace paragraph with:

Under s.20A of the 1979 Act, where there is a contract for the sale of a specified quantity of unascertained goods forming part of an identified bulk, a pre-paying buyer will have transferred to him property in an undivided share in the bulk and he will become an owner in common of the bulk.[438] The effect of s.24 in a situation where the seller of goods sells to successive buyers more than the quantity of goods in the bulk has been discussed in Ch.5 para.5-123 above. Section 24 may also be invoked where, for example, a buyer purchases and pays for a specified quantity of goods from a larger quantity of goods forming the cargo of a named vessel, but the seller continues or is in possession of a bill of lading covering the whole of the cargo and pledges the bill with a bank to secure an advance.[439] In such a case, provided the bank is in good faith and without notice of the sale, it can rely on s.24 to assert the priority of its pledge over the property interest of the buyer. It would appear to be immaterial that the goods which are the subject-matter of the pledge are then unascertained.[440]

7-067

[438] See above, para.5-109.

[439] As in *Re Wait* [1927] 1 Ch. 606 (decided before s.20A was inserted into the 1979 Act).

[440] *Capital and Countries Bank v Warriner* (1896) 12 T.L.R. 216 (on s.25(1) of the 1979 Act: below, para.7-085). But see above, para.5-122; below, para.8-012 (attornment).

7. BUYER IN POSSESSION

Sale, pledge or other disposition

Replace footnote 540 with:

7-079   [540] The entry by the buyer in possession into a bailment with a right to use or consume the goods under a sui generis supply contract of the sort considered in *PST Energy Shipping LLC v OW Bunker Malta Ltd (The Res Cogitans)* [2016] UKSC 23; [2016] A.C. 1034 will be a disposition for present purposes: above, paras 7-041 and 7-064.

8. MOTOR VEHICLES SUBJECT TO A HIRE-PURCHASE OR CONDITIONAL-SALE AGREEMENT

Scope of provisions

Replace footnote 593 with:

7-088   [593] *Kulkarni v Manor Credit (Davenham) Ltd* [2010] EWCA Civ 69; [2012] 2 Lloyd's Rep. 431. See Merrett, [2010] C.L.J. 236.

9. MISCELLANEOUS PROVISIONS

Common law and statutory powers

Replace footnote 648 with:

7-110   [648] See *Bowstead and Reynolds on Agency*, 21st edn, para.4-001.

Replace paragraph with:

7-111   Statutory powers include those of an unpaid seller of goods,[650] an enforcement officer,[651] the trustee for civil recovery,[652] a registrar or other officer of a county court,[653] an administrator,[654] administrative receiver[655] and liquidator[656] of a company, a trustee in bankruptcy[657] and a receiver or manager of a bankrupt's estate,[658] an enforcement agent implementing the commercial rent arrears procedure,[659] a criminal court,[660] the police,[661] a local authority which has taken possession of an abandoned vehicle,[662] a pawnee under the Consumer Credit Act 1974,[663] a bailee of uncollected goods, an innkeeper,[664] and a court ordering the levying of distress on a ship.[665]

[650] Sale of Goods Act 1979 ss.39(1), 48; below, para.15-101.

[651] Insolvency Rules (SI 1986/1925); Insolvency Act 1986 s.346(7) (as amended by the Courts Act 2003 Sch.8); Tribunals, Courts and Enforcement Act 2007 s.72(1) (commercial rent arrears recovery procedure) (effective 6 April 2014)); the Courts Act 2003 Sch.7 para.10; CPR Sch.1, RSC Ords 46, 47. See *Curtis v Maloney* [1951] 1 K.B. 736; *Dyal Singh v Kenyan Insurance Ltd* [1954] A.C. 287. cf. *Jones Bros (Holloway) Ltd v Woodhouse* [1923] 2 K.B. 117.

[652] Proceeds of Crime Act 2002 s.267 and Sch.7 (as amended by the Criminal Finances Act 2017).

[653] Tribunals, Courts and Enforcement Act 2007 ss.62-70 (effective 15 July 2013 for ss.62 and 64, otherwise 6 April 2014) and Sch.12 para.51 (effective 6 April 2014).

[654] Insolvency Act 1986 Sch.B1 paras 59, 70–72, inserted by the Enterprise Act 2002 s.248 and Sch.16.

[655] Insolvency Act 1986 ss.42, 43, Sch.1. But administrative receivership has been abolished (subject to certain exceptions) by s.72A of the 1986 Act, inserted by the Enterprise Act 2002 s.250.

[656] Insolvency Act 1986 ss.165 and 166 (as amended by the Small Business, Enterprise and Employment Act 2016), 167 Sch.4 Pt III.

[657] Insolvency Act 1986 s.134 Sch.5.

[658] Insolvency Act 1986 ss.286, 287.

[659] Tribunals, Courts and Enforcement Act 2007 s.72 and Sch.12; Insolvency Act 1986 s.347 (as amended by the Tribunals, Courts and Enforcement Act 2007). On the 2007 Act, see *Palmer on Bailment*, 3rd edn, paras 43-126 et seq.

[660] Powers of Criminal Courts (Sentencing) Act 2000 s.143.

[661] Police (Property) Act 1897 s.2, as amended by the Police (Property) Act 1997 s.1 and by the Police Reform and Social Responsibility Act 2011 Sch.16(3) para.62, and applied by the Powers of Criminal Courts (Sentencing) Act 2000 s.144. See also s.2A (inserted by the Police Reform Act 2002 s.77).

[662] Road Traffic Regulation Act 1984 s.101 (as amended by the Road Traffic Act 1991 s.67); Removal and Disposal of Vehicles Regulations 1986 (SI 1986/183) Pt III; *Bulbruin Ltd v Romanyszyn* [1994] R.T.R. 273.

[663] Consumer Credit Act 1974 ss.120, 121.

[664] Innkeepers Act 1878 s.1. See also the Hotel Proprietors Act 1956.

[665] Merchant Shipping Act 1995 s.285.

CHAPTER 8

DELIVERY

TABLE OF CONTENTS

1. IN GENERAL

Delivery and payment

Replace footnote 26 with:

26 *Pordage v Cole* (1669) 1 Wms. Saund. 319; *Morton v Lamb* (1797) 7 T.R. 125; *Rawson v Johnson* (1801) 1 East 203 at 212; *Waterhouse v Skinner* (1801) 2 B. & P. 447. See also *Lawrence v Knowles* (1839) 5 Bing. N.C. 399; *Pickford v Grand Junction Ry* (1841) 8 M. & W. 372 at 378; *De Medina v Norman* (1842) 9 M. & W. 820 at 827; *Bankart v Bowers* (1866) L.R. 1 C.P. 484; *Paynter v James* (1867) L.R. 2 C.P. 348; *Re Phoenix Bessemer Steel Co* (1876) 4 Ch. D. 108; *Doherty v Fannigan Holdings Ltd* [2018] EWCA Civ 1615; [2018] 2 B.C.L.C. 623. Previously it was necessary for the buyer expressly to aver that he was ready and willing to pay the price, but this was dispensed with by RSC Ord.18 r.7(4). But see now CPR r.16.4(1)(a). See also below, para.8-054 (instalment deliveries).   **8-004**

Breach by seller

Replace footnote 40 with:

40 See *Chitty on Contracts*, 33rd edn, Vol.1 Ch.24; and below, paras 8-025, 8-066, 8-068.   **8-006**

2. METHODS OF DELIVERY

Symbolic delivery

Replace footnote 54 with:

54 See Bridge, Gullifer, Low and McMeel, *The Law of Personal Property*, 2nd edn paras 17-010 et seq..   **8-008**

4. TIME OF DELIVERY

Express stipulations

Replace paragraph with:

According to the Sale of Goods Act 1979 s.10(2), whether a stipulation as to time   **8-025** (other than as to time of payment) is or is not of the essence of the contract depends on the terms of the contract.[134] The parties are therefore at liberty to stipulate in the contract that time is to be of the essence in relation to the seller's obligation to deliver within an agreed time. If no such stipulation is inserted, but the parties have nevertheless fixed a time for the delivery of the goods, s.10(2) would still require that the nature of this term be determined by reference to the terms of the contract. It was, however, pointed out by McCardie J in *Hartley v Hymans*[135] that the common law and law merchant did not make the question whether time was of the essence depend upon the terms of the contract, unless those terms were express on the point. It looked rather to the nature of the contract and the character of the goods dealt with. There is no presumption or rule of law that stipulations as to time of delivery are of the essence of a contract of sale of goods.[136] But, in commercial contracts, they are frequently so construed, even though this is not expressly stated in the words of the contract.[137] If, in such a case, the seller fails to deliver the goods within the time limited for delivery, there is a breach of condition and the buyer is entitled to reject the goods and treat the contract as repudiated.[138] However, a stipulation as to time of delivery may on its true construction[139] be merely an "innominate" or "intermediate" term,[140] the breach of which entitles the buyer to treat the contract as repudiated only if the delay in delivery is so prolonged as to deprive him of substantially the whole benefit which it was intended he should receive from the contract.[141]

[134] By analogy at common law, this section, along with the case law qualifying it, should apply to sui generis supply contracts of the sort considered in *PST Energy Shipping LLC v OW Bunker Malta Ltd (The Res Cogitans)* [2016] UKSC 23; [2016] A.C. 1034.

[135] *Hartley v Hymans* [1920] 3 K.B. 475 at 483. Contrast Bramwell B in *Tarrabochia v Hickie* (1856) 1 H. & N. 183 at 188. See also *PT Surya Citra Multimedia v Brightpoint Singapore Pte Ltd* [2018] SGHC 245 at [63]–[64] and [74].

[136] *Compagnie Commerciale Sucres et Denrees v Czarnikow (C) Ltd* [1990] 1 W.L.R. 1337 at 1347; *Thunderbird Industries LLC v Simoco Digital UK Ltd* [2004] EWHC 209 (Ch); [2004] 1 B.C.L.C. 541 at [14]; *PT Surya Citra Multimedia v Brightpoint Singapore Pte Ltd* [2018] SGHC 245 at [71] (citing with approval this work). The question was left open in *Spar Shipping AS v Grand China Logistics Holding (Group) Co Ltd (The Spar Capella, Star Vega and Spar Draco)* [2016] EWCA Civ 982; [2016] 2 Lloyd's Rep. 447 at [56].

[137] *Wimshurst v Deeley* (1845) 2 C.B. 253; *Bowes v Shand* (1877) 2 App. Cas. 455 at 463; *Reuter v Sala* (1879) 4 C.P.D. 239 at 246, 249; *Harrington v Brown* (1917) 23 C.L.R. 297; *Hartley v Hymans* [1920] 3 K.B. 475 at 484; *Brooke Tool Manufacturing Co Ltd v Hydraulic Gears Co Ltd* (1920) 89 L.J.K.B. 263; *Finagrain SA Geneva v Kruse (P) Hamburg* [1976] 2 Lloyd's Rep. 508; *United Scientific Holdings Ltd v Burnley BC* [1978] A.C. 904 at 924, 937, 944, 950, 958; *Toepfer v Lenersan-Poortman NV* [1980] 1 Lloyd's Rep. 143; *Cerealmangimi SpA v Toepfer* [1981] 1 Lloyd's Rep. 337; *Bunge Corp v Tradax Export SA* [1981] 1 W.L.R. 711 at 716, 719, 729; *Société Italo-Belge pour le Commerce et l'Industrie v Palm and Vegetable Oils (Malaysia) Sdn. Bhd.* [1981] 2 Lloyd's Rep. 695 at 699; *Compagnie Commerciale Sucres et Denrees v Czarnikow (C) Ltd* [1990] 1 W.L.R. 1337 at 1347; *Westbrook Resources Ltd v Globe Metallurgical Inc* [2009] EWCA Civ 310; [2009] 2 Lloyd's Rep. 224 at [7]. cf. *McDougall v Aeromarine of Emsworth Ltd* [1958] 1 W.L.R. 1126. Contrast *Paton v Payne* (1897) 35 S.L.R. 112 HL. See also below, para.19-064 (tender of documents).

[138] *Plevins v Downing* (1876) 1 C.P.D. 220 at 226; *Coddington v Paleologo* (1867) L.R. 2 Ex. 193 at 196-197. See also the later cases in para.8-025n.137 (above). cf. Vienna Convention on Contracts for the International Sale of Goods Arts 33, 47, 48, 49, 71-73 (above, para.1-024). For delivery by instalments, see below, para.8-065.

[139] Applying the principle stated by Bowen LJ in *Bentsen v Taylor, Sons & Co* [1893] A.C. 274 at 281 (approved in *Bunge Corp v Tradax Export SA* [1981] 1 W.L.R. 711 at 719, 725). See also *Compagnie Commerciale Sucres et Denrees v Czarnikow (C) Ltd* [1990] 1 W.L.R. 1337 at 1347; *Phibco Energy Inc v Coastal (Bermuda) Ltd (The Aragon)* [1991] 1 Lloyd's Rep. 61 (Note). The introduction into an f.o.b. contract of a laycan arrival term from a charterparty contract, where the time of arrival under such a term is not of the essence of the contract, means that time is not of the essence of the f.o.b. contract when it would have been in the case of an ordinary shipment term: *ERG Raffinerie Mediterranee SpA v Chevron USA Inc (The Luxmar)* [2007] EWCA Civ 494; [2007] 2 Lloyd's Rep. 542. See further para.20-037, below.

[140] See below, para.10-033.

[141] *Scandinavian Trading Co A/B v Zodiac Petroleum SA* [1981] 1 Lloyd's Rep. 81 (time for provision of cargo and loading of chartered ships); *Tradax Export SA v Italgrani di Francesco Ambrosio* [1986] 1 Lloyd's Rep. 112 (time for delivery "at buyers' call"); *Soufflet Negoce v Bunge SA* [2009] EWHC 2454 (Comm); [2010] 1 Lloyd's Rep. 718. But contrast *Compagnie Commerciale Sucres et Denrees v Czarnikow (C) Ltd* [1990] 1 W.L.R. 1337.

Notice making time of the essence

Replace paragraph with:

At common law, stipulations as to the time of completion were in general **8-026** regarded as being of "the essence" of a contract of sale of land.[142] But this was not so in equity, which was accustomed to afford relief either by granting specific performance to the party who was out of time or by restraining the other party from enforcing his consequential rights at law.[143] Today the equitable rule prevails.[144] But, even in equity, the innocent party could bring to an end equity's interference with the legal rights of the parties by giving to the party in default a notice requiring him to perform his obligation within a reasonable time.[145] It is, however, submitted that these equitable rules have only a very limited application to contracts of sale of goods,[146] since equity would not ordinarily intervene to relieve a party from the consequences at common law of a breach of a time stipulation in such a contract.[147] Although the extent of equitable intervention outside contracts of sale of land is possibly unclear,[148] there is likely to be little scope for notices making time of the essence in the case of a delay in the delivery of goods in those cases where time was not originally of the essence.[149] If one party is guilty of the breach of a stipulation as to the time of delivery and the stipulation is a condition, the other party is entitled without more to treat the contract as repudiated and there is no need for him to serve a notice giving a further opportunity to deliver within a reasonable time. If the stipulation is not a condition but an intermediate term, then a notice purporting to make time of the essence will not automatically make a failure of performance a repudiatory breach, for one party cannot unilaterally vary the terms of a contract by turning what was previously a non-essential term of the contract into an essential term.[150] Should such a notice be served, the failure to deliver within the time fixed by the notice will not, in itself, constitute a repudiation irrespective of the consequences of the breach.[151]

[142] In the light of intermediate stipulation analysis, there is a need to "adapt" equity's belief that the common law always treated the time of performance as being of the essence of the contract: *Samarenko v Dawn Hill House Ltd* [2011] EWCA Civ 1445; [2013] Ch. 36; [2012] 1 P. & C.R. 14 at [39].

[143] *Tilley v Thomas* (1867) L.R. 3 Ch. App. 61 at 67; *Stickney v Keeble* [1915] A.C. 386 at 415; *Jamshed Khodaram Irani v Burjorji Dhonjibhai* (1915) 32 T.L.R. 156 at 157; *Lock v Bell* [1931] 1 Ch. 35 at 43; *United Scientific Holdings Ltd v Burnley BC* [1978] A.C. 904 at 924, 940; *Raineri v Miles* [1981] A.C. 1050; *British and Commonwealth Holdings Plc v Quadrex Holdings Inc* [1989] Q.B. 842 at 857; *Behzadi v Shaftesbury Hotels Ltd* [1992] Ch. 1. See also Carter, Courtney and Tolhurst, [2017] C.L.J. 63.

[144] Law of Property Act 1925 s.41.

[145] *Stickney v Keeble* [1915] A.C. 386; *Ajit v Sammy* [1967] 1 A.C. 255; *United Scientific Holdings Ltd v Burnley BC* [1978] A.C. 904 at 934, 946; *British and Commonwealth Holdings Plc v Quadrex Holdings Inc* [1989] Q.B. 842 at 857; *Behzadi v Shaftesbury Hotels Ltd* [1992] Ch.1; *Dalkia Utilities Services Plc v Celtech International Ltd* [2006] EWHC 63 (Comm); [2006] 1 Lloyd's Rep. 599; *Sentinel International Ltd v Cordes* [2008] UKPC 60; *BNP Paribas v Wockhardt Operations EU (Swiss) AG* [2009] EWHC 3116 (Comm); (2009) 132 Con. L.R. 177; *Spar Shipping AS v Grand China Logistics Holding (Group) Co Ltd (The Spar Capella, Star Vega and Spar Draco)* [2016] EWCA Civ 982; [2016] 2 Lloyd's Rep. 447 at [104].

[146] Contrast Stannard, (2004) 120 L.Q.R. 137. But: (1) where one party waives timely performance of an obligation by the other party and no period of postponement is fixed, he may give notice that he requires performance within a reasonable time and that time then becomes of the essence (see below, paras 8-030, 9-006); and (2) under s.48(3) of the 1979 Act, an unpaid seller may give notice of his intention to resell and then resell the goods if the buyer does not pay or tender the price within a reasonable time (see below, para.15-119). See also below, para.8-035 (delivery on request).

[147] *Reuter v Sala* (1879) 4 C.P.D. 239 at 249; *Stickney v Keeble* [1915] A.C. 386. But see below, para.15-130 (relief against forfeiture).

[148] *United Scientific Holdings Ltd v Burnley BC* [1978] A.C. 904 at 924, 940, 957.

[149] cf. *Portaria Shipping Co v Gulf Pacific Navigation Co Ltd* [1981] 2 Lloyd's Rep. 180 at 185 (payment); Vienna Convention on Contracts for the International Sale of Goods (above, para.1-024) Arts 47, 48, 63, 64. See Carter, Courtney and Tolhurst, [2017] C.L.J. 63.

[150] *Behzadi v Shaftesbury Hotels Ltd* [1992] Ch. 1 at 12, 24; *Re Olympia & York Canary Wharf Ltd (No.2)* [1993] B.C.C. 159 at 171; *Ocular Sciences Ltd v Aspect Vision Care Ltd* [1997] R.P.C. 289 at 432; *Dalkia Utilities Services Plc v Celtech International Ltd* [2006] EWHC 63 (Comm); [2006] 1 Lloyd's Rep. 599 at [131]; *Multi Veste 226 BV v NI Summer Row Unitholder BV* [2011] EWHC 2026 Ch); (2011) 139 Con. L.R. 23; *Samarenko v Dawn Hill House Ltd* [2011] EWCA Civ 1445; [2013] Ch. 36 at [37]; [2012] 1 P. & C.R. 14; *Urban I (Blonk Street) Ltd v Ayres* [2013] EWCA Civ 816; [2014] 1 W.L.R. 756 at [44]. In *Samarenko*, Lewison LJ at [42] admits that his own earlier judgment in *Multi Veste* may have been too "prescriptive". In *Multi Veste*, when considering the effect of serving a notice, the court did appear to suggest at [201] that the notice itself might change the underlying common law position: "I conclude therefore that the service of notice making time of the essence changes the question from whether delay amounts to a repudiation to the question whether failure to perform the obligation at all amounts to a repudiation". It is submitted that these words should be treated with caution and that a time notice does not recharacterise late performance as non-performance (see *Samarenko v Dawn Hill House Ltd* [2011] EWCA Civ 1445; [2013] Ch. 36 at [65]; [2012] 1 P. & C.R. 14). See further Carter, Courtney and Tolhurst, [2017] C.L.J. 63. See also *Green v Sevin* (1879) 13 Ch. D. 589 at 599.

[151] Nevertheless, even if delivery within the agreed period is not "essential", the Consumer Rights Act 2015 s.28(7), (8) entitles consumer buyers to treat a contract of sale as at an end if the trader fails to deliver within an "appropriate" further period specified by the consumer. See below, para.14-105.

Waiver

Replace footnote 163 with:

8-030   [163] *Ogle v Earl Vane* (1868) L.R. 3 Q.B. 272; *Hartley v Hymans* [1920] 3 K.B. 475; *Besseler Waechter Glover & Co v South Derwent Coal Co* [1938] 1 Q.B. 408; *Rickards (Charles) Ltd v Oppenhaim* [1950] 1 K.B. 616; *Westbrook Resources Ltd v Globe Metallurgical Inc* [2009] EWCA Civ 310; [2009] 2 Lloyd's Rep. 224 at [12]; *Chitty on Contracts*, 33rd edn, Vol.1 paras 22-040 to 22-047. cf. Vienna Convention on Contracts for the International Sale of Goods Art.47 (above, para.1-024).

Abandonment

Replace footnote 175 with:

8-031   [175] *Allied Marine Transport Ltd v Vale do Rio Doce Navegacao SA* [1985] 1 W.L.R. 925 (interpreting *Pearl Mill Co v Ivy Tannery Co Ltd* [1919] 1 K.B. 78). cf. *André et Cie SA v Marine Transocean Ltd* [1981] Q.B. 694 at 700, 713. See also *Tyers v Rosedale and Ferryhill Iron Co* (1875) L.R. 10 Ex. 195; and *Chitty on Contracts*, 33rd edn, Vol.1 para.22-027, Bridge, *The Sale of Goods*, 3rd edn, para.6.23.

Computation of time

Replace the first paragraph with:

8-032   Where one party to a contract of sale is allowed a certain period of time within which to fulfil his obligations under the contract, e.g. to deliver the goods or to pay for them, and this period of time is expressed in terms of years or months, the word "year" is prima facie to be construed as meaning a period of 12 consecutive months[177] and "month" as meaning a calendar month.[178] As a normal rule, a "week" is a period of seven consecutive days; and "day" is a period from midnight to midnight[179] and not a consecutive period of 24 hours.[180] No attention is paid to fractions of a day, so that a number of "days" means a number of complete days, and includes Sundays and holidays.[181] These presumptions may, however, be displaced by a contrary intention appearing from the contract, or by trade custom.[182]

[177] *Bracegirdle v Heald* (1818) 1 B. & Ald. 722.

[178] Sale of Goods Act 1979 s.10(3). See also *Dodds v Walker* [1981] 1 W.L.R. 1027; *Chitty on Contracts*, 33rd edn, Vol.1 para.21-027.

[179] *The Katy* [1895] P. 56; *Cartwright v MacCormack* [1963] 1 W.L.R. 18.

[180] *Chitty on Contracts*, 33rd edn, Vol.1 para.21-023. cf. *Cornfoot v Royal Exchange Assurance Corp* [1904] 1 K.B. 40.

[181] But see the Sale of Goods Act 1979 s.29(5); below, para.8-037.

[182] Sale of Goods Act 1979 s.55(1).

Replace the third paragraph with:

If the period of time is to be computed "from" or "after" a date, act or event, or if something is to be done "in" or "within" a certain period of time "from" or "of" a date, act or event, there is no hard and fast rule as to whether the day of the date, act or event is to be excluded or included.[186] Attempts have been made from time to time to formulate subsidiary rules of construction.[187] It has, for example, been said that, where time is to be computed from the performance of an act, and the act is one to which the party against whom time is to run is privy, there is less hardship in holding that the day of the act should be included, because that party has had the benefit of some part of the day.[188] It has also been stated that, where the computation is to be for the benefit of the person affected as much time should be given as the language admits of, and where it is for his detriment the language should be construed as strictly as possible.[189] However, decisions as to the computation of time with reference to statutes, deeds and contracts reveal no consistent principle[190] and "the rational mode of computation is to have regard in each case to the purpose for which the computation is to be made"[191] and to the precise words used.[192] Nevertheless, in contracts of sale of goods, it is submitted that the computation of the time of performance from a particular date, act or event is prima facie exclusive of the day of the date, act or event[193] and inclusive of the day of performance,[194] although this presumption may be displaced by a contrary intention appearing from the wording of the contract and the circumstances surrounding it.[195]

[186] *Lester v Garland* (1808) 15 Ves. Jun. 248 at 258; *Re North* [1895] 2 Q.B. 264 at 269; *Sheffield Corp v Sheffield Electric Light Co* [1898] 1 Ch. 203 at 209.

[187] See the test of "shortening the period to one day": *Webb v Fairmaner* (1838) 3 M. & W. 473 at 477; *Young v Higgon* (1840) 6 M. & W. 49; *Re Railway Sleepers Supply Co* (1885) 29 Ch. D. 204 at 207; *Carapanayoti v Comptoir Commercial André et Cie SA* [1972] 1 Lloyd's Rep. 139 at 143, 144, 145.

[188] *Lester v Garland* (1808) 15 Ves. Jun. 248 at 256.

[189] *Re North* [1895] 2 Q.B. 264 at 270; *Carapanayoti v Comptoir Commercial André et Cie SA* [1972] 1 Lloyd's Rep. 159 at 143, 144, 146.

[190] For examples of exclusive computation, see *Lester v Garland* (1808) 15 Ves. Jun. 248 ("within"); *Blunt v Heslop* (1838) 8 A. & E. 577 ("after"); *South Staffs Tramways Co Ltd v Sickness and Accident Assurance Assoc* [1891] 1 Q.B. 402 ("from"); *Radcliffe v Bartholomew* [1892] 1 Q.B. 161 ("within"); *Re North* [1895] 2 Q.B. 264 ("for"); *Goldsmith's Co v West Metropolitan Ry* [1904] 1 K.B. 1 ("from"); *Stewart v Chapman* [1951] 2 K.B. 792 ("within"); *Cartwright v MacCormack* [1963] 1 W.L.R. 18 ("from"); *Re Figgis* [1969] Ch. 123 ("from"); *Re Lympne Investments Ltd* [1972] 1 W.L.R. 523 ("thereafter"); *Dodds v Walker* [1981] 1 W.L.R. 1027 ("after"); *Zoan v Rouamba* [2000] 1 W.L.R. 1509 ("after"). For examples of inclusive computation, see *Pugh v Duke of Leeds* (1778) 2 Cowp. 714 ("from"); *English v Cliff* [1914] 2 Ch. 376 at 383 ("from"); *Hare v Gocher* [1962] 2 Q.B. 641 ("beginning with"); *Trow v Ind Coope (West Midlands) Ltd* [1967] 2 Q.B. 899 ("beginning with"); *Zoan v Rouamba* [2000] 1 W.L.R. 1509 ("beginning with"); *R. (Zaporozhchenko) v City of Westminster Magistrates' Court* [2011] EWHC 34 (Admin); [2011] 1 W.L.R 994 ("plainly no distinction to be drawn between 'beginning with' and 'starting with'").

[191] *Re North* [1895] 2 Q.B. 264 at 269.

[192] *Carapanayoti v Comptoir Commercial André et Cie* [1972] 1 Lloyd's Rep. 139 at 144.

[193] *Webb v Fairmaner* (1838) 3 M. & W. 473 (payment for goods). See also *Goldsmith's Co v West Metropolitan Ry* [1904] 1 K.B. 1; *Carapanayoti v Comptoir Commercial André et Cie* [1972] 1 Lloyd's Rep. 139 at 142.

194 But see below, para.8-037.

195 See *Chitty on Contracts*, 33rd edn, Vol.1 para.21-025.

Words and phrases

Replace paragraph with:

8-033   The following words and phrases relating to time have been considered by the courts[197]: "as soon as possible",[198] "directly",[199] "forthwith",[200] "immediately",[201] "prompt",[202] "three working days",[203] "delivery on April 17th, complete 8th May",[204] "One vessel only presenting October 2006 Shipment at Buyer's Option",[205] "not later than",[206] "at latest";[207] "during [February] at buyer's call";[208] and "delivery ... by early 2011".[209]

197 See also *Chitty on Contracts*, 33rd edn, Vol.1 paras 21-022 et seq.; Odgers, *Construction of Deeds and Statutes*, 5th edn, pp.126-140.

198 *Attwood v Emery* (1856) 1 C.B.(N.S.) 110 at 115; *Hydraulic Engineering Co v McHaffie* (1878) 4 Q.B.D. 670; *Société Italo-Belge pour le Commerce et l'Industrie v Palm and Vegetable Oils (Malaysia) Sdn Bhd* [1981] 2 Lloyd's Rep. 695 at 700.

199 *Duncan v Topham* (1849) 8 C.B. 225; *Ministry of Agriculture v Kelly* [1953] N.I. 151.

200 *Simpson v Henderson* (1829) Moo. & M. 300; *Doe d. Pittman v Sutton* (1849) 9 C. & P. 706; *Roberts v Brett* (1865) 11 H.L.C. 337 at 335; *Hudson v Hill* (1874) 43 L.J.C.P. 273; *Re Sillence* (1877) 7 Ch. D. 238; *Re Southam* (1881) 19 Ch. D. 179 at 183; *Keith Prowse & Co v National Telephone Co* [1894] 2 Ch. 147 at 155; *Hillingdon LBC v Cutler* [1968] 1 Q.B. 124. See also *Staunton v Wood* (1851) 16 Q.B. 638 (delivery of goods forthwith and payment within 14 days).

201 *R. v Aston* (1850) 14 Jur. 1045; *Alexiadi v Robinson* (1861) 2 F. & F. 679; *Toms v Wilson* (1862) 4 B. & S. 455; *Massey v Sladen* (1868) L.R. 4 Ex. 13; *Re Burghardt* (1875) 1 Ch. D. 297; *Moore v Shelley* (1883) 8 App. Cas. 285; *Bradley & Sons v Colonial Continental Trading Ltd* [1964] 2 Lloyd's Rep. 52; *Tarkin AG v Thames Steel Ltd* [2010] EWHC 207 (Comm).

202 *European Grain & Shipping Ltd v David Geddes (Proteins) Ltd* [1977] 2 Lloyd's Rep. 591 (GAFTA form 109); *Yam Seng Pte Ltd v International Trade Corp Ltd* [2013] EWHC 111 (QB); [2013] 1 C.L.C. 162.

203 *Vitol SA v Phibro Energy AG* [1990] 2 Lloyd's Rep. 84 (citing *Reardon Smith Line Ltd v Ministry of Agriculture Fisheries and Food* [1963] A.C. 691).

204 *Coddington v Paleologo* (1867) L.R. 2 Ex. 193.

205 *Cereal Investments Co (CIC) SA v Man (ED & F) Sugar Ltd* [2007] EWHC 2843 (Comm); [2008] 1 Lloyd's Rep. 355, where the court interpreted the provision as permitting the vessel to be presented in October even if loading could not be completed until November.

206 *Toepfer v Lenersan-Poortman NV* [1980] 1 Lloyd's Rep. 143.

207 *Gill & Duffus SA v Société pour l'Exportation des Sucres SA* [1986] 1 Lloyd's Rep. 322.

208 *Tradax Export SA v Italgrani di Francesco Ambrosio* [1986] 1 Lloyd's Rep. 112. See also *Compagnie Commerciale Sucres et Denrees v Czarnikow (C) Ltd* [1990] 1 W.L.R. 1337 ("buyer ... shall be entitled to call for delivery").

209 *Kennedy v Newman* [2011] NTSC 27 (Aust).

No time fixed

Replace footnote 212 with:

8-034   212 *Ellis v Thompson* (1838) 3 M. & W. 445 at 456; *Jones v Gibbons* (1853) 8 Ex. Ch. 920 at 922; *Hick v Raymond and Reid* [1893] A.C. 22; *British Motor Body Co Ltd v Thomas Shaw (Dundee) Ltd*, 1914 S.C. 922; *SHV Gas Supply & Trading SAS v Naftomar Shipping and Trading Co Ltd Inc* [2005] EWHC 2528 (Comm); [2006] 1 Lloyd's Rep. 163. See also *Hartwells of Oxford Ltd v British Motor Trade Assoc* [1951] Ch. 50; *Monkland v Jack Barclay Ltd* [1951] 2 K.B. 252 at 260; *Western Union Petro International Co Ltd v Anterra Energy Inc* 2019 ABQB 165 at [32] (Can.) (buyer to be given a reasonable time to collect the goods from the seller). See also Vienna Convention on Contracts for the International Sale of Goods Art.33 (above, para.1-024).

Delivery conditional on buyer's act

Replace footnote 228 with:

[228] On the duty to co-operate, see *Mackay v Dick* (1881) 6 App. Cas. 251 at 263; *Sprague v Booth* [1909] A.C. 576 at 580; *Kleinert v Abosso Gold Mining Co* (1913) 58 S.J. (P.C.) 45; *Terry v Moss's Empires Ltd* (1915) 32 T.L.R. 92; *Colley v Overseas Exporters Ltd* [1921] 3 K.B. 302 at 309; *Pound (AV) & Co Ltd v Hardy (MW) & Co Inc* [1956] A.C. 588 at 608, 611; *Kyprianou v Cyprus Textiles Ltd* [1958] 2 Lloyd's Rep. 60. cf. *Mona Oil Equipment and Supply Co Ltd v Rhodesia Ry* [1949] 2 All E.R. 1014; *Hargreaves Transport Ltd v Lynch* [1969] 1 W.L.R. 215; *Becher (Kurt A) GmbH v Roplak Enterprises* [1991] 1 Lloyd's Rep. 277 at 282-284; *Hudson Bay Apparels Brand LLC v Umbro International Ltd* [2009] EWHC 2861 (Ch) at [117] et seq.; *Swallowfalls Ltd v Monaco Yachting & Technologies SAM* [2014] EWCA Civ 186. See also *Chitty on Contracts*, 33rd edn, Vol.1 para.14-025 (export and import licences).

8-036

5.   QUANTITY OF GOODS DELIVERED

Delivery of the correct quantity

Replace footnote 241 with:

[241] But see below, para.8-044. For the delivery of the wrong quantity in consumer sales, see below, para.14-104.

8-041

Insufficient delivery

Replace footnote 254 with:

[254] Sale of Goods Act 1979 s.36(1)(b). But see s.35(6)(b) (buyer not deemed to have accepted the goods merely because the goods are delivered to another under a sub-sale or other disposition).

8-042

Goods "as required"

Replace the fifth paragraph with:

An "exclusive dealing" agreement under which the buyer promises to purchase the whole of his requirements of goods from a single source and to buy from no other may nevertheless be void and unenforceable as being in unreasonable restraint of trade[311] or be affected by the Competition Act 1998 or by the EC Treaty Art.81 or 82.[312]

8-051

[311] *Esso Petroleum Ltd v Harper's Garage (Stourport) Ltd* [1968] A.C. 269; *Amoco Australia Pty Ltd v Rocca Bros Motor Engineering Co Pty Ltd* [1975] A.C. 561; *Shell UK Ltd v Lostock Garage Ltd* [1977] 1 W.L.R. 1187. cf. *Cleveland Petroleum Ltd v Dartstone Ltd* [1969] 1 W.L.R. 116; *Alec Lobb (Garages) Ltd v Total Oil (Great Britain) Ltd* [1985] 1 W.L.R. 173. See *Chitty on Contracts*, 33rd edn, Vol.1 para.16-106; and above, para.3-037.

[312] See *Chitty on Contracts*, 33rd edn, Vol.2 Ch.43; and above, paras 3-040, 3-041.

Usage

Replace footnote 313 with:

[313] Sale of Goods Act 1979 ss.30(5), 55(1); *Devaux v Conolly* (1849) 8 C.B. 640; *Moore v Campbell* (1854) 10 Exch. 323; *Lister and Biggs v Barry & Co* (1886) 3 T.L.R. 99; *Lomas & Co v Barff Ltd* (1901) 17 T.L.R. 437 (reversed on other grounds, 18 T.L.R. 461); *Société Anonyme l'Industrielle Russo-Belge v Scholefield* (1902) 7 Com. Cas. 114. Contrast *Cross v Elgin* (1831) 2 B. & Ad. 106; *Tancred Arrol & Co v Steel Co of Scotland Ltd* (1890) 15 App. Cas. 125 at 136. See also *Chitty on Contracts*, 33rd edn, Vol.1 paras 13-137 to 13-143, 14-033.

8-052

Exemption clauses

Replace footnote 315 with:

[315] See below, para.13-019; and *Chitty on Contracts*, 33rd edn, Vol.1 paras 15-008, 15-030.

8-053

6. DELIVERY BY INSTALMENTS

Right of discharge

Replace footnote 353 with:

8-060   ³⁵³ See *Chitty on Contracts*, 33rd edn, Vol.1 paras 21-028, 24-045 to 24-046; Glanville Williams, (1941) 57 L.Q.R. 373–375.

Severable contracts

Replace footnote 365 with:

8-062   ³⁶⁵ See *Chitty on Contracts*, 33rd edn, Vol.1 paras 21-028, 24-046.

Repudiation by renunciation

Replace footnote 390 with:

8-066   ³⁹⁰ *Spettabile Consorzio Veneziano di Armamento di Navigazione v Northumberland Shipbuilding Co Ltd* (1919) 121 L.T. 628 at 634-635; *Maple Flock Co v Universal Furniture Products (Wembley) Ltd* [1934] 1 K.B. 148 at 157; *Universal Cargo Carriers' Corp v Citati* [1957] 2 Q.B. 401 at 436 (affirmed in part and reversed in part on different grounds [1957] 1 W.L.R. 979; [1958] 2 Q.B. 254); *The Mihalis Angelos* [1971] 1 Q.B. 164 at 196; *Woodar Investment Development Ltd v Wimpey Construction UK Ltd* [1980] 1 W.L.R. 277 at 287; *Anchor Line Ltd v Keith Rowell Ltd* [1980] 2 Lloyd's Rep. 351 at 353; *Chilean Nitrate Sale Corp v Marine Transportation Co Ltd* [1982] 1 Lloyd's Rep. 570 at 580; *Texaco Ltd v Eurogulf Shipping Co Ltd* [1987] 2 Lloyd's Rep. 541 at 544; *Aktion Maritime Corp of Liberia v Kasmas (S) Bros Ltd* [1987] 1 Lloyd's Rep. 283 at 286; *Nottingham Building Soc v Eurodynamics Systems* [1995] F.S.R. 605; *SK Shipping (S) Pte Ltd v Petroexport Ltd* [2009] EWHC 2974 (Comm); [2010] 2 Lloyd's Rep. 158 at [89]–[97]; *Seadrill Management Services Ltd v OAO Gazprom* [2010] EWCA Civ 691; [2011] 1 All E.R. (Comm) 1077; *Eminence Property Developments Ltd v Heaney* [2010] EWCA Civ 1168; [2011] 2 All E.R. (Comm) 223; *Spar Shipping AS v Grand China Logistics Holding (Group) Co Ltd (The Spar Capella, Star Vega and Spar Draco)* [2016] EWCA Civ 982; [2016] 2 Lloyd's Rep. 447 at [56]; *Regulus Ship Services Pte Ltd v Lundin Services BV* [2016] EWHC 2674 (Comm); [2016] 2 Lloyd's Rep. 612 at [111]–[115]. See also *Forslind v Bechely-Crundall*, 1922 S.C. (HL) 173 at 179.

Repudiation by inability to perform

After "a fundamental breach.*", add:

8-067   The same should apply, it is submitted, in the case of a prospective breach of condition.

Repudiation by failure of performance

Replace footnote 406 with:

8-068   ⁴⁰⁶ *Poussard v Spiers* (1876) 1 Q.B.D. 410 at 414; *Honck v Muller* (1881) 7 Q.B.D. 92 at 100. *Mersey Steel and Iron Co v Naylor Benzon & Co* (1884) 8 App. Cas. 434 at 443-444; *Robert A Munro Ltd v Meyer* [1930] 2 K.B. 312; *Heyman v Darwins Ltd* [1942] A.C. 356 at 397; *Suisse Atlantique Société d'Armement Maritime SA v NV Kolen Centrale* [1967] 1 A.C. 361 at 442; *Decro-Wall International SA v Practitioners in Marketing Ltd* [1971] 1 W.L.R. 361 at 374; *Cehave NV v Bremer Handelsgesellschaft mbH* [1976] Q.B. 44 at 60, 73; *Federal Commerce & Navigation Co Ltd v Molena Alpha Inc* [1979] A.C. 757 at 779. See also *Chitty on Contracts*, 33rd edn, Vol.1 para.24-042. cf. Vienna Convention on Contracts for the International Sale of Goods Art.25 (above, para.1-024).

Replace the second paragraph with:

The most relevant factors in determining whether the breach is or is not of sufficient gravity have been said to be:

"First, the ratio quantitatively which the breach bears to the whole, and secondly the degree of probability or improbability that such a breach will be repeated."⁴¹⁰

The importance of the second factor was emphasised by Bigham J in *Millar's Karri and Jarrah Co v Weddel, Turner & Co,*[411] where he said:

"If the breach is of such a kind, or takes place in such circumstances as reasonably to lead to the inference that similar breaches will be committed in relation to subsequent deliveries, the whole contract may there and then be regarded as repudiated and may be rescinded. If, for instance, a buyer fails to pay for one delivery in such circumstances as to lead to the inference that he will not be able to pay for subsequent deliveries[412]; or if a seller delivers goods differing from the requirements of the contract, and does so in such circumstances as to lead to the inference that he cannot, or will not, deliver any other kind of goods in the future, the other contracting party will be under no obligation to wait and see what may happen; he can at once cancel the contract and rid himself of the difficulty."

The likelihood of a future breach by the seller[412a] is not to be treated in a "fanciful" way; a single breach will not normally of itself justify the apprehension by the buyer of future breaches by the seller. The issue of future breaches and their consequences is "overwhelmingly fact-sensitive".[412b] Judged as of the date of purported termination,[412c] the question whether a contracting party has been deprived of substantially the whole benefit of the contract involves assessing both the likely future consequences of breaches that have already occurred and the likely consequences of probable future breaches.[412d] It has also been said that, the further the parties have proceeded with the performance of the contract, the less likely it is that one party will be entitled to claim that it has been discharged by a single breach,[413] and that the degree to which delivery of one instalment is linked to another is a relevant factor.[414]

[410] *Maple Flock Co Ltd v Universal Furniture Products (Wembley) Ltd* [1934] 1 K.B. 148 at 157. In *Astrazeneca UK Ltd v Albemarle International Corp* [2011] EWHC 1574 (Comm); [2011] 2 C.L.C. 252 at [261], which concerned a requirements contract with a minimum duration of three years, it was said that the seller's failure to deliver 1, possibly even 2, instalments would not amount to a repudiatory breach. Emphasis was laid upon the long-term character of the contract. cf. Vienna Convention on Contracts for the International Sale of Goods Art.25 (above, para.1-024).

[411] *Millar's Karri and Jarrah Co v Weddel, Turner & Co* (1908) 100 L.T. 128 at 129.

[412] See below, para.8-072.

[412a] *Phones 4U Ltd v EE Ltd* [2018] EWHC 49 (Comm); [2018] 1 Lloyd's Rep. 204 at [41].

[412b] *Phones 4U Ltd v EE Ltd* [2018] EWHC 49 (Comm); [2018] 1 Lloyd's Rep. 204 at [42] (and hence is not the proper subject for a summary judgment application).

[412c] *Ampurius Nu Homes Holdings Ltd v Telford Homes (Creekside) Ltd* [2013] EWCA Civ 577; [2013] 4 All E.R. 377 at [44] and [64].

[412d] *Phones 4U Ltd v EE Ltd* [2018] EWHC 49 (Comm); [2018] 1 Lloyd's Rep. 204 at [43].

[413] *Cornwall v Henson* [1900] 2 Ch. 298 at 304. But see *Hoare v Rennie* (1859) 4 H. & N. 19; *Simpson v Crippin* (1872) L.R. 8 Q.B. 14; *Honck v Muller* (1881) 7 Q.B.D. 92; above, para.8-067n.400.

[414] *Warinco AG v Samor SpA* [1977] 2 Lloyd's Rep. 582 at 588 (reversed [1979] 1 Lloyd's Rep. 450).

Effect of repudiation

Replace footnote 416 with:

[416] The innocent party is not bound to accept the repudiation, but may treat the contract as continuing. **8-069** The seller may, in certain circumstances, complete performance of the contract and sue for the price: *White and Carter (Councils) Ltd v McGregor* [1962] A.C. 413; *Tredegar Iron and Coal Co Ltd v Hawthorn Bros & Co* (1902) 18 T.L.R. 716; *Anglo-African Shipping Co of New York Inc v J Mortner Ltd* [1962] 1 Lloyd's Rep. 81 at 610; *Decro-Wall International SA v Practitioners in Marketing Ltd* [1971] 1 W.L.R. 361; *Gator Shipping Corp v Trans-Asiatic Oil Ltd SA* [1978] 2 Lloyd's Rep. 357; *Isabella Shipowner SA v Shagang Shipping Co Ltd (The Aquafaith)* [2012] EWHC 1077 (Comm), [2012] 2 Lloyd's Rep. 61. See also *MSC Mediterranean Shipping Co v Cottonex Anstalt* [2016] EWCA Civ 789; [2016] 2 Lloyd's Rep. 494. But see the qualifications to this principle referred to in paras 16-023, 20-132, below; and in *Chitty on Contracts*, 33rd edn, Vol.1 para.24-011.

7. CLAUSES EXCUSING DELIVERY

Force majeure clauses

Replace the first paragraph with:

8-074   By a clause in the contract of sale, the seller[446] may be entitled[447] to suspend delivery, or extend the time for delivery or even cancel the whole or part of the contract upon the happening of a specified event or events beyond his control. Clauses of this type are often referred to as "force majeure" clauses, and they are frequently found in commercial contracts, where they redress the deficiencies of the common law doctrine of frustration.[448] Such clauses may assume a variety of forms, and a term "the usual force majeure clauses to apply" has been held void for uncertainty.[449] Force majeure clauses have been said not to be exemption clauses,[450] although it is difficult to draw any clear line of demarcation between the two types of clause,[451] since the effect of each may be to relieve a contracting party of an obligation or liability to which he would otherwise be subject, and force majeure clauses may nevertheless be affected by the Unfair Contract Terms Act 1977.[452]

[446] A force majeure clause may also be expressed to operate in favour of the buyer, or of both parties.

[447] The contract may even be cancelled automatically: *Continental Grain Export Corp v STM Grain Ltd* [1979] 2 Lloyd's Rep. 460; *Bremer Handelsgesellschaft mbH v Finagrain SA* [1981] 2 Lloyd's Rep. 259; *Pagnan SpA v Tradax Ocean Transportation SA* [1987] 2 Lloyd's Rep. 342.

[448] *RDC Concrete Ltd v Sato Kogyo (S) Pte Ltd* [2007] 4 S.L.R. 413 (Sing) at [56].

[449] *British Electrical and Associated Industries (Cardiff) Ltd v Patley Pressings Ltd* [1953] 1 W.L.R. 280. But such a term could refer to clauses used in a particular trade.

[450] *Fairclough, Dodd & Jones Ltd v Vantol (JH) Ltd* [1957] 1 W.L.R. 136 at 143. See also *Trade and Transport Inc v Iino Kaiun Kaisha Ltd* [1973] 1 W.L.R. 210 at 230–231; *The Super Servant Two* [1990] 1 Lloyd's Rep. 1 at 7, 12. cf. *Cero Navigation Corp v Jean Lion & Cie* [2000] 1 Lloyd's Rep. 292 at 299.

[451] See Treitel, *Frustration and Force Majeure*, 3rd edn, para.12-022; McKendrick (ed), *Force Majeure and Frustration of Contract*, 2nd edn.

[452] See below, para.8-081; *Seadrill Operations Ghana Ltd v Tullow Ghana Ltd* [2018] EWHC 1640 (Comm); [2018] 2 Lloyd's Rep. 628 at [77] ("in effect an exceptions clause). See also Bridge, *The Sale of Goods*, 3rd edn, para.9.04.

After the first paragraph, add new paragraph:

A further consideration is whether force majeure clauses are drawn as exceptions clauses or as frustration or cancellation clauses. If the clause is an exception clause, then the performing party must show that it was ready and willing to perform but for the event in question. An example of a party unable to rely on an exceptions clause is a seller already unable to supply the contract goods prior to the event. If the clause is a frustration or cancellation clause, the requirement of prior readiness and willingness is dispensed with and the parties are discharged from the contract as a result of the event, sometimes after an agreed period of suspension.[452a] This consideration is to be distinguished from two further considerations. The first of these is whether the event in question could have been prevented or mitigated by the party seeking the protection of the clause. The second further consideration is whether a party who was previously ready and willing to perform does indeed fall within the protective wording of the clause. For example, if the clause refers to a party being "prevented" from performance, the question is whether the event truly prevents performance or has only a lesser impact on performance. Both of these further considerations are dealt with in the following paragraphs.

452a See *Classic Maritime Inc v Limbungan Makmur Sdn Bhd* [2018] EWHC 2389 (Comm); [2019] 1 Lloyd's Rep. 349, affirmed on this point at [2019] EWCA Civ 1102. See also *Bremer Handelsgesellschaft mbH v Vanden-Avenne Izegem PVBA* [1978] 2 Lloyd's Rep. 109; *Continental Grain Export Corp v STM Grain Ltd* [1979] 2 Lloyd's Rep. 460.

Burden of proof

Replace footnote 463 with:

463 *B & S Contracts and Designs Ltd v Victor Green Publications Ltd* [1984] I.C.R. 419; *Channel Island Ferries Ltd v Sealink (UK) Ltd* [1988] 1 Lloyd's Rep. 323 at 327, 328; *Hoecheong Products Co Ltd v Cargill Hong Kong Ltd* [1995] 1 W.L.R. 404 at 409; *Mamidoil-Jetoil Greek Petroleum Co SA v Okta Crude Oil Refinery AD (No.3)* [2003] 2 Lloyd's Rep. 635 at [32]; *RDC Concrete Ltd v Sato Kogyo (S) Pte Ltd* [2007] 4 S.L.R. 413 (Sing) at [64]. See also *Great Elephant Corp v Trafigura Beheer BV (The Crudesky)* [2013] EWCA Civ 905; [2014] 1 Lloyd's Rep. 1 at [34] ("absurd" to allow reliance on a force majeure clause where the force majeure event caused by breach of contract by party seeking to rely upon the clause). **8-075**

"Force majeure"

Replace footnote 528 with:

528 On the need for a causal link between the force majeure event and the inability to perform of the party invoking the clause, see *Seadrill Operations Ghana Ltd v Ghana Ltd* [2018] EWHC 1640 (Comm) (drilling contract), since "the situation and the consequences [have to be]beyond [the] reasonable control" of that party (at [92]). But, in the context of EC Regulations, the European Court has sometimes held that the expression force majeure is not limited to cases where performance is impossible, but extends to unusual circumstances, outside the control of the person concerned, the consequences of which, in spite of the exercise of all due care, could not have been avoided except at the cost of excessive sacrifice: see *Internationale Handelsgesellschaft v Einfuhr-und-Vorratsstelle* [1970] E.C.R. 1125; *De Jong Verenigde v VIB* [1985] E.C.R. 2061. Contrast *Schwarzwaldmilch v Einfuhr-und-Vorratsstelle fur Fette (4/68)* [1968] E.C.R. 377; *Valsabbia v EC Commission* [1980] E.C.R. 907. These cases are discussed in McKendrick (ed), *Force Majeure and Frustration of Contract*, 2nd edn, Ch.17 (Parker). **8-081**

Unfair Contract Terms Act 1977

Replace footnote 547 with:

547 Unfair Contract Terms Act 1977 s.3(2)(b). See *Chitty on Contracts*, 33rd edn, Vol.1 para.15-152. Contrast Treitel, *Frustration and Force Majeure*, 3rd edn, para.12-022. **8-084**

CHAPTER 9

ACCEPTANCE AND PAYMENT

Buyer's duty to accept and pay

Replace footnote 4 with:

⁴ *Sempra Metals Ltd v Inland Revenue Commrs* [2007] UKHL 34; [2008] A.C. 61; *PST Energy Shipping LLC v OW Bunker Malta Ltd (The Res Cogitans)* [2016] UKSC 23; [2016] A.C. 1034 at [48]. The award of damages had earlier been granted in *Wadsworth v Lydall* [1981] 1 W.L.R. 598 under the second limb of the rule in *Hadley v Baxendale* (1854) 9 Exch. 341.

9-001

1. ACCEPTANCE

Acceptance and taking delivery

Replace footnote 12 with:

¹² *Re Redfern Resources Ltd* 2011 BCSC 771 at [53] (Can) ("'Acceptance' means both the physical receipt of the goods by a buyer and the legal duty of the buyer to accept goods properly delivered by the seller"). See also *Western Union Petro International Co Ltd v Anterra Energy Inc* 2019 ABQB 165 at [24] (Can.) ("[n]ormally, the buyer has a duty to accept the goods as much as the seller has a duty to deliver").

9-003

Time of taking delivery

Replace footnote 36 with:

³⁶ Both expressions are used indifferently in the case law. See below, para.10-033.

9-005

Repudiation of the contract

Replace footnote 58 with:

⁵⁸ On the nature of "anticipatory breach", see *The Mihalis Angelos* [1971] 1 Q.B. 64; and *Chitty on Contracts*, 33rd edn, Vol.1 paras 24 022, 24-027, 24-031.

9-010

Repudiation accepted by seller

Replace footnote 97 with:

⁹⁷ *Cooper, Ewing & Co Ltd v Hamel & Horley Ltd* (1922) 13 Ll. L.R. 446; *British and Beningtons Ltd v North Western Cachar Tea Co Ltd* [1923] A.C. 48 at 72. See also *Chitty on Contracts*, 33rd edn, Vol.1 para.24-029. But cf. *Gill & Duffus SA v Berger & Co Inc* [1984] A.C. 382.

9-017

2. PAYMENT

In general

Replace footnote 119 with:

9-020 [119] *PST Energy Shipping LLC v OW Bunker Malta Ltd (The Res Cogitans)* [2016] UKSC 23; [2016] A.C. 1034 at [48]; above, para.9-001.

Amount of payment

Replace footnote 125 with:

9-022 [125] See *Chitty on Contracts*, 33rd edn, Vol.1 para.21–074.

Replace paragraph with:

9-023 As a general rule, the payment by the buyer to the seller of a lesser sum than the full contract price (if indisputably due) will not, even if the seller agrees to accept it in full settlement, discharge his obligation to pay the balance, since there will be no consideration for the seller's promise to forgo the residue of the debt.[127] But payment of a lesser sum at a different place or at an earlier time or by a different method[128] will, if made for the benefit of the seller,[129] operate as a valid discharge.[130] Further, the seller may be estopped[131] from going back on his promise to forgo the residue of the debt if it would be inequitable for him to do so.[132] In such a case, the promise to forgo the balance must be clear and unequivocal[133] and it may well be that the buyer must also have altered his position[134] in reliance on the promise made to him before the seller will be held to be estopped.[135]

[127] *Pinnel's Case* (1602) 5 Co. Rep. 117a; *Foakes v Beer* (1884) 9 App. Cas. 605; *D & C Builders Ltd v Rees* [1966] 2 Q.B. 617; *James Cook Hotel Ltd v Canx Corporate Services Ltd* [1989] 3 N.Z.L.R. 213. See *Chitty on Contracts*, 33rd edn, Vol.1 paras 4-117 to 4-119.

[128] The acceptance of a negotiable instrument issued by the debtor for a smaller amount would at one time suffice (*Goddard v O'Brien* (1882) 9 Q.B.D. 37), but this is no longer so *D & C Builders Ltd v Rees* [1966] 2 Q.B. 617. For the effect of the acceptance of a cheque for part of a debt which is tendered in settlement, see the cases and discussion in McLaughlan, 12 N.Z.U.L.R. 259; and *James Cook Hotel Ltd v Canx Corporate Services Ltd* [1989] 3 N.Z.L.R. 213; *Haines House Haulage Co Ltd v Gamble* [1989] 3 N.Z.L.R. 221.

[129] *Vanbergen v St Edmunds Properties Ltd* [1933] 2 K.B. 223.

[130] *Pinnel's Case* (1602) 5 Co. Rep. 117. cf. *Couldery v Bartrum* (1881) 19 Ch. D. 394 at 399.

[131] The principle of equitable forbearance or "promissory" estoppel: see *Chitty on Contracts*, 33rd edn, Vol.1 paras 4-130 et seq.

[132] *Central London Property Trust Ltd v High Trees House Ltd* [1947] K.B. 130; *Tungsten Electric Co Ltd v Tool Manufacturing Co Ltd* (1950) 69 R.P.C. 108; *Tool Metal Manufacturing Co Ltd v Tungsten Electric Co Ltd* [1955] 1 W.L.R. 761; cf. *Ajayi v Briscoe (RT) (Nigeria) Ltd* [1964] 1 W.L.R. 1326; *D & C Builders v Rees* [1966] 2 Q.B. 617; *Collier v Wright (P&MJ) (Holdings) Ltd* [2007] EWCA Civ 1329; [2008] 1 W.L.R. 643. See *Chitty on Contracts*, 33rd edn, Vol.1 paras 4-086, 4-130, 4-134.

[133] *Woodhouse AC Israel Cocoa Ltd SA v Nigerian Produce Marketing Co Ltd* [1972] A.C. 741; see *Chitty on Contracts*, 33rd edn, Vol.1 para.4-091.

[134] *Société Italo-Belge pour le Commerce et l'Industrie v Palm & Vegetable Oils (Malaysia) Sdn Bhd (The Post Chaser)* [1981] 2 Lloyd's Rep. 695 at 700–702. See also *Tungsten Electric Co Ltd v Tool Metal Manufacturing Co Ltd* (1950) 69 R.P.C. 108 at 112, 115–116; *Combe v Combe* [1951] 2 K.B. 215 at 220, 225; *Tool Metal Manufacturing Co Ltd v Tungsten Electric Co Ltd* [1955] 1 W.L.R. 761 at 764, 784, 799; *Morrow v Carty* [1957] N.I. 174; *Beesly v Hallwood Estates Ltd* [1960] 1 W.L.R. 549 at 560 (affirmed on other grounds [1961] Ch.105);*Ajayi v Briscoe (RT) (Nigeria) Ltd* [1964] 1 W.L.R. 1326 at 1330; *Woodhouse AC Israel Cocoa Ltd SA v Nigerian Produce Marketing Co Ltd* [1972] A.C. 741; *Scandinavian Trading Tanker Co AB v Flota Petrolera Ecuatoriana (The Scaptrade)* [1983] Q.B. 549 (affirmed [1983] 2 A.C. 694). See also *Chitty on Contracts*, 33rd edn, Vol.1 para.4-091.

[135] See also the question of the "suspensive" nature of the doctrine as a necessary limitation to its application: *Chitty on Contracts*, 33rd edn, Vol.1 paras 4-097, 4-131; Wilson, (1951) 67 L.Q.R. 330; [1965] C.L.J. 93.

(a) Methods of Payment

Cash

Replace paragraph with:

Unless otherwise agreed, the buyer must pay or tender[147] the price of the goods to the seller in cash at the time and place indicated by the contract of sale, and the seller need not accept payment or tender otherwise than in lawful money.[148] The parties may, however, expressly or impliedly agree that payment may be made in some other manner, and, in the absence of any express stipulation, the method of payment may be determined by the course of dealing between the parties or by trade custom.[149] Notwithstanding that the method of payment has been agreed in the contract of sale, the seller may waive strict compliance with the contractual terms.[150]

9-027

[147] For the general principles of law relating to tender, see *Chitty on Contracts*, 33rd edn, Vol.1 paras 21-085.

[148] See, e.g. *Gordon v Strange* (1847) 1 Ex. Ch. 477. For legal tender, see the Currency and Bank Notes Act 1954 s.1; Coinage Act 1971 s.2; Currency Act 1983 s.1. See also Bridge, Gullifer, Low and McMeel, *The Law of Personal Property*, 2nd edn, Ch.7.

[149] It is submitted that, in modern conditions, when an account is sent to the buyer, trade custom will permit payment by cheque and by post: see below, para.9-042. See also payment in overseas sales, below, paras 19-076, 20-060 and 22-001.

[150] *Panoutsos v Raymond Hadley Corp of New York* [1917] 2 K.B. 473; *Plasticmoda Societa per Azioni v Davidsons (Manchester) Ltd* [1952] 1 Lloyd's Rep. 527; *Enrico Furst & Co v Fischer (WE)* [1960] 2 Lloyd's Rep. 340; *Alan (WJ) & Co Ltd v El Nasr Export and Import Co* [1972] 2 Q.B. 189; and see below, para.9-055.

Payment by negotiable instrument

After "remedy revives. By", delete "of".*

9-029

Negotiable instrument equivalent to cash

Replace footnote 167 with:

[167] *Fielding & Platt Ltd v Najjar* [1969] 1 W.L.R. 356 at 361 per Lord Denning MR. See also *Brown Shipley & Co Ltd v Alicia Hosiery Ltd* [1966] 1 Lloyd's Rep. 668 at 669; *Cebora SNC v SIP Industrial Products Ltd* [1976] 1 W.L.R. 271 at 274, 278, 279; *Montecchi v Simco (UK) Ltd* [1979] 1 Lloyd's Rep. 509 at 511; *China Export & Credit Insurance Corpn v Emerald Energy Resources Ltd* [2018] EWHC 3740 (Comm) and below, para.22-003.

9-031

In the second paragraph, after "amount in dispute.", add:*

Where the underlying contract of sale contains an arbitration clause, the clause, unless it otherwise provides, will also extend to actions brought by the seller as payee, though not by third party indorsees, on a negotiable instrument.[172a]

[172a] *Uttam Galva Steels Ltd v Gunvor Singapore Pte Ltd* [2018] EWHC 1098 (Comm); [2018] 2 Lloyd's Rep. 152, following Lord Salmon (dissenting on different grounds in *Nova (Jersey) Knit Ltd v Kammgarn Spinnerei GmbH* [1977] 1 W.L.R. 713, 724) and declining to follow *Rals International Pte Ltd v Cassa di Risparmio di Parma e Piacenza Spa* [2016] SGCA 53 (which called for express mention of negotiable instruments in the arbitration clause). See also Lord Hoffmann in *Fiona Trust and Holding Corp v Privalov* [2007] UKHL 40; [2008] 1 Lloyd's Rep. 254 at [13]: "In my opinion the construction of an arbitration clause should start from the assumption that the parties, as rational businessmen, are likely to have intended any dispute arising out of the relationship into which they have entered or purported to enter to be decided by the same tribunal."

Replace title footnote 173:

Payment by credit or charge card[173]

9-032   [173] See Stephenson, *Credit, Debit and Cheque Cards*; Law and Practice (1993); Brindle and Cox, *Law of Bank Payments*, 4th edn, paras 4-001, 5-043; below, para.14-175. For a detailed description of credit card systems and transactions, see *Lancore Services Ltd v Barclays Bank Plc* [2008] EWHC 1264 (Ch); [2008] 1 C.L.C. 1039 at [2]–[6] (approved at [2009] EWCA Civ 752; [2010] 1 All E.R. 763 at [4]–[10]).

Replace paragraph with:

Credit card (or charge card) transactions may involve two parties or three parties.[174] In a two-party transaction, the issuer of the card himself supplies goods to the cardholder and the cardholder undertakes to pay for the goods supplied in accordance with the terms of the credit agreement made between them.[174a] It is clear that, in a two-party situation, the cardholder remains always liable to pay the card issuer/supplier for the goods purchased by use of the card. In a three-party transaction, the card-issuing company is an entity distinct from the supplier of the goods. Three separate contracts exist: (i) the contract of sale between the supplier and the cardholder; (ii) the contract between the card-issuing company and the supplier by which the card-issuing company undertakes to reimburse[175] the supplier the purchase price of the goods as recorded in the sales voucher, less an agreed discount or commission due to the company; and (iii) the contract between the card-issuing company and the cardholder by which the cardholder agrees to reimburse the company in respect of purchases made by use of the card on the terms agreed between them. In *Re Charge Card Services Ltd*,[176] the Court of Appeal held that, unlike payment by negotiable instrument[177] or letter of credit,[178] there was no presumption that the use of the card constituted conditional payment only by the cardholder. Whether the card was accepted by the supplier as conditional or absolute payment depended on the terms of the contract between the supplier and the cardholder, and those terms would have to be inferred from the parties' conduct and the circumstances known to them at the time of the sale. On the facts of the case, which involved a charge card scheme under which participating garages accepted cards of the card-issuing company in payment for fuel supplied to cardholders and charged the price of the fuel so supplied to the card-issuing company, it was held that payment by means of the card was an absolute discharge of the cardholders' liability to the garages. It was not conditional upon the card-issuing company making payment to the garage which supplied the fuel or upon the cardholder making payment to the card-issuing company. Accordingly, where (as in this case) the card-issuing company had sold its receivables to a factor under an invoice discounting agreement and then became insolvent, leaving the garages unpaid, the debts due from cardholders were payable to the factor, and the garages could not call upon cardholders to pay them direct. Although a contrary conclusion could possibly be reached on different facts in a particular case, it is submitted that payment by credit or charge card will normally be taken to discharge the cardholder absolutely from his liability to pay the price of the goods to the supplier. The cardholder's liability will lie only to the card-issuing company.

[174] A variation on the three-party credit card occurs where the "issuer" recruits the supplier to a network of credit card issuers, such as Master Card: *Office of Fair Trading v Barclays Bank Plc* [2006] EWCA Civ 268; [2007] Q.B. 1; affirmed [2007] UKHL 48; [2008] 1 A.C. 316. For a description of the Master Card scheme, see *Deutsche Bahn AG v Mastercard Inc* [2018] EWHC 412 (Ch); [2018] 4 C.M.L.R. 31.

[174a] A credit card is a "payment instrument" for the purposes of the Payment Services Regulations 2017 (SI 2017/752) (in force for the purposes of this work as of 13 January 2018, superseding the Payment Services Regulations 2009 (SI 2009/209) as amended). Liability for unauthorised use arises only where this occurs prior to notification to the card issuer, and liability is limited to £35 except where there has

occurred fraud or gross negligence on the part of the cardholder: regs 2(1) (as amended by the Payment Systems and Services and Electronic Money (Miscellaneous Amendments) Regulations 2017 (SI 2017/1173)), 72 and 77.

[175] In some three-party transactions, the documentation may be so formulated as to give rise to assignment by the supplier to the card-issuing company of the debt of the cardholder to the supplier constituted by the purchase of the goods. But see *Commissioners of Customs and Excise v Diners Club Ltd* [1989] 1 W.L.R. 1196,

[176] *Re Charge Card Services Ltd* [1989] Ch. 497.

[177] See above, para.9-029.

[178] See below, paras 9-040, 23-301.

Payment by debit card

After "or building society).", add new footnote 183a:

[183a] A debit card is a "payment instrument" for the purposes of the Payment Services Regulations 2017 (SI 2017/752) (in force for the purposes of this work as of 13 January 2018), superseding the Payment Services Regulations 2009 (SI 2009/209) as amended). Liability for unauthorised use arises only where this occurs prior to notification to the card issuer, and liability is limited to £35 except where there has occurred fraud or gross negligence on the part of the cardholder: regs 2(1) (as amended by the Payment Systems and Services and Electronic Money (Miscellaneous Amendments) Regulations 2017 (SI 2017/1173)), 72 and 77.

9-034

Replace title footnote 186:

Payment by stored value card[186]

[186] A stored value card is a "payment instrument" for the purpose of the Payment Services Regulations 2017 (in force for the purposes of this work as of 13 January 2018): reg.2(1) (as amended by the Payment Systems and Services and Electronic Money (Miscellaneous Amendments) Regulations 2017 (SI 2017/1173)). See also *Edwards* (ed), The New Legal Framework for E-Commerce in Europe (2005), Ch.6 (Guadamuz and Usher); O'Mahony, Peirce and Tewari, *Electronic Payment Systems for E-Commerce*, 2nd edn; *Ellinger's Modern Banking Law*, 5th edn, p.664; Brindle and Cox, *Law of Bank Payments*, 5th edn, para.5-058.

9-035

Replace paragraph with:

Stored value cards, sometimes referred to as "digital cash cards" or "electronic purses", are cards on which "value" is stored electronically. This card can be used by the cardholder to pay for goods or services supplied, units of value being transferred electronically from buyer to seller. Some cards depend on a magnetic strip, but others carry more complex information stored in a microchip. Some cards are reloadable and can be charged with additional value, while others lack this facility and are considered disposable once the entire value has been spent. In some cases, a stored value card can be used by the cardholder to purchase goods or services only from the card issuer or the card issuer's organisation. In other cases, however, as in three-party credit transactions, the card may be used to effect purchases from any supplier who has agreed to accept payment in this form and the supplier will be reimbursed in accordance with the terms of his agreement in respect of purchases made by use of the card. Since stored value cards are a relatively recent phenomenon, the exact relationship between the participants (the scheme originator, participating banks, supplier and cardholder), and the risks to be borne by each party, have taken time to be established.[187] But the strong analogy between stored value and cash suggests that payment by stored value card would be regarded as absolute, and not conditional, payment.[188] In addition, protection from misuse is afforded to the cardholder by the Payment Services Regulations 2017.[189] A stored value card is a "payment instrument", defined as "any device ... used by the payment service user to initiate a payment order".[190] The payment service provider is liable to refund to the user (the cardholder) the amount of any unauthorised transaction,[191] except where the cardholder has acted fraudulently or with intent or gross negligence in safeguarding the card or notifying the provider of its loss, and except for amounts expended prior to notification of the loss of a card (up to a £50 limit).[192]

[187] See Reed and Davies, *Digital Cash—the Legal Implications* (1995); Finlayson-Brown, (1997) 12 J.I.B.L. 362; Effros (ed), *Current Legal Issues Affecting Central Banks* (1998), Ch.6; Hooley in Rider (ed), *The Realm of Company Law—Essays in Honour of Professor Leonard Sealy* (1998), 245; Brindle and Cox, *Law of Bank Payments*, 5th edn, para.5-060.

[188] Edwards (ed), *The New Legal Framework for E-Commerce in Europe*, Ch.6 (Guadamuz and Usher); Brindle and Cox, *Law of Bank Payments*, 5th edn, para.5-059; *Encyclopedia of Banking Law*, i, DI 315.

[189] Payment Services Regulations 2017 (SI 2017/752) (in force for the purposes of this work as of 13 January 2018), superseding the Payment Services Regulations 2009 (SI 2009/209) (as amended). Since the "value" on the card is pre-purchased by the cardholder, the protection afforded by the Consumer Credit Act 1974 (below, para.9-036) does not apply, as there is no provision of "credit" for purchases. But cf. s.14(1)(b).

[190] Payment Services Regulations 2017 (SI 2017/752) reg.2(1).

[191] Payment Services Regulations 2017 (SI 2017/752) reg.76.

[192] Payment Services Regulations 2017 (SI 2017/752) reg.77.

Replace title footnote 193 with:

Internet payments[193]

9-036   [193] See *Edwards* (ed), The New Legal Framework for E-Commerce in Europe (2005), Ch.6 (Guadamuz and Usher); Brindle and Cox, *Law of Bank Payments*, 5th edn, Ch.5.

Replace paragraph with:

Internet transactions may involve conflict of laws[194] and jurisdictional issues. But, apart from these, payments made online over the internet may give rise to certain special problems. The first and most obvious one is that, since payment is usually in advance of delivery, the buyer is at risk that the goods when delivered may not be in conformity with the contract or may never be delivered at all, and that it will most probably be impractical for him to attempt to recover the payment by legal action, particularly when the seller is in a foreign country. Most business-to-business transactions are paid for in the ordinary way through the banking system. But business-to-consumer transactions will more often be paid for by credit, debit or charge card, the card details being communicated electronically over the internet. Where this method of payment is adopted, then, in the event of non-performance or defective performance of the contract of sale, the consumer may in some cases have a claim against the issuer of the card under the Consumer Credit Act 1974 s.75.[195] Nevertheless this method of payment gives rise to the further risk that the seller or some third party who has acquired knowledge of the consumer's card details may misuse the information obtained to cause unauthorised transactions to be debited to the card account. Again, however, a buyer who is a consumer may (subject to certain conditions) be relieved, in whole or in part, from liability to the card issuer on the card account under the Consumer Credit Act 1974[196] and the Payment Services Regulations 2009.[196a] But the protection afforded by these measures is nevertheless not absolute and in any event the nuisance value of the claims generated by misuse of the card is not inconsiderable. In order to increase consumer confidence in online transactions, the card information may be encrypted. Encryption involves the application to electronic data of a mathematical algorithm, the encryption "key", in order to render the data indecipherable by anyone not having access to the appropriate decryption key.[197] It may be supported or enhanced by a site verification service provided by a Trusted Third Party (TTP) which confirms the identity of the payee and which may also certify that the payee applies acceptable standards of security in protecting payment details.[198] The Electronic Communications Act 2000 Pt I[199] provided for a voluntary approvals regime to cover providers of cryptography support systems.[200] But it is by no means certain whether any liability would arise for financial loss caused to the consumer by failure of encryption and, if so, who would be liable and in what circumstances.[201]

[194] See below, paras 26-053 et seq.

[195] As amended by the Consumer Credit (EU Directive) Regulations 2010 (SI 2010/1010) reg.24 (effective 1 February 2011). See below, para.14-180. But debit card transactions do not qualify for this protection.

[196] Consumer Credit Act 1974 ss.83, 84.

[196a] Payment Services Regulations 2009 (SI 2009/209) (as amended by SI 2009/2475) reg.61. See below, paras 9-032, 9-034, 9-035 and 14-213.

[197] Edwards and Waelde (eds), *Law and the Internet*, 4th edn, Ch.17 (Rauhofer), Ch.3, p.39; Brindle and Cox, *Law of Bank Payments*, 5th edn, paras 5-022 to 5-024.

[198] Brindle and Cox, *Law of Bank Payments*, 5th edn, paras 5-021, 5-027.

[199] Repealed 25 May 2005 further to s.16(4) of the Act.

[200] Edwards and Waelde, *Law and the Internet*, 3rd edn, Ch.17 (Rauhofer).

[201] Edwards and Waelde, *Law and the Internet*, 3rd edn, Ch.17 (Rauhofer); Brindle and Cox, *Law of Bank Payments*, 5th edn, paras 5-039 to 5-041. But see the duty of care imposed in certain circumstances by the Electronic Signatures Regulations 2002 (SI 2002/318) reg.4(1).

Replace footnote 204 with:

[204] See Brindle and Cox, *Law of Bank Payments*, 5th edn, paras 5-021 to 5-030. **9-037**

Use of banking system

Replace footnote 207 with:

[207] On bank transfers, see *Tankexpress A/S v Compagnie Financière Belge des Petroles SA* [1949] A.C. **9-038**
76; *Tenax Steamship Co Ltd v The Brimnes (Owners) (The Brimnes)* [1975] Q.B. 929; *Delbrueck & Co v Barclays Bank International Ltd* [1976] 2 Lloyd's Rep. 341; *Mardorf Peach & Co Ltd v Attica Sea Carriers Corp of Liberia* [1977] A.C. 850; *Momm v Barclays Bank International Ltd* [1977] 1 Q.B. 790; *A/S Awilco of Oslo v Fulvia SpA di Navigazione of Cagliari (The Chikuma)* [1981] 1 W.L.R. 314; *Afovos Shipping Co SA v Romano Pagnan and Pietro Pagnan* [1983] 1 W.L.R. 195; *Jones v Churcher* [2009] EWHC 722 (QB) at [69] et seq.; [2009] 2 Lloyd's Rep. 94. See *Goode on Payment Obligations in Commercial and Financial Transactions*, edited by Proctor, 3rd edn, (2016), paras 5-10 et seq.; *Chitty on Contracts*, 33rd edn, Vol.1 para.21-046, Vol.2, paras 34-380 et seq.; Brindle and Cox, *Law of Bank Payments*, 5th edn, Ch.1.

Direct debits

Replace footnote 208 with:

[208] *Esso Petroleum Co Ltd v Milton* [1997] 1 W.L.R. 938, applied in *Courage Ltd v Crehan* [1999] **9-039**
E.C.C. 455 and *Geldof Metaalconstructie NV v Simon Carves Ltd* [2010] EWCA Civ 667; [2011] 1 Lloyd's Rep. 517, but criticised by Tettenborn, (1997) 113 L.Q.R. 374, Hooley [1997] C.L.J. 500 and Ellinger's *Modern Banking Law*, 5th edn, p.575.

Payment by post

Replace footnote 215 with:

[215] cf. *Tankexpress A/S v Compagnie Financière Belge des Petroles SA* [1949] A.C. 76. For lost instru- **9-042**
ments, see *Chitty on Contracts*, 33rd edn, Vol.2 para.34-145 to 34-146.

Payment to agent

Replace footnote 217 with:

9-043   [217] See, e.g. *Bowstead and Reynolds on Agency*, 21st edn, paras 3-024 and 8-107 et seq.

Payment by agent or third party

Replace footnote 220 with:

9-044   [220] For payment by one of a number of joint (or joint and several) debtors, see *Chitty on Contracts*, 33rd edn, Vol.1 paras 17-001 et seq.

Appropriation of payments

Replace paragraph with:

9-046   Unless otherwise agreed where the buyer owes more than one debt to the seller, he is entitled, when making a payment, to appropriate the sum paid to whichever debt or debts he pleases, and, if the seller receives the payment so made,[225] he must apply it in the manner directed by the buyer.[226] Should the buyer not exercise his right of appropriation, the seller may appropriate the payment to any lawful debt[227] due to him from the buyer,[228] even if such debt is or has become statute-barred.[229] Special rules apply to appropriation of payments where trading is on the basis of a current account[230] and in the case of guaranteed debts.[231]

[225] If the seller is unwilling to apply it to the debt for which it is tendered, he must refuse it and stand upon his rights (whatever they may be) or make a counter-proposal for the appropriation.

[226] See *Chitty on Contracts*, 33rd edn, Vol.1 paras 21-060, 21-061.

[227] See *Chitty on Contracts*, 33rd edn, Vol.1 para.21-062.

[228] See *Chitty on Contracts*, 33rd edn, Vol.1 para.21-063. For appropriation between principal and interest, see para.21-069.

[229] See *Chitty on Contracts*, 33rd edn, Vol.1 para.21-065.

[230] See *Chitty on Contracts*, 33rd edn, Vol.1 para.21-068.

[231] Consumer Credit Act 1974 s.81.

(b)   Place of Payment

Place of payment

Replace footnote 237 with:

9-047   [237] *The Eider* [1893] P. 119 at 131, 136. See also *Sheppard's Touchstone of Common Assurances* (1648), p.136; *Drexel v Drexel* [1916] 1 Ch. 251 at 259; *Fowler v Midland Electric Corp for Power Distribution Ltd* [1917] 1 Ch. 656; *Korner v Witkowitzer* [1950] 2 K.B. 128 at 159 (affirmed sub nom. *Vitkovice Horni a Hutni Tezirstvo v Korner* [1951] A.C. 869); *Commercial Marine Piling Ltd v Pierce Contracting Ltd* [2009] EWHC 2241 (TCC) at [38]. cf. *Fessard v Mugnier* (1865) 18 C.B. (N.S.) 286; *Malik v Narodni Banka Ceskoslovenska* [1946] 2 All E.R. 663. See also *Taurus Petroleum Ltd v State Oil Co of the Iraqi Ministry of Oil* [2017] UKSC 64; [2018] A.C. 690 (situs of a debt).

(c)   Time of Payment

Time of payment

Replace paragraph with:

9-051   The parties to a contract of sale are at liberty to specify in their contract the time at which payment is to be made by the buyer. This time need not necessarily bear any relationship to the time of the transfer of the property in the goods to the buyer, or to the time of delivery.[247] It may be expressed as a reasonable time, which is a question of fact.[248] Where the contract does not stipulate a time for payment, whether directly or by reference to delivery or a delivery date, the Sale of Goods Act 1979 gives no guidance but the buyer, it is submitted, is bound to pay within a reasonable time. By the Sale of Goods Act 1979 s.10(1), unless a different intention appears from the terms of the contract,[249] stipulations as to time of payment are not of the essence of a contract of sale.[250] This means that timely payment is an intermediate term of the contract and s.10(1), in codifying the position at common law, is not a rule peculiar to sale of goods.[250a] Where payment and delivery are to be made concurrently, as is the presumptive rule in s.28 of the Act, the character of the seller's duty to deliver as a condition will lead to the treatment of the buyer's duty to pay in accordance with the contract as a condition too,[251] at least in the sense that the seller can resist delivery to a non-paying buyer.[252] If time is not of the essence, a default by the buyer in making payment at the time specified in the contract will not entitle the seller to treat himself as discharged from further liability and to resell the goods[253] unless the buyer's neglect or refusal to pay the price makes it plain that he is unwilling or unable to perform the contract.[254] However, where there has been undue delay in payment, the seller may give notice requiring payment to be made within a reasonable time.[255] The seller may also in the contract of sale expressly reserve the right of resale in case the buyer should make default,[256] and, by s.48(3) of the Act,[257] an unpaid seller has a statutory right of resale where the goods are of a perishable nature, or where he gives notice to the buyer of his intention to resell, and the buyer does not within a reasonable time pay or tender the price.[258] A resale by the seller in these circumstances effectively rescinds the contract of sale.[259]

[247] cf. *Staunton v Wood* (1851) 16 Q.B. 638 ("delivery forthwith, cash in fourteen days from making of contract"); *Godts v Rose* (1855) 17 C.B. 229 ("free delivered and paid for in fourteen days in cash"); *Minister for Supply and Development v Servicemen's Co-op Joinery Manufacturers Ltd* (1951) 82 C.L.R 621 ("net cash before delivery").

[248] In *Glen Clyde Whisky Ltd v Campbell Meyer & Co Ltd* [2015] CSOH 97, payment to be made in a reasonable time was not dependent upon the seller first supplying the buyer with shipping dates.

[249] *Maclaine v Gatty* [1921] 1 A.C. 376 at 389 ("punctual payment"). cf. *Tenax Steamship Co Ltd v Reinante Transoceanica Navegacion SA (The Brimnes)* [1973] 1 W.L.R. 386 at 409. But see below, paras 19-086, 22-012.

[250] *Dalkia Utilities Services Plc v Celtech International Ltd* [2006] EWHC 63; [2006] 1 Lloyd's Rep. 599 at [130]; *Kuwait Rocks Co v AMN Bulkcarriers Inc* [2013] EWHC 65 (Comm); [2013] 1 C.L.C. 819 at [110]; *Spar Shipping AS v Grand China Logistics Holding (Group) Co Ltd (The Spar Capella, Star Vega and Spar Draco)* [2016] EWCA Civ 982; [2016] 2 Lloyd's Rep. 447 at [56]. See also *Dominion Corporate Trustees Ltd v Debenhams Properties Ltd* [2010] EWHC 1193 (Ch); [2010] 23 E.G. 106 (C.S.). The same rule should apply by analogy to sui generis supply contracts of the sort considered in *PST Energy Shipping LLC v OW Bunker Malta Ltd (The Res Cogitans)* [2016] UKSC 23; [2016] A.C. 1034. cf *Stocznia Gdanska SA v Larvian Shipping Co (No.2)* [2002] EWCA Civ 889; [2002] 2 Lloyd's Rep. 436 at [77] et seq. ("rescission" where payment due on laying the keel not made).

[250a] *Grand China Logistics Holding (Group) Co Ltd v Spar Shipping AS* [2016] EWCA Civ 982 at [56] and [100].

[251] *Berlian (PT) Naju Tanker TBK v Nuse Shipping Ltd (The Aktor)* [2008] EWHC 1330 (Comm); [2008] 2 Lloyd's Rep. 246 at [66], following *Bunge Corp v Tradax Export SA* [1981] 1 W.L.R. 711.

[252] See *Fitzpatrick v Sarcon (No.177) Ltd* [2012] NICA 58, where the court, referring to delivery and payment under the Sale of Goods Act, accepted at [23] that the parties might stipulate that time is of the essence for one of these obligations but not the other. This statement was not explicitly linked to concurrent obligations but counsel for the respondents had at [18] made this link ("It is perfectly possible to have concurrent conditions where time is essential in respect to one of the conditions (delivery) but not of the other (payment)"). See also *Kumar v Station Properties Ltd* [2015] NZSC 34; [2016] 1 N.Z.L.R. 99 (Dawson, (2017) 133 L.Q.R. 183) for the view that, where a term is a condition of the contract but its breach has not yet been accepted as terminating the contract, the non-performance of that term may be treated as a defence to the other party's failure to perform an obligation consequent upon the performance of that condition.

[253] *Martindale v Smith* (1841) 1 Q.B. 389; *Mersey Steel and Iron Co v Naylor* (1884) 9 App. Cas. 434 at 444; *Payzu Ltd v Saunders* [1919] 2 K.B. 581.

[254] *Anchor Line Ltd v Keith Rowell Ltd* [1980] 2 Lloyd's Rep. 351. See also above, para.8-066 (instalment contracts); below, para.9-065. For a discussion of damages for late payment, see below, para.16-030.

[255] See *Chitty on Contracts*, 33rd edn, Vol.1 para.21-014. But see above, para.8-026, on the limitations of making time of the essence.

[256] Sale of Goods Act 1979 s.48(4); below, para.15-128.

[257] See below, para.15-119.

[258] It is doubtful in modern conditions that an analogous common law rule in identical terms would be inferred for sui generis supply contracts of the sort considered in *PST Energy Shipping LLC v OW Bunker Malta Ltd (The Res Cogitans)* [2016] UKSC 23; [2016] A.C. 1034, in those cases where goods remain in the recipient's possession, but the same consequences may flow if the contract is terminated for breach by the seller: below, paras 15-107 et seq.

[259] Sale of Goods Act 1979 s.48(4); *Ward (RV) Ltd v Bignall* [1967] 1 Q.B. 534; below, para.14-127.

Waiver

Replace footnote 272 with:

9-055   [272] cf. *Scandinavian Trader Tanker Co AB v Flota Petrolera Ecuatoriana* [1983] 2 Q.B. 549; affirmed [1983] 2 A.C. 694 (acceptance of late payments on previous occasions creates no estoppel). See also *Chitty on Contracts*, 33rd edn, Vol.1 paras 4-082 to 4-116.

CHAPTER 10

CLASSIFICATION OF STATEMENTS AS TO GOODS

TABLE OF CONTENTS

3.   MISREPRESENTATIONS INDUCING THE CONTRACT

Misrepresentations inducing the contract

Replace footnote 40 with:

[40] See *Chitty on Contracts*, 33rd edn, Vol.1 paras 13-109 et seq.; Treitel, *The Law of Contract*, 14th edn   **10-008**
(Peel), paras 6-014 et seq.; McLauchlan, *The Parol Evidence Rule* (Wellington, N.Z., 1976); Law Com.
No.154, Cmnd.9700 (1986).

Right to rescind in equity

Replace paragraph with:

A full account of the rules as to when the equitable remedy of rescission for   **10-009**
misrepresentation arises should be sought in general works on contract.[47] What
rescinding actually entails, and the further remedies provided by the Misrepresentation Act 1967, are discussed elsewhere in this work.[48] A brief indication as to when
the right arises is, however, appropriate here. The misrepresentation must be of fact
as opposed to opinion[49] or intention.[50] It was formerly regarded as obvious that it
must be of fact not law,[51] though the two could be difficult to distinguish.[52] However
the House of Lords later held that money paid under a mistake of law was as
recoverable as money paid under a mistake of fact,[53] and this decision has prompted
reconsideration of the distinction elsewhere.[54] In the present context, there is a
strong case for abandoning the distinction as regards rescission at least. The
misrepresentation must also be relied on by the person to whom it was made[55]: he
cannot rescind if he did not believe it,[56] or tested its accuracy.[57] But if he does rely
on it, it is immaterial that there were also other inducements to contract.[58] It is also
possible that the misrepresentation must be material in the objective sense that it
would affect the judgment of a reasonable person in deciding whether, or on what
terms, to enter into the contract.[59] There must be a positive misrepresentation:
silence cannot in general constitute misrepresentation[60] unless a representation
arises from conduct,[61] is literally true but misleading,[62] or is falsified by a later event
occurring before the contract is entered into.[63] A duty to disclose may, however,
arise in contracts uberrimae fidei (contracts of insurance and certain family arrange-

[113]

ments[64]), or where there is a fiduciary relationship[65] or a contractual duty of disclosure.[66]

[47] See, e.g. *Chitty on Contracts*, 33rd edn, Vol.1 Ch.7; Treitel, *The Law of Contract*, 14th edn (Peel), Ch.9. The cases usually cited are not sale of goods cases, and indeed many of them do not even concern innocent misrepresentation but the tort of deceit.

[48] Below, paras 12-003, 12-014 et seq.

[49] Above, para.10-006.

[50] Above, para.10-007.

[51] See *Mackenzie v Royal Bank of Canada* [1934] A.C. 468; *Eaglesfield v Marquis of Londonderry* (1876) 4 Ch.D. 693 at 709. But a misrepresentation of foreign law is a misrepresentation of fact: *André & Cie v Ets Michel Blanc & Fils* [1979] 2 Lloyd's Rep. 427.

[52] cf. e.g. *Beattie v Ebury* (1872) L.R. 7 Ch.App. 777; affirmed L.R. 7 H.L. 102; *Cherry and McDougall v Colonial Bank of Australasia* (1869) L.R. 3 P.C. 24.

[53] *Kleinwort Benson Ltd v Lincoln CC* [1999] 2 A.C. 349. See also in general Treitel, *The Law of Contract*, 14th edn (Peel), para.9-017.

[54] See, e.g. *Pankhania v Hackney LBC* [2002] EWHC 2441 (Ch).

[55] *Jennings v Broughton* (1854) 5 De G.M. & G. 126; *JEB Fasteners Ltd v Marks Bloom & Co* [1983] 1 All E.R. 583.

[56] Or in some cases if the truth was known to his agent: *Bawden v London etc Assurance Co* [1892] 2 Q.B. 534. See *Bowstead and Reynolds on Agency*, 21st edn para.8-216.

[57] Even though he did not find out the truth: *Redgrave v Hurd* (1881) 20 Ch.D. 1. *Aliter* if he did not test its accuracy, though he had the opportunity to do so; but cf. *Smith v Eric S Bush* [1990] 1 A.C. 831; Treitel, *The Law of Contract*, 14th edn (Peel), para.9-027. Testing accuracy in one respect may indicate reliance in other respects.

[58] *Edgington v Fitzmaurice* (1885) 29 Ch.D. 459.

[59] See Treitel, *The Law of Contract*, 14th edn (Peel), paras 9-020 et seq.; *Chitty on Contracts*, 33rd edn, Vol.1 paras 7-041, 7-042; *Lonrho Plc v Fayed (No.2)* [1992] 1 W.L.R. 1 at 5–6; *Museprime Properties Ltd v Adhill Properties Ltd* [1990] 2 E.G.L.R. 196.

[60] *Bell v Lever Bros* [1932] A.C. 161 at 227.

[61] *Bodger v Nicholls* (1873) 28 L.T. 441 at 445.

[62] *Nottingham Patent Brick and Tile Co v Butler* (1886) 16 Q.B.D. 778.

[63] *With v O'Flanagan* [1936] Ch. 575; *Awaroa Holdings Ltd v Commercial Securities and Finance Ltd* [1976] 1 N.Z.L.R. 19. If the representation has become false by the time it is acted on, it does not seem that the representor need know this: see the *Awaroa* case at 31. As to the application of this principle to change of intention see Hudson [1984] N.I.L.Q. 1800.

[64] See Treitel, *The Law of Contract*, 14th edn (Peel), paras 9-145 et seq.; *Chitty on Contracts*, 33rd edn, Vol.1 paras 7-158 et seq.

[65] e.g. parent and child, solicitor and client, agent and principal. See Treitel, *The Law of Contract*, 14th edn (Peel), para.9-168.

[66] See *William Pickersgill & Sons Ltd v London etc Insurance Co* [1912] 3 K.B. 614 at 621. There are few indications as to when such a duty will be implied.

7. INTERMEDIATE TERMS

Differences of approach: commercial disputes

Replace footnote 190 with:

10-035   [190] e.g. *Federal Commerce and Navigation Co Ltd v Molena Alpha Inc (The Nanfri)* [1979] A.C. 757 at 785. See also *Ark Shipping Co v Silverburn Shipping (IOM) Ltd* [2019] EWCA Civ 1161; [2019] 1 Lloyd's Rep. 554 at [81] (bareboat charter case: term innominate unless clearly intended to be a condition). For further discussion see Treitel, *The Law of Contract*, 14th edn (Peel), paras 18-052 et seq.

Examples of conditions

Replace paragraph with:

It may be asked what sort of term is likely to be treated as a condition. First, most **10-037** of the statutory implied terms as to the seller's duties in sale of goods (as to title, conformity with description and quality[193]) are designated as conditions. Secondly, the parties may themselves designate terms as conditions, though the court will not be bound by the expressions they use and may hold that notwithstanding the use of the word "condition" its full legal consequences were not intended.[194] Thirdly, the term in question or a similar term may have been held to be a condition in another case: this will be a strong but not conclusive indication that the term is a condition in the instant case.[195] Fourthly, in *Bunge Corp v Tradax Export SA*[196] Lord Roskill refers to a situation:

"... in a mercantile contract, when a term has to be performed by one party as a condition precedent to the ability of the other party to perform another term."[197]

Fifthly, in the same case Lord Wilberforce said in the passage quoted above[198] that the courts should usually interpret "time clauses in mercantile contracts" as conditions[199]; and Lord Lowry justified this as "a practical expedient founded on and dictated by the experience of businessmen".[200] Sixthly, there must also be a residual category of cases where the implementation of the supposed intentions of the parties requires a term to be treated as one any breach of which gives rise to the right to treat the contract as discharged[201]; equally, the overall interpretation of the contract may lead to the conclusion that a term which on isolated criteria might be a condition was not intended as such,[202] and the courts are alert to the risk of "trivial breaches having disproportionate consequences destructive of a long-term contractual relationship".[202a] Most of the residual category of cases will concern large-scale commercial contracts; in this connection it has been said that the court will accord special respect to the findings of commercial arbitrators[203] and reliance placed on the importance of certainty.[204] But the reasoning can be used elsewhere. Thus, in *Harling v Eddy*[205] a statement by the seller of a heifer that there was nothing wrong with the animal sold and that he would take it back if it turned out not to be as he said was held to import a condition because of the undertaking to take back. Where on the other hand a term can be broken in a number of ways involving results of different degrees of gravity, as in the *Hongkong Fir* case itself,[206] that is some indication that it should not be classified as a condition.[207]

---

[193] Above, para.4-001; below, 11-001, 11-024, 11-046, 11-074.

[194] See *Wickman Machine Tool Sales Ltd v L Schuler AG* [1974] A.C. 235 (distributorship contract).

[195] e.g. *Maredelanto Cia Naviera SA v Bergbau-Handel GmbH (The Mihalis Angelos)* [1971] 1 Q.B. 164 ("expected ready to load" in a charterparty: following *Finnish Government v H Ford & Co Ltd* (1921) 6 Ll. L.R. 188 (same term in f.o.b. sale)).

[196] *Bunge Corp v Tradax Export SA* [1981] 1 W.L.R. 711 at 729.

[197] e.g. *Toepfer v Lenersan-Poortman NV* [1980] 1 Lloyd's Rep. 143 (c.i.f. sale: time of tender of documents); *Gill & Duffus SA v Société pour l'Exportation des Sucres SA* [1986] 1 Lloyd's Rep. 322 (f.o.b. sale: nomination of loading port); and see *Greenwich Marine Inc v Federal Commerce and Navigation Co Ltd (The Mavro Vetranic)* [1985] 1 Lloyd's Rep. 580 at 583; *The Aktor* [2008] 2 Lloyd's Rep. 246 (place of payment).

[198] *Bunge Corp v Tradax Export SA* [1981] 1 W.L.R. 711 at 715, quoted above, para.10-035.

[199] *Bunge Corp v Tradax Export SA* [1981] 1 W.L.R. 711 at 716; e.g. *Cie Commerciale Sucres et Denrées v C Czarnikow Ltd (The Naxos)* [1990] 1 W.L.R. 1337 HL (readiness of sugar for delivery) (see Treitel, [1991] L.M.C.L.Q. 147); *Scandinavian Trading Co A/B v Zodiac Petroleum SA (The Al Hofuf)* [1981]

1 Lloyd's Rep. 81 (f.o.b. sale: notice of time of arrival of vessel); *Société Italo-Belge v Palm and Vegetable Oils (Malaysia) Sdn. Bhd. (The Post Chaser)* [1982] 1 All E.R. 19 (c.i.f. sale: declaration of ship "as soon as possible"); cf. *Tradax Export SA v Italgrani* [1986] 1 Lloyd's Rep. 112 (f.o.b. sale: time of delivery to vessel not a condition); *Bremer Handelsgesellschaft v Vanden Avenne-Izegem PVBA* [1978] 2 Lloyd's Rep. 109 (duty to advise "without delay" not a condition); *State Trading Corp of India v M Golodetz Ltd* [1989] 2 Lloyd's Rep. 277 (provision for counter-trade not a condition) (see Treitel, (1990) 106 L.Q.R. 185); *Petrograde Inc v Stinnes Handel GmbH* [1995] 1 Lloyd's Rep. 142 (f.o.b. sale: port of shipment a condition). The precision of the stipulation is obviously relevant, though not conclusive, in determining whether it is a condition. The obligation to make punctual payment of hire was held not to be a condition of a time charterparty in *Spar Shipping AS v Grand China Logistics Holding (Group) Co Ltd* [2016] EWCA Civ 982; [2016] 2 Lloyd's Rep. 447, notwithstanding the presence of an express term permitting withdrawal of the vessel in the event of late payment, overruling the decision to the contrary in *Kuwait Rocks Co v AMN Bulkcarriers Inc (The Astra)* [2013] EWHC 865 (Comm); [2013] 2 Lloyd's Rep. 69.

[200] *Bunge Corp v Tradax Export SA* [1981] 1 W.L.R. 711 at 719.

[201] e.g. *Bergerco v Vegoil Ltd* [1984] 1 Lloyd's Rep. 440 (c. & f. sale: "direct ship"); *Warde v Feedex International Inc* [1985] 2 Lloyd's Rep. 289 (opening of credit).

[202] This was perhaps the basis for the dissenting opinion of Lord Brandon in *The Naxos* [1990] 1 W.L.R. 1337: see Treitel, [1991] L.M.C.L.Q. 147, 152–153. See also *RG Grain Trade LLP v Feed Factors International Ltd* [2011] EWHC 1889 (Comm); [2011] 2 Lloyd's Rep. 432, where arbitrators were found to have assumed (wrongly) that any quality term must be a condition.

[202a] *Ark Shipping Co v Silverburn Shipping (IOM) Ltd* [2019] EWCA Civ 1161; [2019] 1 Lloyd's Rep. 554 at [81] per Gross LJ (bareboat charter).

[203] *State Trading Corp of India v M Golodetz Ltd* [1969] 2 Lloyd's Rep. 277 at 284; *The Naxos* [1990] 1 W.L.R. 1337.

[204] *BS & N Ltd (BVI) v Micado Shipping Ltd (Malta) (The Seaflower)* [2001] 1 Lloyd's Rep. 341 ("majors approval clause" in time charter); *Samarenko v Dawn Hill House Ltd* [2011] EWCA Civ 1445; [2013] Ch. 36 (payment of deposit in land transaction); cf. *Ark Shipping Co v Silverburn Shipping (IOM) Ltd* [2019] EWCA Civ 1161; [2019] 1 Lloyd's Rep. 554 at [48] per Gross LJ (bareboat charter).

[205] *Harling v Eddy* [1951] 2 K.B. 739; see also *Couchman v Hill* [1947] K.B. 554. On this basis, these cases would involve contracts partly written and partly oral. But they may also be explained as cases of collateral contract: see above, para.10-012.

[206] Above, para.10-030.

[207] See *Toepfer v Lenersan-Poortman NV* [1980] 1 Lloyd's Rep. 143; *Aktion Maritime Corp v S Kasmas Bros Ltd (The Aktion)* [1987] 1 Lloyd's Rep. 283.

CHAPTER 11

TERMS AS TO DESCRIPTION AND QUALITY IMPLIED BY THE SALE OF GOODS ACT

TABLE OF CONTENTS

1. CORRESPONDENCE WITH DESCRIPTION

Sale not by description

Replace footnote 53 with:

⁵³ *Harlingdon and Leinster Enterprises Ltd v Christopher Hull Fine Art Ltd* [1991] 1 Q.B. 564. Evidence **11-011**
was given that art dealers do not rely on descriptions by sellers. See Brown, (1990) 106 L.Q.R. 561;
Bridge, [1990] L.M.C.L.Q. 455. See also *Drake v Thomas Agnew & Sons Ltd* [2002] EWHC 294 (QB),
where it was held that an art dealer's attribution of a painting to van Dyck was an expression of opinion
that did not turn the sale into one by description. There is discussion in a recent hire purchase case
concerning the description of a vintage car, *Brewer v Mann* [2012] EWCA Civ 246; [2012] R.T.R. 28;
but the true analysis of the words used was not settled, the matter being remitted for retrial. See also
Walker v Sell [2016] FCA 1259; 245 F.C.R. 308 (model of collectable car not part of description where
buyer inspected vehicle and did not rely on seller's statements).

2. QUALITY AND FITNESS FOR PURPOSE

(b) Satisfactory Quality

Sale through an agent

Replace footnote 170 with:

¹⁷⁰ *Bowstead and Reynolds on Agency*, 21st edn, Art.76. But he would not be personally liable where **11-029**
the existence of a principal was disclosed except under the collateral undertakings entered into by
auctioneers: see *Bowstead and Reynolds on Agency*, 21st edn, para.9-023.

Examples

Replace footnote 229 with:

²²⁹ *Wood v TUI Travel Plc (t/a First Choice)* [2017] EWCA Civ 11; [2018] Q.B. 927 (Supply of Goods **11-039**
and Services Act 1982 s.4).

4. OTHER IMPLIED TERMS

Other implied terms

Replace footnote 440 with:

11-084 440 See *Chitty on Contracts*, 33rd edn, Vol.1 Ch.14; Treitel, *The Law of Contract*, 14th edn (Peel), para.6-032. As to overseas sales, see below, Chs 18-21. On implied terms in general see *Att-Gen of Belize v Belize Telecom Ltd* [2009] UKPC 10; [2009] 1 W.L.R. 1988; *Marks and Spencer plc v BNP Paribas Securities Trust Co (Jersey) Ltd* [2015] UKSC 72; [2016] A.C. 742.

CHAPTER 12

REMEDIES IN RESPECT OF DEFECTS

1. MISREPRESENTATION

Representee may rescind in equity

Replace footnote 7 with:

[7] See in general *Chitty on Contracts*, 33rd edn, Vol.1 paras 7-130 to 7-131; *Whittington v Seale-Hayne* (1900) 82 L.T. 49.

12-003

Powers of court under Misrepresentation Act 1967 s.2(2)

Replace footnote 15 with:

[15] See Treitel, *The Law of Contract*, 14th edn (Peel), para.9-077; *Chitty on Contracts*, 33rd edn, Vol.1 paras 7-108 et seq.; *William Sindall Plc v Cambridgeshire CC* [1994] 1 W.L.R. 1216; Beale, (1995) 111 L.Q.R. 60; *UCB Corporate Services Ltd v Thomason* [2005] EWCA Civ 225; [2005] 1 All E.R. (Comm) 601 (no loss proved).

12-004

Loss of the right to rescind

Replace paragraph with:

In accordance with general principles of equity, the right to rescind is lost where the contract has been affirmed, where restitutio in integrum is impossible, where the subject-matter of the contract has passed into the hands of a third party, and possibly, except where the misrepresentation is fraudulent, by lapse of time.[16] It was formerly probably the law that a contract of sale of a chattel might not be rescinded for innocent misrepresentation where it had been executed,[17] but this rule was much criticised[18] and was abolished by the Misrepresentation Act 1967 s.1(b), which provides that a contract may be rescinded notwithstanding that it has been performed.[19] In such a case, the court may, however, under s.2(2) of the Act[20] refuse rescission and award damages in lieu if this seems more appropriate.

12-005

[16] See *Chitty on Contracts*, 33rd edn, Vol.1 paras 7-124 et seq. The significance of these bars on the right to rescind, particularly that relating to third parties, would be much reduced if the decision in *Car and Universal Finance Co Ltd v Caldwell* [1965] 1 Q.B. 525, para.12-003 n.8 above, were accepted.

[17] *Seddon v North Eastern Salt Co Ltd* [1905] 1 Ch. 326; *Angel v Jay* [1911] 1 K.B. 666.

[18] Hammelmann, (1939) 55 L.Q.R. 90; *Solle v Butcher* [1950] 1 K.B. 671 at 695–696.

[19] *Chitty on Contracts*, 33rd edn, Vol.1 para.7-144.

[20] Above, para.12-004.

Replace title footnote 28 with:

Restitutio in integrum impossible[28]

12-007 [28] *Chitty on Contracts*, 33rd edn, Vol.1 paras 7-124 et seq. For further discussion see Treitel, *The Law of Contract*, 14th edn (Peel), paras 9-105 et seq.

Replace title footnote 39 with:

Third party rights[39]

12-008 [39] *Chitty on Contracts*, 33rd edn, Vol.1 para.7-139. Contrast the position as to assignment of choses in action, where an assignee takes subject to equities. See also below, para.12-053.

Lapse of time

Replace footnote 42 with:

12-009 [42] *Clough v L & N W Ry* (1871) L.R. 7 Ex. 26 at 34; *Aaron's Reefs Ltd v Twiss* [1896] A.C. 273 at 294; *Allen v Robles* [1969] 1 W.L.R. 1193; *Fenton v Kenny* [1969] N.Z.L.R. 552. *Chitty on Contracts*, 33rd edn, Vol.1 paras 7-137 to 7-138.

Liability in tort: deceit

Replace paragraph with:

12-012   The seller may sometimes be liable under the tort of deceit or fraud. This is committed where a statement is made with knowledge of its falsity, or without belief in its truth, or recklessly, careless whether it be true or false; it must be intended to be acted on and in fact acted on by the person to whom it was made, to his prejudice.[53] The statement need not be made directly to the person who relies on it: it is sufficient if it is made to a third person to be communicated to the claimant, or to a class of persons of whom the claimant is one, or to the public generally, with a view to its being acted on.[54] If these criteria are fulfilled, it is irrelevant that there was no wrongful motive and no intention to cause loss.[55] The tort requires the making of a statement, but the active concealment of a defect in goods sold may perhaps sometimes amount to an implied statement.[56] The mere offer to sell defective goods with knowledge that they are defective is not, however, fraud.[57] Where fraud is established, an action for damages in tort will lie against a seller; and it seems clear that the principles of remoteness of damage applicable in cases of intentional tort will apply. These are not limited by notions of foreseeability, but only by the principles of causation: they may therefore lead to a larger award of damages than would be given in an action on the contract, if one was available. It appears that the same principles are applicable to an action under the Misrepresentation Act 1967 s.2(1), discussed below.[58] In *Doyle v Olby (Ironmongers) Ltd*,[59] an ironmongery business was bought on the inducement of fraudulent representations as to its turnover. The damages awardable were held not to be simply such as to cover the difference in value between the price paid and the benefits actually derived from the business, but to cover also consequential loss suffered by the claimant, who had attempted to run it without being able to afford to do so in such a way as to minimise his losses. There will, however, also be cases where an action in tort would yield less damages than one for breach of contract, for contract damages will cover the expectation interest (i.e. loss of bargain) which it is assumed, in England at least, cannot be recovered in deceit.[60] The contract may also be rescinded in equity in cases of fraud,[61] if it is not too late to do so,[62] and it should be noted that some of the limits on the right to rescind are more leniently applied in cases of fraud, and in particular that lapse of time is incapable of itself barring rescission in such a case, but is at most evidence of affirmation.[63]

[53] *Derry v Peek* (1889) 14 App.Cas. 337. See in general *Clerk and Lindsell on Torts*, 22nd edn, Ch.18; and for a recent authoritative discussion see *Hayward v Zurich Insurance Co plc* [2016] UKSC 48; [2017] A.C. 142 (where it was held that belief in the truth of the statement was not an independent ingredient of the tort, though it might be evidence that the statement caused the claimant to act to his detriment in reliance on it).

[54] *Swift v Winterbotham* (1873) L.R. 8 Q.B. 244 at 252–253.

[55] *Polhill v Walter* (1832) 3 B. & Ad. 114; *Brown Jenkinson & Co Ltd v Percy Dalton (London) Ltd* [1957] 2 Q.B. 621.

[56] See *Schneider v Heath* (1813) 3 Camp. 506; cf. *Horsfall v Thomas* (1862) 1 H. & C. 90; *Ward v Hobbs* (1877) 3 Q.B.D. 150; affirmed (1878) 4 App.Cas. 13; *Peters & Co v Planner* (1895) 11 T.L.R. 169. See also *Cottee v Douglas Seaton (Used Cars) Ltd* [1972] 1 W.L.R. 1408; *R. v Ford Motor Co Ltd* [1974] 1 W.L.R. 1220 (Trade Descriptions Act).

[57] *Ward v Hobbs* (1877) 3 Q.B.D. 150. But see *Hurley v Dyke* [1979] R.T.R. 265 at 280–281, 291, 295 (CA) 302, 303 (HL); and below, paras 12-075, 13-092.

[58] Below, para.12-014.

[59] *Doyle v Olby (Ironmongers) Ltd* [1969] 2 Q.B. 158; Treitel, (1969) 32 M.L.R. 526. See also *Archer v Brown* [1985] Q.B. 401; *Smith New Court Securities Ltd v Scrimgeour Vickers (Asset Management) Ltd* [1997] A.C. 254; *Chitty on Contracts*, 33rd edn, Vol.1 paras 7-048 et seq.

[60] But see *Clef Aquitaine SARL v Laporte Materials (Barrow) Ltd* [2001] Q.B. 488; Treitel, *The Law of Contract*, 14th edn (Peel), para.9-068.

[61] Above, para.12-003.

[62] Above, paras 12-005 et seq.

[63] Above, paras 12-075, 12-007.

Negligent misrepresentation

Replace footnote 72 with:

[72] See *Clerk and Lindsell on Torts*, 22nd edn, paras 8-97 et seq.; *Chitty on Contracts*, 33rd edn, Vol.1 paras 7-091 et seq.; Treitel, *The Law of Contract*, 14th edn (Peel), paras 9-037 et seq.; for useful restatements see *James McNaughton Paper Group Ltd v Hicks Anderson & Co* [1991] 2 Q.B. 113 at 125 per Neill LJ; *Bank of Credit and Commerce International (Overseas) Ltd v Price Waterhouse Ltd* [1998] P.N.L.R. 564 at 583–587 per Sir Brian Neill.

12-013

Liability under Misrepresentation Act 1967 s.2(1)

Replace footnote 78 with:

[78] See in general *Chitty on Contracts*, 33rd edn, Vol.1 paras 7-077 et seq.

12-014

"Fiction of fraud"

Replace footnote 86 with:

[86] See *Clerk and Lindsell on Torts*, 22nd edn, paras 18-27 to 18-28. The reference to fraud could also be taken as indicating that the defendant cannot prove contributory negligence for the purposes of application of the Law Reform (Contributory Negligence) Act 1945. However, it seems clear that this can be done, at least where an action for negligence at common law would also lie: see *Gran Gelato Ltd v Richcliff (Group) Ltd* [1992] Ch 560; *Taberna Europe CDO II plc v Selskabet AF I* [2016] EWCA 1262; [2017] Q.B. 633 at [50] et seq.

12-016

2. BREACH OF CONTRACTUAL TERM

Replace title footnote 92 with:

Renunciation by seller[92]

12-019   [92] See in general *Chitty on Contracts*, 33rd edn, Vol.1 paras 24-018 et seq.

Anticipatory breach

Replace footnote 104 with:

12-021   [104] See *Chitty on Contracts*, 33rd edn, Vol.1 paras 24-022 et seq.; Treitel, *The Law of Contract*, 14th edn (Peel), paras 17-074 et seq. The refusal or impossibility must still be such as to affect the whole contract: an anticipatory repudiation in a minor respect would not necessarily amount to a renunciation of the whole contract: *Federal Commerce and Navigation Ltd v Molena Alpha Inc (The Nanfri)* [1979] A.C. 757 at 770, 783; *Woodar Investment Development Ltd v Wimpey Construction UK Ltd* [1980] 1 W.L.R. 277 at 298.

Statutory restriction on right to treat contract as discharged for breach of condition

After "enactment in 1994.", add new footnote 148a:

12-026   [148a] For a brief discussion of the provision, see *Filobake Ltd v Rondo Ltd* [2004] EWHC 695 (TCC) at [121] (affirmed [2005] EWCA Civ 563).

Contractual clauses providing for breach

Replace footnote 158 with:

12-028   [158] See a thorough discussion in *Stocznia Gdynia SA v Gearbulk Holdings Ltd* [2009] EWCA Civ 75; [2009] 1 Lloyd's Rep. 461 per Moore-Bick LJ (sale of ships to be constructed); *Seadrill Management Services Ltd v Oao Gazprom* [2009] EWHC 1530 (Comm); (2009) 126 Con. L.R. 130; *Vinergy International (PVT) Ltd v Richmond Mercantile Ltd FZC* [2016] EWHC 525 (Comm) (notice period in express termination clause inapplicable to common law right to terminate); *Chitty on Contracts*, 33rd edn, Vol.1 paras 22-048 to 22-049; Treitel, *The Law of Contract*, 14th edn (Peel), paras 18-069 to 18-071; Peel, [2013] L.M.C.L.Q. 519. See also the discussion in connection with a withdrawal clause in a time charterparty in *Spar Shipping AS v Grand China Logistics Holding (Group) Co Ltd* [2016] EWCA Civ 982; [2016] 2 Lloyd's Rep. 447.

What constitutes rejection

After "with the goods.", add new footnote 182a:

12-034   [181a] See the discussion in *Fal Oil Trading Co Ltd v Petronas Trading Co* [2002] EWHC 1825.

Waiver

Replace paragraph with:

12-037   The distinction made in the previous paragraph is very relevant when the buyer seeks to retract a waiver. A waiver in the sense of an indication by the buyer that he is satisfied with the defective performance can be regarded as a promise not to sue (or, if promissory terminology is not thought appropriate, as at best an informal release).[191] As such it does not, upon orthodox doctrine, bind for the future unless supported by consideration,[192] and if not so supported can be retracted at any time with reasonable notice; though of course it is effective in the sense that any retraction cannot be retrospective, and it is not possible to treat as broken a duty in respect of which rights have been waived and not resumed.[193] It has even been said that:

"... the only way of establishing [such a waiver] would be to show a separate agreement, binding on the buyer, by which he had agreed to surrender the right to damages which automatically vested in him at the time of the breach."[194]

This dictum seems however too emphatic, for under the principle of *Hughes v Metropolitan Railway Co*[195] the buyer cannot retract where it would be inequitable to do so. This will often mean no more than that he must give notice to enable the seller to resume his former position. Cases may arise where it is inequitable for the buyer ever to retract his waiver, because the seller is not able to resume that position.[196] A clear example in a contract of sale could occur where the seller, in reliance on the buyer's assurances that there was no objection to the goods supplied, has so conducted himself as to prevent himself from making a further, conforming tender, which he could originally have done[197]; or where he for that reason loses an opportunity to tender the goods elsewhere.[198] The exact circumstances in which the principle applies are not yet, however, fully formulated.[199] The prevailing view seems to be that there must be a clear and unequivocal representation that strict legal rights will not be relied on,[200] and:

"... some conduct induced by the representations, differing in some material manner from the way in which the sellers would have conducted themselves if the supposed representation had not been made."[201]

It has been said that "No question arises of any particular knowledge on the part of the representor"[202]; and the doctrine has regularly been stated without any such requirement.[203] But if the representor is not aware, or at least has no obvious means of knowledge, of the facts giving rise to his right to treat the contract as discharged, it may be difficult to establish that the representation was unequivocal.[204]

[191] See Campbell, (1963) 1 N.Z.U.L.R. 232.

[192] Or under seal. The merits of the situation were fully discussed in the famous case of *Foakes v Beer* (1884) 9 App. Cas. 605. A new view of what constitutes consideration for the modification of a contract, considerably more lenient than had hitherto been assumed to be appropriate, was however taken by the Court of Appeal in *Williams v Roffey Bros & Nicholls (Contractors) Ltd* [1991] 1 Q.B. 1; as to which see Treitel, *The Law of Contract*, 14th edn (Peel), para.3-051; and *MWB Business Exchange Centres Ltd v Rock Advertising Ltd* [2016] EWCA Civ 553; [2017] Q.B. 604 (actual decision reversed [2018] UKSC 24; [2019] A.C. 119).

[193] See, e.g. *Panoutsos v Raymond Hadley Corp of New York* [1917] 2 K.B. 473; *Tankexpress A/S v Cie Financière Belge des Petroles SA* [1949] A.C. 76.

[194] *Kwei Tek Chao v British Traders and Shippers Ltd* [1954] 2 Q.B. 459 at 477 per Devlin J. cf. *The Democritos* [1975] 1 Lloyd's Rep. 386 at 398 (affirmed [1976] 2 Lloyd's Rep. 149).

[195] *Hughes v Metropolitan Railway Co* (1877) 2 App.Cas. 439; see *Chitty on Contracts*, 33rd edn, Vol.1 paras 4-086 et seq.

[196] cf. *Birmingham and District Land Co v L & N W Ry* (1888) 40 Ch.D. 268.

[197] An example accepted in *Toepfer v Warinco AG* [1978] 2 Lloyd's Rep. 569 at 576.

[198] An example given in *Société Italo-Belge pour le Commerce et l'Industrie SA v Palm and Vegetable Oils (Malaysia) Sdn Bhd (The Post Chaser)* [1982] 1 All E.R. 19 at 26.

[199] See *Woodhouse AC Israel Cocoa Ltd SA v Nigerian Produce Marketing Co Ltd* [1972] A.C. 741 at 758 per Lord Hailsham LC.

[200] See the *Woodhouse AC Cocoa case* [1972] A.C. 741 at 756, 761, 768, 771. See also *Bremer Handelsgesellschaft mbH v C Mackprang Jr* [1979] 1 Lloyd's Rep. 221 at 228; *Avimex SA v Dewulf & Cie* [1979] 2 Lloyd's Rep. 57 at 67. A misrepresentation may, however, be unequivocal without saying "we hereby waive": *Bremer Handelsgesellschaft mbH v Vanden Avenne-Izegem PVBA* [1978] 2 Lloyd's Rep. 109 at 126 HL. See further *Chitty on Contracts*, 33rd edn, Vol.1 para.4-091.

[201] *Finagrain SA v Kruse* [1976] 2 Lloyd's Rep. 508 at 535 per Megaw LJ.

[202] *Motor Oil Hellas (Corinth) Refineries SA v Shipping Corp of India (The Kanchenjunga)* [1990] 1 Lloyd's Rep. 391 at 399 per Lord Goff of Chieveley.

[203] See *W J Alan & Co Ltd v El Nasr Export and Import Co* [1972] 2 Q.B. 189 at 212–214; *Bremer Handelsgesellschaft mbH v C Mackprang Jr* [1979] 1 Lloyd's Rep. 221 at 226, 230, explaining dicta in *Bremer Handelsgesellschaft mbH v Vanden Avenne-Izegem PVBA* [1978] 2 Lloyd's Rep. 109; *Bremer Handelsgesellschaft mbH v Finagrain, etc. SA* [1981] 2 Lloyd's Rep. 259 at 263.

[204] *Bremer Handelsgesellscheft mbH v C Mackprang Jr* [1979] 1 Lloyd's Rep. 221 at 229; *Avimex SA v Dewulf & Cie* [1979] 2 Lloyd's Rep. 57 at 67.

Ability to return goods to seller

Replace footnote 307 with:

12-053 [307] *Metals Ltd v Diamond* [1930] 3 D.L.R. 886. See also *Filobake Ltd v Rondo Ltd* [2004] EWHC 695 (TCC) at [130] (decision affirmed [2005] EWCA Civ 563).

Rights and duties of buyer and seller as to rejected goods

Replace footnote 406 with:

12-067 [406] See above, para.3-006; *Bowstead and Reynolds on Agency*, 21st edn, Art.33.

Recovery of money paid in cases of short delivery

Replace footnote 429 with:

12-071 [429] See *Goss v Chilcott* [1996] A.C. 788; *David Securities Pty Ltd v Commonwealth Bank of Australia* (1992) 175 C.L.R. 353 at 383; below, para.17-091; *Chitty on Contracts*, 33rd edn, Vol.1 para.29-065; Virgo, *Principles of the Law of Restitution*, 3rd edn, pp.320–323.

3. MISREPRESENTATIONS SUBSEQUENTLY INCORPORATED INTO THE CONTRACT

Both common law and equity applicable

Replace footnote 437 with:

12-073 [437] See *Sycamore Bidco Ltd v Breslin* [2012] EWHC 3443 (Ch) at [204], where Mann J points out the "conceptual problem in characterising provisions *in* the contract as being representations relied on in entering the contract". See also *Idemitsu Kosan Co Ltd v Sumitomo Corp* [2016] EWHC 1909; [2016] 2 C.L.C. 297 (Comm).

4. TORT LIABILITY IN RESPECT OF GOODS

Tort action against seller

Replace paragraph with:

12-075 Where goods supplied cause personal injury or the destruction of or damage to other property, it is also possible for a dissatisfied buyer to sue the seller in tort,[444] though by so doing he takes on the burden of proving negligence. An action in tort may in some circumstances yield more damages[445] (e.g. if expectation of profit cannot be proved,[446] or if the loss claimed is consequential[447]); and the limitation period may run from a different time, viz. in the case of negligence actions the suffering of damage rather than that of the supply of the defective goods.[448] The Law Reform (Contributory Negligence) Act 1945, which permits apportionment, applies to tort claims, but its application to contract claims is not yet certain.[449] Circumstances may arise where an exemption clause covers liability in contract but not in tort.[450] There are also differences in respect of jurisdiction, both local and international, and in other respects such as the conflict of laws, which are beyond the scope of this work. It has been said that there is not "anything to the advantage of the law's development in searching for a liability in tort where the parties are in a contractual relationship".[451] Hence the differences between contract and tort as regards the standard of care required of a seller are unlikely to be of substance. But a tort action may of course lie where there is no privity of contract: indeed, this is its main utility in this context. Hence such an action may lie against a manufacturer or distributor: and also in favour of a non-buyer, e.g. a person to whom the buyer gave the goods in question as a gift.[452]

[444] See *Herschtal v Stewart and Ardern Ltd* [1940] 1 K.B. 155; *Andrews v Hopkinson* [1957] 1 Q.B. 229; *Vacwell Engineering Ltd v BDH Chemicals Ltd* [1971] 1 Q.B. 88 at 108; *Rasbora Ltd v JCL Marine Ltd* [1977] 1 Lloyd's Rep. 645.

[445] As to damages in contract, see below, Ch.17.

[446] e.g. *CCC Films (London) Ltd v Impact Quadrant Films Ltd* [1985] Q.B. 16, though here the damages were recovered in contract.

[447] Under the principles of *The Wagon Mound (No.1)* [1961] A.C. 388; *Clerk and Lindsell on Torts*, 22nd edn, paras 2-152 et seq. But see *H Parsons (Livestock) Ltd v Uttley Ingham & Co Ltd* [1978] Q.B. 791, where consequential loss was recovered in contract: the principle of the case is not clear. As to damages in deceit, see above, para.12-012.

[448] *Battley v Faulkner* (1820) 3 B. & A. 288; *Lynn v Bamber* [1930] 2 K.B. 72 at 74.

[449] *Forsikringsaktieselskapet Vesta v Butcher* [1986] 2 All E.R. 488; affirmed [1989] A.C. 852 CA; for further proceedings see at 880 HL. If it is not applicable the issue turns on causation: see *Lambert v Lewis* [1982] A.C. 225; *Borealis AB v Geogas Trading SA* [2010] EWHC 2789 (Comm); [2011] Lloyd's Rep. 482. See *Chitty on Contracts*, 33rd edn, Vol.1 paras 26-071 et seq.; Treitel, *The Law of Contract*, 14th edn (Peel), paras 20-123 et seq.

[450] e.g. *White v J Warwick & Co Ltd* [1953] 1 W.L.R. 1285; but the significance of such decisions is much reduced by the Unfair Contract Terms Act 1977; below, Ch.13.

[451] *Tai Hing Cotton Mill Ltd v Liu Chong Hing Bank Ltd* [1986] A.C. 80 at 107 per Lord Scarman. See also *Aiken v Stewart Wrightson Members Agency Ltd* [1995] 2 Lloyd's Rep. 618 at 634 et seq. But cf. *Henderson v Merrett Syndicates Ltd* [1995] 2 A.C. 145.

[452] e.g. *Donoghue v Stevenson* [1932] A.C. 562; *Fisher v Harrods Ltd* [1966] 1 Lloyd's Rep. 500.

Manufacturer or distributor

Replace footnote 453 with:

[453] *Donoghue v Stevenson* [1932] A.C. 562; below, paras 14-223 et seq.; as to distributors see *Watson v Buckley, Osborne Garrett & Co Ltd* [1940] 1 All E.R. 174. As to the Contracts (Rights of Third Parties) Act 1999 see *Chitty on Contracts*, 33rd edn, Vol.1 paras 18-090 et seq.　　**12-076**

Care required

Replace footnote 454 with:

[454] See *Clerk and Lindsell on Torts*, 22nd edn, Ch.11.　　**12-077**

Economic loss: goods which threaten damage or are otherwise unsatisfactory

Replace footnote 463 with:

[463] *Murphy v Brentwood DC* [1991] 1 A.C. 398; see also *D & F Estates Ltd v Church Commissioners for England* [1989] A.C. 177; *Department of the Environment v Thomas Bates & Son Ltd* [1991] 1 A.C. 499; *Clerk and Lindsell on Torts*, 22nd edn, paras 8-136 et seq.　　**12-079**

5. MISTAKE AS TO SUBJECT MATTER OF CONTRACT

Mistake

Replace footnote 471 with:

12-081 [471] See *Chitty on Contracts*, 33rd edn, Vol.1 Ch.6; Treitel, *The Law of Contract*, 14th edn (Peel), paras 8-002 et seq.

6. THE VIENNA CONVENTION ON CONTRACTS FOR THE INTERNATIONAL SALE OF GOODS

The Vienna Convention

Replace the second paragraph with:

12-082 Enough has been said to indicate that the Convention, which represents a compromise between common law and civil law techniques, and many parts of which may be understood differently by common lawyers and civil lawyers, is a regime on its own requiring careful study and the use of specialised works. It is more complex than the common law, and from the point of view of a buyer gives less robust remedies, being directed instead to a more balanced adjustment of the positions of the parties. The Sale of Goods Act and the extensive common law overlay on that statute provide little or no guide to its application; much will require to be solved in litigation which will interpret what is in many different countries a completely novel regime. Those who may find the regime unsatisfactory should exclude the operation of the Convention in international transactions to which it would otherwise apply.[490] The Convention is however of some assistance in interpreting the remedies available to consumer buyers under Ch 2 of the Consumer Rights Act 2015.[490a]

[490] As to international sales see below, Chs 18–21.

[490a] Below, paras 14-093 et seq.

EXEMPTION CLAUSES

2. BASIC PRINCIPLES OF FORMATION OF CONTRACT APPLIED TO EXEMPTION CLAUSES

All basic principles of formation applicable in sale

Replace footnote 27 with:

[27] See *Chitty on Contracts*, 33rd edn, Vol.1 Ch.15; Treitel, *The Law of Contract*, 14th edn (Peel), Ch.7; **13-011** Macdonald, *Exemption Clauses and Unfair Terms*, 2nd edn; Lewison, *The Interpretation of Contracts*, 6th edn; McMeel, *The Construction of Contracts: Interpretation, Implication and Rectification*, 3rd edn; Carter, *The Construction of Commercial Contracts* (2013).

Incorporation in contract

Replace footnote 37 with:

[37] See *Chitty on Contracts*, 33rd edn, Vol.1 paras 13–109 et seq. The operation of this principle may **13-012** be affected by an entire agreement clause, as to which see below, paras 13-030, 13-040, 13-059.

Third parties

Replace paragraph with:

In accordance with the normal doctrine of privity of contract, a person who is not **13-016** a party to a contract can at common law neither take the benefit of, nor be bound by, an exemption clause contained in it.[53] This may be very relevant when an action in negligence is brought by or against a third party to the contract of sale.[54] The common law has developed two principal methods of circumventing this rule in the case of exemption clauses.[55] The first involves detecting a separate contract with the third party, incorporating (or even containing no more than) the exemptions of the main contract, made through the agency of one of the parties to the main contract (or more directly if the facts permit of such an inference).[56] If the exemptions are drafted with a view to such interpretation, and if the party to be additionally protected is known from the outset, the separate contract will be easier to infer. The second method involves a promise by one contracting party to the other not to sue the third party; in such a situation an action against the third party would be a breach of contract, and could be stayed[57] or even perhaps made the subject of a claim for damages.[58] Although such a promise could perhaps in some circumstances be inferred,[59] a clearly formulated promise or set of promises ("circular indemnity clauses") are obviously more likely to be effective. Sale of goods situations involve the application of these principles in two different contexts. The first is that of an action against the seller by a person who did not buy the goods, but, for example, for whom they were bought or to whom they were given. Here the claimant will not be affected by exemptions in the contract of sale unless a contract between him and the seller can be detected[60] or there is a contract between the claimant and the actual buyer containing a promise not to sue. The second is that of a claim by the buyer against a person other than the seller, usually the manufacturer.[61] A clause in a contract of sale entered into by a retailer which purports to protect the manufacturer of the goods will again not be effective as such to do so unless it embodies a separate contract with the manufacturer, or a promise to the retailer not to sue the manufacturer. A contract with the manufacturer is sometimes, however, constituted by a separate guarantee. A person buying goods from a retailer is often given with them a document from the manufacturer which may guarantee them in certain respects, but which often also purports to exclude the manufacturer's liability in tort at common law, and sometimes the retailer's liability (which would be contractual) as well. Since the buyer normally has no privity of contract with the manufacturer and deals with the retailer alone, the manufacturer cannot rely on exemption clauses in the contract of sale when sued in tort, and can only rely on the exemption clause in the "guarantee" if a genuine collateral contract can be inferred between him and the buyer. If such a contract can be found, however, it may in principle protect him; though here conversely the exemption cannot operate in favour of the retailer, even if it purports to do so, unless it can be regarded as incorporated also into the main contract of sale, or again if it embodies a promise not to sue the retailer. The problems arising out of such guarantees are discussed together elsewhere.[62]

---

[53] See *Chitty on Contracts*, 33rd edn, Vol.1 paras 15–042 et seq.; Treitel, *The Law of Contract*, 14th edn (Peel), paras 14–057 et seq.; *Dunlop Pneumatic Tyre Co Ltd v Selfridge & Co Ltd* [1915] A.C. 847; *Scruttons Ltd v Midland Silicones Ltd* [1962] A.C. 446.

[54] See above, paras 12-075 et seq.; below, paras 14-223 et seq., 14-242 et seq.; but see below, paras 13-018, 14-242 et seq., 14-243 as to the effect of the Consumer Protection Act 1987.

[55] There is a third, that of bailment on terms, which will not usually be relevant in a sale of goods context. See *Chitty on Contracts*, 33rd edn, Vol.1 paras 15–057 to 15–058.

[56] See *New Zealand Shipping Co Ltd v AM Satterthwaite & Co Ltd (The Eurymedon)* [1975] A.C. 154; *Port Jackson Stevedoring Pty Ltd v Salmond and Spraggon (Australia) Pty Ltd (The New York Star)* [1981] 1 W.L.R. 138 HL; *Celthene Pty Ltd v WKJ Hauliers Pty Ltd* [1981] 1 N.S.W.L.R. 606.

[57] See *Nippon Yusen Kaisha v International Import and Export Co Ltd (The Elbe Maru)* [1978] 1 Lloyd's Rep. 206; *Broken Hill Pty Co Ltd v Hapag-Lloyd Aktiengesellschaft* [1980] 2 N.S.W.L.R. 572; cf. *Gore v Van der Lann* [1967] 2 Q.B. 31; *Gillespie Bros & Co Ltd v Roy Bowles Transport Ltd* [1973] Q.B. 400; *Neptune Orient Lines Ltd v JVC (UK) Ltd (The Chevalier Roze)* [1983] 2 Lloyd's Rep. 438; *Deepak Fertilisers and Petrochemicals Corp v ICI Chemicals and Polymers Ltd* [1998] 2 Lloyd's Rep. 139; [1999] 1 Lloyd's Rep. 387 at 401. For a more radical suggestion, that the defendant can himself plead such a promise in defence, see Birks, (1975) 1 Poly.L.Rev. 39; Birks and Beatson, (1976) 92 L.Q.R. 188, 193 et seq.

[58] cf. *Woodar Investment Development Ltd v Wimpey Construction UK Ltd* [1980] 1 W.L.R. 277 at 300–301 HL.

[59] See *Snelling v John G Snelling Ltd* [1973] 1 Q.B. 87 at 98.

[60] For examples of this problem, see *Lockett v A and M Charles Ltd* [1938] 4 All E.R. 170 (restaurant); *Walls v Centaur Co Ltd* (1921) 126 L.T. 242 (purchase from manufacturer by employee of dealer for employee's personal use); *Cockerton v Naviera Aznar SA* [1960] 2 Lloyd's Rep. 450; *Hollingworth v Southern Ferries Ltd (The Eagle)* [1977] 2 Lloyd's Rep. 70 (boat tickets); *Cooke v Midland Ry Co* (1892) 9 T.L.R. 147; *Hobbs v L & SW Ry Co* (1875) L.R. 10 Q.B. 111 (railway ticket); *MacRobertson Miller Airline Services v Commissioner of State Taxation (WA)* (1975) 133 C.L.R. 125 at 146–147 (airline

ticket); *Varga v John Labatt Ltd* (1956) 6 D.L.R. (2d) 336. See also *Daly v General Steam Navigation Co Ltd (The Dragon)* [1980] 2 Lloyd's Rep. 415; below, para.14-224.

[61] Below, paras 14-223 et seq.

[62] See below, paras 14-215 et seq.

Replace title footnote 63 with:

Contracts (Rights of Third Parties) Act 1999[63]

[63] See *Chitty on Contracts*, 33rd edn, Vol.1 paras 15–042 et seq.; 18–090 et seq;Treitel, *The Law of Contract*, 14th edn (Peel), paras 14–090 et seq.

13-017

Replace footnote 68 with:

[68] In the first situation, a donee from a buyer cannot have the burden of the contract between buyer and seller imposed on him, and the Act does not alter this. However, if the contract of sale is for the benefit of the prospective donee within the wording of the Act, and his action was to be regarded as based on the Act ("in reliance on section 1": s.3(1)), he would only be able to enforce it subject to its terms: s.3(2). It appears however that if he sues on his existing common law right, the existing common law applies: s.7(1). See *Chitty on Contracts*, 33rd edn, Vol.1 paras 15–042 et seq.

3. INTERPRETATION OF EXEMPTION CLAUSES

Strict interpretation

Replace paragraph with:

Exemption clauses are, where (as is common) there is room for argument as to their meaning and coverage, strictly construed contra proferentem.[71] The first justification for this is that a party seeking to rely on such a clause must prove that he comes within it.[72] It can also be said that a person who puts forward a provision that is for his own benefit should only be allowed to rely on it if its meaning is clear, particularly if he participated in its insertion in the contract.[73] It can also be said that there is:

13-019

> "… an inherent improbability that the other party to such a contract including such a clause intended to release the *proferens* from a liability that would otherwise fall on him."[74]

This assumes that there are rules whereby such a liability would arise independently of the contract, which is sometimes (e.g. where a bailment is involved or where there is a potential liability in tort) but by no means always true; and it moves towards the now abandoned doctrine of fundamental breach, which is discussed below.[75] Whatever the basis of this strict interpretation, it is also applied to indemnity clauses[76]; though, as later explained,[77] there is authority for applying less strict criteria to clauses which merely limit the amount recoverable. Such a technique for controlling the effect of exemption clauses is found in many legal systems. There are numerous examples in the area of sale of goods. After the Unfair Contract Terms Act 1977 came into operation, there was less need for stringency, at least in the cases where the Act applies (which include domestic sales of goods). There are indeed clear indications that the courts have taken a more relaxed approach than was sometimes taken before the Act[78]; have not strained to detect ambiguities[79]; have not ascribed "tortured meanings" to exemption clauses[80]; and have in general simply interpreted such clauses in the context of the contract as a whole.[81] But although the Act contains nothing preserving the rules of interpretation, as compared with the rules for formation of contract, which are expressly confirmed,[82] it is clear that the rules of interpretation still operate[83]; and it has been said that the true interpretation of a clause must be ascertained by normal techniques before its reasonableness is assessed.[84] And the fact that the Act looks only to the reasonableness of including a particular clause in the contract rather than reasonableness of reliance on the clause in the case in question[85] means that the rules of interpretation may be particularly useful when the question is not as to whether a clause is reasonable in itself but as to whether it is appropriate that it should be invoked in a specific set of circumstances.[86] It is, however, clear that all decisions prior to the Act of 1977 should be read in the light of the fact that the court has now in many cases the statutory power to declare exemption clauses ineffective on the facts. Furthermore, there are clear signs in cases not involving the sale of goods that the contra proferentem rule is falling out of favour with the courts, at least in a commercial context: in one recent decision concerned with the contracts between the Post Office and sub-postmasters, for example, it was questioned whether the rule survived, and stated that in any case it no longer had "widespread or general applicability to commercial (as opposed to consumer) contracts".[86a]

[71] In view of recent case-law on interpretation of contracts, various attempts have been made to argue for different formulations of the strict interpretation rule, e.g. by identifying the proferens, identifying types of clause affected by the rule, and so forth. A very recent discussion is by Briggs LJ in *Nobuhar-Cookson v The Hut Group Ltd* [2016] EWCA Civ 128, in which he says (at [18]): "Ambiguity in an exclusion clause may have to be resolved by a narrow construction because an exclusion clause cuts down or detracts from the ambit of some important obligation in a contract, or a remedy conferred by the general law such as ... an obligation to give effect to a contractual warranty by paying damages for breach of it." See also Peel, (2017) 133 L.Q.R. 6.

[72] See *Chitty on Contracts*, 33rd edn, Vol.1 para.15–008; Treitel, *The Law of Contract*, 14th edn (Peel), paras 7–033 et seq.

[73] See Staughton LJ in *Youell v Bland, Welch & Co Ltd* [1992] 2 Lloyd's Rep. 127 at 134; see also *Pera Shipping Corp v Petroship SA* [1984] 2 Lloyd's Rep. 363 at 365 per Staughton J.

[74] *Ailsa Craig Shipping Co Ltd v Malvern Fishing Co Ltd* [1983] 1 W.L.R. 964 at 970 per Lord Fraser of Tullybelton. See also *Seadrill Management Services Ltd v OAO Gazprom* [2010] EWCA Civ 691; [2010] 1 C.L.C. 934 at [29]; *Nobuhar-Cookson v The Hut Group Ltd* [2016] EWCA Civ 128; *Bahamas Oil Refining Co International Ltd v Owners of the Cape Bari Tankschiffahrts GmbH & Co KG* [2016] UKPC 20; [2016] 2 Lloyd's Rep. 469 at [31] per Lord Clarke.

[75] Below, paras 13-043 et seq.

[76] See below, para.13-086; *Canada Steamship Lines Ltd v R* [1952] A.C. 192; *Smith v South Wales Switchgear Co Ltd* [1978] 1 W.L.R. 165; *EE Caledonia Ltd v Orbit Valve Co Europe* [1994] 1 W.L.R. 221 and 1515; and see *Stent Foundations Ltd v MJ Gleeson Group Plc* [2001] B.L.R. 134.

[77] Below, para.13-036.

[78] *Howard Marine and Dredging Co Ltd v A Ogden & Sons (Excavations) Ltd* [1978] Q.B. 574 at 594; cf. 599; *Photo Production Ltd v Securicor Transport Ltd* [1980] A.C. 827 at 843, 851; *George Mitchell (Chesterhall) Ltd v Finney Lock Seeds Ltd* [1983] 2 A.C. 803 at 814.

[79] *Ailsa Craig Shipping Co Ltd v Malvern Fishing Co Ltd* [1983] 1 W.L.R. 964 at 966; and see *Livingstone v Roskilly* [1992] 3 N.Z.L.R. 230.

[80] *George Mitchell* case [1983] 2 A.C. 803 at 810.

[81] See *Swiss Bank Corp v Brinks Mat Ltd* [1986] 2 Lloyd's Rep. 79 at 92–93; see also *Darlington Futures Ltd v Delco Australia Pty Ltd* (1986) 161 C.L.R. 500.

[82] See s.11(2); above, para.13-011.

[83] See *Green v Cade Bros Farms* [1978] 1 Lloyd's Rep. 602; *George Mitchell* [1983] 2 A.C. 803.

[84] *Watford Electronics Ltd v Sanderson CFL Ltd* [2001] EWCA Civ 317; [2001] 1 All E.R. (Comm) 696 at [31] et seq.; and see *Granville Oil and Chemicals Ltd v Davies Turner & Co Ltd* [2003] EWCA Civ 570; [2003] 2 Lloyd's Rep. 356 (clause did not purport to cover fraud).

[85] Unfair Contract Terms Act s.11(1).

[86] cf. below, para.13-075.

[86a] *Bates v Post Office Ltd* [2019] EWHC 606 (QB) at [638] per Fraser J. See also *Persimmon Homes Ltd v Ove Arup & Partners Ltd* [2017] EWCA Civ 373; [2017] 2 C.L.C. 28 at [52] per Jackson LJ (role

of rule "very limited" in relation to commercial contracts negotiated between parties of equal bargaining power). For a survey of the recent case law, and a critique of the use of special rules of construction in relation to exemption clauses, see Tofaris, [2019] L.M.C.L.Q. 270.

Negligence

Replace footnote 94 with:

[94] See *Alderslade v Hendon Laundry Ltd* [1945] K.B. 189; *Canada Steamship Lines Ltd v R.* [1952] A.C. 192; *Hollier v Rambler Motors (AMC) Ltd* [1972] 2 Q.B. 71; *Smith v South Wales Switchgear Ltd* [1978] 1 W.L.R. 165 HL. See also *Producer Meats (North Island) Ltd v Thomas Borthwick & Sons (Australia) Ltd* [1964] N.Z.L.R. 700; *Hawkes Bay and East Coast Aero Club Inc v McLeod* [1972] N.Z.L.R. 289; *Lictor Anstalt v Mir Steel UK Ltd* [2012] EWCA Civ 1397 (discussion of Canada Lines case); *Chitty on Contracts*, 33rd edn, Vol.1 paras 15–013 to 15–016; Treitel, *The Law of Contract*, 14th edn (Peel), paras 7–033 et seq.

13-021

Exclusion of warranties

At the end of the paragraph, after "contained in s.14(2).", add:*

It is however questionable whether this particular rule of construction is compatible with the modern approach to contractual interpretation, and a preferable approach may be to adopt a less artificial interpretive approach and instead police attempts to exclude implied conditions by means of the statutory controls on exemption clauses.[118a]

13-024

[118a] Below, paras 13-054 et seq. In support of this view, see Tofaris, [2019] L.M.C.L.Q. 270, 290–292.

Clauses limiting the damages recoverable

Replace footnote 199 with:

[199] See below, paras 16-036 et seq.; *Chitty on Contracts*, 33rd edn, Vol.1 paras 26–190 et seq.; Treitel, *The Law of Contract*, 14th edn (Peel), paras 20–129 et seq.

13-036

Exclusion of indirect or consequential loss

Replace paragraph with:

Commercial contracts frequently include clauses purporting to exclude liability for consequential loss, or indirect loss (which is interpreted as having the same meaning[214]) or both. The purpose of such clauses in a sale of goods context would appear to be to exclude liability beyond the difference in value between that of the goods supplied and the value which they ought to have had, together with direct physical damage caused by the goods; in particular, it may be thought that those who use them seek to exclude liability for loss of profits. The courts have however, interpreted such clauses strictly, regarding a straight claim for loss of profits as being direct rather than indirect or consequential. The current authority is that such clauses only exclude losses covered by the second part of the rule in *Hadley v Baxendale*,[215] that is to say, unusual losses for which the defendant would not be liable unless made aware of the risk of them. It seems that this is now so well established that only the Supreme Court can reconsider the matter.[216] Quite often such clauses reinforce what might be thought to be their purpose by a specific reference to loss of profits.[217] In such cases, a problem of interpretation arises as to whether the loss of profits referred to must be regarded as only covering those arising under the second part of *Hadley v Baxendale*, or whether the reference to profits must be given effect and the exclusion of consequential loss confined to matters outside the express words. There are also problems as to exactly what the second part of the rule in *Hadley v Baxendale* means in practice outside the straightforward

13-037

examples normally given, in particular as to the requirement of special knowledge.[218]

[214] *Saint Line Ltd v Richardsons, Westgarth & Co* [1940] 2 K.B. 99.

[215] *Hadley v Baxendale* (1854) 9 Exch. 341: see *Chitty on Contracts*, 33rd edn, Vol.1 paras 26–119 et seq.; Treitel, *The Law of Contract*, 14th edn (Peel), para.7–017. See also *Scottish Power UK Plc v BP Exploration Operating Co Ltd* [2015] EWHC 2658 (Comm); [2016] 1 All E.R.(Comm) 536 (decision affirmed [2016] EWCA Civ 1043) (sale of gas: exclusion of "loss of use, profits, contracts, production or revenue or for business interruption howsoever caused" did not cover normal loss caused by under-delivery, beyond a specific provision dealing with that).

[216] *Millar's Machinery Co Ltd v David Way & Son* (1935) 40 Com.Cas. 204; *Saint Line Ltd v Richardsons, Westgarth & Co* [1940] 2 K.B. 99; *Wraight Ltd v PH & T (Holdings) Ltd* (1968) 13 B.L.R. 29; *Croudace Construction Ltd v Cawoods Concrete Products Ltd* [1978] 2 Lloyd's Rep. 55 CA (usually taken as the leading case); *British Sugar Plc v NEI Power Products Ltd* (1998) 87 B.L.R. 42; *Deepak Fertilisers and Petrochemicals Corp v ICI Chemicals and Polymers Ltd* [1998] 2 Lloyd's Rep. 139; [1999] 1 Lloyd's Rep. 387; *BHP Petroleum Ltd v British Steel Plc* [1999] 1 Lloyd's Rep. 583 (Rix J.), decision varied [2000] 2 Lloyd's Rep. 277; *Hotel Services Ltd v Hilton International Hotels (UK) Ltd* [2000] B.L.R. 235; *Pegler Ltd v Wang (UK) Ltd* [2000] B.L.R. 218 ("even if Wang shall have been advised of the possibility of such potential loss"); *Watford Electronics Ltd v Sanderson CFL Ltd* [2001] EWCA Civ 317; [2001] 1 All E.R. (Comm) 696. But Lord Hoffmann expressed reservations about this interpretation in *Caledonia North Sea Ltd v British Telecommunications Plc* [2002] UKHL 4; [2002] 1 Lloyd's Rep 553 at [100]. For the suggestion that the Supreme Court should overrule the *Croudace* line of cases, see Tofaris, [2019] L.M.C.L.Q. 270, 288–290.

[217] See *BHP Petroleum Ltd v British Steel Plc* [1999] 1 Lloyd's Rep. 583 at 600. See also the clauses in *Britvic Soft Drinks Ltd v Messer UK Ltd* [2002] 1 Lloyd's Rep. 20 ("losses, costs or expenses of a purely financial or economic nature (including, but not limited to, loss of profits, loss of use or other consequential loss")); and *Bacardi-Martini Beverages Ltd v Thomas Hardy Packaging Ltd* [2002] 1 Lloyd's Rep. 62; affirmed [2002] EWCA Civ 549; [2002] 2 Lloyd's Rep. 379.

[218] See the *BHP* case [1999] 1 Lloyd's Rep. 583, at first instance at 588 et seq. per Rix J. In *Caledonia North Sea Ltd v Norton (No.2) Ltd* [2002] UKHL 4; [2002] All E.R. (Comm) 321 at [100], Lord Hoffmann reserved the question of the correctness of this construction.

Entire agreement clauses

Replace footnote 234 with:

13-040   [234] See *Axa Sun Life Services Plc v Campbell Martin Ltd* [2011] EWCA Civ 133; [2011] 2 Lloyd's Rep.1 and material there considered; *NF Football Investments Ltd v NFFC Group Holdings Ltd* [2018] EWHC 1346 (Ch). As to exclusion of implied terms see *Compass Group UK and Ireland Ltd v Mid-Essex Hospital Services NHS Trust* [2012] EWHC 781 (QB). See also above, para.13-030; below, para.13-060.

Certification and testing clauses

Replace footnote 235 with:

13-041   [235] There are various practical differences between certification and arbitration. There is no general rule of law prohibiting the influencing of certifiers: *Minster Trust Ltd v Traps Tractors Ltd* [1954] 1 W.L.R. 963. Certifiers less frequently perform judicial functions than arbitrators; and it seems that arbitrators acting judicially are not easily liable in negligence. See *Sutcliffe v Thackrah* [1974] A.C. 727; *Arenson v Casson Beckman Rutley & Co* [1977] A.C. 405; *Palacath Ltd v Flanagan* [1985] 2 All E.R. 161; Arbitration Act 1996 ss.29, 74; and generally *Chitty on Contracts*, 33rd edn, Vol.2, para.32–196; Mustill and Boyd, *Commercial Arbitration*, 3rd edn (2001), pp.224–232; Russell, *Arbitration*, 24th edn, paras 2–029 et seq.

Replace title footnote 247 with:

Arbitration clauses[247]

13-042   [247] *Chitty on Contracts*, 33rd edn, Vol.2 Ch.32; Redfern and Hunter, *Law and Practice of International Commercial Arbitration*, 6th edn; Russell, *Arbitration*, 24th edn. Arbitration is now controlled by the Arbitration Act 1996.

4. DOCTRINE OF FUNDAMENTAL BREACH

Doctrine of fundamental breach

Replace footnote 252 with:

[252] See *Chitty on Contracts*, 33rd edn, Vol.1 para.15–023; Treitel, *The Law of Contract*, 14th edn (Peel), **13-043** paras 7–023 et seq.; Coote, *Exception Clauses* (1964). See also Guest, (1961) 77 L.Q.R. 98; Reynolds, (1963) 79 L.Q.R. 534; Lord Devlin, [1966] C.L.J. 192.

5. CONTROL OF EXEMPTION CLAUSES BY STATUTE

Non-reliance provisions

Replace paragraph with:

It has earlier been mentioned that such wording indicating non-reliance or the like **13-060** may create an "evidential estoppel" in favour of a person who actually believed that there had been no reliance, but that this would be rare.[322] More recently decisions, often outside the context of sale, have begun to emphasise the argument that the parties can by such a clause define the basis on which they are acting, creating a "contractual estoppel".[323] From this it might follow that the Misrepresentation Act s.3 (or more generally the Unfair Contract Terms Act) does not apply to such clauses at all, and this is sometimes argued.[324] Other recent cases have affirmed a distinction between "basis clauses" (a new term which is beginning to emerge) and exemption clauses.[325] However, it will be unfortunate if the Act is too easily evaded and the weight of authority now favours the application of a "substance" test.[326] In *Cremdean Properties Ltd v Nash*,[327] estate agents used a clause reading:

> "(a) These particulars are prepared for the convenience of an intending purchaser or tenant and although they are believed to be correct their accuracy is not guaranteed and any error, omission or misdescription shall not annul the sale or be grounds on which compensation may be claimed and neither do they constitute any part of an offer of a contract. (b) Any intending purchaser or tenant must satisfy himself by inspection or otherwise as to the correctness of each of the statements contained in these particulars."

The Court of Appeal rejected arguments that the effect of these words was to bring about a situation as if no representation had been made; and Bridge LJ said that he did not think the courts would be ready "to allow such ingenuity in forms of language to defeat the plain purpose at which section 3 is aimed".[328] More recent cases are (without necessarily finding such clauses unreasonable) consistent with this view. In *First Tower Trustees Ltd v CDS (Superstores International) Ltd*, a landlord and tenant case, Lewison LJ said that section 3 "must be interpreted so as to give effect to its evident policy", which was to prevent contracting parties from escaping from liability for misrepresentation unless it was reasonable for them to do so,[328a] and Leggatt LJ said that whenever a contracting party relied on the principle of contractual estoppel to argue that the other party was prevented from asserting a fact which was necessary to establish liability for a precontractual misrepresentation, the term would fall within section 3.[329] It is difficult to see why such reasoning should not equally apply to "no authority" clauses, at least where the agent concerned is likely to make representations, which is true of many agents for sale such as auctioneers and estate agents. Such clauses will often or even usually be reasonable in commerce,[330] but that should not exclude them from scrutiny.

[322] See above, para.13-040.

323 See *Peekay Intermark Ltd v Australia & New Zealand Banking Group Ltd* [2006] EWCA Civ 386; [2006] 2 Lloyd's Rep. 511; quoted above, para.13-030.

324 See *McGrath v Shah* (1989) 57 P. & C.L.R.452; *Watford Electronics Ltd v Sanderson CFL Ltd* [2001] EWCA Civ 317; [2001] 1 All E.R. (Comm) 696, where Chadwick LJ describes the idea that such a clause is caught by the Act as "bizarre"; *JP Morgan Chase Bank v Springwell Navigation Corp* [2008] EWHC 1186 at [603], where Gloster J said that otherwise "every contract which contains contractual terms defining the extent of each party's obligations would have to satisfy the requirement of reasonableness" (on appeal [2010] EWCA Civ 1221; [2010] 2 C.L.C. 585, see at [179]–[181]); *Titan Steel Wheels Ltd v Royal Bank of Scotland Plc* [2010] EWHC 211 (Comm); [2010] 2 Lloyd's Rep.92, where Steel J said that of several, only one clause (relating to damages) in a contract was a "genuine exclusion clause".

325 See *Thornbridge v Barclays Bank Plc* [2015] EWHC 3430 (QB) at [99] et seq.; *Sears v Minco Plc* [2016] EWHC 433 (Ch) at [76] et seq.; *Carney v NM Rothschild & Sons Ltd* [2018] EWHC 958 (Comm) (all on investment advice, and in all the clause was held, if an exemption clause, in any case reasonable under the Unfair Contract Terms Act); cf. *First Tower Trustees Ltd v CDS (Superstores International) Ltd* [2018] EWCA Civ 1396 per Leggatt LJ at [90] et seq.).

326 See *Inntrepreneur Pub Co (GL) v East Crown Ltd* [2000] 2 Lloyd's Rep. 611 at 614; *Inntrepreneur Estates (CPC) Ltd v Worth* [1996] 1 E.G.L.R. 84; *Thomas Witter & Co Ltd v TBP Industries Ltd* [1996] 2 All E.R. 573 at 597–598; *Government of Zanzibar v British Aerospace (Lancaster House) Ltd* [2000] 1 W.L.R. 2333 at 2341 et seq.; *SAM Business Systems Ltd v Hedley & Co* [2002] EWHC 2733 (TCC); [2003] 1 All E.R. (Comm) 465; *AXA Sun Life Services Plc v Campbell Martin Ltd* [2011] EWCA Civ 133; [2011] 2 Lloyd's Rep. 1 at [48]–[51] (caught by the Unfair Contract Terms Act 1977 s.3: below para.13-083); *Lloyd v Browning* [2013] EWCA Civ. 1637; [2014] 1 P. & C.R. 11.

327 *Cremdean Properties v Nash* (1977) 244 E.G. 547 (also on the unamended wording); see also *South Western General Property Co Ltd v Marton* (1982) 263 E.G. 1090 (new wording) (see below, para.13-075); *St Marylebone Property Co Ltd v Payne* [1994] 2 E.G.L.R. 25.

328 *Cremdean Properties v Nash* (1977) 244 E.G. 547 at 551. Unfair Contract Terms Act 1977 s.13 (below, para.13-065) does not appear to apply, for the reasons given at para.13-066. As to this reasoning in general, see below, paras 13-066 et seq.

328a *First Tower Trustees Ltd v CDS (Superstores International) Ltd* [2018] EWCA Civ 1396 at [51].

329 *First Tower Trustees Ltd v CDS (Superstores International) Ltd* [2018] EWCA Civ 1396 at [111]. For similar reasoning, see *Inntrepreneur Pub Co (GL) v East Crown Ltd* [2000] 2 Lloyd's Rep. 611 at 614; *Inntrepreneur Estates (CPC) Ltd v Worth* [1996] 1 E.G.L.R. 84; *Thomas Witter & Co Ltd v TBP Industries Ltd* [1996] 2 All E.R. 573 at 597–598; *Government of Zanzibar v British Aerospace (Lancaster House) Ltd* [2000] 1 W.L.R. 2333 at 2341 et seq.; *SAM Business Systems Ltd v Hedley & Co* [2002] EWHC 2733 (TCC); [2003] 1 All E.R. (Comm) 465; *Raiffeisen Zentralbank Osterreich AG v Royal Bank of Scotland Plc* [2010] EWHC 1392 (Comm); [2011] 1 Lloyd's Rep 123 (excluding "attempts retrospectively to alter the character of what has gone before", at [315], quoted in *Springwell*, below, at [181]); *Springwell Navigation Corp v JP Morgan Chase Bank* [2010] EWCA Civ 1221; [2010] 2 C.L.C. 585; *AXA Sun Life Services Plc v Campbell Martin Ltd* [2011] EWCA Civ 133; [2011] 2 Lloyd's Rep. 1 at [48]–[51] (caught by the Unfair Contract Terms Act 1977 s.3: below para.13-083); *Avrora Fine Arts Investment Ltd v Christie, Manson & Woods Ltd* [2012] EWHC 298; [2012] P.N.L.R. 35 (fine art auctioneer's terms: Unfair Contract Terms Act s.2).

330 e.g. *EA Grimstead & Son Ltd v McGarrigan* unreported, 27 October 1999 CA; *SAM Business Systems Ltd v Hedley & Co* [2002] EWHC 2733 (TCC); [2003] 1 All E.R. (Comm) 465; *Watford Electronics Ltd v Sanderson CFI Ltd* [2001] EWCA Civ 317; [2005] 1 All E.R. (Comm) 696 (see Peel, (2001) 117 L.Q.R. 546); *Foodco UK LLP v Henry Boot Developments Ltd* [2010] EWHC 358 (Ch); *Springwell Navigation Corp v JP Morgan Chase Bank* [2010] EWCA Civ 1221; [2010] 2 C.L.C. 585 at [179]–[181]; *AXA Sun Life Services Plc v Campbell Martin Ltd* [2011] EWCA Civ 133; [2011] 2 Lloyd's Rep. 1 (most clauses). As to "authority" clauses see above, para.13-058. See also below, para.13-061.

Replace title footnote 344 with:

Methods used by the 1977 Act[344]

13-064   344 See in general *Chitty on Contracts*, 33rd edn, Vol.1 paras 15–062 et seq; Treitel, *The Law of Contract*, 14th edn (Peel), paras 7–049 et seq.; Coote, (1978) 41 M.L.R. 312. Part II of the Act applies to Scotland; and Pt III to the whole UK. Discussion here is confined to the law applicable in England, Wales and Northern Ireland. As to international sales, see below, paras 18-328 et seq.

Guidelines

Replace footnote 417 with:

[417] Sch.2. Decisions are allocated to these guidelines in *Chitty on Contracts*, 33rd edn, Vol.1 para.15– **13-077** 097.

Present wording

Replace paragraph with:

After a slow start cases on reasonableness now appear quite frequently. Useful **13-079** general criteria in the context of carriage, but plainly relevant elsewhere, have been set out by Potter LJ in *Overseas Medical Supplies Ltd v Orient Transport Services Ltd*[427] as follows:

- the way in which the relevant conditions came into being and are used generally;
- the five guidelines as to reasonableness set out in Sch.2;
- in relation to the question of equality of bargaining position the court will have regard not only to the question of whether the customer was obliged to use the services of the supplier, but also to the question of how far it would have been practicable and convenient to go elsewhere;
- the question of reasonableness must be assessed having regard to the relevant clause viewed as a whole: it is not right to take any particular part of the clause in isolation, although it must also be viewed against a breach of contract which is the subject of the case;
- the reality of the consent of the customer to the supplier's clause will be a significant consideration;
- in cases of limitation rather than exclusion of liability, the size of the limit compared with other limits in widely used standard terms may also be relevant;
- while the availability of insurance to the supplier is relevant, it is by no means a decisive factor;
- the presence of a term allowing for an option to contract without the limitation clause but with a price increase in lieu is important; however, if the condition works in such a way as to leave little time to put such option into effect, this may effectively eliminate the option as a factor indicating reasonableness.

Clauses held unreasonable in the context of sale and related contracts include clauses having very wide application in view of the facts of the case,[428] limiting liability to repair or replacement, or containing a specific warranty with onerous terms,[429] time bars,[430] limits on amount recoverable,[431] exclusion of liability for consequential loss[432] and some clauses excluding or significantly restricting rights of set-off.[433] It has been held that availability of insurance, which is specifically made relevant in the case of limits on amount[434] is also more generally relevant to reasonableness; but this refers to general availability rather than the actual position between the parties concerned, at least unless the question of insurance was taken into account by the parties at the time the contract was made.[435] It has been held also that clauses in tripartite situations excluding or reducing the financier's liability as seller may still be unreasonable though the financier has not seen the goods.[436] Cases on the Misrepresentation Act 1967 s.3 are also relevant.[437] It can be said that the most recent trend is to regard terms in arm's length commercial transactions between parties judged able to look after themselves as reasonable, especially when a commercial need for such an arrangement can be demonstrated or inferred.

[427] *Overseas Medical Supplies Ltd v Orient Transport Services Ltd* [1999] 2 Lloyd's Rep. 273 at 276. There is extended discussion of reasonableness in a recent case on a company auditor's disclaimer of liability to third parties: *Barclays Bank Plc v Grant Thornton UK LLP* [2015] EWHC 320 (Comm); [2015] 2 B.C.L.C. 180.

[428] *Edmund Murray Ltd v BSP International Financiers Ltd* (1992) 33 Con. L.R. 1 (drill rig); *Lease Management Services Ltd v Purnell Secretarial Services Ltd* (1993) 13 Tr L.R. 337 (photocopier); *Pegler Ltd v Wang (UK) Ltd* [2000] B.L.R. 218 (computer hardware and software); *Britvic Soft Drinks Ltd v Messer UK Ltd* [2002] 1 Lloyd's Rep. 20; affirmed on this point [2002] EWCA Civ 548; [2002] 2 Lloyd's Rep. 368; *Bacardi-Martini Beverages Ltd v Thomas Hardy Packaging Ltd* [2002] 1 Lloyd's Rep. 62; affirmed [2002] EWCA 549; [2002] 2 Lloyd's Rep. 379 (both on bulk carbon dioxide); *Balmoral Group Ltd v Borealis (UK) Ltd* [2006] EWHC 1900 (Comm); [2006] 2 Lloyd's Rep. 629 (clause excluding core terms and with one exception denying buyer any redress if the goods are defective, held unreasonable: see at [419]). cf. *Regus (UK) Ltd v Epcot Solutions Ltd* [2008] EWCA Civ 361; [2009] 1 All E.R. (Comm) 586 (exclusion of liability for consequential loss reasonable; not true that no remedy left to hirer (of serviced office accommodation) for inefficiency of air conditioning). See also *J Murphy & Sons Ltd v Johnston Precast Ltd* [2008] EWHC 3024 (TCC), where an exclusion of the fitness for purpose obligation was held reasonable; *Air Transworld Ltd v Bombardier Inc* [2012] EWHC 243 (Comm); [2012] 1 Lloyd's Rep. 349, where an elaborate scheme of duties effectively superseding the normal duties of a seller in a contract for the sale of an aircraft was held reasonable on the general basis that commercial parties should be free to negotiate their own terms.

[429] *Charlotte Thirty Ltd v Croker Ltd* (1990) 24 Con. L.R. 46 (industrial plant); *Edmund Murray Ltd v BSP International Financiers Ltd* (1992) 33 Con. L.R. 1; *AEG (UK) Ltd v Logic Resources Ltd* [1996] C.L.C. 265; but cf. *British Fermentation Products Ltd v Compair Reavell Ltd* (1999) 66 Con L.R. 1 (centrifugal air compressor), where such a clause was held reasonable. See also *Stag Line Ltd v Tyne Shiprepair Group (The Zinnia)* [1984] 2 Lloyd's Rep. 211 (ship repair contract: clause requiring return of vessel to yard in case of unsatisfactory work unreasonable); *Sterling Hydraulics Ltd v Dichtomatik Ltd* [2006] EWHC 2004 (QB); [2007] 1 Lloyd's Rep. 8 ("hidden defects": one week unreasonable); *Avrora Fine Arts Investment Ltd Christie Manson & Woods Ltd* [2012] EWHC 2198 (Ch); [2012] P.N.L.R. 35 (5-year warranty accompanied by exemptions regarding attribution of painting: reasonable).

[430] *Rees-Hough Ltd v Redland Reinforced Plastics Ltd* (1984) 27 B.L.R. 136 (piping: three months); *Knight Machinery (Holdings) Ltd v Rennie*, 1995 S.L.T. 166 (printing machine: seven days); *Pegler Ltd v Wang (UK) Ltd* [2000] B.L.R. 218 (computer hardware and software: two years); *Bacardi-Martin Beverages Ltd v Thomas Hardy Packaging Ltd* [2002] 1 Lloyd's Rep. 62 (bulk carbon dioxide: five days); cf. *Expo Fabrics (UK) Ltd v Martin* [2003] EWCA Civ 1165 (textiles: 20 days reasonable). See also *Whitecap Leisure Ltd v John H Rundle Ltd* [2008] EWCA Civ 429; [2008] 2 Lloyd's Rep. 216 (time limit for claims reasonable: but decision not under the statute); *Rohlig (UK) Ltd v Rock Unique Ltd* [2011] EWCA Civ 18; [2011] 2 All E.R. (Comm) 1161 (freight forwarder: reasonable).

[431] *Salvage Association v CAP Financial Services Ltd* [1995] F.S.R. 654 (computer software: £25,000: insurance taken into account); *St Albans City and District Council v International Computers Ltd* [1995] F.S.R. 686; affirmed on this point [1996] 4 All E.R. 481 (computer software: £100,000); but cf. holdings of reasonableness in *Watford Electronics Ltd v Sanderson CFL Ltd* [2001] EWCA Civ 317; [2001] 1 All E.R. (Comm) 696 (computer software: sum paid); *Britvic Soft Drinks Ltd v Messer UK Ltd* [2002] 1 Lloyd's Rep. 20; *Bacardi-Martin Beverages Ltd v Thomas Hardy Packaging Ltd* [2002] 1 Lloyd's Rep. 62 (both on bulk carbon dioxide: £2 million, £500,000); *Sterling Hydraulics Ltd v Dichtomatik Ltd* [2006] EWHC 2004 (QB); [2007] 1 Lloyd's Rep. 8 (seals for use with brake fluid: limitation to amount of contract price in "low value high volume contract" reasonable); *Regus (UK) Ltd v Epcot Solutions Ltd* [2008] EWCA Civ 361; [2009] 1 All E.R. (Comm) 586 (serviced office accommodation: 125 per cent of fees or £50,000 reasonable: insurance possible).

[432] *Charlotte Thirty Ltd v Croker Ltd* (1990) 24 Con. L.R. 46 (industrial plant); *Edmund Murray Ltd v BSP International Financiers Ltd* (1992) 33 Con. L.R. 1 (drill rig); *Pegler Ltd v Wang (UK) Ltd* [2000] B.L.R. 218 (computer hardware and software); *Bacardi-Martini Beverages Ltd v Thomas Hardy Packaging Ltd* [2002] 1 Lloyd's Rep. 62; but cf. *British Fermentation Products Ltd v Compair Reavell Ltd* (1999) 66 Con. L.R. 1 (centrifugal air compressor); *Watford Electronics Ltd v Sanderson CFL Ltd* [2001] EWCA Civ 317 and *Goodlife Foods Ltd v Hall Fire Protection Ltd* [2018] EWCA Civ 1371; 178 Con. L.R. 1 (goods and services: fire suppression system), where such clauses were held reasonable. The *Watford Electronics* case contains strong dicta by Chadwick LJ (at 158) that "unless satisfied that one party has, in effect, taken advantage of the other—or that a term is so unreasonable that it cannot properly be understood or considered—the court should not interfere". These dicta seem to bring unreasonableness close to unconscionability, a connection explicitly made by Coulson LJ in the *Goodlife Foods* case (at [93]), where it was also said that "the trend in the UCTA cases decided in recent years has been towards upholding terms freely agreed, particularly if the other party could have contracted elsewhere and has, or was warned to obtain, effective insurance cover". See also Peel, (2001) 117 L.Q.R. 545. A clause excluding liability for consequential loss was also held reasonable in *Regus (UK) Ltd v Epcot Solutions Ltd* [2008] EWCA Civ 361; [2009] 1 All E.R. (Comm) 586 (supply of serviced office accom-

modation) and in *Allen Fabrications Ltd v ASD Metal Services* [2012] EWHC 2213 (TCC). See also above, para.12-038.

433 *Stewart Gill Ltd v Horatio Myer & Co Ltd* [1992] Q.B. 600 (goods and services: overhead conveyor system); *AXA Sun Life Services Plc v Campbell Martin Ltd* [2011] EWCA Civ 133; [2011] 2 Lloyd's Rep. 1 (insurance representative, some clauses unreasonable); but cf. *Schenkers Ltd v Overland Shoes Ltd* [1998] 1 Lloyd's Rep. 498 (freight forwarding: reasonable); *Surzur Overseas Ltd v Ocean Reliance Shippiloan*: Misrepresentation Act 1967, above, para.13-055); *Skipskedittforeningen v Emperor Navigation* [1998] 1 Lloyd's Rep. 66 (loan: reasonable: Misrepresentation Act 1967); *WRM Group Ltd v Wood* [1998] C.L.C. 189 (reasonable in loan and financial agreements); *Rohlig (UK) Ltd v Rock Unique Ltd* [2011] EWCA Civ 18; [2011] 2 All E.R. (Comm) 1161 (freight forwarder: reasonable); *F.G. Wilson (Engineering) Ltd v John Holt & Co* [2012] EWHC 2477 (Comm); [2012] 2 Lloyd's Rep 479 (sale: reasonable).

434 Below, para.13-080.

435 *Flamar Interocean Ltd v Denmac Ltd (The Flamar Pride)* [1990] 1 Lloyd's Rep. 434 at 440. See also *Trustees of Ampleforth Abbey Trust v Turner and Townsend* [2012] EWHC 2137 (TCC). cf. *Goodlife Foods Ltd v Hall Fire Protection Ltd* [2018] EWCA Civ 1371; 178 Con. L.R. 1 at [76] et seq., where the actual insurance position of the parties was also taken into account.

436 *Lease Management Services Ltd v Purnell Secretarial Services Ltd* (1993) 14 Tr.L.Rep. 337, followed in *Sovereign Finance Ltd v Silver Crest Furniture Ltd* [1997] C.C.L.R. 76; and *Scania Finance Ltd v Monteum Ltd* unreported, 30 January 2001 QBD; and not following dicta in *R & B Customs Brokers Ltd v United Dominions Trust Ltd* [1988] 1 W.L.R. 321 at 332.

437 See above, para.13-061.

Limits on amount

Replace footnote 440 with:

440 See above, para.13-079.   **13-080**

Standard terms

Replace paragraph with:

The notion of standard terms is undefined, and is unfamiliar to English law, **13-084** though it has been used in other countries to identify terms requiring control.454 There is no provision as to burden of proof.455 Various problems may arise in connection with the notion. It would seem, first, that the terms, though they must be written, need not be printed; and that they may be incorporated into the contract orally,456 by a notice or by course of dealing.457 If the terms otherwise qualify as standard terms they must rank as such even when used for the first time.458 Where standard terms are used with extra clauses added, whether by hand or in typescript, and even if they are added for the particular transaction in question only, unless the addition is the result of individual negotiation it is submitted that all the terms should rank as standard terms: there is no need to seek reasons for restricting the category, for the terms can always be held reasonable. If the additions are negotiated but the dispute concerns the remainder of the contract, the parties may be regarded as dealing on standard terms.459 Questions may arise as to whether the terms must be intended for use in a large or indefinite number of transactions: although this will usually be so, it is submitted that sometimes terms prepared for quite a small group of transactions may justifiably be classed as standard. The terms obviously need not be prepared by or on behalf of one of the parties to the contract. The proponent may use a set of terms prepared by his or his agent's trade or professional organisation; or by an organisation representing both sides to a transaction (e.g. suppliers and buyers); or by an independent organisation representing neither (e.g. the International Chamber of Commerce, which prepared INCOTERMS). In all these cases it may be that adoption of the terms by one party will constitute them his written standard terms of business.460 In Scotland it has been said that the phrase "standard form contract" in s.17 of the Scottish part of the Act:

"... is ... wide enough to include any contract, whether wholly written or partly oral, which includes a set of fixed terms or conditions which the proponer applies, without material variation to contracts of the kind in question."[461]

The object of the notion of standard terms must in fact be to identify contracts which are not individually negotiated.[462] Nevertheless, a person may deal on standard terms even where there has been negotiation.[463] The notion provides protection for small businesses dealing with larger businesses, but it may also operate between large concerns—though here there may be difficulties, where both use standard terms, in determining which deals on the other's terms[464]: for standard terms may obviously be used by buyers as well as by sellers.

[454] See Law Com. No.69 (1975), paras 153–157. A useful definition is to be found in s.1 of the German AGB-Gesetz (Standard Contract Terms Law) of 1976 (now contained in s.305(1) BGB): "(1) Standard contract terms are all such conditions of contract as are formulated in advance for a large number of contracts, which one contracting party (the proponent) presents to the other at the conclusion of the contract. It is immaterial whether the conditions form a physically separate part of the contract or are set out in the contractual document itself, what scope they have, in what type of writing they are set out, or what form the contract takes. (2) Standard contract terms are not present in so far as the conditions of contract are individually negotiated between the contracting parties". The Israeli Standard Contracts Law of 1982 provides that standard contract "means the text of a contract, all or part of the terms of which have been determined in advance by one party in order to serve as conditions of many contracts between him and persons unidentified as to number or identity": see Deutch, (1985) 30 McGill L.J. 458.

[455] In *African Export-Import Bank v Shebah Exploration and Production Co* [2017] EWCA Civ 845; [2018] 1 W.L.R. 487, a case on a syndicated loan facility, it is said that "A party who wishes to contend that it is arguable that a deal is on standard business terms must ... produce some evidence that it is likely to have been so done" (at [33]).

[456] *McCrone v Boots Farms Sales Ltd*, 1981 S.C. 68.

[457] *McCrone v Boots Farms Sales Ltd*, 1981 S.C. 68.

[458] In *Hadley Design Associates v Westminster City Council* [2003] EWHC 1617 (TCC); [2004] T.C.L.R.1 it is said that the terms "should exist in written form prior to the possibility of the making of the relevant agreement arising" (at [78]); but this was said not to be conclusive in *University of Wales v London College of Business Ltd* [2015] EWHC 1280 (QB).

[459] *Salvage Assoc v CAP Financial Services Ltd* [1995] F.S.R. 654; *St Albans City and DC v International Computers Ltd* [1995] F.S.R. 686; affirmed on this point [1996] 4 All E.R. 481; *Pegler Ltd v Wang (UK) Ltd* [2000] B.L.R. 218; cf. *Flamar Interocean Ltd v Denmac Ltd (The Flamar Pride)* [1990] 1 Lloyd's Rep. 434.

[460] *Chester Grosvenor Hotel Co Ltd v Alfred McAlpine Management Ltd* (1991) 56 B.L.R. 115; *British Fermentation Products Ltd v Compair Reavell Ltd* (1999) 66 Con. L.R. 1 (requiring "proof that the model form is invariably or at least usually used by the party in question. It must be shown that either by practice or by express statement a contracting party has adopted a model form as his standard terms of business"). This may be putting the matter too narrowly: cf. *Overseas Medical Supplies Ltd v Orient Transport Services Ltd* [1999] 2 Lloyd's Rep. 273, above, para.13-079, where applicability of the BIFA Standard Terms and Conditions appears to have been assumed to bring the section into operation. But in *African Export-Import Bank v Shebah Exploration and Production Co* [2017] EWCA Civ 845; [2018] 1 W.L.R. 487, a case on a syndicated loan facility, it is said that it is not enough "to show that a model form has, on the particular occasion, been used; the party relying on the Act has to show that such model form is habitually used by the other party" (at [20]; see also at [37]).

[461] *McCrone v Boots Farm Sales Ltd*, 1981 S.C. 68 at 74 per Lord Dunpark. In *African Export-Import Bank v Shebah Exploration and Production Co* [2017] EWCA Civ 845; [2018] 1 W.L.R. 487, a case on a syndicated loan facility, Longmore L.J. (at [25]) approved this statement and said that if there have been "substantial variations" to the terms which may otherwise have been habitually used by the party in question, then it was unlikely that the contract would be considered to have been made on that party's written standard terms of business. See also *Chester Grosvenor Hotel Co Ltd v Alfred McAlpine Management Ltd* (1991) 56 B.L.R. 115; *Pegler Ltd v Wang (UK) Ltd* [2000] B.L.R. 218.

[462] See *Salvage Assn v CAP Financial Services Ltd* [1995] F.S.R. 654.

[463] *St Albans City and DC v International Computers Ltd* [1996] 4 All E.R. 481; affirming on this point [1995] F.S.R. 686; *Salvage Assn v Cap Financial Services Ltd* [1995] F.S.R. 654; but cf. *Flamar Interocean Ltd v Denmac Ltd (The Flamar Pride)* [1990] 1 Lloyd's Rep. 434; *Yuanda (UK) Co Ltd v WW Gear Construction Ltd* [2010] EWHC 720 (TCC); [2010] 1 C.L.C. 491 at [23] et seq. (construction contract: but containing a useful discussion of the notion of standard terms); *African Export-*

Import Bank v Shebah Exploration and Production Co [2017] EWCA Civ 845; [2018] 1 W.L.R. 487, a case on a syndicated loan facility, but also containing a useful discussion of this notion.

[464] See *Butler Machine Tool Co v Ex-Cell-O Corp (England) Ltd* [1979] 1 W.L.R. 401; *Edmund Murray Ltd v BSP International Financiers Ltd* (1992) 33 Con. L.R. 1.

Liability in tort

Replace footnote 487 with:

[487] Though it is arguable that the defence of volenti has no application to negligence simpliciter: **13-092**
Wooldridge v Sumner [1963] 2 Q.B. 43 at 69–70; *Clerk and Lindsell on Torts*, 22nd edn, paras 3–107 et seq.

Replace footnote 501 with:

[501] The matter is further discussed above, paras 13-066, 13-067. See a useful discussion in *Clerk and* **13-093**
Lindsell on Torts, 22nd edn, para.8–133, 8–134.

CHAPTER 14

CONSUMER PROTECTION

TABLE OF CONTENTS

[141]

1. INTRODUCTION

(b) The significance of EU law

The UK's exit from the EU ("Brexit")

Replace paragraph (including title, above) with:

14-006   After a national referendum held on 23 June 2016 at which a majority voted in favour of the UK leaving the EU, the UK Conservative Government formed on 16 July 2016 declared its intention to end the UK's membership of the EU ("Brexit") and on 29 March 2017 the then Prime Minister, the Right Hon. Mrs Theresa May MP, set in motion the process of doing so under Art.50 of the Treaty of the European Union (TEU).[21] The Conservative Government formed on 16 July 2016 by Mrs May set out its intentions as to the position of existing EU law (including on consumer protection) in the UK in two white papers, *The United Kingdom's exit from and new partnership with the European Union*[22] and *Legislating for the United Kingdom's withdrawal from the European Union.*[23] After a general election held on 8 June 2017, the Conservative Government formed by Mrs May remained in office. On 26 June 2018 the European Union (Withdrawal) Act 2018 received Royal Assent. The Act makes provision for repeal of the European Communities Act 1972 and further provision in connection with the withdrawal of the UK from the EU.[24] The Act is accompanied by Explanatory Notes ("Explanatory Notes to the 2018 Act"). The Act made detailed provision for the coming into force of its own provisions,[24a] but the intention at the time was that the UK would leave the EU on 29 March 2019 ("exit day").[24b] Mrs May's government made an agreement with the EU Council on 25 November 2018 (the "Withdrawal Agreement", together with a "Political Declaration") relating to the withdrawal of the UK from the EU, but this agreement was not approved by the UK Parliament. The UK and the European Council therefore agreed a first extension (until 12 April 2019 at the latest)[24c] and then a second, flexible extension with a cut-off of 31 October 2019. The 2018 Act was therefore amended so as to redefine "exit day" as 31 October 2019 at 11pm.[24d] On 24 May 2019 Mrs May announced her resignation as Prime Minister and on 24 July 2019 the Right Hon. Mr Boris Johnson MP became Prime Minister. Mr Johnson has made clear that his government would intend to leave the EU by 31 October 2019 with or without a withdrawal agreement with the EU.[24e]

[21] The Prime Minister's authority to do so was given by the European Union (Notification of Withdrawal) Act 2017 s.1.

[22] Department for Exiting the European Union, Cm 9417 (February 2017).

[23] Department for Exiting the European Union, Cm 9446 (March 2017).

[24] Section 25 of the 2018 Act makes detailed provision for the coming into force of its own provisions.

[24a] See 2018 Act s.25.

[24b] 2018 Act s.20(1) "exit day".

[24c] Put into effect in the UK by the European Union (Withdrawal) Act (Exit Day) (Amendment) Regulations 2019 (SI 2019/718).

[24d] European Union (Withdrawal) Act 2018 (Exit Day) (Amendment) (No. 2) Regulations 2019 (SI 2019/859) reg.2(2).

[24e] See *https://www.bbc.co.uk/news/uk-politics-48496082* (23 July 2019).

After paragraph 14-006, add new paragraph 14-006A:

The impact of Brexit on English contract law   In terms of the likely impact of   **14-006A**
Brexit on English consumer protection law, there are two sets of legislative sources which should be considered: first, the terms of the 2018 Act itself (as amended where this applies) and, secondly, the considerable number of statutory instruments made under the 2018 Act which seek to give effect to the general policy of the preservation of the UK's EU legislative acquis, while amending and, where necessary, replacing certain legislative instruments or particular legislative provisions in the light of the UK's exit from the EU.[24f] The following paragraphs (as updated in August 2019) will note the general approach of the 2018 Act to the EU legislative acquis and the changes made by statutory instruments made under the 2018 Act affecting the UK legislation discussed in this chapter.

[24f] These powers are contained in the 2018 Act s.8.

The general preservation of the UK's EU legislative acquis

Replace paragraph with:
The 2018 Act repeals the European Communities Act 1972 on "exit day",[25] re-   **14-007**
defined as "October 31, 2019 at 11.00 p.m.",[26] but with a continuing power in a Minister of the Crown to amend this definition so as "to ensure that the day and time specified in the definition are the day and time that the Treaties are to cease to apply to the United Kingdom."[27] Despite this repeal, the 2018 Act would in principle retain the EU legislative acquis as part of UK law and, taken together, these laws are referred to by the Act as "retained EU law".[28] There are, however, two types of qualifications on the resulting preservation in UK law of the EU legislative acquis. First, the 2018 Act itself sets out certain exceptions for this purpose.[29] Secondly, the 2018 Act provides for the later amendment or repeal of legislation (primary or secondary) whose source is in EU legislation, distinguishing for this purpose

between "retained direct principal EU legislation" and "retained direct minor EU legislation".[30] In the course of 2018 and 2019 a considerable number of regulations have been made under the Act for this purpose, and in the context of contracts they have in common that their operative provisions are generally due to come into force on "exit day" as defined by the 2018 Act while leaving unaffected contracts entered into before "exit day".

[25] 2018 Act s.1.

[26] 2018 Act s.20(1) "exit day" as amended by SI 2019/859 reg.2(2).

[27] 2018 Act s.20(4) and see also s.20(2)–(3) and (5).

[28] 2018 Act s.6(7) defines "retained EU law" by reference to "anything which, on or after exit day, continues to be, or forms part of, domestic law by virtue of" ss.2, 3, 4 or 6(3) or (6) of the Act, "as that body of law is added to or otherwise modified by or under the Act or by other domestic law from time to time".

[29] 2018 Act s.5 (exceptions provided by the Act itself, e.g. s.5(4) states that "the Charter of Fundamental Rights is not part of domestic law on or after exit day").

[30] 2018 Act ss.7 and 8. Section 7(6) defines the "retained direct principal EU legislation" and "retained direct minor EU legislation" for this purpose, "retained direct EU legislation" being defined by s.20(1) as any direct EU legislation which forms part of domestic law by virtue of s.3 (as modified) and s.7(1)–(5) provides for the modification of these two categories of retained direct legislation itself and by reference to other powers in the Act.

After paragraph 14-007, add new paragraph 14-007A:

14-007A **Examples of the impact on consumer protection legislation** The 2018 Act distinguishes three categories of legislation which forms part of or which is derived from EU law.[31]

First, in principle "EU-derived domestic legislation, as it has effect in domestic law immediately before exit day, continues to have effect in domestic law on and after exit day".[32] This provision would in principle preserve important UK consumer protection legislation affecting consumer sales of goods enacted as secondary legislation under the European Communities Act 1972, as in the case of the Consumer Contracts (Information, Cancellation and Additional Charges) Regulations 2013[33] and the Consumer Protection from Unfair Trading Regulations 2008.[34]

Secondly, "[d]irect EU legislation, so far as operative immediately before exit day, forms part of domestic law on or after exit day".[35] Such direct EU legislation in principle includes EU regulations[36] and therefore concerns such instruments as the Rome I Regulation on the law applicable to contractual obligations[37] in the area of private international law and the Denied Boarding Regulation in the area of consumer protection.[37a] As presently foreseen, the Rome I Regulation is to be retained though subject to amendment,[37b] as is also the Denied Boarding Regulation.[37c] Other EU regulations which are discussed later in this chapter and which put in place various mechanisms of intra-EU co-operation (such as the Regulation on cooperation in the area of consumer protection[37d]) or co-ordination (for example, the Regulation on consumer ODR[37e]) are set not to be retained on "exit day".

Thirdly, the 2018 Act contains provision for the preservation of UK primary legislation enacted for the purpose of implementing EU obligations, (such as the Consumer Rights Act 2015 Pts 1 and 2,[37f] which are due to be subject to some amendment[37g] and the Consumer Protection Act 1987[37h])[37i] or secondary legislation with the same purpose but made under statutory powers other than those contained in s.2(2) of the 1972 Act.[37j]

[31] 2018 Act ss.2 and 3.

[32] 2018 Act s.2(1). Section 2(2) defines "EU-derived domestic legislation" to include, in particular, any enactment made under s.2(2) of the European Communities Act 1972. The exceptions to this general position are set out by s.5 and Sch.1.

[33] SI 2013/3134 implementing Directive 2011/83/EU on consumer rights [2011] O.J. L304/64 on which see below, paras 14-195 et seq. The 2013 Regulations are amended on "exit day" by the Consumer Protection (Amendment etc.) (EU Exit) Regulations 2018 (SI 2018/1326) reg.8 (making modest and merely technical amendments): reg.1(3)).

[34] The 2008 Regulations (on which see below, paras 14-269 et seq.) are amended on "exit day" by the Consumer Protection (Amendment etc.) (EU Exit) Regulations 2018 (SI 2018/1326) reg.6 (making modest amendments): reg.1(3)).

[35] 2018 Act s.3(1).

[36] 2018 Act s.3(2).

[37] Regulation 593/2008 on the law applicable to contractual obligations ("Rome I") [2008] O.J. L177/6, on which see below, paras 26-015 et seq.

[37a] Regulation (EC) 261/2004 establishing common rules on compensation and assistance to passengers in the event of denied boarding and of cancellation or long delay of flights [2004] O.J. L46/1 on which see *Chitty on Contracts* (33rd edn, 2018), Vol.II, paras 35-045—35-059.

[37b] The Law Applicable to Contractual Obligations and Non-Contractual Obligations (Amendment etc.) (EU Exit) Regulations 2019 (SI 2019/834) reg.10 (the Rome I Regulation) and see similarly reg.11 (amendment of Regulation 864/2007 of the European Parliament and of the Council law applicable to non-contractual obligations ("Rome II Regulation") [2007] O.J. L199/40).

[37c] Air Passenger Rights and Air Travel Organisers' Licensing (Amendment) (EU Exit) Regulations 2019 (SI 2019/278) reg.8 (in force on "exit day": reg.1(3)).

[37d] Regulation (EC) 2006/2004 on cooperation between national authorities responsible for the enforcement of the consumer protection law [2004] O.J. L364/1 (on which see below, para.14-313) is to be revoked by the Consumer Protection (Enforcement) Amendment etc.) (EU Exit) Regulations 2019 (SI 2019/203) reg.8.

[37e] Regulation (EU) No 524/2013 of the European Parliament and of the Council of 21 May 2013 on online dispute resolution for consumer disputes etc (Regulation on consumer ODR) on which see below, para.14-249) is to be revoked on "exit day" by SI 2018/1326 reg.10.

[37f] The 2015 Act implements Directive 1999/44/EC on certain aspects of the sale of consumer goods and associated guarantees [1999] O.J. L171/12 (principally in Pt 1 Ch.2 of the Act); Directive 93/13/EEC of April 5, 1993 on unfair terms in consumer contracts [1993] O.J. L95/29 (principally in Pt 2 of the Act) and certain aspects of Directive 2011/83/EU on consumer rights [2011] O.J. L304/64 (ss.11(4)–(6), 12; ss.36(3)–(4) and 37; and s.50(3)–(4) of the Act). On this see below, paras 14-034 et seq. and 14-130 et seq.

[37g] Consumer Protection (Amendment etc.) (EU Exit) Regulations 2018 (SI 2018/1326) reg.3 (in force on "exit day": reg.1(3)). The most significant of these amendments concern ss.32 and 74 of the 2015 Act at present governing contracts applying the law of a non-EEA State and, as amended, governing "contracts applying law of a country other than the UK".

[37h] The 1987 Act implements Directive 1985/374/EEC concerning liability for defective products, [1985] OJ L 210/29, and see below, paras 14-277 et seq. The 1987 Act is subject to relatively minor amendments on "exit day" by the Product Safety and Metrology etc. (Amendment etc.) (EU Exit) Regulations 2019 (SI 2019/696) reg.6 and Sch.3.

[37i] 2018 Act s.2(2) and see Explanatory Notes to 2018 Act para.77.

[37j] 2018 Act s.2(2) and see Explanatory Notes to 2018 Act para.77, which gives as an example domestic health and safety law implementing EU obligations made under powers in the Health and Safety at Work etc. Act 1974 rather than the European Communities Act 1972.

Further issues arising from Brexit

Replace paragraph with:

Three further issues in particular should be noted. First, the 2018 Act makes **14-008** provision to ensure that any remaining EU rights and obligations which are not preserved in the way just explained[38] continue to be recognized and available in domestic law after the UK leaves the EU and these include directly effective rights contained in the European Treaties themselves.[39] Secondly, on leaving the EU, the 2018 Act would end the general supremacy of EU law, but this would take effect only prospectively in the sense that any conflict between two pre-exit laws (one EU-derived, one not) would be resolved in favour of the EU-derived law.[40] Thirdly, provision is made for the future authoritative interpretation of the UK legislation whose source is EU legislation before and after the UK has left the EU ("exit day"). For this purpose a distinction is drawn between the case law of, or principles laid down by, the Court of Justice of the EU *before* and *after* the UK's leaving the EU. As regards the former, "retained EU law"[41] is in principle to be interpreted "in accordance with any retained case law and any retained general principles of EU law[42], and, having regard (among other things) to the limits, immediately before exit day, of EU competences".[43] However, the Act then provides that "the Supreme Court is not bound by any retained EU case law"[44] and explains that "[i]n deciding whether to depart from any retained EU case law, the Supreme Court ... must apply the same test as it would apply in deciding whether to depart from its own case law."[45] As the Government's second white paper earlier foresaw, this would therefore treat "retained EU case law" as "normally binding" but it would allow the Supreme Court to depart from it "when it appears right to do so".[46] As regards the position of EU case law and principles after the UK has left the EU, the Act provides that "[a] court or tribunal ... is not bound by any principles laid down, or any decisions made, on or after exit day by the European Court"[47] but adds that, subject to qualifications which are there set out, "a court or tribunal may have regard to anything done on or after exit day by the European Court, another EU entity or the EU so far as it is relevant to any matter before the court or tribunal." Although this form of words is more positive than the equivalent provision in the 2017 Bill as drafted, it still means that UK courts would not be required even to *consider* case law of the Court of Justice made after exit day, though they may do so if they consider it appropriate.[48-49] In this respect, the position will differ from the duty of UK courts under the Human Rights Act 1998 s.2(1) of which provides that in determining a question which has arisen in connection with a right under the European Convention on Human Rights a court "must take into account any ... judgment, decision, declaration or advisory opinion of the European Court of Human Rights."

[38] Above, para.14-007.

[39] 2018 Act s.4 and Explanatory Notes to 2018 Act, paras 92-99.

[40] 2018 Act s.5; Cm 9446 (March 2017) paras 2.19 to 2.20.

[41] See above.

[42] Defined in terms of temporal origin by s.6(7) of the 2018 Act as those which are made or laid down immediately before exit day: s.6(7) "retained EU case law" and "retained general principles of EU law".

[43] 2018 Act s.6(3).

[44] 2018 Act s.6(4)(a). Further provision is made as regards the (Scottish) High Court of Justiciary.

[45] 2018 Act s.6(5).

[46] Cm 9446 (March 2017) para.2.16 quoting the House of Lords Practice Statement (Judicial Precedent) of 1966, [1966] 1 W.L.R. 1234; and see also Explanatory Notes to 2018 Act, paras 113 and 115.

[47] 2018 Act s.6(1)(a).

[48-49] Explanatory Notes to 2018 Act, para.110.

Present position

Replace paragraph with:

However, until the UK leaves the EU (whether on 31 October 2019 or on some **14-008A** other date), the UK remains a full member of the EU and the status of EU law remains the same as it has been since the UK's becoming a Member State in 1972 and the enactment of the European Communities Act.[50] This chapter continues, therefore, to be written on the premise that the UK is a Member of the EU and that the status of EU law in the UK remains the same until such time as the UK leaves the EU, while noting, where relevant and practicable at this stage, the principal changes that will take effect on exit day.

[50] This follows from the remaining in force of the European Communities Act 1972 and is acknowledged by Cm.9446 (March 2017) para.1.10.

The particular role of UK courts in relation to EU consumer protection

Replace paragraph with:

At this point it is convenient to note a particular feature of the role of national **14-009** courts in relation to the rights for consumers which are provided by national legislation implementing EU consumer protection directives, for the European Court of Justice has held that the national court may have a duty to raise the issue of the consumer's rights of its own motion. This was seen clearly first in the context of the Unfair Terms in Consumer Contracts Directive 1993, where the European Court of Justice has held that a national court has a duty to raise of its own motion the question of the unfairness of a term in a consumer contract falling within the scope of that Directive,[51] provided that it "has available to it the legal and factual elements necessary for that task"[52] and that "the consumer, after having been informed of it by that court, does not intend to assert its unfair or non-binding status".[53] This duty in the national court is justified by the Court of Justice by the need to ensure that the consumer enjoys effective protection in view of the real risk that he is unaware of his rights or encounters difficulties in enforcing them.[54] More recently, this requirement has been subsumed under its general approach to the question whether a national court must raise an issue of EU law of its own motion under *Van Schijndel*,[55] according to which national procedural rules on this question must not be less favourable than those governing similar domestic actions nor render virtually impossible or excessively difficult the exercise of rights conferred by EU law.[56] The Court of Justice has also recognised such a duty in national courts in relation to the Consumer Credit Directive 1986[57] and the Doorstep Selling Directive 1985.[58] As will be seen, the Consumer Rights Act 2015 gives legislative expression to this duty of the national court to raise the unfairness of a term in a consumer contract of its own motion.[59] Moreover, recently, the Court of Justice has applied this approach to the Consumer Sales Directive 1999 and, in doing so, has appeared to go further in its requirements of national courts. In *Faber v Autobedrijf Hazet Ochten BV*,[60] the Court of Justice of the EU held in the context of the 1999 Directive, that:

> "it is, in principle, for the national court, for the purpose of identifying the legal rules applicable to a dispute which has been brought before it, to assign a legal classification to the facts and acts on which the parties rely in support of their claims."[61]

As a result, where national procedural rules do not provide the national court with the means of classifying a party to litigation as a "consumer" and where "that classification has not been expressly invoked by the parties themselves in support of their claims"[62]:

> "the principle of effectiveness requires a national court before which a dispute relating to a contract which may be covered by that directive has been brought to determine whether the purchaser may be classified as a consumer, even if the purchaser has not expressly claimed to have that status, as soon as that court has at its disposal the matters of law and of fact that are necessary for that purpose *or may have them at its disposal simply by making a request for clarification.*"[63]

For this purpose, the Court of Justice held that it is irrelevant whether or not a consumer is assisted by a lawyer.[64] This judgment makes clear that a court must in principle consider the possibility of a party to litigation being a "consumer" for the purposes of those provisions of the 2015 Act which implement the 1999 Directive, as well as those provisions in Pt 2 relating to unfair contract terms for which this duty is expressly stated by the Act.[65] But, secondly, and more radically from the point of view of English law, where a national court cannot on the facts as otherwise available to it determine whether a case before it falls within the scope of national legislation implementing an EU consumer protection directive, this judgment appears to require the national court to request a party to clarify the factual position.[66]

---

[51] *Océano Grupo Editorial SA v Murciano Quintero* (C-240/98 to C-244/98) [2000] E.C.R. I-4941; *Mostaza Claro v Centro Móvil Milenium SL* (C-168/05) [2006] E.C.R. I-10421. On this case law see generally *Chitty on Contracts*, 33rd edn (2018) paras 38–329 to 38–333.

[52] *Pannon GSM Zrt v Erzsébet Sustikné Györfi* (C-243/08) [2009] E.C.R. I-4713 at [32]; *Bucura v SC Bancpost SA* (C-348/14) of 9 July 2015 at [44].

[53] *Pannon GSM Zrt v Erzsébet Sustikné Györfi* (C-243/08) [2009] E.C.R. I-4713 at [33] and see similarly at [35].

[54] *Océano Grupo Editorial SA v Murciano Quintero* (C-240/98 to C-244/98) [2000] E.C.R. I-4941 at [26].

[55] *Van Schijndel v Stichting Pensioenfonds voor Fysiotherapeuten* (C-430/93 and C-431/93) [1995] E.C.R. I-4705 esp. at 17; *Peterbroeck, Van Campenhout & Ci e SCS v Belgium* (C-312/-9) [1995] E.C.R. I-4615; *Heemskerk BV and Firma Schaap v Productschap Vee en Vlees* (C-455/06) [2008] E.C.R. I-8763. For a comparative discussion see Whittaker in Leczykiewicz and Weatherill (eds) *The Involvement of EU Law in Private Relationships* (2013), Ch.6.

[56] *Asturcom Telecommunicaciones SL v Rodriquez Nogueira* (C-40/08) [2009] E.C.R. I-9579; *Banco Español de Crédito, SA v Calderón Camino* (C-618/10) of 14 June 2012.

[57] *Rampion v Franfinance SA* (C-429/05) [2007] E.C.R. I-8017; Directive 87/102/EEC [1987] O.J. L 42/48 (replaced by Directive 2008/48/EC on consumer credit [2008] O.J. L133/66 on which see para.14-321); *Radlinger v Finway a.s.* (C-377/14) [2016] 3 C.M.L.R. 28 at [62]–[74] (information duties under Directive 2008/48/EC Art.10). A. G. Kokott has argued that, where relevant to the fairness of a term of a consumer contract under the Unfair Terms in Consumer Contracts Directive 1993, a national court has an obligation to raise the unfairness of any *commercial practice* within the meaning of the Unfair Commercial Practices Directive 2005: *Margarit Panicello v Hernández Martinez* (C-503/15) A.G. Opinion of 15 September 2016 at [127]–[128]. The CJEU (judgment of 16 February 2017) did not comment on these issues as it ruled that it had no jurisdiction to hear the request for a preliminary ruling as it did not come from a "court or tribunal" within the meaning of TFEU Art.267.

[58] *Martín Martín v EDP Editores SL* (C-227/08) [2009] E.C.R. I-11939 at [18]; Directive 85/577/EEC, which was replaced by Directive 2011/83/EU on consumer rights [2011] O.J. L304/64 (Consumer Rights Directive 2011), as implemented in UK law by the Consumer Contracts (Information, Cancellation and Additional Charges Regulations 2013 (SI 2013/3134) on which see paras 14-195 et seq.

[59] 2015 Act s.71, below, para.14-152.

[60] *Faber v Autobedrijf Hazet Ochten BV* (C-497/13) of 4 June 2015.

[61] *Faber v Autobedrijf Hazet Ochten BV* (C-497/13) of 4 June 2015 at [38].

[62] *Faber v Autobedrijf Hazet Ochten BV* (C-497/13) of 4 June 2015 at [41].

[63] *Faber v Autobedrijf Hazet Ochten BV* (C-497/13) of 4 June 2015 at [46] (emphasis added).

[64] *Faber v Autobedrijf Hazet Ochten BV* (C-497/13) of 4 June 2015 at [47].

[65] 2015 Act s.71.

[66] cf. the more cautious approach of A. G. Sharpston, advising that the national court should not have a duty to go beyond the ambit of the dispute as defined by the parties and not, therefore, where the legal and factual elements are neither already part of the file or are obtainable in accordance with *national* procedural law: Opinion in *Faber* (C-227/08) of 27 November 2014, esp. at [70] to [73].

2. Rights Under the Civil Law: the Consumer Rights Act 2015

(a) The development of the legislation

Replace title footnote 101 with:

Consumer Sales Directive of 1999[101]

[101] Directive 1999/44/EC on certain aspects of the sale of consumer goods and associated guarantees **14-013** [1999] O.J. L171/12 (Consumer Sales Directive or 1999 Directive). For discussion of the Directive and its implementation, see Bianca and Grundmann (eds), *EU Sales Directive* (2002); Whittaker, *Liability for Products* (2005), Ch.19; Willett, Morgan-Taylor and Naidoo, [2004] J.B.L. 94; and *DTI Consultation Papers on the Sale of Goods Directive* of January 4, 2001 and February 26, 2002; Watterson, (2001) 9 Euro. Rev. of Private Law 197; Twigg-Flesner and Bradgate, [2000] Web J. C.L.1; Twigg-Flesner, [1999] Consum. L.J. 177. The Directive had its origins in a much more ambitious *Green Paper on Guarantees for Consumer Goods and After-Sales Services* COM (93) 509 final. For comments on an earlier draft, see the Report of the House of Lords Select Committee on the European Communities, *Consumer Guarantees* (1996–97 H.L. 57); Bradgate, [1995] Consum. L.J. 94; Beale and Howells, (1997) 12 J.C.L. 21; Shears, Zollers and Hurd, [2000] J.B.L. 262. The scope of the Directive and various issues which arise in relation to it, including the position with respect to recurring defects, the burden of proof and remedies, were considered by the Commission's Green Paper on the Review of the Consumer Acquis COM (2006) 744 final (2007/C 61/01). The Commission had originally proposed that Directive 1999/44/EC be repealed and replaced (Proposal for a Directive of the European Parliament and of the Council on consumer rights COM (2008) 614/3) published on 8 October 2008), but this aspect of the proposal was not proceeded with and was replaced by limited reporting requirements: see Directive 2011/83/EU on consumer rights Art.33. However, in 2019, the EU enacted Directive (EU) 2019/771 of the European Parliament and of the Council of 20 May 2019 on certain aspects concerning contracts for the sale of goods, etc [2019] O.J. L 136/28 which will revoke and replace the 1999 Directive, on this see below, para.14-022.

(b) Overview of the 2015 Act

Introduction

After "of "digital content").", add new footnote 119a:

[119a] On the UK's leaving the EU on "exit day" (on which see generally, above, paras 14-006 et seq.), **14-016** the 2015 Act is due to be amended as noted below where relevant: see 2015 Act ss.32 (below, para.26-111), 59 (below, para.14-072), 73 (below, para.14-141) and 74 (below, para.26-111) (amendments to be made by the Consumer Protection (Amendment etc.) (EU Exit) Regulations 2018 (SI 2018/1326) reg.3) and Sch.5 (Investigatory Powers etc.) (below, para.14-176) amendments to be made by the Consumer Protection (Enforcement) (Amendment etc.) (EU Exit) Regulations 2019 (SI 2019/203) reg.4; Consumer Rights Act 2015 (Enforcement) (Amendment) Order 2019 (SI 2019/1074) arts 2 and 3 (in force 23 July 2019).

Temporal application of Pts 1 and 2 of the 2015 Act

Replace footnote 151 with:

[151] The Consumer Rights Act 2015 (Commencement No.3, Transitional Provisions, Savings and **14-021** Consequential Amendments) Order 2015 (2015/1630) Art.3 brought into force the relevant sections of Pts 1 and 2 of the Act (as there specified) on 1 October 2015, though Art.4 (as amended by SI 2016/484) made an exception as regards Pt 1 Ch.4's provisions governing services contracts which did not apply to "consumer transport services" (as defined by the Order) until 1 October 2016. Article 6(1) of Order 2015/1630 provides that the provisions brought into force on 1 October 2015 do not apply to any contract entered into before 1 October 2015 which would, apart from its provisions, be covered by Pts

1 or 2 nor to any notice provided or communicated before 1 October 2015 which would constitute a "consumer notice" and so be covered by Pt 2 of the Act. Article 6(3) of the 2015 Order therefore preserves the effect of the amendments to the law required by the Sale and Supply of Goods to Consumers Regulations 2002 (especially as regards the Unfair Contract Terms Act 1977 and the Sale of Goods Act 1979 on which see above, para.14-014) in relation to any contract entered before 1 October 2015 despite the revocation of those Regulations by the Act; and Art.6(4) preserves the effect of the Unfair Terms in Consumer Contracts Regulations 1999 in relation to "any contract or notice relating to any contract" entered into before 1 October 2015 which is provided or communicated before 1 October 2015 and which would otherwise be covered by Pts 1 or 2 of the Act, despite the revocation of those Regulations by the 2015 Act.

New EU Directives on contracts for the sale of goods and on contracts for the supply of digital content

Replace paragraph (including title, above) with:

14-022   In May 2019, the EU enacted directives governing contracts of sale of goods and contracts for the supply of digital content both of which require implementation by Member States by 1 July 2021 so as to apply from 1 January 2022. The Directive on aspects of the law governing sales of goods[152] repeals the Consumer Sales Directive 1999[153] and, if the UK were still a Member State at the relevant time,[154] would require it to amend Ch.2 of Pt 1 of the 2015 Act so as to accord with its new requirements.[155] The directive on certain aspects concerning contracts for the supply of digital content and digital services[156] is new to EU law, and, subject to the same condition, would require the amendment of Ch.3 of Pt 1 of the 2015 Act.[156a] Both directives require "full harmonization"[156b] and this would make their implementation in English law more difficult. On the other hand, even if the UK were no longer a Member State on 1 July 2021, it could decide to amend the 2015 Act in the light of the directives provisions.

[152] Directive (EU) 2019/771 of the European Parliament and of the Council of 20 May 2019 on certain aspects concerning contracts for the sale of goods, etc [2019] O.J. L 136/28 ("Directive (EU) 2019/771").

[153] Directive (EU) 2019/771 Art.23.

[154] See above, paras 14-006 et seq.

[155] On this law see below, paras 14-052 et seq.

[156] Directive (EU) 2019/770 of the European Parliament and of the Council of 20 May 2019 [2019] O.J. L.136/1 ("Directive (EU) 2019/770").

[156a] On this law, see below, paras 14-113—14-117.

[156b] Directive (EU) 2019/771 art.4; Directive (EU) 2019/770 art.4.

(c)   Parties to "consumer contracts"

"Consumer" in the 2015 Act

Replace footnote 168 with:

14-025   [168] It is not clear whether in EU law a person contracting *mainly* but not wholly for purposes outside his or her business or profession counts as a "consumer" for the purposes of the 1993 and the 1999 Directives. The decision of the ECJ in *Gruber v Bay Wa AG* (C-464/01) [2005] E.C.R. I-439 at [54] in the context of the Brussels Convention on jurisdiction and the enforcement of judgments in civil or commercial matters 1968 Art.13 suggests that such a person does not, but it is submitted that the CJEU is likely to distinguish *Gruber* on the basis that it relates to special (and therefore exceptional) jurisdiction under the Convention and is likely instead to follow the 2011 Directive's recital 17 interpretative lead and hold that the definition of "consumer" in EU consumer protection directives also protects persons acting mainly for non-business purposes: see to this effect Advocate General Crux Villalón in *Costea v SC Volksbank România SA* (C-110/14) of 23 April 2015 esp. at [35]–[47] (The CJEU in its judgment of 3 September 2015 did not address this issue). cf. *Schrems v Facebook Ireland Ltd.* (C-498/16) of 25 January 2018 in which the CJEU appears to be moving towards including as a "consumer" a person who acts predominantly for non-business purposes, on which see *Chitty on Contracts*, 33rd edn (2018), Vol.II para.38–037.

English case law on "consumer" under the 1999 Regulations

Replace footnote 195 with:

195 *Maple Leaf Macro Volatility Master Fund v Rouvroy* [2009] EWHC 257 (Comm) at [209] and [270]. **14-027** The Brussels Convention on jurisdiction and the enforcement of judgements in civil and commercial matters 1968 Art.13 is now replaced by Regulation (EU) 1215/2012 of 12 December 2012 on jurisdiction and the recognition and enforcement of judgments in civil and commercial matters (recast) (the Brussels Ibis Regulation) Art.17. In commenting on the contrast between the *Apostolakis* and *Rouvroy* decisions, the HC in *AMT Futures Ltd v Mazillier, Dr Meier & Dr Guntner Rechnsanwaltsgesellschaft mbH* [2014] EWHC 1085 (Comm); [2015] 2 W.L.R. 187 at [58] considered that the dividing line between investors who count as "consumers" and those who do not "is likely to be heavily dependent on the circumstances of each individual and the nature and pattern of investment". (This point was not discussed on appeal to the CA or the SC: [2015] Civ 143; [2015] Q.B. 699; [2017] UKSC 13; [2017] 2 W.L.R. 853); *Ang v Reliantco Investments Ltd* [2019] EWHC 879 (Comm); [2019] 3 W.L.R. 161 at [23]–[70] especially at [63] and [65], the HC considering that a private individual making investments of her personal surplus wealth in the hope of generating good returns does not generally count as business activity, and expressly approving the view just noted of the HC in *AMT Futures Ltd*, though adding that the spread, regularity and value of investment activity cannot determine the issue as this would replace the non-business purpose test in the Regulation. See also the Opinion of A.G. Tanchev *Petruchová v FIBO Group Holdings Ltd* (C-2018/18) of 11 April 2019 at paras [58]–[63], explicitly preferring the approach of the HC in *Standard Bank London Ltd v Apostolakis (No.1)* [2000] I.L. Pr. 766 to that taken in *AMT Futures Ltd v Mazillier, Dr Meier & Dr Guntner Rechtsanwaltsgesellschaft mbH*. See also *Barclays Bank Plc v Kufner* [2008] EWHC 2319 at [31]; [2009] 1 All E.R. (Comm) 1 (person entering guarantee contract to acquire (through an offshore company) the component parts of a ship chartering business not a "consumer"); *Heifer International Inc v Christiansen* [2007] EWHC 3015 (TCC); [2008] All E.R. (D) 120 (Jan) at [243]–[250] (offshore company set up to purchase a residential property for its beneficial owners acted "for purposes outside [its] trade, business, or profession" when it entered contracts for the purchase and renovation of the property in question); *Wilson v MF Global UK Ltd* [2011] EWHC 138 (QB) at [129]–[131] (claimant trading through defendant in volatile financial market apparently held not a "consumer"); *Turner & Co (GB) Ltd v Abi* [2010] EWHC 2078 (QB); [2011] 1 C.M.L.R. 17 at [42] (shareholder director of a business commissioning an agent to sell the business not acting as a "consumer" but for the purposes of that business); *The Office of Fair Trading v Foxtons Ltd* [2009] EWHC 1681 (Ch); [2009] 29 E.G. 98 (C.S.) at [28] (owners of property seeking to lease it acted as "consumers" in entering a letting agency contract with an estate agent, although other "professional" or "commercial" landlords would not); *RTA (Business Consultants) Ltd v Bracewell* [2015] EWHC 630 (QB); [2015] Bus. L.R. 800 at [51]–[60] (person contracting with estate agent for the sale of his business not a "consumer" for the purposes of the Cancellation of Contracts made in a Consumer's Home or Place of Work etc Regulations 2008 (SI 2008/1816)); *R. (on the application of Bluefin Insurance Services Ltd v Financial Ombudsman Service Ltd* [2014] EWHC 3413 at [121]–[128] (director of company taking out a Directors and Officers Insurance Policy was not a "consumer" for the purposes of the Financial Ombudsman Service's jurisdiction (which was defined by reference, inter alia, to the definition of "consumer" in the 1993 Directive) as the insurance concerned his liability for acts in the course of his trade, business, or profession). cf. *Evans v Cherry Tree Finance Ltd* unreported, 13 April 2007 Ch. D. (concession that if any purposes for which the claimant contracted were outside his trade or business, then he was a consumer as defined by the regulations).

Consumers as the supplier of goods or services?

Replace paragraph with:

Typically, a "consumer" is a person who receives goods or services from a **14-029** trader,[211] but the standard definition of consumer (both in the 2015 Act and in the relevant EU directives[212]) is not itself restricted in this way, since an individual who acts for purposes that are (wholly or mainly[213]) outside his or her trade, business, craft or profession may equally *supply* goods or services to a trader, for example, in the case of a person who sells his or her second-hand car or jewellery to a dealer or a person who guarantees a relative's debts to a bank. In the case of the rules contained in Pt 1 of the 2015 Act, the position is clear, as they are stated clearly as applying only to contracts under which a trader supplies goods, digital content or services to the consumer.[214] This restriction makes sense, of course, given that these provisions create rights for *buyers* and other consumer customers.[215] On the other hand, the question whether the general controls on unfair terms in consumer contracts set out by Pt 2 of the 2015 Act[216] which implement the 1993 Directive can apply to individuals who supply goods or services to traders is left more open by the legislation. While the English version of Arts 1 and 2 of the 1993 Directive describe the business party to the contract as the "seller or supplier" and this implies an understanding of a consumer as "recipient", other language versions of these articles do not have this implication, instead using terms to describe the non-consumer party to the contract such as *professionnel* in the French and *Gewerbetreibender* in the German. Moreover, the justification for the protection of consumers against unfair terms by the Directive which is accepted by the Court of Justice of the EU is that "consumers" are weaker than traders in their bargaining power and level of knowledge and that this leads to their agreeing to terms whose content they cannot influence, and this justification applies with equal force to "consumers" who supply as to those who receive.[217] This was the main reason why the Court of Justice in *Tarcău v Banca Comercială Intesa Sanpaolo România SA*[218] rejected any restriction according to which the trader must supply the goods or service to the consumer, since the contracts to which the 1993 Directive applies are defined by reference to the capacity of the contracting parties, that is, according to whether or not they are acting for purposes relating to their trade, business or profession.[219] It held, therefore, that the Directive could apply to a contract under which a natural person (the potential "consumer") guaranteed the debt of a commercial company.[220] As a result, an individual acting for purposes that are wholly or mainly outside their trade, business, craft or profession who concludes a contract of sale of goods may be protected by the controls on unfair terms in Pt 2 of the 2015 Act, whether they do so as seller or as buyer.

[211] cf. "dealing as consumer" under the Unfair Contract Terms Act 1977 before this concept was abolished by the Consumer Rights Act 2015. Under the 1977 Act, a person might "deal as consumer" in supplying goods or services to a person contracting in the course of business: Treitel, *The Law of Contract*, 13th edn (Peel, 2012) para.7–053.

[212] i.e. 1993 Directive Art.2(b); 1999 Directive Art.1(2)(a); 2011 Directive Art.2(1).

[213] On this point, see above, para.14-025.

[214] 2015 Act ss.1(1), 3(1) ("goods contracts"), 33(1) and (2) ("digital content contracts"), 48(1) ("services contracts").

[215] The main exception to this is 2015 Act s.51's provision regarding the imposition of a reasonable price on the consumer under "services contracts": below, para.14-121.

[216] Below, para.14-130 et seq.

[217] cf. above, para.14-026.

[218] *Tarcău v Banca Comercială Intesa Sanpaolo România SA* (C-74/15) (Order of CJEU) of 19 November 2015. See also *Dumitraş v BRD Groupe Société Générale* (C-534/15) Order of the CJEU of 14 September 2016;*Bachman v FAER IFN SA* (C-535/16) (Order of the CJEU of 27 April 2017, available in French).

[219] *Tarcău v Banca Comercială Intesa Sanpaolo România SA* (C-74/15) (Order of CJEU) of 19 November 2015 at [23]. See similarly *Dumitraş v BRD Groupe Société Générale* (C-534/15) Order of the CJEU of 14 September 2016; *Bachman v FAER IFN SA* (C-535/16) (Order of the CJEU of 27 April 2017, available in French). See also *Harvey v Dunbar Assets Plc* [2017] EWCA Civ 60; [2017] Bus. L.R. 784 at [69]–[70].

[220] *Tarcău v Banca Comercială Intesa Sanpaolo România SA* (C-74/15) (Order of CJEU) of 19 November 2015 at [25].

"Trader"

Replace the second paragraph with:

Taken together these definitions follow the definition of "trader" in the Consumer **14-032** Rights Directive 2011[230] but also reflect the definition of "seller or supplier" in the 1993 Directive[231] and "seller" in the 1999 Directive.[232] One consequential advantage of using "trader" is that it avoids the implication that contracts by which consumers supply goods or services *to* traders are necessarily excluded from the controls on unfair contract terms.[233] The Court of Justice of the EU has held that the very similar definition of "trader" for the purposes of the Unfair Commercial Practices Directive 2005[234] is "particularly broad", not excluding "either bodies pursuing a task of public interest or those which are governed by public law" and must be determined "in relation to the related but diametrically opposed concept of 'consumer', which refers to any individual not engaged in commercial or trade activities".[235] And recently the Court of Justice has followed this earlier approach to the definition of "trader" for the purposes of the 1993 Directive.[236] As a result, "trader" is wide enough to include not-for-profit organisations, such as charities, mutual societies and cooperatives, where they carry on a business.[237] Moreover, there is no need for the contract to relate to the main activity of the would-be "trader".[237a] Finally, in *Kamenova* the question arose before the Court of Justice as to the circumstances in which a natural person who simultaneously offers to sell new and second-hand goods through a website may be classified as a "trader" for the purposes of the Unfair Commercial Practices Directive or the Consumer Rights Directive.[237b] This depends on whether that person acts "for purposes relating to his trade, business or profession", a question which requires a "case-by-case approach".[237c] For this purpose, the Court set out a non-exhaustive list of criteria for the context: whether the platform was organised and set up for profit; whether the seller had technical information and expertise relating to the products offered for sale not necessarily possessed by the consumer; whether the seller had a legal status enabling her to engage in commercial activities[237d] and the extent to which the online sale was connected to the seller's commercial or professional activity; whether the seller was subject to VAT; whether the seller, acting on behalf of a particular trader or on her own behalf or through another person acting in her name and on her behalf, received remuneration or an incentive (as in the case of "influencers"); whether the seller purchased new or second-hand goods in order to resell them, so as to make it a regular, frequent and/or simultaneous activity when compared to her usual commercial or business activity; whether the goods for sale were all of the same type or value, and, in particular, whether the offer was concentrated on a small number of goods.[237e] The Court explained that compliance with one or more of these criteria (such as selling with the view to profit) does not, in itself, mean that the online seller is a "trader".[237f]

[230] Directive 2011/83/EU on consumer rights O.J. L 304/64 Art.2(2); Explanatory Notes 2015 para.34.

[231] 1993 Directive Art.2(c).

[232] 1999 Directive Art.1(2)(c). One difference between the two definitions is that the Act refers expressly to a trader acting either "personally or through another person acting in the trader's name or on the trader's behalf", but it is submitted that such a situation should also be read into the definition in 1993 Directive Art.2(c). A "person" is sufficiently broad to include both a "natural" and "legal" person as specified by Art.2(c).

[233] cf. above, para.14-029.

[234] 2005 Directive Art.2(b).

[235] *BKK Mobil Oil Körperschaft des öffentlichen Rechts v Zentrale zur Bekämpfung unlauteren Wettbewerbs eV* (C-59/12) of 3 October 2013 at [32]–[33] citing by analogy *Shearson Lehman Hutton* (C-89–91) [1993] E.C.R. I-139 at 22 on the Brussels Convention Art.13 on jurisdiction and the enforcement of judgments in civil and commercial matters.

[236] *Šiba v Devėnas* (C-537/13) of 15 January 2015 and see also *Karel de Grote–Hogeschool Katholieke Hogeschool Antwerpen VZW v Kuijpers* (C-147/16) of 17 May 2018; *Pouvin and Dijoux v Electricite de France (EDF)* (C-590/17) EU:C:2019:23 of 21 March 2019 at paras [34]–[35].

[237] Explanatory Notes 2015 para.35.

[237a] *Pouvin and Dijoux v Electricite de France (EDF)* (C-590/17) EU:C:2019:23 of 21 March 2019 at paras [40]–[41] (employer whose main activity was the supply of energy rather than the provision of financial services held to be a "seller or supplier" under the 1993 Directive art.2(b) in relation to a contract of loan made to its employee and his spouse to finance the purchase of property for their private purposes).

[237b] *Komisiaza zashtita na potrebeitelite v Kamenova* (C-105/17) EU:C:2018:80 of 4 October 2018 ("*Kamenova* (C-105/17)") at [24].

[237c] *Kamenova* (C-105/17) at [36]–[37].

[237d] In some national laws, "commercial activities" (translating "*actes de commerce*") are defined by law and may be restricted to persons enjoying the status to do so.

[237e] *Kamenova* (C-105/17) at [37]–[38] following the Opinion of A.G. Szpunar at [50]–[51].

[237f] *Kamenova* (C-105/17) at [39]–[40].

Traders as "intermediaries" of non-traders

Replace footnote 247 with:

14-033 [247] See *Chitty on Contracts*, 33rd edn (2018), Vol.I para.31–063. The general law of agency applies to contract for the sale of goods: Sale of Goods Act 1979 s.62(2); above, para.3-002.

(d) Consumer rights in respect of goods contracts

(i) Introductory

Common law and equity

Replace footnote 331 with:

14-049 [331] See generally *Chitty on Contracts*, 33rd edn (2018), Vol.I Chs 7 and 8.

(ii) "Goods Contracts"

"Goods" and "digital content"

Replace paragraph with:

14-055 The 2015 Act defines "digital content" as "data which are produced and supplied in digital form"[360] and this may include software, music, computer games and applications (or "apps").[361]Chapter 3 of the Act applies both to contracts for a trader to supply digital content to a consumer for a price paid by the consumer and to contracts for a trader to supply digital content to a consumer where it is supplied free with goods or services or other digital content for which the consumer pays a price, and it is not generally available to consumers unless they have paid a price for it or for goods or services or other digital content.[362]Chapter 3 makes provision, inter alia, for dedicated statutory terms as to the satisfactory quality and fitness for particular purpose of digital content (modelled very broadly on those in "goods contracts") and for the consumer's rights to enforce the statutory terms.[363] It is clear, therefore, that a digital content contract within the meaning of Ch.3 may also be a "goods contract" within the meaning of Ch.2, that is, where both goods and digital content are supplied under the contract or where goods are supplied under the contract and digital content is supplied for free in the circumstances set out above. This reflects the general position provided by the 2015 Act governing "mixed contracts"[364] and is explicitly recognised by s.16 of the Act, which makes particular provision for the case where goods do not conform to the contract if the goods consist of an item that includes digital content and the digital content does not conform to the contract.[365] This regulatory overlap of the rules governing "goods contracts" and "digital content contracts" in the 2015 Act contrasts with the position under the Consumer Contracts (Information, Cancellation and Additional Charges) Regulations 2013, which distinguish between sales contracts (defined as relating to tangible moveable items, which may *include* digital content, as in the case of a CD) and contracts for the supply of digital content not in a tangible medium; the 2013 Regulations then regulate these two categories distinctly.[366]

[360] 2015 Act s.2(9).

[361] Explanatory Notes 2015 para.166. cf. the illustrations of "digital content" provided by the Consumer Rights Directive 2011 recital 19 and see also the different treatment of "digital content" under the Proposal for a Directive of the European Parliament and of the Council on certain aspects concerning contracts for the supply of digital content COM (2015) 634 final.

[362] 2015 Act s.33(1) and (2). On the other hand the category of "digital content contracts" in the 2013 Regulations (following the 2011 Directive) is broader, as there is no requirement there that the digital content be supplied for a price. This is reflected in the treatment of information supplied by the trader to the consumer: see 2013 Regulations regs 10(5) and 13(6) and also reg.9(3) (though not required by the 2011 Directive art.6(5)).

[363] 2015 Act ss.34–45. For detailed discussion of the law in the 2015 Act Ch.3, see *Chitty on Contracts*, 33rd edn (2018), Vol.II paras 38–540 to 38–566.

[364] 2015 Act s.1(4)–(6), above, para.14-038.

[365] Below, para.14-081. This overlap is also noted by the 2015 Act s.42(3) for the case where "an item including the digital content is supplied".

[366] SI 2013/3134 Regulations reg.5 "sales contract" and "goods". The distinctness of the regulation is found most clearly in reg.37 (supply of digital content during cancellation period). On the 2013 Regulations generally see below, para.14-195 et seq. cf. *Software Incubator Ltd v Computer Associates UK Ltd* [2016] EWHC 1587 (QB) at [35]–[69] holding that a contract for the supply of software may constitute a "sale of goods" for the purposes of the Commercial Agents (Council Directive) Regulations 1993 (SI 1993/3053), the court distinguishing the position in the law of sale of goods. On computer software and "goods" within the meaning of the 1979 Act see above, para.1-086.

Certain contracts for work and materials as "sales contract"

Replace paragraph (including title, above) with:

The 2015 Act includes within "sales contracts" certain contracts which would **14-057** traditionally be treated by English law as contracts for work and materials,[376] thereby implementing the Consumer Sales Directive 1999.[377] The 2015 Act therefore provides that a contract is a sales contract (whether or not it would be under its general definition[378]) "if under the contract—

(a) goods are to be manufactured or produced and the trader agrees to supply them to the consumer,

(b) on being supplied, the goods will be owned by the consumer, and

(c) the consumer pays or agrees to pay the price."[379]

So, for example, a contract under which a tailor produces a made-to-measure suit for a consumer is a sales contract.[380] On the other hand, the Court of Justice of the EU has confirmed that the Consumer Sales Directive 1999 does not apply to contracts for the provision of work and materials other than the two types of such contract which it specifically includes.[380a] First, the Directive specifically deems contracts of sale of goods to include "contracts for the supply of consumer goods to be manufactured or produced."[380b] Secondly, the Directive provides that "[a]ny lack of conformity resulting from incorrect installation of the consumer goods shall be deemed to be equivalent to lack of conformity of the goods if installation forms part of the contract of sale of the goods and the goods were installed by the seller or under his responsibility."[380c] This means that a contract of sale which includes an obligation to install on the part of the seller also falls within a "contract of sale of goods" within the meaning of the Directive.[380d] As regards both contracts for goods to be manufactured and for goods to be installed, the Court of Justice held that "in order for those categories of contract involving a supply of services to be classified as 'contracts of sale' within the meaning of that directive, the supply of services must be ancillary to the sale."[380e] This being the case, the 1999 Directive was held not extend to a contract for the renovation of a swimming pool even where this includes the supply of goods as the goods did not have to be manufactured by the would-be "seller".[380f] As noted earlier in this paragraph, the Consumer Rights Act deems contracts for goods to be manufactured or produced to be a "sales contract".[380g] In the case of contracts which require the installation of goods supplied, this installation forms part of the conformity of the goods, without providing that such a contract is one of sale rather than, notably, a contract for transfer of goods.[380h] Under the scheme of the 2015 Act, such a "non-conformity of the goods" gives rise to the four special rights for consumers as required by the 1999 Directive for the contracts within its scope.[380i] Moreover, to the extent that there is a services element within a contract for the supply of goods by a trader to a consumer, the provisions governing services contained in Ch.4 of Pt 1 of the Act may also apply.[380j]

[376] cf. above paras 1-031, 1-041 to 1-042 on the general position.

[377] 1999 Directive Art.1(4).

[378] This definition is provided in 2015 Act s.5(1), above, para.14-053.

[379] 2015 Act s.5(2).

[380] Explanatory Notes 2015 para.58.

[380a] *Schottelius v Seifert* (C 247/16) of 7 September 2017.

[380b] Consumer Sales Directive 1999 art.1(4).

[380c] Consumer Sales Directive 1999 art.2(5).

[380d] *Schottelius v Seifert* (C 247/16) at paras 36–37.

[380e] *Schottelius v Seifert* (C 247/16) at para.38.

[380f] *Schottelius v Seifert* (C 247/16) at para. 46.

[380g] Consumer Rights Act 2015 s.5(2).

[380h] 2015 Act s.15 and see below, para.14-080. On contracts for transfer of goods see 2015 Act s.8 and below, para.14-061.

[380i] 2015 Act s.19(4); 1999 Directive art.3 and see below, paras 14-067 and 14-069.

[380j] 2015 Act s.1(6) which specifically refers to contracts under which goods are installed as a "mixed contract": see above, paras 14-038 (mixed contracts) and below, 14-118 et seq. (services contracts).

"Sales contracts", reservation of title and the *Res Cogitans*

After "they were not", replace " "transparent" " with:

14-063   "transparent and prominent"

Replace paragraph with:

14-064   However, if the relevant contract term or terms fell within the core exclusion in s.64 or, even if they did not, were found to be fair under the test in s.62, the contract would fall to be classified for the purposes of the 2015 Act Pt 1 on its terms as agreed, that is, a contract providing for possession of goods to be given, coupled with a legal entitlement to use or consume them before the property in them is transferred upon payment. Given that the forms of words of the definitions of "sales contracts" under Ch.2 of Pt 1 of the 2015 Act and contracts of sale of goods under the 1979 Act are all but identical, it may be thought that the Supreme Court's decision in the *Res Cogitans* holds good for the purposes of "sales contracts" under the 2015 Act.[406a] It is submitted, however, that this is by no means necessarily the case. It will be recalled that a number of provisions of Ch.2 of Pt 1 of the 2015 Act implement the Consumer Sales Directive 1999,[407] and that the significance of "sales contracts" to which Ch.2 applies must therefore be understood to include as a minimum those contracts contained within the "autonomous" European meaning of "sales of consumer goods".[408] For this purpose, it is likely that the Court of Justice of the EU would not follow the UK Supreme Court in holding that a consumer contract providing for possession of goods to be given, coupled with a legal entitlement to use or consume them before the property in them is transferred upon payment fell outside the European meaning of "consumer sales contracts", as the Court of Justice would seek to ensure that the rights for consumers which the 1999 Directive provides could not be avoided by a trader reserving for itself title in the goods. For this purpose, the Court of Justice is likely to note that the rights for consumers provided by the 1999 Directive are mandatory for the contracting parties, as it provides that any contract terms "which directly or indirectly waive or restrict the rights resulting from this Directive shall, as provided for by national law, not be binding on the consumer".[409] Although formally this provision applies only to contracts which fall within the scope of the Directive (which is the question which the Court of Justice would have to decide), the mandatory character of the consumer's rights provided by the 1999 Directive is likely to be seen by the court as arguing against a trader's characterisation of the contract which is in substance one of sale in a way which avoids its application. If EU law does indeed require the definition of "sales of consumer goods" under the 1999 Directive to include consumer contracts providing for possession of goods to be given by the trader to the consumer, coupled with a legal entitlement in the consumer to use or consume them before the property in them is transferred upon payment, then a UK court would have to include them within the definition of "sales contracts" for the purposes of Ch.2 of Pt 1 of the 2015 Act even though they are not "contracts of sale of goods" within the meaning of the 1979 Act.

[406a] See Low (2018) J.B.L. 229 at 251 who observes that such a contract is "presumably" not a "sales contract" under the definition of "sales contract" under the 2015 Act s.5.

[407] In particular, ss.9–11, 19, 23–24 and 31(1). Other provisions (notably, ss.11(4)–(6), 12, 28 and 29 implement aspects of the Consumer Rights Directive 2011, below, paras 14-076, 14-106 to 14-109.

[408] Consumer Sales Directive 1999 Art.1.

[409] Consumer Sales Directive 1999 Art.7(1).

(iii)   The statutory terms and "goods conforming to a contract"

Goods to be of satisfactory quality

Replace footnote 469 with:

[469] 2015 Act s.59(1); 1999 Directive Art.1(2)(d). It will be noted that the definition of "producer" for the purposes of the 2015 Act is stated as being "in relation to goods or digital content", unlike the   **14-072**

Directive's reference to "goods". This difference reflects the fact that the Directive applies only to the "conformity" of goods, whereas the 2015 Act makes parallel provision to s.9 on "goods contracts" in s.34 on "digital content contracts": see in particular, 2015 Act s.34(5)–(7) and below, para.14-115. On the UK's exit from the EU (on which see above, paras 14-006 et seq.), in the definition of "producer" in s.59(1) of the 2015 Act, the "United Kingdom" will be substituted for the "European Economic Area": Consumer Protection (Amendment etc.) (EU Exit) Regulations 2018 (SI 2018/1326) regs 1(3) and 3(3).

Information as to the "main characteristics of the goods"

Replace footnote 494 with:

14-076 494 2015 Act s.11(4)–(5). In contrast to the general position, for the purposes of s.11(4)–(5) goods contracts include contracts where the goods are second-hand goods and are sold at public auction: 2015 Act s.11(6) referring to s.2(5) and (6). Until 2015, similar provision was made by the 2013 Regulations themselves (reg.9(3) (on-premises contracts); reg.10(5)(off-premises contracts) and reg.13(6) (distance contracts), but on the coming into force of the 2015 Act, these provisions were amended so as to apply only to contracts for "the supply of digital content other than for a price paid by the consumer", a category of contract which falls outside Pt 1 of the 2015 Act (and specifically its Ch.3) but within the scope of the 2011 Directive and therefore of the 2013 Regulations: see 2013 Regulations regs 9(3), 10(5) and 13(6) as amended SI 2015/1629 regs 4–6.

Other pre-contractual information included in contract

Replace paragraph with:

14-077 Section 12 of the 2015 Act applies to all goods contracts[498] and provides that where a trader was required to provide information under the Consumer Contracts (Information, Cancellation and Additional Charges) Regulations 2013[499] any of that information that was provided by the trader other than the information concerning the main characteristics of the contract[500] "is to be treated as included as a term of the contract".[501] Section 12(3) provides that a change to any of that information, made before entering into the contract or later, is not effective unless expressly agreed between the consumer and the trader.[502] As will be seen, the 2015 Act therefore distinguishes between information concerning the main characteristics of the contract (which becomes a statutory term under s.11) and other information (which becomes a statutory term under s.12). The significance of this treatment lies in the differences in remedies available for breach of the terms in the two sections. As has been seen, breach of a statutory term inserted by s.11 makes available (subject to their own conditions) the short-term right to reject, the right to repair or replacement and the right to a price reduction or the final right to reject,[503] as well as any "other remedies" available under the general law.[504] However, breach of any statutory term inserted by s.12 does not render the goods "non-conforming" within the meaning of s.19.[505] Instead, s.19(5) provides that:

> "If the trader is in breach of a term that section 12 requires to be treated as included in the contract, the consumer has the right to recover from the trader the amount of any costs incurred by the consumer as a result of the breach, up to the amount of the price paid or the value of other consideration given for the goods."

This is clearly a very much more restricted remedy than the set of remedies available in respect of breach of the terms treated as included more generally[506] as it is restricted to "the amount of any costs incurred by the consumer as a result of the breach." The notion of "costs" is not explained by the Act, but it is helpful to recall that s.12 concerns the provision of information other than relating to the main characteristics of the goods, and this includes or may include a variety of matters, including the identity of the trader and its address, the total price of the goods, and other charges, the trader's complaints handling arrangements.[507] Where this information becomes a term of the contract under s.12, a trader's failure to abide by the information as provided would constitute breach of the term. The idea of recovery by the consumer for "any costs incurred ... as a result of the breach" appears therefore to be intended to provide a simple capped remedy for the consumer's out-of-pocket expenses incurred in these circumstances. The Explanatory Notes to the Act state that this new remedy could be supplemented by a claim for damages under the general law where the consumer has incurred costs or losses above this amount,[508] but if this is right, it is difficult to see what practical role the restriction in s.19(5) is intended to play.[509]

[498] On which see above, para 14-052 et seq.

[499] SI 2013/3134 reg.9 (on-premises contracts), reg.10 (off-premises contracts) and reg.13 (distance contracts). As earlier noted, while the 2011 Directive Art.6(1)(a) and (5) requires information provided before the conclusion of off-premises and distance contracts to form part of the contract, it does not make the same requirement as regards information provided by the trader in respect of other contracts (governed by Art.5 and termed "on-premises contracts" by the 2013 Regulations) but the 2013 Regulations reg.9 and the 2015 Act (as is explained in the text) do so require.

[500] Any information which concerns the main characteristics of the goods which is to be treated as a term of the contract under 2015 Act s.11(4), as noted above, para.14-076.

[501] 2015 Act s.12(1) and (2). Until 2015, similar provision was made by the 2013 Regulations themselves (reg.9(3) (on-premises contracts); reg.10(5)(off-premises contracts) and reg.13(6) (distance contracts), but on the coming into force of the 2015 Act, these provisions were amended so as to apply only to contracts for "the supply of digital content other than for a price paid by the consumer", a category of contract which falls outside Pt 1 of the 2015 Act (and specifically its Ch.3) but within the scope of the 2011 Directive and therefore of the 2013 Regulations: see 2013 Regulations regs 9(3), 10(5) and 13(6) as amended by SI 2015/1629 regs 4–6

[502] Until 2015, similar provision was made by the 2013 Regulations themselves (reg.9(3) (on-premises contracts); reg.10(5)(off-premises contracts) and reg.13(6) (distance contracts), but on the coming into force of the 2015 Act, these provisions were amended so as to apply only to contracts for "the supply of digital content other than for a price paid by the consumer", a category of contract which falls outside Pt 1 of the 2015 Act (and specifically its Ch.3) but within the scope of the 2011 Directive and therefore of the 2013 Regulations: see 2013 Regulations regs 9(3), 10(5) and 13(6) as amended by SI 2015/1629 regs 4–6

[503] 2015 Act s.19(3) above, paras 14-067 and 14-076.

[504] 2015 Act s.19(9), as explained and restricted by s.19(10)–(13), below, para.14-103.

[505] This follows from the terms of s.19(1)(a) and s.19(3) which do not include s.12 in their lists of relevant terms.

[506] i.e. under 2015 Act ss.9–11, 13 and 14 and in respect of non-conformity under s.16.

[507] 2013 Regulations reg.9(1) ("on-premises contracts" referring to the categories of information listed by Sch.1); ss.10(1) and 13(1) ("off-premises contracts" and "distance contracts" respectively, referring to the categories of information listed by Sch.2). On these see below, paras 14-198, 14-203 and 14-207.

[508] 2015 Act ss.19(9)(a), (10) and 11(a); Explanatory Notes 2015 para.89. A consumer could not, however, rely on the general law so as to terminate the contract for breach of any terms inserted by s.12: 2015 Act s.19(12)–(13). The Explanatory Notes 2015 para.89 explain in relation to the recovery of costs that where there is other consideration given instead of a price, the cap on the recoverable costs would be the value of that consideration.

[509] On the other hand, if the Explanatory Notes are wrong and the consumer's claim for compensation for breach (including by way of damages) is restricted as s.19(5) suggests, there would be a question whether the Act properly implements the 2011 Directive Art.6(5).

Goods not conforming to contract if digital content does not conform

Replace paragraph with:

Part 1 of the 2015 Act defines "digital content" as "data which are produced and **14-081** supplied in digital form"[530] and distinguishes generally between "contracts for a

[159]

trader to supply digital content to a consumer" (which are regulated specially by Pt 1 Ch.3[531]) and contracts where the digital content is included within goods, which may be regulated by Ch.2 of the Act.[532] This appears from s.16(1) of the Act which provides explicitly that:

"Goods (whether or not they conform otherwise to a contract to supply goods) do not conform to it if—

(a) the goods are an item that includes digital content, and
(b) the digital content does not conform to the contract to supply that content (for which see section 42(1))."

As a result, where digital content is included within goods (for example, a CD) and the digital content does not conform to the contract,[533] then the goods themselves will not conform to the contract. This position reflects the likely position under the wider law under the 1979 Act, where, for example, the lack of satisfactory quality or reasonable fitness for particular purpose of digital content included within the goods are likely to render the goods themselves not satisfactory or reasonably fit, subject to the considerations more generally which these implied terms themselves require.[534] Under the 2015 Act, non-conformity of digital content included within goods leads to the non-conformity of the goods themselves and this means that the consumer may enjoy (subject to their own conditions) the short-term right to reject, the right to repair or replacement and the right to a price reduction or the final right to reject,[535] as well as any "other remedies" available under the general law.[536] This range of remedies includes the short-term and final right to reject which are not available under Ch.3 in respect of digital content supplied other than where included in goods.[537]

[530] 2015 Act s.2(9).

[531] cf. below, paras 14-113 to 14-117. The 2015 Act s.33(4) further specifies that "[a] trader does not supply digital content to a consumer for the purposes of this Part merely because the trader supplies a service by which digital content reaches the consumer."

[532] cf. 2015 Act s.42(3) which refers to s.16 as applying "if an item including digital content is supplied."

[533] For this purpose, s.42(1) of the 2015 Act provides that digital content does not conform to the contract where it does not conform to the statutory terms imposed by s.34 (satisfactory quality), s.35 (fit for particular purpose) and s.36 (description).

[534] *St Albans City and DC v International Computers Ltd* [1997] F.S.R.251 at 266.

[535] 2015 Act s.19(1)(b) and s.19(3) referring to ss.20 and 22 (short-term right to reject, on which see below, paras 14-094 and 14-097); s.23 (right to repair or replacement, on which see below, para.14-098) and s.24 (the right to a price reduction or the final right to reject, on which see below, para.14-099 to 14-100).

[536] 2015 Act s.19(9)(b), as explained and restricted by s.19(10)–(13), below, para.14-103.

[537] On which see 2015 Act s.42(2) and see below, para.14-116.

Privity of contract

Replace footnote 543 with:

14-083   [543] Contracts (Rights of Third Parties) Act 1999 s.1(1) and (2). On the 1999 Act generally see *Chitty on Contracts*, 33rd edn (2018), Vol.1 paras 18-090 et seq.

No other terms "treated as included" about quality or fitness except express terms

After "meaning of s.18(1)", replace "." with:

, as well as to any other stipulation (requirement) as to the goods (such as their **14-084** place of manufacture or their colour).

Rights for consumer in respect of goods failing to conform to requirements stated in the contract

Replace footnote 561 with:

[561] See above, paras 10-024 et seq and *Chitty on Contracts*, 33rd edn (2018), Vol.I paras 24-039 to 24- **14-085** 041.

(iv)   The scheme of remedies for the consumer

Right to price reduction or final right to reject

Replace paragraph with:

These rights reflect the second level of remedies required by the 1999 Directive **14-099** and formerly implemented in UK law by the 2002 Regulations.[619] Under the right to a price reduction, the consumer may require the trader to reduce the price[620] which the consumer is required to pay under the contract "by an appropriate amount"[621] (and the legislation makes clear that this may lead to the extinction of the price,[622]) and/or to receive a refund from the trader for anything already paid by the consumer above such a reduced amount.[623] In this respect, neither the 1999 Directive nor the 2015 Act explain the precise purpose of a price reduction (beyond referring to reduction by an "appropriate amount"[623a]), but it would seem that (following its origins in the civil law[623b]) in general the reduction should reflect the difference in value between what was received by the consumer compared to what he should have received if the goods had conformed to the contract.[623c] However, s.24(5) of the Act provides that:

> "A consumer who has the right to a price reduction and the final right to reject may only exercise one (not both), and may only do so in one of these situations—
>
> (a)   after one repair or one replacement, the goods do not conform to the contract;
> (b)   because of section 23(3) the consumer can require neither repair nor replacement of the goods; or
> (c)   the consumer has required the trader to repair or replace the goods, but the trader is in breach of the requirement of section 23(2)(a) to do so within a reasonable time and without significant inconvenience to the consumer."[624]

For the purposes of subs.(5)(a) there has been a repair or replacement if the consumer has requested or agreed to repair or replacement of the goods (whether in relation to one fault or more than one), and the trader has delivered goods to the consumer, or made goods available[625] to the consumer, in response to the request or agreement.[626]

[619]   1999 Directive Art.3(5)–(6).

[620]   "Price reduction" may also apply to anything else the consumer is required to transfer under the contract: s.24(1) and (2). However, where this is the case, the right to a price reduction does not apply where what the consumer is (before the reduction) required to transfer under the contract (whether or not already transferred) cannot be divided up so as to enable the trader to receive or retain only the

reduced amount, or if anything transferred which cannot be the subject of substitution cannot be given back in its original state: s.24(4) referring to s.20(12) in this respect. While in some circumstances the general law may reach the same result as the remedy of price reduction by way of a claim for damages (the relevant measure being the value of the goods at the time of delivery and the value they would have been if they had been as contracted under s.53(3) of the 1979 Act), this measure of damages applies only prima facie and may be displaced, e.g. where it was in the contemplation of the parties that the goods would be sold on: *Bence Graphics International Ltd v Fasson UK Ltd* [1998] Q.B. 87 on which see below, paras 17-057 and 17-082.

[621] 2015 Act s.24(1)(a).

[622] This is the effect of s.24(2)'s provision that "[t]he amount of the reduction may, where appropriate, be the full amount of the price or whatever the consumer is required to transfer". From the fact that the 2015 Act s.42 does not allow a right of rejection in respect of digital content, it would appear that the drafters of the Act took the view that there can be no right to reject where the consumer has nothing physical to hand back. Where the consumer is in this position as regards a "goods contract", a consumer could recover a 100% reduction in price.

[623] 2015 Act s.24(1). Section 24(3) provides that s.20(10)–(17) applies to the consumer's right to receive a refund as outlined above, para.14-095.

[623a] 1999 Directive art.3(2) and (5) ("appropriate reduction"); 2015 Act s.24(1)(a) (reduction by an "appropriate amount").

[623b] In Roman law, the *actio quanti minoris* in sale, which is reflected, e.g., in art.1644 of the French *Code civil*. Cf. the "right to a discount" under the 2008 Regulations, below, para.14-298.

[623c] Cf. *Principles, Definitions and Model Rules of European Private Law, Draft Common Frame of Reference (DCFR)* prepared by the Study Group for a European Civil Code and the Research Group on EC Private Law (Acquis Group) (2010) art.III.-3:601 Right to reduce price. See also below, para.14-126 in relation to the 2015 Act s.56 (price reduction in relation to services contracts). See also Directive (EU) 2019/771 of the European Parliament and of the Council of 20 May 2019 on certain aspects concerning contracts for the sale of goods, etc [2019] O.J. L.136/28 (which repeals and replaces the Consumer Sales Directive 1999, above, para.14-022), art.15 of which provides that "[t]he reduction of price shall be proportionate to the decrease in the value of the goods which were received by the consumer compared to the value the goods would have if they were in conformity".

[624] On which see above, para.14-098. The County Court at Nottingham has held that a requirement made by a consumer to repair a car by the car dealer can satisfy the condition set by s.24(5), even though the car was sold by the dealer's associated finance house (the "trader" for this purpose), as long as the dealer acted on behalf of the finance house in relation to handling defects in the cars sold: *Gordon v Volkswagen Financial Services (UK) Ltd (t/a Audi Finance)*, unreported, 30 April 2019 especially at [28]–[34].

[625] For these purposes goods that the trader arranges to repair at the consumer's premises are made available when the trader indicates that the repairs are finished: 2015 Act s.24(7).

[626] 2015 Act s.24(6).

Limitation of actions

Replace footnote 633 with:

14-101   [633] Limitation Act 1980 s.5 (6 years from accrual of the cause of action). The general rule in contract is that the cause of action accrues when the breach takes place rather than when any damage may have been suffered: *Chitty on Contracts*, 33rd edn (2018), paras 28-032 et seq.

Enforcement of consumer's specific remedies and discretion as to appropriate remedy

Replace paragraph (including title, above) with:

14-102   The 2015 Act s.58 provides that in any proceedings in which one of the special remedies provided for consumers by Ch.2[636] is sought, the court may act under two additional powers which it provides.[637] First, on the application of the consumer, the court may make an order requiring specific performance by the trader of any obligation imposed on the trader in respect of repair or replacement of the goods.[638] Secondly, where a consumer claims the right to repair or replacement or the right to a price reduction or the final right to reject (termed the "relevant remedies" by s.58), but the court decides that the provisions governing these rights "have the effect that exercise of another of these rights is appropriate", "the court may proceed as if the consumer had exercised that other right".[639] The court may make an order under s.58 unconditionally or on such terms and conditions as to damages, payment of the price and otherwise as it thinks just.[640] It is submitted, though, that in the case of contracts for the sale of goods (sales contracts), the consumer's right to repair or replacement of goods in the Act reflects requirements of the Consumer Sales Directive 1999 and so the provisions of the Act relating to them must be interpreted with this in mind and in the light of the principle of effectiveness, here, of the consumer's protection.[641] For this purpose, in *Weber & Putz* the Court of Justice of the EU assumed that the consumer's specific rights under the Directive were enforceable in kind against the seller, holding that national law must not allow replacement to be refused by a trader on the ground of disproportionality with regard to the value of the goods as conforming and the significance of the nonconformity, even though in the circumstances this meant that the trader had to bear the costs of the removal of goods installed by the consumer and the reinstallation of the replacement goods.[642] This suggests that an English court should not refuse specific performance in support of the consumer's right to repair or replacement of goods sold on the ground that damages would be an adequate remedy, as this would to this extent replace the consumer's "European rights" with damages and so render them ineffective. It could also mean that the court should not take into account other traditional elements governing the availability of specific performance stemming from its equitable nature on the basis that the Directive itself provides only two circumstances (impossibility and disproportionality compared to the other specific remedy) where the trader is entitled to refuse to repair or replace,[643] although it could be argued that the Court of Justice would allow a national court to refuse the right to repair or replacement where the consumer had not acted in good faith.[644] The judgment of the Court of Justice in *Weber & Putz* also suggests that, in the case of "sales contracts", the court's power to substitute another "appropriate right" under s.58 is incompatible with the 1999 Directive. Finally, on their terms, the court's powers under the 2015 Act s.58 do not extend to the consumer's "other remedies" as this is understood by the Act and as explained in the following paragraph.

[636] 2015 Act s.58(1), referring to s.19(3) and (4) and therefore to the legal grounds of the consumer's rights in respect of the statutory terms as to quality, fitness for purpose etc, under the special rules governing conformity of the goods or for breach of requirements that are stated in the contract as there provided: above, para.14-067. The powers of the court in s.58 therefore do not extend to proceedings brought in respect of the costs incurred by the consumer under s.19(5) in relation to breach of the statutory terms under s.12, nor to the right of rejection foreseen by s.19(6) as regards breach of the statutory term as to the trader's right to supply under s.17. Moreover, while the remedies for consumers foreseen by s.19(3) and (4) are the short-term right to reject, the right to repair or replacement and the right to a price reduction or the final right to reject, s.58's provisions affect only the latter four of these remedies.

[637] These powers in the court were earlier provided by the 1979 Act s.48E (as inserted by the 2002 Regulations), even though they were not foreseen by the 1999 Directive.

[638] 2015 Act s.58(2) referring to s.23 of the Act, above, para.14-098.

[639] 2015 Act s.58(4) and (5). The "relevant remedies" are defined by s.58(8)(a), referring to ss.23 and 24. For this purpose, if the consumer has claimed to exercise the final right to reject, the court may order that any reimbursement to the consumer is reduced by a deduction for use, to take account of the use the consumer has had of the goods in the period since they were delivered to the extent provided by s.24(9) and (10): 2015 Act s.58(5) and (6).

[640] 2015 Act s.58(7).

[641] On the Consumer Sales Directive 1999 generally, see above, para.14-013. On "sales contracts" see above, paras 14-053 to 14-057, 14-062 to 14-065.

[642] *Gebr. Weber GmbH v Wittmer, Putz v Medianess Electronics GmbH* (C-65/09 and C-87/09) [2011] 3 CMLR 27 at [63]–[78]; Whittaker (2017) L.Q.R. 47, 63–64. cf. the stated position of the EEC Commission to the HL Select Committee of the European Communities in relation to the (differently drafted) Proposal for a European Parliament and Council Directive on the sale of consumer goods and associated guarantees Com (95) 520 final. According to the Select Committee's 10th Report, *Consumer Guarantees* (1997) para.97 "the Commission told the Committee that the Directive would not require the national court to order specific performance of the repair or replacement of the goods", on the basis that the Proposal's intention would not be "to alter national judicial procedures and practice". It is submitted, however, that the availability of specific performance to enforce the right to repair or replace is not, viewed from the perspective of EU law, a matter merely of "procedure and practice" but is the mechanism by which English law can give effect to these rights as opposed merely to a right to damages.

[643] 1999 Directive Art.3(3) reflected in 2015 Act s.23(3)–(4) and see above, para.14-098.

[644] The EEC Commission expressed the view to the HL Select Committee of the European Communities in relation to the (differently drafted) Proposal for a European Parliament and Council Directive on the sale of consumer goods and associated guarantees Com (95) 520 final that "the consumer would be required to act in good faith" in relation to the exercise of his various remedies: Select Committee's 10th Report, *Consumer Guarantees* (1997) para.98. This could be supported by the CJEU's references to the good faith of the consumer in installing goods which were later discovered to be non-conforming and therefore in need of replacement and re-installation: *Gebr. Weber GmbH v Wittmer, Putz v Medianess Electronics GmbH* (C-65/09 and C-87/09) [2011] 3 C.M.L.R. 27 at [56] and [62]. The ECJ has referred to good faith as a "principle of civil law", although in a way which is not explicitly clear whether this principle is a principle of EU law or merely of the national law before the court: *Messner v Krüger* (C-489/07) [2009] E.C.R. I–7315 at [26]. cf. *Gruber v Bay Wa AG* (C-464/01) [1997] E.C.R. I–3767 at [53] where the European Court used good faith in the application of the special jurisdiction provisions in the Brussels Convention Art.13. On the use of good faith in EU law and by civil law systems see *Chitty on Contracts*, 33rd edn (2018), paras 1-047–1-048.

Other remedies for the consumer

Replace footnote 647 with:

14-103   [647] On this law see on damages see below, paras 16-031 et seq. (general rules for the assessment of damages) and on specific performance see *Chitty on Contracts*, 33rd edn (2018), Ch.27. Note that the 2015 Act disapplies the 1979 Act s.51 (damages for non-delivery), s.52 (specific performance), s.53 (remedy for breach of warranty) and s.54 (interest) from contracts to which Ch.2 of Pt 1 of the 2015 applies: 2015 Act s.60 Sch.1 paras 38–32 as noted above, para.14-046. In the absence of specific provision in the 2015 Act paralleling these disapplied provisions in the 1979 Act, it is submitted that the issues with which they are concerned are governed by the general common law. On the other hand, in the case of contracts of sale of goods, the question whether a consumer buyer may rely on the trader seller's breach in resisting the seller's claim for the price remains governed by the law surrounding ss.27, 28 and 49 of the 1979 Act (none of which the 2015 Act amends): on this law see below, paras 16-016, 16-021 to 16-024. This law does not, however, apply to the other "goods contracts" governed by Ch.2 of the 2015 Act where the question is governed by the general common law, on which see *Chitty on Contracts*, 33rd edn (2018), Vol.I paras 21-028 to 21-039.

(v)   Other rules about goods contracts

Delivery of goods in sales contracts

Replace footnote 691 with:

14-107   [691] 2015 Act s.28(3). Although s.28 implements Art.18 of the 2011 Directive, it would appear that the time of the conclusion of the contract must be determined in accordance with the general rules of English contract law: 2011 Directive Art.3(5), on which see *Chitty on Contracts*, 33rd edn (2018), Vol.II paras 38-015, 38-063 to 38-065.

Replace footnote 713 with:

14-108   [713] See *Chitty on Contracts*, 33rd edn (2018), Vol.1 Chs 26 and 27.

(vi)   Exclusion of liability

Enforcement of Pt 1 more generally

Replace footnote 734 with:

⁷³⁴ Enterprise Act 2002 s.212; Sch.13 Pt 1 paras 8 and 9F. On the UK's leaving the EU on "exit day", **14-112** "Community infringements" are to be replaced by "Schedule 13 infringements" and the relevant provisions of Pt 1 of the 2015 Act are included within the substituted Sch.13 of the 2002 Act for this purpose: Consumer Protection (Enforcement) (Amendment etc.)(EU Exit) Regulations 2019 (SI 2019/203) reg.3(20) and Sch, para.1 inserting new 2002 Act Sch.13 para.27. On this change more generally see below, para.14-313A.

(e)   Consumer rights in respect of digital content contracts and services contracts

(i)   "Digital content contracts"

Introduction

Replace footnote 737 with:

⁷³⁷ Explanatory Notes 2015 para.169 referring to Bradgate, "*Consumer rights in digital products: A* **14-113** *research report prepared for the UK Department for Business, Innovation and Skills*", Institute for Commercial Law Studies, Sheffield and BIS, available at: *https://www.scribd.com/document/262297762/10-1125-Consumer-Rights-in-Digital-Products* [Accessed 19 September 2017] and see above, para.1-086. For detailed discussion of the provisions in the 2015 Act governing digital content contracts see *Chitty on Contracts*, 33rd edn (2018), paras 38–535 et seq.

Definition of "digital content contracts"

Replace footnote 743 with:

⁷⁴³ 2015 Act s.33(1) and (2). Cf. the position under the 2013 Regulations, whose requirements also ap- **14-114** ply to contracts for digital content other than for a price paid by the consumer, following the requirements of the Consumer Rights Directive 2011 which the Regulations implement. This is reflected in particular in the treatment of the information requirements in the 2013 Regulations: see regs 10(3) (on-premises contracts), 10(5) (off-premises contracts) and 13(6) (distance contracts).

Exclusion of liability; enforcement

Replace footnote 759 with:

⁷⁵⁹ Enterprise Act 2002 s.212(3); Enterprise Act 2002 (Part 8 EU Infringements) Order 2014 (SI 2014/ **14-117** 2908) Art.4; Schedule (as amended by the Enterprise Act 2002 (Part 8 Community Infringements and Specified UK Laws) (Amendment) Order 2015 (SI 2015/1628) Art.3(2)) listing, inter alia, 2015 Act ss.36(3) to (4), 37, 38 and 42. On the UK's leaving the EU on "exit day", "Community infringements" within the meaning of s.212 of the 2002 Act are to be replaced by "Schedule 13 infringements" and ss.36(3) and (4), 37, 38 and 40 of the 2015 Act are included within the substituted Sch.13 of the 2002 Act for this purpose: Consumer Protection (Enforcement) (Amendment etc.) (EU Exit) Regulations 2019 (SI 2019/203) reg.3(20) and Sch, para.1 inserting new 2002 Act Sch.13 para.27. On this change more generally see below, para.14-313A.

(ii)   "Services Contracts"

Introduction

Replace the first paragraph with:

    Contracts for the supply of services provide further examples of areas where there **14-118** is a potential source of consumer dissatisfaction. Many different types of services are involved, including repairs and servicing, bailment (as in the case of home removals and storage, laundry and dry cleaning), film processing, car washes, and the provision of holidays, whether package or tailor-made. Package holidays are subject to detailed control under the Package Travel and Linked Travel Arrangements Regulations 2018,[761] implementing the EU Directive (EU) 2015/2302 on package travel and linked travel arrangements.[762] Professional services are also relevant, including surveying, insurance and medical, legal and banking services. Many of these areas have their own specialist literature.[763]

[761] (SI 2018/634). The 2018 Regulations (in force generally on 1 July 2018) revoked and replaced the earlier Package Travel, Package Holidays and Package Tours Regulations 1992 (SI 1992/3288), though they preserved the 1992 Regulations as regards contracts made on or after 1 July 1998 and before 1 July 2018: 2018 Regulations regs 1(2) and 37. The 2018 Regulations substitute the 2015 Directive for the Package Travel Directive 1990 in the list of instruments which may give rise to a "Community infringement" and so apply Pt 8 of the Enterprise Act 2002 for their purposes; and they substitute the 2018 Regulations as the regulations specified as the UK law giving effect to the 2015 Directive for these purposes: 2018 Regulations reg.38(3) referring to 2002 Act, Sch.13, Pt 1 para.4; 38(7) amending the Enterprise Act 2002 (Part 8 Community Infringements Specified UK Laws) Order 2003/1374 Sch.1.

[762] Directive (EU) 2015/2302 on package travel and linked travel arrangements [2015] O.J. L326/1 repealing Directive 90/314/EEC of 13 June 1990 on package travel, package holidays and package tours [1990] O.J. L158/59.

[763] See generally Dugdale and Stanton, *Professional Negligence*, 4th edn; Harvey and Parry, *Law of Consumer Protection and Fair Trading*, 6th edn, Ch.7; as to bailment, see Palmer, *Bailment*, 3rd edn.

Replace footnote 764 with:

14-119   [764] For more detailed discussion of these provisions see *Chitty on Contracts*, 33rd edn (2018), Vol.II paras 38-567 et seq. On the coming into force of these provisions, see above, para.14-021.

No statutory definition of "services contracts"

Replace footnote 772 with:

14-120   [772] See *Chitty on Contracts*, 33rd edn (2018), Vol.II paras 40-002, 40-005, 40-010 et seq. In common with the 1982 Act s.12(4)–(5), s.48(5)–(8) of the 2015 Act empowers the Secretary of State to provide by Order that a provision within Ch.4 does not apply in relation to a service of a description specified in the order. It has been seen that s.15 of the 2015 Act provides specially that the incorrect installation of goods (a form of the provision of a service) renders the goods themselves non-conforming: see above, para.14-080.

The statutory terms reflecting the 1982 Act and remedies for their breach

Replace footnote 782 with:

14-121   [782] See *Chitty on Contracts*, 33rd edn (2018), Vol.I para.26-009 (though ex hypothesi, the trader's claim for enforcement of the statutory term inserted by s.51 would not be for an *agreed* sum).

A right to repeat performance

Replace footnote 793 with:

14-125   [793] See *Chitty on Contracts*, 33rd edn (2018), Vol.I Ch.27.

Exclusion of liability for breach of the statutory terms; enforcement

Replace footnote 807 with:

14-129   [807] Enterprise Act 2002 s.212(3); Enterprise Act 2002 (Part 8 Community Infringements Specified UK Laws) Order 2003 Art.3; Schedule, as amended by the Enterprise Act 2002 (Part 8 Community Infringements and Specified UK Laws) (Amendment) Order 2015 (SI 2015/1628) Art.3 listing 2015 Act ss.50 and 54. On the UK's leaving the EU on "exit day", "Community infringements" within the meaning of s.212 of the 2002 Act are to be replaced by "Schedule 13 infringements" and ss.50 and 54 of the 2015

Act are included within the substituted Sch.13 of the 2002 Act for this purpose: Consumer Protection (Enforcement) (Amendment etc.)(EU Exit) Regulations 2019 (SI 2019/203) reg.3(20) and Sch, para.1 inserting new 2002 Act Sch.13 para.27. On this change more generally see below, para.14-313A.

(f) The general scheme of control of unfair contract terms

(i) Introductory

Amendment of the 1977 Act

Replace footnote 825 with:

825 It does not include all the law, either at common law (such as the rule rendering ineffective an attempted exclusion of liability for personal fraud: see *Chitty on Contracts*, 33rd edn (2018), Vol.1 para.7-145) or in legislation creating rules governing consumer contracts whose effect cannot be excluded or restricted (e.g. the Package Travel and Linked Travel Arrangements Regulations 2018 (SI 2018/634) reg.30(3) (in force 1 July 2018, protecting "travellers" and not merely "consumers") or the Timeshare, Holiday Products, Resale and Exchange Contracts Regulations 2010 (SI 2010/2960) reg.19). Moreover, provisions in other UK legislation make the rules (or some of the rules) which they set out incapable of exclusion by contract: e.g. Consumer Protection Act 1987 s.7 (no exclusion of product liability imposed by Pt 1 of that Act) on which see generally below, paras 14-227 et seq especially at para.14-230.

14-132

Interpretation by CJEU of 1993 Directive implemented by the 2015 Act

Replace footnote 833 with:

833 *Freiburger Kommunalbauten GmbH Baugesellschaft & Co KG v Hofstetter* (C-237/02) [2004] 2 C.M.L.R. 13; *Nemzeti Fogyasztóvédelmi Hatóság v Invitel Távközlési Zrt* (C-472/10) 26 April 2012 at [21]–[22]; *Aziz v Caixa d'Estalvis de Catalunya, Tarragona i Manresa* (C-415/11) 14 March 2013 at [66]–[67]; *RWE Vertrieb AG v Verbraucherzentrale Nordrhein-Westfalen eV* (C-92/11) 21 March 2013 at [48]–[54]; *Constructora Principado SA v Menéndez Álvarez* (C-226/12) 16 January 2014 at [20]–[25]; *Sebestyén v Kovári* (C-342/13) 3 April 2014 at [25]–[35]. For an overview of the CJEU's case-law on the 1993 Directive see EU Commission, *Guidance on the interpretation and application of Council Directive 93/13/EEC of 5 April 1993 on unfair contract terms in consumer contracts* (22 July 2019) C(2019) 5325 final.

14-135

(ii) Scope of controls on contract terms and notices in the Consumer Rights Act Pt 2

"Consumer contract"

Replace footnote 844 with:

844 2015 Act s.61(2). This reflects the exclusion from the scope of the 1993 Directive of "contracts relating to employment": 1993 Directive, recital 10; Art.1; *Pouvin and Dijoux v Electricite de France (EDF)* (C-590/17) EU:C:2019:23 of 21 March 2019 especially at [32]. On the question whether the CJEU would adopt an autonomous European definition of "contract" or would leave the interpretation of this concept to national law, see *Chitty on Contracts* (33rd edn, 2018) Vol. II, paras 38-229—38-230.

14-139

Terms or notices reflecting "mandatory statutory or regulatory provisions" or international conventions

Replace paragraph with:

The Consumer Rights Act 2015 adopts the exclusion from the scope of the controls set out by Art.1(2) of the 1993 Directive and included in the 1999 Regulations851 by excluding from Pt 2 terms which reflect "mandatory statutory or regulatory provisions" or the provisions or principles of an international convention to which the UK or the EU is a party, but it extends this exclusion to "consumer notices".852 This exclusion is not significant in the context of contracts of sale of goods and will not be further discussed here.853

14-141

851 1999 Regulations reg.4(2).

852 2015 Act s.73 (due to be amended on the UK's leaving the EU (on which see above, paras 14-006 et seq.) by the Consumer Protection (Amendment etc.) (EU Exit) Regulations 2018 (SI 2018/1326) reg.3(4)). See also 1993 Directive Art.1(2) recital 13 and *RWE Vertrieb AG v Verbraucherzentrale Nordrhein-Westfalen eV* (C-92/11) 21 March 2013; *Kušionová v SMART Capita asl* (C-34/13) of 10 September 2014; *Engilbertsson v Íslandsbanki hf* (E-25/13) 28 August 2014 (EFTA Court); *Jones v Roundlistic Ltd* [2018] EWCA Civ 2284; [2019] 1 W.L.R. 4461.

853 On this provision generally see *Chitty on Contracts*, 33rd edn, paras 38-233 to 38-240.

(iii)   Contract terms and notices not binding on the consumer where assessed as unfair

(aa)   Terms of consumer contracts

General test of unfairness

Replace footnote 859 with:

14-143 859 2015 Act s.62(4); 1993 Directive Art.3(1); 1999 Regulations reg.5(1). In *Kiss v Kiss* (C-621/17) EU:C:2019:411 A.G. Hogan in his Opinion of 15 May 2019, [50] advised that "term" for the purposes of the 1993 Directive "must be understood in a substantial and not in a formal sense, i.e. referring to a specific right or obligation laid down in a contract and not to a particular paragraph of the contract. As a result a clause may contain several terms and a term may take the form of several clauses". The particular context for this view was the proper approach to the exclusion in art.4(2) of the Directive (on which see below, paras 14-155 et seq.), but it could also affect a court's approach to art.6's stipulation that "unfair terms" are not binding on the consumer: see below, para.14-162.

Interpretation of the test of fairness

Replace paragraph with:

14-144 While general works on contract law discuss the relevant case law in more detail, the following points can be noted here.863 First, the basic test of unfairness is one of significant imbalance in the rights and obligations of the parties to the detriment of the consumer, but this is qualified by the clause "contrary to the requirement of good faith", and recital 16 of the Directive suggests that the role of this qualification is intended to ensure that a court makes an "overall evaluation of the different interests involved". The open nature of the test is further supported by the very wide range of circumstances which are specified for taking into account.864

863 See *Chitty on Contracts*, 33rd edn (2018), paras 38–265 et seq. The CMA has also published guidance on the provisions in the Consumer Rights Act 2015 governing unfair contract terms: CMA, *Unfair contract terms guidance, Guidance on the unfair terms provisions in the Consumer Rights Act*, CMA37 31 July 2015. For relevant English cases apart from those discussed in the text see: *Munkenbeck & Marshall v Harold* [2005] EWHC 356 (TCC); [2005] All E.R. (D) 227 (term charging interest rate for unpaid sums); *Domsalla v Dyason* [2007] EWHC 1174 (TCC) at [77] (wide range of contracts related to the consumer contract in question relevant to fairness of term as part of "all the circumstances"); *West v Ian Finlay & Associates* [2014] EWCA Civ 316; [2014] B.L.R. 324 ("net contribution clause" in contract of appointment of architects held fair); *Spreadex Ltd v Cochrane* [2012] EWHC 1290 (Comm) at [17] (term of contract under which the consumers were deemed to have authorised all trading under their account number in on-line trading platform held unfair); *Bryen & Langley Ltd v Boston* [2004] EWHC 2450 (TCC); 98 Con. L.R. 82 at [45]; [2005] EWCA Civ 973, [2005] All E.R. (D) 507 (July) (appeal allowed on other grounds) (relevance of unusual and costly nature of contract); *UK Housing Alliance (North West) Ltd v Francis* [2010] EWCA Civ 117; [2010] Bus. L.R. 1034 esp. at [27]–[29] (term in sale and leaseback contract between landlord and tenant not unfair in the circumstances); *Office of Fair Trading v Ashbourne Management Services Ltd* [2011] EWHC 1237 (Ch); [2011] E.C.C. 32 (series of terms in gym membership contract); *Du Plessis v Fontgary Leisure Parks Ltd* [2012] EWCA Civ 409 (terms in licence agreement of space at holiday caravan park); *Boyde v Clipper Ventures Plc* 2013 S.C.L.R. 313; 2013 G.W.D. 12–243 (a term allowing a person agreeing to participate in a world voyage by clipper to cancel the contract at a charge of 75% of the price held fair); *RWE Vertrieb AG v Verbraucherzentrale Nordrhein-Westfalen eV* (C-92/11) 21 March 2013 (guidance on variation clauses in contract for the domestic supply of gas); *The Office of Fair Trading v Foxtons Ltd* [2009] EWHC 1681

(Ch); [2009] 29 E.G. 98 (C.S.) at [91]–[95], [101], [103]–[106] (renewal commission clauses held unfair in the circumstances).

864 1993 Directive Art.4(1), 2015 Act s.62(5) and see above, para.14-144. "The unfairness of a contractual term is to be assessed by reference to the time of conclusion of the contract at issue, taking account of all the circumstances which could have been known to the seller or supplier at that time, and which were of such a nature that they could affect the future performance of the contract, since a contractual term may give rise to an imbalance between the parties which only manifests itself during the performance of the contract": *Andriciuc v Banca Românească* (C-186/16) of 20 September 2017 at para.54.

The decisions in *Aziz* and *Menéndez Álvarez*

Replace footnote 875 with:

875 *Aziz v Caixa d'Estalvis de Catalunya, Tarragona i Manresa* (C-415/11) 14 March 2013 at [69]. The **14-147** approach in *Aziz* was followed closely in the order of the CJEU in *Sebestyén v Kovári* (C-342/13) 3 April 2014 at [27]–[28]. Cf *Toth v ERSTE Bank Hungary Zrt* (C-34/18) (Opinion of 29 March 2019), [55]–[62] especially at [58] where A.G. Hogan took the view (which he admitted was not reflected in the case law of the CJEU) that the phrase "contrary to the requirement of good faith" is not distinct from the overall criterion of "significant imbalance", but is instead "essentially descriptive of the state of affairs" where there is a significant imbalance. See similarly *Kiss v Kiss* (C-621/17) Opinion of A.G. Hogan of 15 May 2019, at [66].

The relevance of transparency

Replace footnote 880 with:

880 *RWE Vertrieb AG v Verbraucherzentrale Nordrhein-Westfalen eV* (C-92/11) 21 March 2013 at [43]– **14-148** [44] referring to 1993 Directive Art.5 and recital 20; *Mylcrist Builders Ltd v Buck* [2008] EWHC 2172 (TCC); [2009] 2 All E.R. (Comm) 259 at [56]. The CJEU has emphasised the importance of the quality of pre-contractual information to the requirement of plain intelligible language in Art.5 of the Directive (implemented by 2015 Act s.68): see below, paras 14-160 to 14-161, 14-172 to 14-173. At times the CJEU has come close to seeing the lack of transparency of a term as justifying a finding of unfairness (e.g. *Verein fur Konsumenteninformation v Amazon EU Sarl* (C-191/15) EU:C:2016:61, 28 July 2016 where the CJEU identified the unfairness of a choice of foreign law clause in its failure to conform to the requirement of plain and intelligible language by the trader in failing to inform the consumer that the effects of such a term are qualified by the mandatory statutory provisions of the consumer's place of residence provided for his protection), but in *Toth v ERSTE Bank Hungary Zrt* (C-34/18) (Opinion of 29 March 2019) at [86] A.G. Hogan emphasised that art.5's requirement of plain, intelligible language "does not constitute an alternative test of unfairness: it rather simply provides an interpretative rule in order to determine the legal effect produced by such terms."

ParkingEye Ltd v Beavis

Replace footnote 887 with:

887 *ParkingEye Ltd v Beavis* [2015] UKSC 67 at [108] (referring for this purpose to A.G. Kokott's **14-149** Opinion in *Aziz v Caixa d'Estalvis de Catalunya, Tarragona i Manresa* (C-415/11) 14 March 2013 at [75], though her reference was to "an objective reason for the term" rather than specifically an objective approach to the hypothetical test) cf. above, para.14-147. This approach to the requirement of good faith was followed by the CA in *Jones v Roundlistic Ltd* [2018] EWCA Civ 2284; [2019] 1 W.L.R. 4461 at [47]–[49], [50].

Burden of proof as to fairness of a contract term

Replace footnote 925 with:

925 See *Chitty on Contracts*, 33rd edn (2018), Vol.I paras 38–335 to 38-335 and 38–393. **14-153**

The "core exclusion" from the assessment of fairness

Replace footnote 934 with:

934 See generally *Chitty on Contracts*, 33rd edn (2018), Vol.II paras 38–245 to 38-264; 38–394–38– **14-155** 400.

Comments; relationship to recent case law of the CJEU

Replace paragraph with:

14-159   It will be seen, therefore, that s.64 follows a number of the recommendations of the Law Commissions. First, it adopts the view that the nature of the two limbs of Art.4(2) of the 1993 Directive differs: the first limb excludes from assessment for its fairness "a term ... to the extent that it specifies the main subject matter of the contract"; whereas the second limb excludes a term from assessment for its fairness "to the extent that the assessment is of the appropriateness of the price payable under the contract by comparison with the goods, digital content or services supplied under it". This view finds clear support in the judgments of the Court of Justice in *Kásler* and *Matei*.[971]

[971] *Kásler v OTP Jelzálogbank Zrt* (C-26/13) 30 April 2014 at [43], [49]–[51] and [52]–[55]; *Matei v SC Volksbank România SA* (C-143/13) 26 February 2015 at [70]. For further decisions of the CJEU on the exclusion in art.4(2) of the 1993 Directive, see *Van Hove v CNP Assurances SA* (C-96/14) of 26 April 2015; *Bucura v SC Bancpost SA* (C-348/14) 9 July 2015; *Andriciuc v Banca Românească* (C-186/16) of 20 September 2017; and *OTP Bank Nyrt v Ilyes and Kiss* (C-51/17) EU:C:2018:75 of 20 September 2018.

Replace paragraph with:

14-160   Secondly, s.64(3) explains the condition of transparency of a term as concerning both its expression in plain and intelligible language and, in the case of written terms, legibility, but, contrary to the recommendation of the Law Commissions, s.64 does not also require that the term be "readily available".[972] It is submitted, however, that this omission makes no substantive difference, as the Court of Justice in *Kásler* held that Arts 4(2) and 5 of the 1993 Directive reflect the same requirement of plain and intelligible language and that, for these purposes, recital 20 states that "the consumer should actually be given an opportunity of examining all the terms of the contract".[973] As a result, an English court would have to give effect to this aspect of the condition of the transparency of terms under Art.4(2) in its interpretation of s.64(3). Indeed, the Court of Justice in *Kásler* went much further, holding that the requirement of transparency does not merely require that the term is "formally and grammatically intelligible",[974] but also that the "consumer is in a position to evaluate, on the basis of clear, intelligible criteria, the economic consequences for him which derive from" the term in question: the trader's reasons for using the term and its relationship with other contractual terms should be clear and intelligible.[975] For this purpose, the Court of Justice set as the standard for evaluation "the average consumer, who is reasonably well informed and reasonably observant and circumspect".[976]

[972] cf. above, para.14-156.

[973] *Kásler v OTP Jelzálogbank Zrt* (C-26/13) 30 April 2014 at [66]–[68]. According to the CJEU in *Andriciuc v Banca Românească* (C-186/16) of 20 September 2017 at para.47, the requirement of plain intelligible language requires a national court to consider whether "all the information likely to have a bearing on the extent of his commitment have been communicated to the consumer".

[974] *Kásler v OTP Jelzálogbank Zrt* (C-26/13) 30 April 2014 at [71].

[975] *Kásler v OTP Jelzálogbank Zrt* (C-26/13) 30 April 2014 at [75].

[976] *Kásler v OTP Jelzálogbank Zrt* (C-26/13) 30 April 2014 at [74]. See further *Van Hove v CNP Assurances SA* (C-96/14) 23 April 2015; *Bucura v SC Bancpost SA* (C-348/14) 9 July 2015 at [57]–[63]; *Andriciuc v Banca Românească* (C-186/16) of 20 September 2017 at para.47.

Replace paragraph with:

14-161   Thirdly, s.64(4) explains the new condition of "prominence" as recommended by the Law Commissions in terms of it being "brought to the consumer's attention in such a way that an average consumer would be aware of the term".[977] The Law Commissions apparently assumed that this additional condition would go beyond the condition of "plain intelligible language" set by Art.4(2) of the Directive,[978] but this assumption is open to doubt given the very broad interpretation of this condition in *Kásler*, for the Court of Justice there requires national courts to consider not merely whether a relevant term had been "brought to the consumer's attention in such a way that an average consumer would be aware of the term",[979] but that the average consumer "is in a position to evaluate, on the basis of clear, intelligible criteria, the economic consequences for him which derive from that term".[980] In sum, the additional condition of "prominence" set by the 2015 Act may not go far enough to give proper effect to the interpretation of the Court of Justice without the aid of the principle of conforming interpretation by national courts of legislation implementing EU law.[981] On the other hand, if and to the extent to which the Act's condition of "prominence" goes further than the 1993 Directive in the interests of providing greater protection for consumers than it requires, then the Act's compatibility with EU law is covered by the Directive's "minimum harmonisation" clause as regards its "contract law effects", though it may not be so covered as to its provision of enforcement measures.[982] Fourthly, the strategy of the 2015 Act in dealing with the problem of "hidden price terms" by requiring that they must be "prominent" rests on the Law Commission's very broad interpretation of the expression "price and remuneration" found in Art.4(2) of the Directive[983] so as to cover all terms which impose money obligations on consumers.[984] This view is reflected directly in s.64(1)(b) of the 2015 Act which excludes from the assessment of the term "the appropriateness of the price payable under the contract by comparison with the goods, digital content or services supplied" under the contract. It is submitted that this reformulation of the second limb of the exclusion in Art.4(2) of the Directive may be broader in its effect than the interpretation given to that limb by the Court of Justice. In *Kásler*, the court considered whether a term in a contract of consumer credit denominated in a foreign currency which set the exchange rate for repayment by the consumer of the loan at the creditor bank's "selling rate" could be assessed for its unfairness, where another term set the exchange rate for repayment of the original sums lent by the bank to the consumer at the bank's "buying rate". It held that the second limb of the exclusion in Art.4(2) *could not apply* to the repayment term, as such a term "in so far as it contains a pecuniary obligation for the consumer to pay, in repayment instalments of the loan, the difference between the selling rate of exchange and the buying rate of exchange of the foreign currency, *cannot be considered as 'remuneration'*, the adequacy of which as consideration for a service supplied by the lender cannot be subject of an examination as regards unfairness under Article 4(2)" of the Directive,[985] apparently on the basis that this difference did not constitute something in return ("consideration") for any foreign exchange service supplied by the lender.[986] The Court of Justice therefore saw the second limb of the exclusion in Art.4(2) as ruling out comparison of the sum payable under a contract term (there, the repayment term) as against any services provided for such a sum, thereby implicitly rejecting the Supreme Court's approach in *OFT v Abbey National Plc* which looked globally at the sums payable (or contingently payable) under the term as against the package of services provided by the trader in respect (in part) of those sums.[987] Moreover, this contrast between the approach of the Court of Justice and the Supreme Court in *OFT v Abbey National Plc* was made clearer by the Court of Justice's judgment in *Matei*, where it again required the identification of a distinct service in exchange for which the "price or remuneration" is to be paid.[988] It is submitted that in these circumstances English courts should seek to give effect to the interpretation and guidance of the Court of Justice of the EU in their application of s.64(1)(b) of the 2015 Act following the principle of the conforming interpretation of UK legislation implementing EU directives, though the difficulty in doing so would turn on whether the English court would consider this "possible" given the wording of s.64(1)(b) and its background in the Law Commissions' earlier Advice.[989]

[977] The Explanatory Notes to the Act provide as an example of this condition that terms governing the price or subject matter are "in the small print": Explanatory Notes 2014 para.314.

[978] Above, para.14-155.

[979] 2015 Act s.64(4).

[980] *Kásler v OTP Jelzálogbank Zrt* (C-26/13) 30 April 2014 at [75].

[981] On which, see above, para.14-135.

[982] See below, para.14-176 and *Chitty on Contracts*, 33rd edn (2018) paras 38–421 to 38–426. This would also apply to the three added examples of terms which may be unfair of terms in the "indicative list" as membership of this list excludes the application of the exclusion in s.64 of the Act: s.64(6).

[983] The Law Commissions saw their view as reflecting the position of the SC in the *Bank Charges* case, see above, paras 14-155 to 14-156.

[984] Law Com. *Advice* (2013) para.4.61, above, para.14-156.

[985] *Kásler v OTP Jelzálogbank Zrt* (C-26/13) 30 April 2014 at [59] (emphasis added).

[986] *Kásler v OTP Jelzálogbank Zrt* (C-26/13) 30 April 2014 at [58].

[987] Above, para.14-155.

[988] *Matei v SC Volksbank România SA* (C-143/13) 26 February 2015 at [70] and [71]. Cf, the very different interpretation given to *Matei* by A.G. Hogan in *Kiss v Kiss* (C-621/17) EU:C:2019:41, Opinion of 15 May 2019 at [35]–[38]. There, a contract of consumer credit included two terms under which a "disbursement commission" (a fixed sum of about 250 Euros) and a "management charge" of 2.4% per annum were payable by the consumer borrower. Even though the contract did not specify the services for which it was made, A.G. Hogan advised that the term providing for the management charge could fall within the second limb of art.4(2) of the 1993 Directive on the basis that the charge formed "one element of the price to be paid" in return for the loan: "a single service may give rise to several price clauses" without taking the clauses outside the exclusion, and "a clause may contain several terms and a term may take the form of several clauses": ibid. at [50]. However, he further advised that the terms were not in "plain intelligible writing": ibid., [44]. The decision of the CJEU is pending at the time of writing.

[989] On the principle of "conforming interpretation" and its limits, see above, para.14-135. But see *Casehub Ltd v Wolf Cola Ltd* [2017] EWHC 1169 (Ch); [2017] 5 Costs L.R. 835 where the High Court rejected the invitation of the claimant consumer that it should not follow the Supreme Court's decision in *Abbey National Plc* in relation to the exclusion in Art.4(2) implemented by s.64 of the 2015 Act on the basis that Supreme Court's decision was inconsistent with the later decisions of the CJEU in *Kásler* and *Matei* on the ground that it was bound by the Supreme Court's decision as a matter of precedent and that it was "far from clear that the CJEU cases … have the effect for which [the claimant] contends": [2017] EWHC 1169 (Ch) at [53]–[54]. With respect, however, it is doubtful whether the High Court's approach to the authority of the Supreme Court's decision is correct given the requirement in s.3(1) of the European Communities Act 1972 that questions of the meaning of EU law (here, Art.4(2) of the 1993 Directive) must be determined in accordance with the principles laid down by and any relevant decision of the European Court" and given that the High Court did not explain how the European case-law did not have the effect contended for in relation to the Supreme Court's decision.

Effects of a finding of unfairness of a contract term

Replace the first paragraph with:

14-162   The effects of a finding by a court that a term of a consumer contract is unfair under the Consumer Rights Act follow closely the position under the 1999 Regulations and the 1993 Directive.[990] As a result, "[a]n unfair term of a consumer contract is not binding on the consumer",[991] it being clarified that "[t]his does not prevent the consumer from relying on the term or notice if the consumer chooses to do so".[992] On the other hand:

"Where a term of a consumer contract is not binding on the consumer as a result of [Part 2 of the Act], the contract continues, so far as practicable, to have effect in every other respect."[993]

Where a contract term is held unfair and "not binding" on a consumer, the Court of Justice of the EU allows a national court to apply a national supplementary rule (that is, one applicable in the absence of other or contrary agreement) to govern an issue regulated by that term only where otherwise the contract would fail to the prejudice of the consumer and where such an application would enable a "real balance between the rights and obligations of the parties to be restored".[994] Where these conditions are not satisfied, a national court must *not* apply any national supplementary law to govern the issue which the unfair contract term attempted to govern. For example, where a national court held unfair a contract term setting an interest rate in respect of late payments under a contract of consumer credit, the Court of Justice held that the national court must not apply the interest rate applicable to late payments otherwise applicable under the general national law.[995] And where a court declares a penalty clause in a consumer contract to be unfair, the 1993 Directive "cannot be interpreted as allowing the national court ... to reduce the amount of the penalty imposed on the consumer instead of excluding entirely the application of the clause".[996] In the context of English law, this appears to mean that where a contract term imposing a penalty on a consumer for breach of a contractual obligation is held unfair under the 2015 Act, that consumer could not be liable in damages at common law in respect of that breach, unlike the position at common law as regards unenforceable penalty clauses.[997] On the other hand, the Court of Justice has also held that a consumer who has paid money under a contract term held unfair and not binding on him under national legislation implementing the 1993 Directive, must be able to recover that money, as Art.6 of the 1993 Directive (which provides for that unfair terms are not binding on the consumer) "must be interpreted as meaning that a contractual term held to be unfair must be regarded, in principle, as never having existed, so that it cannot have any effect on the consumer".[998]

[990] See similarly 1993 Directive Art.6(1) and 1999 Regulations reg.8(1).

[991] 2015 Act s.62(1). See further *Chitty on Contracts*, 33rd edn (2018) paras 38–401 et seq. (in relation to the 1999 Regulations). For discussion of the effect of a finding of unfairness in a "secondary contract" under s.72 of the Act see below, paras 14-163 to 14-165.

[992] 2015 Act s.62(2). This also follows the CJEU's ruling that where a court raises the issue of fairness of a term of its own motion and finds it unfair, then it must not apply it unless "the consumer, after having been informed of it, does not intend to assert its unfair or non-binding status": *Pannon GSM Zrt v Erzsébet Sustikné Győrfi* (C–243/08) [2009] E.C.R. I–4713 at [33].

[993] 2015 Act s.67. See similarly 1993 Directive Art.6(1) and 1999 Regulations reg.8(2).

[994] *Kásler v OTP Jelzálogbank Zrt* (C-26/13) 30 April 2014 at [82]–[84]; *Unicaja Banco, SA v Hidalgo Rueda* (C-482/13, C-484/13, C-485/12 and C-487/13) 21 January 2015 at [33]; *Albanca Corporación Bancaria SA v Salamanca Santos*; *Bankia SA v Rodríquez Ramirez* (C-701/17 and C-179/17) EU:C:2019:250 26 March 2019 at [57].

[995] *Banco Bilbao Vizcaya Argentaria SA v Quintano Ujeta* (C-602/13) Order of 11 June 2015 (available in French); *Banco Grupo Cajatres SA v Manjón Pinilla* (C-90/14) 8 July 2015 at [33]–[38]. On the other hand, a national court may impose interest under a term of a consumer credit contract imposing "ordinary interest" not itself held unfair and therefore still binding on the consumer, even where the unfair interest provision and the fair interest provision are contained in a single term: *Banco Santander v Demba*; *Cortés v Banco de Sabadell SA* (C-96/16 and C-94/17) EU:C:2018:643 at [73]–[79].

[996] *Banco Bilbao Vizcaya Argentaria SA v Quintano Ujeta* (C-602/13) Order of 11 June 2015 at [34] and see [35]–[39].

[997] For the position at common law see *McGregor on Damages*, 19th edn (2014), paras 15–026–15–027; *Cavendish Square Holding BV v El Makdessi* [2015] UKSC 67; [2015] 3 W.L.R. 1373 at [9]. On the common law of penalties see below, para.16-036.

[998] *Gutiérrez Naranjo v Cajasur Banco SAU, Palacios Martinez v Banco Bilbao Vizcaya Argentaria SA (BBVA), Banco Popular Español, SA v Irles López* (C-154/15, C-307/15 and C-308/15) 21 December 2016 at [61].

(bb)   Certain types of term of "secondary contracts"

Extending the controls of Pt 2 of the 2015 Act to certain types of term in "secondary contracts"

Replace the first paragraph with:

14-163   The Consumer Rights Act 2015 s.72 applies the rules of Pt 2 to "a term of a contract ('the secondary contract')" that "reduces the rights or remedies or increases the obligations of a person under another contract ('the main contract')",[1001] "that would apply to the term if it were in the main contract".[1002] For these purposes, it does not matter "whether the parties to the secondary contract are the same as the parties to the main contract" or "whether the secondary contract is a consumer contract".[1003] On the other hand, these rules do not apply "if the secondary contract is a settlement of a claim arising under the main contract".[1004] This provision has no counterpart in the 1999 Regulations (nor the 1993 Directive), but is related to the Unfair Contract Terms Act 1977 s.10,[1005] which provides that:

> "A person is not bound by any contract term prejudicing or taking away rights of his which arise under, or in connection with the performance of, another contract, so far as those rights extend to the enforcement of another's liability which [Part I of the Act] prevents that other from excluding or restricting."

The purpose of this anti-evasion provision has been said to prevent a person (A) from enforcing against another person (B) a clause in a contract between them (the "secondary contract") which provides that B is not to sue a third person (C) under a contract between B and C and which would have been ineffective under the 1977 Act if it had been contained in the contract between B and C (the "main contract").[1006] It therefore applies, for example, to the case where a term in a direct contract between a manufacturer of goods and a buyer purports to affect the rights of that buyer under the Sale of Goods Act 1979 against the retailer from whom he or she purchases the goods[1007] or to the case where a supplier (B) contracts to supply a customer (C) with a product under a contract (the main contract) containing no exemption clause, but the customer (C) also enters a servicing contract with A (the secondary contract) under which C is precluded from exercising his rights against B under the main contract.[1008] While the scope of s.10 has been described as "enigmatic",[1009] it has been held not to apply to the compromise or waiver of an existing contractual claim such as the release by a person of rights which have accrued to him as the result of the breach of another contract to which he is party[1010] nor to the case where the parties to the main contract and the secondary contract are the same.[1011]

[1001] 2015 Act s.72(1).

[1002] 2015 Act s.72(2).

[1003] 2015 Act s.72(3).

[1004] 2015 Act s.72(4).

[1005] On which see above, para.13-086.

[1006] *Treitel, The Law of Contract*, 14th edn (Peel, 2015) p.315 para.7–084. This lack of enforceability could result either directly from a provision of the Act (e.g. s.2(1), s.6(2)) or from a finding of "unreasonableness" of such a term (e.g. s.2(2) or s.6(3) as assessed under s.11).

[1007] See *Chitty on Contracts*, 33rd edn (2018), Vol.1 para.15-128.

[1008] *Tudor Grange Holdings Ltd v Citibank NA* [1992] Ch. 53 at [66].

[1009] *Chitty on Contracts*, 33rd edn (2018), Vol.I para.15-128.

[1010] *Tudor Grange Holdings Ltd v Citibank NA* [1992] Ch. 53; *Chitty on Contracts*, 33rd edn (2018), Vol.1 para.15-128.

[1011] *Tudor Grange Holdings Ltd v Citibank NA* [1992] Ch. 53 at [66]; *Treitel, The Law of Contract*, 14th edn (Peel, 2015), p.316.

(cc) Consumer notices

The test of unfairness

Replace footnote 1022 with:

[1022] But see the argument that the control of non-contractual notices as understood at common law may be required as a matter of the autonomous interpretation of "contract" for the purposes of the 1993 Directive: *Chitty on Contracts*, 33rd edn (2018), Vol.II para.38–387 (note).

14-166

(iv) The requirement for transparency

"Consumer notices in writing"

Replace footnote 1049 with:

[1049] 2015 Act s.68(1). cf. *Chitty on Contracts*, 33rd edn (2018), Vol.II para.38–356 (note) on the possibility that "consumer notices" do fall within the 1993 Directive's autonomous definition of contract terms. On the definition of "consumer notice" see above, para.14-140.

14-174

Effects of failure to fulfil requirement for transparency

Replace paragraph with:
First, s.69(1) of the 2015 Act provides:

14-175

"If a term in a consumer contract, or a consumer notice, could have different meanings, the meaning that is most favourable to the consumer is to prevail."

This seeks to implement the requirement of the 1993 Directive (earlier implemented in reg.7(2) of the 1999 Regulations), with the difference that this rule of interpretation is not restricted to the interpretation of written terms (as was reg.7(2)[1050]) and that it extends to "consumer notices". This effect does not seem to add much to the traditional general rule at common law according to which an ambiguous written instrument shall be construed against the person who made it (*contra proferentem*), but recent cases suggest that, under the general common law, construction *contra proferentem* will be used by courts only where recourse to the context of the contract (its, "matrix of fact") has been exhausted, whereas the requirement in the 1993 Directive (and s.69 of the 2015 Act) is expressed as a legal rule applicable to cases where a term in a consumer contract "could have different meanings".[1051] Secondly, the 2015 Act provides that the enforcement measures provided for regulators for the enforcement of the law of unfair terms applies to the enforcement of the requirement of transparency of terms and notices as it does to the requirement of fairness,[1052] a position which was not stated in the 1999 Regulations.[1053] Following the 1993 Directive (and the 1999 Regulations), the 2015 Act provides that the special rule of construction does not apply for the purposes of proceedings for an injunction under this enforcement regime.[1054]

[1050] The position under the 1993 Directive in this respect is not entirely clear. The first sentence of Art.5 (which requires plain, intelligible writing), is restricted expressly to "contracts where all or certain terms offered to the consumer are in writing"; while the second sentence ("[w]here there is doubt about the meaning of a term, the interpretation most favourable to the consumer shall prevail") is not so restricted, it could be thought that its scope remains restricted by what has been stated in the first sentence.

[1051] See *Chitty on Contracts*, 33rd edn (2018) Vol. I para.15-012 referring, inter alia, to *Persimmon Homes Ltd v Ove Arup & Partners Ltd* [2017] EWCA Civ 373 at [52], where it is explained that this more recent approach focusses on that aspect of construction *contra proferentem* which concerns the construction of exclusion clauses rather than the related aspect of construction against the person who has drawn up an instrument.

[1052] 2015 Act s.70(1) referring to "the enforcement of this Part", i.e. Pt 2.

[1053] For argument that these measures did extend to the requirement of transparency, see *Chitty on Contracts*, 33rd edn (2018), Vol.II para.38–355; Law Com. *Advice* (2013) paras 6.60–6.63.

[1054] 2015 Act s.69(2); 1993 Directive Art.5; 1999 Regulations reg.7(2).

(v) Enforcement

Enforcement of Pt 2 of the 2015 Act

Replace paragraph with:

14-176   The approach of the 2015 Act to the enforcement of the controls which it requires for unfair terms and notices extends the special scheme required by the 1993 Directive[1055] (earlier set out by the 1999 Regulations and now set out by Sch.3 of the Act) to the Act's controls on terms generally[1056] as well as providing that the investigatory powers needed for these purposes are the same as for the enforcement of consumer protection legislation more widely.[1057] Under Sch.3 of the Act, the CMA and other "regulators"[1058] (who are the same as the "qualifying bodies" previously foreseen by the 1999 Regulations[1059]) possess a power to apply for an injunction against a person if it thinks that the person is "using, or proposing or recommending the use of, a term or notice" in the following circumstances:[1060] where a term or notice purports to exclude or restrict liability imposed by Pt 1 (for example, in respect of the satisfactory quality of goods supplied) or business liability for death or personal injury resulting from negligence[1061]; where a term or notice is unfair within the meaning of Pt 2 "to any extent"[1062]; and where a term or notice fails the requirement for transparency.[1063] Schedule 3 also provides regulators with powers to consider complaints about a term or notice in the same circumstances,[1064] and to accept an undertaking from a person against whom it has applied, or thinks it is entitled to apply for an injunction.[1065] Courts may grant an injunction on such conditions, and against such respondents to the proceedings, as it thinks appropriate.[1066] The powers in regulators are therefore wider than those earlier contained in the 1999 Regulations in three principal ways: first, they apply to those provisions in the 2015 Act which reflect provisions in the 1977 Act and which render terms not binding on consumers without any assessment of their fairness[1067]; secondly, they apply to terms assessed as unfair under the general test even where (owing to the extended character of the scope of this test) they would not fall to be assessed under the 1999 Regulations (or the 1993 Directive)[1068]; and, thirdly, they apply to "consumer notices" in the same way as they apply to contract terms.[1069] While it is clear that the 1993 Directive allows Member States to extend the "contract law" consequences of their national laws governing unfair terms in consumer contracts in this way,[1070] it is less clear whether they are entitled to extend the enforcement measures against use or recommendation for use beyond the requirements of the 1993 Directive (and other special EU law requirements, such as those contained in the 1999 Directive), as this may fall within the scope of the "full harmonisation" required by the Unfair Commercial Practices Directive 2005.[1071]

[1055] 1993 Directive Art.7.

[1056] 2015 Act ss.31(7), 47(5), 57(7) and 70(1). The provisions providing enforcement powers regarding a trader's use, proposal for use or recommendation for use of unfair contract terms foreseen by s.70(1) of the Act and contained in Sch.3 came into force on 1 October 2015: Consumer Rights Act 2015 (Commencement No.3, Transitional Provisions, Savings and Consequential Amendments) Order 2015 (SI 2015/1630) Art.3(a)–(c). The powers themselves concern the actions of a trader expressed in the present tense ("using, or proposing, or recommending the use" of a term or notice (2015 Act Sch.3 para.3(1)(a)) and this indicates that, as regards conduct by the trader falling within these categories which takes place on or after 1 October 2015, the new powers in Sch.3 of the 2015 Act apply, even though the 2015 Order makes no explicit provision to this effect. However, the 2015 Order makes special transitional and saving provision in respect of investigatory powers in relation to Schs 5 and 6 of the Act: 2015 Order Art.8.

[1057] 2015 Act s.70(2), applying the investigatory powers in Sch.5 (which replace the special provisions on investigatory powers in the 1999 Regulations, reg.13): see esp. s.77 and Sch.5 paras 2(d), 6 ("unfair contract terms enforcer"), and 13(7) and (8). Schedule 5 is due to be amended on the UK's leaving the EU on "exit day" (on which see above, paras 14-006 et seq.) so as to replace references to "Community infringement" with "Schedule 13 infringement" and "EU enforcer" with "Schedule 13 enforcer": reg.4. This harmonises the provisions in the 2015 Act Sch.5 with the changes to be made to the Enterprise Act 2002 Pt 8, on which see below, para.14-313A.

[1058] The 2015 Act replaces the expression "qualifying body" and instead refers to all those empowered to enforce its provisions governing unfair contract terms (including the CMA) as "regulators": 2015 Act Sch.3 para.8(1).

[1059] 2015 Act Sch.3 para.8(1), though para.8(2) allows the Secretary of State to amend this list. (The Director General of Electrical Supply of Northern Ireland and the Director General of Gas for Northern Ireland were replaced by the Northern Ireland Authority for Utility Regulation).

[1060] 2015 Act Sch.3 para.3(1).

[1061] 2015 Act Sch.3 para.3(2) referring to ss.31, 47, 57 and 65(1) of the Act and see above, paras 14-110, 14-117, 14-129 and 14-169 respectively.

[1062] 2015 Act Sch.3 para.3(3). This includes both terms or notices assessed as unfair under s.62 and terms deemed to be unfair under s.63(6) or the Arbitration Act 1986 s.91.

[1063] 2015 Act Sch.3 para.3(5) and see s.68, above, para.14-175.

[1064] 2015 Act Sch.3 para.2 (reflecting 1999 Regulations reg.10).

[1065] 2015 Act Sch.3 para.6(1).

[1066] 2015 Act Sch.3 para.5(1). This broadly reflects 1999 Regulations reg.12(3) and (4).

[1067] 2015 Act Sch.3 para.3(2), referring to ss.31, 47, 57 and 65(1) of the 2015 Act.

[1068] The scope of the test of unfairness is widened in the following ways: the definition of "consumer" is (possibly) extended by ss.2(3) and 76(2), above, para.14-025; the subjection of terms which have been individually negotiated to the test of unfairness by s.62, above, para.14-142; the exclusion from the assessment of fairness of terms which specify the main subject matter of the contract etc in reg.64 is subjected to an additional condition of "prominence", above, para.14-158 to 14-161 (where it is argued that this is not in fact an extension). The 2015 Act does not expressly apply the Sch.3 enforcement regime to its controls on the effectiveness of certain terms on choice of applicable law as set out in s.74, as the latter is not expressed as rendering such terms unfair or otherwise not binding on consumers so as to fall within one of the categories in Sch.3 para.(2), (3) or (5) as required by para.3(1)(b), but Art.6(2) of the 1993 Directive requires Member States to "take the necessary measures to ensure that the consumer does not lose the protection granted" by it and so such an effect could possibly be achieved by way of "conforming interpretation" as explained above, para.14-135.

[1069] 2015 Act ss.62(2), (6) and (7), 65 and 68; Sch.3 para.3(3) and (5).

[1070] This follows from the minimum harmonisation required by the 1993 Directive Art.8 and by the exclusion from the scope of the Unfair Commercial Practices Directive 2005 Art.3(2) of "contract law".

[1071] On this question see *Chitty on Contracts*, 33rd edn (2018), paras 38–421 to 38–426.

Replace paragraph with:

14-177   In addition, the 2015 Act does not affect the possibility of enforcement measures being taken under Pt 8 of the Enterprise Act 2002 in respect of "Community infringements" which harm the collective interests of consumers and these include acts or omissions which contravene the 1993 Directive[1072] or which contravene laws of an EEA State (including the UK) which give effect to that Directive and which "provide additional permitted protections" beyond its minimum requirements and "such additional protection is permitted by that Directive".[1073] Moreover, the whole of Pts 1 and 2 of the 2015 Act have been designated as capable of giving rise to "domestic infringements" within the meaning of the Enterprise Act 2002 Pt 8, again allowing the possibility of enforcement measures which the 2002 provides.[1074] As is later explained, the 2015 Act enhanced the consumer measures which are available under the Enterprise Act so as to include, for example, measures offering compensation or other redress to consumers who have suffered loss as a result of the conduct which has given rise to the enforcement order.[1075] Thirdly, although not mentioned by the 2015 Act, in principle the use or recommendation for use of an unfair term or notice by a trader in its commercial practices with consumers can constitute an "unfair commercial practice" within the meaning of the Consumer Protection from Unfair Trading Regulations 2008.[1076]

[1072] Enterprise Act 2002 s.212(1)(a), Sch.13 para.5.

[1073] Enterprise Act 2002 s.212(1)(b) and (2). On the UK's leaving the EU on "exit day", "Community infringements" are to be replaced by "Schedule 13 infringements" and ss.61 to 64, 67 to 70, 71 to 74 and Schs 2 and 3 and Pt 3 of Sch.5 of the 2015 Act are to be included within the substituted Sch.13 of the 2002 Act for this purpose: Consumer Protection (Enforcement) (Amendment etc.) (EU Exit) Regulations 2019 (SI 2019/203) reg.3(20) and Sch. para.1 inserting new 2002 Act Sch.13 para.27. On this change more generally see below, para.14-313A.

[1074] Enterprise Act 2002 s.211; Enterprise Act 2002 (Part 8 Domestic Infringements) Order 2015 (SI 2015/1727) Art.2 and see below, paras 14-309 et seq.

[1075] 2015 Act s.79 Sch.7 inserting new s.219A to 219C in the Enterprise Act 2002. The example is found in the new s.219A(2)(a). See generally below, para.14-315. These amendments to the Enterprise Act 2002 effected by s.79(1) and Sch.7 of the 2015 Act came into force on 1 October 2015 (SI 2015/1630 Art.3(e)), but s.79(2) provides expressly that they "have effect only in relation to conduct which occurs, or which is likely to occur, after the commencement of [s.79]".

[1076] On this possibility see *Chitty on Contracts*, 33rd edn (2018), paras 38–362 to 38–364, 38–422. On the 2008 Regulations generally, see below, para.14-269 et seq.

3.   RIGHTS UNDER THE CIVIL LAW: COMMON LAW AND OTHER LEGISLATION

(b)   Duress, undue influence and "aggressive commercial practices"

The general common law

Replace footnote 1142 with:

14-193   [1142] For the general law see above, para.3-010 and *Chitty on Contracts*, 33rd edn (2018), Vol.1 Ch.8.

(c)   "Off-premises Contracts", "Distance Contracts" and "On-premises Contracts"

(i)   Introduction

Background

Replace footnote 1153 with:

1153 These categories of contract are defined by the 2013 Regulations reg.5 and noted below, paras 14-197 et seq., 14-201 et seq. and 14-206 et seq. For further discussion of the information requirements and cancellation rights under the 2013 Regulations see *Chitty on Contracts*, 33rd edn (2018), Vol.II paras 38-059 et seq.

14-195

The scope of the 2013 Regulations

Replace paragraph with:

Although this is not formally stated by the 2013 Regulations, in principle they apply to all types of "consumer contracts", defined by reference to the now standard definitions of "trader" and "consumer" in UK consumer protection legislation.[1154] The breadth of scope of the 2013 Regulations is apparent from the Consumer Rights Directive 2011 Art.3(1) which they implement, as Art.3(1) states that:

14-196

> "This Directive shall apply, under the conditions and to the extent set out in its provisions, to any contract concluded between a trader and a consumer. It shall also apply to contracts for the supply of water, gas, electricity or district heating, including by public providers, to the extent that these commodities are provided on a contractual basis."

There are, however, several types of contract which are excluded from the scope of the Regulations, some of which are relevant to the supply of goods to consumers.[1155] The list is lengthy, but the more important include contracts for the services of a banking, credit, insurance, personal pension, investment or payment nature; contracts for the creation of immovable property or of rights in such property[1156]; contracts for rental of accommodation for residential purposes; contracts for the construction of new buildings (or the construction of substantially new buildings by the conversion of existing buildings); contracts for the supply of foodstuffs, beverages or other goods intended for current consumption in the household and which are supplied by a trader on frequent and regular rounds to the consumer's home, residence or workplace; and contracts concluded by means of automatic vending machines. Contracts within the scope of Directive (EU) 2015/2302 on package travel and linked travel arrangements[1157] or Directive 2008/122/EC on the protection of consumers in respect of certain aspects of timeshare, long-term holiday product, resale and exchange[1158] are similarly excluded.[1159] Certain other contracts, including off-premises contracts (but not distance contracts) under which the payment to be made by the consumer does not exceed £42 are excluded from particular substantive aspects of the Regulations.[1160]

1154 "Trader" is defined as "a person acting for purposes relating to that person's trade, business, craft or profession, whether acting personally or through another person acting in the trader's name or on the trader's behalf"; "Consumer" is defined as "an individual acting for purposes which are wholly or mainly outside that individual's trade, business, craft or profession": 2013 Regulations reg.4. See further above, paras 14-023 et seq.

1155 See 2013 Regulations reg.6. Some of the contracts so excluded appear to be of more obvious relevance to distance, as opposed to off-premises, contracts and vice versa.

[1156] See 2013 Regulations reg.6. For a decision concerning the scope of the exclusion for contracts for the sale of immovable property in the context of Directive 1985/577, see *Schulte v Deutsche Bausparkasse Badenia AG* (C-350/03) [2005] E.C.R. I-9215; [2006] 1 C.M.L.R. 11; also, *Crailscheimer Volksbank EG v Conrads* (C-229/004) [2005] E.C.R. I-9273; [2006] 1 C.M.L.R. 21.

[1157] [2015] O.J. L326/1 repealing Directive 90/314/EEC of 13 June 1990 on package travel, package holidays and package tours [1990] O.J. L158/59. For discussion of this law and its implementation in the UK see *Chitty on Contracts*, 33rd edn (2018), Vol.II paras 38-138–38-142.

[1158] Directive 2008/122/EC on the protection of consumers in respect of certain aspects of timeshare, long-term holiday product, resale and exchange [2009] O.J. L33/10. See also the Timeshare, Holiday Products, Resale and Exchange Contracts Regulations 2010 (SI 2010/2960). For discussion of timeshare and similar contracts see *Chitty on Contracts*, 33rd edn (2018), Vol.II paras 38-148–38-154.

[1159] 2013 Regulations reg.6(1)(g) and (h).

[1160] See 2013 Regulations regs 7(4) (information requirements) and 27(3) (right to cancel).

(ii) "Off-premises Contracts"

"Off-premises contract"

Replace footnote 1164 with:

14-197 [1164] For "business" and "business premises", see 2013 Regulations reg.5. See also the definition, explanation and illustrations in the Consumer Rights Directive 2011 Art.2(9), recitals 22 and 23 and *Verbraucherzentrale Berlin v Unimatic Vertriebs GmbH* (C-485/17) EU:C:2018:64 of 7 August 2018.

Information to be provided

Replace paragraph with:

14-198 Where the 2013 Regulations apply,[1165] the trader must, before the consumer is bound by an off-premises contract, give the consumer the information listed in Sch.2 in a clear and comprehensible manner.[1166] Schedule 2 to the 2013 Regulations[1167] lists the information so required:

"(a) the main characteristics of the goods, services or digital content[1168], to the extent appropriate to the medium of communication and to the goods, services or digital content[1169];

(b) the identity of the trader (such as the trader's trading name);

(c) the geographical address at which the trader is established and, where available, the trader's telephone number, fax number and e-mail address, to enable the consumer to contact the trader quickly and communicate efficiently;

(d) where the trader is acting on behalf of another trader, the geographical address and identity of that other trader;

(e) if different from the address provided in accordance with paragraph (c), the geographical address of the place of business of the trader, and, where the trader acts on behalf of another trader, the geographical address of the place of business of that other trader, where the consumer can address any complaints;

(f) the total price of the goods, services or digital content inclusive of taxes, or where the nature of the goods, services or digital content is such that the price cannot reasonably be calculated in advance, the manner in which the price is to be calculated,

(g) where applicable, all additional delivery charges and any other costs or, where those charges cannot reasonably be calculated in advance, the fact that such additional charges may be payable;

(h) in the case of a contract of indeterminate duration or a contract containing a subscription, the total costs per billing period or (where such contracts are charged at a fixed rate) the total monthly costs;

(i) the cost of using the means of distance communication for the conclusion of the contract where that cost is calculated other than at the basic rate;

(j) the arrangements for payment, delivery, performance, and the time by which the trader undertakes to deliver the goods, to perform the services or to supply the digital content;

(k) where applicable, the trader's complaint handling policy;

(l) where a right to cancel exists, the conditions, time limit and procedures for exercising that right in accordance with regulations 27 to 38;

(m) where applicable, that the consumer will have to bear the cost of returning the goods in case of cancellation and, for distance contracts, if the goods, by their nature, cannot normally be returned by post, the cost of returning the goods;

(n) that, if the consumer exercises the right to cancel after having made a request in accordance with regulation 36(1), the consumer is to be liable to pay costs in accordance with regulation 36(4);

(o) where under regulation 28, 36 or 37 there is no right to cancel or the right to cancel may be lost, the information that the consumer will not benefit from a right to cancel, or the circumstances under which the consumer loses the right to cancel;

(p) in the case of a sales contract, a reminder that the trader is under a legal duty to supply goods that are in conformity with the contract;

(q) where applicable, the existence and the conditions of after-sale customer assistance, after-sales services and commercial guarantees;

(r) the existence of relevant codes of conduct, as defined in regulation 5(3)(b) of the Consumer Protection from Unfair Trading Regulations 2008, and how copies of them can be obtained, where applicable;

(s) the duration of the contract, where applicable, or, if the contract is of indeterminate duration or is to be extended automatically, the conditions for terminating the contract;

(t) where applicable, the minimum duration of the consumer's obligations under the contract;

(u) where applicable, the existence and the conditions of deposits or other financial guarantees to be paid or provided by the consumer at the request of the trader;

(v) where applicable, the functionality[1170], including applicable technical protection measures, of digital content[1171];

(w) where applicable, any relevant compatibility of digital content with hardware and software that the trader is aware of or can reasonably be expected to have been aware of[1172];

(x) where applicable, the possibility of having recourse to an out-of-court complaint and redress mechanism, to which the trader is subject, and the methods for having access to it."[1173]

The information relating to the consumer's cancellation right in paras (l), (m) and (n) above may be provided by means of the "model instructions on cancellation" set out by the 2013 Regulations, and if the trader uses this model correctly filled in, this is to be treated as compliance with those requirements.[1174] The 2013 Regulations also provide that, if a right to cancel exists, the trader must give the consumer a cancellation form which they set out[1175] and that the information and any cancellation form must be given on paper or, if the consumer agrees, on another durable medium and must be legible.[1176] As we have earlier seen, any information which is required to be provided by the trader under reg.10 is to be treated as included as a term of the contract by the Consumer Rights Act 2015.[1177] Under the 2013 Regulations, separate and less restrictive provision is made for service contracts involving the carrying out of repairs or maintenance which are to be performed immediately and which have been requested by the consumer.[1178] By reg.12(1) the trader is required to give the consumer a copy of the signed contract or confirmation of the contract and, unless the trader has already provided it in the appropriate form, the confirmation must include all the information referred to in Sch.2.[1179] The copy or confirmation must be provided within a reasonable time after the conclusion of the contract and, in any event, not later than the time of delivery of any goods supplied under the contract and before performance begins of any service supplied under the contract.[1180] In the event of a dispute about the trader's compliance with any provision of regs 10–16, the onus of proof lies on the trader to show that the provision was complied with.[1181] Moreover, a trader who enters into an off-premises contract to which reg.10 applies without providing the information listed in Sch.2 paras (l), (m) or (n) is guilty of an offence.[1182] It is likely that the courts have a duty to consider of their own initiative whether the information requirements imposed by the 2013 Regulations have been fulfilled and, if not, the legal consequences which follow from this infringement.[1183]

[1165] The 2013 Regulations reg.6 makes certain general exclusions, see above, para.14-196.

[1166] See 2013 Regulations reg.10(1)(a).

[1167] As amended by SI 2014/870.

[1168] "Digital content" means "data which are produced and supplied in digital form": 2013 Regulations reg.5.

[1169] On the special significance of this requirement under the Consumer Rights Act 2015 s.11(4) (goods contracts) and s.36(3)(digital content contracts), see above, paras 14-076 and 14-115 respectively.

[1170] 2013 Regulations reg.5 provides that "'functionality' in relation to digital content includes region coding, restrictions incorporated for the purposes of digital rights management, and other technical restrictions".

[1171] On the particular significance of this category of information under the Consumer Rights Act 2015 s.36(3), see above, para.14-115.

[1172] On the particular significance of this category of information under the Consumer Rights Act 2015 s.36(3), see above, para.14-115.

[1173] 2013 Regulations Sch.2, which notes that in the case of a public auction (as defined by reg.5 "public auction" and explained by the 2011 Directive recital 24) the information listed in paras (b) to (e) may be replaced with the equivalent details for the auctioneer.

[1174] 2013 Regulations reg.10(3) (off-premises contracts); reg.13(3) (distance contracts), referring to the "Model instructions for cancellation" in Sch.3(a).

[1175] 2013 Regulations reg.10(1)(b) (off-premises contracts) 13(1)(b) (distance contracts); Sch.3(b).

[1176] 2013 Regulations reg.10(2). Regulation 10(3), (4), and (6) makes further incidental provision as to these requirements. Regulation 11 makes special provision for the provision of information in connection with repair or maintenance contracts. The 2013 Regulations reg.5 defines "durable medium" as meaning "paper or email, or any other medium that—(a) allows information to be addressed personally to the recipient, (b) enables the recipient to store the information in a way accessible for future reference for a period that is long enough for the purposes of the information, and (c) allows the unchanged reproduction of the information stored".

[1177] 2015 Act ss.11(4) and (5), 12 replacing earlier provision in the 2013 Regulations reg.10(5) which was therefore amended so as to apply only to contracts for the supply of digital content other than for a price paid by the consumer (which are not governed by the 2015 Act): 2015 Act s.33. See above, paras 14-076 and 14-077.

[1178] 2013 Regulations reg.11.

[1179] 2013 Regulations reg.12(2).

[1180] 2013 Regulations reg.12(4).

[1181] 2013 Regulations reg.17(1).

[1182] 2013 Regulations reg.19(1). Until March 12, 2015 the maximum fine available on summary conviction was £5,000 (level 5 on the standard scale), but on that date this was changed to an unlimited fine by the Legal Aid, Sentencing and Punishment of Offenders Act 2012 s.85. Regs 24–26 of the 2013 Regulations (powers of investigation, obstruction of authorised officers, and freedom from self-incrimination, respectively) were revoked by the Consumer Rights Act 2015 (Consequential Amendments) Order 2015 (SI 2015/1726) art.2, Sch. Pt 2, para.7 and the 2015 Act was amended so as to include the 2013 Regulations in the list of legislation to which the investigatory powers in that Act (Sch.5) apply: SI 2015/1726 art.2, Sch. Pt 1 para.6 and 7. Note, however, that reg.17 (burden of proof) does not apply to proceedings for an offence under reg.19(1) or relating to compliance with an injunction under reg.45: see reg.17(2).

[1183] This follows from the decision of the CJEU in *Radlinger v Finway a.s.* (C-377/14) [2016] 3 C.M.L.R. 28 at [62]–[74] where it held that national courts bear such duties in relation to information requirements under Directive 2008/48/EC concerning credit agreements for consumers [2008] O.J. L133/66 Art.10. The relevant information duties imposed by the 2013 Regulations implement those required by Directive 2011/83/EU on consumer rights Art. 6. On national courts' duties to raise issues of EU consumer protection law generally see above, para.14-009.

Replace title footnote 1184 with:

The right to cancel[1184]

[1184] For a detailed discussion see *Chitty on Contracts*, 33rd edn (2018), Vol.II paras 38-112–38-131. **14-199**

Replace footnote 1191 with:

[1191] See 2013 Regulations reg.30(1) and (3). The 2011 Directive (which the 2013 Regulations implement) uses the notion of goods "coming into the physical possession of the consumer" in relation to sales contracts in the context of the consumer's right of cancellation (art.9(2)(b)) and in relation to its provisions governing the delivery of goods and the passing of risk (arts 18 and 20). In the case of the passing of risk, recital 55 of the Directive explains that "a consumer should be considered to have acquired the physical possession of the goods when he has received them". In order to achieve a coherent interpretation of the Directive, this explanation should also be used as regards "coming into physical possession of the consumer" for the purposes of the consumer's right of cancellation. On this basis, the question when goods have come into the physical possession of a consumer would become when he has received them, but the precise significance of the latter in a particular case would remain for national courts as a matter of the application of the law to the facts as they find them. The end of the period is calculated differently in the cases of sales contracts falling within reg.30(4) to (6) (multiple goods or multiple lots delivered on different days and contracts for regular delivery of goods during a defined period etc).

(iii) "Distance Contracts"

Background

Replace paragraph with:

For long the paradigm case of the sale of goods to consumers was one in which   **14-201** buyer and seller were in the physical presence of each other. However, more recently there has been a marked shift towards distance selling, whether through methods which have long been familiar (mail order catalogues, press advertising with accompanying order forms, and the like) or such modern counterparts as telephone sales, television shopping, email and the internet or online selling. Such transactions create difficulties in applying the traditional rules as to contract formation, for example, as to the so-called "click-wrap" contracts formed through clicking in a box or on an icon on the computer screen. These have been considered in an earlier chapter.[1207] There are also significant problems of consumer protection in that the buyer will not have seen the specific goods and, depending on the type of transaction, may be susceptible to pressure (as with "cold calling" on the telephone) or prone to buy on impulse (as with internet shopping). The temptation of the double-glazing trader offering "interest-free" terms, or the convenience of clicking on an icon, may not be easy to resist. After a protracted period of debate the Distance Selling Directive was agreed in 1997[1208] and was implemented in the UK by the Consumer Protection (Distance Selling) Regulations 2000.[1209] As earlier noted, the 1997 Directive was revoked and replaced by the Consumer Rights Directive 2011 and the latter's provisions relative to the information and cancellation requirements governing distance contracts were implemented in the UK by the Consumer Contracts (Information, Cancellation and Additional Charges) Regulations 2013[1210] which apply in relation to contracts entered into on or after 13 June 2014.[1211] It should be noted that there may be further reform in this area of the law as the EU has enacted directives affecting sales of goods and contracts for the supply of digital content.[1212] In both cases, the directives would make significant new substantive provision in relation to the categories of contract to which they would apply.

[1207] See paras 2-002, 2-012, 2-015. See also in relation to conflict of laws issues, below, paras 26-047 to 26-061, 26-116 to 26-117.

[1208] Directive 1997/7 [1997] O.J. L144/19. The 1997 Directive laid down only minimum requirements, so that laws which are more favourable to the consumer were permissible provided that they were compatible with the "free trade" provisions of the Treaty (notably, Arts 28–30): the relationship between the two was considered by the ECJ in *Criminal Proceedings against Gysbrechts* (C-205/07) [2009] 2 C.M.L.R. 2. However, the position in this respect was changed on the adoption of the Consumer Rights Directive 2011/83/EU which repeals and replaces the 1997 Directive and which in principle requires "full harmonization" (Art.4).

[1209] Consumer Protection (Distance Selling) Regulations 2000 (SI 2000/2334), as amended by SI 2004/2095, SI 2005/55, SI 2005/689, SI 2008/1277, SI 2009/209 and SI 2010/2960.

[1210] Consumer Contracts (Information, Cancellation and Additional Charges) Regulations 2013 (SI 2013/3134) reg.2(a).

[1211] 2013 Regulations reg.1(2). For contracts which continue to be governed by the 2000 Regulations, reference may be made to the previous (8th) edition of this work, paras 14-057 to 14-063.

[1212] Directive (EU) 2019/770 of the European Parliament and of the Council of 20 May 2019 on certain aspects concerning contracts for the supply of digital content and digital services [2019] O.J. L.136/1, above, para.14-022. In the case of sales of goods, the Commission first proposed a directive applicable only to online and other distance contracts (Proposal for a Directive of the European Parliament and of the Council on certain aspects concerning contracts for the online and other distance sales of goods Com (2015) 635 final), but this was later amended so as to apply to contracts of sale of goods more generally: Directive (EU) 2019/771 of the European Parliament and of the Council of 20 May 2019 on certain aspects concerning contracts for the sale of goods, etc [2019] O.J. L 136/28.

"Distance contracts" and the scope of application of the 2013 Regulations

Replace paragraph with:

14-202   The 2013 Regulations apply to a "distance contract" which is defined to mean, "a contract concluded between a trader and a consumer[1213] under an organised distance sales or service-provision scheme without the simultaneous physical presence of the trader and the consumer, with the exclusive use of one or more means of distance communication up to and including the time at which the contract is concluded".[1214] Hence the Regulations do not apply to private sales from one consumer to another, nor to business-to-business transactions. The requirement that the distance selling be via an "organised scheme" is also apt to exclude a business which does not operate an interactive website, but which responds to an isolated request from a consumer.[1214a] As earlier noted, certain contracts are wholly outside the 2013 Regulations,[1215] but in addition the Regulations set out a further list of circumstances in which a right of cancellation in the consumer is excluded.[1216] The list is lengthy, but examples include certain supplies of medicinal products or of products by a health care professional and a supply of passenger transport services[1217]; contracts for the supply of goods that are made to the consumer's specifications or are clearly personalised or are liable to deteriorate or expire rapidly[1218]; contracts where the consumer has specifically requested a visit from the trader for the purpose of carrying out urgent repairs or maintenance[1219]; contracts for the supply of a newspaper, periodical or magazine with the exception of subscription contracts for such publications[1220]; contracts concluded at a public auction (which would include an internet auction)[1221]; and contracts for the supply of accommodation, transport of goods, vehicle rental services, catering or services related to leisure activities if the contract provides for a specific date or period of performance (for example, air travel, concert performances or events).[1222] Finally, cancellation rights will cease to be available in the case of a contract for the supply of sealed goods which, for health protection or hygiene reasons, are not suitable for return if they become unsealed after delivery; or of sealed audio or sealed video recordings or, importantly, sealed computer software, if the goods become unsealed after delivery; or, in the case of any sales contract, if the goods become mixed inseparably with other items after delivery.[1223]

[1213] For the definition of these terms see 2013 Regulations reg.4 and above, paras 14-196 and 14-022 to 14-033.

[1214] 2013 Regulations reg.5. The corresponding provision in the 2000 Regulations contained an indicative list which referred to unaddressed printed matter, addressed printed matter, letter, press advertising with order form, catalogue, telephone with human intervention, telephone without human intervention (automatic calling machine, audiotext), radio, videophone (telephone with screen), videotext (microcomputer and television screen) with keyboard or touch screen, electronic mail, facsimile machine (fax) and television (teleshopping) (reg.3, Sch.1).

[1214a] European Commission, DG Justice Guidance Document concerning Directive 2011/83/EU etc. (June 2014) para.5.1 and see *Christopher Linnett Ltd v Harding (t/a MJ Harding Contractors)* [2017] EWHC 1781 (TCC); [2018] Bus. L.R. 179 at [86].

[1215] 2013 Regulations reg.6 above, para.14-196. However, some such contracts seem to be of more obvious relevance to distance, as opposed to, off-premises, contracts and vice versa.

[1216] 2013 Regulations Pt 3 (Right to cancel). See below, para.14-205.

[1217] 2013 Regulations reg.27(1) and (2).

[1218] 2013 Regulations reg.28(1)(b) and (c).

[1219] 2013 Regulations reg.28(1)(e) to which there are qualifications as specified in reg.28(2).

[1220] 2013 Regulations reg.28(1)(f).

[1221] 2013 Regulations reg.28(1)(g).

[1222] 2013 Regulations reg.28(1)(h). The ECJ has held, construing the equivalent provision in Art.3(2) of the 1997 Directive, that "contracts for the provision of transport services" includes car rental agreements: see *easyCar (UK) Ltd v Office of Fair Trading* (C-336/03) [2005] E.C.R. I-1947; [2005] 2 C.M.L.R. 2.

[1223] 2013 Regulations reg.28(3). For the approach of the CJEU to these exceptions (found in the 2011 Directive Art.16) and, in particular, the exclusion of goods which have been unsealed and are therefore unsuitable for return for health protection etc reasons see *slewo-schlafen leben wohnen GmbH v Ledowski* (C-681/17) EU:C:2019:255, 27 March 2019, [34]–[48].

Information to be provided

Replace paragraph with:

One of the central concerns of the 2013 Regulations is to require that before a **14-203** consumer is bound by a distance contract the trader must give, or make available to, the consumer the information listed in Sch.2 (as quoted in full above in the context of off-premises contracts)[1224] and do this in a clear and comprehensible manner and in a means appropriate to the type of distance communication used.[1225] In so far as the information is provided on a durable medium, it must be legible.[1226] The appropriateness of the means adopted will vary according to whether the information was given or made available in an advertisement or catalogue, on a website or over the phone, or in some other manner. If a right to cancel exists[1227] the trader must also give, or make available to, the consumer a cancellation form as set out in the model cancellation form contained in Pt B of Sch.3. As is to be expected, the necessary requirements as to the provision of information and the ways in which they may be satisfied overlap considerably with those which are required in the case of off-premises contracts.[1228] However, there are differences. In particular, in the case of a "means of distance communication which allows limited space or time to display the information", the Regulations require the trader to comply with a "minimum set of information requirements" while referring the consumer to another source of information, such as a free telephone number or a hypertext link to a webpage of the trader where the information is directly available and easily accessible".[1228a] Moreover, in cases where the distance contract is concluded by electronic means and the contract places the consumer under an obligation to pay, the trader must make the consumer aware in a clear and prominent manner, and directly before the consumer places the order, of information listed in various paragraphs of Sch.2.[1229] Further, the trader must also ensure that, when placing the order, the consumer explicitly acknowledges that it implies an obligation to pay[1230] and also that any trading website indicates clearly and legibly, at the latest at the beginning of the ordering process, whether any delivery restrictions apply and which means of payment are accepted.[1231] Another safeguard applies to telephone sales so that when a trader makes a telephone call to a consumer with a view to concluding a distance contract the trader must, at the beginning of the conversation with the consumer, disclose (a) the trader's identity; (b) where applicable, the identity of the person on whose behalf the trader makes the call; and (c) the commercial purpose of the call.[1232] Although this provision may sometimes benefit consumers, it may not always be easy to apply where the attempted conversation begins with requests to take part in "a survey" which later leads to an attempted sale. More generally, it is likely that the courts have a duty to consider of their own initiative whether the various information requirements set by the 2013 Regulations have been fulfilled and, if not, the legal consequences which follow from this infringement.[1233] Where a trader seller has supplied information as set out in Sch.2 of the 2013 Regulations, the Consumer Rights Act 2015 provides that this information "is to be treated as included as a term of the contract", as earlier explained.[1234]

[1224] See above, para.14-198.

[1225] See 2013 Regulations reg.13(1)(a). For this purpose, information is "made available to" a consumer only if "the consumer can reasonably be expected to know how to access it": see 2013 Regulations reg.8. For discussion of how "making information available" differs from "providing it" see *Chitty on Contracts*, 33rd edn (2018) Vol.II paras 38-091 to 38-093.

[1226] See 2013 Regulations reg.13(2). For the definition of "durable medium", see reg.5 and above, para.14-198 (note)

[1227] See above, para 14-202 and below, para.14-205.

[1228] See above, para.14-198. Note also this is also true of the burden of proof as to the trader's compliance with the relevant provisions affecting information requirements: see reg.17(1).

[1228a] 2013 Regulations reg.13(4) implementing the Consumer Rights Directive art.8(4) as explained in *Walbusch Walter Busch GmbH & Co KG v Zentrale zur Bekämpfung unlauteren Wettbewerbs Frankfurt am Main eV* (C-430/17) EU:C:2019:47, 23 January 2019, especially at [37].

[1229] 2013 Regulations reg.14(2). This information covers such matters as the main characteristics of the goods or services or digital content; their total price inclusive of taxes or the manner in which it is to be calculated; where applicable, all additional delivery charges; where the contract is one of a indeterminate duration or one containing a subscription, the total cost per billing period or, as the case may be, per month; where applicable, the duration of the contract or, if the contract is one of indeterminate duration or is to be extended automatically the conditions for terminating it; and, where applicable, the minimum duration of the consumer's obligation under the contract: see 2013 Regulations Sch.2 paras (a), (f), (g), (h), (s), and (t) and above, para.14-198.

[1230] 2013 Regulations reg.14(3). This is reinforced in cases where placing an order entails activating a button or similar function (reg.14(4)). The consequence of a failure to comply with reg.14(3) and (4) is that the consumer will not be bound by the contract or order: reg.14(5).

[1231] 2013 Regulations reg.14(6).

[1232] 2013 Regulations reg.15.

[1233] This follows from the decision of the CJEU in *Radlinger v Finway as* (C-377/14) [2016] 3 C.M.L.R. 28 at [62]–[74] where it held that national courts bear such duties in relation to information requirements under Directive 2008/48/EC concerning credit agreements for consumers [2008] O.J. L133/66 Art.10. The information duties imposed by the 2013 Regulations implement those required by Directive 2011/83/EU on consumer rights Art.6. On national courts' duties to raise issues of EU consumer protection law generally see above, para.14-009.

[1234] Consumer Rights Act 2015 ss.11(3)-(4) and 12 ("goods contracts") and see above, paras 14-076 to 14-077. The 2013 Regulations as originally enacted themselves contained provision (in reg.13(6) and (7)) giving contractual force to this information, but (except as regards certain digital content contracts) this is now contained in the 2015 Act.

Confirmation of distance contracts

Replace footnote 1235 with:

[1235] 2013 Regulations reg.16(1). For the definition of "durable medium", see reg.5 and above, para.14-198 (note). The equivalent provision in Directive 97/7/EC Art.5(1) required that the consumer "receive written confirmation". In *Content Services Ltd v Bundesarbeitskammer* (C-49/11) [2012] 2 All E.R. (Comm) 1019 the ECJ ruled that the requirement was not satisfied when the relevant information was accessible to the consumer only by clicking on a hyperlink on a website of the undertaking since in such circumstances the information was neither "given" by the undertaking nor "received" by the consumer.

14-204

Cancellation rights

Replace footnote 1241 with:

[1241] See paras 14-199 to 14-200 and for further discussion see *Chitty on Contracts*, 33rd edn (2018), Vol.II paras 38-086–38-089.

14-205

(v)   Enforcement

Enforcement measures

Replace footnote 1272 with:

[1272] Enterprise Act 2002 ss.210 and 212, Sch.13 Pt 1 para.9F; Enterprise Act 2002 (Part 8 EU Infringements) Order 2014 (SI 2014//2908) para.4. On the UK's leaving the EU on "exit day", "Community infringements" within the meaning of s.212 of the 2002 Act are to be replaced by "Schedule 13 infringements" and the 2013 Regulations are included within the substituted Sch.13 of the 2002 Act for this purpose: Consumer Protection (Enforcement) (Amendment etc.) (EU Exit) Regulations 2019 (SI 2019/203) reg.3(20) and Sch. para.1 inserting new 2002 Act Sch.13 para.25. On this change more generally see above, para.14-313A.

14-208

(d)   The Directive on Electronic Commerce

The Directive on Electronic Commerce

Replace paragraph with:

This Directive,[1274] which was implemented by the Electronic Commerce (EC Directive) Regulations 2002,[1275] is expressed as complementing information requirements established in a range of consumer protection measures, particularly the Distance Selling Directive.[1276] The overall objective is to contribute to the proper functioning of the internal market by ensuring the free movement of information society services between the Member States.[1277] Since these include selling goods online they are relevant in the present context. The Directive covers such matters as basic general information which must be provided (name and address of the

14-209

service provider including his electronic mail address etc),[1278] information to be provided in commercial communications (including promotional offers and competitions),[1279] and unsolicited commercial communications (which must be clearly identified as such).[1280] Further provisions apply to contracts concluded by electronic means. These include obligations of ensuring that the conclusion of such contracts is not deprived of legal effectiveness,[1281] information to be provided prior to the order being placed (e.g. the technical steps to follow to conclude the contract and to correct input errors)[1282] and principles which are applicable where orders are placed by technological means. This includes such matters as acknowledging the receipt of the order and the ability to identify and correct input errors before the order is placed.[1283] While these duties apply for the benefit of all "recipients" of the service, they may be excluded by agreement only where the parties are not consumers.[1284] The 2002 Regulations provide that the duties which they impose on service providers in this respect[1285] shall be enforceable by the recipient of the service in the tort of breach of statutory duty[1286] and that, in the case of a failure in the service provider to make available means of allowing a person to identify and correct input elements, a person may rescind any contract made, unless a court orders otherwise on the former's application.[1287] Apart from the last provision, the service provider's failures to perform these duties are not stated as affecting the validity of any contract made, but as a "Community infringement" they may attract enforcement measures under the Enterprise Act 2008 Pt 8.[1288]

[1274] Directive 2000/31 [2000] O.J. L178/1.

[1275] Electronic Commerce (EC Directive) Regulations 2002 (SI 2002/2013), as amended by, inter alia, SI 2003/115, SI 2003/2500 and SI 2004/1178. The scope of the Regulations is subject to a range of exclusions, e.g. in relation to taxation and data protection (reg.3) and there are alternative sources of control in the broad area of financial services and markets. On the UK's leaving the EU on "exit day" (on which generally see above, paras 14-006 et seq.), the 2002 Regulations are due to be amended: Electronic Commerce (Amendment etc.) (EU Exit) Regulations 2019 (SI 2019/87) ("SI 2019/87"). These amendments are noted below where relevant to the discussion.

[1276] Directive 1997/7 [1997] O.J. L144/19, implemented by the Consumer Protection (Distance Selling) Regulations 2000 (SI 2000/2334). The Distance Selling Directive was revoked and replaced by the Consumer Rights Directive 2011, which was implemented in UK law by the Consumer Contracts (Information, Cancellation and Additional Charges) Regulations 2013 (SI 2013/3134) as explained above, paras 14-201 to 14-205.

[1277] Directive 2000/31 Art.1.1.

[1278] Directive 2000/31 Art.5 and the corresponding provision in reg.6 (due to be amended by SI 2019/87 reg.3(6)). The requirements for compliance with Art.5(1) were considered by the ECJ in *Bundesverband der Verbraucherzentralen v Deutsche Internet Versicherung* (C-298/07) [2008] E.C.R. I-7841.

[1279] Directive 2000/31 Art.6 and reg.7.

[1280] Directive 2000/31 Art.7 and reg.8.

[1281] Directive 2000/31 Art.9.

[1282] Directive 2000/31 Art.10 and reg.9. This does not apply to contracts concluded exclusively by exchange of electronic mail or by equivalent individual communications (reg.9(4)).

[1283] Directive 2000/31 Art.11 and reg.11. The same exception for electronic mail is applicable as noted in previous note: reg.11(3).

[1284] Electronic Commerce (EC Directive) Regulations 2002 reg.9(1) and (2).

[1285] i.e. Electronic Commerce (EC Directive) Regulations 2002 regs 6–8, 9(1) and 11(1)(a).

[1286] Electronic Commerce (EC Directive) Regulations 2002 reg.13.

[1287] Electronic Commerce (EC Directive) Regulations 2002 reg.15 referring to the duty in reg.11(1)(b).

[1288] Enterprise Act 2002 s.210(6) and 212; Sch.13 Pt 1 para.9. On these enforcement powers see below, paras 14-306 to 14-316. On the UK's leaving the EU on "exit day", "Community infringements" within the meaning of s.212 of the 2002 Act are to be replaced by "Schedule 13 infringements" and regs 6–9 and 11 of the 2002 Regulations are included within the substituted Sch.13 of the 2002 Act for this purpose: Consumer Protection (Enforcement) (Amendment etc.) (EU Exit) Regulations 2019 (SI 2019/203) reg.3(20) and Sch. para.1 inserting new 2002 Act Sch.13 para.11. On this change more generally see above, para.14-313A.

(e) Payment Surcharges, Additional Payments, Help-Line Charges and Payment Services

Payment surcharges

Replace paragraph with:

A significant qualification on the general reluctance both of the legislature and **14-210** of the courts to inquire into the adequacy of the consideration furnished by the provider of goods and services is contained in the Consumer Rights (Payment Surcharges) Regulations 2012.[1289] Regulation 4 provides that: "A trader must not charge consumers,[1290] in respect of the use of a given means of payment, fees that exceed the cost borne by the trader for the use of that means". The prohibition applies only if "the use is as a means for the consumer to make payments for the purposes of a contract with the trader, and only to the extent that that contract—(a) is a sales or service contract,[1291] or a contract (other than a sales or service contract) for the supply of water, gas, electricity, district heating or digital content and (b) is not an excluded contract".[1292] Regulation 4's prohibition does not refer to any particular method of payment (such as a credit or debit card) and therefore applies to any means of payment that a trader decides to accept, including cash, cheques, prepaid cards, charge cards etc and this means that any new methods of paying will also be subject to this prohibition as the technology relating to payments develops.[1293-1294]

[1289] Consumer Rights (Payment Surcharges) Regulations 2012 (SI 2012/3110), as amended (with effect from 13 June 2014) by SI 2013/3134 reg.47, Sch.4 para.15; and implementing Directive 2011/83/EU on consumer rights [2011] O.J. L304/64 Art.19. See Reifa (2018) E.L.Rev. 343. See also the further controls on payment surcharges on the coming into force of amendments to the 2012 Regulations described below, para.14-210A. On the UK's leaving the EU on "exit day" (on which generally see above, paras 14-006 et seq.), the 2012 Regulations are due to be subject to minor amendment: Consumer Protection (Amendment etc.) (EU Exit) Regulations (SI 2018/1326) ("SI 2018/1326") reg.7.

[1290] For the definitions of "trader" and "consumer", see reg.2, as substituted in the case of the definition of "trader" by SI 2013/3134 reg.47, Sch.4 para.15(2); also, a definition of "business" was inserted to include "the activities of any government department or local or public authority" (para.15(3)(a)).

[1291] For the definitions of "sales contract" and "service contract", see reg.3, as amended in the case of "sales contract", by SI 2013/3134 reg.47, Sch.4 para.15(3)(b).

[1292] 2012 Regulations reg.5(1) and see 2012 Regulations reg.5(2) (due to be amended on "exit day" by SI 2018/1326 reg.7(2)), which lists those contracts which are excluded.

[1293-1294] Department of Business, Energy & Industrial Strategy, The Consumer Rights (Payment Surcharges) Regulations 2012, Guidance (June 2018) para.8.5.

Abolition of charges for use of non-commercial payment instruments; extension of protections to other "payers"

Replace paragraph (including title, above) with:

The protection for consumers set out in the previous paragraph was sup- **14-210A** plemented by a very wide prohibition on payment surcharges on the coming into force of amendments to the Consumer Rights (Payment Surcharges) Regulations 2012 made by the Payment Services Regulations 2017.[1295] These amendments implement a requirement imposed by the Second Payment Services Directive

2015,[1296] under which a payee, such as a retailer, "shall not request charges for the use of payment instruments" where their interchange fees are capped under the Interchange Fees Regulation 2015,[1297] this including the majority of consumer debit and credit cards.[1298] However, the UK's implementation of this aspect of the 2015 Directive went further than this requirement, as the Directive permits where a Member State considers that this is needed to encourage competition and promote the use of efficient payment instruments.[1299] As a result, under reg.6A(1) of the 2012 Regulations (as inserted by the 2017 Regulations), "a payee[1300] must not charge a payer[1301] any fee in respect of payment by means of a payment instrument as long as it is not a commercial card or other commercial payment instrument,[1301a] whether or not it is a card-based payment instrument within the meaning of the Interchange Fees Regulation 2015; nor must a payee charge in respect of a payment service (such as a direct debit) in euro[1301b]. As a result (and subject to territorial limitations[1301c]), under the 2012 Regulations as amended, reg.6A(1) imposes a ban on surcharging applicable to all non-commercial retail payment instruments, including means such as PayPal as well as credit and debit cards[1301d]; and where reg.6A(1) does not apply (and subject to its own conditions), reg.4 prohibits traders from charging consumers more than the direct cost borne by them for use of the relevant means of payment. Finally, reg.6A(2)[1301e] imposes the same control in respect of most payments between businesses made with commercial payment instruments. The new rules contained in reg.6A of the 2012 Regulations apply to *charges made* on or after 13 January 2018, except for charges under *contracts entered into* before 18 July 2017 (the date on which the 2017 Regulations were made).[1301f]

[1295] SI 2017/752 ("2017 Regulations") reg.156; Sch.8 Pt 3 para.12. The 2017 Regulations are due to be amended on the UK's exit from the EU, though these amendments apply only marginally to the provisions discussed here: Electronic Money, Payment Services and Payment Systems (Amendment and Transitional Provisions) (EU Exit) Regulations 2018 (SI 2018/1201) Sch.2, Pt 2.

[1296] Directive (EU) 2015/2366 of the European Parliament and of the Council of 25 November 2015 on payment services in the internal market [2015] O.J. L337/35 ("2015 Directive"), art.62(3)–(4).

[1297] Regulation (EU) 2015/251 of the European Parliament and of the Council of 29 April 2015 on interchange fees for card-based payment transactions [2015] O.J. L123/1 ("Interchange Fees Regulation 2015"). On the UK's exit from the EU on "exit day" (on which generally see above, paras 14-006 et seq.) the Interchange Fees Regulation 2015 (which will generally form part of "retained EU law") is due to be amended: Interchange Fee (Amendment) (EU Exit) Regulations 2019 (SI 2019/284) ("SI 2019/284") Pt 3. These amendments restrict the scope of the retained Regulation to the UK rather than the EU.

[1298] Explanatory Memorandum to the 2017 Regulations, para.7.16.

[1299] 2015 Directive art.62(5).

[1300] A "payee" for the purposes of reg.6A is defined in reg.3 of the 2012 Regulations (as inserted) by reference to reg.2(1) of the 2017 Regulations as "a person who is the intended recipient of funds which have been the subject of a payment transaction." Unlike reg.4, reg.6A is not, therefore, restricted to payments made to traders.

[1301] Under reg.3 of the 2012 Regulations (as inserted and referring to reg.2(1) of the 2017 Regulations) ""payer" means— (a) a person who holds a payment account and initiates, or consents to the initiation of, a payment order from that payment account; or (b) where there is no payment account, a person who gives a payment order". Unlike the protections in reg.4, there is no restriction to "payers" being consumers, but reg.6A excludes payment instruments which are "commercial cards".

[1301a] 2012 Regulations reg.6A(1)(a)(ii) and (b)(ii). "Commercial card" is defined by art.2(6) of the Interchange Fees Regulation 2015 as "any card-based payment instrument issued to undertakings or public sector entities or self-employed natural persons which is limited in use for business expenses where the payments made with such cards are charged directly to the account of the undertaking or public sector entity or self-employed natural person".

[1301b] "Payment service" is defined by reg.3 of the 2012 Regulations (as amended) by reference to the

2017 Regulations reg.2(1), which refers to lists in its Sch.1 (due to be amended on the UK's exit from the EU by SI 2018/1201 Sch.2, Pt 2, para.69).

[1301c] These are contained in the 2012 Regulations reg.6B which as enacted in 2017 refers to the location in "an EEA State" of the payment service provider of the payer or the payment service provider of the payee. On the UK's exit from the EU on "exit day" (on which see generally, above, para.14-006 et seq.), these references to "an EEA State" are to be replaced by references to "the United Kingdom": SI 2018/1326 reg.7(3).

[1301d] Explanatory Memorandum to the 2017 Regulations, para.7.16; Department of Business, Energy & Industrial Strategy, The Consumer Rights (Payment Surcharges) Regulations 2012, Guidance (June 2018) para.3.2.

[1301e] This is the effect of reg.6A(2)'s use of the very general terms "payer" and "payee" as earlier noted.

[1301f] 2012 Regulations reg.1(3) as inserted by the 2017 Regulations Sch.8(3) (as regards the temporal effect on contracts of reg.6A); 2017 Regulations reg.1(6) (in relation to the prohibition on charging in reg.6A).

After paragraph 14-210A, add new paragraph 14-210B:

Enforcement of rules on payment surcharges Enforcement of the controls on   **14-210B**
payment charges in reg.4 and of the new controls in reg.6A of the 2012 Regulations is primarily through applications by an enforcement authority for an injunction.[1301g] Where a trader charges a fee in contravention of reg.4 or any payee charges a fee in contravention of reg.6A, any provision of a contract requiring the payment of the fee is unenforceable to the extent that the charging of the fee contravenes those regulations and "the contract for the purposes of which the payment is made is to be treated as providing for the fee to be repaid to the extent that the charging of the fee contravenes regs 4 or 6A.[1301h] In addition, the relevant provisions of the 2012 Regulations have been designated as the "specified UK law" for the purposes of "Community infringements" under s.212 of the Enterprise Act 2002[1301i] and this means that the various powers provided by Pt. 8 of the 2002 Act are available for their enforcement.[1301j]

[1301g] See 2012 Regulations regs 7 and 8 (as amended in particular by SI 2017/752 Sch.8(3) para.12(7). Note also that an enforcement authority is under a duty (albeit a qualified one) to consider a complaint based on contravening reg.4. It does not simply have a power to do so.

[1301h] 2012 Regulations reg.10 (as amended by SI 2017/752 Sch.8(3) para.12(8)).

[1301i] Enterprise Act 2002 (Part 8 EU Infringements) Order 2014 (SI 2014/2908) art.3 and Sch. The Consumer Rights Directive 2011 and art.62(3) (second sentence), (4) and (5) of the Payment Services Directive 2015 are listed in the 2002 Act Sch.13 paras 9F and 16 respectively. On the UK's leaving the EU on "exit day", "Community infringements" are to be replaced by "Schedule 13 infringements" and the 2012 Regulations regs 4 and 6A to 10 are included within the substituted Sch.13 of the 2002 Act for this purpose: Consumer Protection (Enforcement) (Amendment etc.) (EU Exit) Regulations 2019 (SI 2019/203) reg.3(20) and Sch. para.1 inserting new 2002 Act Sch.13 para.24. On this change see generally below, para.14-313A.

[1301j] See below, paras 14-308–14-316.

Help-line charges

Replace footnote 1310 with:

[1310] *Zentrale zur Bekämpfung unlauteren Wettbewerbs Frankfurt am Main eV v comtech GmbH* (C-568/   **14-212**
15) 2 March 2017 at [27]–[32]. The prohibition applies regardless of the type of telephone number by which the consumer customer can contact the trader and therefore applies equally to a speed dial number at a rate higher than the basic rate even if the trader also provides another telephone number at the basic rate so that it can be said that the consumer to have chosen to use the higher rate number: *Starman v Tarbijakaitseamet* (C-332/17) EU:C:2018:72 of 13 September 2018 at [30]–[33].

Unauthorised payment transactions

Replace paragraph with:

In all categories of sales or the provision of services to consumers (whether off-   **14-213** premises, distance or on-premises[1311]) the consumer may benefit from additional protections provided by the Payment Services Regulations 2017.[1312] If the consumer denies having authorised an executed payment transaction or claims that a payment transaction has not been correctly executed, it is for "the payment service provider to prove that the payment transaction was authenticated, accurately recorded, entered in the payment service provider's accounts and not affected by a technical breakdown or some other deficiency in the service provided by the payment service provider."[1313] Moreover, in principle, the payment service provider must immediately refund the amount of any unauthorised payment transaction to the payer and, where applicable, restore the debited payment account to the state it would have been in had the unauthorised payment transaction not taken place.[1314] The general rule is that a payment service provider potentially liable to refund in this way may require that the payer is liable up to a maximum of £35 for any losses incurred in respect of unauthorised payment transactions arising from the use of a lost or stolen payment instrument, or from the misappropriation of a payment instrument, but the payer is liable for all losses incurred in respect of an unauthorised payment transaction where he or she has acted fraudulently or has with intent or gross negligence failed to comply with his or her obligations in respect of use or notification of loss etc. of a payment instrument and in relation to "personalised security credentials".[1315]

[1311] On these categories see above, paras 14-195 et seq.

[1312] SI 2017/752 ("2017 Regulations") implementing Directive (EU) 2015/2366 on payment services in the internal market [2015] O.J. L337/35. On the dates of the coming into force of the provisions of these regulations see reg.1. The 2017 Regulations repealed and replaced the Payment Services Regulations 2009 (SI 2009/209) regs 59–62, which implemented Directive 2007/64/EC [2007] O.J. L319/1 (itself repealed and replaced by Directive (EU) 2015/2366).

[1313] 2017 Regulations reg.75(1) (in force 13 January 2018). Cf. 2009 Regulations reg.60.

[1314] 2017 Regulations reg.76 (in force 13 January 2018). Cf. 2009 Regulations reg.61.

[1315] 2017 Regulations reg.77 (in force 13 January 2018, except for reg.77(4)(c) and (6) which are not in force), which makes further provision in respect of the relative responsibilities of payment service provider and payer. Cf. 2009 Regulations reg.62.

(f) "Inertia selling"

Unordered goods

Replace footnote 1319 with:

14-214 [1319] 2008 Regulations reg.3(4)(1) and 4(d). "Inertia selling" is described in the list of "commercial practices which are in all circumstances considered unfair" in Sch.1 para.29 (amended by the Consumer Contracts (Information, Cancellation and Additional Charges) Regulations 2013 (SI 2013/3134) reg.47, Sch.4 para.9 and subsequently corrected by the Consumer Protection (Amendment) Regulations 2014 (SI 2014/870) reg.9 (5)(b), which came into force on 13 June 2014 (reg.1(2)). This prohibition reflects the requirement of Directive 2005/29 concerning unfair business-to-consumer commercial practices in the internal market Art.5(1) and (5); Annex I para 29. The CJEU has held that the sale of SIM (Subscriber Identity Module) cards by a telecommunications operator on which services such as internet browsing services and voicemail services are pre-loaded and pre-activated, the fees for those services being charged to the user if the services were not deactivated at the user's express request, without sufficiently informing the consumer in advance of that pre-loading and pre-activation nor of the cost of those services, falls within the definition of inertia selling within the meaning of para.29 as the services are thereby "unsolicited". "For a service to be solicited the consumer must have made a free choice" and "[t]hat supposes, in particular, that the information provided by the trader to the consumer is clear and adequate" and for this purpose information about the price is of fundamental importance: *Autorità Garante della Concorrenza e del Mercato v Wind Tre SpA and Vodafone Italia SpA* (Joined Cases C-54/17 and C-55/177) EU:C:2018:710 of 13 September 2018 at [45]–[47].

(g) Manufacturers' Guarantees

The Consumer Sales Directive 1999 and the Consumer Rights Act 2015 s.30

Replace paragraph with:

Important modifications were introduced into the English law governing goods **14-218** under guarantee as a result of implementing the Consumer Sales Directive Art.6.[1337] The relevant implementing provisions were first contained in the Sale and Supply of Goods to Consumers Regulations 2002 reg.15,[1338] but the 2015 Act revoked the 2002 Regulations and the implementation of Art.6 of the 1999 Directive now appears in s.30 of the 2015 Act. While the drafting differs between the two UK implementing provisions, the substance remains the same. Accordingly, s.30 applies where there is a contract to supply goods, and there is a guarantee in relation to the goods.[1339] A "guarantee" for these purposes is:

> "an undertaking to the consumer given without extra charge by a person acting in the course of the person's business (the 'guarantor'[1340]) that, if the goods do not meet the specifications set out in the guarantee statement or in any associated advertising—
>
> (a)   the consumer will be reimbursed for the price paid for the goods, or
> (b)   the goods will be repaired, replaced or handled in any way."[1341]

The Act provides that the guarantee "takes effect, at the time the goods are delivered, as a contractual obligation owed by the guarantor" on its terms and on any associated advertising.[1342] The guarantor must ensure that the guarantee sets out in plain and intelligible language[1343] the contents of the guarantee and the essential particulars for making claims under the guarantee and that it states that the consumer has statutory rights in relation to the goods and that those rights are not affected by the guarantee.[1344]Section 30 makes further detailed provision as to the contents and availability to the consumer of the guarantee.[1345] These duties on guarantors and other traders may be enforced by injunction on the application of the CMA or a local weights and measures authority.[1346] Moreover, as s.30 implements the 1999 Directive, it attracts the enforcement measures put in place for "Community infringements" which harm the collective interests of consumers under the Enterprise Act 2002 Pt 8.[1347]

[1337]   Directive 1999/44 on certain aspects of the sale of consumer goods and associated guarantees [1999] O.J. L172/12.

[1338]   Sale and Supply of Goods to Consumers Regulations 2002 (SI 2002/3045).

[1339]   2015 Act s.30(1) and see 2015 Act s.3(1) and (2), above, para.14-052 et seq. on "contracts for a trader to supply goods to a consumer".

[1340]   There is no definition of "guarantor" in the 2015 Act except the designation in s.30(2), with the result that any person who gives a guarantee as is described there (whether the trader party to the goods contract, the producer of the goods or any other person) can be a "guarantor" subject to the condition that they act in the course of their business. On the definition of "business" for this purpose see 2015 Act s.2(7) and above, para.14-032.

[1341]   2015 Act s.30(2).

[1342]   2015 Act s.30(3). This would mean that any failure in respect of the undertakings in the guarantee would give rise to the normal remedies for breach of contract (and notably damages) provided under the general law: on damages see *Chitty on Contracts*, 33rd edn (2018), Vol.I Ch.26.

[1343]   As the 2015 Act s.30 implements Art.6 of the 1999 Directive, it is submitted that the interpretation of this requirement should follow the approach taken by the CJEU for the purposes of the Unfair Terms in Consumer Contracts Directive 1993 Arts 4(2) and 5, as explained above, paras 14-172 to 14-173.

[1344] 2015 Act s.30(4)(a) and (b). Where the goods are offered within the territory of the UK, the guarantee must be written in English: ibid. s.30(4)(c).

[1345] These contents must include the name and address of the guarantor and the duration and territorial scope of the guarantee. The guarantor and any other person who offers to supply to consumers the goods which are the subject of the guarantee must, on request by the consumer, make the guarantee available to the consumer within a reasonable time, in writing and in a form accessible to the consumer: 2015 Act s.30(5)–(7).

[1346] 2015 Act s.30(8)–(10).

[1347] Enterprise Act 2002 s.212; Sch.13 Pt 1 para.8; s.30 is specified as a provision giving effect to the 1999 Directive by the Enterprise Act 2002 (Part 8 Community Infringements Specified UK Laws) Order 2003 (SI 2003/1374) Art.3 and Sch. (as amended by SI 2015/1628 Art.2(2)(b) and has also been specified as capable of giving rise to a "domestic infringement" for the purposes of s.211 of the 2002 Act: Enterprise Act 2002 (Part 8 Domestic Infringements) Order 2015 Art.2 and see below, paras 14-309 et seq. On the UK's leaving the EU on "exit day", "Community infringements" are to be replaced by "Schedule 13 infringements" and s.30 of the 2015 Act is included within the substituted Sch.13 of the 2002 Act for this purpose: Consumer Protection (Enforcement) (Amendment etc.) (EU Exit) Regulations 2019 (SI 2019/203) reg.3(20) and Sch. para.1 inserting new 2002 Act Sch.13 para.27. On this change generally, see below, para.14-313A.

(h)   Product liability

(iii)   Liability under the Consumer Protection Act 1987 Pt I

Introduction

In the first paragraph, after "be construed accordingly.", add new footnote 1411a:

14-228   [1411a] On the UK's leaving the EU on "exit day" (on which see above, para.14-006 et seq.), s.1(1) is due to be amended so as to read: "This Part was enacted for the purpose of making such provision as was necessary in order to comply with the product liability Directive and shall be construed accordingly": Product Safety and Metrology etc. (Amendment etc.) (EU Exit) Regulations (SI 2019/696) ("SI 2019/696") reg.6 and Sch.3, para.2(2).

Replace the second paragraph with:

The final point is that the High Court has held, in the context of a case involving an allegedly defective prosthetic hip implant which, it was claimed, had caused damage in other jurisdictions, that neither the 1987 Act nor the Directive on which it is based provided for claims to be brought in respect of damage suffered by persons outside the territory of the EU or EEA who have no connection with the EEA, and where the marketing and supply of the defective product was outside the EEA.[1417]

[1417] *Allen v Depuy International Ltd* [2014] EWHC 753 (QB); [2014] All ER (D) 235 (Mar.) at [32] (Stewart J). On the UK's leaving the EU on "exit day" (on which see generally above, para.14-006 et seq.), the question would arise whether the territorial application of Pt 1 of the 1987 Act would be restricted to the UK rather than the EEA. For this purpose, it would be relevant that references to the EU in the 1987 Act are due to be replaced with ones to the UK, e.g. the 1987 Act s.2(2)(c)'s reference to importing "into a member State from a place outside the member States" will be replaced with importing "into the United Kingdom": SI 2019/696 reg.6, Sch.3, para.3.

Persons subject to liability

Replace footnote 1425 with:

14-230   [1425] 1987 Act s.2(2)(c). See, e.g. *Ide v ATB Sales Ltd* [2008] EWCA Civ 424; [2009] R.T.R. 85 (importer of mountain bike held liable when handlebar fractured and broke off, causing rider to fall to the ground and sustain injury). On the UK's leaving the EU on "exit day" (on which see generally above, para.14-006 et seq.), the reference to importing "into a member State from a place outside the member States" will be replaced with importing "into the United Kingdom": SI 2019/696 reg.6, Sch.3, para.3.

The definition of a defect

Replace paragraph with:

The issue of defectiveness was considered by Burton J. against the background **14-233** of tragic circumstances in *A v National Blood Authority*.[1444] The claimants had been infected with hepatitis C through blood transfusions or blood products, usually in the course of undergoing surgery. The source of the infection was not contamination by an outside agent, but came, rather, from a donor's blood. In the relevant period, the risk of infection was known to the medical profession in general terms, but it was impossible to avoid in any given case—whether because the virus had not been identified or, at a later stage, because it was undetectable through a screening test. Burton J held that persons generally were entitled to expect that blood would be free from what was, in effect, an unavoidable risk and that "avoidability of the harmful characteristic" was not a relevant circumstance to take into account when determining whether a product was defective.[1445] A cover to be attached to a child's pushchair by an elasticated buckle was also held to be defective in *Abouzaid v Mothercare (UK) Ltd*[1446] even though the danger of the attachment snapping back had not previously been contemplated or appeared in accident statistics.[1447] By contrast, in *Wilkes v Depuy International Ltd.*[1448] Hickinbottom J held that the fracture of a steel femoral shaft (the "C-Stem") after insertion into the claimant by way of hip-replacement did not render it defective in the circumstances. In his view, under the 1987 Act, "safety is inherently and necessarily a relative concept" and "no medicinal product, if effective, can be absolutely safe"; moreover, "however consumer expectations are defined and gauged, there cannot be a sensible expectation that any medicine or medicinal product is entirely risk-free" and the "potential benefits (including potential utility) of such a product have to be balanced against its risks."[1449] What persons generally are "entitled to expect" must be understood objectively, and not from the point of view of a particular patient or even a notional individual or group of individuals.[1450] For this purpose, the avoidability of the risk of harm should be seen in the broader context of the risk-benefit balance.[1451] The learned judge concluded that the C-Stem was not defective in design, taking into account in particular the very low failure rate as a result of fatigue fractures (0.004%), that the risk of fracture had been warned against, that a suggested change in design may have had design dis-benefits, that the C-Stem complied with all relevant mandatory standards, and that the consequences of the fracture of the C-Stem are relatively limited, that is, the need for the patient to undergo a further replacement hip operation.[1452] The approach to the interpretation and application of defect taken by Hickinbottom J in *Wilkes v Dupuy International Ltd.* was followed by Andrews J in *Gee v Depuy International Ltd.*[1452a] In his view, a court is entitled to have regard for this purpose to "all circumstances which may have a bearing on the assessment of the safety of the product" although those "circumstances may differ, depending on the nature of the product and the nature of the complaint about it".[1452b] In particular, the relative costs or benefits of a product "may sometimes play a legitimate part in the evaluation of the degree of safety risk that the public would be expected to tolerate, because there may be cases in which one cannot fairly or sensibly evaluate the latter without looking at the former."[1452c] For example, "where a product includes a feature which gives it a potential functional advantage, or eliminates a perceived deficiency in design, but by doing so necessarily introduces a risk, it is artificial to prevent the Court from considering that actual or potential benefit when making an assessment of whether the product is defective."[1452d] Moreover, the fact that a product creates a risk of injury does not itself render it defective unless the risk created is abnormal.[1452e] On the facts before the court in *Gee*, it was held that the claimants had failed to show that the product (a hip replacement prosthesis) was defective in that it entailed a materially worse failure rate (actual or expected) than comparator products.[1452f]

[1444] *A v National Blood Authority* [2001] 3 All E.R. 289. See Howells and Mildred, (2002) 65 M.L.R. 95; Hodges, (2001) 117 L.Q.R. 528; Goldberg, (2002) 10 Med. L. Rev. 165.

[1445] The infected blood was classified as a "non-standard" product in the sense of one which had not been produced as intended. Cf. *Wilkes v Depuy International Ltd* [2016] EWHC 3096 (QB); [2017] 3 All E.R. 589 at [94] where Hickinbottom J considered the distinction between standard and non-standard products to be "as a classification unnecessary and undesirable": it is not present in the 1987 Act nor the 1985 Directive and the question whether a particular product is within the producer's specification and compliant with relevant standards may be *relevant* to the level of safety to which persons generally are entitled to expect. See also *Gee v Depuy International Ltd., "The Depuy Pinnacle Metal on Metal Hip Litigation"*, [2018] EWHC 1208 (QB); unreported, at [157]–[160] where it was considered that the distinction between standard and non-standard products may, but will not necessarily, be relevant to the assessment of defect.

[1446] *Abouzaid v Mothercare (UK) Ltd* [2002] All E.R. (D) 2436; *Times,* 20 February 2001 (the Cosytoes case). See also *Ide v ATB Sales Ltd* [2008] EWCA Civ 424; [2009] R.T.R. 85 (handlebar of mountain bike fractures when in use: importer held liable for resultant injury).

[1447] An elder brother's retina was badly damaged; cf. *Richardson v LRC Products Ltd* [2000] Lloyd's Rep. Med. 280 (bursting condom leading to pregnancy: no liability); *B (a Child) v McDonald's Restaurants Ltd* [2002] EWHC 490 (burns from scalding coffee: no liability). See also *Palmer v Estate of Palmer* [2006] EWHC 1284 (QB) ("Klunk klip" device which was designed to introduce slack into inertia reel seatbelt held to be defective).

[1448] [2016] EWHC 3096 (QB); [2017] 3 All E.R. 589.

[1449] [2016] EWHC 3096 (QB) at [65].

[1450] [2016] EWHC 3096 (QB) at [69].

[1451] [2016] EWHC 3096 (QB) at [88] and [89].

[1452] [2016] EWHC 3096 (QB) at [114]–[134].

[1452a] *"The Depuy Pinnacle Metal on Metal Hip Litigation"* [2018] EWHC 1208 (QB); [2018] Med. L.R. 347.

[1452b] [2018] EWHC 1208 (QB) at [160].

[1452c] [2018] EWHC 1208 (QB) at [152] (original emphasis).

[1452d] [2018] EWHC 1208 (QB) at [153] (therefore rejecting at [154] – [155] "rigid rules of more general application pertaining to the circumstances that fall to be legally excluded from consideration when evaluating safety" as Burton J. had apparently laid down in *A v National Blood Authority* [2001] 3 All E.R. 289 at [68]).

[1452e] [2018] EWHC 1208 (QB) at [101]–[134], referring to *Baker v KTM Sportmotorcycle UK Ltd.* [2017] EWCA Civ 378 at [36] (defect found in the susceptibility of motorcycle brakes to corrode after limited and normal use and notwithstanding proper servicing, cleaning and maintenance).

[1452f] [2018] EWHC 1208 (QB) at [498]–[500].

Boston Scientific Medizintechnik GmbH

Replace paragraph with:

14-234   In *Boston Scientific Medizintechnik GmbH*, the Court of Justice of the EU considered for the first time directly the proper interpretation of the concept of "defect" within the meaning of the Product Liability Directive Art.6 on unusual facts.[1453] There, a company imported and marketed cardiac pacemakers and implantable cardioverter defibrillators in the EU. In the case of the pacemakers, the company informed treating physicians that a component used in them might experience gradual degradation which might result in loss of pacing without warning and it therefore recommended that they should consider replacing them for the patients affected and undertook to make replacement devices available free of charge. Following this recommendation, the pacemakers implanted in two patients were replaced and then destroyed without any expert opinion as to their functioning. The company wrote in similar terms concerning the defibrillators, which it was said might be affected by a defect in one of their components which could lead to it operating in the patient in a way which could be fatal. In both situations, the medical insurers of the patients (as subrogated to the latters' claims) claimed damages against the company in respect of the costs incurred in effecting the medical procedures by which replacement medical devices were implanted. In these circumstances, it could not be established that the particular medical devices originally implanted in the patients themselves suffered from the defects in question and so the question for the Court of Justice was whether the medical devices affected by the potential defect were thereby "defective" within the meaning of Art.6. For this purpose, the court observed that:

> "The safety which the public at large is entitled to expect, ... must ... be assessed by taking into account, inter alia, the intended purpose, the objective characteristics and properties of the product in question and the specific requirements of the group of users for whom the product is intended."[1454]

In the case of medical devices such as pacemakers, the "particularly vulnerable situation of patients using such devices, the safety requirements for those devices which such patients are entitled to expect are particularly high".[1455] Moreover, "the potential lack of safety which would give rise to liability" on the producer stems for products of this type "from the abnormal potential for damage which those products might cause to the person concerned".[1456] As a result:

> "where it is found that products [of this type] belonging to the same group or forming part of the same production series have a potential defect, it is possible to classify as defective all the products in that group or series, without there being any need to show that the product in question is defective."[1457]

This interpretation was seen as consistent with the Directive's objective in ensuring a fair appointment of the risks inherent in modern technological production between the injured person and the producer.[1458] While decided in a very particular context, this judgment appears to reflect more generally a concern that the Directive should be interpreted in a way which takes proper account of its purpose in furthering consumer protection as well as in integrating the internal market through the harmonisation of liability rules.[1459] On the other hand, according to Andrews J in *Gee v Depuy International Ltd*, the decision of the Court of Justice in *Boston Scientific Medizintechnik GmbH* did not establish that a defect in a product should be identified in its potential for damage and that when this potential crosses a threshold of what persons generally are entitled to expect, the product is to be regarded as defective.[1459a] In *Boston Scientific Medizintechnik GmbH* some (but not all) of the products in the group were clearly defective as failing the objective standard of safety, and it was in this special context that the Court of Justice had held that a product with such a potential defect could be classified as defective as itself failing to achieve the level of safety that the general public would expect.[1459b]

[1453] *Boston Scientific Medizintechnik GmbH v APL Sachsen-Anhalt – Die Gesundheitskasse, Betriebskrankenkasse RWE* (C-503/13 and C-504/13) [2015] 3 C.M.L.R. 6.

1454 *Boston Scientific Medizintechnik GmbH v APL Sachsen-Anhalt – Die Gesundheitskasse, Betriebskrankenkasse RWE* (C-503/13 and C-504/13) [2015] 3 C.M.L.R. 6 at [38].

1455 *Boston Scientific Medizintechnik GmbH v APL Sachsen-Anhalt – Die Gesundheitskasse, Betriebskrankenkasse RWE* (C-503/13 and C-504/13) [2015] 3 C.M.L.R. 6 at [39].

1456 *Boston Scientific Medizintechnik GmbH v APL Sachsen-Anhalt – Die Gesundheitskasse, Betriebskrankenkasse RWE* (C-503/13 and C-504/13) [2015] 3 C.M.L.R. 6 at [39].

1457 *Boston Scientific Medizintechnik GmbH v APL Sachsen-Anhalt – Die Gesundheitskasse, Betriebskrankenkasse RWE* (C-503/13 and C-504/13) [2015] 3 C.M.L.R. 6 at [41].

1458 *Boston Scientific Medizintechnik GmbH v APL Sachsen-Anhalt – Die Gesundheitskasse, Betriebskrankenkasse RWE* (C-503/13 and C-504/13) [2015] 3 C.M.L.R. 6 at [42].

1459 For the CJEU's decision on the application of Art.9 of the 1985 Directive, see below, para.14-235. In his opinion of 7 March 2017 in *W and others v Sanofi Pasteur MSD SNC* (C-621/15) A.G. Bobek at [87] expressed the view that the notion of defect under Art.6 of the Directive "essentially refers to baseline expectations of the product under normal conditions of use. It does not mean that where the product is used normally and causes serious harm in an individual case, that a conclusion of defectiveness necessarily requires a balancing of the costs and benefits of the product". The CJEU in its judgment of 21 June 2017, at [32] and [41], did not explain the concept of defect except by reference to its earlier judgment in *Boston Scientific Medizintechnik GmbH v APL Sachsen-Anhalt - Die Gesundheitskasse, Betriebskrankenkasse RWE* (C-503/13 and C-504/13).

1459a *"The Deputy Pinnacle Metal on Metal Hip Litigation"* [2018] EWHC 1208 (QB), [2018] Med. L.R. 347 at [120].

1459b [2018] EWHC 1208 (QB) at [125]–[126].

Defences available

Replace paragraph with:

14-236   Section 4 of the Act makes provision for some six defences which mitigate the strict liability otherwise imposed. Most are relatively uncontroversial. Thus by s.4(1)(a) it is a defence to prove that the defect is attributable to compliance with a requirement imposed by or under any enactment or with any EU obligation.1469a This defence is therefore restricted in its scope and does not mean that a defendant will have a defence merely if he complies with the applicable regulatory safety or other standard. Section 4(1)(b) provides a defence on proof that the defendant did not at any time supply1470 the product to another, while s.4(1)(c) provides a defence on showing that any such supply was otherwise than in the course of a business.1471 A further defence in s.4(1)(d) is based on proving that the defect did not exist in the product at "the relevant time" which, broadly speaking, is the time of supply.1472 The defence is unlikely to assist manufacturers when, for example, foreign objects are found in bottles or tins, but it may be more helpful when they can plausibly suggest that the defect was caused by a lack of servicing or incorrect storage or installation by a third party.

1469a On the UK's leaving the EU on "exit day" (on which see generally above, para.14-006 et seq.), "any EU obligation" in s.4(1)(a) is due to be replaced with "any retained EU obligation": SI 2019/696 reg.6, Sch.3, para.4.

1470 See the 1987 Act s.46. The equivalent provision in Art.7(a) of the Directive confers a defence on proving that the producer did not "put the product into circulation". This expression has been discussed in *Veedfald v Arhus Amtskommune* (C-203/99) [2001] E.C.R. I-3569; see Taschner, (2002) 39 C.M.L. Rev. 385; also, below para.n.1494.

1471 By the 1987 Act s.4(1)(c)(ii) it must further be proved that the defendant is not within s.2(2) and, if he is, is so by virtue only of things done otherwise than with a view to profit. As to "business", see s.45(1).

1472 See the 1987 Act s.4(2) which, however, makes special provision both for electricity and (in subs.(2)(b)) for a person who is not within s.2(2). For a decision in which s.4(1)(d) was successfully pleaded, see *Piper v JRI Manufacturing Ltd* [2006] EWCA Civ 1344; [2006] All E.R. (D) 181 (Oct) (hip prosthesis which had sheered requiring replacement).

(iv)   Civil Liability for Breach of Statutory Duty

Illegality affecting contract

Replace footnote 1509 with:

[1509] *Anderson Ltd v Daniel* [1924] 1 K.B. 138. See also *B and B Viennese Fashions v Losane* [1952] 1 All E.R. 909; cf. *Marles v Philip Trant & Sons* [1954] 1 Q.B. 29 (successful action by buyer). But cf. *St John Shipping Corp v Joseph Rank Ltd* [1957] 1 Q.B. 267. See further, Enonchong, *Illegal Transactions* (1998), Ch.15; Law Commission Consultation Paper (No.154), *Illegal Transactions: The Effect of Illegality on Contracts and Trusts* (1999); Law Commission Consultative Report, The Illegality Defence (L.C.C.P 189 (2009)); Treitel, *The Law of Contract*, 14th edn (Peel), Ch.11; *Chitty on Contracts*, 33rd edn (2018), Vol.I Ch.16 and above, paras 3-027 et seq.

14-245

4.   CONSUMER REDRESS

Replace title footnote 1519 with:

Arbitration[1519]

[1519] *Chitty on Contracts*, 33rd edn (2018), Vol.II Ch.32 esp. para.32-013.

14-248

"ADR" and "ODR"

Replace paragraph with:

EU legislation has provided for the establishment of a European online dispute resolution (ODR) platform[1529] and has required Member States to ensure that ADR (alternative dispute resolution) is available for consumer disputes by the "ADR Directive",[1530] although the legislation does not make ADR mandatory.[1531] As part of this scheme, the ADR Directive required Member States to impose on traders a duty to inform consumers as to the availability of ADR.[1532] Following the scope of the Directive as a whole, this requirement applies to domestic and cross-border disputes[1533] relating to contractual obligations stemming from sales contracts or service contracts[1534] between traders and consumers, where the consumer claims against the trader.[1535] This requirement was implemented in the UK by the Alternative Dispute Resolution for Consumer Disputes (Competent Authorities and Information) Regulations 2015.[1536] However, on the UK's leaving the EU on "exit day" the 2015 Regulations are due to be amended, inter alia, so as to restrict their scope to "domestic disputes"[1536a] and the ODR Regulation is to be revoked so that it will not form part of the "retained EU law".[1536b]

14-249

[1529] Regulation (EU) 524/2013 of 21 May 2013 on online dispute resolution for consumer disputes (Regulation on consumer ODR) [2013] O.J. L165/1. The European ODR platform was established by the EU Commission and is available to allow consumers and traders in the EU and the EFTA states to resolve disputes relating to the online purchase of goods and services without going to court: see *https ://ec.europa.eu/consumers/odr/main/?event=main.home.show*. On the UK's leaving the EU on "exit day" (on which see above, para.14-006 et seq.) the Regulation on consumer ODR is to be revoked: Consumer Protection (Amendment etc.) (EU Exit) Regulations 2018 (SI 2018/1326) reg.10.

[1530] Directive 2013/11/EU of 21 May 2013 on alternative dispute resolution for consumer disputes [2013] O.J. L165/63.

[1531] ADR Directive Art.1 referring to the availability of ADR procedures to consumers "on a voluntary basis", though adding that the Directive is without prejudice to national legislation making participation in such procedures mandatory, provided that such legislation does not prevent the parties from exercising their right of access to the judicial system: see further *Menini and Rampanelli v Banco Populare Società Cooperativa* (C-75/16) of 14 June 2017 at paras 45 et seq. See further generally Hodges, *Consumer ADR in Europe* (2012).

[1532] ADR Directive Art.13.

[1533] ADR Directive Art.2(1). The Directive is implemented in UK law by the Alternative Dispute Resolution for Consumer Disputes (Competent Authorities and Information) Regulations 2015 (SI 2015/542) (the 2015 Regulations), as amended by the Alternative Dispute Resolution for Consumer Disputes (Amendment) Regulations 2015 (SI 2015/1392).

[1534] "Sales contracts" and "services contracts" are defined by the ADR Directive Art.4(1)(c) and (d) (as implemented by the 2015 Regulations reg.5). Recital 16 explains that this means that the Directive applies to disputes between traders and consumers "in all economic sectors, other than the exempted sectors" and includes "disputes arising from the sale or provision of digital content for remuneration".

[1535] ADR Directive recital 16; Art.2 (with exclusions there made), especially Art.2(2)(g).

[1536] Alternative Dispute Resolution for Consumer Disputes (Competent Authorities and Information) Regulations 2015 (SI 2015/542) (as amended by SI 2015/1392) reg.19 (in force July 9, 2015).

[1536a] See notably the Consumer Protection (Amendment etc.) (EU Exit) Regulations 2018 (SI 2018/1326) reg.9(9)(b) and (10) amending the 2015 Regulations regs 14A (ADR entity's duty to co-operate) and 14B (agreement to submit disputes to an ADR entity). On "exit day" see above, para.14-007.

[1536b] Consumer Protection (Amendment etc.) (EU Exit) Regulations 2018 (SI 2018/1326) reg.10. On "retained EU law" see above, para.14-007.

Small claims proceedings

Replace footnote 1545 with:

14-250 [1545] CPR r.27.8(1), which states: "The court may adopt any method of proceeding at a hearing that it considers to be fair". On not allowing cross-examination, cf. *Chilton v Saga Holidays* [1986] 1 All E.R. 841.

Civil litigation

Replace footnote 1550 with:

14-251 [1550] See the High Court and County Courts Jurisdiction Order 1991 (SI 1991/724) as amended by SI 1993/1407, SI 1995/205, SI 1996/3141, SI 1999/1014, SI 2001/1387, SI 2001/2685, SI 2005/587, SI 2008/2934, SI 2009/577, SI 2011/2222, SI 2014/821, SI 2014/2947 and SI 2015/1641. On the UK's leaving the EU (on which see above, para.14-006 et seq.) amendments are to be made so as to remove reference to the European order for payment and small claims procedures: European Enforcement Order, European Order for Payment and European Small Claims Procedure (Amendment etc.) (EU Exit) Regulations 2018 (SI 2018/1311).

Powers of Criminal Courts (Sentencing) Act 2000

Replace paragraph with:

14-255 The power to make a compensation order (which is not of course confined to consumer situations, but may prove of value to consumers) is exercisable by magistrates' courts and Crown Courts.[1583] There is no set procedure and the court may even make such an order of its own motion. It must give reasons if an order is not made.[1584] The amount is such as the court considers appropriate having regard to any evidence and to any representations that are made by or on behalf of the accused or the prosecutor.[1585] In making an order the offender's means must be taken into account, so far as they appear or are known to the court,[1586] and, where the offender has insufficient means to pay both an appropriate fine and appropriate compensation, preference must be given to the latter.[1587] The power is applicable where an offence has been committed, even though there would be no civil liability,[1588] as, for example, in the case of a misleading omission by a trader which constitutes an offence under the Consumer Protection from Unfair Trading Regulations 2008 but which does not give rise to a "right to redress" for a consumer under Pt 4A of the same Regulations.[1589] In determining compensation under the 2000 Act, fine questions of causation will not be taken into account[1590]; and the court may make assessments where the evidence is scanty or incomplete.[1591] But it may not do so unless the right itself is clear.[1592] Where civil proceedings have been settled it is not appropriate to make an order in respect of costs payable by the buyer.[1593] Provision is also made for the effect of a compensation order on a subsequent award of damages in civil proceedings. Such damages are to be assessed without regard to the order. However, the claimant may only recover a sum equal to any amount by which they exceed such compensation and any portion of the compensation which he fails to recover.[1594]

[1583] In the case of young offenders though the jurisdiction of the magristrates' courts is limited to £5,000 for each offence of which the accused is convicted: Powers of Criminal Courts (Sentencing) Act 2000 s.131(1).

[1584] 2000 Act s.130(3).

[1585] 2000 Act s.130(4).

[1586] 2000 Act s.130(11).

[1587] 2000 Act s.130(12). Where the offender is without means it is recognised that there is no point making a compensation order (see *R. v Goodall* [2002] EWCA Crim 511; citing *R. v Jorge* [1999] 2 Cr. App. R. (S) 7.

[1588] *R. v Chappell* (1984) 80 Cr. App. R. 31.

[1589] 2008 Regulations regs 6, 10, 27A and 27B and see below, paras 14-289 et seq.

[1590] *R. v Thomson Holidays Ltd* [1974] Q.B. 592; *Bond v Chief Constable of Kent* [1983] 1 W.L.R. 40.

[1591] *R. v Horsham JJ Ex p. Richards* [1985] 1 W.L.R. 986 at 993. See also *R. v Stapylton* [2012] EWCA Crim 728; [2013] 1 Cr. App. R. (S.) 12 (noting that a compensation order could not be made for general inconvenience).

[1592] *R. v Horsham JJ Ex p. Richards* [1985] 1 W.L.R. 986; *R. v Chappell* (1984) 80 Cr. App. R. 31 at 35; *R. v Stapylton (Ben)* [2012] EWCA Crim 728; [2013] 1 Cr. App. R. (S.) 12.

[1593] *Hammertons Cars Ltd v Redbridge London BC* [1974] 1 W.L.R. 484.

[1594] Powers of Criminal Courts (Sentencing) Act 2000 s.134.

5. CRIMINAL LAW

(b) Food safety

The Food Safety Act 1990

Replace paragraph with:

The Food Safety Act 1990 repealed and replaced earlier legislation, notably much **14-258** of the Food Act 1984. The main provisions are to be found in Pt II (ss.7–26), as much amended.[1609] This both creates and largely re-enacts offences previously contained in the 1984 Act and empowers the Secretary of State to make regulations for inter alia, general food safety and consumer protection,[1610] special provisions for particular foods,[1611] and for the registration and licensing of food premises.[1612] considerable use has been made of these extensive enabling powers. Section 7 re-enacts the substance of a previous prohibition[1613] against rendering food injurious to health by adding or abstracting articles or constituent parts with intent that the food should be sold for human consumption. By s.8 it is an offence to sell[1614] food which does not comply with food safety requirements as being unsafe within the meaning of Art.14 of Regulation 178/2002.[1615] Section 14 re-enacts a long-standing prohibition[1616] against selling to the purchaser's prejudice food which is not of the nature or substance or quality demanded, while s.15 creates offences based on falsely describing or presenting food.[1617] Part II also contains important provisions covering the inspection and seizure of suspected food (s.9), the service of improvement notices (s.10) and prohibition orders (s.11) on proprietors of food businesses. There are provisions also for emergency prohibition notices and orders (s.12) and for the Secretary of State to issue emergency control orders (s.13). Overall, the powers are very extensive, as may be thought appropriate in an area where there is such an obvious need for consumer protection.

1609 Food Standards Act 1999 s.40(1) Sch.5. See also the General Food Regulations 2004 (SI 2004/3279), as amended by SI 2005/2626, SI 2011/1043 and SI 2013/2996 which provide for the enforcement of certain provisions of Regulation 178/2002 [2002] O.J. L31/1 laying down the general principles and requirements of food law, establishing the European Food Safety Authority and laying down procedures in matters of food safety; and the Food Safety Act 1990 (Amendment) Regulations 2004 (SI 2004/2990). The General Food Regulations 2004 are to be amended on the UK's leaving the EU (on which see above, para.14-006 et seq.): Food and Feed Hygiene and Safety (Miscellaneous Amendments) (Wales) (EU Exit) Regulations 2019 (SI 2019/434) reg.2.

1610 Food Safety Act 1990 s.16. Regulations may also be made to implement EC Directives or enforce EU directly applicable regulations (s.17).

1611 1990 Act s.18.

1612 1990 Act s.19.

1613 Previously contained in s.8 of the 1984 Act.

1614 The word "sell" is given an extended meaning by s.2.

1615 O.J. [2002] L 31/1. Article 14(2) provides that: "Food shall be deemed to be unsafe if it is considered to be: (a) injurious to health; (b) unfit for human consumption". Various factors which are relevant in making this assessment are listed in Art.14.3–14.9. On the UK's leaving the EU (on which see above, para.14-006 et seq.) the 2002 Regulation is to form part of "retained EU law" with amendments: General Food Law (Amendment etc.) (EU Exit) Regulations 2019 (SI 2019/642) Pt 3.

1616 Previously contained in s.2 of the 1984 Act.

1617 Previously contained in s.6 of the 1984 Act. Further offences linked to contravention of or failure to comply with certain provisions of Regulation 178/2002 are provided for by SI 2004/3279 regs 4 and 5 (Wales) and SI 2013/2996 reg.19 (England).

(d) General powers relating to the safety of goods and the general safety requirement

Safety regulations

Replace paragraph with:

14-261 The Consumer Protection Act 1987 s.11, confers on the Secretary of State powers to make regulations[1633] for the purposes of securing: (a) that goods are safe; (b) that goods which are unsafe (or would be unsafe in the hands of persons of a particular description) are not made available to persons generally or, as the case may be, to persons of that description; and (c) that appropriate information is provided and inappropriate information is not provided in respect of goods.[1634] In particular, such regulations may contain provision with respect to the composition or contents, design, construction, finish or packing of goods[1635] or they may require that goods satisfy certain specified standards[1636] or are tested or inspected in prescribed ways.[1637] By s.11(2)(j) regulations may also (and typically will) prohibit persons from supplying,[1638] or offering or agreeing to supply, or exposing or possessing for supply, specified goods and component parts and raw materials for such goods. A contravention of such a prohibition is an offence under s.12 and, as has been noted, a civil action will also lie.[1639] A considerable number of regulations has now been made under s.11[1640] or under an equivalent provision and in order to implement the requirements of EU Directives.[1641] A comprehensive list of such regulations may be found elsewhere,[1642] but the more important cover the following goods: filament lamps for vehicles,[1643] pedal bicycles,[1644] asbestos products,[1645] nightwear,[1646] furniture and furnishings,[1647] food imitations,[1648] tobacco products,[1649] construction products,[1650] simple pressure vessels,[1651] machinery,[1652] personal protective equipment,[1653] medical devices,[1654] electric plugs and sockets,[1655] motor vehicle tyres,[1656] electrical equipment,[1657] toys,[1658] rubber teats and dummies,[1659] recreational craft,[1660] cosmetic products,[1661] lifts,[1662] fireworks,[1663] cigarette lighter refills,[1664] pressure equipment,[1665] road vehicle brake linings,[1666] pressure systems,[1667] biocidal products,[1668] and blood.[1669] Regulations governing various other types of goods (including bunk beds and fireguards for heating appliances) were revoked by the Product Safety (Revocation) Regulations 2012.[1670]

[1633] Usually, there is a requirement of consultation under the Consumer Protection Act 1987 s.11(5). In *R. v Secretary of State for Health Ex p. United States Tobacco International Inc* [1992] Q.B. 353 failure to consult led to the Oral Snuff (Safety) Regulations 1989 (SI 1989/2347) being declared void following an application for judicial review. Subsequently they were replaced by the Tobacco for Oral Use (Safety) Regulations 1992 (SI 1992/3134). Consultation is not required where the regulations are of no more than 12 months' duration.

[1634] Consumer Protection Act 1987 s.11(1)(a)–(c). Earlier powers to issue product safety regulations had been contained in the Consumer Protection Act 1961 and the Consumer Safety Act 1978.

[1635] Consumer Protection Act 1987 s.11(2)(a).

[1636] Consumer Protection Act 1987 s.11(2)(f).

[1637] Consumer Protection Act 1987 s.11(2)(g).

[1638] Comprehensively defined in Consumer Protection Act 1987 s.46.

[1639] Consumer Protection Act 1987 s.41(1); see above, para.14-243.

[1640] Regulations made under the 1961 Act continue in force notwithstanding the repeal of that Act by the Consumer Protection Act 1987 s.48(3) and Sch.5: Consumer Protection Act 1987 (Commencement No.1) Order 1987 (SI 1987/1680) Arts 6–9.

[1641] They will then also be made or, as the case may be, made exclusively under the European Communities Act 1972 s.2(2). The notion of "safety" brings in further measures not entirely directed at consumers nor at sales. Examples include health and safety regulations made under the Health and Safety at Work, etc. Act 1974 s.15: see, e.g. the Chemicals (Hazard Information and Packaging for Supply) Regulations 2009 (SI 2009/716), as amended. Further important examples include the Control of Asbestos Regulations 2012 (SI 2012/632).

[1642] See, e.g. Miller, *Product Liability and Safety Encyclopaedia* 1979–2014, Div.IV, which contains the relevant texts.

[1643] SI 1982/444.

[1644] SI 2010/198.

[1645] SI 2012/632.

[1646] SI 1985/2043, as amended by SI 1987/286.

[1647] SI 1988/1324, as amended by SI 1989/2358, SI 1993/207 and SI 2010/2205.

[1648] SI 1989/1291.

[1649] Tobacco and Related Products Regulations 2016 (SI 2016/507) (amendments due on the UK leaving the EU (on which see above, para.14-006 et seq.), by SI 2019/41 reg.6).

[1650] SI 2013/1387 (amendments due on the UK leaving the EU (on which see above, para.14-006 et seq.) by SI 2019/465 reg.4 and Sch.2).

[1651] SI 2016/1092 (amendments due on the UK leaving the EU (on which see above, para.14-006 et seq.), by SI 2019/696 reg.24 and Sch.21).

[1652] SI 2008/1597, as amended by SI 2011/2157 (amendments due on the UK leaving the EU (on which see above, para.14-006 et seq.) by SI 2019/696 reg.25 and Sch.12).

[1653] SI 2018/390 (amendments due on the UK leaving the EU (on which see above, para.14-006 et seq.) by SI 2019/696 reg.38 and Sch.35).

1654 SI 2002/618, as amended by SI 2003/1400, SI 2003/1697, SI 2005/2759, SI 2005/2909, SI 2007/400, SI 2008/530, SI 2008/2936, SI 2010/557, SI 2012/1426, SI 2013/2327 and SI 2017/207 (amendments due on the UK leaving the EU (on which see above, para.14-006 et seq.) by SI 2019/791 Pt 1 reg.3).

1655 SI 1994/1768, as amended by SI 2016/1101.

1656 SI 1994/3117, as amended by SI 1996/3227, SI 1997/815, SI 2003/1316 and SI 2003/2762.

1657 SI 2016/1101 (amendments due on the UK leaving the EU (on which see above, para.14-006 et seq.) by SI 2019/696 reg.26 and Sch.23).

1658 SI 2011/1881 (amendments due on the UK leaving the EU (on which see above, para.14-006 et seq.) by SI 2019/696 reg.18 and Sch.15).

1659 SI 1995/1012.

1660 SI 2017/737 (amendments due on the UK leaving the EU (on which see above, para.14-006 et seq.) by SI 2019/696 reg.31 and Sch.28).

1661 SI 2013/1478 (amendments due on the UK leaving the EU (on which see above, para.14-006 et seq.) by SI 2019/696 reg.37 and Sch.34).

1662 SI 2016/1093 (amendments due on the UK leaving the EU (on which see above, para.14-006 et seq.) by SI 2019/696 reg.25 and Sch.22).

1663 SI 2004/1836, as amended by SI 2004/3262, SI 2010/1554 and SI 2012/2963. See also Fireworks Act 2003; SI 2010/1554, SI 2013/1950 and SI 2015/1553.

1664 SI 1999/1844.

1665 SI 2016/1105 (amendments due on the UK leaving the EU (on which see above, para.14-006 et seq.) by SI 2019/696 reg.27 and Sch.24).

1666 SI 1999/2978, as amended by SI 2003/3314.

1667 SI 2000/128, as amended by SI 2001/1426, SI 2004/568, SI 2005/2092 and SI 2007/1573.

1668 Regulation (EU) 528/2012, [2012] O.J. L167/1. On the UK leaving the EU (on which see above, para.14-006 et seq.), this EU regulation will form part of "retained EU law" as amended by SI 2019/720 reg.2(2) and Sch.2.

1669 SI 2005/50, as amended by SI 2005/1098, SI 2005/2532, SI 2005/2898, SI 2006/2013, 2007/604, SI 2008/941, SI 2010/554, SI 2010/1881, SI 2011/2581, SI 2013/235 and SI 2016/604. Further amendments are due on the UK's leaving the EU (on which see above, para.14-006 et seq.): SI 2019/4.

1670 SI 2012/1815. See also in the case of pencils and graphic instruments the Product Safety Amendment and Revocation Regulations 2012 (SI 2012/2963) reg.3.

Replace title footnote 1681 with:

The General Product Safety Regulations 2005[1681]

14-264   1681 General Product Safety Regulations 2005 (SI 2005/1803) amended principally by SI 2011/1881, SI 2012/3032, SI 2012/1848 and SI 2015/1630. On the UK's leaving the EU (on which see above, para.14-006 et seq.), the 2005 Regulations are due to be subject to amendment: Product Safety and Metrology etc. (Amendment etc.) (EU Exit) Regulations 2019 (SI 2019/696) reg.12 and Sch.9.

Replace footnote 1691 with:

1691 2005 Regulations reg.3(1) and (2) (amendments due on the UK leaving the EU (on which see above, para.14-006 et seq.) by SI 2019/696 reg.12 and Sch.9).

The "general safety requirement" imposed on "producers"

Replace the first paragraph with:

14-265   The central obligation imposed by reg.5(1) requires that: "No producer shall place a product on the market unless it is a safe product".[1693] For this purpose the word "producer" is defined broadly to include manufacturers, own-branders, persons who recondition products and other professionals in the supply chain in so far as their activities may affect the safety properties of a product.[1694] Where the manufacturer is not established in a Member State the "producer" is his representative who is so established, or, if there is no such person, the importer of the product from a state that is not a Member State into a Member State.[1695] A "safe product" is defined as one which:

"... under normal or reasonably foreseeable conditions of use including duration and, where applicable, putting into service, installation and maintenance requirements, does not present any risk or only the minimum risks compatible with the product's use, considered to be acceptable and consistent with a high level of protection for the safety and health of persons."[1696]

[1693] See also the 2005 Regulations reg.5(4) which covers the "supply" (as defined in reg.2) of products which are not safe products. There are further provisions (see reg.5(2) and (3)) covering preparatory acts (e.g. offering or agreeing to place such a product on the market, etc or exposing or possessing it for such a purpose). For penalties, see reg.20(1)–(3). A standard "due diligence" defence is contained in reg.29.

[1694] 2005 Regulations reg.2. On the UK leaving the EU (on which see above, para.14-006 et seq.) the definition of "producer" is to be amended so as, in particular, to replace references to "Member State" with "the UK" SI 2019/696 reg.12 and Sch.24 para.2.

[1695] See 2005 Regulations reg.2 and see previous note.

[1696] 2005 Regulations reg.2. In turn, a "dangerous product" is defined as "a product other than a safe product".

Replace the second paragraph with:

In determining whether this standard has been achieved various matters must be taken into account, including the characteristics and presentation of the product and the category of consumers at risk when using it, particularly children and the elderly.[1697] Producers are also subject to other obligations, including the provision of relevant information to consumers and the requirement to notify enforcement authorities of known risks associated with products which they have placed on the market or supplied.[1698]

[1697] 2005 Regulations reg.2. See also reg.6, which contains a limited presumption of conformity where a product complies with mandatory health and safety requirements or with certain national UK standards and makes further reference to other relevant factors, including recommendations of the European Commission and codes of good practice. On the UK leaving the EU (on which see above, para.14-006 et seq.), reg.6 is due to be amended so as to replace references to the EU: SI 2019/696 reg.12 and Sch.24 para.4).

[1698] See, respectively, the 2005 Regulations regs 7 and 9 (latter to be amended on the UK leaving the EU by SI 2019/696 reg.12 and Sch.24 para.5).

The obligations of "distributors"

Replace footnote 1702 with:

[1702] See, respectively, the 2005 Regulations regs 8(1)(b) and 9 (latter to be amended on the UK leaving the EU by SI 2019/696 reg.12 and Sch.24 para.5). For penalties, see reg.20(1)–(3). A standard "due diligence" defence is contained in reg.29.   **14-266**

Enforcement

Replace footnote 1709 with:

[1709] Consumer Rights Act 2015 s.77(1), Sch.5 Pt 2 para.10 (defining 'enforcer's legislation' to include the duties and powers arising under the 2005 Regulations reg.10(1)). While not relevant here, Sch.5 is due to be amended on the UK leaving the EU (on which see above, para.14-006 et seq.) by the Consumer Protection (Enforcement) (Amendment etc.) (EU Exit) Regulations 2019 (SI 2019/203) reg.4.   **14-267**

The exchange of information about product safety

Replace paragraph with:

The General Product Safety Regulations 2005 Pt 4 contains important provi-   **14-268** sions, the purpose of which is to implement the General Product Safety Directive 2001 Arts 11, 12 and 13.[1712a] In broad outline, the general scheme is for enforcement authorities to inform the Secretary of State of product-related risks which have been notified to them[1713] and, where appropriate, for the Secretary of State to pass the information on to the competent authorities in Members States where the product in question is or has been marketed or otherwise supplied to consumers.[1714] obligations are also imposed on enforcement authorities to notify the Secretary of State of measures taken to restrict the placing on the market of products or to require their withdrawal or recall and the Secretary of State must in turn notify the European Commission.[1715] In the event of a "serious risk",[1716] notification to the Commission must be through the Community Rapid Information System, known as "RAPEX".[1717] Although it is primarily a matter for individual Member States to take appropriate measures with regard to dangerous products located within their territory, Art.13 of the Directive provides for situations in which such states differ in their approach to dealing with the risks posed by products. In the event of a serious risk, where urgent action is required and not forthcoming, the Commission may as a last resort adopt a decision to require Member States to take measures from among those listed in Art.8(1)(b)–(f).[1718] This includes banning the marketing of products and ordering their withdrawal and recall. Prior consultation with Member States is required and in general the decision is valid for a period not exceeding one year, which may, however, be extended.[1719] For this purpose, by Art.13(3) of the 2001 Directive:

"Export from the Community of dangerous products which have been the subject of [such as decision] shall be prohibited unless the decision provides otherwise."[1720]

However, on the UK's leaving the EU on "exit day",[1720a] this scheme for the exchange of information is due to be amended. In particular, instead of a combination of national and EU exchanges of information, the Secretary of State must established a database containing information relating to market surveillance and product safety, with notifications of risk to be received by it from enforcement authorities.[1720b] Moreover, decisions made by the EU Commission under art.13 of the Directive will cease to have effect in the UK.[1720c]

[1712a] See, however, text at the end of this paragraph as to the position on the UK's leaving the EU when Pt 4 of the 2005 Regulations is due to be subject to amendment.

[1713] See the 2005 Regulations reg.33(1). For the obligation of producers and distributors to notify an enforcement authority, see reg.9(1). Guidelines for the notification of dangerous consumer products to the competent authorities of the Member States are to be found in Commission Decision 2004/905 of 14 December 2004.

[1714] 2005 Regulations reg.33(1).

[1715] 2005 Regulations reg.33(2)–(4).

[1716] Defined by the 2005 Regulations reg.2 as "a serious risk including one the effects of which are not immediate, requiring rapid intervention".

[1717] 2005 Regulations reg.33(5). See also General Product Safety Directive 2001 recital 25 Art.10.

[1718] See the General Product Safety Directive 2001 recitals 30, 31 and 32 and Art.13(1); also 2005 Regulations reg.35.

[1719] There is no time limit where the decision concerns specific, individually identified products or batches of products: General Product Safety Directive 2001 Art.13(2).

[1720] For implementation of this provision, see the 2005 Regulations reg.35(4).

[1720a] On which see generally, above, para.14-006 et seq.

[1720b] 2005 Regulations reg.33 (as to be amended by SI 2019/696 Sch.9, para.6).

[1720c] This is the effect of the revocation on "exit day" of reg.35 of the 2005 Regulations by SI 2019/696 Sch.9, para.8.

(e) The Consumer Protection from Unfair Trading Regulations 2008

(i) The prohibition of unfair commercial practices

Unfair Commercial Practices Directive 2005

Replace footnote 1731 with:

[1731] 2005 Directive Art.4; *VTB-VAB NV Total Belgium NV* (C-261/07 and C-299/07) [2009] E.C.R. I-2949 at [63]; *Mediaprint Zeitungs- und Zeitschriftenverlag GMBH & Co KG v 'Österreich'-Zeitungsverlag GmbH* (C-540/08) [2010] E.C.R. I-10909 at [27]; *Zentral sur Bekämpfung unlauteren Weebewerbs eV v Plus Warenhandelsgessellschaft mbh* (C-304/08) [2010] E.C.R. I-00217 at [41]; *Wamo BVBA v JBC NV* (C-288/10) [2011] E.C.R. I-5835 at [33]. *Europamur Alimentación SA v Dirección General de Commercio y Protección del Consumidor de la Comunidad Autónoma de la Región de Murcia* (C-295/16) 19 October 2017 at paras 34 -35, and 43. There is an important exception to "full harmonisation" in relation to "financial services": 2005 Directive Art.3(9).

14-270

Consumer Protection from Unfair Trading Regulations 2008

Replace footnote 1742 with:

[1742] SI 2008/1277. See *Butterworths Trading and Consumer Law*, Div.1A. The OFT and the Department for Business Enterprise and Regulatory Reform (as they both then were) issued a document entitled *Guidance on the Consumer Protection from Unfair Trading Regulations 2008* (May 2008). On the UK's leaving the EU (on which see generally above, para.14-006 et seq.), the 2008 Regulations will be subject to minor amendments: Consumer Protection (Amendment etc.) (EU Exit) Regulations 2018 (SI 2018/1326) reg.6.

14-272

Scope of the 2008 Regulations

Replace footnote 1751 with:

[1751] See further on the definition of "commercial practice" *RLvS Verlagsgesellschaft mbH v Stuttgarter Wochenblatt GmbH* (C-391/12) EU:C:2013:66; of 17 October 2013 at [37]; *UAB 'Gelvora' v Valstybine vartotoų teisių apsaugos tarnyba* (C-357/16) of 20 July 2017; *Komisiaza zashtita na potrebeitelite v Kamenova* (C-105/17) EU:C:2018:80; of 4 October 2018 at [42]; *Openbarr Ministerie v Kirschstein* (C-393/17) EU:C:2019:56; of 4 July 2019; and *Chitty on Contracts*, 33rd edn (2018), Vol.II para.38-167.

14-273

"Trader", "consumer" and "product"

Replace paragraph with:

Under the 2008 Regulations, "trader" means "a person acting for purposes relating to that person's business,[1752] whether acting personally or through another person acting in the trader's name or on the trader's behalf," and (except for the purposes of the consumer's rights to redress in Pt 4A[1753]) "includes a person acting in the name of or on behalf of a trader"[1754]; and a "consumer" means "an individual acting for purposes that are wholly or mainly outside that individual's business".[1755] Finally, the word "product" is defined broadly to include "goods, services, digital content, immoveable property, rights and obligations".[1756] As a consequence of these definitions, traders whose activities do not involve any actual or potential dealing with consumers (whether directly or indirectly) are not subject to these Regulations[1757]; nor do the Regulations apply to straightforward consumer-to-consumer transactions between private individuals.

14-274

1752 2008 Regulations reg.2(1) (as amended by SI 2014/870 reg.2(1)(a)) provides that "business includes–(a) a trade, craft or profession, and (b) the activities of any government department or local or public authority." In *R. (on the application of Surrey Trading Standards) v Scottish & Southern Energy Plc* [2012] EWCA Crim 539 it was held that a non-trading entity such as a holding company could be a "trader" for the purposes of the Regulations even though it did not did not directly supply the product (electricity) which was the subject of the allegedly misleading commercial practice. On the definition of "trader" in the Unfair Commercial Practices Directive see *BKK Mobil Oil Körperschaft des öffentlichen Rechts v Zentrale zur Bekämpfung unlauteren Wettbewerbs eV* (C-59/12) 3 October 2013 and the discussion above, paras 14-032 to 14-033.

1753 See below, paras 14-284 et seq.

1754 2008 Regulations reg.2(1) (as amended by SI 2014/870 reg.2(7)).

1755 2008 Regulations reg.2(1) (as amended by SI 2014/870 reg.2(3)). On this increasingly standard definition of "consumer" which is also found in the Consumer Rights Act 2015 s.2(3) see above, paras 14-023 et seq.

1756 2008 Regulations reg.2(1). The definition also includes as the supply of a "product" the full or partial settlement of a consumer's liabilities in response to demand by the trader for payment in this respect: 2008 Regulations reg.2(1A) and 2(1B). In *UAB 'Gelvora' v Valstybine vartotoų teisių apsaugos tarnyba* (C-357/16) of 20 July 2017 at [21]–[25] the CJEU held that where claims assigned to a debt collection agency originated in the supply of a service (the provision of credit at interest), its debt recovery activities may be regarded as a "product" within the meaning of art.2(c) of the 2005 Directive and may constitute an unfair "commercial practice" as the measures which it adopts are liable to influence the consumer's decision in respect of payment of the product. The definition of "product" is qualified for the purposes of the "rights to redress" in Pt 4A of the Regulations (SI 2014/870 reg.2(6)): 2008 regs 27C and 27D and see below, para.14-288n.1893.

1757 An "indirect" dealing might typically occur where a manufacturer of consumer goods with (say) misleading labelling or advertising sells them through wholesalers or retailers, etc. rather than to consumers directly.

Practices considered unfair in all circumstances

Replace footnote 1793 with:

14-278 1793 2008 Regulations Sch.1 para.29. On this unfair commercial practice see *Autoritá Garante della Concorrenza e del Mercato v Wind Tre SpA and Vodafone Italia SpA* (Joined Cases C-54/17 and C-55/77) EU:C:2018:71 of 13 September 2018, noted above, para.14-214 note. Other, civil consequences of this commercial practice are regulated by 2008 Regulations reg.27M on which see above, para.14-214.

"Misleading action"

Replace paragraph with:

14-280   A practice may be prohibited as constituting a "misleading action" within reg.5 in two alternative ways. The first such way[1797] is: (a) if it contains false information in relation to any of a long list of matters specified in reg.5(4) or if it or its overall presentation in any way deceives or is likely to deceive the average consumer[1798] in relation to any such matters, even if the information is factually correct[1799]; *and* (b) it causes or is likely to cause the average consumer to take a transactional decision[1800] he would not have taken otherwise.[1801] The list of matters specified in reg.5(4) covers:

"(a)   the existence or nature of the product;
(b)   the main characteristics of the product (as defined in paragraph 5);
(c)   the extent of the trader's commitments;
(d)   the motives for the commercial practice;
(e)   the nature of the sales process;
(f)   any statement or symbol relating to direct or indirect sponsorship approval of the trader or the product;
(g)   the price or the manner in which the price is calculated;
(h)   the existence of a specific price advantage;

(i)   the need for a service, part, replacement or repair;
(j)   the nature attributes and rights of the trader (as defined in paragraph (6);
(k)   the consumer's rights or the risks he may face."

There is also a substantial list of what is included within "the main characteristics of the product" in reg.5(4)(b)[1802] and the "nature, attributes and rights" as far as they concern the trader in reg.5(4)(j).[1803] The second alternative way in which a commercial practice may be prohibited as being a "misleading action" is when the conditions of reg.5(3) are satisfied. This will be so when the practice causes or is likely to cause the average consumer to take a transactional decision he would not have taken otherwise *and* it involves *either*: (a) any marketing of a product (including comparative advertising) which creates confusion with any products, trade marks, trade names or other distinguishing marks of a competitor; *or* (b) non-compliance by the trader with firm and verifiable commitments contained in a code of conduct[1804] (or practice) by which he has undertaken to be bound, the trader having indicated that he is bound by the code. In general, any such unfair commercial practice will constitute an offence.[1805]

[1797] 2008 Regulations reg.5(1) and (2). On the definition of "misleading action" in art.6(2) and its relationship to "misleading omission" in art.7 of the 2005 Directive see *Criminal Proceedings against Canal Digital Denmark A/S* (C-611/14) of 26 October 2016. In particular, the CJEU's judgment (at paras 43–44) makes clear that the omission of some information regarding an aspect of the "product" may form part of a misleading action and that the same commercial practice may constitute both a misleading action and a misleading omission, subject in either case to its satisfying the particular conditions and taking into account the particular factors which are required by the 2005 Directive.

[1798] As to the "average consumer", see above, para.14-028, 14-276.

[1799] 2008 Regulations reg.5(2)(a).

[1800] A "transactional decision" means "any decision taken by a consumer, whether it is to act or refrain from acting, concerning: (a) whether, how and on what terms to purchase, make payment in whole or in part for, retain or dispose of a product; or (b) whether, how and on what terms to exercise a contractual right in relation to a product": 2008 Regulations reg.2(1). This definition does not apply for the purposes of the consumer's rights to redress under Pt 4A, which provides its own definition: 2008 Regulations reg.2(1) (as amending by SI 2014/870 reg.2(8)); reg.27B(2) and see below, para.14-292.

[1801] 2008 Regulations reg.5(2)(b).

[1802] 2008 Regulations reg.5(5).

[1803] 2008 Regulations reg.5(6). See also reg.5(7) which provides (as amended by SI 2015/1630 Sch.1 para.3) that the "consumer's rights" referred to in reg.5(4)(k) "include rights the consumer may have under sections 19 and 23 or 24 of the Consumer Rights Act 2015", on which see above, paras 14-067 and 14-098 to 14-099.

[1804] Defined as "an agreement or set of rules (which is not imposed by legal or administrative requirements), which defines the behaviour of traders who undertake to be bound by it in relation to one or more commercial practices or business sectors": 2008 Regulations reg.2(1).

[1805] See the 2008 Regulations reg.9. However, this is not so in the case of those falling within reg.5(3)(b) (non-compliance with commitments made in code of conduct). For an example of offences under reg.9 involving "misleading" conduct, see *Motor Depot Ltd v Kingston Upon Hull City Council* [2012] EWHC 3257 (Admin); [2013] All E.R. (D) 77 (Jan) (vehicles advertised for sale "interest free"); *Warwickshire CC v Halfords Autocentres Ltd* [2018] EWHC 3007 (Admin); [2019] 1 W.L.R. 3597 (invoice by trader for full service of a car whereas various faults in the vehicle were not rectified or reported).

"Misleading omission"

Replace footnote 1806 with:

[1806] 2008 Regulations reg.6(1). See *Criminal Proceedings against Canal Digital Denmark A/S* (C-611/ 14) of 26 October 2016 and above, para.14-280. **14-281**

Aggressive commercial practices

Replace footnote 1814 with:

14-282 ¹⁸¹⁴ 2008 Regulations reg.7(1). For this purpose, "coercion" includes the use of physical force and "undue influence" means "exploiting a position of power in relation to the consumer so as to apply pressure, even without using or threatening to use physical force, in a way which significantly limits the consumer's ability to make an informed decision" (reg.7(3)). On "undue influence" for this purpose see *Prezes Urzedu Ochrony Konkurencji i Konsumentow v Orange Polska SA* (C-628/17) EU:C:2019:48 of 12 June 2019.

Offences, defences, penalties and enforcement

Replace paragraph with:

14-283 With the exception of the offence of contravening reg.3(3) (the general prohibition), the various offences outlined above (practices considered unfair in all circumstances, misleading actions and omissions and aggressive commercial practices) do not require proof of any specific or free-standing mental element.¹⁸¹⁸ However, it should not be overlooked that a mental element is sometimes embodied within the definition of the prohibited conduct itself. For example, in the list of commercial practices which are in all circumstances considered unfair, "bait and switch" selling requires "an intention of promoting a different product"¹⁸¹⁹ and other specified circumstances envisage deliberately misleading the consumer¹⁸²⁰ or intentionally inducing the consumer to acquire the product at less favourable conditions.¹⁸²¹ Subject to this, liability is strict, albeit subject to a common form due diligence defence.¹⁸²² In the case of contravening the general prohibition, the trader is guilty of an offence only if:

> "(a) [H]e knowingly or recklessly engages in a commercial practice which contravenes the requirements of professional diligence under regulation 3(3)(a)¹⁸²³; and (b) the practice materially distorts or is likely to materially distort the economic behaviour of the average consumer with regard to the product under regulation 3(3)(b)."

In all cases, on summary conviction a unlimited fine may be imposed and on conviction on indictment a term of imprisonment not exceeding two years may be imposed in addition to or instead of an unlimited fine.¹⁸²⁴ In relation to enforcement, local weights and measures authorities are under a duty to enforce the Regulations¹⁸²⁵ and the Competition and Markets Authority has a power, although not a duty, to enforce them.¹⁸²⁶ Investigative powers in relation to these offences (which were formerly contained in the 2008 Regulations themselves¹⁸²⁷) have since 1 October 2015 been contained in the Consumer Rights Act 2015 Sch.5.¹⁸²⁸ The 2005 Directive has been added to the Schedule of listed Directives under the Enterprise Act 2002 Pt 8,¹⁸²⁹ thus enabling enforcement under that Act. As earlier noted, the Unfair Commercial Practices Directive 2005 does not require any "contract law" consequences for the unfair commercial practices which it prohibits and this approach was followed by the 2008 Regulations as originally enacted.¹⁸³⁰ However, on the recommendation of the Law Commission and the Scottish Law Commission,¹⁸³¹ in 2014 the 2008 Regulations were amended so as to provide for consumers three possible "rights to redress" in respect of a misleading action or aggressive commercial practice which is a significant factor in a consumer's decision to enter into a contract or to make a payment.¹⁸³² This new law is discussed in the following section.

¹⁸¹⁸ 2008 Regulations regs 9–12.

¹⁸¹⁹ 2008 Regulations Sch.1 para.6.

[1820] 2008 Regulations Sch.1 para.13.

[1821] 2008 Regulations Sch.1 para.18.

[1822] 2008 Regulations reg.17. A further defence is available to the innocent publisher of advertisements (reg.18) and there are common form provisions for time-limits for prosecutions (reg.14), offences committed by bodies of persons (reg.15) and offences due to the default of another person (reg.16).

[1823] 2008 Regulations reg.8(1)(a). Of itself, the meaning of this requirement is by no means self-evident. However, the position is clarified by reg.8(2) which states that "a trader who engages in a commercial practice without regard to whether the practice contravenes the requirements of professional diligence shall be deemed recklessly to engage in the practice, whether or not the trader has reason for believing that the practice might contravene those requirements". Note, however, that the "trader" will usually be a corporate body and it will often be a matter of inference as to whether knowledge or recklessness can be established at the corporate level: see *R. v X Ltd* [2013] EWCA Crim 818; [2013] 3 All E.R. 995 at [28]–[35].

[1824] 2008 Regulations reg.13. Although reg.13(a) refers in relation to summary conviction to "a fine not exceeding the statutory maximum" on 12 March 2015 the maximum fine available on summary conviction was changed to an unlimited fine by the Legal Aid, Sentencing and Punishment of Offenders Act 2012 s.85(1). Note that although the promotion of any unfair commercial practice by a code owner in a code is prohibited (reg.4), it does not constitute an offence under the Regulations.

[1825] 2008 Regulations (SI 2008/1277) reg.19(1), as substituted by SI 2013/783 Art.13(4). In Northern Ireland, the duty is imposed on the Department of Enterprise, Trade and Investment in Northern Ireland.

[1826] 2008 Regulations (SI 2008/1277) reg.19(1A), as inserted by SI 2013/783 Art.13(4) and amended by SI 2014/549 Art.2 Sch.1(2) para.35(3).

[1827] 2008 Regulations regs 20–25.

[1828] 2015 Act s.77; Order 2015/1630 Sch.2 para.115.

[1829] See the 2008 Regulations reg.26, which inserts the Directive as a new para.9C of Sch.13 to that Act and reg.27 which inserts a new s.218A into the 2002 Act (Evidence as to factual claims in applications for enforcement or interim enforcement orders). See also reg.30(1) Sch.2 para.100, which adds the Directive to the Enterprise Act 2002 (Pt 8 Community Infringements Specified UK Laws) Order 2003 (SI 2003/1374); as to the 2002 Act more generally, see below, paras 14-306 et seq. On the UK's leaving the EU on "exit day", "Community infringements" are to be replaced by "Schedule 13 infringements" and the 2008 Regulations are included within the substituted Sch.13 of the 2002 Act for this purpose: Consumer Protection (Enforcement) (Amendment etc.) (EU Exit) Regulations 2019 (SI 2019/203) reg.3(20) and Sch. para.1 inserting new 2002 Act Sch.13 para.19. On this change generally, see below, para.14-313A.

[1830] 2005 Directive Art.3(2); 2008 Regulations reg.29 (as enacted) and see above, para.14-270.

[1831] See *Consumer Redress for Misleading and Aggressive Practices* (Law Com. No.332, Scot Law Com. No.226 Cm.8323, 2012).

[1832] 2008 Regulations, new Pt 4A esp. regs 27A and 27B (as inserted by SI 2014/870).

(ii)   Rights to civil redress for consumers

(aa)   Introduction

The structure of the new law

Replace footnote 1847 with:

[1847] Consumer Protection (Amendment) Regulations 2014 (SI 2014/870). On the consumer's rights to redress under the 2008 Regulations see Bant and Paterson (2018) 80 M.L.R. 895 and *Chitty on Contracts*, 33rd edn, (2018) Vol.II, paras 38-172 et seq.   **14-285**

(bb)   General conditions for the availability of the rights to redress

Second condition: "prohibited practice"

Replace paragraph with:

Here, the 2008 Regulations require either that the "trader engages in a prohibited   **14-289** practice in relation to the product" or that, in the case of contracts of sale of goods or the supply of digital content, the "producer" does so in certain circumstances.[1867] For both purposes, the Regulations restrict "prohibited practice" to "misleading actions" under reg.5 and "aggressive commercial practices" under reg.7 and, following the Law Commissions' recommendations, therefore they do not extend the availability of consumer rights to redress to commercial practices qualifying as unfair under the general test[1868] nor to "misleading omissions" under reg.6.[1869] In the case of commercial practices designated by the Regulations in general as unfair in all circumstances,[1870] the rights to redress are therefore available only if the commercial practice in question satisfies the evaluative tests for misleading action or aggressive commercial practice.[1871] This means in particular that they must cause or be likely to cause the average consumer to take a transactional decision he would not have taken otherwise.[1872] The definitions of misleading actions and aggressive commercial practices have been outlined earlier,[1873] but the following paragraphs will note certain differences between these concepts and those found in the general law of contract.

[1867] 2008 Regulations reg.27A(4)(b) provides that "in a case where a consumer enters into a business to consumer contract for goods or digital content—(i) a producer engages in a prohibited practice in relation to the goods or digital content, and (ii) when the contract is entered into, the trader is aware of the commercial practice that constitutes the prohibited practice or could reasonably be expected to be aware of it". The Regulations then define "producer" to include a manufacturer, EEA importer or a person who presents themselves as a producer: 2008 Regulations reg.27A(5). On the UK's leaving the EU (on which see above, paras 14-006 et seq), reg.27A(5)(b) is to be amended so as refer to an importer into the UK rather than into the EEA: SI 2018/1326 reg.6(2).

[1868] See above, para.14-276 (on the general test) and para.14-284 (for the Law Commissions' views).

[1869] Above, paras 14-281 and 14-284.

[1870] 2008 Regulations reg.3(4)(d); Sch.1, above, para.14-278.

[1871] 2008 Regulations regs 5 and 7 and above, para.14-280 and 14-282.

[1872] 2008 Regulations reg.5(2)(b), 5(3) and 7(1)(b). Moreover, "transactional decision" is redefined specially for these purposes as: "any decision taken by a consumer to enter into a contract with a trader for the sale or supply of a product by the trader, or for the sale of goods to the trader, or to make a payment to a trader for the supply of a product": reg.27B(2). This redefinition for the purposes of the rights to redress is necessary in order to link the definitions of misleading actions and aggressive practices to the circumstances governed by the first condition of the availability of these rights: see 2008 Regulations reg.27A(2) and (3) and above, para.14-288.

[1873] Above, paras 14-280 and 14-282.

"Misleading action" and "misrepresentation"

Replace footnote 1875 with:

14-290 [1875] See *Chitty on Contracts*, 33rd edn (2018), Vol.I paras 7-006 et seq.

"Duress", "undue influence", unconscionable bargains and "aggressive commercial practices"

Replace paragraph with:

14-291 The list of practices unfair in all the circumstances illustrates the sort of practices which could fall within the category of aggressive practices: creating the impression that the consumer cannot leave the premises until a contract is formed, conducting personal visits to the consumer's home and ignoring the consumer's legitimate request to leave or not to return, and making persistent and unwanted solicitations by telephone, fax, email or other remote media except in circumstances and to the extent justified to enforce a contractual obligation.[1878] The Law Commissions recommended that the definition of an aggressive practice for the purposes of the consumer's rights to redress should track the definition in reg.7 with some modifications so as, in particular, to avoid reference to "undue influence" which would cause confusion with the doctrine of undue influence under the general law, to define "harassment" as "unreasonable behaviour which is likely to cause alarm, distress or serious annoyance and inconvenience" and to make clear that no "course of conduct" is required for there to be harassment for this purpose.[1879] These recommendations are not, however, reflected in the law as made, which simply adopts the definition of "aggressive commercial practice" in the Regulations generally without change as the basis of the consumer's new rights, except in relation to the definition of "transactional decision".[1880] This has the advantage of relative simplicity, but it does allow the confusion which the Law Commissions foresaw between "undue influence" for the purposes of the new rights for consumers and "undue influence" under the general law, the main difference being that the latter typically involves the abuse of a special relationship of trust between the parties,[1881] which is unlikely to be the case in the context of consumer contracts. Moreover, the idea of "undue influence" in the 2008 Regulations (following the Unfair Commercial Practices Directive which they generally implement) is much broader and less technical than undue influence under the general law, though the significance of vulnerable groups of consumers (notably, by reason of "age, physical or mental infirmity or credulity"[1882]) for the purposes of "average consumer" and the may sometimes have a similar resonance to some of the traditional concerns of the general law of undue influence or, indeed, equitable relief against unconscionable bargains.[1883] Indeed, the Regulations' reference to "the exploitation of a position of power"[1884] without limiting it to a relationship of trust and confidence suggests that the exploitation of a consumer's urgent need for the product may amount to an aggressive practice. The contrast between the definition of "aggressive practices" and the facts which would attract the common law doctrine of duress is also marked, as the latter typically involves an illegitimate threat to the person, goods or economic interests of the party to the contract.[1885] Finally, the definition of "aggressive commercial practice" in the 2008 Regulations is much clearer than the doubtful law governing the circumstances in which equity can relieve on the ground of unconscionable bargains.[1886]

[1878] 2008 Regulations Sch.1 paras 24, 25 and 26.

[1879] Law Commissions' Report (2012) paras 7.67–7.82.

[1880] 2008 Regulations reg.27B(1)(b), (2) and see above, n.1872.

[1881] Law Commissions' Report (2012) para.7.65 and see *Chitty on Contracts* 33rd edn (2018), Vol.I paras 8-058 et seq. where the complexities of the general law are explained.

[1882] 2008 Regulations reg.2(5)(a), above, para.14-276. For discussion of the significance of aggressive commercial practice and undue influence for the purposes of the 2005 Directive, see *Prezes Urzedu Ochrony Konkurencji i Konsumentow v Orange Polska SA* (C-628/17) EU:C:2019:48 of 12 June 2019.

[1883] See *Chitty on Contracts* Vol.I paras 7-130 et seq.

[1884] 2008 Regulations reg.7(3)(b).

[1885] See *Chitty on Contracts* 33rd edn (2018) Vol.1 paras 8-003 et seq. esp. 8-010 – 8-011.

[1886] On this law see *Chitty on Contracts* 33rd edn (2018) Vol.I paras 8-132 et seq..

(cc)   The three rights to redress

The right to unwind the contract: business to consumer contracts

Replace paragraph with:
If a consumer has entered a "business to consumer" contract[1906] and the three   **14-295**

conditions of the general availability of the consumer's rights to redress[1907] are fulfilled, the consumer will have a right to "unwind" the contract provided that (i) the consumer indicates to the trader that he or she rejects the product within a limited period,[1908] (ii) that the "product" remains "capable of rejection"[1909] and (iii) the consumer has not already exercised the right to discount for the same contract and prohibited practice.[1910] The period is 90 days from the later of the day on which the contract was made or, in effect, on which the consumer first received delivery or performance.[1911] The "product" is incapable of rejection only if (as the case may be) the goods have been fully consumed, services have been fully performed,[1912] digital content was available to the consumer for a fixed period that has expired,[1913] the lease has expired or the right conferred on the consumer has been fully exercised.[1914] If the consumer has a right to unwind (which, as stated above, requires that the consumer has notified the trader that he or she rejects the product), the contract comes to an end and the consumer and the trader are released from their obligations under it[1915]; the trader must give the consumer a refund[1916]; and, if the contract was for the sale or supply of goods, the consumer must make the goods available for the trader to collect.[1917] Where the consumer has paid money under the contract, in principle the amount paid must be refunded without any deduction for use,[1918] though this is qualified by detailed provisions governing cases in which the consumer has transferred something other than money[1919] and also where the contract was for the sale or supply of goods on a regular basis.[1920] This general position is to be compared with the effects of cancellation by a consumer of an off-premises or distance contract, as cancellation also brings to an end the obligations of the parties to the contract, but generates an obligation in the trader to reimburse all payments received from the consumer other than payments for delivery (subject to a possible qualification for diminution in value through their handling) and in principle also an obligation in the consumer to return any goods supplied.[1921]

[1906] i.e. one under which the trader is to supply a product to the consumer: see above, para.14-288.

[1907] See above, paras 14-287 to 14-292.

[1908] 2008 Regulations reg.27E(1)(a). The drafting of the 2008 Regulations is curious: rather than conferring a right to unwind that the consumer may exercise and that will expire if the consumer does not exercise it within a limited period, the consumer will have a right only if he or she exercises it within the period. If the consumer has the right and exercises it, the contract comes to an end: 2008 Regulations reg.27E(1)(a) and 27F(1).

[1909] 2008 Regulations reg.27E(1)(b).

[1910] 2008 Regulations reg.27E(10).

[1911] See 2008 Regulations reg.27E(3)-(7). cf. the 30-day period for the consumer's "short-term right to reject" goods under the Consumer Rights Act 2015 s. 20 and 22, below, paras 14-094 to 14-095 and 14-097.

[1912] Law Commissions Report (2012) paras 8.77 considered that a consumer who abandons services mid-performance (e.g. a consumer who is misled about a theatre performance and who leaves before the final curtain call) should have a right to a full refund. However, the reason for excluding the right to unwind (with consequential refund) where services have been fully performed is far from clear, given that the prohibited practice may have resulted in the consumer contracting for services that were of no value to him or her even though fully completed, while in other cases a consumer may derive a considerable benefit from services that have only been performed in part yet be entitled to a refund of the whole price. Note, however, that in some circumstances the consumer may obtain a 100% discount of the price (below, para.14-298) as foreseen by Law Commissions Report (2012) para.8.78.

[1913] Note that the 2008 Regulations clearly contemplate the consumer being entitled to reject digital content, whereas under the Consumer Rights Act 2015 Ch.3, a consumer who has been supplied digital content that does not conform to the statutory requirements has no right to reject, the drafters having taken the view that there cannot be a right to reject when there is nothing to give back: see Consumer Rights Act 2015 s.42 esp. at 42(7), above, para.14-116. It is not clear how digital content that is supplied on a tangible medium is to be treated under the 2008 Regulations, as goods or as digital content.

It seems better to view them as goods, so that the consumer must make the tangible medium available for collection by the trader, but if the digital content was to be available to the consumer for only a limited period to regard the goods as "fully consumed" when the period expires, so that the consumer will lose the right to unwind just as with other types of digital content. This distinction would accord with the treatment of digital content under the Consumer Contracts (Information, Cancellation and Additional Charges) Regulations 2013 SI 2013/3134 (above, para.14-195 et seq.). The 2013 Regulations provide a consumer who has concluded an off-premises or distance contract for the supply of digital content not on a tangible medium with a right of cancellation, but then qualify this where the trader begins performance with the express consent of the consumer and with an acknowledgement that the right to cancel will be lost: 2013 Regulations reg.37(1) and (2), above, paras 14-199 to 14-200.

[1914] 2008 Regulations reg.27E(8)-(9).

[1915] 2008 Regulations reg.27F(1)(a). It is not clear whether this would affect obligations that are normally intended to survive termination or avoidance of the contract, such as obligations of confidentiality.

[1916] 2008 Regulations reg.27F(1)(b).

[1917] 2008 Regulations reg.27F(1)(b). Under other legislation the term "contract for the supply of goods" includes contracts for work and materials, which will result in the goods being incorporated into other goods (as when parts are used to repair a car) or land (as in a building contract) (e.g. under the Supply of Goods and Services Act 1982 s.1); under the Consumer Rights Act 2015, the contract will be regarded as a mixed contract, partly for the supply of goods and partly for services, see ss.1(3)-(5). The 2008 Regulations also refer to a "mixed contract", i.e. "a contract relating to a product which consists of any two or more of goods, a service, digital content, immoveable property or rights", but only for the purposes of setting the "relevant day" for start of the 90 day period for the right to unwind: reg.27E(5) and (6). If the goods cannot readily be detached (cf. *Borden (UK) Ltd v Scottish Timber Products, Ltd* [1979] 3 W.L.R. 672 CA; *Hendy Lennox (Industrial Engines) Ltd v Grahame Puttick* [1984] 2 All E.R. 152 (QBD)), it can be said that they will have ceased to have an independent existence and therefore should be treated as "fully consumed" within reg.27E(8)(a), with the result that the consumer has no right to redress.

[1918] 2008 Regulations reg.27F(3). Law Commissions Report (2012) paras 8.83–8.96 rejecting an analogy with the then applicable position under Sale of Goods Act 1979 s.48(C)(3). This provision is reflected in the "final right to reject" in the Consumer Rights Act 2015 s.24(8)–24(10).

[1919] 2008 Regulations reg.27F(4)-(6).

[1920] 2008 Regulations reg.27F(7)-(10).

[1921] Consumer Contracts (Information, Cancellation and Additional Charges) Regulations 2013 (SI 2013/3134) regs 33–38 above, paras 14-200 and 14-205.

The right to unwind the contract: consumer to business contracts

Replace footnote 1924 with:

[1924] 2008 Regulations 27K(5), applying the general six-year period applicable to actions founded on simple contract under the Limitation Act 1980 s.6. It seems unlikely that the consumer will lose this right by inaction unless it is possible to infer an agreement (for good consideration) to abandon the right, or possibly promissory estoppel prevents the consumer from enforcing the right (see *Chitty on Contracts*, 33rd edn, Vol.I, paras 4-130 et seq.), but see below, para.14-305 on the question whether these general exclusions of a claim by a consumer apply in the context of Pt 4A rights.

14-296

Unwinding payments

Replace footnote 1927 with:

[1927] 2008 Regulations reg.27H. The Law Commissions Report (2012) para.8.102 acknowledged that a payment made as a result of misleading actions or threats could be recovered under the general law of unjust enrichment, but this law was seen by consumer groups as "complex and difficult" and so the new law should make this recovery "more accessible". On the general law see *Chitty on Contracts*, 33rd edn (2018), Vol.I paras 29-033 et seq. (mistake) and 29-094 et seq. (compulsion).

14-297

The right to a discount

Replace footnote 1929 with:

[1929] The drafting in reg.27I(1)(b) seems inconsistent with earlier provisions. In the case of a business to consumer contract, the consumer does not have a right to unwind at all unless the consumer notifies

14-298

the trader within the stated period, etc. If the consumer has this right, unwinding then seems to follows automatically. (See above, para.14-295 n.1908.) But the intention behind the words "if the consumer has not exercised the right to un-wind" seems clear enough.

Nature of the right to a discount

Replace footnote 1942 with:

14-299 [1942] See *Chitty on Contracts*, 33rd edn (2018), Vol.I para.26-049. Law Commission Report, *Aggravated, Exemplary and Restitutionary Damages* Law Com. No.247 (1997), Pt II.

Damages

Replace paragraph with:

14-300 A consumer who has entered a contract as the result of a prohibited practice by the trader, whether or not the consumer unwinds the contract or claims a discount, may recover damages for financial loss other than "the difference between the market price of a product and the amount payable for it under a contract",[1946] and for "alarm, distress or physical inconvenience or discomfort"[1947] that would not have occurred otherwise,[1948] provided that the loss was reasonably foreseeable at the time of the prohibited practice[1949] and subject to what amounts to a defence of due diligence on the part of the trader and which was intended to reflect the position under the Misrepresentation Act 1967 s.2(1), though using the language of the defence to the criminal offences as set out by the Regulations.[1950] Moreover, the right to damages under Pt 4A of the Regulations extends to consumers who have made a payment to the trader in respect of a product as the result of a prohibited practice and this includes not only payments that were not in fact due but also payment of sums that were due.[1951] There will seldom be a viable claim for financial loss in such cases,[1952] but it is not hard to imagine cases in which the consumer should be compensated for distress caused by an aggressive practice, which consists of "harassment, coercion or undue influence".[1953]

[1946] Regulation 27(1)(a) and (3). The Law Commissions described the loss recoverable as "consequential economic loss", giving the example of a consumer "who is sold a new bed in an aggressive way and then throws away the old bed to make room for it": Report (2012) para.8.148. The relevant measure of damages under Pt 4A therefore follows the "reliance measures" rather than the "expectation measure" of damages: Report (2012) para.8.3–8.15. See further on the measure of damages under reg.27J of the 2008 Regulations *Chitty on Contracts*, 33rd edn (2018), Vol.II, paras 38-199.

[1947] Regulation 27J(1)(b).

[1948] See reg.27J(1)(a) and (b).

[1949] Regulation 27J(4). The criterion of reasonable foreseeability reflects the position under the general law of remoteness in the tort of negligence and for breach of contract (below, para.16-031 (breach of contract), *Overseas Tankship (UK) Ltd. v Morts Dock & Engineering Co. (The Wagon Mound no 1)* [1961] A.C. 388 (tort of negligence)) rather than the special rule of directness applicable to damages in the tort of deceit and applied by the Court of Appeal to liability under s.2(1) of the Misrepresentation Act 1967 (*Doyle v Olby (Ironmongers) Ltd.* [1969] 2 Q.B.158. *Royscot Trust Ltd v Rogerson* [1991] 2 Q.B. 297. On the other hand, the Regulations require that the consumer's loss was reasonably foreseeable, rather than (as under the the general law governing the tort of negligence and breach of contract) his or her type or kind of loss. The form of words in the Regulations is therefore apparently more restrictive than the general law, as a type of loss may be reasonably foreseeable even where the particular loss suffered by the consumer was not so foreseeable at the time of the prohibited practice.

[1950] 2008 Regulations reg.27J(5); Law Commissions Report (2012) 8.165–8.173. On the defence to the criminal offence see 2008 Regulations reg.17(1), above, para.14-283.

[1951] See above, para.14-288. There is no right to unwind nor to a discount if the payment was in fact due: above, para.14-297 to 14-298.

[1952] In the case of a debt paid, the amount was already due, so there is unlikely to be financial loss, unless, possibly, in order to pay the trader the consumer resorts to an (even more) expensive form of credit such a pay-day loan. In the case of a payment of a sum that was not due, the normal remedy would be to unwind the settlement agreement. In addition, the exclusion of damages for the difference between the market price of a product and the amount payable for it under a contract (reg.27J(3)), read with the definition of "product" in cases of payment (reg.2(9)), seems to preclude an award under reg.27J for loss caused by paying sums that were not due.

[1953] 2008 Regulations reg.7, above, para.14-282.

Relationship to existing law

Replace footnote 1955 with:

[1955] A possible exception could be punitive damages, but these are not awarded in claims for breach of contract, though they may exceptionally be awarded for claims in tort: *Chitty on Contracts*, 33rd edn (2018), Vol.I para.26-048. **14-301**

Misrepresentation Act 1967 s.2 disapplied

Replace paragraph with:

However, the 2014 Regulations, which inserted Pt 4A into the 2008 Regula- **14-302** tions, amended the Misrepresentation Act 1967 so that a consumer who has a right to redress under Pt 4A in respect of the conduct constituting misrepresentation is not entitled to damages under s.2 of the Act.[1958] The thinking behind this disapplication was that leaving two possible grounds for consumer claims would lead to greater complexity in litigation.[1959] Nevertheless, the disapplication in the 2014 Regulations is a very strange provision. Its effect is not merely to prevent consumers from claiming damages under s.2 of the 1967 Act where they have a right to *damages* under the 2008 Regulations, but where they have a right to *redress*, that is, including a right to unwind the contract or to a discount. This would not matter if it were not for the fact that a consumer could have a right to unwind the contract or to a discount but no right to damages under the 2008 Regulations, notably, where his or her loss was not foreseeable by the trader at the time of engaging in the prohibited practice. In this situation, the consumer would almost certainly have a right to a discount[1960] (the right to unwind may have expired[1961]) and therefore could not rely on s.2 in order to recover damages under the more generous (if criticised) rule of remoteness there applicable.[1962] Moreover, apart from different rules of remoteness of damage, other differences between claims under s.2 and claims for damages under the 2008 Regulations may make them more or less attractive to a consumer depending on context. So, while the right to damages under the Regulations may compensate the consumer's "alarm, distress or physical inconvenience or discomfort" these heads of loss are less clearly recoverable under s.2[1963]; on the other hand, while the limitation periods for rights to redress and claims under s.2 are both six years, the time of accrual may differ.[1964] And while contributory negligence may be a defence to a claim under s.2,[1965] it is less clear that such a defence would apply to a claim for damages under Pt 4A.[1966] Certainly, the drawing of an exclusive line between claims under s.2 and the consumer's right to redress under the 2008 Regulations places considerable stress on the scope of availability of the new rights, which, as has been seen, is complex. In particular, where the contract does not concern a "product" as redefined for the purposes of Pt 4A,[1967] the consumer may claim only under s.2 and not under the 2008 Regulations.

[1958] SI 2014/870 reg.5. It is provided that this disapplication does not affect claims under the Consumer Credit Act 1974 s.75(1) against a creditor under a debtor-creditor-supplier agreement. See below, para.14-333. On the possible significance of s.2(4) of the 1967 Act on the court's discretion to refuse rescission and award damages in lieu in s.2(2) of the same Act, see below, para.14-304 (note).

[1959] Law Commissions Report (2012) paras 7.133 to 7-134.

[1960] The exception would be where the prohibited practice is not sufficiently serious to qualify as "minor" in the first band of reg.27I(4)(a), above, para.14-298.

[1961] Above, para.14-295.

[1962] Under this rule, damages may be recoverable even though the claimant's loss was not of a foreseeable kind: see further *Chitty on Contracts*, 33rd edn (2018), Vol.1 para.7-078.

[1963] They are recoverable in the tort of deceit (*Chitty on Contracts*, 33rd edn (2018), Vol.I paras 7-079-7-080) and the fiction of fraud in the Misrepresentation Act 1967 s.2(1) (para.7-078) suggests that they should therefore equally be recoverable in this context.

[1964] 2008 Regulations reg.27K provides that the period is "as if it were an action founded on simple contract", thereby attracting a six-year period from the time of accrual of the cause of action, which is normally the breach of contract: *Chitty on Contracts*, 33rd edn Vol.I para.28-032. Accrual of the cause of action in tort for the purposes of Misrepresentation Act s.2 is often the date when the contract is entered into, but may be a later date: para.28-034.

[1965] *Gran Gelato Ltd v Richcliff (Group) Ltd.* [1992] Ch. 560 and see *Chitty on Contracts*, 33rd edn Vol.I para.7-084.

[1966] The question would turn on whether the trader's liability to damages under reg.27J qualifies as "fault" as being an "act or omission which gives rise to a liability in tort" within the meaning of the Law Reform (Contributory Negligence) Act 1945 s.1(1) and s.4. At no point do the 2008 Regulations classify the trader's liability under reg.27J as tortious, and the limitation period designated is the period applicable to claims under a simple contract (reg.27K(5)); on the other hand the consumer's rights to damages under reg.27J arises from the commission of a "prohibited practice" rather than from any breach of contract.

[1967] Above, para.14-288.

Rescission for misrepresentation, duress or undue influence

Replace footnote 1973 with:

14-304 [1973] The relationship between a consumer's right to redress and the application of s.2(2) of the 1967 Act which provides courts with a power to award damages in lieu of rescission is not clear. Section 2(4) of the 1967 Act provides that "this *section* does not entitle a person to be paid damages in respect of a misrepresentation if the person has a right to redress ... in respect of the conduct constituting the misrepresentation" (emphasis added). While this could be thought to rule out the possibility of an award of damages under s.2(2) as well as damages under s.2(1), it is submitted that s.2(4) should not be so interpreted, as its unattractive consequence would be that where a consumer would have a right to redress under the Regulations, then the court would lose its power to refuse rescission (for example, in respect of an insignificant and purely innocent misrepresentation), as the court would not be in a position to "declare the contract subsisting and award damages in lieu of rescission" as provided by s.2(2). This consequence would be avoided if s.2(2) were interpreted as not "entitling" the misrepresentee/consumer to damages given that the award of damages is subject to the discretion of the court, as this would then mean that the disapplication in s.2(4) would not affect s.2(2) at all.

Waiver or contractual exclusion of rights to redress

To the end of the paragraph, add:

14-305 In particular, in the case of the consumer's right to unwind, the Regulations provide that the consumer enjoys this right only for a very short period (90 days) and further provide that, if the consumer has exercised the right to a discount, the consumer no longer enjoys the right to unwind. This structure argues that, within the 90 day period and unless the consumer has opted for a discount, he should not lose his right to unwind by action which would constitute affirmation under the general law.

6. ADMINISTRATIVE PROTECTION

Enterprise Act 2002 Pt 8

At the end of the paragraph, after ""enhanced consumer measures".", add:*

14-309 As will be noted, on the UK's exit from the EU on "exit day" (set at the time of writing at 31 October 2019), there are due to be significant amendments to the Pt 8 scheme.[2004a]

[2004a] See below, para.14-313A.

The definitions of "consumer"

Replace footnote 2008 with:

[2008] Or listed Regulation (s.210(6), (7) and (7A), as amended by SI 2006/3363, regs 3, 4 and 5) and SI 2011/1043 Art.4(1). The relevant Directives and Regulations are as specified in Sch.13. See further, below, para.14-312. On the UK's leaving the EU on "exit day", "Community infringements" are to be replaced by "Schedule 13 infringements" with consequential amendments, inter alia, to the 2002 Act s.210: Consumer Protection (Enforcement) (Amendment etc.) (EU Exit) Regulations 2019 (SI 2019/203) reg.3(2). On these changes more generally see below, para.14-313A   **14-310**

Add new title footnote 2014a:

Community infringements[2014a]

[2014a] On the UK's leaving the EU on "exit day", "Community infringements" are to be replaced by "Schedule 13 infringements" see below, para.14-313A.   **14-312**

Replace paragraph with:

Section 212(1) of the Act, defines a "Community infringement" as:

"An act or omission which harms the collective interests of consumers[2015] and which— (a) contravenes a listed Directive,[2016] as given effect by the laws, regulations or administrative provisions of an EEA State,[2017] (b) contravenes such laws, regulations or administrative provisions which provide additional permitted protections,[2018] (c) contravenes a listed Regulation, or (d) contravenes any laws, regulations or administrative provisions of an EEA State which give effect to a listed Regulation.[2019]

By s.212(3) the Secretary of State may by order specify the corresponding laws of the UK and this was done in the Enterprise Act 2002 (Pt 8 Community Infringements Specified UK Laws) Order 2003 (as much amended).[2020] The relevant "listed Directives" and "listed Regulations" are set out in Sch.13 to the 2002 Act (as much amended) and the corresponding UK laws are as stated in the Schedule to the 2003 Order. The lists are lengthy and detailed and cover such areas as unfair business to consumer commercial practices,[2021] consumer credit,[2022] package travel and linked travel arrangements,[2023] unfair terms in consumer contracts,[2024] timeshares and similar arrangements,[2025] off-premises contracts, distance contracts, and "on-premises contracts",[2026] aspects of the sale of consumer goods and associated guarantees,[2027] and the distance marketing of consumer financial services.[2028]

[2015] On the definition of "consumer" see Enterprise Act 2002 s.210(6)–(7A), above, para.14-310. Note that this is not limited to consumers in the UK.

[2016] See the 2002 Act s.210 and Sch.13.

[2017] For the meaning of "EEA State", see the 2002 Act s.212(5) referring to the Interpretation Act 1978 Sch.1.

[2018] Such additional permitted protection may exist where the relevant Directive is one of minimum harmonisation, as with Directive 1999/44 on certain aspects of the sale of consumer goods and associated guarantees.

[2019] 2002 Act s.212(1)(c) and (d) were added by SI 2006/3363 reg.7. For "listed Regulation", see s.210(7A), added by SI 2006/3363 reg.5"

[2020] Enterprise Act 2002 (Pt 8 Community Infringements Specified UK Laws) Order 2003 (SI 2003/1374) (2003 Order). The list, which is set out in Sch.1 to the Order, has been added to or amended by SI 2004/2095 reg.27, SI 2005/2418 Art.2(2), SI 2008/1277 Sch.2 para.100 and Sch.4 Pt 2 (but note also the savings in Sch.3 paras 13 and 14) and SI 2008/1816 reg.3 and Sch.1, SI 2010/1010 reg.69, SI 2010/2960 reg.36, Sch.6 and 8, SI 2011/1208 reg.17, SI 2012/1916 reg.348, SI 2013/472 Art.2, SI 2013/3168 Art.2, 2015/1392 Pt 4 reg.9(4)(b), and SI 2015/1628 Art.2(2)(b).

2021 See Directive 2005/29/EC concerning unfair business-to-consumer commercial practices [2005] O.J. L149/22 (listed by the 2002 Act Sch.13 Pt 1 para.9C) and the corresponding provisions in the Consumer Protection from Unfair Trading Regulations 2008 (SI 2008/1277).

2022 See Directive 2008/48/EC concerning credit agreements for consumers [2008] O.J. L133/66, replacing Directive 87/102/EEC concerning consumer credit O.J. L 42/48 (listed by the 2002 Act Sch.13 Pt 1 para.9D) and the corresponding provisions in the Consumer Credit Act 1974 and secondary legislation made thereunder (not including hire-purchase agreements): see the Consumer Credit (EU Directive) Regulations 2010 (SI 2010/1010) reg.69.

2023 Directive (EU) 2015/2302 on package travel and linked travel arrangements [2015] O.J. L326/1 (listed by the 2002 Act Sch.13 Pt 1 para.4); Enterprise Act 2002 (Pt 8 Community Infringements Specified UK Laws) Order 2003 (SI 2003/1374) Sch. listing the 2015 Directive and the Package Travel and Linked Travel Arrangements Regulations 2018 (SI 2018/634) (in force 1 July 2018). These instruments replaced an earlier directive of 1990 and its UK implementing regulations of 1992 as noted above, para.14-118.

2024 See Directive 1993/13/EEC on unfair terms in consumer contracts [1993] O.J. L95/29 (listed by the 2002 Act Sch.13 Pt 1 para.5) and the Consumer Rights Act 2015 Pt 2, on which see above, esp. paras 14-130 et seq.

2025 See Directive 2008/122/EC [2008] O.J. L33/10 on timeshare and related contracts (listed by 2002 Act Sch.13 Pt 1 para.9E) and the corresponding provisions in the Timeshare, Holiday Products, Resale and Exchange Contracts Regulations 2010 (SI 2010/2960).

2026 See Directive 2011/83/EU on consumer rights [2011] O.J. L304/64 (listed by the 2002 Act Sch.13 Pt 1 para.9F) and the corresponding provisions in the Consumer Contracts (Information, Cancellation and Additional Charges) Regulations 2013 (SI 2013/3134), above, paras 14-195 et seq.

2027 See Directive 1999/44/EC [1999] O.J. L171/12 (listed by the 2002 Act Sch.13 Pt 1 para.9E) implemented in UK law by the Consumer Rights Act 2015 Pt 1, Ch.2 as discussed above, paras 14-013 to 14-014 et seq.

2028 See Directive 2002/65/EC concerning the distance marketing of financial services [2002] O.J. L271/16 (listed by the 2002 Act Sch.13 Pt 1 para.9A) and the corresponding provisions in the Financial Services (Distance Marketing) Regulations 2004 (SI 2004/2095).

Replace paragraph with:

14-313   Section 213 of the 2002 Act (as amended) establishes the various categories of "enforcers" for the purposes of the Pt 8 provisions.[2028a] First, there are "general enforcers" (notably the CMA and local weights and measures authorities)[2029]; general enforcers may apply for an enforcement order in respect of any infringement.[2030] Secondly, there are "designated enforcers", that is, enforcers which have been designated by order as having as one of their purposes the protection of the collective interests of consumers.[2031] This category comprises both independent public bodies[2032] and private organisations which meet designated criteria and enforcers may be designated in respect of all infringements or such infringements as may be specified.[2033] Designated enforcers may apply for an enforcement order in respect of an infringement to which the designation relates.[2034] Thirdly, there are "Community enforcers", that is bodies which are neither a general enforcer nor a designated enforcer but which are qualified entities for the purposes of the Injunctions Directive[2035] and which are listed as such in the *Official Journal of the European Union*.[2036] There are also provisions for enabling enforcers to take proceedings in other EEA states and for co-operating with Community enforcers.[2037] This may be important when a trader is operating from another EEA state but in such a way as to harm the collective interests of consumers in the UK.[2038] Fourthly, there are "CPC enforcers" (named after the "CPC Regulation" which required their creation[2039]) which are established and listed by s.213(5A) of the Act and which include such bodies as the CMA, weights and measures authorities and the Financial Conduct Authority. CPC enforcers may make an application for an enforcement order in respect of a Community infringement.[2040] CPC enforcers possess enforcement powers which are required in order to comply with the CPC Regulation, including powers of entry on premises backed up by associated offences of obstruction.[2041]

[2028a] On the UK's leaving the EU on "exit day", the categories of "enforcers" are to be amended as noted below, para.14-313A.

[2029] 2002 Act s.213(1). In Northern Ireland, the enforcement authority is the Department of Enterprise, Trade and Investment in Northern Ireland.

[2030] 2002 Act s.215(2).

[2031] 2002 Act s.213(2).

[2032] 2002 Act s.213(3).

[2033] 2002 Act s.213(6). The Enterprise Act 2002 (Part 8 Designated Enforcers: Criteria for Designation, Designation of Public Bodies as Designated Enforcers and Transitional Provisions) Order 2003 (SI 2003/1399), as amended by SI 2014/549, designates the relevant public bodies including utility and other industry regulators (Art.5 and Sch.) and establishes criteria for designating non-public bodies (Arts 3 and 4). See also SI 2013/478 (designation of the Financial Conduct Authority) and SI 2005/917 (Designation of the Consumers' Association), the Enterprise Act 2002 (Water Services Regulation Authority) Order 2006 (SI 2006/522) Art.3(2) (substituting a designation of "The Water Services Regulation Authority" for "The Director General of Water Services".

[2034] 2002 Act s.215(3).

[2035] Originally Directive 98/27 [1998] O.J. L166/51 which was repealed and replaced on 29 December 2009 by Directive 2009/22 [2009] O.J. L110/30. Community enforcers may apply for an enforcement order in respect of a Community infringement (s.215(4)), as may CPC enforcers (2002 Act s.215(4A).

[2036] 2002 Act s.213(5). For the bodies so listed, see the Commission Communication concerning Art.4(3) of Directive 2009/22/EC [2012] O.J. C97/01.

[2037] 2002 Act s.221.

[2038] Hence the OFT used its cross-border enforcement powers to secure binding undertakings preventing a Dutch marketing company from publishing and distributing misleading mailings to UK residents (see *Butterworths Consumer Law Bulletin*, Issue No.225, June 2005, p.4).

[2039] Regulation 2006/2004 on co-operation between national authorities responsible for the enforcement of consumer protection laws [2004] O.J. L364/1 Arts 4(6) and 13(4) (as amended by the Unfair Commercial Practices Directive 2005). The amendments to the 2002 Act were made by the Enterprise Act 2002 (Amendment) Regulations 2006 (SI 2006/3363). Regulation (EC) 2006/2004 is repealed and replaced with effect from 17 January 2020 by Regulation (EU) 2017/2394 of the European Parliament and of the Council of 12 December 2017 on cooperation between national authorities responsible for the enforcement of consumer protection laws and repealing Regulation (EC) No 2006/2004 O.J. L 345/1.

[2040] See the 2002 Act s.215(4A), which was added by SI 2006/3363 reg.12. The list of CPC enforcers is set out by the 2002 Act s.213(5A) as inserted by SI 2006/3363 reg.11 and amended by the Consumer Rights Act 2015 s.79, Sch.7 para.4.

[2041] These powers are now contained in the Consumer Rights Act 2015 s.77 Sch.5: see Enterprise Act 2002 s.223A (as inserted by the 2015 Act Sch.6 para.78).

After paragraph 14-313, add new paragraph 14-313A:

Amendments to Pt 8 of the 2002 Act on the UK's exit from the EU   As outlined   **14-313A** in the previous paragraphs, the scheme of control set out in Pt 8 of the 2002 Act distinguishes between "domestic infringements" and "Community infringements" and sets out a series of categories of enforcers which includes "Community enforcers" and "CPC enforcers". However, on the UK's leaving the EU on "exit day" (which is currently defined as 31 October 2019 at 11.00 pm[2041a]), this scheme is due to be subject to significant change,[2041b] reflecting in particular the fact that European cross-border enforcement of EU consumer protection legislation will no longer apply. First, the category of "Community infringement" is replaced with one of "Schedule 13 infringement" and the existing lists of EU legislation (and UK legislation implementing EU legislation) giving rise to Community infringements are replaced with a substituted Sch.13 to the 2002 Act.[2041c] Accordingly, a "Schedule 13 infringement" is defined as "an act or omission which contravenes a listed enactment and which harms the collective interest of consumers", it being provided that "[a]n enactment is a listed enactment if it is specified in Schedule 13 or to the extent that it is so specified."[2041d] Secondly, while the Act's recognition of "general enforcers" and "designated enforcers" remains,[2041e] its inclusion of "Community enforcers" is deleted as is its reference to the Secretary of State designating persons under the CPC Regulation,[2041f] there being substituted instead a list of "Schedule 13 enforcers".[2041g] As this scheme foresees, the content of Sch.13 of the 2002 Act is therefore replaced with a list of enactments which can give rise to "Schedule 13 infringements", these consisting of 27 UK legislative instruments, both primary and secondary and whether or not they implemented EU legislation,[2041h] and two EU regulations "retained" after the UK's exit from the EU by the European Union (Withdrawal) Act 2018,[2041i] notably, the Denied Boarding Regulation.[2041j] The UK legislation contained in Sch.13 includes the Consumer Contracts (Information, Cancellation and Additional Charges) Regulations 2013 (SI 2013/3134), as well as the Consumer Protection from Unfair Trading Regulations 2008 (SI 2008/1277) and many provisions in Pts 1 and 2 of the Consumer Rights Act 2015[2041k].

[2041a] European Union (Withdrawal) Act s.20(1) "exit day" as amended by SI 2019/859 reg.2(2). On the UK's exit from the EU generally see above, paras 14-006 et seq.

[2041b] These changes are contained in the Consumer Protection (Enforcement) (Amendment etc.) (EU Exit) Regulations 2019 (SI 2019/203) ("SI 2019/203"), which come into force on "exit day": reg.1.

[2041c] As a result, the orders specifying the relevant UK and EU laws) are to be revoked: SI 2019/203 reg.7 specifying the following orders: SI 2003/1374; SI 2005/2418; SI 2006/3372; SI 2014/2098; SI 2015/1628. Transitional provision is also made by SI 2019/203 for Community infringements or suspected Community infringments occurring before exit day: regs 9 and 10.

[2041d] Enterprise Act 2002 s.212 as amended by SI 2019/203 reg.3(3), referring to the s.212(6A) and (6B) as inserted by reg.3(2)(b).

[2041e] Enterprise Act 2002 s.213(1)–(4).

[2041f] i.e. Regulation (EC) 2006/2004 on cooperation between national authorities responsible for the enforcement of consumer protection laws which is itself revoked on "exit day": SI 2019/203 reg.8.

[2041g] Enterprise Act 2002 s.213(5) (deleted by SI 2019/203 reg.3(4)(a); s.213(5A) amended by SI 2019/203 reg.3(4)(b); s.213(10) and (11) deleted by SI 2019/203 reg.3(4)(c). Other references in the Act to Community infringement, Community enforcer and CPC infringement are also replaced accordingly or the relevant provision deleted: SI 2019/203 reg.3(5)–(19).

[2041h] SI 2019/203 reg.3(20) referring to the Schedule to these regulations. Some of these UK regulations are themselves revoked except as regards contracts made before their date of revocation, as in the case of the Unfair Terms in Consumer Contracts Regulations 1999 (SI 1999/2083): SI 2019/203 Sch. para.1 inserting new 2002 Act Sch.13, para.9. Others remain fully in force: e.g. the Consumer Protection from Unfair Trading Regulations 2008 (SI 2008/1277): SI 2019/203 Sch. para.1 inserting new 2002 Act Sch.13, para.19.

[2041i] 2018 Act s.3(1) and (2) on which see above, para.14-007.

[2041j] SI 2019/203 Sch. para.15 referring to Regulation (EC) No 261/2004. Otherwise, Sch.13 para.28 (as substituted by SI 2019/203 SI 2019/203 Sch. para.1) refers to art.10(4) of Regulation (EU) 2015/751 of the European Parliament and of the Council of 29 April 2015 on interchange fees for card-based payment transactions.

[2041k] SI 2019/203 Sch. para.1 inserting new 2002 Act Sch.13, paras 25, 19 and 27 respectively.

Enforcement orders: cessation of the infringement

Replace paragraph with:

14-314   Where an enforcer contemplates bringing proceedings for an enforcement order the usual requirement is one of trying to achieve the cessation, non-repetition or, in the case of a Community infringement, the non-occurrence of the infringement through an appropriate consultation with the apparent offender.[2042] Attempts to achieve cessation may be dispensed with where the CMA thinks that an application for an order should be made "without delay"[2043] and, in any event, the period of grace will expire within 14 days after the request for consultation is received.[2044] Applications for an enforcement order may be made to the High Court or a county court[2045] and are subject to a significant amount of control in the form of directions by the CMA,[2046] one purpose of which is to prevent multiple applications in respect of the same infringement in different parts of the country. The court may make an order where it finds that the person named in the application has engaged in the conduct which constitutes the infringement or, in the case of a Community infringement, is likely to do so.[2047] An enforcement order must indicate the nature of the conduct to which the finding of an infringement or likely infringement relates and must direct the person not to continue or repeat the conduct (in the case of an infringement that has already occurred), not to engage in such conduct in the course of his business or another business and/or not to consent to or connive in the carrying out of such conduct by a body corporate with which he has a special relationship.[2048] Breach of such an order will attract the usual sanctions of the law of contempt.

[2042] 2002 Act s.214(1)(a). The CMA must also be consulted where it is not the enforcer (s.214(b)). On the UK's leaving the EU on "exit day", "Community infringements" are to be replaced by "Schedule 13 infringements" as noted above, para.14-313A.

[2043] 2002 Act s.214(3).

[2044] 2002 Act s.214(4)(a). Or 7 days in the case of an application for an interim enforcement order (s.214(4)(b)). The grace period is 28 days where the person against whom the enforcement order would be made is a member of, or is represented by, a representative body, and that body operates a consumer code which has been approved by (a) an enforcer, other than a designated enforcer which is not a public body, (b) a body which represents an enforcer mentioned in para.(a), (c) a group of enforcers mentioned in para.(a), or (d) a community interest company whose objects include the approval of consumer codes: see 2002 Act s.214(4)(a), (4A) and (4B) as amended and inserted by the Consumer Rights Act 2015 s.79, Sch.7 para.5.

[2045] 2002 Act s.215(5)(za) and (5)(a). No doubt in practice it will normally be a county court. Note the Enterprise Act 2002 s.218A (as inserted by the Consumer Protection from Unfair Trading Regulations 2008 (SI 2008/1277) reg.27), which contains special provisions covering evidence as to factual claims on an application for enforcement orders in respect of alleged Community infringements based on Directive 2005/29 (unfair commercial practices).

[2046] 2002 Act s.216 which does not, however, prevent an application for an enforcement order being made by a Community enforcer (s.216(6)).

[2047] 2002 Act s.217(1) and (2). There are provisions also for interim enforcement orders (s.218) and for accepting undertakings in lieu of an order (s.219). For enforcement orders against bodies corporate and accessories, see ss.222 and 223. For an example of an interim enforcement order being made both against a company and its directors, see *Office of Fair Trading v MB Designs (Scotland) Ltd* 2005 S.L.T. 691 (Outer House: Lord Drummond Young). The decision also confirms the important point that it is permissible to have regard to conduct which occurred before the Pt 8 provisions came into force. On the UK's leaving the EU on "exit day", "Community infringements" are to be replaced by "Schedule 13 infringements" as noted above, para.14-313A.

[2048] 2002 Act s.217(5)–(7).

Enforcement orders: "enhanced consumer measures"

Replace paragraph with:

In general, it may be said that the Pt 8 procedures are helpful in establishing a **14-316** framework to deal with persons who are in breach of criminal or civil obligations and who thereby harm the collective interests of consumers. However, the procedures are not free from complexity, not least because of the central distinction between "domestic infringements" and "Community infringements" falling within the scope of the Injunctions Directive.[2058] Again, whilst the CMA is able to act under all these enactments there is no common list of others who may do so.

[2058] For "domestic" and "Community" infringements, see, respectively, above, paras 14-311 and 14-312 and 14-313A (noting the abolition of the category of "Community infringement on the UK's leaving the EU).

Codes of practice; advice to consumers

Replace the second paragraph with:

14-319   Of course, there are limits to what can be achieved through such codes. Sanctions for non-compliance may not be fully effective and less-reputable traders may not in any event belong to the association which draws up the code; but there are indications that the codes reduced the number of consumer complaints and provided significant protection to consumers, especially in areas which do not lend themselves to a stricter form of regulation through the criminal or civil law.[2072] However, the Enterprise and Regulatory Reform Act 2013 repealed s.8 of the 2002 Act,[2073] although existing codes may remain influential and further informal codes of practice may be adopted.[2074] Instead, in 2001 the OFT introduced a voluntary scheme, the Consumer Codes Approval Scheme (CCAS), and in 2012 the Government asked the Chartered Trading Standards Institute (CTSI, a not-for-profit membership organisation supporting and representing trading standards professionals in the UK and abroad) to develop a successor to the OFT's scheme on the abolition of the OFT. The management of CCAS was transferred by the CTSI to a new Consumer Codes Approval Board supported by the CTSI in 2013. According to its Annual Report for 2017:

> "CCAS is facilitated self-regulation. It aims to promote consumer interests by setting out the principles of effective customer service and protection. It goes above and beyond consumer law obligations and sets a higher standard, giving consumers a clear indication—through the right to display the CTSI Approved Code logo—that code members can be trusted."[2075]

The Enterprise Act 2002's provisions concerning the acquisition of information, its provision to the public and the provision of information and advice to Ministers, remain in force with the relevant functions being exercised by the CMA.[2076]

[2072] It was recognised by the European Commission Green Paper, European Union Consumer Protection COM(2001) 531 final (see para.4.4) that many problems are not suitable for regulatory action and effective self-regulation is more appropriate.

[2073] Enterprise and Regulatory Reform Act s.26(3), Sch.5 Pt 2 paras 59, 63.

[2074] Enterprise and Regulatory Reform Act 2013 s.26(3), Sch.5 Pt 2 paras 59, 60, 61 and 62.

[2075] CTSI, *Consumer Codes Approval Scheme*, Annual Report (2017) p.4 at *https://www.tradingstandards.uk/* [Accessed September 4, 2018].

[2076] Enterprise Act 2002 ss.5, 6 and 7.

7. CONSUMER CREDIT TRANSACTIONS

The regulation of consumer credit.

After "made under it.", add new footnote 2077a:

14-320   [2077a] On the UK's leaving the EU (on which generally see above, para.14-006 et seq.) the 1974 Act and related secondary legislation are due to be subject to amendment: see the Consumer Credit (Amendment) (EU Exit) Regulations 2018 (SI 2018/1038) and the Financial Services and Markets Act 2000 (Amendment) (EU Exit) Regulations 2019 (SI 2019/632) reg.194.

Regulated credit agreements

Replace footnote 2095 with:

[2095] The 1974 Act s.8(3), cross-referring to the definition in the FSMA 2000 (Regulated Activities) Order **14-322**
2001 (SI 2001/544) Pt 2 Ch.IVA. On the UK's leaving the EU (on which generally see above, paras 14-006 et seq.), these definitions are to be amended: Financial Services and Markets Act 2000 (Amendment) (EU Exit) Regulations 2019 (SI 2019/632) regs 194 and 138–142 respectively. See also 1974 Act s.15, cross-referring to the definition in the FSMA 2000 (Regulated Activities) Order 2001 (SI 2001/544) Pt 2 Ch.IVB which defines a "consumer hire agreement" as "an agreement between a person ("the owner") and an individual or relevant recipient of credit (the "hirer") for a bailment or, in Scotland, the hiring of goods to the hirer, being an agreement which—(a) is not a hire-purchase agreement, and (b) is capable of subsisting for more than three months" (reg.60N). In *TRM Copy Centres (UK) Ltd v Lanwall Services Ltd* [2009] UKHL 35; [2009] 4 All E.R. 33 it was held that an agreement under which a photocopier was located in a retailer's shop was not a consumer hire agreement for the purposes of the Act. The photocopier was not being hired by the retailer as bailee as it did not pay for the bailment in either cash or kind.

Exempt agreements

Replace paragraph with:

A number of credit agreements are "exempt agreements" and hence escape **14-323**
control.[2099] First, although there is now generally no financial limit for regulated agreements,[2100] agreements entered into "wholly or predominantly" for the debtor's "business purposes", where the credit provided exceeds £25,000, are exempt.[2101] Secondly, debtors certified as "high net worth" may opt out of regulation in certain[2102] circumstances.[2103] Thirdly, exemption is also provided for certain agreements where there is no or a low charge for credit.[2104] Finally,[2105] certain agreements where the number of payments is small, are exempt.[2106]

[2099] But (with one exception, FCA regulated land mortgages and home purchase plans), the "unfair relationship" provisions in ss.140A–140C (see para.14-330, below), apply to exempt agreements.

[2100] See para.14-322, above.

[2101] See the FSMA 2000 (Regulated Activities) Order 2001 (SI 2001/544) art.60C(3)–(7) (ex–1974 Act s.16B (inserted by the Consumer Credit Act 2006 s.4)) for the detailed requirements.

[2102] As this exemption is incompatible with the Consumer Credit Directive (see para.14-321, above), it is now only available for credit agreements outside the scope of the Directive: agreements secured on land and agreements where credit in excess of £60,260 is provided.

[2103] See the FSMA 2000 (Regulated Activities) Order 2001 (SI 2001/544) art.60H (ex–1974 Act s.16A (inserted by the Consumer Credit Act 2006 s.2)) for the detailed requirements (amendments due on the UK's exit from the EU (on which see above, para.14-006 et seq.): SI 2019/632 reg.141).

[2104] See the FSMA 2000 (Regulated Activities) Order 2001 (SI 2001/544) art.60G (ex–1974 Act s.16(5)(b)) for the detailed requirements. (Amendments are due on the UK's leaving the EU: SI 2019/632 reg.140.)

[2105] A large number of credit agreements secured on land are also exempt (although many are regulated under the FSMA 2000). See the FSMA 2000 (Regulated Activities) Order 2001 (SI 2001/544) arts 60C, 60E (ex–1974, Act s.16) and art.60D (ex–1974 Act s.16C (inserted by the Legislative Reform (Consumer Credit) Order 2008 (SI 2008/2826) art.3)) for the detailed requirements (with amendments due on the UK's leaving the EU by SI 2019/632 regs 138 and 139). Implementation of the Mortgage Credit Directive (Directive 2014/17/EU [2014] O.J. L60/34 required considerable changes for this context and these have been made by the FCA by the Mortgage Credit Directive Order SI 2015/910 (as amended). The details of these rules lies beyond the scope of the present work.

[2106] The provisions are extremely complex: see the FSMA 2000 (Regulated Activities) Order 2001 (SI 2001/544) art.60F (ex–1974 Act s.16(5)(a)) for the detailed requirements.

Outline of control

Replace paragraph with:

14-324   The 1974 Act makes provision for the form, content, and signing of regulated agreements[2107] and of security instruments,[2108] for example, guarantees and indemnities,[2109] given in respect of regulated agreements, and for the supply of copies of the agreement to the debtor and sureties.[2110] In some circumstances, the credit agreement will be subject to a "cooling-off period" during which it may be cancelled by the debtor.[2111] Restrictions are placed upon the power of the creditor to enforce a regulated agreement, to terminate it or to exercise his rights under it in the event of the debtor's default.[2112] Should the debtor fall into arrears, "notices of sums in arrears", accompanied by FCA-drafted information sheets on arrears and default,[2113] need to be served.[2114] The sanctions for breach of these requirements vary, but generally they render the agreement unenforceable, except on an order or court.[2115] The debtor has a statutory right to settle the agreement, in whole or in part, early if he so wishes,[2116] and upon early settlement he becomes entitled to a rebate of future interest and charges.[2117] The county court[2118] is given wide discretionary powers to control regulated agreements,[2119] including the power to make a "time order" whereby a debtor will be permitted to pay any sum owed by him by such instalments and at such times as the court, having regard to his means, considers reasonable, or to remedy any other breach of the agreement within such period as the court may specify.[2120] The debtor is also entitled, while the agreement continues, upon request and the payment of £1[2121] to a copy of the agreement and a statement of his account with the creditor.[2122] A creditor who fails to comply with these obligations will not be entitled to enforce the agreement while the default continues.[2123] The creditor is also obliged to provide periodic statements of account in various circumstances.[2124]

[2107] 1974 Act ss.60, 61 (as amended). As a result of the Consumer Credit Directive (see para.14-321, above) there are two sets of Agreement Regulations: (a) for "non-Directive" agreements, see the Consumer Credit (Agreements) Regulations 1983 (SI 1983/1553, as amended); and (b) for "Directive" agreements, see the Consumer Credit (Agreements) Regulations 2010 (SI 2010/1014, as amended). In relation to disclosure requirements made under the 1974 Act s.55, again there are two sets of regulations: (a) for "non-Directive" agreements, see the Consumer Credit (Disclosure of Information) Regulations 2004 (SI 2004/1481, as amended); and (b) for "Directive" agreements, see the Consumer Credit (Disclosure of Information) Regulations 2010 (SI 2010/1013, as amended, with further amendments on the UK leaving the EU by SI 2018/1038 reg.3).

[2108] 1974 Act s.105.

[2109] Consumer Credit (Guarantees and Indemnities) Regulations 1983 (SI 1983/1556), as amended by SI 2004/3236.

[2110] 1974 Act ss.61A–63 (amended).

[2111] 1974 Act ss.67–73; also s.66A (right to withdraw from consumer credit agreement within 14 days, inserted as from February 1, 2011 by SI 2010/1010 reg.13). Note also that s.67 does not apply where s.66A applies: see SI 2010/1010 reg.14.

[2112] 1974 Act ss.76, 87, 98. See also Consumer Credit (Enforcement, Default and Termination Notices) Regulations 1983 (SI 1983/1561, as amended).

[2113] 1974 Act s.86A, inserted by the Consumer Credit Act 2006 s.8.

[2114] 1974 Act ss.86B–86F, inserted by the Consumer Credit Act 2006 ss.9–14. Failure to serve these "NOSIAs" gives rise to a "period of non-compliance" during which the creditor may not charge interest or enforce the agreement. The Consumer Credit (Information Requirements and Duration of Licences and Charges) Regulations 2007 (SI 2007/1167), as amended by SI 2008/1751 and SI 2008/2826, make provision for the contents of such notices and associated matters.

[2115] 1974 Act s.65 (and see 127(1)). In relation to "NOSIAs", see previous footnote. Originally certain agreements were "irredeemably" unenforceable (i.e. no order of court was available: now repealed 1974

Act s.127(3)–(4)) and this was challenged as being incompatible with the European Convention on Human Right Art.6. This challenge was rejected (at least in the case of a loan under £25,000), obiter, by the House of Lords in *Wilson v Secretary of State for Trade and Industry* [2003] UKHL 40; [2004] 1 A.C. 816 but (when the financial limit was abolished, see para.14-322, above) those provisions were repealed on 6 April 2007 (see the Consumer Credit Act 2006 (Commencement No.2 and Transitional Provisions and Savings) Order 2007 (SI 2007/123) Art.3(2) Sch.2); but as noted in *Heath v Southern Pacific Mortgage Ltd* [2009] EWHC 103 (Ch); [2009] 2 All E.R. (Comm) 687 at [6], the repeal does not have retrospective effect.

[2116] 1974 Act ss.94–97A (as amended).

[2117] 1974 Act ss.95–95A (as amended). The detail is in the Consumer Credit (Early Settlement) Regulations 2004 (SI 2004/1483), as amended.

[2118] Actions to enforce a regulated agreement must be brought in the county court: 1974 Act s.141.

[2119] 1974 Act Pt IX.

[2120] 1974 Act s.129.

[2121] Raised by SI 1998/997.

[2122] See 1974 Act ss.77, 78 (criminal sanction removed by SI 2008/1277 Sch.4 Pt 1) and ss.107, 108 (information to sureties) (criminal sanction removed by SI 2008/1277 Sch.4 Pt 1). See also s.77B (statements of account to be provided on request for instalment credit).

[2123] 1974 Act ss.77(4)(a), 78(6)(a). The creditor's rights are not extinguished but are unenforceable during the period of default and the creditor is not precluded from reporting the debtor's outstanding indebtedness to credit reference agencies: see *McGuffick v Royal Bank of Scotland Plc* [2009] EWHC 2386 (Comm); [2010] 1 All E.R. 634 (Flaux J). See also *Carey v HSBC Bank Plc* [2009] EWHC 3417 QB; [2010] Bus. L.R. 1142 (considering the relationship between non-compliance with s.78 and the provisions of ss.140A–140C providing relief to the debtor where there is an "unfair relationship" with the creditor (below, para.14-330).

[2124] 1974 Act s.77A (fixed-sum agreements) and s.78(4) (running-account credit agreements). The Consumer Credit (Information Requirements and Duration of Licences and Charges) Regulations 2007 (SI 2007/1167, as amended by SI 2008/1751, SI 2008/2826, SI 2010/1010, SI 2012/2798, SI 2013/1881, SI 2014/2369 and SI 2014/366) contain the details of the content of statements to be provided.

Authorisation

Replace paragraph with:

Originally, a licence was required to carry on a consumer credit business and **14-325** certain "ancillary credit businesses", for example, credit brokerage. Since the transfer of consumer credit regulation to the FCA,[2125] such businesses now require authorisation under the FSMA 2000 Pt 4A. Hence entering into a regulated agreement by way of business as lender and other related activities such as credit broking are "regulated activities" under that Act.[2126] Trading without authorisation attracts both a criminal penalty[2127] and renders any regulated agreement made when the lender was not authorised unenforceable against the borrower and voidable at his instance unless the FCA orders otherwise.[2128] Authorised persons are subject to the extensive regulatory powers of the FCA. As well as deciding whether to authorise those wishing to undertake credit-related activities, the FCA has the power to make rules and guidance,[2129] to monitor and investigate their activities[2130] and to discipline (for example, by imposing penalties[2131])[2132] and ordering redress to be made.[2133] Moreover, the Financial Ombudsman Service, established under the Financial Services and Markets Act 2000[2134] with power to make determinations "by what is, in the opinion of the ombudsman, fair and reasonable in all the circumstances of the case"[2135] applies to consumer credit disputes.[2136]

[2125] See para.14-320, above.

[2126] They are "regulated activities" by virtue of FSMA 2000 s.22 (amendments by SI 2018/135 reg.38 due on UK's leaving EU) and the FSMA 2000 (Regulated Activities) Order 2001 (SI 2001/544) arts 36A–36G (credit broking), arts 36H–36J (peer-to peer lending), arts 39D–39M (activities in relation to debt), arts 60B–60M (credit business), arts 60N–60R (hire) and arts 89A –89E (credit reference agencies). Undertaking such activities without being an authorisation (or exempt) person is a breach of the "general prohibition" in FSMA 2000 s.19. These provisions are likely to be amended on the UK's leaving the EU: see Electronic Commerce and Solvency 2 (Amendment etc.) (EU Exit) Regulations 2019 (Draft) reg.5.

[2127] FSMA 2000 s.23. The FCA may also apply to court for various orders against miscreants and those "knowingly concerned" in the contravention: FSMA 2000 ss.380, 382 (amendments due on the UK leaving the EU: SI 2019/632 regs 70 and 71).

[2128] FSMA 2000 ss.26, 26A, 28A. Agreements made by authorised lenders through unauthorised persons (e.g. an unauthorised broker) are also unenforceable: FSMA 2000 ss.27, 28A.

[2129] Under FSMA 2000 Pt IXA. Those particularly relevant to consumer credit are in the "CONC" Module of the FCA Handbook (see *https://www.the-fca.org.uk/* [Accessed 19 August 2019]). For rulemaking power specific to this sector, see s.137C (cost of credit).

[2130] See FSMA 2000 Pt XIA.

[2131] FSMA 2000 s.206.

[2132] FSMA 2000 ss.205–211.

[2133] FSMA 2000 s.384. It may also apply to court for various orders: FSMA 2000 ss.380, s.382. These provisions are due to be amended on the UK's leaving the EU: SI 2019/632 regs 138–140.

[2134] See s.225(4) and Sch.17.

[2135] FSMA s.228(2). The determinations need not be in accordance with the strict legal position: *R. (Heather Moor & Edgecomb) v FOS* [2008] EWCA Civ 642; [2008] Bus. L.R.1486.

[2136] Credit activities are "regulated activities", the general "compulsory" jurisdiction applies under ss.225–226 of the 1974 Act, above, para.14-322.

Credit cards, etc

Replace footnote 2160 with:

14-328 [2160] See the Consumer Credit Act 1974 s.84, (as amended in particular by the Payment Services Regulations 2017/752 Sch.8(1) para.1(b))(maximum £35 liability in the debtor to the creditor or loss to the creditor arising from use of the credit-token by other persons). See further above, paras 14-210–14-210B (controls on payment surcharges) and para.14-213 (unauthorized payment transactions).

Extent of protection

Replace footnote 2161 with:

14-329 [2161] See para.14-320 note, above.

Liability of creditor for acts of supplier

Replace footnote 2198 with:

14-333 [2198] But it (unlike s.75) applies where the cash price is over £30,000. See para.14-333 above, in relation to s.75(3).

Promotion of credit

Replace paragraph with:

14-334 The advertising of consumer credit was originally regulated by the Consumer Credit Act 1974 and regulations made thereunder but it is now covered by the "financial promotion" provisions of FSMA 2000,[2201] including the Financial Promotion Order[2202] made under it, which sets out which "promotions" are exempt from regulation. The detailed requirements concerning the form and content of credit "promotions" are now contained in the "CONC" Module of the FCA Handbook.[2203]

[2201] FSMA 2000 s.21 (as amended by the Financial Guidance and Claims Act 2018 s.27(3)).

[2202] The FSMA 2000 (Financial Promotion) Order 2005 (SI 2005/1529) as amended.

[2203] The *FCA Handbook* is at *https://www.the-fca.org.uk/* [Accessed 20 August 2019].

Enforcement

Replace footnote 2208 with:

[2208] See s.212 of the Act and the Enterprise Act 2002 (Part 8 Community Infringements Specified UK **14-335** Laws) Order 2003 (SI 2003/1374) Art.3 and Sch.; above, para.14-312 and, more generally, paras 14-309 et seq. On the UK's leaving the EU on "exit day", "Community infringements" are to be replaced by "Schedule 13 infringements" and the Consumer Credit Act 1974 and "secondary legislation made under that Act excluding requirements relating to consumer hire agreements" are included within the substituted Sch.13 of the 2002 Act for this purpose: Consumer Protection (Enforcement) (Amendment etc.) (EU Exit) Regulations 2019 (SI 2019/203) reg.3(20) and Sch, para.1 inserting new 2002 Act Sch.13 para.2. On this change more generally see below, para.14-313A.

CHAPTER 15

THE SELLER'S REMEDIES AFFECTING THE GOODS

TABLE OF CONTENTS

1.   INTRODUCTION

(a)   Remedies of Unpaid Seller

Effect on third parties

Replace paragraph with:

The remedies of the unpaid seller against the goods are not affected by the fact **15-005** that the buyer has resold the goods to a sub-buyer, or made some other disposition of the goods to a third person. The rights of the unpaid seller therefore in principle prevail over those of a sub-buyer (although this rule is subject to a number of exceptions[37]). Furthermore, these remedies against the goods may be exercised in such a way as to affect third parties (viz. persons who are not parties to the contract of sale or claiming under such a party). The title of the claimant to bring proceedings for wrongful interference based on trespass to goods must, and that based on conversion may, be founded on the claimant's being in possession of the goods at

[231]

the time of the defendant's interference with the goods.[38] The title of the claimant to bring proceedings for wrongful interference in respect of conversion may also be based on the claimant's right to immediate possession of the goods at the time of the defendant's refusal to return the goods, or his interference with them.[39] Since the exercise of the remedies against the goods set out in s.39 may determine the issues of who has possession of the goods and who is entitled to possess them, it may affect the entitlement of both the seller and the buyer to bring proceedings for wrongful interference with the goods against third parties.[40] For instance, the liability of the carrier of the goods to an action of this kind may be affected by the seller's exercise of his right of stoppage in transit.[41]

[37] 1979 Act s.47 (below, paras 15-092 et seq., where the exceptions to this rule are examined).

[38] *Clerk and Lindsell on Torts*, 22nd edn, paras 17–44 et seq.; para.17-136.

[39] *Clerk and Lindsell on Torts*, 22nd edn, paras 17–59 et seq.

[40] See below, paras 16-093, 17-102, 17-103. The action for detinue was abolished by the Torts (Interference with Goods) Act 1977 s.2(1).

[41] See the 1979 Act s.46(4) (below, para.15-088).

Agency

Replace footnote 49 with:

15-008   [49] *Bird v Brown* (1850) 4 Ex. 786. This proviso is in accordance with a general principle of agency: *Bowstead and Reynolds on Agency*, 21st edn, paras 2-062 to 2-070.

(b)   Definition of "Seller"

Extended meaning of "seller"

Replace footnote 82 with:

15-013   [82] *Imperial Bank v London and St Katherine Docks Co* (1877) 5 Ch. D. 195. See *Bowstead and Reynolds on Agency*, 21st edn, paras 7-100 to 7-102.

Surety

Replace paragraph with:

15-014   At common law before the 1893 Act, a surety for the payment of the price under the contract of sale had no right to exercise the remedy of stoppage in transit against the goods.[89] It is submitted that a surety for the buyer is, when he has paid the seller, a "person who is in the position of a seller" within the meaning of subs.(2) above.[90] Before the buyer has defaulted in paying the price, the surety has only a contingent liability to pay the price[91]; but after payment he is subrogated to the rights of the seller against the defaulting buyer.[92]

[89] *Siffken v Wray* (1805) 6 East 371.

[90] The Mercantile Law Amendment Act 1856 s.5, may also lead to the same result: *Imperial Bank v London and St Katherine Docks Co* (1877) 5 Ch. D. 195 (sed quaere whether the right of lien or stoppage is a "security" within this section: it may, however, be covered by the wide words "shall be entitled to stand in the place of the creditor, and to use all the remedies ... of the creditor". See Benjamin, *Sale of Personal Property*, 8th edn, pp.882–883.) See also *Chitty on Contracts*, 33rd edn, Vol.2 para.45-145.

[91] *Chitty on Contracts*, 33rd edn, Vol.2 paras 45-001, 45-008.

[92] *Chitty on Contracts*, 33rd edn, Vol.2 paras 45-144 et seq.

(c) When Seller is "Unpaid"

Payment by negotiable instrument

Replace footnote 114 with:

[114] *Gunn v Bolckow, Vaughan & Co* (1875) L.R. 10 Ch. App. 491 at 501 (dishonour by non-payment: a **15-018**
fortiori in the case of non-acceptance of the draft). See further the authorities cited above, para.9-029
n.158.

Tender of the price

Replace the first paragraph with:

In the case of all three remedies against the goods the relevant section specifies **15-022**
"until payment or tender of the price",[129] or uses the verbs "pay or tender" the
price,[130] to indicate the purpose of the remedies and the circumstances justifying
them. The general principles of the law on tender of money to pay a debt should
be sought elsewhere.[131] For a valid tender, the full[132] amount of the price must be
tendered; the tender must be in legal currency[133] (unless the seller waives[134] his right
to legal tender and is willing to accept another form of payment, e.g. a cheque[135]);
and the tender must be unconditional.[136] But a valid tender may be made by an agent
of the buyer, and to an agent of the seller, provided that the agent has actual or
ostensible authority from his principal to pay, or to receive, the price.[137]

[129] Lien: 1979 Act s.41(1); stoppage in transit: s.44.

[130] Resale: 1979 Act s.48(3) ("… and the buyer does not within a reasonable time pay or tender the price
…").

[131] *Chitty on Contracts*, 33rd edn, Vol.1 paras 21-085 to 21-098. See also above, para.9-027.

[132] *Chitty on Contracts*, 33rd edn, Vol.1 para.21-087.

[133] Coinage Act 1971 s.2; Currency and Bank Notes Act 1954 s.1(2) and (6); Currency Act 1983 s.1(3).
See *Chitty on Contracts*, 33rd edn, Vol.1 para.21-088.

[134] *Chitty on Contracts*, 33rd edn, Vol.1 paras 21-088 to 21-089.

[135] *Cubitt v Gamble* (1919) 35 T.L.R. 223; *Cohen v Roche* [1927] 1 K.B. 169 at 180 (below, para.15-023).

[136] *Chitty on Contracts*, 33rd edn, Vol.1 paras 21-093 to 21-094.

[137] *Chitty on Contracts*, 33rd edn, Vol.1 paras 21-096 to 21-097; *Bowstead and Reynolds on Agency*,
21st edn, paras 3-003 to 3-005, 3-024 to 3-026.

Waiver of tender

Replace footnote 142 with:

[142] *Chitty on Contracts*, 33rd edn, Vol.1 paras 21-088 to 21-089. **15-023**

(d) Insolvency

The time when the buyer becomes insolvent

Replace footnote 167 with:

[167] This submission is supported by the words "he may resume possession of the goods *as long as* they **15-026**
are in course of transit" (1979 Act s.44: emphasis added).

2. LIEN

(b) When the Lien Arises

Possession of the goods

Replace footnote 239 with:

15-038 [239] 1979 Act s.41(1); and see *Re Redfern Resources Ltd* 2011 BCSC 711 (Can) where the court held that the seller could not rely on its lien because possession of the goods had passed to the buyer's agent (at [39]). The decision was affirmed on appeal: 2012 BCCA 189. See also *Svebois Aktiebolag v Dawco Ltd*, CA, unreported, 15 April 1986 (1986 WL 1255017), where the Court emphasises the requirement that the seller be in possession.

Replace footnote 258 with:

15-039 [258] *Valpy v Oakeley* (1851) 20 L.J.Q.B. 380. But see para.15-056, below and cases cited at nn.360 and 361: there may be an argument that the wrongful repudiation acts as a waiver of the lien.

3. STOPPAGE IN TRANSIT

(a) In General

Right of stoppage in transit

Replace footnote 383 with:

15-061 [383] Defined in the 1979 Act s.61(4): see above, paras 15-024 et seq. The time when the buyer becomes insolvent is examined, above, para.15-026. Where the buyer is placed into administration under the Insolvency Act 1986, Sch.1B, para.43 of that Act prevents enforcement of a security: the reasoning in *Uniserve v Croxen* [2012] EWHC 1190 (Ch); [2013] B.C.C. 825 suggests that an unpaid seller exercising a right of stoppage is enforcing its security and requires the consent of the administrator or the permission of the court. See further above paras 5-164 and 5-165.

Purpose of the right of stoppage

Replace footnote 394 with:

15-062 [394] cf. retention of title clauses, above, paras 5-143 et seq. especially at paras 5-164 and 5-165.

(b) Duration of Transit

Delivery to the buyer's ship

Replace footnote 487 with:

15-073 [487] 1979 Act s.19(2) (see above, para.5-139; below, para.18-265). The seller in this situation may often have retained the property in the goods, so that he is not limited to a right of stoppage in transit and can give directions to the carrier irrespective of the buyer's insolvency (see below, paras 18-262 et seq.).

Acknowledgment to the buyer

Replace paragraph with:

15-077 Section 45(3) provides:

"If, after the arrival of the goods at the appointed destination,[502] the carrier or other bailee or custodier acknowledges to the buyer or his agent that he holds the goods on his behalf and continues in possession of them as bailee or custodier for the buyer or his agent, the transit is at an end, and it is immaterial that a further destination for the goods may have been indicated by the buyer."

This subsection deals with an acknowledgment by the carrier to the buyer which creates the relationship of bailment between them. Such an acknowledgment is an illustration of the doctrine of attornment,[503] which is often associated with the concept of estoppel: a bailee who acknowledges to the claimant that the claimant has title to[504] a chattel is estopped at common law from denying the claimant's title and becomes the bailee of the claimant.[505] The subsection codifies the common law before the 1893 Act; thus, it was said in 1866:

> "A carrier may and often does become a warehouseman for the consignee; but that must be by virtue of some contract or course of dealing between them, that, when arrived at their destination, the character of the carrier shall cease, and that of warehouseman supervene."[506]

The buyer's request to the carrier to hold the goods in the carrier's warehouse pending further instructions from the buyer is strong evidence that the carrier thereupon becomes the buyer's agent and transit ends.[507]

[502] See below, para.15-080. And see *Re Redfern Resources Ltd*, 2011 BCSC 771 (Can) where the court held that the transit was at an end (at [42]), when the equipment was stored by the carrier as the agent of the buyer and the buyer was billed for storage. The decision was affirmed on appeal: 2012 BCCA 189.

[503] *Chitty on Contracts*, 33rd edn, Vol.2 para.33-030.

[504] By the Torts (Interference with Goods) Act 1977 s.8(1) a bailee may now set up the title of a third person in reply to the bailor's demand for redelivery of the chattel: see *Chitty on Contracts*, 33rd edn, Vol.2 paras 33-015 to 33-016.

[505] *Henderson & Co v Williams* [1895] 1 Q.B. 521; *Dublin City Distillery Ltd v Doherty* [1914] A.C. 823 at 847–848. See above, paras 5-065, 7-008 et seq.

[506] *Bolton v Lancs and Yorks Railway* (1866) L.R. 1 C.P. 431 at 438. See also *Ex p. Cooper* (1879) 11 Ch. D. 68 at 78.

[507] *Johann Plischke und Sohne GmbH v Allison Brothers Ltd* [1936] 2 All E.R. 1009. (This construction was not precluded by the fact that the contract provided for "Freehouse, London", i.e. that the seller would pay charges on the goods until delivered at the buyer's premises in London.)

(c)   Exercise of the Right of Stoppage

Duties of the parties after notice is given

Replace footnote 579 with:

[579] *The Tigress* (1863) 32 L.J.P.M. & A. *Mechan & Sons Ltd v North Eastern Railway*, 1911 S.C. 1348; **15-088** *Toll Holdings Ltd v Stewart* [2016] FCA 256. The action will fall under s.60 of the 1979 Act (below, para.16-096) and is classified as an action in tort, not in contract: *Pontifex v Midland Railway* (1877) 3 Q.B.D. 23; it will be governed by the Torts (Interference with Goods) Act 1977.

5.   RESALE

(a)   Introduction

Wrongful resale

Replace footnote 704 with:

[704] Goff and Jones, *The Law of Restitution*, 7th edn, paras 36-001 et seq.; *Chitty on Contracts*, 33rd edn, **15-104** Vol.1 paras 29-147 to 29-157.

Replace title footnote 716 with:

Agency of necessity[716]

15-106 [716] See *Bowstead and Reynolds on Agency*, 21st edn, paras 3-006, 4-001 to 4-013; Goff and Jones, *The Law of Unjust Enrichment*, 9th edn, paras 18-46 et seq.

(b) Termination of Contract upon Buyer's Repudiation or Breach

Repudiation by the buyer entitling the seller to terminate the contract

Replace footnote 726 with:

15-107 [726] See *Chitty on Contracts*, 33rd edn, Vol.1 paras 24-001 et seq.

Insolvency

Replace footnote 734 with:

15-108 [734] *Re Phoenix Bessemer Steel Co* (1876) 4 Ch. D. 108 (see the quotation, above, para.15-025); *Ex p. Stapleton* (1879) 10 Ch. D. 586; *Morgan v Bain* (1874) L.R. 10 C.P. 15; *Mess v Duffus* (1901) 6 Com. Cas. 165; *Phones 4U Ltd (in Administration) v EE Ltd* [2018] EWHC 49 (Comm); [2018] 1 Lloyd's Rep 204.

Fundamental breach by the buyer

Replace footnote 747 with:

15-109 [747] See above, paras 15-016 to 15-023. On general principles, in order to justify a termination for actual breach the seller will need to show, either that there has been a breach of an essential term (condition), or that the consequences of the breach will or have deprived the seller of substantially the whole benefit of the contract: *Cehave NV v Bremer Handelsgesellschaft mbh* [1976] 1 QB 44 (CA); *Hong Kong Fir Shipping Ltd v Kawasaki Kisen Kaisha Ltd* [1962] 2 QB 26 (CA). It will obviously be difficult for a seller who has been paid the price to establish that he has been deprived of substantially the whole benefit of the contact so in practice the important obligations referred to in the text will need to be conditions. See generally *Lombard North Central Plc v Butterworth* [1987] QB 527 (CA) and *Phones 4U Ltd (In Administration) v EE Ltd* [2018] EWHC 49 (Comm); [2018] 1 Lloyd's Rep 204.

Alternative remedies of the seller

Replace footnote 758 with:

15-110 [758] e.g. an arbitration clause: *Heyman v Darwins Ltd* [1942] A. C. 356. See *Chitty on Contracts*, 33rd edn, Vol.1 paras 24-049 to 24-054. On the effect of termination for breach upon an exemption clause, see above, paras 13-043 et seq.

Specific restitution of the goods

After "order for delivery*", replace "),￼" with:

15-116 ,

(c) Statutory Resale of Perishable Goods or Upon Giving Notice

Resale of perishable goods

Replace footnote 845 with:

15-121 [845] See *Chitty on Contracts*, 33rd edn, Vol.1 paras 21-011 to 21-015.

Resale upon giving notice to the buyer

Replace footnote 856 with:

15-123 [856] See *Chitty on Contracts*, 33rd edn, Vol.1 para.21-014.

Revesting of the immediate right to possession

Replace footnote 870 with:

[870] This is not intended to be an exhaustive list: e.g. the seller's right to immediate possession may also arise where the contract is held void for mistake (*Chitty on Contracts*, 33rd edn, Vol.1 para.3-009) or in some instances of illegality (*Chitty on Contracts*, 33rd edn, Vol.1 para.16-218).

15-125

(d)   Express Right to Resell

Express reservation of the right of resale

Replace footnote 890 with:

[890] See below, paras 16-064 et seq., 16-088 to 16-090.

15-128

(e)   The Method of Reselling

The method of reselling

Replace footnote 908 with:

[908] *Chitty on Contracts*, 33rd edn, Vol.1 paras 26-087 et seq.; see below, paras 16-056 to 16-062.

15-131

(f)   Forfeiture of Deposits or Other Prepayments

Forfeiture of deposits

Replace footnote 915 with:

[915] *Commission Car Sales (Hastings) Ltd v Saul* [1957] N.Z.L.R. 144 at 146 (following the principles laid down in cases on contracts for the sale of land: *Ockenden v Henley* (1858) E.B. & E. 485; *Howe v Smith* (1884) 27 Ch D 89 at 104–105l *Shuttleworth v Clews* [1910] 1 Ch. 176). See *Chitty on Contracts*, 33rd edn, Vol.1, paras 29-068 to 29-069. cf. the proposals of the *Law Commission's Working Paper* No.61 (1975), paras 49-67.

15-132

Replace footnote 923 with:

[923] *Linggi Plantations Ltd v Jagatheesan* [1972] 1 M.L.J. 89, 94 (PC); *Garratt v Ikeda* [2002] 1 N.Z.L.R. 577 (NZCA) at [33]–[39]. cf. however, the decision of the Privy Council where the deposit in a sale of land of 25% was unreasonable in amount: *Workers Trust and Merchant Bank Ltd v Dojap Investments Ltd* [1993] A.C. 573 and *Cavendish Square Holding BV v Makdessi* [2015] UKSC 67; [2016] A.C. 1172 at [16] and [35].

15-133

CHAPTER 16

OTHER REMEDIES OF THE SELLER

1.   THE CLAIM FOR THE PRICE

(a)   In General

Scope of s.49

Replace footnote 26 with:

[26] cf. *Minister for Supply and Development v Servicemen's Cooperative Joinery Manufacturers Ltd* **16-003**
(1951) 82 C.L.R. 621 (HCA) in which the High Court held that parties could reach their own agreement as to when the price was payable and could be recovered as a debt. See also *Garmin Australasia Pty Ltd v B&K Holdings (Qld) Pty Ltd* [2018] QCA 353 after consideration of the *Res Cogitans*, where it is suggested at [37] and [39] that the terms of the contract should do more than specify a time for payment and should provide for the recovery of the price.

Distinction between a claim for the price and a claim for damages

Replace footnote 31 with:

[31] Below, para.16-036. See *Chitty on Contracts*, 33rd edn, Vol.1 para.26-230.   **16-004**

Replace footnote 34 with:

34 See below, paras 16-040, 16-061. cf. *Jervis v Harris* [1996] Ch. 195, *Doherty v Fannigan Holdings Ltd* [2018] EWCA Civ 1615 (for insolvency purposes whether a debt is owing for a liquidated sum).

(b) Interest

Replace title footnote 43 with:

Power to award interest[43]

16-007   43 See *McGregor on Damages*, 20th edn, Ch.19; *Chitty on Contracts*, 33rd edn, Vol.1 paras 26-187 et seq., Vol.2 paras 39-285 et seq. See *The Law Commission's Report on Interest* (Law Com. No.88, 1978), Cmnd. 7229. In *Clarkson v Whangamata Metal Supplies Ltd* [2007] NZCA 590; [2008] 3 NZLR 31, the New Zealand Court of Appeal distinguished between: (1) an award of damages for loss of use of money assessed by reference to interest which would have been earned on the money (whether such damages are recoverable depends on the application of the ordinary rules of remoteness); and (2) an order that interest be paid upon an award of damages (this requires statutory authority); see at [22]–[24]. See also *Hungerfords v Walker* (1989) 171 C.L.R. 125 at [2] per Brennan and Deane JJ.

Replace the first paragraph with:

Section 54 of the Act[44] provides that:

"Nothing in this Act shall affect the right of the buyer or the seller to recover interest or special damages in any case where by law interest or special damages may be recoverable ... ."

At common law,[45] interest was payable on a debt, such as the price of goods sold, where there was contractual provision for it to be paid[46]; although the courts held that there was no term to be implied as a matter of law that interest was payable, they were prepared to infer an agreement to pay interest on the price of goods sold where this could be based on the course of dealing between the parties[47] or a relevant trade usage.[48] In the absence of such an express or implied agreement for interest to be paid for late payment, the claimant might recover damages caused by the late payment of monies by the application of the ordinary principles of the law on damages for breach of contract.[49] Damages will be awarded for losses resulting from late payment where the losses are within the contemplation of the parties as likely to result from the non-payment of the debt and it is reasonable to assume that the defendant was accepting responsibility for such losses. The law will not assume that delay in payment of a debt will of itself cause damage,[50] and the fact that the parties have chosen not to insert a provision for interest when they could have done so may prima facie lead to the inference that such liability was not intended to be assumed by the defendant and is too remote.[51] Where however the terms and the nature of a transaction make it clear that loss of interest was within the contemplation of the parties as likely to result, loss of interest may be recoverable as damages.[52]

44 This section no longer applies to consumer sales: Consumer Rights Act 2015 Sch.1 para.32. The relevant provision now is s.15 of the 2015 Act.

45 cf. the practice of the court in its equitable jurisdiction: *Wallersteiner v Moir (No.2)* [1975] Q.B. 373 at 388, 406; *O'Sullivan v Management Agency and Music Ltd* [1985] Q.B. 428. In *Westdeutsche Landesbank Girozentrale v Islington London BC* [1996] A.C. 669, the HL held that in equity compound interest may be awarded only in cases of fraud or against a trustee (or other person in a fiduciary position) in respect of profits improperly made by him. In *Sempra Metals Ltd v Inland Revenue Commissioners* [2007] UKHL 34; [2008] 1 A.C. 561, a majority of their Lordships considered *Westdeutsche* wrongly decided (see at [111]–[112], [184] and [236]–[240]).

46 Or where a bill of exchange was dishonoured (which is now covered by the Bills of Exchange Act 1882 s.57; in the enactment of general powers to award interest (discussed below), this provision has

been preserved: the Law Reform (Miscellaneous Provisions) Act 1934 s.3(1)(c); the Senior Courts Act 1981 s.35A(8) (formerly the Senior Courts Act, the title of this Act was modified by the Constitutional Reform Act 2005 Sch.11(1) para.1(2)); and the County Courts Act 1984 s.69(7)).

[47] *Re Anglesey* [1901] 2 Ch. 548. See also *Great Western Insurance Co v Cunliffe* (1874) L.R. 9 Ch. 525; *Re Duncan & Co* [1905] 1 Ch. 307.

[48] *Ikin v Bradley* (1818) 8 Taunt. 250; *Page v Newman* (1829) 9 B. & C. 378 at 381. On implied terms see *Sheikh Mohamed Bin Issa Al Jaber v Sheikh Walid Bin Ibrahim Al Ibrahim* [2018] EWCA Civ 1690.

[49] *Sempra Metals Ltd v Inland Revenue Commissioners* [2007] UKHL 34; [2008] 1 A.C. 561 at [16]–[17], [74]–[92], [132], [164]–[165] and [215]. Although the *Sempra Metals* case related to restitution for money paid under mistake, their Lordships took the opportunity to review previous authority on the right of a claimant to seek damages for late payment of a debt. The House of Lords earlier decisions in *London, Chatham and Dover Railway Co v South Eastern Railway Co* [1893] A.C. 429 (that damages are not available for late payment of a debt); and in *President of India v La Pintada Cia Navigacion SA* [1985] A.C. 104 (which had affirmed the *London, Chatham* case) were both not followed. The distinction drawn in the *President of India* case between a claim for interest by way of general damages and a claim for special damages under the second rule in *Hadley v Baxendale* (1854) 9 Ex. 341 was rejected as unsound.

[50] *Sempra Metals Ltd v Inland Revenue Commissioners* [2007] UKHL 34; [2008] 1 A.C. 561 at [96]. The losses must be particularised and proved. It follows that the *London Chatham* rule still prevents an award of damages for an un-particularised and unproved claim for interest losses.

[51] *Sempra Metals Ltd v Inland Revenue Commissioners* [2007] UKHL 34; [2008] 1 A.C. 561 at [216]. And see *Transfield Shipping Inc v Mercator Shipping Inc (The Achilleas)* [2008] UKHL 48; [2009] 1 A.C. 61. See however para.16-010, below. (Interest on commercial debts).

[52] *Trans Trust SPRL v Danubian Trading Co Ltd* [1952] 2 Q.B. 297; *Wadsworth v Lydall* [1981] 1 W.L.R. 598. Such losses must be pleaded and proved: *Sempra Metals Ltd v Commissioners of Inland Revenue* [2007] UKHL 34; [2008] 1 A.C. 561 at [96]. Depending on the circumstances compound interest may be recoverable: see *Sempra Metals Ltd v Inland Revenue Commissioners* [2007] UKHL 34; [2008] 1 A.C. 561; *JSC BTA Bank v Ablyazov* [2013] EWHC 867 (Comm) at [18] ("to require actual interest losses to be specifically pleaded might be regarded ... as unrealistic and unduly formalistic. But Lord Nicholls expressly accepted this 'reproach' to the common law and said that in the absence of a specific plea of actual interest losses the remedy lay in the statutory provisions for interest ..."). But compare *Equitas Ltd v Walsham Bros & Co Ltd* [2013] EWHC 3263 at [123] esp. at sub-paras (ii)-(iv) thereof suggesting that unless there is some positive reason to do otherwise the law will proceed on the basis that a claimant kept out of his money has suffered loss and that the loss is the cost of borrowing represented by compound interest at a conventional rate.

Interest due as of right

Replace footnote 82 with:

[82] For illustrations, see *Chitty on Contracts*, 33rd edn, vol.2, para 39-270 The Consumer Credit Act 1974 ss.140A to 140D enable the court to reopen certain transactions: see above, para.14-330.   **16-009**

Interest on commercial debts

Replace paragraph with:

Interest is payable on certain debts under a term implied into contracts by the Late   **16-010** Payment of Commercial Debts (Interest) Act 1998.[86] The Act applies to "a contract for the supply of goods or services"[87] where both parties are acting in the course of a business.[88] It is an implied[89] term in any such contract that any "qualifying debt"[90] created by the contract carries simple interest (called "statutory interest" in the Act).[91] The rate of statutory interest (or the formula for calculating it) is to be prescribed by order of the Secretary of State.[92]

[86] The Act is considered in *Ruttle Plant Hire Ltd v Secretary of State for Environment, Food and Rural Affairs* [2009] EWCA Civ 97 at [19]. See *Chitty on Contracts*, 33rd edn, Vol.1, paras 26-277 et seq.

[87] Defined by the Late Payment of Commercial Debts (Interest) Act 1998 s.2(2), (3) and (4). (Some other relevant definitions are found in s.2(5): consumer credit agreements; mortgages, pledges, charges or other securities; s.12 makes provision for the conflict of laws. See *Martrade Shipping and Transport GmbH v United Enterprises Corp* [2014] EWHC 1884 (Comm); [2015] 1 W.L.R. 1 where it was held that the Act does not have effect in relation to a contract governed by the law of England and Wales by choice

of the parties if there is no significant connection between the contract and England and Wales and but for that choice of law the contract would have been governed by a foreign law.

[88] 1998 Act s.2(1). In *Christopher Linnett Ltd v Matthew J Harding* [2017] EWHC 1781 (TCC); [2018] Bus. L.R. 179, it was held that the defendant contractor, in entering into a contract for the adjudication of a building dispute, was acting in the course of business because the defendant contractor was acting in a business capacity to determine the building dispute, notwithstanding that the defendant contractor had only entered into three previous adjudications in 32 years. The meaning of "business" includes a profession and the activities of any government department or local or public authority (s.2(7)). Initially, only businesses with 50 or fewer employees were entitled to claim under the Act: SI 1998/2479 Art.2(2); see also SI 1998/2481. By the Late Payment of Commercial Debts (Interest) Act 1998 (Commencement No.5) Order 2002 (SI 2002/1673) the provisions of the Act apply to businesses of all sizes and to the public sector.

[89] In cases where the contract provides "a substantial remedy" (as defined in the 1998 Act s.9) for late payment of the debt, s.1(3) and Pt II of the Act (ss.7–10) permit the parties to oust or vary the right to statutory interest conferred by s.1(1).

[90] As defined by s.3(1) of the 1998 Act. Section 3(2) and (3) exclude debts where any other enactment or any rule of law confers a right to interest or to charge interest. By s.13, the Act applies to a qualifying debt despite any assignment of the debt or the transfer of the duty to pay it, or any change in the identity of the parties, whether by assignment, operation of law or otherwise.

[91] 1998 Act s.1(1).

[92] 1998 Act s.6. In *Martrade Shipping and Transport GmbH v United Enterprises Corp* [2014] EWHC 1884 (Comm); [2015] 1 W.L.R. 1; [2014] 2 Lloyd's Rep. 198 it was said that the policy underlying the Act was to provide a statutory rate of interest to promote the prompt payment of commercial debts. The current rate is fixed at 8% over the official dealing rate of the Bank of England (SI 2002/1675). In addition to interest, the Late Payment of Commercial Debts (Interest) Act 1998 s.5A (as introduced by the Late Payment of Commercial Debts Regulations 2002 (SI 2002/1674), provides for fixed sums to be payable as well as statutory interest. The Late Payment of Commercial Debts Regulations 2013 (SI 2013/395) (s.5A(2A)) allow a right to compensation for the reasonable costs of recovering the debt if that amount exceeds the sums provided in s.5A(2).

Period and rate of statutory interest

Replace footnote 100 with:

16-011   [100] 1998 Act s.5(1) and (2). By s.5(3) a reduced rate of statutory interest may apply if "the interests of justice require". See *Ruttle Plant Hire Ltd v Secretary of State for Environment, Food and Rural Affairs* [2009] EWCA Civ 97 at [46]; *Rowles-Davies v Call 24 - 7 Ltd* [2010] EWHC 1443 (Ch) at [75]; and *First Personnel Services Ltd v Halford's Ltd* [2016] EWHC 3220 (Ch) at [164] et seq.

(c)   Wrongful Failure to pay the Price

Wrongful neglect or refusal to pay

Replace footnote 127 with:

16-016   [127] See below, paras 16-021 et seq.; *Doherty v Fannigan Holdings Ltd* [2018] EWCA Civ 1615 (sale of shares).

The effect of tender

Replace footnote 134 with:

16-017   [134] *Chitty on Contracts*, 33rd edn, Vol.1 paras 21-085 to 21-098.

(d) Entitlement to Sue for the Price

(i) Where the Property has Passed to the Buyer

Action for price when property has passed

Replace footnote 158 with:

[158] *Caterpillar (NI) Ltd v John Holt & Co (Liverpool) Ltd* [2013] EWCA Civ 1232. Delivery is normally concurrent with payment of the price: s.28 of the 1979 Act (see above, para.8-004). In *Abraaj Investment Management Ltd v Bregawn Jersey Ltd* [2010] EWHC 630 (Comm) at [19], Teare J held that unless otherwise agreed, delivery of the goods and payment of the price are concurrent conditions so that no claim for the price could be maintained in the absence of delivery: "Since Abraaj is not able to deliver the goods and has not offered to do so, it cannot establish a right to the price". And see *Doherty v Fannigan Holdings Ltd* [2018] EWCA Civ 1615 (sale of shares). See further para.16-016 above and para.19-240, below.

16-021

(ii) Price Payable on "a Day Certain"

Action for price due on "a day certain"

Replace footnote 181 with:

[181] "Delivery" is defined in s.61(1) of the 1979 Act. See above, paras 8-002 et seq. In *Ledger v Cleveland Nominees Pty Ltd* [2001] WASCA 369 (sale of car—term of the contract that price payable on or before 1 June 1997), the Full Court of Western Australia held that the words "irrespective of delivery" cannot be ignored and require that the agreement be in terms adequate to demonstrate a right to payment irrespective of delivery. See also *Otis Vehicle Rentals Ltd v Cicely Commercials Ltd* [2002] EWCA Civ 1064 at [16]; *Pala v BTC Group Ltd* [2015] NZCA 487 at [35] to [36]. In *Garmin Australasia Pty Ltd v B & K Holdings (Qld) Pty Ltd* [2018] QCA 353, it was held that where the payment terms related payment to delivery by the provision of invoices on shipment the price was not payable "irrespective of delivery".

16-025

Meaning of "a day certain"

Replace footnote 196 with:

[196] *Otis Vehicle Rentals Ltd v Cicely Commercials Ltd* [2002] EWCA 1064; *Caterpillar (NI) Ltd v John Holt & Co (Liverpool) Ltd* [2013] EWCA 1232; [2014] 1 W.L.R. 2365 at [50]; *Garmin Australasia Pty Ltd v B&K Holdings (Qld) Pty Ltd* [2018] QCA 353; but see *The Res Cogitans* [2016] UKSC 23 at [45].

16-027

(e) Claims for Consequential Loss

Claim for consequential loss in addition to the price

Replace the first paragraph with:

The seller may wish to claim damages in addition to his claim for the agreed price, on the ground that the buyer's failure to pay the price at the agreed time caused consequential loss to the seller. Although a claim for interest may also arise under the terms of the contract itself,[208] or by statute,[209] the question whether damages are recoverable for the mere failure to pay an agreed sum of money on the due date turns on the ordinary principles governing awards of damages for breach of contract.[210] The law does not assume that delay in payment of a debt beyond the date when it was contractually due will cause damage, and the fact that parties have chosen not to include a term as to payment for interest may be some evidence to infer that the parties did not intend that the defendant should assume liability for such losses.[211] But where the surrounding circumstances and the terms of the contract make it clear that such losses were within the contemplation of the parties as likely to result and it is reasonable to assume that the defendant was accept-

16-030

ing responsibility for such losses, then damages may be recovered for interest paid and other expenses incurred by the claimant in arranging alternative finance as the result of the buyer's failure to pay a debt on the fixed date.[212]

[208] *Chitty on Contracts*, 33rd edn, Vol.2 paras 39-284 to 39-286; above, para.16-009.

[209] See above, para.16-007.

[210] *Sempra Metals Ltd v Commissioner of Inland Revenue* [2007] UKHL 34; [2008] 1 A.C. 561 at [16]–[17], [74]–[92], [132], [164]–[165] and [215]. See *Chitty on Contracts*, 33rd edn, Vol.1 para.26-275; *McGregor on Damages*, 20th edn, paras 19-058 et seq.

[211] *Sempra Metals Ltd v Commissioner of Inland Revenue* [2007] UKHL 34 at [96] and [216]; and *Transfield Shipping Inc v Mercator Shipping Inc (The Achilleas)* [2008] UKHL 48; [2009] 1 A.C. 61.

[212] *Sempra Metals Ltd v Commissioner of Inland Revenue* [2007] UKHL 34; *Wadsworth v Lydall* [1981] 1 W.L.R. 598; *Trans Trust Sprl v Danubian Trading Co Ltd* [1952] 2 Q.B. 297.

2.   GENERAL RULES ON DAMAGES

(a)   Introduction

General rules for the assessment of damages

Replace the first paragraph with:

16-031   A detailed examination of the general rules for the assessment of damages for breach of contract must be sought elsewhere.[215] In this work, the general principles on damages will be summarised and examined in detail only to the extent that they have been applied to contracts for the sale of goods. Accordingly, this section does not examine matters such as appeals against the assessment of damages,[216] the liability of damages to tax or the effect of tax liability on assessment of damages.[217] The rules discussed in this section are applicable both to the seller's and to the buyer's claim for damages.

[215] *Chitty on Contracts*, 33rd edn, Vol.1 Ch.26; *McGregor on Damages*, 20th edn, Chs 1–36; Waddams, *The Law of Damages*, 5th edn. For a comparison between the common law and the civil law, see Treitel, *Remedies for Breach of Contract* (1988), Chs IV–VII. On the question of a claim for damages which are calculable in a foreign currency, see below, paras 26-193 and 26-194.

[216] *Chitty on Contracts*, 33rd edn, Vol.1 para.26-021; *McGregor on Damages*, 20th edn, Ch.53.

[217] *Chitty on Contracts*, 33rd edn, Vol.1 paras 26-262–26-271; *McGregor on Damages*, 20th edn, Ch.18.

In the third paragraph, replace footnote 227 with:

[227] See *Chitty on Contracts*, 33rd edn, Vol.1 paras 26-134 to 26-136; and see *Grébert-Borgnis v Nugent* (1885) 15 Q.B.D. 85.

The scope of the compensatory principle

Replace footnote 240 with:

16-033   [240] *Flame SA v Glory Wealth Shipping Pte Ltd* [2013] EWHC 3153 (Comm); [2013] 2 Lloyd's Rep. 653; and contrast *Classic Maritime Inc v Limbungan Makmur Sdn Bhd* [2019] EWCA Civ 1102.

Expectation, Reliance and Restitution Interest

Replace footnote 255 with:

16-035   [255] *Att-Gen v Blake* [2001] 1 A.C. 268; *Experience Hendrix LLC v PPX Enterprises Inc and Edward Chaplin* [2003] EWCA Civ 323; [2003] 1 All E.R. (Comm) 830. See *Chitty on Contracts*, 33rd edn, Vol.1 paras 26-039 to 26-041. And see *Morris-Garner v One Step (Support) Ltd* [2018] UKSC 20; [2018] 1 Lloyd's Rep 495 at [111] (claimant in *Blake* entitled to recover more than its pecuniary loss as its non-pecuniary governmental interest extended beyond pecuniary loss).

(b)   Liquidated Damages and Penalties

Clauses fixing sums payable upon breach

Replace footnote 274 with:

[274] *Cine Bes Filmcilik ve Yapimcilik AS v Universal International Pictures* [2003] EWCA Civ 1669; **16-036**
[2004] 1 CLC 401; *General Trading Co (Holdings) Ltd v Richmond Corp Ltd* [2008] EWHC 1479
(Comm); [2008] 2 Lloyd's Rep. 475; *Lordsvale Finance Plc v Bank of Zambia* [1996] QB 752; *Murray v Leisureplay Plc* [2005] EWCA Civ 963; [2005] IRLR 946; *Azimutt-Benetti SPA v Healey* [2010]
EWHC 2234; [2011] 1 Lloyd's Rep. 473. And see *Paciocco v Australia & New Zealand Banking Group
Ltd* [2016] HCA; (2016) 258 CLR 525 (HCA) (late payment fee not out of all proportion to contracting party's legitimate interests given its cost of capital).

The scope of the law on penalties

In the first paragraph, replace footnote 287 with:

[287] *Export Credit Guarantee Department v Universal Oil Products Co* [1983] 1 W.L.R. 399; *Cavendish* **16-039**
Square Holding BV v Talal El Makdessi [2015] UKSC 67; [2016] A.C. 1172; [2016] 1 Lloyd's Rep. 55
at [12], [129]–[130], [239]. As the joint opinion of Lords Neuberger and Sumption observed, there is
an important difference between a jurisdiction to review the fairness of a contractual obligation and a
jurisdiction to regulate a remedy for contractual breach. The penalty rules are confined to regulating
agreed remedies for breach of a primary obligation, and not the primary obligations themselves. If were
otherwise, the doctrine will be transformed into a jurisdiction which reviewed the content of substantive obligations. *Dana Gas PJSC v Dana Gas Sukuk Ltd* [2017] EWHC 2928 (Comm); [2018] 1 Lloyd's
Rep. 177 at [71] (rule against penalties only applies to sums payable on breach). In *Polymers Ltd v
Imerys Minerals Ltd* [2008] EWHC 344 (Comm); [2008] 1 Lloyd's Rep. 541 it was held that a take or
pay clause ("the buyers will pay for the minimum quantities of products ... even if they have not ordered
the indicated quantities during the relevant monthly period") was subject to the law on penalties but did
not offend against the law because the clause was commercially justifiable, not oppressive, was freely
negotiated between parties of comparable bargaining power, and did not have the predominant purpose
of deterring a breach of contract. As *Chitty on Contracts*, 33rd edn, Vol.1 para.26-234 n.1298 observes,
whether a take or pay clause is subject to the penalty rules must depend on the wording of the clause. It
will not be a penalty clause if the buyer is obliged to pay for a minimum quantity with an option whether
or not to take delivery of the goods. But see *Andrews v ANZ Banking Group Ltd* [2012] HCA 30; (2012)
290 A.L.R. 595 (noted Peel, (2013) 129 L.Q.R. 152), where the High Court of Australia held that bank
charges were capable of being characterised as penalties even though they did not arise upon a breach
of contract but also indicated at [80] that there is a valid distinction between a penalty clause and an
alternative stipulation—i.e. between a sum payable on the breach of a stipulation and the right to do an
act on the payment of an agreed sum.

Replace the second paragraph with:

The law on penalties may apply to an obligation to transfer property to the innocent party,[292] but it does not apply, as such, to "forfeiture" clauses, in respect of
which a limited form of relief may be available.[293] But the law on penalties may apply to a clause which entitles the innocent party to withhold a payment which would
otherwise be due to the contract-breaker.[294] An express power to terminate the
contract following breach of a term classified as a condition[295] entitles the innocent party both to terminate and to sue for damages for loss of the contract as a
whole,[296] not simply for loss suffered through any breaches up to the date of the
termination[297]: the law on penalties does not apply to such a clause.[298]

[292] *Johnson v Jobson* [1989] 1 W.L.R. 1026; *Cavendish Square Holding BV v Talal El Makdessi* [2015]
UKSC 67; [2016] A.C. 1172; [2016] 1 Lloyd's Rep. 55 at [16], [157]–[158], [230] where it was said
that the doctrine was sufficiently broad to embrace obligations to pay in kind; cf. *Forestry Commission
of NSW v Stefanetto* (1976) 133 C.L.R. 507.

[293] Below, paras 16-042 to 16-043. On the question of the interrelationship between the penalty doctrine
and equity's jurisdiction to relieve against forfeiture see *Cavendish Square Holdings BV v Talal El
Makdessi* [2015] UKSC 67; [2016] A.C. 1172; [2016] 1 Lloyd's Rep. 55 at [10], [17]–[18], [160]–
[161], [227], [291], and [292]. On "acceleration" clauses, see *Chitty on Contracts*, 33rd edn, Vol.1
para.26-232.

²⁹⁴ *Cavendish Square Holding BV v Talal El Makdessi* [2015] UKSC 67; [2016] A.C. 1172; [2016] 1 Lloyd's Rep. 55 at [70]–[72], [154], [226]; *Gilbert Ash (Northern) Ltd v Modern Engineering (Bristol) Ltd* [1974] A.C. 689. And see *Cavendish Square Holdings BV v El Makdessi* [2012] EWHC 3582 (Comm) [2013] 1 All E.R. (Comm) 787 at [29]–[32]; and *General Trading Co (Holdings) Ltd v Richmond Corp Ltd* [2008] EWHC 1479 (Comm); [2008] 2 Lloyd's Rep. 475 at [113].

²⁹⁵ viz. where any breach of the term entitles the innocent party to terminate, e.g. a clause making compliance with time "of the essence".

²⁹⁶ viz. in respect of all the outstanding obligations of the contract breaker.

²⁹⁷ *Lombard North Central Plc v Butterworth* [1987] Q.B. 527. See Treitel, [1987] L.M.C.L.Q. 143; Beale, (1988) 104 L.Q.R. 355; and *Chitty on Contracts*, 33rd edn, Vol.1 para.26-233.

²⁹⁸ The *Lombard* case [1987] Q.B. 527. Agreed damages clauses do not bar the remedy of rejection of the goods. Above, para.13-036.

Purchase by instalments and pre-payment of price

Replace footnote 318 with:

16-042 ³¹⁸ *Re Dagenham (Thames) Dock Co* (1873) L.R. 8 Ch. App. 1022; *John H Kilmer v British Columbia Orchard Lands Ltd* [1913] A.C. 319; *Steedman v Drinkle* [1916] 1 A.C. 275; *Mussen v Van Diemen's Land Co* [1938] Ch. 253. See Lang, (1984) 100 L.Q.R. 427; *Chitty on Contracts*, 33rd edn, Vol.1 para.26-245.

(c)   Remoteness of Damage and Causation

Remoteness of damage

Replace the first paragraph with:

16-045   The Sale of Goods Act 1979 lays down the basic principle for remoteness of damage in language derived from the leading case of *Hadley v Baxendale*³⁴¹ where the main proposition was:

> "Where two parties have made a contract which one of them has broken, the damages which the other party ought to receive in respect of such breach of contract should be such as may fairly and reasonably be considered either as arising naturally, i.e. according to the usual course of things, from such breach of contract itself, or such as may reasonably be supposed to have been in the contemplation of both parties, at the time they made the contract, as the probable result of the breach of it."³⁴²

In the Act, the language of s.50(2) is:

> "The measure of damages is the estimated loss directly and naturally resulting,³⁴³ in the ordinary course of events, from the buyer's breach of contract."³⁴⁴

The principles in *Hadley v Baxendale*, above, have been interpreted and restated in the Court of Appeal in 1949³⁴⁵, in 1978,³⁴⁶ and in 2013³⁴⁷ and in the House of Lords in 1967, 2005, and 2008. The language used in the cases has departed somewhat from the language used in the Act (e.g. the word "directly" is not used, and some emphasis is placed on the "reasonable contemplation" of the parties), but it is submitted that the courts, when interpreting the Act, will be strongly influenced by the common law on remoteness of damage.³⁴⁸ Although their Lordships in *Koufos v C Czarnikow Ltd*³⁴⁹ did not agree upon a common formula,³⁵⁰ their slightly differing formulations of the common law principle for remoteness of damage in contract are still based on *Hadley v Baxendale*, above. Lord Reid said that Alderson B in *Hadley v Baxendale*:

> "... clearly meant that a result which will happen in the great majority³⁵¹ of cases should

fairly and reasonably be regarded as having been in the contemplation of the parties, but that a result which, though foreseeable as a substantial possibility, would only happen in a small minority of cases should not be regarded as having been in their contemplation."[352]

Lord Reid continued:

"The crucial question is whether, on the information available to the defendant when the contract was made, he should, or the reasonable man in his position would, have realised that such loss was sufficiently likely to result from the breach of contract to make it proper to hold that the loss flowed naturally from the breach or that loss of that kind should have been within his contemplation."[353]

In *Transfield Shipping Inc v Mercator Shipping Inc (The Achilleas)*,[354] a majority of their Lordships have indicated that the extent of a promisor's liability for damages should be worked out in terms of the kinds of losses to which it may fairly be presumed the promisor would have assented and that the remoteness rules reflected the presumed intention of the parties. Lord Hope stated:

"The policy of the law is that effect should be given to the presumed intention of the parties. That is why the damages that are recoverable for breach of contract are limited to what happens in ordinary circumstances—in the great multitude of cases as Alderson B put it in *Hadley v Baxendale*—where an assumption of responsibility can be presumed, or what arises from special circumstances known to or communicated to the party who is in breach at the time of entering into the contract which because he knew about he can be expected to provide for."[355]

Lord Hoffmann said that it was logical to found liability for damages upon the intention of the parties because contractual liability was voluntarily undertaken, and that the principles in *Hadley v Baxendale* were intended to give effect to the presumed intention of the parties.[356] Lord Walker said that it may be that the rather precise formulation of the notion of assumption of responsibility applies to cases within the second limb of *Hadley v Baxendale*, but that its underlying idea, what was the common basis on which the parties were contracting, applies to the rule as a whole.[357] It follows from the foregoing that Lord Reid's test in the *Heron II* stated above remains the prima facie rule governing questions of remoteness.[358] But it is not determinative and is capable of being rebutted in cases in which the context, surrounding circumstances, or general understanding in the relevant market show that a party would not have been regarded as assuming liability for the type of losses claimed.[359] Thus in the *Transfield Shipping* case, the normal and usual measure of damages for the kind of breach involved (late redelivery of a vessel) was loss of user damages for the period of delay. Damages of the type claimed (losses derived from a follow-on charter) were too remote because having regard to the surrounding circumstances, the general view in the market, and the fact that the quantum of this loss was unpredictable, the defendant charterer could not reasonably be viewed as having assumed liability for that type of loss.

[341] *Hadley v Baxendale* (1854) 9 Ex. 341. (For a discussion of this case, see *Chitty on Contracts*, 33rd edn, Vol.1 paras 26-119 to 26-120; *McGregor on Damages*, 20th edn, paras 8-160 et seq.).

[342] *Hadley v Baxendale* (1854) 9 Ex. 341 at 354 (per Alderson B).

[343] On causation, see below, para.16-051.

[344] A similar provision in s.51(2) of the 1979 Act is enacted for the seller's breach. See below, paras 17-021 et seq. This provision does not apply to sui generis supply contracts of the sort considered in *PST Energy Shipping LLC v OW Bunker Malta Ltd (The Res Cogitans)* [2016] UKSC 23; [2016] A.C. 1034 but analogous common law principles should apply.

[345] *Victoria Laundry (Windsor) Ltd v Newman Industries Ltd* [1949] 2 K.B. 528 (below, paras 17-040 to 17-041) (Some of the propositions in this case were cited with approval in *East Ham Corp v Bernard Sunley & Sons Ltd* [1966] A.C. 406 at 440, 445, 450–451; as well as in *Koufos v C Czarnikow Ltd* [1969] 1 A.C. 350).

[346] *Parsons (H) (Livestock) Ltd v Uttley Ingham & Co Ltd* [1978] Q.B. 791. See also *Brown v KMR Services Ltd* [1995] 4 All E.R. 598 at 621, 642–643; *Kpohraror v Woolwich Building Society* [1996] 4 All E.R. 119.

[347] *John Grimes Partnership Ltd v Gubbins* [2013] EWCA Civ 37; [2013] B.L.R. 126.

[348] *Parsons (H) (Livestock) Ltd v Uttley Ingham & Co Ltd* [1978] Q.B. 791 at 807 and 809.

[349] *Koufos v C Czarnikow Ltd* [1969] 1 A.C. 350 (the case is also known as *"The Heron II"*): *Jackson v Royal Bank of Scotland* [2005] UKHL 3; [2005] 1 W.L.R. 377; *Transfield Shipping Inc v Mercator Shipping Inc (The Achilleas)* [2005] UKHL 48; [2009] 1 A.C. 61.

[350] In *Koufos v C Czarnikow Ltd* [1969] 1 A.C. 350, Lords Morris (at 399), Hodson (at 410–411), and Pearce (at 414, 415, 417) gave general approval to the propositions of the Court of Appeal in the *Victoria Laundry* case [1949] 2 K.B. 528 but Lord Reid (at 389, 390) rejected parts of these propositions. See *Aruna Mills Ltd v Dhanrajmal Gobindram* [1968] 1 Q.B. 655 at 668.

[351] Lord Hodson, [1969] 1 A.C. 350 at 411, also adopted the expression used in *Hadley v Baxendale* (1854) 9 Ex. 341, "in the great multitude of cases": at 355, 356. Also considered helpful by each of Lord Hope and Lord Rodger in *Transfield Shipping Inc v Mercator Shipping Inc (The Achilleas)* [2005] UKHL 48 at [33] and [36] and [49].

[352] *Koufos v C Czarnikow Ltd* [1969] 1 A.C. 350 at 384. Both Lords Reid and Upjohn criticised the words "foreseeable" or "reasonably foreseeable" in the Victoria Laundry formulations: at 389, 423; Lord Upjohn, at 422–423, expressly preferred "contemplate" or "contemplation" for cases in contract, and these are the words used by Lord Reid at 384, 385.

[353] *Koufos v C Czarnikow Ltd* [1969] 1 A.C. 350 at 385.

[354] *Transfield Shipping Inc v Mercator Shipping Inc (The Achilleas)* [2008] UKHL 48; [2009] 1 A.C. 61.

[355] *Transfield Shipping Inc v Mercator Shipping Inc (The Achilleas)* [2008] UKHL 48; [2009] 1 A.C. 61 at [36].

[356] *Transfield Shipping Inc v Mercator Shipping Inc (The Achilleas)* [2008] UKHL 49 at [24]. And see also *Supershield Ltd v Siemens Building Technologies FE Ltd* [2010] EWCA 7; [2010] 1 Lloyd's Rep. 20 at [43]. In *MFM Restaurants Pte Ltd v Fish & Co Restaurants Pte Ltd* [2010] SGCA 36 (not a sale of goods case) the Singapore Court of Appeal considered the speeches in *The Achilleas* (above) at length and considered the extent to which assumption of responsibility was a distinct requirement or merely an aspect of the existing doctrine of remoteness. At [103] of the opinion the court suggests that the first limb in *Hadley v Baxendale* (1854) 9 Ex. 341 embodies an implied undertaking or assumption of responsibility and (at [107] and [115]) that the criterion of knowledge in the second limb in *Hadley v Baxendale* furnishes the basis on which to premise the existence of an implied obligation or assumption of responsibility by the defendant. It then suggests (at [109]) that the two limbs in *Hadley v Baxendale* are in substance what the parties would have agreed to had they thought about a situation in which the contract was breached. Accordingly, an assumption of responsibility was an aspect of the existing doctrine and it followed that the two limbs set out in *Hadley v Baxendale* continue to be the governing principles in relation to the doctrine of remoteness.

[357] *Transfield Shipping Inc v Mercator Shipping Inc (The Achilleas)* [2008] UKHL 48 at [68].

[358] *Wellesley Partners LLP v Withers LLP* [2015] EWCA Civ 1146 at [69]. In *John Grimes Partnership Ltd v Gubbins* [2013] EWCA Civ 37; [2013] B.L.R. 126 at [20] Keene J (with whom Laws and Tomlinson LLJ agreed) commented that Lord Hoffmann was not seeking to depart wholesale from the usual test of remoteness. See *Sylvia Shipping Co Ltd v Progress Bulk Carriers Ltd* [2010] EWHC 542 (Comm) at [49]–[50] ("In my judgment, it is important that it be made clear that there is no new generally applicable legal test of remoteness ... In the vast majority of cases tribunals of fact can and should be able to apply the well established remoteness test with which they are familiar and which, in the vast majority of cases, works perfectly well."); and *Borealis AB v Geogas Trading SA* [2010] EWHC 2789 (Comm); [2011] 1 Lloyd's Rep. 482 at [48] and *Maestro Bulk Ltd v Cosco Bulk Carrier Co Ltd (The Great Creation)* [2014] EWHC 3978 (Comm); [2015] 1 Lloyd's Rep. 315 at [56]–[67]. And see *Chitty on Contracts*, 33rd edn, Vol.1 para.26-144.

[359] *John Grimes Partnership Ltd v Gubbins* [2013] EWCA Civ 37; [2013] B.L.R. 126 at [20]. *Transfield Shipping Inc v Mercator Shipping Inc (The Achilleas)* [2008] UKHL; [2009] 1 A.C. 61 at [9] per Lord Hoffmann.

The degree of probability

Replace footnote 367 with:

[367] *Koufos v C Czarnikow Ltd* [1969] 1 A.C. 350 at 406. See *Hi-Lite Electrical Limited v Wolseley UK* **16-046**
Ltd [2011] EWHC 2153; [2011] B.L.R. 629 at [215]: "The correct question … is whether at the time of
the contract, a fire was not unlikely to result from a manufacturing defect in the cable or that there was
a serious possibility of loss by fire arising from that manufacturing defect". See below at para.17-072.

Non-pecuniary losses

Replace footnote 401 with:

[401] *Addis v Gramophone Co Ltd* [1909] A.C. 488 (wrongful dismissal of an employee). But see *Malik* **16-049**
v BCCI [1998] A.C. 20. In *Eastwood v Magnox Electric Plc* [2004] UKHL 35; [2005] 1 A.C. 503, Lord
Nicholls said (at [11]) that if the facts of *Addis* occurred today, the claimant would have a remedy at
common law for breach of contract. See *Chitty on Contracts*, 33rd edn, Vol.1, paras 26-155 et seq.

Loss of amenity

Replace footnote 404 with:

[404] See *Harris, Ogus and Phillips*, (1979) 95 L.Q.R. 581 (on the "consumer surplus") cited in the *Ruxley* **16-050**
case [1996] 1 A.C. 344 at 360; and in *Farley v Skinner* [2002] 2 A.C. 732 at 748. See also *Morris-*
Garner v One Step (Support) Ltd [2018] UKSC 2; [2018] 1 Lloyd's Rep. 495 at [39-40]: "That approach is consistent with the logic of damages for breach of contract: they are a substitute for the end-
result of performance, not for the economic end-result of performance."

Causation

Replace the first paragraph with:

The word "resulting" in ss.50 (2) and 51 (2), above, assumes that there is a causal **16-051**
link between the "loss" and the "breach of contract" in question. This was clearly
the draftsman's intention as the early common law on damages in contract was built
around the idea that damages were recoverable if they were a natural consequence
of the breach.[406] Whether any particular loss was a natural consequence of the
breach was a question of fact for the jury to decide.[407] The decision in *Hadley v
Baxendale*[408] refined the common law test to enable the court to control awards of
the jury by making it clear that the natural consequences of the breach were
confined to those which arose naturally according to the usual course of things or
those which could be contemplated as arising as the probable result of the breach.
Although the power of the factfinder to find that particular losses had been caused
by a breach was somewhat curtailed the opinion in *Hadley v Baxendale* remained
faithful to the underlying idea that recoverable losses had to be those which were
the natural consequence of the breach. As a result, principles of causation remain
an integral part of the law of damages for breach of contract, although they are at
times subsumed into the larger question of remoteness. It follows that the
defendant's breach of contract must have been an effective cause of the claimant's
loss[409] and, as at common law the application of this test is a matter of common
sense for the finder of fact.[410]

[406] *Black v Baxendale* (1847) 1 Ex 410; *Bridge v Wain* (1816) 1 Stark. 504; Washington (1931) 47
L.Q.R. 345; 48 L.Q.R. 90.

[407] *Black v Baxendale* (1847) 1 Ex. 410.

[408] *Hadley v Baxendale* (1854) 9 Ex. 341.

[409] *Monarch SS Co Ltd v Karlshamns Oljefabriker (A/B)* [1949] A.C. 196, 212, 227–22; *Carlos Soto
SAU v AP Moller Maersk (The Seahawk)* [2015] EWHC 458 (Comm); [2015] 1 Lloyd's Rep. 537 at [32]
(where a breach of contract is one of two causes both co-operating and both of equal efficacy in causing loss to the claimant it was not necessary for a claimant to prove that the breach was the effective

cause as long as it was an effective cause). The legal burden of proof rests throughout on the claimant to prove that the defendant's breach caused its loss: see *Borealis AB v Geogas Trading SA* [2010] EWHC 2789 (Comm); [2011] 1 Lloyd's Rep. 482 at [43]. *McGregor on Damages*, 20th edn, paras 8-140 to 8-157; Hart and Honoré, *Causation in the Law*, 2nd edn, Ch.11; *Chitty on Contracts*, 33rd edn, Vol.1 paras 26-066 et seq.

[410] *Galoo Ltd v Bright Grahame Murray* [1994] 1 W.L.R. 1360 at 1374–1375 CA. The approach to the question must always be that the claimant must prove the cause of the damage on the balance of probabilities: See *Hi-Lite Electrical Ltd v Wolseley UK Ltd* [2011] EWHC 2153 (TCC); [2011] B.L.R. 629 at [131]–[135]; *Dundee City Council v D Geddes (Contractors) Ltd* [2017] CSOH 108 (goods not shown to be the cause of the loss suffered).

Replace footnote 418 with:

[418] *Quinn v Burch Bros (Builders) Ltd* [1966] 2 Q.B. 370. (It was held that the breach of contract merely gave the claimant the opportunity to injure himself by using unsuitable equipment.) cf. *Vacwell Engineering Co Ltd v BDH Chemicals Ltd* [1971] 1 Q.B. 88 and *A. Ehrentreu v IG Index Ltd* [2018] EWCA Civ 79 (breach the opportunity for the loss not its cause); *Claire Busby v Berkshire Bed Company Ltd* [2018] EWHC 2976 (QB) (defective bed not cause of plaintiff's physical injury).

Loss of chance

Replace footnote 425 with:

16-052 [425] *The Allied Maples case* [1995] 1 W.L.R. 1602. See *Chitty on Contracts*, 33rd edn, Vol.1 paras 26-067 to 26-082.

Replace subsection title footnote 439:

(d) Mitigation of Damage[439]

16-054 [439] See *McGregor on Damages*, 20th edn, Ch.9; *Chitty on Contracts*, 33nd edn, Vol.1 paras 26-087 et seq.

No recovery for loss which should have been avoided

Replace footnote 442 with:

[442] *British Westinghouse Electric and Manufacturing Co Ltd v Underground Electric Rys* [1912] A.C. 673 at 689 (for the facts, see below, para.17-055). *Bunge SA v Nidera BV* [2015] UKSC 43; [2015] 2 Lloyd's Rep. 469 at [81] ("the so called duty to mitigate …is an aspect of the principle of causation..") ; and see *A Ehrentreu v IG Index Ltd* [2018] EWCA Civ 79 at [52]. The claimant is debarred from recovering only the net gain from his mitigating action viz. he may set off against the substitute profits the reasonable expenses incurred in making them: *Westwood v Secretary of State for Employment* [1985] A.C. 20 at 44.

Replace footnote 449 with:

[449] 1979 Act ss.50(3) and 51(3) (below, paras 16-064 et seq., paras 17-001 et seq.). *Bunge SA v Nidera BV* [2015] UKSC 43; [2015] 2 Lloyd's Rep. 469 at [78]–[80]. *Deutsche Bank AG v Total Global Steel Ltd* [2012] EWHC 1201 (Comm) at [160] where the court observed that the explanation for the general rule is that the injured party should ordinarily go out into the market to make a substitute contract to mitigate and generally thereby to crystallise its loss. See further *Dampskibsselskabet "Norden" A/S v Andre & Cie SA* [2003] 1 Lloyd's Rep. 287 at [41]–[42]. *Spar Shipping AS v Grand China Logistics Holding (Group) Co Ltd* [2015] EWHC 718; [2015] 2 Lloyd's Rep. 407 at [220]; *Scottish Power UK Plc v BP Exploration Operating Co Ltd* [2015] EWHC 2658 (Comm) at [121]

Actual knowledge of the claimant's impecuniosity

Replace footnote 466 with:

16-057 [466] *Wadsworth v Lydall* [1981] 1 W.L.R. 598; *Bacon v Cooper* [1982] 1 All E.R. 397; *Wroth v Tyler* [1974] Ch. 30. In *Compania Financiera "Soleada" SA v Hamoor Tanker Corp Inc* [1981] 1 W.L.R. 274 the principle was accepted by the Court of Appeal but not applied on the facts. See *Chitty on Contracts*, 33rd edn, Vol.1 paras 26-091 to 26-094.

No recovery for loss which is in fact avoided

Replace the first paragraph with:

The second rule of mitigation is that if the claimant in fact avoids or mitigates **16-058** his potential loss consequent upon the defendant's breach, he cannot recover for such avoided loss,[470] even though the steps he took were more than could be reasonably required of him under the first (the "avoidable loss") rule.[471] One illustration of this rule is discussed later, viz. where the seller resells immediately upon the buyer's breach, but at a price higher than the market price.[472] But if the seller could, but does not, resell immediately, and the market price later rises, the increased price which the seller obtains on his actual resale is not taken into account to reduce the damages payable by the buyer: the seller chooses to retain the goods at his own risk, and the benefit does not arise directly[473] from his acting in mitigation.[474] The benefit to the claimant must arise out of[475] his attempts to mitigate his potential loss resulting from the breach: if it arises from his actions which were independent of his mitigating steps, it should not lead to a reduction in his damages.[476]

[470] *Lowick Rose LLP (In Liquidation) v Swynson* [2017] UKSC 32; [2017] 2 W.L.R. 1161. The claimant's actual loss is assessed by taking account of all the items in his notional "profit and loss" calculation for the whole transaction: *Westwood v Secretary of State for Employment* [1985] A.C. 20 at 44. Thus, in *Omak Maritime Ltd v Mamola Challenger Shipping Co Ltd* [2010] EWHC 2026 (Comm); [2011] 1 Lloyd's Rep. 47, a charterer wrongfully repudiated a five-year charterparty early in its term. The shipowner accepted the repudiation and relet the vessel. The charter rates were less than the market rates obtained on mitigation and over the balance of the term of the charter the shipowner would have earned significantly more than under the contract. The shipowner had incurred substantial expenditure and sought to argue that it was entitled to recover its wasted expenditure as reliance losses. It was held that the shipowner's position had to be looked at on a net overall basis and since the excess earnings were greater than the wasted expenditure the shipowner was not entitled to recover damages for the wasted expenditure: "where steps have been taken to mitigate the loss which would otherwise have been caused by a breach of contract, principle requires the benefits obtained by mitigation to be set against the loss which would otherwise have been sustained": at [65].

[471] *British Westinghouse Electric and Manufacturing Co Ltd v Underground Electric Rys* [1912] A.C. 673 at 689, 690 (see below, para.17-055). See also *Erie County Natural Gas and Fuel Co Ltd v Carroll* [1911] A.C. 105 (below, para.17-024); *Hill v Showell* (1918) 87 L.J.K.B. 1106. cf. *Harbutt's "Plasticine" Ltd v Wayne Tank and Pump Co Ltd* [1970] 1 Q.B. 447 at 467–468, 473, 475–476 (see below, n.477, where it is noted that the case has been overruled on another point). *Thai Airways International Public Co Ltd v K I Holdings Co Ltd* [2015] EWHC 1250 (Comm).

[472] Below, paras 16-077 to 16-078. cf. *Melachrino v Nickoll and Knight* [1920] 1 K.B. 693 at 698 (below, para.17-015).

[473] cf. *Jebsen v East and West India Dock Co* (1875) L.R. 10 C.P. 300.

[474] *Campbell Mostyn (Provisions) Ltd v Barnett Trading Co* [1954] 1 Lloyd's Rep. 65 (below, para.16-078) (distinguished in *Pagnan (R) & Fratelli v Corbisa Industrial Agropacuaria Limitada* [1970] 1 W.L.R. 1306: see below, para.17-020). See also *Jones v Just* (1868) L.R. 3 Q.B. 197 (breach by seller but loss avoided by buyer when market price later rose); *Jamal v Moolla Dawood* [1916] 1 A.C. 175 (below, para.16-078).

[475] *The British Westinghouse case* [1912] A.C. 673 at 689. In *Fulton Shipping Inc. of Panama v Globalia Business Travel SAU (formerly Travelplan SAU) of Spain (The New Flamenco)* [2015] EWCA Civ 1299; [2016] 1 W.L.R. 2450, benefits accruing from the owners' reasonable act of mitigation in selling a capital asset (a vessel) on repudiation of a charter where there was no available market to refix the vessel, were required to be taken into account. This was a surprising result, not only because the asset employed in the performance of the contract for its term was the depreciation value of the capital asset rather than the whole value of that asset, but also because the corollary of the decision would appear to be that losses on the capital sale would be for the defendant's account. The decision of the Court of Appeal has now been reversed by the Supreme Court ([2017] UKSC 43; [2017] 1 W.L.R. 2581) for briefly stated reasons emphasising that the owners' decision was a commercial one that they took at their own risk which had nothing to do with the charterers, and because their interest in the capital value of the vessel had nothing to do with the interest injured by the charterers' repudiatory breach.

[476] *Hussey v Eels* [1990] 2 Q.B. 227 (sale of land); *Mobil North Sea Ltd v PJ Pipe and Valve Co* [2001] EWCA Civ 741; [2001] 2 All E.R. (Comm) 289; *Prestige Marine Services Pte Ltd v Marubeni International Petroleum (S) Pte Ltd* [2011] SGHC 270 at [52]. There is a valuable summary of principles

on this point contained in *Fulton Shipping Inc of Panama v Globalia Business Travel SAU* [2014] EWHC 1547 (Comm); [2014] 2 Lloyd's Rep. 230 at [64] at first instance (see above n.475).

Replace the second paragraph with:

However, a contract-breaker cannot have the damages reduced in respect of advantages gained by the claimant from wholly independent transactions,[477] as, for example, from a sum due to the claimant under an insurance policy.[478] So where the claimant, by another contract with a third party entered into before the defendant's breach of his contract with the claimant, has made an arrangement which should or does in fact prevent loss to the claimant from the defendant's breach, the defendant cannot rely on that other contract to reduce his damages[479]; it is an extraneous circumstance, *res inter alios acta.*

[477] See below, paras 17-019 to 17-020, 17-028. cf. *Lavarack v Woods of Colchester* [1967] 1 Q.B. 278; *Harbutt's "Plasticine" Ltd v Wayne Tank and Pump Co Ltd* [1970] 1 Q.B. 447 at 468, 473, 476 (overruled on another point: *Photo Productions Ltd v Securicor Transport Ltd* [1980] A.C. 827); *Hussey v Eels* [1990] 2 Q.B. 227. *Thai Airways International Public Co Ltd v K I Holdings Co Ltd* [2015] EWHC 1250 (Comm) at [178] (credits granted on purchase of new aircraft); *Rimpacific Navigation Inc v Daehan Shipbuilding Co Ltd* [2011] EWHC 2618 (Comm) at [26] (sale of capital asset where available market held irrelevant-before the sale they had the capital value of the vessels. After the sale they had realised that capital value); *Lowick Rose LLP (In Liquidation) v Swynson* [2017] UKSC 32; [2017] 2 W.L.R. 1161 overruling [2015] EWCA Civ 629; [2016] 1 W.L.R. 1045 (the repayment of an original debt incurred as a result of negligent advice and eliminated as a result of a corporate restructuring not regarded as a collateral matter and could not be ignored in the assessment of losses); *Fulton Shipping Inc. of Panama v Globalia Business Travel SAU (formerly Travelplan SAU) of Spain* [2017] UKSC 43; [2017] 1 W.L.R. 2581 (benefit accruing from a sale of a capital asset held to be res inter alios acta).

[478] *Bradburn v GW Ry* (1874) L.R. 10 Ex. 1.

[479] *Haviland v Long* [1952] 2 Q.B. 80 at 84. See also *Joyner v Weeks* [1891] 2 Q.B. 31 (below, para.17-019); *Slater v Hoyle and Smith* [1920] 2 K.B. 11 (buyer of defective goods able to avoid loss on sub-sale). On several recent occasions, courts have had to consider whether a sub-sale entered into prior to the defendant's breach should be ignored as an extraneous circumstance or whether it should be taken into account on the ground that when the contract of sale was entered into it was within the contemplation of the parties that a sub-sale was likely to be entered into so that the resultant gains or losses flowed as a natural consequence of the breach: *Bear Stearns Bank Plc v Forum Global Equity Ltd* [2007] EWHC 1576 (Comm); *Bence Graphics Ltd v Fasson* [1998] Q.B. 87; *Euro-Asian Oil SA v Credit Suisse* [2018] EWCA Civ 1720. The exact inter-relationship between the rules on mitigation relating to sub-contracts entered into prior to breach and the principles in *Hadley v Baxendale* (1854) 9 Ex. 341 is still in the course of refinement. It may therefore be necessary to qualify the proposition that the defendant cannot rely on a sub-contract entered into prior to the date of breach to reduce losses with the qualification, "except perhaps where the subcontract in question was within the contemplation of the parties at the time of contracting, as likely to have been entered into and it is reasonable to infer that the defendant was assuming liability for such losses": see also *Re R and H Hall and WH Pim (Junior) & Co's Arbitration* [1928] All E.R. 763; *Biggin & Co Ltd v Permanite* [1951] 1 K.B. 314; *Bence Graphics Ltd v Fasson* [1998] Q.B. 87.

Replace title footnote 480 with:

Release of resources for other uses[480]

16-059 [480] The arguments in this paragraph are developed more fully in *Chitty on Contracts*, 33rd edn, Vol.1 paras 26-110 and 26-111.

3. THE SELLER'S CLAIM FOR DAMAGES

(b) An Available Market

Suggested tests for an "available market"

Replace footnote 534 with:

16-065 [534] *Heskell v Continental Express Ltd* [1950] 1 All E.R. 1033 at 1056 ("A market for this purpose means more than a particular place. It also means a particular level of trade"). See also *The Arpad* [1934] P. 189 at 191 ("Market means buyers and sellers"); at 202; and *Gunvor SA v Sky Oil & Gas Ltd* [2018]

EWHC 1189 (Comm) (no available market in Yemen due to the paucity of participants in the market at the time).

The meaning of "available market"

Replace the first paragraph with:

It is submitted that the courts are likely to eschew formal limitations on the meaning of "available market",[556] especially in the light of the fact that the concept provides only a prima facie measure of damages which need not be applied whenever there is some justification for not doing so.[557] The availability of buyers and sellers, and their ready capacity to supply or to absorb the relevant goods[558] is the basic concept of an "available market": it is submitted that there is no need to add to this the test of a price liable to fluctuations in accordance with supply and demand, as occurs in official exchanges or certain commodity markets. A fixed market price may render s.50(3) ineffective as a ground for substantial damages, but it should not make the term "available market" inapplicable.[559] A fluctuating market price indicates the existence of an available market, but it should not be a necessary test: "there must be sufficient traders, who are in touch with each other".[560]

16-068

[556] *Charrington & Co Ltd v Wooder* [1914] A.C. 71 at 82 ("market" is "a term of no fixed legal significance": per Lord Dunedin). See also *Charter v Sullivan* [1957] 2 Q.B. 117 at 128; and *ABD (Metals and Waste) Ltd v Anglo-Chemical Ore Co Ltd* [1955] 2 Lloyd's Rep. 456 at 466 ("It is not necessary to establish a market that it should have a fixed place or building"); *Panwah Steel Pte Ltd v Burwill Trading Pte Ltd* [2006] SGCA 34 at [33]–[34].

[557] See *Bence Graphics International Ltd v Fasson UK Ltd* [1998] QB 87.

[558] *Marshall & Co v Nicoll & Son*, 1919 S.C. 244 at 253 (affirmed 1919 S.C. (HL) at 129); *Thompson (WL) Ltd v Robinson (Gunmakers) Ltd* [1955] Ch. 177 at 187 (cited above in para.16-066); *Gunvor SA v Sky Oil and Gas Ltd* [2018] EWHC 1189 (Comm) at [55]. cf. *Lazenby Garages Ltd v Wright* [1976] 1 W.L.R. 459.

[559] Waters, (1958) 36 Can. Bar Rev. 360, 371; Lawson, (1969) 43 A.L.J. 106, 110 ("The essential nature of a market requires potentially speedy buyers or sellers"). cf. *McGregor on Damages*, 20th edn, paras 25-118 to 25-120.

[560] *ABD (Metals and Waste) Ltd v Anglo-Chemical Ore Co Ltd* [1985] 2 Lloyd's Rep. 456 at 466 (followed in *Shearson Lehman Hutton Inc v Maclaine Watson & Co Ltd (No.2)* [1990] 3 All E.R. 723 at 730: "sufficient traders potentially in touch with each other to evidence a market in which the actual or notional seller could if he wished sell the goods". So "if the seller actually offers the goods for sale there is no available market unless there is one actual buyer on that day at a fair price"). And see *AerCap Partners 1 Ltd v Avia Asset Management Ltd* [2010] EWHC 2431 (Comm); [2010] 2 C.L.C. 578 at [107] ("If the goods are offered for sale and there is no buyer at a fair price, it is difficult to conclude that there was an available market at the time in question"). And see *Air Studios (Lyndhurst) Ltd v Lombard North Central Plc* [2012] EWHC 3162 (QB); [2013] 1 Lloyd's Rep. 63 at [96].

The extent of the market area

Replace footnote 572 with:

[572] *Gunvor SA v Sky Oil & Gas Ltd [* 2018] EWHC 1189 (Comm) (no market for oil in Yemen; sale at Fujairah nearest accessible market). It is submitted that *Wertheim v Chicoutimi Pulp Co* [1911] A.C. 301 (below, para.17-039: delayed delivery) which is often cited in this connection, really concerns the question of reaching a market value in one place by basing the calculation on the market price elsewhere; it did not decide that the latter place constituted an available market.

16-070

Proof of "the market or current price"

Replace footnote 621 with:

[621] This is a result of the rules of mitigation, and is the position under the case law before the Act: *Barrow v Arnaud* (1846) 8 Q.B. 595. In *Vitol SA v Beta Renowable Group SA* [2017] EWHC 1734 (Comm); [2017] 2 Lloyd's Rep 338 on a seller's refusal to deliver diesel oil in Bilbao, the market price was

16-076

established by reference to the price at which the buyer acquired a substitute cargo having comparable specifications at the place of delivery.

(d) Anticipatory Breach

Acceptance of the buyer's anticipatory repudiation

Replace footnote 662 with:

16-083 [662] *Roth & Co v Taysen Townsend & Co* (1895) 73 L.T. 628 at 629–630 (affirmed on appeal (1896) 12 T.L.R. 211 at 212); *Tredegar Iron and Coal Co (Ltd) v Hawthorn Bros & Co* (1902) 18 T.L.R. 716; *Sudan Import and Export Co (Khartoum) Ltd v Société Générale de Compensation* [1958] 1 Lloyd's Rep. 310 at 316. And see *Gunvor SA v Sky Oil and Gas Ltd* [2018] EWHC 1189 (Comm) (sale in nearest available market on termination of the contract after a refusal by the buyer to make payment). The rule is similar in the case of the buyer's acceptance of the seller's anticipatory repudiation: *Melachrino v Nickoll and Knight* [1920] 1 K.B. 693 at 697; *Garnac Grain Co Inc v HMF Faure and Fairclough Ltd* [1966] 1 Q.B. 650 at 687 (on appeal [1968] A.C. 1130 at 1140) (see below, para.17-015, for other analogous cases on the seller's anticipatory repudiation).

4. MISCELLANEOUS REMEDIES

Mistake and misrepresentation

Replace footnote 727 with:

16-092 [727] See above, paras 3-011 to 3-026; *Chitty on Contracts*, 33rd edn, Vol.1 paras 6-001 et seq.

Special remedies

Replace footnote 747 with:

16-096 [747] *Chitty on Contracts*, 33rd edn, Vol.2 Ch.32.

CHAPTER 17

THE REMEDIES OF THE BUYER

[255]

1. Damages for Non-delivery

(b) An Available Market

(ii) The Time for taking the Market Price

Damages when price paid in advance

Replace footnote 80 with:

17-009   80 *Shepherd v Johnson* (1802) 2 East 211; *McArthur v Seaforth* (1810) 2 Taunt. 257. See *McGregor on Damages*, 20th edn, para.25-015.

(iv) The Market Price

The relevant prices

Replace footnote 137 with:

17-017   137 Above, para.16-072; and see *Vitol SA v Beta Renowable Group SA* [2017] EWHC 1734 (Comm); [2017] 2 Lloyd's Rep 338.

Substitute goods bought at less than market price

Replace footnote 148 with:

17-019   148 *Rodocanachi v Milburn* (1886) 18 Q.B.D. 67; *Williams Bros v Ed T Agius Ltd* [1914] A.C. 510; *Bear Stearns Bank Plc v Forum Equity Ltd* [2007] EWHC 1576 (Comm); but see *McGregor on Damages*, 20th edn, paras 9-170 et seq.

(c) The Absence of an Available Market

Cost of procuring the nearest equivalent

Replace footnote 173 with:

17-023   173 *Vitol SA v Beta Renowable Group SA* [2017] EWHC 1734 (Comm); [2017] 2 Lloyd's Rep 338 (acquisition by buyer of substitute cargo having slightly superior specifications accepted). Contrast the similar rule in the case of a seller's claim for damages (above, paras 16-079 to 16–081).

Is the buyer obliged to buy the nearest equivalent?

Replace footnote 192 with:

17-025   192 cf. the obligation of a wrongfully dismissed employee to accept a reasonable opportunity for alternative employment, although it would never be an exact substitute for the post from which he was dismissed: see *Chitty on Contracts*, 33rd edn, Vol.2 paras 40-201 and 40-202.

(d) Resale by the Buyer

Relevance of sub-contracts

Replace the second paragraph with:

17-028   In the exceptional cases where the seller is liable for loss of profits or expenses under the sub-sale, his liability is based on the parties' reasonable contemplation of the consequences of a breach of the contract,[209] which depends on the knowledge, actual or imputed, of the seller at the time of the contract, and an inference that the defaulting party assumed responsibility for the consequences of the breach.[210] Thus in *Euro-Asian Oil SA v Credit Suisse*,[210a] the claimant entered into a contract to buy a quantity of diesel oil on c.i.f. terms. To the knowledge of the seller the buyer agreed to sell an identical quantity of diesel oil to an affiliate of the seller. The purpose of the transaction was to enable the seller's group of companies to access larger quantities than its resources would ordinarily permit. The buyer's fee for participating in the transaction was the difference between the purchase price and the onsale price to the seller's affiliate. The contract provided for payment by letter of credit against specified documents and further provided that, if bills of lading were not available, payment was to be made on presentation of an invoice and a letter of indemnity signed by the seller and its bankers. The seller obtained payment but the buyer never received the goods.

[209] *Biggin & Co Ltd v Permanite Ltd* [1951] 1 K.B. 422 at 435–436.

[210] See above, paras 16-045 to 16-048; and see *Transfield Shipping Inc v Mercator Shipping Inc (The Achilleas)* [2008] UKHL 48; [2009] 1 A.C. 61.

[210a] [2018] EWCA Civ 1720; [2019] 1 Lloyd's Rep. 444.

After the second paragraph, add new paragraph:

The buyer claimed the market value of the goods pursuant to a term contained in the letter of indemnity, but the Court of Appeal affirming the lower court[210b] held that damages should be measured by reference to the subcontract as both parties had contracted with reference to the subsale and both parties contemplated that the goods acquired under the contract would be used to perform the subcontract. Simon LJ said[210c]:

"The normal measure of damages for a failure to deliver goods is the estimated loss directly and naturally resulting, in the ordinary course of events from the seller's breach of contract, see s. 51(2). Where there is an available market for the goods, the measure of damages is prima facie the difference between the contract price and the market or current price of the goods at the time or times when they ought to have been delivered or (if no time was fixed) at the time of the refusal to deliver, see s. 51 (3). However the application of s.51 (2) may mean that the prima facie rule in s. 51(3) is not applied, or may be 'displaced' in the particular circumstances of the case... The issue in each case depends on the particular circumstances... In the present case, the sale contracts formed part of a series of what were effectively financing transactions...[T]here was a proper factual foundation... for the Judge's conclusion that 'it was always contemplated' that Euro-Asian would nominate the same cargo to perform the Real Oil contracts that Abilo nominated to perform the sale contracts, so that he was entitled to his view that the damages he awarded was the measure of loss contemplated by the parties."

[210b] [2016] EWHC 3340 (Comm); [2017] 1 Lloyd's Rep 287.

[210c] [2018] EWCA Civ 1720; [2019] 1 Lloyd's Rep. 444 at [72]. King LJ and Dame Elizabeth Gloster DBE agreed.

Hall v Pim

Replace footnote 220 with:

[220] *Re R and H Hall Ltd and WH Pim (Junior) & Co's Arbitration* [1928] All E.R. Rep. 763; *Patrick v Russo-British Grain Export Co Ltd* [1927] 2 K.B. 535 at 540 ("... it is enough if both parties contemplate that the buyer will probably resell and the seller is content to take the risk"). cf. above, para.16-046. And see *Seven Seas Properties Ltd v Al-Essa (No.2)* [1993] 1 W.L.R. 1083, 1087-1088 (sale of land case) for an exposition and application of the relevant principles. **17-030**

Damages payable by the buyer to the sub-buyer

Replace footnote 269 with:

17-036   269 cf. *Agius v Great Western Colliery Co* [1899] 1 Q.B. 413 at 420 (analogous case where seller delayed delivery: below, para.17-045); and the analogous cases where the goods were defective in quality (below, paras 17-077, 17-084). On the assessment of such costs see below, para.17-077.

3.   DAMAGES FOR DEFECTIVE QUALITY

(a)   In General

Introduction

Replace footnote 357 with:

17-047   357 *Hadley v Baxendale* (1854) 9 Ex. 341 (the first rule: see above, para.16-045); *H Parsons (Livestock) Ltd v Uttley Ingham & Co Ltd* [1978] Q.B. 791 at 800, 807. Section 53 of the Act will not apply to sui generis supply contracts of the sort considered in *PST Energy Shipping LLC v OW Bunker Malta Ltd* [2016] UKSC 23; [2016] A.C. 1034, but analogous common law principles should apply.

(b)   Diminution in Value

Buyer performing sub-contract despite seller's breach

Replace footnote 443 with:

17-057   443 *OMV Petrom SA v Glencore International AG* [2016] EWCA Civ 778 at [43]; [2016] 2 Lloyd's Rep. 432. And see the criticism of *Bence Graphics International Ltd v Fasson UK Ltd* [1998] Q.B. 87 by Treitel, (1997) 113 L.Q.R. 188 summarised below, para.17-082. See also Hawes, (2005) 121 L.Q.R. 389 (commenting on a New Zealand case which followed *Bence Graphics*). See further *Bear Stearns Bank Plc v Forum Global Equity Ltd* [2007] EWHC 1576 (Comm) at [208], where the court observed that the cases are hard to reconcile. See also *Oxus Gold v Templeton Insurance Ltd* [2007] EWHC 770 (Comm) at [66]–[83]; and *Transfield Shipping Inc v Mercator Shipping Inc (The Achilleas)* [2008] UKHL 48; [2009] 1 A.C. 61.

(c)   Losses other than Diminution in Value

(ii)   *Additional or Wasted Expenditure*

Other additional or wasted expenses

Replace footnote 476 with:

17-061   476 *Smith v Johnson* (1899) 15 T.L.R. 179 (mortar supplied by a builder was below standard; it was used for a building which the local authority later condemned as unsafe, and the owner recovered from the builder the cost of pulling it down and of rebuilding; he also recovered damages for loss of ground-rent). See *Chitty on Contracts*, 33rd edn, Vol.1 paras 26-025.

Expenditure incurred in reliance on the contract

Replace paragraph with:

17-062   Incidental expenditure may be incurred by the buyer in reliance on the seller's promise to deliver goods which meet the contractual description or standard. Provided the buyer's expenditure was within the reasonable contemplation of the parties at the time of making the contract, he may recover damages in respect of this expenditure if it has been rendered futile by the seller's breach of contract.[484] But the buyer can recover his wasted expenditure only to the extent that it would have been covered by the gross return which he would have made from his use of the goods if the seller had fully performed his contract[485]; the onus of proof is on the seller to show[486] that the buyer would not have recouped all of his expenditure if the contract had been fully performed by the seller.[487] It is unsettled how far the buyer can recover damages in respect of both his "expectation interest" (the profit or gain which he expected to receive from performance of the contract but which was prevented by the seller's breach of contract) and of his "reliance interest" (wasted expenditure).[488] But it is clear that the buyer may recover one or the other[489] and that he is free to elect between them: if he claims his wasted expenditure, he need not show that he cannot prove his loss of expected profits.[490] Where, however, there is an available market in which the buyer could buy substitute goods, a claim for wasted expenditure will not be possible if the court holds that the "prima facie" rule in s.53(3)[491] is the proper measure of damages.

[484] Illustrations of this type of recovery are *Cullinane v British "Rema" Manufacturing Co Ltd* [1954] 1 Q.B. 292 (discussed below, para.17-069); *Molling & Co v Dean & Son Ltd* (1901) 18 T.L.R. 217 (in respect of the freight to New York: see above, para.17-061); *Richard Holden Ltd v Bostock & Co Ltd* (1902) 18 T.L.R. 317 (below, para.17-065); *Bostock & Co Ltd v Nicholson & Sons Ltd* [1904] 1 K.B. 725 (below, paras 17-065, also 17-074, 17-076). See also above, para.12-042 and, on pre-contract expenditure, below, para.17-063. And see *Idas Group Ltd v Syntech New Zealand Ltd* [2014] NZHC 3188 (price paid by buyer recoverable since the goods were held worthless).

[485] *Mcrae v Commonweath Disposals Commission* (1951) 84 C.L.R. 377 (HCA), 411–419; *C & P Haulage v Middleton* [1983] 1 W.L.R. 1461 at 1468; *CCC Films (London) Ltd v Impact Quadrant Films Ltd* [1985] 1 Q.B. 16 at 32. And see *Grange v Quinn* [2013] EWCA Civ 24; [2013] P.&C.R. 18 at [27] and [102]–[103]. (The latter cases are not sale of goods cases.) The sentence in the text refers only to wasted expenditure which the claimant intended to recoup from the gross return.

[486] On a balance of probabilities.

[487] *Mcrae v Commonweath Disposals Commission* (1951) 84 C.L.R. 377 (HCA), 411–419; *CCC Films (London) Ltd v Impact Quadrant Films Ltd* [1985] 1 Q.B. 16 at 39–40. In the absence of such proof, it will be assumed in favour of the buyer that he would have recouped his expenditure.

[488] See the discussion below, para.17-069. The distinction between the two types of interest is made by Fuller and Perdue, (1937) 46 Yale L.J. 52, 373. See also above, para.16-031.

[489] See below, para.17-069.

[490] *CCC Films (London) Ltd v Impact Quadrant Films Ltd* [1985] 1 Q.B. 16.

[491] See above, paras 17-047, 17-050 et seq.

(iv)   Loss of Amenity

Loss of amenity

Replace footnote 553 with:

[553] *Ruxley Electronics and Construction Ltd v Forsyth* [1996] A.C. 344. *Ruxley* was distinguished in **17-071** *Peebles v Rembrand Builders Merchants Ltd* [2017] ScotSC 28 at [90], where roof tiles were defective and subject to discolouration. The contract in question was characterized as an ordinary sale of goods contract and not one for pleasure or peace. But the Court at [91] allowed damages for inconvenience as remedial works had to be carried out on the roof of the house.

(v)   Physical Injury to the Buyer or his Property

Physical injury to the buyer, his family or his property

Replace footnote 559 with:

[559] The physical damage must have been caused by the breach: see *Claire Busby v Berkshire Bed Co* **17-072** *Ltd* [2018] EWHC 2976 (QB) (plaintiff's injury not caused by the breach). See below, para.17-075 for the situation where the defective goods cause injury to a third person or his property, and the buyer is compelled to compensate the third person.

Replace footnote 568 with:

568 *Priest v Last* [1903] 2 K.B. 148; *Frost v Aylesbury Dairy Co Ltd* [1905] 1 K.B. 608; *Jackson v Watson & Sons* [1909] 2 K.B. 193; *Square v Model Farm Dairies (Bournemouth) Ltd* [1939] 2 K.B. 365 at 374. cf. the recovery of damages in respect of loss suffered by third parties, *Linden Gardens Trust Ltd v Lenesta Sludge Disposals Ltd* [1994] 1 A.C. 85; *Darlington BC v Wiltshier Northern Ltd* [1995] 1 W.L.R. 68; *Alfred McAlpine Construction Ltd v Panatown Ltd* [2001] 1 A.C. 518; *Swynson Ltd v Lowick Rose LLP* [2017] UKSC 32; [2018] A.C. 313. In *BV Nederlandse Industrie Van Eiprodukten v Rembrandt Enterprises Inc* [2019] EWCA Civ 596; [2019] 1 Lloyd's Rep 491 the plaintiff seller was held unable to recover damages on the principle of transferred loss as it had not been established that it was part of the contract to benefit the third party.

(viii) Compensation Paid in a Chain of Sub-sales

Compensation paid to sub-buyers in a series of "string contracts"

Replace footnote 656 with:

17-081 656 *Chitty on Contracts*, 33rd edn, Vol.2 para.44-434 (which is virtually identical with the first paragraph of the present para.17-081—the then same editor being responsible for both paragraphs); was cited in *Louis Dreyfus Trading Ltd v Reliance Trading Ltd* [2004] EWHC 525 (Comm); [2004] 2 Lloyd's Rep. 243 at [24].

Damages limited by reference to sub-sale

Replace footnote 661 with:

17-082 661 *Bence Graphics International Ltd v Fasson UK Ltd* [1998] Q.B. 87 (see above, para.17-057). In this case, the CA departed from the decision of the CA in *Slater v Hoyle and Smith Ltd* [1920] 2 K.B. 11 (above, para.17-056). It may be observed that in *Slater v Hoyle and Smith Ltd* (p.14) it was not suggested that the seller had any knowledge of the buyer's contract with the sub-buyer. By contrast in *Bence Graphics* the sellers were aware of the precise use to which the buyers would put the film. The contemplated extent of the liability assumed in respect of the sub-contract by the seller was therefore markedly different in the 2 cases and explains the outcomes. See *Euro-Asian Oil SA v Credit Suisse* [2018] EWCA Civ 1720 where an analysis similar to that used in *Bence Graphics* can be found and it was held that, since the defaulting party can fairly be said to have contracted with reference to the sub-contract, the Court in calculating the loss should not ignore the sub-contract. But in (1997) 113 L.Q.R. 188, Treitel strongly supports the decision in *Slater v Hoyle* and criticises the decision in the *Bence Graphics* case, on the ground that when the buyer is not seeking damages for consequential loss (e.g. arising under a resale) but claiming the "difference in value" (under s.53(3) of the 1979 Act)) the remoteness rules are not relevant. See also Hawes, (2005) 121 L.Q.R. 389 (commenting on a New Zealand case which followed *Bence Graphics*).

5. REPAYMENT OF THE PRICE OR ADVANCE PAYMENTS

Restitution: recovery of money paid to the seller

Replace the first paragraph with:

17-090 Section 54 of the Act provides that: "Nothing in this Act affects the right of the buyer ... to recover money paid where the consideration for the payment of it has failed". The claim referred to in this provision is one in restitution[707] where the claimant has failed to receive the benefit of the other party's performance[708]:

"... subject always to special provisions in a contract, payments on account of a purchase price are recoverable if the consideration for which that price is paid wholly fails."[709]

Thus, the buyer has a claim in restitution to recover the price he has paid to the seller if the seller, in breach of his obligation under s.12(1),[710] failed to pass a good title to the goods sold.[711] The "consideration" for the payment of the price is treated as the transfer of the property in the goods to the buyer, and the buyer may sue in restitution to recover the price on the ground of a total failure of consideration, despite the fact that he enjoyed some use[712] of the goods.[713] Similarly, if the seller failed to deliver the goods, or delivered goods which the buyer was entitled to, and did reject, the buyer may recover the deposit he paid to the seller.[714]

[707] Goff and Jones, *The Law of Unjust Enrichment*, 9th edn, paras 3.37 to 3.39; *Chitty on Contracts*, 33rd edn, Vol.1 paras 29-057 to 29-069. In a sui generis supply contract of the sort encountered in *PST Energy Shipping LLC v OW Bunker Malta Ltd (The Res Cogitans)* [2016] UKSC 23; [2016] A.C. 1034 failure of consideration might occur where the recipient does not obtain an effective permission to use and consume the goods and is in consequence potentially liable for conversion of the goods: see *PST Energy Shipping LLC v OW Bunker Malta Ltd* [2015] EWHC 2022 (Comm) at [48].

[708] Actual "performance of the promise" is the sense in which "consideration" is used in this context: *Fibrosa Spolka Akcyjna v Fairbairn Lawson Combe Barbour Ltd* [1943] A.C. 32 at 48, 61, 72 ("... the failure of consideration which justifies repayment is a failure in the contract performance": at 72).

[709] *Fibrosa Spolka Akcyjna v Fairbairn Lawson Combe Barbour* [1943] A. C. 32 at 75 (quoting *Ockenden v Henly* (1858) E.B. & E. 485 at 492). See also below, para.20-117.

[710] Above, paras 4-002 et seq.

[711] *Rowland v Divall* [1923] 2 K.B. 500. See the examination and criticism of this case, above, paras 4-006 et seq., where further authorities are cited; and Treitel, *The Law of Contract*, 14th edn, paras 22-007 et seq.

[712] *Rowland v Divall* [1923] 2 K.B. 500 cf. *Yeoman Credit Ltd v Apps* [1962] 2 Q.B. 508 (accumulation of defects in a vehicle constituted breach of a fundamental term: but some use of the vehicle prevented a total failure of "consideration"); cf. also *Barber v NSW Bank Plc* [1996] 1 W.L.R. 641; see above, paras 13-052 to 13-053. See the Law Commission's Report No.160 (1987), paras 6.1–6.5.

[713] For a thorough examination of the authorities on the recovery of monies paid where the consideration for the payment has failed, see *Giedo van der Garde BV v Force India Formula One Team* [2010] EWHC 2373 (QB) at [233]–[367].

[714] *Fitt v Cassanet* (1842) 4 M. & G. 898 (wrongful resale of the goods by the seller: the buyer also recovered damages for non-delivery).

6. REMEDIES OTHER THAN CLAIMS TO MONEY

(c) Specific Performance for Delivery of the Goods

The types of goods for which the remedy is appropriate

Replace footnote 784 with:

[784] *Chitty on Contracts*, 33rd edn, Vol.1, para 27-025; Jones and Goodhart, *Specific Performance*, 2nd edn, pp.148–149. See also Sharpe, *Injunctions and Specific Performance*, paras 8-390 to 8-510, 9-130 to 9-200. And see *Thomas Borthwick & Sons (Australia) Ltd v South Otago Freezing Co Ltd* [1978] 1 N.Z.L.R. 538 at 548. In some cases injunctions have been granted which have the practical effect of an order to perform the contract: see *Land Rover Group Ltd v UPF (UK) Ltd (In Administrative Receivership)* [2002] EWHC 3183 (QB); [2003] 2 B.C.L.C. 222 at [52] (interim injunction to enforce obligation to supply car chassis to manufacturer where it appeared to have been accepted that the goods were specific goods); *Sky Petroleum Ltd v V.S.P. Petroleum Ltd* [1974] 1 W.L.R. 576 (interim injunction to stop cutting off of supplies where alternative supplies not available and goods unascertained). **17-098**

(d) Injunctions and Declarations

Injunction

Replace the first paragraph with:

Whereas specific performance is a remedy for the positive promise of the seller to deliver the goods, the remedy of an injunction is usually the order of the court restraining the breach of a purely negative promise by the seller.[799] Like specific performance,[800] an injunction is an equitable remedy,[801] but, unlike specific performance, it is not expressly referred to in the Act.[802] Section 62(2) preserves "the rules of common law" except where inconsistent with the express provisions of the Act, and it has been suggested earlier[803] that the rules of equity are included in this **17-100** phrase. The court may use an injunction in support of an order for specific performance. In *Behnke v Bede Shipping Co Ltd*,[804] in addition to making the order for specific performance against the sellers, as set out in an earlier paragraph,[805] the court also granted an injunction restraining the sellers from parting with the ship to anyone but the buyer.[806] Similarly, the court has power by injunction to prevent a specific chattel from being removed out of the jurisdiction until a question relating to the chattel has been decided by the court.[807] So where the buyer sought specific performance of the sale to him of a German ship, which was in an English port, the court restrained the seller and the master of the ship from removing her, so that she could be delivered under the contract if the court later so ordered.[808] In some circumstances, an injunction may be granted which has much the same effect as an order of specific performance.[809] Thus, where the goods sold to the buyer are on the land of the seller, and the contract gives the buyer a right to enter the land to remove the goods, the court may grant an injunction to restrain the seller from preventing the due execution of the contract.[810]

[799] The order of the court must define clearly what should or should not be done by the seller. In *Simon Carves Ltd v Ensus UK Ltd* [2011] EWHC 657 (TCC); [2011] B.L.R. 340 at [33], the court granted an interim injunction to restrain payment being made under an on-demand performance bond on the ground that there was an express negative covenant in the underlying contract restricting the circumstances in which the grantee of the performance bond could seek payment.

[800] Above, paras 17-095 to 17-099.

[801] *Kerr on Injunctions*, 6th edn, pp.409 et seq.; Sharpe, *Injunctions and Specific Performance*, 3rd edn, Pt I; Spry, *The Principles of Equitable Remedies*, 9th edn, Chs 4 and 5; *Ashburner's Principles of Equity*, 2nd edn, pp.384–387; *Snell's Equity*, 33rd edn, Ch.16; *Doherty v Allman* (1878) 3 App. Cas. 709 at 719–721.

[802] cf. s.60 of the 1979 Act (above, para.16-096).

[803] Above, paras 1-007 to 1-011.

[804] *Behnke v Bede Shipping Co Ltd* [1927] 1 K.B. 649.

[805] Above, para.17-098.

[806] *Behnke v Bede Shipping Co Ltd* [1927] 1 K.B. 649 at 662. The Privy Council in *Dominion Coal Co Ltd v Dominion Iron and Steel Co Ltd* [1909] A.C. 293 at 310 (above, para.17-096) envisaged the granting of an injunction to prevent the sellers from discriminating against the buyers in the selection of the quality of the coal to be supplied to the buyers.

[807] *Hart v Herwig* (1873) L.R. 8 Ch. App. 860.

[808] *Hart v Herwig* (1873) L.R. 8 Ch. App. 860. cf. *North v Great Northern Railway* (1860) 2 Giff. 64 (claimant hired coal wagons of special value to him; railway company could be restrained from selling them).

[809] Above para.17-098 n 784 and cf. *Astro Exito Navegacion SA v Southland Enterprises (No.2)* [1983] 2 A.C. 787 (injunction to buyers to sign document needed by sellers to comply with letter of credit; Master of Supreme Court to sign if buyers failed to do so). And see *Lauritzen Cool AB v Lady Navigation Inc* [2005] EWCA 579; [2006] 1 All E.R. 866 (injunction granted to restrain shipowner from employing vessel inconsistently with terms of time charter contract and restraining owner from fixing vessel with third party during term of charter).

[810] *James Jones & Sons Ltd v Tankerville* [1909] 2 Ch. 440 (timber growing on the seller's land: by s.61(1) of the 1979 Act "goods" are defined as including industrial growing crops which are to be severed under the contract of sale: see above, paras 1-090 to 1-094).

(e)   Proprietary Claims to Possession or Damages

Wrongful resale or retaking by the seller

Replace the first paragraph with:

17-103   In *Chinery v Viall*,[835] where the unpaid seller, without a right to resell,[836] wrongfully resold the goods at a time when the original buyer was entitled to possession of them[837] (the sale being on credit terms[838]), the seller was held liable to the original buyer for damages for non-delivery,[839] or for conversion.[840] But it was held that the damages for the conversion did not amount to the full value of the goods, because the buyer had not paid the price[841]: the buyer could recover only his actual loss, which was the difference between the market price of the goods at the time of the conversion[842] and the contract price.[843]

[835] *Chinery v Viall* (1860) 5 H. & N. 288.

[836] See above, para.15-105.

[837] The seller had remained in possession of the goods after the original sale.

[838] Even where the buyer had failed to pay the price on the date fixed by the contract, he would be entitled to possession of the goods if he tendered the price to the seller within a reasonable time and before the seller had justifiably resold or terminated the contract: *Martindale v Smith* (1841) 1 Q.B. 389. See also *Bloxam v Sanders* (1825) 4 B. & C. 941.

[839] *Fitt v Cassanet* (1842) 4 M. & G. 898. See s.51 of the 1979 Act (above, paras 17-001 et seq.).

[840] *Bloxam v Sanders* (1825) 4 B. & C. 941 at 949.

[841] Since he had not delivered the goods, the seller could not sue for the price: *Lamond v Davall* (1847) 9 Q.B. 1030 (above, paras 15-128, 16-020).

[842] The basic measure of damages in conversion is the value of the item at the time of the conversion (this measure applies even where the tortfeasor replaces the item at a later date—its value at that date should be deducted from its value at the time of conversion): *BBMM Finance (Hong Kong) Ltd v Eda Holdings Ltd* [1990] 1 W.L.R. 409 PC (a case concerning shares).

[843] *Chinery v Viall* (1860) 5 H. & N. 288 (applied in *Butler v Egg and Egg Pulp Marketing Board* (1996) 114 C.L.R. 185). The position is the same in the case of a wrongful taking, sale or pledge by a pledgee: *Johnson v Stear* (1863) 15 C.B.(N.S.) 330; *Brierly v Kendall* (1852) 17 Q.B. 937; or a wrongful sale and purchase of goods held on hire-purchase terms: *Wickham Holdings Ltd v Brooke House Motors Ltd* [1967] 1 W.L.R. 295 (distinguished in *Chubb Cash Ltd v John Crilley & Son* [1983] 1 W.L.R. 599). See *McGregor on Damages*, 20th edn, paras 38-058 to 38-063; *Clerk and Lindsell on Torts*, 22nd edn, paras 17-115 to 17-118. On waiver of tort, see above, paras 1-073, 15-104.

Replace footnote 847 with:

[847] *Stephens v Wilkinson* (1831) 2 B. & Ad. 320 at 327; *Page v Cowasjee Eduljee* (1866) L.R. 1 P.C. 127 at 147. See *McGregor on Damages*, 20th edn, para.38-063. The claim will be made by proceedings for wrongful interference under the Torts (Interference with Goods) Act 1977.

CHAPTER 18

OVERSEAS SALES IN GENERAL

TABLE OF CONTENTS

1. PRELIMINARY

INCOTERMS

Replace footnote 7 with:

18-002   ⁷ e.g. in *The Albazero* [1977] A.C. 774: see at 782; *BV Oliehandel Jongkind v Coastal International Ltd* [1983] 2 Lloyd's Rep. 463; *The Forum Craftsman* [1985] 1 Lloyd's Rep. 291; *P & O Oil Trading Ltd v Scanoil AB (The Orient Prince)* [1985] 1 Lloyd's Rep. 389; *ERG Petroli SpA v Vitol SA (The Ballenita)* [1992] 2 Lloyd's Rep. 455; *Trasimex Holdings SA v Addax BV (The Red Sea)* [1999] 1 Lloyd's Rep. 610; *Geofizika v MMB International Ltd* [2010] EWCA Civ 459; [2010] 2 Lloyd's Rep. 1 at [4] and passim; *Great Elephant Corp v Trafigura Beheer BV* [2013] EWCA Civ 905; [2013] 2 All E.R. (Comm) 415 at [15], [35]. See also *Scottish & Newcastle International Ltd v Othon Ghalanos Ltd* [2006] EWCA Civ 1750; [2007] 2 Lloyd's Rep. 341, where forms issued by the sellers stated that "delivery will be in accordance with INCOterms" (at [7]), but counsel for the sellers "did not rely on Incoterms" (at [32]); affirmed [2008] UKHL 11; [2008] 1 Lloyd's Rep. 462, where no reference was made to *INCOTERMS*. See also *KG Bominflot Bunkergesellschaft für Mineralöle mbH & Co v Petroplus Marketing AG (The Mercini Lady)* [2010] EWCA Civ 1145; [2011] 1 Lloyd's Rep. 442, where an f.o.b. contract expressly incorporated *INCOTERMS* 2000, but nothing seems to have turned on this point; similarly *Nidera BV v Venus International Free Zone for Trading & Marine Services SAE* [2014] EWHC 2013 (Comm); [2014] 1 C.L.C. 1001 (CPT contract). See also the comment below, at para.19-002 n.12, on *Euro-Asian Oil SA (formerly Euro-Asian Oil AG) v Abilo (UK) Ltd Euro-Asian Oil SA (formerly Euro-Asian Oil AG) v Credit Suisse AG* [2016] EWHC 3340 (Comm); [2017] 1 Lloyd's Rep. 287; varied [2018] EWCA Civ 1720; [2019] 1 Lloyd's Rep. 444.

2. DOCUMENTS OF TITLE TO GOODS

(a) Bills of Lading

(iii) Bill of Lading as a Contractual Document

Bill of lading as evidence of contract of carriage

At the end of the first paragraph, after "have contractual force.", add:

18-073   A person who becomes a party to a contract on bill of lading terms ("the matrix contract") may thereby also become a party to a separate contract governed by different rules from those governing the "matrix" contract, e.g., an arbitration agreement concluded by virtue of an arbitration clause in the matrix contract.⁶¹⁴ᵃ

⁶¹⁴ᵃ *Sea Master Shipping Inc v Arab Bank (Switzerland) Ltd* [2018] EWHC 1902 (Comm); [2019] 1 Lloyd's Rep. 101.

Bill of lading transferred to charterer

Replace footnote 646 with:

[646] See *Bowstead and Reynolds on Agency*, 21st edn, Art.98.

18-079

(iv) Bill of Lading as a Document of Title

Shipped bill made out to bearer or order

Replace footnote 752 with:

[752] In *Laemthong International Lines Co Ltd v Artis (The Laemthong Glory)* [2005] EWCA Civ 519; **18-090**
[2005] 1 Lloyd's Rep. 688, goods were carried in a chartered ship in circumstances giving rise to a
contract of carriage with the shipowners and not with the charterers as carriers (see below, para.18-
169). The goods were delivered under a letter of indemnity addressed to the *charterer* but it was held
that this letter, on its true construction, purported to confer a benefit on the *shipowner* within the
Contracts (Rights of Third Parties) Act 1999 s.1(1)(b) and was therefore enforceable by the shipowner
as a third party by virtue of that Act (see above, para.18-005 n.25). See also *Great Eastern Shipping Co
Ltd v Far East Chartering Ltd (The Jag Ravi)* [2012] EWCA Civ 180; [2012] 1 Lloyd's Rep. 637, where
such a letter of indemnity amounting to a contract between the prospective receivers of goods (A) and
the charterers of the carrying ship (B) was held to be enforceable by the owners of that ship (C) by virtue
of the 1999 Act. For this case, see further *Chitty on Contracts*, 33rd edn, Vol.1 para.18-095. For a further
decision whether, on the facts, a person is receiving goods in his proper capacity, see *Songa Chemicals
AS v Navig8 Chemicals Pool Inc (The Songa Winds)* [2018] EWHC 397 (Comm); [2018] 2 Lloyd's Rep
47; affd sub nom *Navig8 Chemicals Pool Inc v Glencore Agriculture BV (The Songa Winds)* [2018]
EWCA Civ 1901; [2018] 2 Lloyd's Rep. 374.

(v) Contractual Effects of Transfer of Bill of Lading: Introductory

Carriage of Goods by Sea Act 1992

Replace footnote 1343 with:

[1343] Below, para.18-180. See also *Sea Master Shipping Inc v Arab Bank (Switzerland) Ltd* [2018] EWHC   **18-142**
1902 (Comm); [2019] 1 Lloyd's Rep. 101 (ante, para 18-074) (entry into a bill of lading contract with
an arbitration clause may result in entry into a separate arbitration agreement).

(vi) Acquisition of Contractual Rights

Good faith

Replace footnote 1378 with:

[1378] *Aegean Sea Traders Corp v Repsol Petroleo SA (The Aegean Sea)* [1998] 2 Lloyd's Rep. 39 at 60.   **18-146**
See also *Overseas-Chinese Banking Corp Ltd v Owner and/or Demise Charterer of the vessel Yue You
902 (The Yue You 902)* [2019] SGHC 106.

Bill of lading transferred to charterer

At the end of the paragraph, after "before the 1992 Act.", add:

At common law, a bill of lading holder is entitled to sue for damages in full for   **18-153**
loss occurring to the cargo during the voyage if he owned them at the time of the
loss or received damaged goods, and is not obliged to make a deduction for loss
indemnified by another person, e.g. a seller from whom he has bought them.[1418a]

[1418a] *Sevylor Shipping & Trading Corp v Atfadul Co for Foods, Fruits & Livestock (The Baltic Strait)*
[2018] EWHC 629 (Comm); [2018] 2 Lloyd's Rep 33 ("Question (iii)"].

Spent bill of lading

At the end of the first paragraph, after "a "spent" bill.", add new footnote 1424a:

18-155   ¹⁴²⁴ᵃ Nevertheless, the meaning of a "spent" bill of lading is the same both at common law and under the 1992 Act: *Overseas-Chinese Banking Corp Ltd v Owner and/or Demise Charterer of the vessel Yue You 902 (The Yue You 902)* [2019] SGHC 106.

In the third paragraph, replace footnote 1429 with:

¹⁴²⁹ See *Borealis AB v Stargas Ltd (The Berge Sisar)* [2001] UKHL 17; [2002] 2 A.C. 205 at [31], where the actual decision was that, for reasons discussed in para.18-173 below, the transferee was not liable on the bill. cf. *Primetrade AG v Ythan Ltd (The Ythan)* [2005] EWHC 2399 (Comm); [2006] 1 All E.R. 367 at [68]. The actual decision was that the alleged transferee had not acquired rights of suit under the bill as he had not become the "holder" of it (see above, para.18-145); and that therefore, for the reason given in para.18-166 below, he had not incurred any liability under it. cf. *Euro-Asian Oil SA v Abilo (UK) Ltd* [2016] EWHC 3340 (Comm); [2017] 1 Lloyd's Rep. 287 esp. at [387] (no rights acquired where right to possession preceded the transaction or other arrangement); the decision was varied at [2018] EWCA Civ 1720; [2019] 1 Lloyd's Rep. 444.

In the fourth paragraph, replace footnote 1432 with:

¹⁴³² *Standard Chartered Bank v Dorchester LNG (2) Ltd (The Erin Schulte)* [2014] EWCA Civ 1382; [2015] 1 Lloyd"s Rep. 1382; reversing on this point [2013] EWHC 808 (Comm); [2013] 2 Lloyd's Rep. 388. See also *Overseas-Chinese Banking Corp Ltd v Owner and/or Demise Charterer of the vessel Yue You 902 (The Yue You 902)* [2019] SGHC 106.

Rights of original shipper

At the end of the fourth paragraph, after "a mere receipt.", add:

18-156   A third, and common, possibility is that entry into a contract on bill of lading terms containing an arbitration clause results in an arbitration agreement, which, being a separate contract from the bill of lading contract, is neither transferred nor extinguished on transfer of the bill of lading and so continues to govern the relationship between its parties.¹⁴⁷¹ᵃ

¹⁴⁷¹ᵃ *Sea Master Shipping Inc v Arab Bank (Switzerland) Ltd* [2018] EWHC 1902 (Comm); [2019] 1 Lloyd's Rep. 101.

Loss suffered by person other than lawful holder

Replace the first paragraph with:

18-161   Section 2(4) of the 1992 Act deals with the situation in which rights under the contract of carriage are transferred to A by virtue of s.2(1), but the loss resulting from a breach of that contract is suffered by B. The subsection provides that:

"… where, in the case of any document to which this Act applies—(a) a person with any interest or right in or in relation to goods to which the document relates sustains loss or damage in consequence of a breach of the contract of carriage; but (b) subsection (1) above operates in relation to that document so that rights of suit in respect of that breach are vested in another person, the other person shall be entitled to exercise those rights for the benefit of the person who sustained the loss or damage to the same extent as they could have been exercised if they had been vested in the person for whose benefit they are exercised."

The purpose of this subsection is to avoid the consequences which might, but for the subsection, flow from the general principle of English law¹⁵⁵⁵ that damages in a contractual action can be recovered only in respect of the claimant's own loss.¹⁵⁵⁶ That general principle was also subject to exceptions at common law,¹⁵⁵⁷ and these exceptions could still apply in the present context even in cases which did not fall squarely within s.2(4).[1558] For s.2(4) to apply, it is not necessary that the party who suffered the loss previously had rights under the contract of carriage contained in, or evidenced by, the bill of lading (e.g., where goods have been bought from a charterer).[1558a] However, it will not enable a claimant to recover under the Carriage of Goods by Sea Act 1992, s.2 for a loss suffered by a previous cargo-owner who did not have a claim under s.2(1) (e.g. where the claimant bought cargo from a charterer in whose hands the bill of lading was merely a receipt).[1558b]

[1555] Above, para.18-156.

[1556] This appears to be what is meant by the Law Commissions' somewhat puzzling statement in Law Com. No.196, Scot Law Com. No.130, para.2.8 that, but for s.2(4), "the decision in *The Albazero* [1977] A.C. 774 [above, para.18-158], could prevent those holders of bills of lading who do not themselves sustain loss from recovering anything other than nominal damages". The reason for the actual result in *The Albazero* was that the claimants had transferred the bill of lading so as to vest contractual rights in the transferee. Where this is done by a person whose only contract with the carrier is on bill of lading terms, that person's rights under the contract of carriage would now be extinguished under s.2(5) of the 1992 Act.

[1557] Above, para.18-156.

[1558] Below, para.18-162 n.1579.

[1558a] *Sevylor Shipping & Trading Corp v Atfadul Co for Foods, Fruits & Livestock (The Baltic Strait)* [2018] EWHC 629 (Comm); [2018] 2 Lloyd's Rep 33 ("Question (i) (obiter)"].

[1558b] *Sevylor Shipping & Trading Corp v Atfadul Co for Foods, Fruits & Livestock (The Baltic Strait)* [2018] EWHC 629 (Comm); [2018] 2 Lloyd's Rep 33 ("Question (ii) (obiter)"].

(vii)   Imposition of Contractual Liabilities

Introductory

At the end of the paragraph, after "point of delivery.", add:

It must also be noted that the effect of becoming a party to a contract on bill of lading terms may be that, independently of the rules applying specifically to contracts of carriage of goods by sea, the parties may automatically acquire certain rights and liabilities separate from those applying by virtue of their relationship under the contract of carriage of goods by sea. Thus, a bill of lading arbitration clause may entitle and oblige them to have disputes determined by arbitration, whether or not they assert rights under the bill of lading contract and even after the bill of lading has been transferred.[1603a]   **18-165**

[1603a] *Sea Master Shipping Inc v Arab Bank (Switzerland) Ltd* [2018] EWHC 1902 (Comm); [2019] 1 Lloyd's Rep. 101.

Liabilities of original contracting parties

Replace footnote 1682 with:

[1682] "The contract" in s.3(3) clearly refers back to "the contract of carriage" in s.3(1) and (2). In *Sea Master Shipping Inc v Arab Bank (Switzerland) Ltd* [2018] EWHC 1902 (Comm); [2019] 1 Lloyd's Rep 101, the court left to be decided on the facts the question whether a bank holding a bill of lading as security and which assented to the bills' substitution by switch bills, making the cargo deliverable to a different consignee, was an original party to the switch bill.   **18-176**

3. PASSING OF PROPERTY

"Agents" in fact sellers or buyers

Replace footnote 2399 with:

18-283 2399 *Ireland v Livingston* (1871) L.R. 5 H.L. 395; and see generally *Bowstead and Reynolds on Agency*, 21st edn, para.1-036.

6. BULK SHIPMENTS

(a) Shipping Documents

Tender of documents

Replace footnote 2774 with:

18-334 2774 *SIAT di del Ferro v Tradax Overseas SA* [1978] 2 Lloyd's Rep. 470 at 480. cf. *Noble Resources Ltd v Cavalier Shipping Corp (The Atlas)* [1996] 1 Lloyd's Rep. 642 at 644, describing the practice of issuing such "switch" bills as "fraught with danger" since it gives opportunities for fraud. See also *Trafigura Beheer BV v Kookmin Bank Co (No.2)* [2006] EWHC 1929 (Comm); [2007] 1 Lloyd's Rep. 669. The facts relating to the substitute bills are stated in para.18-123 n.1170 above. No doubt, those bills would have been a bad tender under the contract of sale if they had been tendered under that contract. For difficulties with switch bills, arbitration clauses and the Carriage of Goods by Sea Act 1992, see *Sea Master Shipping Inc v Arab Bank (Switzerland) Ltd (The Sea Master)* [2018] EWHC 1902 (Comm); [2019] 1 Lloyd's Rep. 101.

8. SUPERVENING PROHIBITION OF EXPORT OR IMPORT

(a) Discharge by Supervening Prohibition

Self-induced frustration

Replace footnote 3151 with:

18-389 3151 *William Cory & Son Ltd v London Corporation* [1951] 2 K.B. 476; *Chitty on Contracts*, 33rd edn, Vol.1 para.11-007.

(b) Prohibition of Export or Import Clauses

(i) Effects

Construction

Replace footnote 3166 with:

18-392 3166 See the following discussion and esp. below, paras 18-394 to 18-400. cf. *Classic Maritime Inc v Limbungan Makmur Sdn Bhd* [2019] EWCA Civ 1102; varying [2018] EWHC 2389 (Comm); [2019] 1 Lloyd's Rep. 349.

(ii) Burden of Proof

Where the embargo is absolute

Replace footnote 3209 with:

18-395 3209 *Bremer Handelsgesellschaft mbH v C Mackprang Jr* [1979] 1 Lloyd's Rep. 221 at 227–228. cf. *Classic Maritime Inc v Limbungan Makmur Sdn Bhd* [2019] EWCA Civ 1102; varying [2018] EWHC 2389 (Comm); [2019] 1 Lloyd's Rep. 349.

Seller must show that no excepted goods available

In the second paragraph, after "with the contract.", add new footnote 3226a:

^{3226a} cf. *Classic Maritime Inc v Limbungan Makmur Sdn Bhd* [2019] EWCA Civ 1102; varying [2018] **18-397**
EWHC 2389 (Comm); [2019] 1 Lloyd's Rep. 349. The Court of Appeal distinguished between a
contractual cancellation clause with automatic effect, as in *Bremer v Vanden*, and an exception clause
which relieved a pary from liability from non-performance only where he would have been ready and
willing to perform.

(iv)   Notice of Supervening Events

Waiver of defects in the notice

Replace footnote 3316 with:

³³¹⁶ *Chitty on Contracts*, 33rd edn, Vol.1 paras 4-091 to 4-093, stating this requirement for so-called **18-406**
"promissory estoppel"; an expression now often used interchangeably with this kind of "waiver": see
below at para.18-406 nn.3325 and 3326.

Replace the third paragraph with:

The operation of the kind of waiver here under consideration is illustrated by
Bremer Handelsgesellschaft mbH v Vanden Avenne-Izegem PVBA,[3322] where the
seller gave a notice, which was out of time, claiming an extension of the shipment
period. The buyer, while objecting to the quantity of goods specified in the notice,
did not raise any point as to its being out of time. He continued to press for delivery
in the extended period and during it the seller made efforts to appropriate goods to
the contract. It was held that the buyer had waived the seller's breach in giving
notice out of time, so that the seller was entitled, in spite of the defect in the notice,
to rely on the force majeure clause[3323] and the buyer's claim for damages for non-
delivery failed. Such a result may also be explained on the grounds of estoppel or
promissory estoppel[3324]; indeed, in the context of abandonment of rights, the expressions "waiver" and "promissory estoppel" are now often used interchangeably[3325]
and have been described as "two ways of saying exactly the same thing".[3326] In
whatever way the rule may be described, a buyer is not prevented by it from relying on a defect in the notice merely because he fails to object to the notice on account of the defect when he first receives the notice[3327]; or merely because he calls
for proof of force majeure after receipt of the notice[3328]; or merely because, after
receipt of the notice, he accepts an appropriation of part of the quantity sold (which
the seller was allowed to export under an exception to the embargo).[3329] In none of
these cases is there any "unequivocal representation" by the buyer that he is treating the notice as valid and does not intend to rely on the defect in it; and even if
there is such a representation the argument that the defect in the notice has been
waived will still fail if the seller's alleged action in reliance consists of some act
(such as applying for an export licence) that he would have done anyway, even if
the representation had not been made.[3330]

³³²² *Bremer Handelsgesellschaft mbH v Vanden Avenne-Izegem PVBA* [1978] 2 Lloyd's Rep. 109; cf.
Intertradex SA v Lesieur-Torteaux SARL [1978] 2 Lloyd's Rep. 509; *Bremer Handelsgesellschaft mbH
v C Mackprang Jr* [1979] 1 Lloyd's Rep. 221.

³³²³ The case was described in *Glencore Grain Ltd v Flacker Shipping Ltd (The Happy Day)* [2002]
EWCA Civ 1068; [2002] 2 Lloyd's Rep. 487 at [64] as one of "waiver by election" (sc. of remedies)
but the description may, with respect, be doubted. The buyer in *Bremer Handelsgesellschaft mbH v
Vanden Avenne-Izegem PVBA* [1978] 2 Lloyd's Rep. 109 was seeking to enforce the contract of sale and
so could have had no interest in rescinding (as opposed to affirming) it. The issue was not whether he
had lost his right *to rescind* by election between remedies but whether he had abandoned his right *to
delivery* (or to damages for non-delivery).

3324 *Bremer Handelsgesellschaft mbH v Finagrain etc SA* [1981] 2 Lloyd's Rep. 259 at 263.

3325 See *Chitty on Contracts*, 33rd edn, Vol.1 para.4-105.

3326 *Prosper Homes v Hambro's Bank Executor and Trustee Co* (1979) 39 P. & C.R. 395 at 401. In *Glencore Grain Ltd v Flacker Shipper Ltd (The Happy Day)* [2002] EWCA Civ 1068; [2002] 2 Lloyd's Rep. 487 the two doctrines are described as "closely associated" (at [67]) but nevertheless distinct in that "waiver looks principally to the position and conduct of the person who is said to have waived his rights" while estoppel "looks chiefly at the position of the person relying on the estoppel" (at [64]). The guarded nature of the latter statement, however, shows that the distinction is far from clear-cut. Waiver in the sense of election between remedies is certainly distinct from estoppel in that such waiver requires no action in reliance by the person invoking it: see Treitel, *The Law of Contract*, 14th edn (Peel), para.18-087; but waiver in the sense of abandonment of a right does require such action in reliance: *Chitty on Contracts*, 33rd edn, para.4-094. Our present concern is with the latter kind of waiver.

3327 *V Berg & Sons Ltd v Vanden Avenne-Izegem PVBA* [1977] 1 Lloyd's Rep. 499; cf. *Bunge SA v Companie Euopéenne de Céréales* [1983] 1 Lloyd's Rep. 307, where the sellers' defence failed, not because of defects in the notice, but because he could not identify the "relevant shipper": above, para.18-398.

3328 *Bremer Handelsgesellschaft v Deutsche Conti-Handelsgesellschaft mbH* [1983] 1 Lloyd's Rep. 339.

3329 *Bremer Handelsgesellschaft mbH v Bunge Corp* [1983] 1 Lloyd's Rep. 476.

3330 *Bremer Handelsgesellschaft mbH v Bunge Corp* [1983] 1 Lloyd's Rep. 476.

C.I.F. CONTRACTS

1. Nature of a C.I.F. Contract

Importance of tender of documents

Replace the second paragraph with:

19-002   It follows from the statement that the seller performs his part of the bargain by tendering documents, that he is not obliged actually to deliver the goods at the agreed destination[9]; he is only under a negative duty not to prevent the goods from being delivered to the buyer at that destination, by (for example) diverting them elsewhere, or by ordering the carrier not to deliver them to the buyer.[10] If the contract does impose an affirmative obligation on the seller to deliver the goods at the agreed destination, or in respect of their discharge there,[11] it is not a c.i.f. contract, even though the letters "c.i.f." occur in the contract. The question whether a contract obliges the seller to deliver goods or only to tender documents depends on the construction of the contract as a whole. The presence or absence of the expression c.i.f. or its equivalent is not conclusive. Thus, on the one hand, it has been said that "Not every contract which is expressed to be a c.i.f. contract is such".[12] On the other hand, a contract for the sale of goods "*delivered* Harburgh, cost freight and insurance" has been held to be a c.i.f. contract, so that the seller's obligations were performed by tender of documents even though the goods did not arrive.[13]

[9] *Parker v Schuller* (1901) 17 T.L.R. 299; cf. *Bowden Bros & Co Ltd v Little* (1907) 4 C.L.R. 1364; as to deterioration in transit see above, paras 18-294 et seq.

[10] *Peter Cremer v Brinkers Groudstoffen NV* [1980] 2 Lloyd's Rep. 605; *Empresa Exportadora de Azucar v Industria Azucarera Nacional SA (The Playa Larga)* [1983] 2 Lloyd's Rep. 171; *Gatoil International Inc v Tradax Petroleum Ltd (The Rio Sun)* [1985] 1 Lloyd's Rep. 351; *Établissements Soules et Cie v Intertradex SA* [1991] 1 Lloyd's Rep. 379 at 386; *Birkett Sperling & Co v Engholm & Co* (1871) 10 M (Ct. of Sess.) 170 at 174; below, paras 19-008, 19-074.

[11] *Soon Hua Seng Co Ltd v Glencore Grain Ltd* [1996] 1 Lloyd's Rep. 398 at 401; *Y P Barley Ltd v E C Robertson Pty Ltd* [1927] V.L.R. 194 at 199–202, where the expression "c.i.f." was said at 200 to be "nothing more … than a provision as to price".

[12] *The Julia* [1949] A.C. 293 at 309; *Manbré Saccharine Co Ltd v Corn Products Co Ltd* [1919] 1 K.B. 198; *Gardano and Giampieri v Greek Petroleum Co* [1962] 1 W.L.R. 40; as to this case, see para.18-156 n.1463. See also *Euro-Asian Oil SA (formerly Euro-Asian Oil AG) v Abilo (UK) Ltd* [2018] EWCA Civ 1720; [2019] 1 Lloyd's Rep. 444, [46]. cf. *Scottish & Newcastle International Ltd v Othon Ghalanos Ltd* [2008] UKHL 11; [2008] 1 Lloyd's Rep. 462 where invoices referred to "delivery … cost and freight Limassol". In the Court of Appeal, Rix LJ had said ([2006] EWCA Civ 1750 at [9]) that "the contract differed very little from a form of F.O.B. contract although it was expressed to be CFR" (i.e. cost and freight, or c. & f.: see at [3]). Some of his later discussion (e.g. at [23]) is based on the assumption that the contract was a c. & f. contract; except in the respect discussed in para.21-012, below, such contracts are governed by the same rules as c.i.f. contracts. In the House of Lords, the contract in the *Scottish & Newcastle* case was classified as an f.o.b. contract: see [2008] UKHL 11; [2008] 1 Lloyd's Rep. 462 at [33] and [36] and below, paras 19-008 and 20-010. In *Euro-Asian Oil SA (formerly Euro-Asian Oil AG) v Abilo (UK) Ltd Euro-Asian Oil SA (formerly Euro-Asian Oil AG) v Credit Suisse AG* [2016] EWHC 3340 (Comm); [2017] 1 Lloyd's Rep. 287 the court had to interpret the effect of a cocktail of ingredients of a contract described as a CIF contract (general rules of law of CIF contracts, INCOTERMS 2000, the practice of the oil trade, express terms and the parties' intentions) but appeared to presume that description as a CIF contract was determinative unless clearly contradicted. The decision has been affirmed on this point on the ground that the buyer consistently intended that the contract should be performed as a conventional c.i.f. contract: [2018] EWCA Civ 1720; [2019] 1 Lloyd's Rep. 444.

[13] *Tregelles v Sewell* (1862) 7 H. & N. 574.

Provisions for tender of delivery order or other alternative document

Replace the third paragraph with:

19-003   As *The Julia* illustrates, it may be a difficult process to determine whether, even though parties adopt the familiar description c.i.f., particular practical arrangements and the employment of documents that vary from the simple model of a c.i.f. contract mean that the contract does not have the legal consequences of c.i.f. contract. In the *Euro-Asian Oil* case,[23] the seller under a "c.i.f." contract traded in a "carousel" of various shipments of oil that were delivered to a terminal at the port of destination which issued "holding certificates". The buyer contracted to pay, by means of an irrevocable documentary letter of credit, 120 days after the bill of lading date, against presentation of original documents, including a commercial invoice and a "full set 3/3 clean on board ocean bills of lading". In the event that the original shipping documents were not available when payment became due, the contract provided, conventionally, that payment was to be effected against presentation of the commercial invoice and seller's letter of indemnity. In fact, it was contemplated that, as an oil trader, the buyer would not take possession of the oil but would acquire constructive possession by receiving a holding certificate for oil held by the terminal, which could result in the buyer's receiving oil held by the terminal other than the oil that was the subject-matter of the contract. The evidence was that the practice in oil trading is that the bill of lading is not used at the time of presentation. Accordingly, it was held that presentation in that situation of a commercial invoice and a letter of indemnity in lieu of the shipping documents could not per se transform the contract into something other than a c.i.f. contract; nor did the contract's provision for deferred payment, which did not permit deferred presentation of documents. What preserved its character as a c.i.f. contract was that (curiously despite a term that title would pass from the seller to the buyer when the goods "passed the vessel's permanent hose connection at the loading port"[24]) passing of property was held to be dependent upon transfer of the agreed documents.[25] The trial judge's decision was affirmed on this point on the ground that he had held as a fact that, whatever the circumstances to enable performance in practice, there was no departure from the parties' intention that the contract should not be performed other than as a c.i.f. contract or that the buyer should not forgo the rights afforded to him by such a contract.[25a]

[23] *Euro-Asian Oil SA (formerly Euro-Asian Oil AG) v Abilo (UK) Ltd Euro-Asian Oil SA (formerly Euro-Asian Oil AG) v Credit Suisse AG* [2016] EWHC 3340 (Comm); [2017] 1 Lloyd's Rep. 287.

[24] It was said, without explanation, that "That clause cannot sensibly be given wide import": *Euro-Asian Oil SA (formerly Euro-Asian Oil AG) v Abilo (UK) Ltd Euro-Asian Oil SA (formerly Euro-Asian Oil AG) v Credit Suisse AG* [2016] EWHC 3340 (Comm); [2017] 1 Lloyd's Rep. 287 at [26].

[25] It was observed, somewhat elliptically, that the contract "did not intend that property pass: (1) only upon payment 120 days after the bill of lading date; or (2) upon a transfer of the bill of lading after discharge of the cargo at Constanza following a conforming tender of a letter of indemnity": *Euro-Asian Oil SA (formerly Euro-Asian Oil AG) v Abilo (UK) Ltd Euro-Asian Oil SA (formerly Euro-Asian Oil AG) v Credit Suisse AG* [2016] EWHC 3340 (Comm); [2017] 1 Lloyd's Rep. 287 at [24]. cf. *The Delfini* [1990] 1 Lloyd's Rep. 252; *Filiatra Legacy* [1991] 2 Lloyd's Rep. 337; *The Future Express* [1992] 2 Lloyd's Rep. 79 (on appeal [1993] 2 Lloyd's Rep. 542).

[25a] [2018] EWCA Civ 1720; [2019] 1 Lloyd's Rep. 444.

Provision for performance guarantee

Replace footnote 28 with:

[28] e.g. *Enichem Anic SpA v Ampelos Shipping Co Ltd (The Delfini)* [1990] 1 Lloyd's Rep. 252; *Euro-Asian Oil SA (formerly Euro-Asian Oil AG) v Abilo (UK) Ltd Euro-Asian Oil SA (formerly Euro-Asian Oil AG) v Credit Suisse AG* [2016] EWHC 3340 (Comm); [2017] 1 Lloyd's Rep. 287; varied [2018] EWCA Civ 1720; [2019] Lloyd's Rep. 444 (above, para.19-003).

19-005

2. DUTIES OF THE SELLER

(c) Tender of Documents

"String" contracts

Replace footnote 480 with:

19-068 ⁴⁸⁰ e.g. *Enichem Anic SpA v Ampelos Shipping Co Ltd (The Delfini)* [1990] 1 Lloyd's Rep. 252; *Euro-Asian Oil SA (formerly Euro-Asian Oil AG) v Abilo (UK) Ltd Euro-Asian Oil SA (formerly Euro-Asian Oil AG) v Credit Suisse AG* [2016] EWHC 3340 (Comm); [2017] 1 Lloyd's Rep. 287; varied [2018] EWC Civ 1720; [2019] 1 Lloyd's Rep. 444 (above, para.19-003).

3. DUTIES OF THE BUYER

(a) Payment of the Price

Duty to pay price on tender of documents

Replace footnote 523 with:

19-076 ⁵²³ e.g. *Enichem Anic SpA v Ampelos Shipping Co Ltd (The Delfini)* [1990] 1 Lloyd's Rep. 252; *Euro-Asian Oil SA (formerly Euro-Asian Oil AG) v Abilo (UK) Ltd Euro-Asian Oil SA (formerly Euro-Asian Oil AG) v Credit Suisse AG* [2016] EWHC 3340 (Comm); [2017] 1 Lloyd's Rep. 287; varied [2018] EWC Civ 1720; [2019] 1 Lloyd's Rep. 444 (above, para.19-003). See also *Newland Shipping and Forwarding Ltd v Toba Trading FZC* [2014] EWHC 661 (Comm) esp. at [25]–[33] (the lots argument).

Time of payment

Replace footnote 602 with:

19-086 ⁶⁰² Above, paras 19-070, 19-075. cf. *Euro-Asian Oil SA (formerly Euro-Asian Oil AG) v Abilo (UK) Ltd Euro-Asian Oil SA (formerly Euro-Asian Oil AG) v Credit Suisse AG* [2016] EWHC 3340 (Comm); [2017] 1 Lloyd's Rep. 287; varied [2018] EWC Civ 1720; [2019] 1 Lloyd's Rep. 444 (above, para.19-003).

Other payments to be made by buyer

Replace footnote 621 with:

19-089 ⁶²¹ *Fal Oil Co Ltd v Petronas Trading Corp (The Devon)* [2004] EWCA Civ 822; [2004] 2 Lloyd's Rep. 282 at [42]; in this case there was a difference of judicial opinion on the point. In *Profindo Pte Ltd v Abani Trading Pte Ltd (The MV Athens)* [2013] SGHC 10; [2013] 1 Lloyd's Rep. 370 the sellers claimed by way of demurrage no more than the amount actually paid by them (after negotiations) to the carrier. This was less than the amount which would have been due to the sellers if the formula set out in the contract of sale for calculating it had been applied. Judith Prakash J said at [31] that "it could have been argued that the demurrage clause in the … sale contract … was a free-standing provision of an independent contract unconnected with the contractual arrangements between the sellers and the shipowners …"; but as this issue had not been "properly ventilated" she awarded only the lower sum actually claimed by the sellers. See also *Glencore Energy UK Ltd v OMV Supply and Trading Ltd* [2018] EWHC 895 (Comm); [2018] 2 Lloyd's Rep 223.

5. PASSING OF PROPERTY

On shipment

Replace footnote 753 with:

19-100 ⁷⁵³ A dictum at first instance in *Anonima Petroli Italiani SpA v Marlucidez Armadora SA (The Filiatra Legacy)* [1990] 1 Lloyd's Rep. 354 at 358 refers to shipment as one possible point at which property passed under a c.i.f. contract, but on appeal property was evidently regarded as having passed at a later stage: see [1991] 2 Lloyd's Rep. 337 at 343. The latter view is, with respect, to be preferred since there was no indication that the seller had intended at the time of shipment to relinquish his right of disposal.

For the passing of property in this case, see above, para.18-270. In *Euro-Asian Oil SA (formerly Euro-Asian Oil AG) v Abilo (UK) Ltd Euro-Asian Oil SA (formerly Euro-Asian Oil AG) v Credit Suisse AG* [2016] EWHC 3340 (Comm); [2017] 1 Lloyd's Rep. 287, the contract provided that title would pass from the seller to the buyer when the goods "passed the vessel's permanent hose connection at the loading port" but it was held, without explanation, that "That clause cannot sensibly be given wide import": [26]. The judgment on this point was affirmed on the facts at [2018] EWCA Civ 1720; [2019] 1 Lloyd's Rep. 444.

On transfer of documents

Replace footnote 766 with:

19-103

[766] *Sanders Bros v Maclean & Co* (1883) 11 Q.B.D. 327 at 341; cf. *Karslhamns Oljefabriker v Eastport Navigation Corp (The Elafi)* [1981] 2 Lloyd's Rep. 679 at 686 ("upon the negotiation of the documents"). See also *Euro-Asian Oil SA (formerly Euro-Asian Oil AG) v Abilo (UK) Ltd Euro-Asian Oil SA (formerly Euro-Asian Oil AG) v Credit Suisse AG* [2016] EWHC 3340 (Comm); [2017] 1 Lloyd's Rep. 287; varied [2018] EWCA Civ 1720; [2019] 1 Lloyd's Rep. 444 (above, para.19-003).

On payment

Replace footnote 800 with:

19-104

[800] A provision for deferred payment does not prevent a contract from being a c.i.f. contract: *Euro-Asian Oil SA (formerly Euro-Asian Oil AG) v Abilo (UK) Ltd Euro-Asian Oil SA (formerly Euro-Asian Oil AG) v Credit Suisse AG* [2016] EWHC 3340 (Comm); [2017] 1 Lloyd's Rep. 287; varied [2018] EWCA Civ 1720; [2019] 1 Lloyd's Rep. 444.

8. REMEDIES OF THE BUYER

(a) Rejection

Ground of rejection must exist at time of rejection

Replace footnote 1232 with:

19-177

[1232] This possibility was discussed in the 9th edn of this book at paras 19-171 to 19-175. cf. *Classic Maritime Inc v Limbungan Makmur Sdn Bhd* [2019] EWCA Civ 1102; varying [2018] EWHC 2389 (Comm); [2019] 1 Lloyd's Rep. 349.

(b) Damages for Non-delivery

Is there a "market"?

At the end of the paragraph, after "it, too remote.", add:

If there is a market but the parties always contemplated that the contract cargo would be nominated to perform a sub-sale, the buyer's loss may properly be calculated by reference to the contemplated sub-sale rather than to the available market rule.[1346a]

19-193

[1346a] *Euro-Asian Oil SA (formerly Euro-Asian Oil AG) v Abilo (UK) Ltd* [2018] EWCA Civ 1720; [2019] 1 Lloyd's Rep. 444 ("Issue 2").

9. REMEDIES OF THE SELLER

(c) Action for Damages

Damages for non-acceptance: the market rule

Replace the second paragraph with:

The concept of a "market" for goods sold on c.i.f. terms is here, as in the case of a seller's breach,[1706] a somewhat restricted one: it has, for example, been held that

19-242

there was no "market" within subs.50(3) for manioc or tapioca to be shipped *to specified ports*[1707]; and there would similarly be no such market for goods shipped or to be shipped *on a named ship*. Where there is a market, and in particular where there are no publically available guidelines, the courts will adopt a flexible and comprehensive approach to consider the evidence indicating the market price for the goods in the circumstances.[1708] To ensure that it is properly compensated for the purposes of s.50(3), it is also necessary to take into account the hypothetical cost to the claimant of accessing the nearest available market.[1708a]

[1706] Above, para.19-193.

[1707] *Bem Dis A Turk Ticaret S/A TR v International Agri Trade Co (The Selda)* [1999] 1 Lloyd's Rep. 729 at 733.

[1708] *Glencore Energy UK Ltd v Cirrus Oil Services Ltd* [2014] EWHC 87 (Comm); [2014] 2 Lloyd's Rep. 1 (CFR contract). (The court in *Glencore v Cirrus* also held that the contract/market differential in s.50(3) took account of, but was not identical to, the seller's lost profit—see above, para.16-066; cf. *Somasteel SARL v Coresteel DMCC* [2015] EWHC 1234 (Comm) (CFR contract and Sale of Goods Act 1979 s.51(3)); above, para.19-194.)

[1708a] See *Gunvor SA v Sky Oil & Gas Ltd* [2018] EWHC 1189 (Comm), especially at [61].

Anticipatory breach

Replace footnote 1716 with:

19-243 [1716] *Vitol SA v Norelf Ltd (The Santa Clara)* [1996] A.C. 800. The case was treated in the lower courts as one of anticipatory breach but, except in quotations from the judgments of those courts, no reference to this aspect of the case was made in the House of Lords. The *Santa Clara* was applied in *Vitol SA v Beta Renewable Group SA* [2017] EWHC 1734 (Comm); [2017] 2 Lloyd's Rep 338 (need for unequivocal acceptance of repudiatory anticipatory breach of f.o.b. contract).

CHAPTER 20

F.O.B. CONTRACTS

1.   DEFINITION AND CLASSIFICATION

Definition

Replace footnote 2 with:

[2] *Stock v Inglis* (1884) 12 Q.B.D. 564 at 573; *J Raymond Wilson & Co Ltd v Norman Scatchard Ltd*   **20-001**
(1944) 77 Ll. L.R. 373 at 374. More broadly, it may be said that the contract involves carriage from one
place to another. See, e.g., *Trafigura Beheer BV v Renbrandt Ltd* [2017] EWHC 3100 (Comm); [2018]
2 Lloyd's Rep 437, where delivery was by way of ship-to-ship transfer.

2. DUTIES OF THE SELLER

In general

Replace paragraph with:

20-014   The duties of an f.o.b. seller are hard to state in general terms, for the obvious reason that they vary according to the type of f.o.b. contract in question. A further difficulty in discussing the duties of the seller results from the fact that shipment under an f.o.b. contract is in many respects a collaborative enterprise, involving co-operation between buyer and seller. It follows that there can be no neat separation between discussions of the duties of the two parties, so that, in discussing the duties of the seller reference necessarily has to be made to those of the buyer; and conversely. Subject to these difficulties it can, however, be said that the principal duties normally undertaken by an f.o.b. seller are to put goods which conform with the contract on board ship in accordance with the shipping instructions (if any) received from the buyer, and to bear the expense of doing so.[104] Additional duties may, of course, be undertaken by the contract.[105] As with contracts generally, a party to an f.o.b. contract may commit a repudiatory or renunciatory breach, entitling the other party to terminate performance of the contract. The nature of the relationship (with continuing duties by both parties) makes it particularly important to clarify whether a party alleging a repudiatory breach by the other party demonstrates an unequivocal intention to terminate. Thus, where a seller indicates that it will not deliver on time, the buyer's failure to nominate a vessel on time may not amount to termination, though a notice of termination should do so when that is given.[105a] It has been suggested, further, that, for an effective termination, there must be not only objective evidence of the innocent party's intention to terminate performance but a subjective belief that that is the case, by the party in breach[105b]; however, this view has not been accepted.[105c]

[104] *Henderson and Glass v Radmore & Co* (1922) 10 Ll. L.R. 727; *J Raymond Wilson & Co Ltd v Norman Scatchard Ltd* (1944) 77 Ll. L.R. 373 at 374.

[105] See above, para.20-007.

[105a] *Vitol SA v Beta Renowable Group SA* [2017] EWHC 1734 (Comm); [2017] 2 Lloyd's Rep 338.

[105b] *SK Shipping (S) Pd Ltd v Petroexport Ltd (The Pro Victor)* [2009] EWHC 2974 (Comm); [2010] 2 Lloyd's Rep 158, [90-97].

[105c] See *Vitol SA v Beta Renowable Group SA* [2017] EWHC 1734 (Comm); [2017] 2 Lloyd's Rep 338; ante, para 12-021 n 106.

3. DUTIES OF THE BUYER

(a) Shipping Instructions

Duty to give shipping instructions

After "damages for non-acceptance.", add:

20-047   However, a failure to nominate a loading vessel is not per se a repudiatory breach or an unequivocal acceptance of a repudiatory breach by the seller.[395a]

[395a] *Vitol SA v Beta Renowable Group SA* [2017] EWHC 1734 (Comm); [2017] 2 Lloyd's Rep 338.

Divided option as to time of shipment

Replace paragraph with:

20-055   The judgments in *Forrestt & Son Ltd v Aramayo* are based on the assumption that the case was one in which, in accordance with the normal rule, the seller was under no obligation to deliver unless the buyer first nominated an effective ship. But the contract in that case was for goods to be manufactured by the seller, who was not bound to deliver before the end of the shipment period. In such a case, it is submitted that the buyer is not bound to nominate a ship until he has been notified by the seller, within that period, that the goods are ready for shipment[457]; a term to this effect should be implied to give business efficacy to the contract, for unless this were done the buyer might be legally obliged to make a perfectly useless nomination. But this argument would not affect the actual decision; for even if the seller had been under an obligation to give notice of readiness to deliver within the shipment period, this obligation would have been waived, in respect of time, by the buyer's letter of 14 December.

In principle, whether a buyer's failure to nominate a vessel relieves the seller of his duties to tender delivery and to pay damages for not doing so is a question of construction of the contract. In *Vitol SA v Beta Renowable Group SA*,[457a] the buyer recovered damages where it had failed to nominate but was ready and willing to do so and the seller indicated that it could not deliver within the contract period.

[457] cf. above, para.20-040. It does not follow that the option as to the time of shipment is wholly the seller's as the buyer may have the whole rest of the shipment period to ship the goods, after notice that they are ready: above, para.20-054.

[457a] [2017] EWHC 1734 (Comm); [2017] 2 Lloyd's Rep 338, esp [52]–[60].

Substitution of a nominated ship

Replace footnote 461 with:

[461] In *JJ Cunningham Ltd v Robert A Munro & Co Ltd* (1922) 28 Com.Cas. 42 at 46 Lord Hewart CJ **20-056** said that it was "not exactly estoppel" and based it on a principle analogous to that in *Hughes v Metropolitan Ry* (1877) 2 App.Cas. 439, with the addition that the claimant must "suffer damage". Normally that principle would not in English law give rise to a cause of action but only to a defence: see *Chitty on Contracts*, 33rd edn, Vol.1 paras 4-100 to 4-101.

(b)   Payment of the Price

Payment

After "as an invoice,", add new footnote 481a:

[481a] See, e.g. *K v A (The Sea Commander)* [2019] EWHC 1118 (Comm).   **20-060**

8.   REMEDIES OF THE BUYER

(b)   Action for Damages

Damages for non-delivery: commercial sales

Replace footnote 916 with:

[916] cf. above, para.19-200. See also *Vitol SA v Beta Renowable Group SA* [2017] EWHC 1734 (Comm);   **20-122** [2017] 2 Lloyd's Rep 338, where the buyer's claim for actual loss suffered because of its use of hedging instruments was denied as not representing a fair or proper basis of compensation.

CHAPTER 21

OTHER SPECIAL TERMS AND PROVISIONS IN OVERSEAS SALES

3.   C. & F. CONTRACTS

Duties of the parties

Replace footnote 43 with:

[43] For use of the letters "cfr" to refer to this type of contract, see *Scottish & Newcastle International*   **21-012**
Ltd v Othon Ghalanos Ltd [2006] EWCA Civ 1750; [2007] 2 Lloyd's Rep. 341 at [3] ("cfr (or cost and
freight ...)"); affirmed [2008] UKHL 11; [2008] 1 Lloyd's Rep. 462, where the contract was classified
as an f.o.b. contract. For the usage, see also *Fortis Bank SA/NV v Indian Overseas Bank* [2011] EWHC
538 (Comm); [2011] 2 Lloyd's Rep. 190 at [2] ("CFR CY ...—viz Cost and Freight Container Yard");
Profindo Pte Ltd v Abani Trading Pte Ltd (The MV Athens) [2013] SGHC 10; [2013] 1 Lloyd's Rep.
370 at [1] (a "cost and freight (CFR) sale contract"); and [4] ("on a CFR (i.e. cost and freight) basis");
Carlos Soto SAU v AP Møller-Maersk AS (The SFL Hawk) [2015] EWHC 458 (Comm); [2015] 1
Lloyd's Rep. 537; and *Glencore Energy UK Ltd v Cirrus Oil Services Ltd* [2014] EWHC 87 (Comm);
[2014] 2 Lloyd's Rep. 1. See also *The Cape Elise* [2016] LOFA 12.09.16 (para.21-013 n.48). In
*Overseas-Chinese Banking Corp Ltd v Owner and/or Demise Charterer of the vessel Yue You 902 (The
Yue You 902)* [2019] SGHC 106 at [76], Pang Khang Chau JC explained that "'CNF' is the old abbrevia-
tion for 'cost & freight', now abbreviated as 'CFR' under the International Chamber of Commerce's rules
on the use of domestic and international trade terms ('Incoterms 2010')."

For the use of the letters "CPT" (carriage paid to) to refer to this type of contract, see *Newland Shipping and Forwarding Ltd v Toba Trading FZC* [2014] EWHC 661 (Comm) esp. at [9]; *Public Co Rise
v Nibulon SA* [2015] EWHC 684 (Comm); [2015] 2 Lloyd's Rep. 108 (where the carriage was ter-
restrial, to a transshipment terminal; and, it seems, not involving, but prior to, sea carriage).

4. EX SHIP AND ARRIVAL CONTRACTS

Stipulations as to arrival

Replace footnote 109 with:

21-023   [109] See *Mackay v Dick* (1881) 6 App.Cas. 251; *Chitty on Contracts*, 33rd edn, Vol.1 para.2-160.

7. CONVENTIONS ON INTERNATIONAL CARRIAGE OF GOODS

In general

Replace footnote 247 with:

21-049   [247] e.g. Scrutton, *Charterparties and Bills of Lading*, 23rd edn; *Carver on Bills of Lading*, 4th edn; Shawcross and Beaumont, *Air Law*, 4th edn; McNair, *Law of the Air*, 3rd edn; M. A. Clarke, *Contracts of Carriage by Air*, 2nd edn (2010); Kahn-Freund, *Law of Inland Transport*, 4th edn, pp.408-455; *Chitty on Contracts*, 33rd edn, Vol.1 Chs 35 and 36; Clarke, *International Carriage of Goods by Road: CMR*, 6th edn, (2014).

(b) International Carriage of Goods by Road

Consignment note

Replace footnote 335 with:

21-061   [335] Carriage of Goods by Road Act 1965 Sch. Art.4, which provides that the Convention can apply although no consignment note is issued: see *Gefco UK Ltd v Mason* [1998] 2 Lloyd's Rep. 585. The Additional Protocol to the Convention on the Contract for the International Carriage of Goods by Road (CMR) Concerning the Electronic Consignment Note 2008 (e-CMR) (to which the UK has not yet acceded) provides for the use of electronic consignment notes.

8. CONTAINER TRANSPORT

(b) Multimodal Transport Document

(i) Contractual Effects

Contracts (Rights of Third Parties) Act 1999

Replace footnote 520 with:

21-079   [520] *Port Line Ltd v Ben Line Steamers Ltd* [1958] Q.B. 146 at 166; and see generally *Chitty on Contracts*, 33rd edn, Vol.1 paras 18-023, 18-147 to 18-153.

(c) Liability of Carrier

(i) Package or Unit Limitation

Introduction

Replace footnote 627 with:

21-089   [627] In *Vinnlustodin HF v Sea Tank Shipping AS (The Aqasia)* [2016] EWHC 2514 (Comm); [2016] 2 Lloyd's Rep. 510, a case of a bulk cargo, which was part of a larger cargo but apparently carried in separate tanks, it was held that "package" in the Hague Rules Art.IV(5) did not did not apply to bulk or liquid cargo and that "unit" should be similarly construed, so that "unit" means a "physical unit", not a unit of measurement, and probably not a "freight unit", though if it could be a "freight unit" that would not help the defendant in the case, where "2,000 tons cargo of fishoil in bulk" was carried for a lump sum freight. However, the Hague-Visby Rules Art.IV(5)(a) has an alternative limitation for "units of account per kilogramme of gross weight". This decision has been affirmed sub nom *Sea Tank Shipping*

AS v Vinnlustodin HF (The Aqasia) [2018] EWCA Civ 276; [2018] 1 Lloyd's Rep. 530. The Court of Appeal acknowledged that parties were free to displace the meaning accorded to "unit" or "package" by incorporating in the charterparty some form of deeming provision giving Article IV.5 and "unit" a different meaning from what they would have had in the absence of the deeming provision: ibid, [97].

Hague Rules

At the end of the paragraph add:

The issue has recently been revisited in *Kyokuyo Co Ltd v AP Møller-Maersk* **21-090**
A/S.[651a] The relevant contract was held to be governed by the Hague-Visby Rules but, given that the position under the Hague Rules had been fully argued, the Court of Appeal expressed its view, albeit necessarily as obiter dicta. In its view, the word "unit" was capable of applying to frozen tuna loins that were stuffed into a container; and, for this purpose, it was not necessary for cargo owners to show that the tuna loins could have been shipped "as is" break bulk without being packaged in some way. In particular, such an interpretation was objectionable as seeking to revive the discredited "functional economics" test.

[651a] [2018] EWCA Civ 778; [2018] 2 Lloyd's Rep 59 ("Issue 2").

Hague-Visby Rules

At the end of the second paragraph add:

However, the approach in the Australian case has been disapproved in *Kyokuyo* **21-091**
Co Ltd v AP Møller-Maersk A/S.[663a] The contracts were governed by the Hague-Visby Rules, though bills of lading were not issued. As substitutes, sea waybills were issued in respect of three containers, each waybill referring to "1 Container Said to Contain [no] PCS FROZEN BLUEFIN TUNA LOINS", the number of individual frozen tuna loins being stated, respectively, as 206, 520 and 500. It was held that there was sufficient enumeration of the frozen tuna loins in the waybills that each loin was a separate "unit" for the purposes of Art.1V(c) and that it was neither necessary nor appropriate to add the gloss that the shipping document should specify how the packages and units were packed in the container.

[663a] [2018] EWCA Civ 778; [2018] 2 Lloyd's Rep 59 ("Issue 3").

PAYMENT IN INTERNATIONAL SALES

After Section 5 (Collections) and paragraph 22-060, add new section:

5A.   ELECTRONIC COLLECTIONS

1 July 2019 saw the advent of the eURC, a supplement to the URC designed to   **22-060A**
enable collections to function electronically. Just as the eURC has, therefore, to be
read in conjunction with the URC, so the discussion in this section must be read in
conjunction with that in the previous section.

(a)   Introduction

Role of the eURC   The official title of the eURC is the "Uniform Rules for Col-   **22-060B**
lections (URC 522) Supplement for Electronic Presentation ('eURC')". As this
indicates, the eURC is not a free-standing set of rules for collections. It serves
instead as an optional supplement to the URC to enable the latter to accommodate
a presentation entirely of electronic records or of a combination of electronic
records and paper documents.[197a] Its focus, therefore, is narrow: the structure of collections and principles of law and practice as articulated by the URC remain
unchanged. Instead, the eURC modifies definitions within the URC to permit
presentation of documents in the form of electronic records and addresses a number

[287]

of additional and consequential issues arising from electronic presentation. To distinguish the articles of the eURC from those of the URC, the numbers of the former are prefaced by an "e".

22-060C Applicability The eURC prescribes that it should apply only where the remitting bank on the one hand and the collecting or presenting bank on the other hand have previously entered into an agreement for the handling of collections involving electronic records, either exclusively or in combination with paper documents. This agreement should address the format in which each electronic record should be presented and the place for presentation to the collecting or presenting bank (meaning an electronic address of a data processing system).[197b]

The eURC applies only if specifically incorporated into the collection instruction. Since the eURC cannot function independently of the URC, incorporation of the eURC automatically renders the collection subject also to the URC.[197c] The converse does not apply: the eURC will not apply, and electronic presentation will not be available, unless the collection instruction indicates it is subject to the eURC.[197d] That an eURC collection will be subject to both the URC and the eURC raises the possibility of conflict between the two. In such a case, the eURC prevails.[197e]

22-060D Successive revisions The eURC introduced in 2019 has, of course, no predecessor and is denominated Version 1.0. Over time, revised versions will inevitably follow, raising the question of which version is applicable. This should be indicated by the collection instruction. If, however, the instruction is silent, the collection is subject to whichever version is in effect on the date of issuance of the collection instruction, or, if the credit is made subject to the eURC by an amendment, on "the date of that amendment".[197f]

(b) Electronic Instruments

22-060E Modified definitions Collections operate by reference to three key categories of instrument: the collection instruction, the documents that are to be presented under the collection, and various forms of advice of fate. The eURC modifies relevant provisions of the URC to expand each of these three concepts to embrace electronic versions. Accordingly, the term "collection instruction" includes "an instruction issuing from a data processing system",[197g] and a document or an advice can take the form of an "electronic record".[197h]

22-060F eURC collection instruction An eURC collection instruction should incorporate the eURC into the collection and must indicate the format of each electronic record, namely the method of organising the data either contained in or referred to by the electronic record, as stipulated in the precursor agreement between the participating banks.[197i]

22-060G Electronic records The term "electronic record" is defined by eURC Art.e4(b)(iii). The definition has three elements. First, the term is defined expansively to embrace "data created, generated, sent, communicated, received or stored by electronic means, including, where appropriate, all information logically associated with or otherwise linked together so as to become part of the record, whether generated contemporaneously or not". According to the ICC Banking Commission, this does not include a scanned version of a paper document or a fax where the fact of having been scanned or being a fax is apparent to an examiner.[197j] Secondly, the definition requires that the data can be authenticated as to three matters: the apparent identity of the sender, the apparent source of the data in the record, and whether the data has remained complete and unaltered. If such authentication is not possible, the data does not constitute an electronic record under the eURC, is not, therefore, a legitimate document under the collection, and, consequently, is deemed not to have been presented.[197k] Thirdly, the definition further requires that the data can be viewed to ensure that it represents the type and/or description of electronic record listed on the collection instruction.

(c)   Realisation of an eURC Collection

Responsibilities of banks in respect of documents   As discussed above, in the   **22-060H** context of a collection, the responsibilities of banks with respect to documents are limited to verifying whether the documents as presented to them appear on their face to be the documents as stipulated in the collection instruction. There is no obligation to examine the data content of the documents.[197l] With respect to electronic records, the required verification appears to include authentication with respect to the matters specified in the definition of that expression.[197m]

Availability of documents   Electronic records may be sent or simply rendered ac-   **22-060I** cessible at a specified electronic location, and either by the presenter or by a third party. A presentation under an eURC collection, whether entirely of electronic documents or of a mixture of paper and electronic documents, may therefore become available to a collecting or presenting bank at different times. Such a bank must check the presentation to verify that it contains the documents as stipulated in the collection instruction. It is therefore necessary to co-ordinate a presentation both temporally and by connecting the various documents to the same collection.

With respect to timing, receipt of the eURC collection instruction is the critical moment. All electronic records must be accessible to the collecting or presenting bank at the time it receives the eURC collection instruction, which, in the case of a mixed presentation, will itself be accompanied by the paper documents.[197n] It is at that time that it must be possible to effect the authentication specified in the definition of an electronic record, otherwise the record is deemed not to have been presented.[197o]

With respect to connection to the collection, the remitting bank must ensure that each presentation whether of one or more electronic records or one or more paper documents identifies the eURC collection instruction to which it relates. In relation to electronic records, this may be effected by specific reference in the record, in accessory metadata, or by the terms of the collection instruction itself. Absent such linkage, the relevant document, whether paper or electronic, may be treated as not received.[197p] Unlike the situation where it is not possible to authenticate an electronic record, the recipient bank has a discretion whether to request the presenter of the documents in question to identify the relevant collection, but any refusal so to request must be consistent with the banks' general duty of good faith under the URC.[197q]

Format of electronic records   The required format for an electronic record should   **22-060J** be stipulated, first, in the previous agreement between the participating banks[197r] and, secondly, in the eURC collection instruction.[197s] Any electronic record presented in connection with that instruction should therefore adopt that format. This is not, however, part of the definition of electronic record, so that a record presented in a different format can still qualify as an electronic record, and therefore as a legitimate document, under the eURC collection. Nevertheless, the collecting or presenting bank in receipt of an electronic record in a format not previously agreed is at liberty[197t] to treat the record as not received and notify the remitting bank.[197u]

22-060K **Corruption of documents** Corruption of an electronic record on receipt is likely to preclude either authentication or determination of whether it is the correct type of document. The corrupted record, therefore, will not qualify as an electronic record under the eURC and as a legitimate document under the URC. There will, accordingly, be a disparity between the documents as received and as listed in the collection instruction.[197v] Suppose, however, that an electronic record becomes corrupted after receipt. This is the electronic equivalent of losing a presented paper document.[197w] The URC is silent on this point. However, the eURC provides that the recipient remitting, collecting or presenting bank may inform the party from which it received the electronic record and request re-presentation. Should a collecting or presenting bank not receive a replacement electronic record within 30 calendar days, it may treat the electronic record as never having been presented and dispose of the remaining records in any manner considered appropriate and without any assumption of responsibility. Inherent in this provision, therefore, is an exclusion of liability for the record having become corrupted after receipt, however that occurred. The collecting or presenting bank is not obliged to act in this manner, but any alternative course of conduct should accord with its general duty of good faith.[197x]

(d) Dishonour

22-060L **Advice of fate** In the event of dishonour of the collection by non-payment or non-acceptance, a corresponding advice of fate should be given to the bank from which the collection instruction was received. In the absence of instructions from that bank within 60 days with respect to the disposition of paper documents, the URC provides that they may be returned to that bank without any further responsibility.[197y] The eURC provides that the absence of instructions within 60 days entitles disposition of electronic records in any manner considered appropriate with no assumption of liability.

[197a] eURC Art.e2(a).

[197b] eURC Arts e1, e4(a)(iv).

[197c] eURC Art.e3(a).

[197d] eURC Art.e2(b).

[197e] eURC Art.e3(b).

[197f] eURC Art.e2(c). It is unclear how this date is to be ascertained. A parallel cannot be drawn between a principal's request to amend a collection instruction and the offer of an amendment by a bank participating in a documentary credit (discussed below, para.23-075). It is obviously desirable that all parties to a collection should be subject to the same rules.

[197g] eURC Art.e4(a)(ii). "Data processing system" is itself broadly defined: Art.e4(b)(ii).

[197h] eURC Art.e4(a)(i), (iii).

[197i] eURC Arts e1(a), e2(b), e6.

[197j] *Unpublished Opinions* 1995–2994, R 596 (Ref.400).

[197k] eURC Art.e7(c). Authentication does not entail any assumption of liability for any of the matters mentioned in art.e4(b)(iii) "other than that which is apparent in the electronic record received by the use of a data processing system for the receipt, authentication, and identification of electronic records": Art.e12(a).

[197l] See above, para.22-042.

[197m] See above, para.22-060G

[197n] eURC Art.e7(a), (b).

[197o] eURC Art.e7(c).

[197p] eURC Art.e7(d). The text refers to "each presentation of an electronic record", but it is clear that the identification requirement attaches to a presentation as a whole and not separately to each and every electronic record or paper document included within the same presentation.

[197q] URC Art.9. See above, para.22-037. A developing case law, moreover, recognises that contractual discretions in principle must not be exercised capriciously or arbitrarily, but in a manner consistent with their purpose: e.g. *Braganza v BP Shipping Ltd (The British Unity)* [2015] UKSC 17; [2015] 1 W.L.R. 1661.

[197r] See above, para.22-060C

[197s] eURC Art.e6(a), (b)(i).

[197t] Although see the point about good faith in the preceding paragraph.

[197u] eURC Art.e6(b)(ii).

[197v] See above, para.22-042.

[197w] *Unpublished Opinions* 1995–2994, R 596 (Ref.400).

[197x] URC Art.9. See above, para.22-037.

[197y] On advice of fate and dishonour, see above, paras 22-048, 22-058.

CHAPTER 23

DOCUMENTARY CREDITS

[293]

2. THE UNIFORM CUSTOMS AND PRACTICE FOR DOCUMENTARY CREDITS

ICC guidance on interpretation

Replace footnote 10 with:

23-005 [10] The ICC has published a series of volumes of opinions. Four significant volumes (G. Collyer and R. Katz (eds)) are: *ICC Banking Commission, Collected Opinions 1995–2001* (2002, ICC Publication No.632)(*"Collected Opinions 1995–2001"*); *ICC Banking Commission, Unpublished Opinions 1995–2004* (2005, ICC Publication No.660)(*"Unpublished Opinions 1995–2004"*); *ICC Banking Commission, Opinions 2005–2008* (2009, ICC Publication No.697)(*"Opinions 2005–2008"*); *ICC Banking Commission, Opinions 2009–2011* (2012, ICC Publication No. 732E)(*"Opinions 2009–2011"*). Two further collections (G. Collyer (ed)) are: *ICC Banking Commission, Opinions 2012–2016* (2016, ICC Publication No.785E)(*"Opinions 2012–2016"*); *ICC Banking Commission, Opinions 2016* (2018, ICC Publication No. 799E)(*"Opinions 2016"*). The volumes include opinions on uniform rules relating not just to documentary credits but also to collections (discussed above in Ch.22) and to autonomous guarantees (discussed below in Ch.24).

Status and applicability of the UCP

Replace footnote 13 with:

23-006 [13] *Alaska Textile Co Inc v Chase Manhattan Bank NA*, 982 F.2d 813 at 816 (2nd Circuit, 1992); *Collected DOCDEX Decisions 2009–2012*, Decisions Nos 316, 317.

3. THE CONCEPT OF A DOCUMENTARY CREDIT

The issuing bank's undertaking

Replace the first paragraph with:

An issuing bank's undertakings under a credit, assuming always a presentation **23-018** of the stipulated documents in compliance with the terms and conditions of the credit, depend on the terms of the credit as to its availability. First, a credit is always available with the issuing bank,[70a] which, accordingly, incurs a primary obligation to honour, in accordance with the terms of the credit, by making payment at sight, or by incurring a deferred payment undertaking and duly paying on maturity, or by accepting a bill of exchange and paying on maturity.[71] An issuing bank does not promise to negotiate documents.[72]

[70a] A credit that states it is available with a nominated bank is also available with the issuing bank: UCP 600 Art.6(a).

[71] UCP 600 Art.7(a)(i).

[72] UCP 600 Art.7(a). See also Art.2 (definitions of "credit", "honour", and "confirmation").

Replace the second paragraph with:

Secondly, where the credit provides that it is available with a nominated bank in any of the four ways described in the preceding paragraphs and the nominated bank, despite a complying presentation, fails to honour or negotiate in accordance with the terms and conditions of the credit, the issuing bank incurs a default obligation to honour.[73] This obligation of the issuing bank to the beneficiary arises irrespective of whether the failure constitutes a breach of contract, where the nominated bank is a confirming bank, or a lawful refusal to perform, in the case of any non-confirming nominated bank.[74] The issuing bank selects and appoints the nominated bank and, as against the beneficiary, takes the consequences of that bank's acts or omissions.[75] The UCP does not, however, specify the form of honour involved. Subject to contrary intention, it may be inferred that where the credit is available by honour the form of default obligation will mirror the form of payment by which the credit is available with the nominated bank. However, if the credit is available with the nominated bank by negotiation and the nominated bank fails to negotiate, the issuing bank, which does not negotiate, must still honour. In such a case, by inference from the obligation undertaken by a confirming bank that promises to negotiate,[76] it is suggested that the issuing bank must honour by sight payment.

[73] UCP 600 Art.7(a)(ii)–(v).

[74] *Grains & Industrial Products Trading Pte Ltd v Bank of India* [2016] SGCA 32; [2016] 3 S.L.R. 1308 at [50], [55(a)], [56].

[75] *Grains & Industrial Products Trading Pte Ltd v Bank of India* [2016] SGCA 32; [2016] 3 S.L.R. 1308 at [57], [64].

[76] See below, para.23-020.

Confirmation: the obligations engendered

At the start of the second paragraph, after "The", replace "primary undertaking of a confirming bank mirrors that of an issuing bank. In the event of a complying presentation to the confirming bank or any other nominated bank, Art.8(a)(i) provides that a confirming bank must" with:

undertakings of a confirming bank mirror, to a considerable extent those of an **23-020** issuing bank. First, in accordance with Art.8(a)(i), where the credit provides that it is available with the confirming bank, that bank incurs a primary obligation to

At the start of the third paragraph, replace "A confirming bank also" with:
Secondly, the confirming bank

Credits as "bank" instruments

After "an issuing bank.", add:

23-025   Where, therefore, a credit subject to the UCP is issued or confirmed by a non-bank, references in the UCP to a bank must be read as including the non-bank party to the credit, so that the non-bank issuer or confirmer is held to the same obligations and standards as if it were a bank.[113a]

[113a] *Opinions 2016*, R 873.

6.   TWO FUNDAMENTAL PRINCIPLES: IRREVOCABILITY AND AUTONOMY

(a)   The Irrevocability of Documentary Credits

Time at which credits and amendments binding on the banks

Replace the fourth paragraph with:

23-073   It is suggested, therefore, that issuing and confirming banks are bound from the moment that the advice communicating the issuing or confirming of a credit or of any amendment is sent or transmitted by the relevant bank. As a matter of legal analysis, at that point the bank is bound by an irrevocable unilateral offer. There is no need for communication to or acceptance by the beneficiary. Nor is there any requirement for the beneficiary to provide consideration in return for the banks' promises, which would be impossible prior to receipt of the relevant advice.[245] This of course is incompatible with the principles of orthodox contract law, but documentary credits constitute a sui generis exception to such principles, based on internationally recognised mercantile usage.[246] It is inconceivable that an English court would defy this accepted international commercial practice on the strength of an argument based on domestic rules of contract formation, even if pleaded by the liquidator of an insolvent bank.[246a]

[245] In *Urquhart Lindsay & Co Ltd v Eastern Bank Ltd* [1922] 1 K.B. 318, Rowlatt J suggested that the beneficiary provided consideration by performing the underlying contract in response to notification of the credit. However, this would mean that the bank was free to revoke its undertaking at any point before such acts, which is clearly contrary to commercial understanding. An argument of absence of consideration was initially advanced but withdrawn in *Dexters Ltd v Schenker & Co* (1923) 12 Ll. L.R. 586. Greer J considered that consideration lay in the perfecting of the seller's liability to perform obligations on the underlying contract to which the opening of the credit was a condition precedent. Such analysis fails, however, to explain the binding nature of a proposed amendment to a credit. The better view is that the doctrine of consideration simply has no place in the context of an international banking instrument governed by universally applied international soft law rules.

[246] *Bank of Nova Scotia v Angelica Whitewear Ltd* (1987) 36 D.L.R. (4th) 161 at 176; *Alaska Textile Co Inc v Chase Manhattan Bank NA*, 982 F.2d 813 at 816 (2nd Circuit, 1992); *Taurus Petroleum Ltd v State Oil Co of the Ministry of Oil, Republic of Iraq* [2015] EWCA Civ 835; [2016] 1 Lloyd's Rep. 42 at [61].

[246a] See *Taurus Petroleum Ltd v State Oil Marketing Company of the Ministry of Oil, Republic of Iraq* [2015] EWCA Civ 835; [2016] 1 Lloyd's Rep. 42 at [13]; [2017] UKSC 64; [2017] 3 W.L.R. 1170 at [25] ("loath to hold, particularly in a commercial context, that a promise which both parties intended should be relied on was unenforceable for want of consideration" per Moore-Bick LJ, approved by Lord Clarke).

(b)　The Autonomy of Documentary Credits

Freezing orders

Replace footnote 268 with:

268 *Intraco Ltd v Notis Shipping Corp of Liberia (The Bhoja Trader)* [1981] 2 Lloyd's Rep. 256; *Z Ltd*　**23-080**
v A–Z & AA–LL [1982] Q.B. 558 at 574; *Czarnikow-Rionda Sugar Trading Inc v Standard Bank London
Ltd* [1999] 2 Lloyd's Rep. 187 at 203. The availability of a freezing order was common ground in *Britten Norman Ltd v State Ownership Fund of Romania* [2000] Lloyd's Rep. Bank. 315. The critical distinction between a freezing order and an injunction preventing payment or, on the facts, preventing the beneficiary from calling for payment appears to have been overlooked in *Sunderland Association
Football Club v Uruguay Montevideo FC* [2001] 2 All ER (Comm) 828 (ex parte interim injunction
discharged for failure to prove fraud although balance of convenience satisfied by inadequacy of assets
within the jurisdiction).

7.　Time and Place of Presentation

Contractual presentation requirement

Replace footnote 311 with:

311 *Alternative Power Solutions Ltd v Central Electricity Board* [2014] UKPC 31; [2015] 1 W.L.R. 697　**23-092**
at [9] (within 15 days of shipment); *Euro-Asian Oil SA v Credit Suisse AG* [2018] EWCA Civ 1720
("documents presented more than 21 days from bill of lading date but within documentary credit validity acceptable").

Presentation to a bank other than the issuing or nominated bank

After "with the UCP.", add:

The presenting bank, moreover, does not become the beneficiary and has no　**23-095**
rights under the UCP, but only pursuant to its agreement with the beneficiary.322a

322a *Opinions 2016*, R 868.

9.　Compliance: General Principles

(d)　Of Presentations Generally

Non-original documents

Replace the first paragraph with:

The ICC Banking Commission Decision provided, by way of example, that a　**23-118**
document does not qualify as an original:

"... if it (i) appears to be produced on a telefax machine; (ii) appears to be a photocopy
of another document which has not otherwise been completed by hand marking the
photocopy or by photocopying on what appears to be original stationary; or (iii) states in
the document that it is a true copy of another document or that another document is the
sole original."

A copy does not need to be signed or dated,436a unless the credit explicitly states to
the contrary.

436a ISBP 2013 para.A31(b); *Opinions 2016*, R 881.

Replace the second paragraph with:

A requirement for presentation of a copy will be satisfied by presentation of either
an original or a copy,437 unless the credit expressly prohibits presentation of an

original.[438] It may be noted that a credit that permits presentation of any document by telefax waives the originality requirement in respect of that document.[439]

[437] UCP 600 Art.17(d); ISBP 2013 para.A29(d)(iii), (iv). Likewise where the credit calls for a duplicate, so that a requirement for a document "in original and duplicate" will be satisfied by either two originals (and see ISBP 2013 para.A28: that a document is marked "duplicate" does not prevent it from constituting an original) or one original and one copy, and a requirement for a document "in duplicate" will be satisfied by two originals, one original and one copy, or two copies: *Opinions 2012–2016*, R 841.

[438] ISBP 2013 para.A30(a). A credit that requires presentation of a copy of a transport document and contains a disposal instruction for all originals is considered to prohibit presentation of an original: ISBP 2013 para.A30(b).

[439] *ICC Banking Commission Decision*, Pt 3 "Telefaxed Presentation of Documents".

(e)   Compliance of Documentary Data (1): Compliance with the Credit

Error in the credit

At the start of the second paragraph, replace "A" with:

23-127   It is, furthermore, arguable that, a

After the second paragraph, add new paragraph:

No such concession to the beneficiary is recognised, however, by American case law. On the contrary, "the beneficiary must inspect the letter of credit and is responsible for any negligent failure to discover that the credit does not achieve the desired commercial ends",[489a] a principle that reflects the beneficiary's ability to assess whether the credit as issued meets the requirements of the underlying contract and, if not, to request appropriate amendments. A beneficiary that overlooks this opportunity takes the consequences and forfeits all rights to recourse arising out of the erroneous terms of the credit to which the beneficiary should and could have objected.[489b]

[489a] *Mutual Export Corp v Westpac Banking Corp*, 983 F.2d 420 at 423 per Oakes CJ (2nd Circuit, 1993).

[489b] *Mutual Export Corp v Westpac Banking Corp*, 983 F.2d 420 at 423, 426 (2nd Circuit, 1993) (incorrect termination date); *Hanil Bank v Pt Bank Negara Indonesia (Persero)*, 2000 U.S. Dist. LEXIS 2444 (S.D.N.Y., 2000) (beneficiary's name rendered as "Sung Jin Electronics Co Ltd" instead of its correct name of "Sung Jun Electronics Co Ltd").

(g)   Compliance of Documentary Data (3): To Be Disregarded

Typographical errors

After the first paragraph, add new paragraph:

23-131   The conclusion that a minor disparity should not be considered as generating a conflict of data may be assisted by the compliance of other data in the document. Where an invoice contained the correct letter of credit number, and the description, quantity and unit price of the goods in accordance with the terms of the credit, the insertion of an additional numeral in an otherwise correct eight-digit contract number constituted a typographical error and did not render the invoice discrepant.[521a]

[521a] *Opinions 2016*, R 871.

(h) Description

Correspondence

Replace footnote 551 with:

[551] ISBP 2013 para.C8. See also *Collected Opinions 1995–2001*, R 237 (Ref.222), R 362 (Ref.226). **23-137**
There is, however, flexibility as to where in the invoice it is stated: *Opinions 2016*, R 884; *Collected DOCDEX Decisions 2013–2016*, Decision No.337.

Additional wording

After "than those described.", add:

In contrast, where the credit described the goods as "Steering Gear Poseidon 900- **23-138**
35", the Banking Commission considered that adding the phrase "spare parts" would not generate a discrepancy as not indicating a difference in nature, classification or category of goods.[560a]

[560a] *Opinions 2016*, R 875.

(j) Particular Aspects of Documents

Issuer of documents

After "the Inspectorate Group.", add:

Indeed, provided the document appears to have been issued by the issuer speci- **23-144**
fied in the credit, that the document features the letterhead of another party does not render it non-compliant.[585a]

[585a] *Opinions 2016*, R 867.

After paragraph 23-148, add new paragraph 23-148A:

Designated spaces for data   Merely because a document contains a box, field or **23-148A**
space designated for the insertion of specified data does not, of itself, require such data to be to be inserted in that space or indeed recorded in the document at all.[615a] A signature box, for example, need not be completed with a signature.[615b] It follows that there is no discrepancy where the signature of a party signing a document is required to indicate the capacity of the signatory, the signature box contains the signature, but the capacity in which the document is being signed is stated elsewhere in the document.[615c]

[615a] ISBP 2013 para.A17.

[615b] ISBP 2013 para.A37.

[615c] *Opinions 2016*, R 877. On signature and capacity, see below, para.23-165.

10. Compliance: Specific Documents

(b) Transport Documents

(i) General Provisions Relating to Transport Documents

Requirement for a clean transport document

Replace footnote 672 with:

23-160   672 A clause stating "vessel under arrest" does not speak to the condition of the goods or their packaging and does not render a bill of lading unclean: *Opinions 2012–2016*, R 839. A container does not constitute packaging for the purposes of art.27: *Opinions 2016*, R 878.

(ii) Multimodal Transport Documents

Identity of carrier and signature

Replace footnote 702 with:

23-165   702 UCP 600 Art.19(a)(i); ISBP 2013 para.D5. And see *Abani Trading Pte Ltd v BNP Paribas* [2014] SGHC 111; [2014] 3 S.L.R. 909 at [33]–[34] (signature as agent for carrier identified elsewhere held compliant under credit pre-dating ISBP 2013, referring to *Opinions 2009–2011*, R 734, which is now reflected in ISBP 2013). That signature requirements need not be inserted in a signature box or other designated space for signature but may be present elsewhere in the document, see above, para.23-148A.

(iii) Bills of Lading

Shipment and discharge

After the fourth paragraph, add new paragraph:

23-171   It follows from the requirement in art.20(a)(iii) that the bill of lading evidence shipment from the port of loading that where the bill of lading indicates pre-carriage at the port of loading on a feeder vessel to an ocean going vessel, the bill must attest to shipment in the latter vessel. Where the bill provides the date of shipment on board the feeder vessel, a dated on-board notation in relation to the ocean going vessel will be required.724a

724a *Opinions 2016*, R 876.

After the sixth paragraph, add new paragraph:

If a city or other location of the port of loading or discharge contains more than one port, it suffices for the bill of lading to designate the port by referring to the city or location unless the credit clearly requires greater specificity.728a

728a *Opinions 2016*, R 880.

Transhipment

Replace paragraph with:

23-172   With respect to transhipment, Art.20 adopts the same permissive approach as Art.19. First, transhipment is defined by Art.20(b) as meaning:

"… unloading from one vessel and reloading to another vessel during the carriage from the port of loading to the port of discharge stated in the credit."

Transhipment from a feeder vessel to an ocean-going vessel at the port of loading stated in the credit, or from the ocean-going vessel to a further conveyance at the port of discharge stated in the credit, does not constitute transhipment for the purposes of Art.20(b).[731] Secondly, under Art.20(c)(i) a clause indicating that the goods will or may be transhipped is acceptable provided that the entire carriage is covered by a single bill of lading. Thirdly, Art.20(c)(ii) provides that such a clause is acceptable even if the credit prohibits transhipment if the bill evidences shipment in a container, trailer or LASH barge. Effectively prohibiting transhipment where the bill evidences such shipment requires express exclusion of Art.20(c)(ii) by the terms of the credit.[732] Fourthly, Art.20(d) states that a clause reserving the right to tranship shall be disregarded, so that a prohibition in a credit on transhipment is not infringed by such a clause on the basis that, as noted above in the context of Art.19,[733] reserving a right to do something is not to be equated with doing it. The bill will be acceptable provided it does not evidence that transhipment will indeed occur.[733a]

[731] See also ISBP 2013 para.E17.

[732] See the comment on Art.19(c)(ii), above, para.23-169.

[733] See above, para.23-169.

[733a] For the same position at common law, see *Soproma SpA v Marine & Animal By-Products Corp* [1966] 1 Lloyd's Rep. 367 at 388–389.

(vi) Air Transport Documents

Air transport documents

Replace footnote 752 with:

[752] UCP 600 Art.23(a)(iii); ISBP 2013 para.H8; *Opinions 2012–2016*, R 859; *Opinions 2016*, R 882.   **23-178**

(d) Drafts

Maturity

Replace the first paragraph with:

The tenor of the draft must accord with the terms of the credit.[811] If the credit calls   **23-192** for a draft available "at sight", a draft that states simply "sight" will be compliant.[811a] If the draft is drawn at a tenor other than sight or a specified period after sight, the maturity date must be ascertainable from the data stated in the draft itself.[812] A tenor of a specified period after the date of the bill of lading (or other transport document) is calculated by reference to the on-board date, not the date of issuance of the bill of lading.[813] Where the bill of lading shows more than one on-board notation at ports of loading within the terms of the credit, the maturity date is calculated by reference to the earliest on-board notation where the multiple notations arise from transhipment,[814] and the latest where they arise from multiple shipments in different ports of parts of the overall consignment of goods.[815] Where more than one set of bills of lading is presented under one draft, the maturity date is calculated from the date of the last bill of lading.[816]

[811] ISBP 2013 para.B2(a).

[811a] *Opinions 2016*, R 867.

[812] ISBP 2013 para.B2(b). For guidance on ways of indicating a tenor of a certain number of days after the bill of lading date, see further para.B2(b).

[813] ISBP 2013 para.B2(c).

814 ISBP 2013 para.B2(e)(i).

815 ISBP 2013 para.B2(e)(ii).

816 ISBP 2013 para.B2(e)(iii).

12. DETERMINATION THAT PRESENTATION IS NON-COMPLIANT

(a) Consultation of the Applicant

The liberty to consult

Replace footnote 863 with:

23-204   863 Expert evidence to this effect tendered in *Bankers Trust Co v State Bank of India* [1991] 2 Lloyd's Rep. 443 is corroborated by an empirical survey in the US in which discrepancies were found in 73% of presentations sampled and waiver was forthcoming in every case (subject to slight deduction in one case): R. Mann, (2000) 98 Mich. L. Rev. 2494. For an example of notification of discrepancy followed by waiver and taking of documents by the applicant, see *Carlos Soto SAU v AP Møller-Maersk AS* [2015] EWHC 458 (Comm); [2015] 1 Lloyd's Rep. 537 at [13].

(c) Preclusion

Failure to handle documents in accordance with the notice of refusal

Replace footnote 943 with:

23-225   943 *Fortis Bank SA/NV v Indian Overseas Bank (Nos 1 & 2)* [2011] EWCA Civ 58; [2011] 1 C.L.C. 276 at [36]–[45]; *Opinions 2016*, R 873. Consequently, the change in wording between UCP 500 Art.14(e), which expressly applied preclusion to a failure to act in accordance with a refusal notice and UCP 600 Art.16(f), which contains no such statement, is of no import. For preclusion following a failure to handle documents in accordance with a refusal notice under UCP 500, see, e.g. *Unpublished Opinions 1995–2004*, R 546 (Ref.350) (preclusion under UCP 500 followed when issuing bank rejected documents, stating they were held at the presenter's disposal, but then released three of them to the applicant); *Bayerische Vereinsbank Aktiensgesellschaft v National Bank of Pakistan* [1997] 1 Lloyd's Rep. 59 at 70.

(d) In the Aftermath of a Refusal

Re-presentation of documents

Replace the third paragraph with:

23-231   Submitting a re-presentation revised to take account of discrepancies asserted by a presentee bank in its refusal notice does not, however, import a waiver of the right to dispute the correctness of the bank's determination of non-compliance, and still less does a request to the refusing bank to seek a waiver of discrepancies or to forward the documents to the issuing bank to seek acceptance.957

957 *Opinions 2016*, R 871; *Collected DOCDEX Decisions 2009–2012*, Decision No.310. On requesting waiver or forwarding, see below, paras 23-233, 23-235.

Remittance of documents pursuant to collateral agreement

Replace footnote 968 with:

23-233   968 *Harlow and Jones Ltd v American Express Bank Ltd* [1990] 2 Lloyd's Rep. 343 at 348; *Unpublished Opinions 1995–2004*, R 547 (Ref.351). This was stated expressly in UCP 500 Art.14(f). It was omitted from UCP 600 purely on the basis that it addressed a contract between nominated bank and beneficiary falling outside the credit, rather than because its provisions were no longer considered appropriate: G. Collyer, *Commentary on UCP 600* (2007, ICC Publication No.680), p.74. The presentation is sometimes said to be forwarded "on a collection basis" or "for collection". Such expressions are unlikely to invoke the collection instrument discussed in the previous chapter, but indicate rather that the issuing bank is being requested to seek a waiver from the applicant under Art.16(b): *Alaska Textile Co Inc v Chase*

Manhattan Bank NA , 982 F.2d 813 at 818-820 (2nd Circuit, 1992); *United Bank Ltd v Banque Nationale de Paris* [1992] 2 S.L.R. 64 at 76; *Unpublished Opinions 1995–2004*, R 537 (Ref.342).

13.   ELECTRONIC LETTERS OF CREDIT: THE eUCP

Replace paragraph with:
Technological development in the field of international trade finance has **23-238** presented challenges of adaptation for documentary credits. The process has not been smooth, notably in the context of original documents. Adopted in its original version in 2001, the eUCP is designed as a supplement to the UCP to permit the latter to function in relation to an entirely or partially electronic credit. This accommodation of electronic records is, however, limited to the UCP. Other legal norms applicable to any stipulated document may fail to accommodate such dematerialisation, a significant practical problem that may inhibit use of electronic credits.

(a)   Introduction

Role of the eUCP

After "the eUCPis the", replace ""Supplement to the Uniform Customs and Practice for Documentary Credits" with:
"Uniform Customs and Practice for Documentary Credits (UCP 600) Supple- **23-239** ment

Successive revisions

Replace paragraph with:
The original eUCP (Version 1.0) was adopted in 2001. The advent of UCP 600 **23-241** heralded the slightly revised Version 1.1. This was succeeded in turn as from 1 July 2019 by Version 2.0. The question may arise, therefore, as to which version is applicable. This should be indicated by the credit. If, however, the credit is silent, Art.e1(c) provides that the credit is subject to whichever version is in effect on the date of issuance of the credit, or, if the credit is made subject to eUCP by an amendment, on "the date of that amendment".[986]

[986] This is presumably a reference to the date when the amendment is issued and becomes binding on the issuing bank: as to which, see above, para.23-075.

After subsection (a) (Introduction) and paragraph 23-241, add new sub-section:

(a1)   Opening an eUCP Credit

Physical location   An electronic credit may naturally operate entirely in **23-241A** cyberspace, but regulatory and sanctions issues require the participating banks to be geographically located in the physical world. An eUCP credit must, therefore, state the physical location of the issuing bank and of any nominated bank if known to the issuing bank at the time of issuance of the credit. If not already stated in the credit, moreover, the location of any advising bank, confirming bank, or non-confirming nominated bank must be indicated to the beneficiary no later than the time of advising or confirming the credit, or agreeing to act on its nomination.[987]

[987] eUCP Art.e1(d).

(b)   Realisation of an eUCP Credit

23-242   *Change title of paragraph:*

What must be presented: electronic records

Replace paragraph with:
The traditional documentary credit requires the presentation of paper documents. Incorporation of the eUCP means that the term "document" in the UCP is read as including an "electronic record",[988] the definition of which in Art.e3(b)(iii) has three elements. First, the term is defined expansively to embrace "data created, generated, sent, communicated, received or stored by electronic means, including, where appropriate, all information logically associated with or otherwise linked together so as to become part of the record, whether generated contemporaneously or not". According to the ICC Banking Commission, this does not include a scanned version of a paper document or a fax where the fact of having been scanned or being a fax is apparent to an examiner.[989] Secondly, the definition requires that the data can be authenticated as to three matters: the apparent identity of the sender, the apparent source of the data in the record, and whether the data has remained complete and unaltered.[990] If such authentication is not possible, the data does not constitute an electronic record under the eUCP, is not, therefore, a legitimate document under the credit, and, consequently, is deemed not to have been presented.[991] Thirdly, the definition further requires that the data is "capable of being examined" to determine whether the presentation is compliant.Where, therefore, data corruption prevents examination to determine compliance, the presented data does not constitute an electronic record within the meaning of the eUCP, and therefore is not a document for the purposes of meeting the requirements of the UCP.

[988]   eUCP Art.e3(a)(ii).

[989]   *Unpublished Opinions* 1995–2994, R 596 (Ref.400).

[990]   eUCP Art.3(b)(i).

[991]   eUCP Art.e6(f). Authentication does not entail any assumption of liability for any of the matters mentioned in Art.e3(b)(i) "other than that which is apparent in the electronic record received by the use of a data processing system for the receipt, authentication, and identification of electronic records": Art.e13(a).

A nominated bank that forwards electronic records, irrespective of whether the bank is acting on its nomination and therefore even if the bank has not examined the documents to determine compliance, thereby signifies that it has satisfied itself as to the records' apparent authenticity: Art.e7(d)(i). Consequently, an issuing or confirming bank to which the records have been forwarded that is unable to authenticate them from their original source can rely on authentication by the nominated bank.

After this, add new paragraph:
Any requirement for an electronic record to be signed is satisfied by an electronic signature.[992-996]

[992-996]   eUCP Art.e3(a)(v).

23-243   *Delete paragraph "Records on external systems".*

Originals and copies

Replace footnote 998 with:

23-244   [998] eUCP Art.e9.

Paper and/or electronic presentation

At the end of the paragraph, after "to that presentation.*", add:

If a credit incorporates the eUCP but permits presentation of paper documents **23-245** only, the credit will be governed by the UCP.[999a]

[999a] Ibid. eUCP is inapplicable to paper documents, leaving the UCP whether incorporated expressly or derivatively by virtue of Art.e2(a).

Place of presentation

Replace paragraph with:

The key to payment under a traditional documentary credit is, of course, presenta- **23-246** tion of the stipulated paper documents at a permissible place and time. With respect to place of presentation, the documents must be presented at a bank at which the credit states it is available.[1000] The eUCP requires the credit to state a place of presentation of electronic records, provides that for electronic records the place of presentation means an electronic address of a data processing system, and further provides that this place may differ for paper documents and electronic records in the case of a credit calling for, or permitting, a combination of the two.[1001] Moreover, should a credit require electronic records to be presented on a physical storage device, a physical address will again be required.

[1000] UCP 600 Art.6(a), (d)(ii).

[1001] eUCP Arts e3(a)(iii), e5(a).

After this, add new paragraph:

As discussed above, a credit may involve obligations being assumed to the beneficiary by not only the issuing bank but also a confirming bank and contemplate the possibility of a credit being honoured by a non-confirming nominated bank.[1001a] The possibility of presentation to any one of a number of banks, or to a second bank under a default obligation, requires references to "a" place of presentation of electronic records to be understood as a separate place for each bank assuming an obligation or agreeing to act on its nomination.[1001b]

[1001a] See above, paras 23-018, 23-020, 23-023.

[1001b] Likewise the concept of "received", as defined in eUCP Art.e3(b)(vii).

Time of presentation

Replace paragraph with:

The documents must be presented before the credit ceases to be available. The **23-247** UCP provides that this is the close of business on the earlier of the expiry date and the last date for presentation after the date of issuance of a transport document.[1002] In case of bank closure on the last date for presentation other than for reason of force majeure, the UCP provides for the extension of the last date for presentation until the first following banking day when the bank is open.[1003] The eUCP applies the same approach to the situation where a bank is open on the last date for presentation, but its systems are unable to receive a transmitted electronic record. In such a case, the last date is extended to the first following banking day on which the bank's systems have been restored to enable it to receive an electronic record.[1003a] As in the case of paper presentations, a confirming or non-confirming nominated bank that honours the credit on such an extension day must so state on its covering schedule when seeking reimbursement from the confirming or issuing bank.[1003b]

[1002] UCP 600 Arts 33, 6(d)(i), (e), 14(c); discussed above, paras 23-088 to 23-093. With respect to electronic records as transport documents, the date of shipment or dispatch of the goods is deemed, in the absence of contrary indication, to be the date of issuance of the electronic record or, as the case may be, the date of a notation in the record evidencing shipment or dispatch: Art.e11. In the latter case, it is the date of the notation rather than any date contained in the data content of the notation that counts. An electronic record must provide evidence of its date of issuance: Art.e10.

[1003] UCP 600 Art.29(a). See above, para.23-093.

[1003a] eUCP Art.e6(e)(i).

[1003b] eUCP Art.e6(e)(ii). For discussion under the UCP, see below, paras 23-261 to 23-264.

Presentation in parts

Replace paragraph with:

23-248   As already discussed, UCP 600 in practice encourages a single act of presentation of stipulated documents.[1004] eUCP, however, adopts a different approach. First, Art.e6(b) provides that "electronic records may be presented separately and need not be presented at the same time". Consequently, where the stipulated records will be created by different issuers, the beneficiary can arrange for the issuers to send the records directly to the issuing or nominated bank to which it intends to make the presentation. Secondly, in order to facilitate the collation of independent presentations, Art.e6(d) requires that each presentation of one or more electronic records identifies the eUCP credit under which it is presented[1004a] and provides by way of sanction that any presentation lacking such identification "may be treated as not received". This wording is not as strong as that attaching under UCP 600 to non-stipulated documents, which "will be disregarded",[1005] but the potential for refusal of the overall presentation for want of a stipulated document remains.

[1004] See above, para.23-103.

[1004a] Art.e6(d) refers to "each presentation of an electronic record" but it is clear that the identification requirement attaches to a presentation as a whole and not separately to each and every electronic record included within the same presentation. Earlier versions of eUCP applied this identification requirement also to presentations of paper documents (Version 1.1, Art.e5(d)(i)). This has been removed under Version 2.0. This is consistent with the demise of a general requirement of linkage under the UCP: see above, para.23-130.

[1005] UCP 600 Art.14(g).

Notice of completeness of presentation

Replace the first paragraph with:

23-249   The prospect of electronic records arriving at different times from one another and/or on different days from the moment of presentation of any stipulated paper documents raises the question of from precisely which day time runs for the recipient bank to examine and, if appropriate, refuse the presentation. Consequently, Art.e6(c) provides that, whenever a credit permits presentation of one or more electronic records (and not only when stipulated documents are presented separately), presentation is deemed not to be made until the bank receives a notice from the "presenter" signifying that the presentation is complete. Such notice of completeness may itself be either electronic or in paper and must identify the eUCP credit to which it relates. It follows that the day of receipt of the notice of completeness constitutes the "day of presentation" for the purposes of the examination and refusal rules.[1006] For these purposes, an electronic record is received when it enters the information system of the recipient in a form capable of being accepted by that system. The risk of incompatibility preventing acceptance by the intended recipient's system is, therefore, carried by the presenter.

[1006] eUCP Art.7(a)(i).

After the first paragraph, add new paragraph:
The term "presenter" is defined as meaning "the beneficiary, or any party acting on behalf of the beneficiary who makes a presentation to a nominated bank, confirming bank, if any, or to the issuing bank directly."[1006a] The requirement of a notice of completeness does not, therefore, apply to the forwarding of documents by a bank that has honoured or negotiated in connection with a claim for reimbursement from another bank participating in the credit. Where, however, a presentation is rejected but the rejecting bank is persuaded to forward the documents to the issuing bank on a collection basis, the forwarding bank is acting on behalf of the beneficiary in presenting the documents directly to the issuing bank and a notice of completeness is required.

[1006a] eUCP Art.e3(a)(iv).

In the (former) second paragraph, after "is extended under", replace "Art.e5(e) and the only outstanding electronic record is the notice of completeness, Art.e5(e)" with:
Art.e6(e) and the only outstanding electronic record is the notice of completeness, Art.e6(e)

Time for examination

Replace paragraph with:
Under UCP 600, the period available to a bank for examining a presentation is **23-250** "five banking days following the day of presentation".[1007] This applies whether the presentation is made on or before the original last date for presentation or, pursuant to UCP 600 Art.29(a), on an extended last date for presentation in cases of closure (other than by reason of force majeure as indicated by Art.36) of the bank to which presentation is made on the original last date. Under eUCP, the same approach is adopted where the notice of completeness is received on or before the original last date for presentation: Art.e7(a)(i) provides that the period for examination "commences on the banking day following the day" of receipt of the notice. Where presentation is made on an extended last date for presentation, there is only one day when presentation can be made before time expires. In such a case, Art.e7(a)(ii) accordingly provides that:

> "... the time for the examination of documents commences on the next banking day following the day on which the bank to which presentation is to be made is able to receive the notice of completeness, at the place for presentation."

[1007] UCP 600 Art.14(b). See above, para.23-100.

Replace title of paragraph: **23-251**

Format of electronic records

Replace paragraph with:
The "format" of an electronic record refers to the way data is organised in the record, including in external sources incorporated into the record.[1008] A particular

data processing system will not be able to access each and every format in which an electronic record may be presented. To address the possibility of incompatibility between the format of a presented electronic record and the data processing system of a participating bank, the eUCP first dictates that an eUCP credit "must" indicate the required format for each electronic record.[1009] A bank that issues or confirms an eUCP credit with a stipulated format is then not permitted to claim an inability to examine a presented electronic record adopting that format.[1010] The record must nevertheless still be "capable of being examined for compliance"[1011]; consequently, a record with the correct format but in which data was corrupted before presentation so that compliance could not be determined would not constitute an electronic record as defined by eUCP, resulting in the presentation lacking a stipulated document.

[1008] eUCP Art.e3(b)(v).

[1009] eUCP Art.e5.

[1010] eUCP Art.e7(c).

[1011] eUCP Art.e3(b)(iii).

After this, add new paragraph:

If an eUCP credit fails to specify the required format, an electronic record may be presented in any format[1012] and, again, an issuing or confirming bank would not be permitted to assert an inability to examine the record on the basis of its format.[1013] The bank would be considered as having assumed the risk of incompatibility between the format of the presented record and its own data processing system. The normal period for examination of presented documents and giving a timely notice of refusal would apply, within which the bank would need to find a means of accessing the data content of the electronic record or prove that the record was not capable of examination by reason, for example, of data corruption, and duly give the requisite refusal notice, or otherwise incur preclusion from alleging non-compliance.

[1012] eUCP Art.e5.

[1013] eUCP Art.e7(c).

After paragraph 23-251, add new paragraph 23-251A:

23-251A Records on external systems An electronic record may contain a hyperlink to an external system or a presentation may incorporate an electronic record on an external system. In which case, the record at the hyperlink or on the external system constitutes an integral part of the presentation to be examined to determine compliance. Should the external system fail to afford access to the examining bank at the time of examination, the presentation will be discrepant.[1013a] By way of exception, however, where a nominated bank examines records that include data on external systems and makes a determination of compliance, an inability or the part of a confirming or issuing bank to which the records are forwarded to access an external system to check the data for itself does not constitute a ground for refusal.[1013b]

[1013a] eUCP Art.e7(b).

[1013b] eUCP Art.e7(d)(ii).

Corruption of documents

Replace the first paragraph with:

If an electronic record is corrupted when presented so that it cannot be examined **23-252** for compliance, it will not qualify as a legitimate electronic record under eUCP,[1014] and because it will not be capable of authentication it will be deemed not to have been presented.[1015] Indeed, it is likely that the bank's systems would prevent receipt of such a record. A stipulated document will, therefore, be absent and the bank will have to proceed on the basis of a non-compliant presentation. Suppose, however, that an electronic record becomes corrupted after receipt. This is the electronic equivalent of losing a presented paper document.[1016-1017] The UCP is silent on this point. However, Art.e12(a) provides that an examining bank that determines that an electronic record appears to have been corrupted after receipt may, if it so elects, inform the presenter and request re-presentation of the relevant electronic record. Assuming that a bank adopts this option, Art.e12(b) then addresses the consequences.

[1014] eUCP Art.e3(b)(iii).

[1015] eUCP Art.e6(f).

[1016-1017] *Unpublished Opinions 1995–2994*, R 596 (Ref.400).

At the start of the second paragraph, after "First,", replace "Art.e11(b)(i)" with:
Art.e12(b)(i)

Replace the third paragraph with:

Secondly, where re-presentation is requested by a non-confirming nominated bank, Art.e12(b)(ii) provides that such a bank "must provide any confirming bank and the issuing bank with notice of the request for the electronic record to be re-presented and inform it of the suspension". This is similar to the requirement in cases of extension of the last permitted day for presentation under Art.29(a) placed on a nominated bank under UCP 600 Art.29(b) to provide a statement on its covering schedule that the presentation was made under such an extension of the presentation time limits. Two points may be made in comparison. First, Art.e12(b) is clear that the requirement of a re-presentation notice is confined to a nominated bank that is not the confirming bank, while Art.29(b) would appear to apply to all nominated banks, including the confirming bank when remitting documents to the issuing bank. Secondly, it is suggested below that the provision of such an extension statement constitutes a contingent condition precedent to the nominated bank's entitlement to reimbursement,[1018] and there is no reason why the requirement for a re-presentation notice under Art.e12(b) should not enjoy the same status.

[1018] See below, paras 23-260 to 23-264.

Replace the fourth paragraph with:

Thirdly, Art.e12(b)(iii) provides that in the event of failure to comply with the request for re-presentation within 30 calendar days, and, in any event, no later than the last permitted date for presentation under the credit, the bank may treat the electronic record as not presented, in which case the presentation will fall to be treated as non-compliant. The language of para.(iii) is however permissive, so that a bank could still accept a later re-presentation. Ultimately, however, the risk of post-presentation corruption of electronic records lies with the presenter, not the recipient bank in whose systems the record has become corrupted.

Delete the fifth paragraph.

(c)   Discrepant Documents

Retention of refused documents

Replace paragraph with:

23-253   Banking transactions that fail sometimes leave banks holding documents in which they have no interest. Under the Uniform Rules for Collections, a bank that has given advice of fate indicating dishonour is required to hold the documents pending further instructions for a period of 60 days, after which it is free to return them to the party from which it received them.[1019] Under the UCP, a bank that refuses a presentation must indicate what it will do with the documents from the range of options offered by the UCP. This includes holding the documents pending further instructions from the presenter.[1020] Assuming that option is chosen, however, for how long must the bank then retain the documents in the absence of further instructions? UCP 500 provides no answer to this. UCP 600 Art.16(e) does provide an answer: the bank may return the documents to the presenter at any time. eUCP Art.e8 also provides an answer but a different one: the bank must retain the electronic records and any paper documents for 30 calendar days from the date the notice of refusal is given. In the absence of any instructions from the presenter, the bank is required to return any paper documents to the presenter and has the option of disposing of the electronic records in any manner the bank considers appropriate and without any responsibility. In the context of a credit incorporating UCP 600 and eUCP, Art.e7(b) will prevail[1021] unless the credit affords the presenter the option of presenting only paper documents and the presenter takes that option.[1022]

[1019] *Uniform Rules for Collections* (URC 522) Art.26(c)(iii). See above, para.22-058. Likewise under eURC: above, para.22-060L

[1020] UCP 500 Art.14(d)(ii) ("at the disposal of ... the presenter"); UCP 600 Art.16(c)(iii)(a).

[1021] eUCP Art.e2(b).

[1022] eUCP Art.e2(c).

15.   REIMBURSEMENT OF A NOMINATED BANK

(a)   The Entitlement to Reimbursement

Forwarding of documents and bills of exchange

Replace footnote 1061 with:

23-267   [1061] It is, accordingly, suggested that contrary dicta in *Société Générale SA v Saad Trading* [2011] EWHC 2424 (Comm); [2011] 2 C.L.C. 629 are incorrect. On a bill of exchange as a financial instrument and not a document, see also *Opinions 2016*, R 883.

Additional requirements

Replace the first paragraph with:

23-268   The UCP confers an entitlement to reimbursement where the nominated bank has paid against a complying presentation and forwarded the documents. The credit, however, can clearly impose additional conditions precedent to an entitlement to reimbursement. No difficulty arises where the requirement comprises a simple statement of matters within the knowledge of the nominated bank.[1061a] Otherwise, the commercial context may militates against such characterization, rendering pertinent the reasoning of Mance J in *Bayersiche Vereinsbank*, discussed above.[1062]

[1061a] *Opinions 2016*, R 869.
[1062] See above, para.23-263.

CHAPTER 24

AUTONOMOUS GUARANTEES

1. INTRODUCTION: ORTHODOX AND AUTONOMOUS GUARANTEES

Orthodox v autonomous guarantees

In the first paragraph, after "discharges the guarantee.", add new footnote 5a:

5a *Holme v Brunskill* (1878) 3 Q.B.D. 495 (although many guarantees contain an "indulgence clause" **24-003**
contracting out of this principle).

Whether autonomous or secondary guarantee

In the first paragraph, after "the underlying contract.", add:

Commonly, again, the guarantee will contain an undertaking to pay on demand **24-005**
any amount certified by the beneficiary as due in consequence of breach of the
underlying contract. Such certification clearly denotes autonomy; arguments that
such a clause precludes disputes only about quantum while leaving open the possibility of disputing liability have been firmly rejected.[13a]

13a *Dobbs v National Bank of Australasia Ltd* (1935) 53 C.L.R. 643 at 651; *Bitumen Invest AS v
Richmond Mercantile Ltd FZC* [2016] EWHC 2957 (Comm); [2017] 1 Lloyd's Rep. 219 at [22]-[27]
(especially in combination with a no set-off clause).

At the end of the third paragraph, after "an autonomous undertaking.", add:

Inevitably, therefore, everything depends on the precise wording of the
instrument. A "guarantee" given by the chairman and managing director of the
primary debtor undertaking "unconditionally and irrevocably" to pay on the "first
written demand ... a sum equivalent to" the original primary indebtedness, in turn

quantified as a specific sum, and to do so without contesting or defending any enforcement proceedings constituted an autonomous guarantee giving rise to a primary liability, which was consequently unaffected by partial repayment by the primary debtor.[25a]

[25a] *Ultrabulk A/S v Jagatramka* [2017] EWHC 2792 (Comm); [2018] 1 Lloyd's Rep. 384 at [16].

Replace the fourth paragraph with:

Sixthly, effect will be given to a conclusive evidence clause, whereby presentation of a demand that complies with the terms of the instrument is conclusive evidence of the fact that the liability that the guarantee is designed to secure has indeed been incurred on the underlying transaction.[26] Such a clause may either reinforce autonomy or render autonomous an instrument that is otherwise an orthodox secondary guarantee. It has been held to rebut the presumption against a non-bank guarantee being an autonomous instrument.[27] It is in no way undermined by a requirement that the demand must specify the facts allegedly giving rise to the relevant liability.[28] In the light, however, of the potentially dramatic impact of such clauses, they are construed strictly and any ambiguity is resolved in favour of the guarantor (and therefore in favour of characterisation of the instrument as an orthodox guarantee).[28a] In particular, courts will enquire closely to see whether the evidence to which the clause speaks is conclusive evidence of the existence of liability (so that the guarantee functions as an autonomous instrument) or merely of the quantum of liability in the event that liability is proved (consistent with the guarantee being orthodox in character).[29] To similar effect is a clause requiring payment against certification, in whatever form specified in the guarantee, by the beneficiary of an amount due under the guarantee, such clause dispensing with the need to establish the guaranteed liability on the facts.[29a]

[26] *Bache & Co (London) Ltd v Banque Vernes et Commerciale de Paris SA* [1973] 2 Lloyd's Rep. 437; *Harbottle (RD) (Mercantile) Ltd v National Westminster Bank Ltd* [1978] 1 Q.B. 146 at 156.

[27] *IIG Capital LLC v Van Der Merwe* [2008] EWCA Civ 542; [2008] 2 Lloyd's Rep. 187 at [32].

[28] *Rainy Sky SA v Kookmin Bank* [2009] EWHC 2624 (Comm); [2010] 1 All E.R. (Comm) 823.

[28a] *Bache & Co (London) Ltd v Banque Vernes et Commerciale de Paris SA* [1973] 2 Lloyd's Rep. 437 at 440; *Carey Value Added SL v Grupo Urvasco SA* [2010] EWHC 1905 (Comm); [2011] 2 All E.R. (Comm) 140 at [41]; *North Shore Ventures Ltd v Anstead Holdings Inc* [2011] EWCA Civ 230; [2012] Ch 31 at [46]; *Autoridad del Canal de Panama v Sacyr SA* [2017] EWHC 2228 (Comm); [2017] 2 Lloyd's Rep. 351 at [81(6)].

[29] *Vossloh Aktiengesellschaft v Alpha Trains (UK) Ltd* [2010] EWHC 2443 (Ch); [2011] 2 All E.R. (Comm) 307 at [50]–[51]; *Autoridad del Canal de Panama v Sacyr SA* [2017] EWHC 2228 (Comm); [2017] 2 Lloyd's Rep. 351 at [100(3)].

[29a] *Bitumen Invest AS v Richmond Mercantile Ltd FZC* [2016] EWHC 2957 (Comm) at [27].

5. TWO FUNDAMENTAL PRINCIPLES: IRREVOCABILITY AND AUTONOMY

(b) **Autonomy**

24-024 *Change title of paragraph:*

Meaning of fraud

Replace the first paragraph with:

A claim under a letter of credit is fraudulent where it amounts to deceit on the part of the beneficiary, namely where the beneficiary does not or cannot honestly believe in the validity of the claim.[87] Although not the subject of decision, it is probable that fraud carries the same meaning as in the tort of deceit and therefore embraces not only intentional falsehood but also recklessness in the sense of subjective awareness of a real possibility of falsehood.[87a] A strict distinction must however be drawn between fraud and any allegation that the beneficiary ought to have known of the falsehood, which, however compellingly formulated, amounts to no more than negligence and does not constitute fraud. A beneficiary that presents documents does not thereby impliedly represent that it has reasonable grounds for believing in the genuineness of the documents presented.[87b]

[87] *GKN Contractors Ltd v Lloyd's Bank Plc* (1985) 30 B.L.R. 48 at 63; *Consolidated Oil Ltd v American Express Bank Ltd* [2002] C.L.C. 488 at 495.

[87a] *Derry v Peek* (1889) L.R. 14 App. Cas. 337.

[87b] *DBS Bank Ltd v Carrier Singapore* [2008] SGHC 53; [2008] 3 S.L.R. 261 at [99].

Replace the second paragraph with:

In the context of a documentary credit, fraud connotes the absence of an honest belief in the genuineness and validity of the documents tendered or in the truthfulness of the statements made in those documents. In the context of an autonomous guarantee, fraud connotes the absence of an honest belief in either the entitlement to claim under the guarantee or in the amount claimed. A mistaken belief in the legitimacy of the claim is not fraud.[88]

[88] *AES-3C Maritza East 1 EOOD v Crédit Agricole Corporate and Investment Bank* [2011] EWHC 123 (TCC); [2011] B.L.R. 249 at [48].

After paragraph 24-024, add new paragraph 24-024A:

Fraud requires dishonesty of the beneficiary   The autonomy principle insulates   24-024A
the beneficiary's rights under the credit from the underlying reality; the fraud exception pierces that insulation to the beneficiary's detriment, and therefore the exception requires the dishonesty of the beneficiary itself.[89] It follows that where a document prepared by a third party conforms on its face to the terms of the credit, the beneficiary cannot be denied payment on the ground that, unknown to the beneficiary at the time of presentation, the document was fraudulently issued. The documentary integrity of the credit, which focuses upon the appearance of the presented documents on their face at the time of their presentation, is not denied to a beneficiary by virtue of the beneficiary's being a victim of fraud.[90] It follows likewise that the documentary integrity of a letter of credit is not overridden by the status as a total nullity of a presented document that appears on its face to comply with the credit. The beneficiary is not prejudiced by the fact that the third party fraud extends beyond the creation of a document that contains a fraudulent misstatement to the total forgery of a required document, nor by the fact that the nullity is the unwitting result of an act of the beneficiary itself.[91] Of course, a beneficiary that presents as genuine and truthful a document that, at the time of presentation, the beneficiary knows contains one or more fraudulent statements or knows to be a forgery will itself commit fraud even where the beneficiary is not itself responsible for the original making of the statements or creation of the document but is instead an innocent purchaser of documents from a third party that may be responsible for the fraud or forgery or that may itself be the victim of a fraud perpetrated by a more remote party.[91a]

[89] *GKN Contractors Ltd v Lloyd's Bank Plc* (1985) 30 B.L.R. 48 at 65.

[90] *United City Merchants (Investments) Ltd v Royal Bank of Canada* [1983] A.C. 168 at 187; *Bank of Nova Scotia v Angelica-Whitewear Ltd* (1987) 36 D.L.R. (4th) 161 at 177; *Korea Industry Co Ltd v*

Andoll Ltd [1990] 2 Lloyd's Rep. 183 at 189. This would also appear to cover the situation of the original beneficiary under a transferred credit where the transferee tenders a document it knows to be fraudulent that the original beneficiary unknowingly uses to claim the balance of the credit. On transferable credits generally, see above, paras 23-313 et seq.

[91] *Montrod Ltd v Grundkötter Fleischvertriebs GmbH* [2001] EWCA Civ 1954; [2002] 1 W.L.R. 1975 (applicant's certificate signed and presented by the beneficiary under mistaken belief that it had the applicant's authority to sign held to be a compliant document). For the possibility that a beneficiary might be prejudiced by an innocent but recklessly careless involvement in the creation of a fraudulent document rendering the beneficiary culpable in facilitating, albeit not complicit in, the fraud of another, see *Montrod* at [59].

[91a] *Lambias (Importers & Exporters) Co Pte Ltd v Hong Kong & Shanghai Banking Corp* [1993] 2 S.L.R. 751 at [67]; *Montrod Ltd v Grundkötter Fleischvertriebs GmbH* [2001] EWCA Civ 1954; [2002] 1 W.L.R. 1975 at [43]. See also *Group Josi Re v Walbrook Insurance Co Ltd* [1996] 1 W.L.R. 1152 at 1161 per Staughten LJ: "It is the time of presentation that is crucial" (albeit by way of disregarding knowledge gained by the beneficiary after the time of presentation).

Enjoining a beneficiary from claiming or receiving payment

Replace the quotation with:

24-034   "The effect on the lifeblood of commerce will be precisely the same whether the bank is restrained from paying or the beneficiary is restrained from asking for payment."

Fraud in the transaction

After "a freezing order,", add new footnote 145a:

24-035   [145a] See above, para.23-080.

Unconscionability as the basis for enjoining the beneficiary under an autonomous guarantee

Replace footnote 170 with:

24-038   [170] For an extended defence of a controlled use of unconscionability, see *BS Mount Sophia Pte Ltd v Join-Aim Pte Ltd* [2012] SGCA 28; [2012] 3 S.L.R. 352. An unconscionability exception to autonomy has been rejected in Malaysia: *Esso Petroleum Malaysia Inc v Kago Petroleum Sdn Bhd* [1996] 1 M.L.J. 149; *LEC Contractors (M) Sdn Bhd v Castle Inn Sdn Bhd* [2000] 3 A.M.R. 2625; *Nam Fatt Corp Bhd v Petrodar Operating Co Ltd* [2011] 7 M.L.J. 305. An argument that English law should develop an unconscionability defence in the context of autonomous guarantees was rejected with respect to first instance hearings: *National Infrastructure Development Co Ltd v Banco Santander SA* [2016] EWHC 2990 (Comm) at [26]-[27] (and leave to appeal on the point was refused by the Court of Appeal).

8.   Compliance

Compliance at common law

After the third paragraph, add new paragraph:

24-056   In *Crystal Handy C SA v Woori Bank*,[216a] a refund guarantee covering advance payments made to a shipbuilding company by the customer (the beneficiary) operated as an on demand guarantee unless the company furnished the guarantor with notification and written confirmation that the beneficiary's request for refund was disputed and had been referred to arbitration, in which case the beneficiary was entitled only to such sum as was awarded in the arbitration proceedings once the award was finalised. In proceedings brought by the beneficiary against the guarantor seeking payment under the guarantee, the guarantor sought summary judgment on the basis that the company had instituted the deferral mechanism by providing the requisite notification and confirmation and instituting arbitration proceedings. Summary judgment was, however, refused: the beneficiary had a real prospect of successfully arguing that the company had not properly instituted the deferral mechanism. First, it was arguable whether the company had capacity under the relevant law to institute arbitration proceedings, as it was in insolvency at the time. Secondly, the customer had been introduced to the transaction by novation, but the notice of intention to arbitrate named the original customer as the defendant, precluding any arbitration award being made against the customer. Thirdly, the notice failed to identify the issue to be arbitrated, contrary to the terms of the refund guarantee or contractual arbitration clause. Fourthly, in so far as defects in the notice or confirmation might be rectified by reading the two documents together, such document handling was precluded by the terms of the guarantee which required two separate documents.

216a [2018] EWHC 1991 (Comm).

After paragraph 24-056 add new paragraph 24-056A:

Conclusive evidence clauses and manifest error   A conclusive evidence clause   **24-056A**
in an autonomous guarantee may provide for a certificate stating an amount due and owing under the guarantee to be conclusive of that fact subject only to "manifest error". An error will be manifest if "obvious or easily demonstrable without extensive investigation",[217a] may be established by reference to evidence extrinsic to the document containing it,[217b] and need not be manifest at the time of issuing of the certificate.[217c] The manifest error exception does not require an absence of any dispute as to the correct interpretation of the provisions of the guarantee relied on by the guarantor in identifying a manifest error.[217d]

217a *IIG Capital LLC v Van der Merwe* [2007] EWHC 2631 (Ch) at [52] per Lewison J; affd [2008] 2 All E..R (Comm) 1185 at [35].

217b *Axa Sun Life Services Plc v Campbell Martin Ltd* [2011] EWCA Civ 133; [2011] 2 Lloyd's Rep. 1 at [72]; *IG Index v Colley* [2013] EWHC 748 (QB) at [813]-[814].

217c *North Shore Ventures Ltd v Anstead Holdings Inc* [2011] EWCA Civ 230; [2012] Ch. 31 at [53].

217d *North Shore Ventures Ltd v Anstead Holdings Inc* [2011] EWCA Civ 230; [2012] Ch. 31 at [61].

9.   THE DEMAND FOR PAYMENT

"Extend or pay" demand

After the fourth paragraph, add new paragraph:
   UCP 600, being intended for payment credits rather than autonomous guarantees,   **24-074**
does not contemplate an extend or pay demand. In the absence of an express contractual regime for such a demand, it will be handled as a demand for payment.

10.   CONSEQUENCES OF A DETERMINATION OF COMPLIANCE

Inadequate payment

Replace footnote 288 with:

288 *Comdel Commodites Ltd v Siporex Trade SA* [1997] 1 Lloyd's Rep. 424 at 431; *Pun Serge v Joy Head*   **24-079**
Investments Ltd [2010] SGHC 182; [2010] 4 S.L.R. 478; *Fluor v Shanghai Zhenhua Heavy Industry Co Ltd* [2018] EWHC 490 (TCC) at [40]–[41].

EXPORT CREDIT GUARANTEES

1. INTRODUCTION

Objects

Replace footnote 1 with:

[1] See Z. Salcic, *Export Credit Insurance and Guarantees: A Practitioner's Guide*; M. Stephens, *The Changing Role of Export Credit Agencies*; D.E. Gianturco, *Export credit agencies: the unsung giants of international trade and finance*; OECD, *Smart Rules for Fair Trade: 50 years of Export Credits* (2011: OECD Publishing, Paris), *https://doi.org/10.1787/9789264111745-en*.   **25-001**

Insurance and guarantee providers

Replace footnote 7 with:

[7] The OECD maintains a list of (some) official ECA websites on: *https://www.oecd.org/trade/topics/export-credits/documents/links-of-official-export-credit-agencies.pdf* [Accessed 23 July 2019]. The ECAs also provide: (i) "investment insurance" covering investment overseas against political risks; and (ii) "project finance" (or "limited recourse finance") financing major projects on the basis of the income they are expected to generate. These will be noted below (see para.25-046), although this chapter will focus on support for the export of goods.   **25-003**

2. EXPORT AND INVESTMENT GUARANTEES ACT 1991

Powers of UK Export Finance

Replace footnote 19 with:

[19] See *British American Tobacco Co v IRC* [1943] A.C. 339 at 340 per Simon LC (on meaning of "control" and "controlling interest" in Finance Act 1937 Sch.IV). Cases considering the meaning of "control" in the taxation context are likely to be helpful (see, e.g. *IRC v Bibby & Sons Ltd* [1945] 1 All E.R. 667 at 670 (on Finance (No.2) Act 1939 s.13(3), (9)); *IRC v Harton Coal Co* [1960] Ch. 563 (on Finance Act 1922 s.21(6)); *Barclays Bank Ltd v IRC* [1961] A.C. 509 at 523 (on Finance Act 1940 s.55)).   **25-008**

"Control" was defined in the Income and Corporation Taxes Act 1988 ss.416(2), considered in *Kellogg Brown & Root Holdings (UK) Ltd v Revenue and Customs Commissioners* [2010] EWCA Civ 118 and replaced by Corporation Tax Act 2010 s.450(2). Contrast the definition of "controller of body corporate" in the Enterprise Act 2002 s.222(4). Note also the meaning of "control", in the company law definitions of a "subsidiary" company in Companies Act 2006 ss.1159 and 1162; and see *Lonhro Ltd v Shell Petroleum Co Ltd* [1980] 1 W.L.R. 627 HL; *Re Technicon Investments Ltd* [1985] B.C.L.C. 434.

3. Supplier Credit Policies

(a) General Principles

Uberrimae fidei

Replace paragraph with:

25-013   As the supplier credit policy constitutes an insurance contract, the seller is under a duty to disclose any matters that are material to the risk.[27] Apart from specific clauses in the policy requiring such disclosure, this duty is established at law in regard to insurance policies.[28] Moreover, the policy incorporates the seller's proposal form and is based on it. Thus, the statements made by the seller in the proposal form constitute warranties of the policy; an incorrect statement entitles the insurer to avoid the policy even if the statement has been made in good faith.[29] The insurer, too, is subject to a duty of disclosure. In *Culford Metal Industries v Export Credits Guarantee Department*,[30] Neill J held the ECGD (which, at that time, issued such policies) liable where it gave the policy-holder negligent advice concerning the insurance effected. His Lordship based his decision on the duty of care established in *Hedley, Byrne & Co Ltd v Heller and Partners Ltd*.[31] In appropriate cases, a similar decision could be based on a breach of the *uberrimae fidei* duty, which is imposed on both parties to an insurance contract.

[27] And note that the duty is of a continuing nature remaining intact throughout the relationship involved: *Formica Ltd v Export Credits Guarantee Department* [1995] 1 Lloyd's Rep. 692 at 701–703 (concerning also the issue of the discovery of documents in proceedings against the ECGD). For a nondisclosure decision concerning the Italian ECA (SACE) and Italian law, see *Morgan Grenfell & Co Ltd v SACE* [2001] EWCA Civ 1932.

[28] See, generally, *Chitty on Contracts*, 33rd edn, Vol.2 paras 42-034 et seq. Moreover, a clause making full disclosure a condition precedent to the insurer's liability is included in most standard supplier's credit policies.

[29] *Chitty on Contracts*, 33rd edn, Vol.2 para.42-042; and especially *Dawsons v Bonnin* [1922] 2 A.C. 413.

[30] *Culford Metal Industries v Export Credits Guarantee Department* unreported, 16 March 1981 QB, Commercial Court; *Times,* 25 March 1981.

[31] *Hedley, Byrne & Co Ltd v Heller and Partners Ltd* [1964] A.C. 465.

(b) Policies Available

UK Export Finance's policies

Replace footnote 38 with:

25-016   [38] Copies of specimen policies are available on the UK Export Finance website, see para.25-004 n.8. The wording was updated in January 2017 to take account of the Insurance Act 2015.

(c) Common Provisions in Comprehensive Policies

Credit limit

After "a "credit limit"", add new footnote 47a:

47a For case law (on the applicability of a variable credit limit), see *Moore Large & Co Ltd v Hermes* **25-019**
Credit & Guarantee Plc [2003] EWHC 26 (Comm); [2003] 1 Lloyd's Rep. 163. And see *Hill and Lichtenstein Ltd v Export Guarantee General Manager* [1972] N.Z.L.R. 802 SC; affirmed [1973] 2 N.Z.L.R. 730 CA, para.25-021, below: credit limit defined the maximum recoverable in respect of one debtor and the 85% cap applied to each such claim.

(d) Assignment of Credit Insurance Policies

Disadvantage of assignment

Replace footnote 55 with:

55 See, generally, *Chitty on Contracts*, 33rd edn, Vol.1 para.19-071. **25-028**

Not a bill of sale

Replace footnote 64 with:

64 A Law Commission report (*Report No.369 Bills of Sale*, September 2016) recommended the repeal **25-030**
of the Bills of Sale Acts 1878-1882 and their replacement by a new Goods Mortgages Act, which was not to apply to UK Export Finance policies. However, the Government has announced that this recommendation will not be taken forward.

4. GUARANTEES

(a) Guarantees for Supplier Credit Financing

Legal nature

Replace paragraph with:

The "direct guarantee" given by UK Export Finance to the supplier's bank **25-033**
constitutes a guarantee[70] and not an insurance policy. This conclusion is supported by two arguments. First, the guarantee is given to the bank in order to induce it to make an advance to the supplier. In effect, UK Export Finance guarantees the payment of a debt incurred by the buyer which, under the agreement between the bank and the supplier, becomes payable to the bank. Secondly, the bank does not submit a proposal form or an application for the direct guarantee; it is given to it at the request and at the expense of the supplier. It is therefore wrong to regard the bank as a person who effects insurance against a credit risk.[71] As the contract between the bank and UK Export Finance is not an insurance policy, the bank does not owe UK Export Finance a duty of full disclosure. Longmore J's decision in *Credit Lyonnais Bank Nederland v Export Credits Guarantee Department*[72] illustrates the point. In this case one C, who had moved to London from Singapore, induced an employee of the ECGD to grant the claimant bank a direct guarantee covering the payment of bills of exchange to be drawn by him under contracts purported to be made with Nigerian importers. In reality, there were no such importers in existence. The transactions were shams and the importers' purported acceptances of the bills were forgeries executed thereon by C. One of the defences raised by the ECGD to the bank's action to enforce the guarantee was that certain aspects of C's transactions should have raised the bank's suspicions and, further, that the bank ought to

have disclosed certain irregularities when it lodged the application for the ECGD's cover. Rejecting this argument, Longmore J said:

"I do not accept that there is any such general duty on a banker in making applications for guarantees to ECGD. To so hold would be to apply the duties of an insured to a creditor and, for that, there is no authority. It may be that, in general, there is an implied representation that unusual matters, material to the guarantee, do not exist but the scope for any such general implication must be limited where explicit questions are asked and answers given."[73]

His Lordship concluded, however, that, on the facts, the ECGD was entitled to rescind the guarantee because the bank had given incomplete and hence incorrect answers to certain questions raised in the relevant standard documents. Thus, although concealment is not, in itself, a cause for the rescission of a direct guarantee, it can, on occasions, constitute a misrepresentation. This is particularly so where an answer to a given question conceals certain facts and, accordingly, conveys the wrong impression.

[70] As such guarantees are invariably reduced into writing, it seems unnecessary to consider whether they constitute guarantees strictu sensu or indemnities. Contrast *Chitty on Contracts*, 33rd edn, Vol.2 para.45-007. Moreover, questions of the main debtor's capacity and the validity of his contract, in relation to which it is important to determine whether an instrument is a guarantee or an indemnity, are not likely to arise in the case of transactions covered by UK Export Finance.

[71] For the definition of an insurance policy, see *Chitty on Contracts*, 33rd edn, Vol.2 para.42-001. See also *Chitty on Contracts*, 33rd edn, Vol.2 para.45-001 as regards the definition of a guarantee.

[72] *Credit Lyonnais Bank Nederland v Export Credits Guarantee Department* [1996] 1 Lloyd's Rep. 200. The decision was upheld on appeal, but without reference to this issue: [2000] A.C. 486.

[73] *Credit Lyonnais Bank Nederland v Exports Credits Guarantee Department* [1996] 1 Lloyd's Rep. 200 at 216. That a contract of suretyship is not an *uberrimae fidei* contract, see *Chitty on Contracts*, 33rd edn, Vol.1 para.7-177.

7. INTERNATIONAL ASPECTS

25-050 *Change title of paragraph:*

The Berne Union and Prague Club Committee

Replace the first paragraph with:

The International Union of Credit and Investment Insurers—the "Berne Union"—was established in Berne in 1934,[110] with four export credit insurers members from the UK, France, Italy and Spain. It is now a worldwide association of credit insurers (both ECAs and private companies, large and small) with 84 members from 73 countries.[111] Just over one-third of the members come from non-OECD countries. In 1993, the Berne Union, with funding from the EBRD (European Bank for Reconstruction and Development), founded the "Prague Club", an information exchange network initially for new agencies in Central and Eastern Europe, with a view to helping them towards satisfying the entrance requirements for the Berne Union (which some did, although remaining active in the Prague Club). Later, certain Asian and African agencies joined the Prague Club and presently membership stands at 38. The Prague Club initially shared a Secretariat with and enjoyed close links with the Berne Union. It has now become part of the Berne Union as a committee of that institution: the Prague Club Committee.

[110] As an association under the Swiss Civil Code. Its secretariat is in London and its website is *http://www.berneunion.org.uk* [Accessed 25 July 2017].

[111] There are also two "multilateral" members: the Islamic Corporation for the Insurance of Investment and Export Credit (ICIEC, a multinational ECA established by the Islamic Development Bank Group) and the World Bank Group.

The OECD Arrangement

Replace the first paragraph with:

In order to discourage the distortion of competition by government subsidy of export credit guarantees—an "export credit race"—the OECD produced an "Arrangement on Officially Supported Export Credits", then known as the "OECD Consensus", in April 1978.[112] This provides an institutional framework for an orderly market for officially supported export credit with repayment terms of two years or more and is regularly revised, the last version being dated January 2018. Annexed to it are six "Sector Understandings" which set out special guidelines for certain sectors, namely ships, nuclear power plants, civil aircraft and renewable energies and water projects, rail infrastructure and (most recently) coal-fired electricity generation projects. However, the Arrangement does not apply to other sectors such as military equipment and agricultural commodities. The Arrangement is not an OECD Act (although it receives the administrative support of the OECD Secretariat, which monitors its implementation) but is a "Gentlemen's Agreement" among its "Participants" whereby "Participants" agree to be bound by it.[113] The EU is a "Participant",[114] and the Arrangement has been incorporated into EC law by a Council Decision.[115]

25-051

[112] See generally, the OECD website is *http://www.oecd.org* [Accessed 25 July 2017]. It published a 20 year anniversary report in 1998 (updated in 2008): OECD (1998), The Export Credit Arrangement: Achievements and Challenges 1978/1998, OECD Publishing, Paris,*https://doi.org/10.1787/9789264163867-en*.

[113] In addition, Israel and Turkey are observers to Participants' meetings and other organisations, such as the Berne Union (see para.25-050, above), EBRD, IMF, UNEP, World Bank and WTO, are invited to meetings when issues of mutual interest are discussed.

[114] The others are Australia, Canada, Japan, Korea (Republic of), New Zealand, Norway, Switzerland and the US.

[115] See below, para.25-052 n.123.

EU harmonising measures

Replace the first paragraph with:

As noted above, the EU has been concerned with official export credit support since its inception[119] and has issued a series of legislative instruments in this area, aimed primarily at eliminating distortions in competition resulting from differences between official guarantee and insurance systems in different Member States of the EU. The most significant harmonising measure is the Directive on medium- and long-term export credit insurance.[120] In the area of short-term export credit insurance, an (amended[121]) Communication[122] has been issued by the Competition Directorate which defines "marketable risks" and precludes these being covered with official support. In addition, a Regulation has incorporated the OECD Arrangement.[123]

25-052

[119] The Council, by a Decision, created a Policy Co-ordination Group for Credit Insurance, Credit Guarantees and Financial Credits (the Export Credits Group) in 1960 [1960] O.J. Spec. Ed. 66.

[120] Directive 1998/29 [1998] O.J. L148/22, amended by Council Regulation 806/2003 of 14 April 2003. The Annexe sets out the common principles for export credit support. It repeals and replaces Directives 1970/509 [1970] O.J. L254/1 and 1970/510 [1970] O.J. L254/26.

[121] By 2012/C 398/02 which alters the definition of "marketable risk". See also the amendments made by Communications 2015/C 28/01, 2015/C 215/01 and 2016/C 244/01.

[122] 2012/C 392/01. As this expires at the end of 2020, the Commission is presently consulting on its future.

[123] See above, para.25-051. See Regulation (EU) No 1233/2011 of the European Parliament and of the Council of 16 November 2011 on the application of certain guidelines in the field of officially supported export credits and Annual review by the Commission of Member States' Annual Activity Reports on Export Credits in the sense of Regulation (EU) No 1233/2011 (COM(2017) 67 final) Previously, Decisions incorporated previous versions of (and amendments to) the OECD Consensus/Agreement but the Regulation now enables the EU Commission to amend the annexed OECD Arrangement by delegated act: see art.2 of Regulation.

Replace footnote 126 with:

[126] MEMO/08/795, dated December 17, 2008. These "temporary" measures remained in place for a number of years, see the Commission's Communication "Temporary Union framework for State aid measures to support access to finance in the current financial and economic crisis" (2011/C 6/05). See its *State aid Scoreboard 2012 Update* {Com (2012) 778 final}.

CHAPTER 26

CONFLICT OF LAWS

1. PRELIMINARY CONSIDERATIONS

Scope and arrangement of this chapter

Replace footnote 2 with:

26-001   ² This chapter does not consider the distinct topic of the jurisdiction of English courts in sale of goods cases. For the general principles of English jurisdiction in personam see Fawcett, Harris and Bridge, *International Sale of Goods in the Conflict of Laws*, Chs 2–10; and generally, Dicey, Morris and Collins, *The Conflict of Laws*, 15th edn, Chs 11 and 12; Cheshire, North and Fawcett, *Private International Law*, 15th edn (2017), Chs 10–14; Fentiman, *International Commercial Litigation*, 2nd edn, Pt IV; Rogerson, *Collier's Conflict of Laws*, 4th edn (2013), Chs 5 and 6. Other topics omitted from this chapter, include the recognition and enforcement of foreign judgments as to sales (see Fawcett, Harris and Bridge, *International Sale of Goods in the Conflict of Laws*, Ch.11; and generally, Dicey, Morris and Collins, *The Conflict of Laws*, 15th edn, Chs 14 and 15; Cheshire, North and Fawcett, *Private International Law*, 15th edn, Chs 15–16; Fentiman, *International Commercial Litigation*, 2nd edn, Ch.18; and Rogerson, *Collier's Conflict of Laws*, 4th edn, Ch.8; and the conflicts aspects of arbitration of disputes arising out of sales contracts (see Dicey, Morris and Collins, *The Conflict of Laws*, 15th edn, Ch.16; and *Cheshire, North and Fawcett*, Private International Law, 15th edn, Ch.17).

Replace the third paragraph with:

The future legal relationship of the UK to the EU remains to be determined in the light of the UK's decision to withdraw from the EU. In the absence of any arrangements which include the UK remaining bound by EU law, the impact on conflict of laws is potentially very significant. Most significantly for the purposes of this chapter, the Rome I Regulation, which applies to all contracts entered into on or after 17 December 2009, and whose rules form the main subject matter of this chapter, would no longer be directly effective EU law. One possibility is that the UK would return to the position under the Contracts (Applicable Law) Act 1990, which implemented the Rome Convention into English law. However, the status of those rules following the UK's exit from the EU raises difficult issues of international law and UK statutory law. Alternatively, as choice of law rules are unilateral (not requiring reciprocity, unlike rules of jurisdiction) it would be possible for the UK to enact national legislation which substantially mirrors the Rome I Regulation.[17a] All of these issues remain to be determined and the discussion of conflict of laws in this chapter remains written on the premise that the status of EU law in UK law remains unchanged.[17b]

[17a] From an early stage post referendum, the UK Government has made it clear that the Rome I and Rome II Regulations will form part of retained EU law. On 29 March 2019, the Government enacted the Law Applicable to Contractual Obligations and Non Contractual Obligations (Amendment etc.) (EU Exit) Regulations (SI 2019/834) (under powers granted by s.8 of the European Union (Withdrawal) Act 2018). These Regulations will incorporate the provisions of the Rome I and Rome II Regulations into domestic law with only minor or consequential amendments necessary to prevent, remedy or mitigate any failure of retained EU law to operate effectively or any other deficiency of retained EU law, arising from the withdrawal of the UK from the EU.

[17b] For a discussion see A. Dickinson, "Back to the future: the UK's EU exit and the conflict of laws" [2016] J.P.I.L. 195; P. Rogerson, "Litigation post-Brexit" [2017] N.L.J 2016; J. Harris "How will Brexit impact on cross-border litigation?" [2016] S.J. 160; "Brexit & cross-border dispute resolution" [2016] N.L.J. 166; P. Gross, "A good forum to shop in: London and English law post-Brexit" [2018] L.M.C.L.Q. 222; Final Report of the House of Lords Justice Sub-Committee, *Implications of Brexit for the justice system*, 14 March 2017.

The characterisation of "goods" in conflict of laws

Replace footnote 33 with:

26-004   ³³ As well as with the provisions of Regulation 864/2007 on the law applicable to non-contractual obligations (the "Rome II Regulation"). On the meaning of "sale of goods" in the context of the Judgments Regulation see *Car Trim GmbH v KeySafety Systems Srl* (C-381/08) unreported, 25 February

2010, discussed below. See further Fawcett, Harris and Bridge, *International Sale of Goods in the Conflict of Laws*, paras 3.146–3.163; Cheshire, North and Fawcett, *Private International Law*, pp.255–257.

2. COMMON LAW BACKGROUND: THE RELEVANCE AND ROLE OF THE PROPER LAW DOCTRINE

Implied choice of proper law

Replace title of paragraph 26-007 and footnote 51 with:

⁵¹ See cases cited in para.26-007 above.

26-007

Replace section title footnote 97 with:

3. THE ROME I REGULATION AND THE ROME CONVENTION⁹⁷

⁹⁷ There is an extensive body of literature on the Convention. The following are among the more significant contributions in English: Fawcett, Harris and Bridge, *International Sale of Goods in the Conflict of Laws* (2005), Chs 13 and 14; Plender and Wilderspin, *The European Contracts Convention*, 2nd edn; Kaye, *The New Private International Law of Contract of the European Community* (1993); Lasok and Stone, *Conflict of Laws in the European Community* (1987), Ch.9; North (ed), *Contract Conflicts* (1982); Cheshire, North and Fawcett, *Private International Law*, 15th edn, Ch.19; Anton, *Private International Law*, 2nd edn (1990), Ch.11; North, (1990) 220 *Hague Recueil, I*, 3, 176–205; Diamond, (1986) 216 *Hague Recueil, IV*, 233; Williams, (1986) 35 I.C.L.Q. 1; Nadelmann, (1985) 33 Am. J. Comp. L. 297; Jaffey, (1984) 33 I.C.L.Q. 531; Morse, (1982) 2 Ybk. Eur. L. 107; North, (1980) J.B.L. 382.

26-015

(a) General Considerations

Replace title footnote 128 with:

Interpretation¹²⁸

¹²⁸ Plender and Wilderspin, *European Private International Law of Obligations*, 4th edn paras 1-090–1-126; Kaye, *The New Private International Law of Contract of the European Community*, pp.77–83; Dicey, Morris and Collins, *The Conflict of Laws*, 15th edn, paras 32-013 to 32-014; Cheshire, North and Fawcett, *Private International Law*, pp.687–689.

26-018

Meaning of "law of a country"

Replace footnote 154 with:

¹⁵⁴ cf. the controversy at common law which emerged in *James Miller & Partners v Whitworth Street Estates (Manchester) Ltd* [1970] A.C. 583; above, para.26-008.

26-021

Situations to which the Regulation and the Convention apply

Replace footnote 166 with:

¹⁶⁶ Compare the similar wording in the Rome II Regulation Art.1(1) (discussed by Cheshire, North and Fawcett, *Private International Law*, pp.786–802; Dickinson, *The Rome II Regulation*, paras 3.75–3.145.

26-023

Specific exclusions

Replace footnote 167 with:

¹⁶⁷ The excluded matters which are unlikely to arise directly in relation to sales of goods are contractual obligations relating to wills and succession, rights in property arising out of a matrimonial relationship and rights and duties arising out of a family relationship, parentage, marriage or affinity, including maintenance obligations in respect of children who are not legitimate: Rome I Regulation Art.1(2)(b) and (c); Recital (8). Compare the Rome Convention Art.1(2)(b). For general discussion of the matters excluded from the Regulation, see Dicey, Morris and Collins, *The Conflict of Laws*, 15th edn, paras 32-

26-024

020 to 32-021; Plender and Wilderspin, *The European Private International Law of Obligations*, 4th edn, Ch.5. For discussion of the exclusions under the Rome Convention, see Dicey, Morris and Collins, *The Conflict of Laws*, 14th edn, paras 32-031 to 32-053. For a comparison between the exclusions in the Rome I Regulation and the Rome Convention, see Cheshire, North and Fawcett, *Private International Laws*, pp.697-705.

Replace footnote 197 with:

26-025   [197] Any such Conventions are likely to be negotiated by the EU on behalf of all Member States and to be subject to specific provisions on their relationship to the Rome I Regulation. The Hague Choice of Court Convention 2015 came into force on 1 October 2015 when it was ratified by the EU on behalf of all Member States except for Denmark. The other States which have ratified the Convention are Mexico, Singapore and Montenegro. The effect of the Convention on agreements which also potentially fall within the Brussels regime is set out in Art.26(6). On 28 December 2018, the UK acceded to the Convention in its own right allowing the Convention to remain in force in the UK in the event of a no-deal Brexit.

(b)   Choice of Law by the Parties

Making the choice of law

Replace footnote 257 with:

26-031   [257] cf. *Travellers Casualty and Surety Company of Europe Ltd v Sun Life Assurance Co of Canada (UK) Ltd* [2004] Lloyd's Rep. I.R. 846. Note, however, that no reference is made to choice of law in favorem negotii as being a potentially relevant factor: see Plender and Wilderspin, *The European Private International Law of Obligations*, 4th edn, para.6–047; cf. above, para.26-010.

Replace footnote 266 with:

26-032   [266] Compare the views of Lords Diplock and Wilberforce in *Amin Rasheed Shipping Corp v Kuwait Insurance Co* [1984] A.C. 50. See above, para.26-008.

Severability

Replace footnote 275 with:

26-034   [275] Rome Convention Art.3(1) is in materially equivalent terms. For discussion, see Plender and Wilderspin, *The European Contracts Convention*, 2nd edn, paras 6-044 to 6-045; Morse, (1982) 2 Ybk. Eur. L. 107, 117–118. See also Maclachlan, (1990) 61 B.Y.I.L. 311; Dicey, Morris and Collins, *The Conflict of Laws*, 15th edn, paras 32-024 to 32-027; Cheshire, North and Fawcett, *Private International Law*, pp.707–709.

Varying the choice of law

Replace paragraph with:

26-036   Further uncertainty existed in the common law as to what law determined whether the parties might change the law which governed the contract to a new and different governing law.[285] The Rome I Regulation Art.3(2) (which is materially the same as the Rome Convention Art.3(2)) provides a specific rule on this question in the following terms:

> "The parties may at any time agree to subject the contract to a law other than that which previously governed it, whether as a result of an earlier choice made under this Article or of other provisions of this Regulation. Any change in the law to be applied that is made after the conclusion of the contract shall not prejudice its formal validity under Article 11[286] or adversely affect the rights of third parties."

Subject to the proviso as to formal validity,[287] and the need to preserve the rights of third parties which might be adversely affected by a change in the governing law,[288] the parties are left with maximum freedom as to the time when the ultimate choice of law is made because of this wide freedom to change the applicable law.[289] The freedom extends to changing the applicable law when the law was expressly chosen by the parties or applicable because of the absence of a choice of law according to the provisions of Art.4.[290] To be effective, however, the choice of law which purports to vary or change the original governing law must itself satisfy the requirements of Art.3(1).[291]

[285] See Fawcett, Harris and Bridge, *International Sale of Goods in the Conflict of Laws*, paras 13-107 to 13-111; Dicey, Morris and Collins, *The Conflict of Laws*, 15th edn, para.32-053; Cheshire, North and Fawcett, *Private International Law*, pp.709–711; Plender and Wilderspin, *The European Private International Law of Obligations*, 4th edn, paras 6-050 to 6-058; Hill, (2004) 53 I.C.L.Q. 325, 332–333; Morse, (1982) 2 Ybk. Eur. L. 107, 119–122; Diamond, (1986) 216 *Hague Recueil*, IV, 233, 261–264; F. A. Mann, (1954) 31 B.Y.B.I.L. 216, 222; North in *Multum non Multa, Festschrift für Kurt Lipstein* (1980), p.205, reprinted in North, *Essays in Private International Law* (1993), p.51. In *Mauritius Commercial Bank Ltd v Hestia Holdings Ltd* [2013] EWHC 1328; [2013] 2 All E.R. (Comm) 898, the court held that English common law authorities suggested there was nothing objectionable about prospective changes (although left open the position in relation to retrospective change) ([21]–[29]). Furthermore, any other conclusion would be a triumph of form over substances because the parties could simply enter into a new agreement ([19]) and also did not accord with the policy identified in the Rome I Regulation Art.3.2 in favour of party autonomy.

[286] In the case of the Rome Convention, the relevant provision on formal validity is Art.9.

[287] See below, para.26-097.

[288] "In certain legal systems, a third party may have acquired rights in consequence of a contract concluded between two other persons. These rights cannot be affected by a subsequent change in the choice of the applicable law": *Giuliano-Lagarde Report*, p.18.

[289] *Giuliano-Lagarde Report*, p.18. This power to vary the applicable law is distinct from and in addition to any power which may exist as a matter of procedure, in national law (such as English law) to make, or change, a choice of law in the course of legal proceedings: *Giuliano-Lagarde Report*, p.18. Further it must be stressed that the provision is only concerned with changing the applicable law and may not affect the principle of the common law that there must be a law governing the contract at the outset of the contract so that the applicable law cannot "float": see above, para.26-006. However, now that the Rome I Regulation makes it clear that the parties are permitted retrospectively to change the applicable law it is hard to see what the objection could be to such contingent choice of law clauses. Prior to the choice being made, the contract would be governed by the law applicable in the absence of choice identified under Art.4, thus there would be no vacuum. See further Fentiman, *International Commercial Litigation*, 2nd edn, paras 5.50–5.55; and *Mauritius Commercial Bank Ltd v Hestia Holdings Ltd* [2013] EWHC 1328; [2013] 2 All E.R. (Comm) 898, noting that one of the objections to such clauses at common law was perhaps the problem of potential uncertainty caused by the retrospective change of applicable law ([24]).

[290] *Giuliano-Lagarde Report*, p.18.

[291] *Giuliano-Lagarde Report*, p.18; *Aeolian Shipping SA v ISS Machinery Services Ltd* [2001] EWCA Civ 1162; [2001] 2 Lloyd's Rep. 641.

Provisions of law that cannot be derogated from by agreement: Art.3(3)

Replace footnote 294 with:

[294] North, (1990) 220 *Recueil des Cours*, I, 13, 184. For general discussion of Art.3(3) of the Regulation (and the Rome Convention Art.3(3)), see Plender and Wilderspin, *The European Private International Law of Obligations*, 4th edn, paras 6-059 to 6-071; Morse, (1982) 2 Ybk. Eur. L. 107, 122–124; Philip in *Contract Conflicts*, pp.81, 95–97; Dicey, Morris and Collins, *The Conflict of Laws*, 15th edn, paras 32-083 to 32-090; Cheshire, North and Fawcett, *Private International Law*, pp.711–713.

26-038

Overriding mandatory provisions of English law

Replace footnote 329 with:

[329] See Fentiman, *International Commercial Litigation*, 2nd edn, paras 4.23–4.27; A Bonomi, (2008) Yearbook of PIL 285, 289; cf. Plender and Wilderspin, *The European Private International Law of Obligations*, 4th edn, para.12-012; and Cheshire, North and Fawcett, *Private International Law*, p.745-746. See also *United Antwerp Maritime Agencies (Unamar) NV v Navigation Maritime Bulgare* (C-184/12) and *Eurobank Ergasias SA v Kallirio Navigation Co Ltd* [2015] EWHC 2377 (Comm).

26-044

Replace footnote 330 with:

³³⁰ *Giuliano-Lagarde Report*, p.38. Other examples given are rules on cartels, competition and restrictive practices. In *Roberts (A Child) v Soldiers, Sailors, Airmen and Families Association-Forces Help* [2019] EWHC 1104 (QB); [2019] 3 W.L.R. 343 the Civil Liability (Contribution) Act 1978 was held to have mandatory or overriding effect and accordingly to apply to all proceedings for contribution brought in England and Wales regardless of the otherwise applicable law.

Overriding mandatory provisions of the law of the place of performance

Replace footnote 347 with:

26-045   ³⁴⁷ See, e.g. *Foster v Driscoll* [1929] 1 K.B. 470; *Regazzoni v KC Sethia (1944) Ltd* [1958] A.C. 301; *Dana Gas PJSC v Dan Gas Sukuk Ltd* [2017] EWHC 2921 (Comm) and [2018] EWHC 278 (Comm). cf. *Deutsche Bank AG v Unitech Global Ltd* [2013] EWHC 2793 (Comm); [2013] 2 Lloyd's Rep. 629.

Contracts governed by the Rome Convention: the three conditions of Art.5(2)

Replace footnote 385 with:

26-051   ³⁸⁵ cf. The similar phraseology in the Brussels Convention Art.13(3): see *Rayner v Davies* [2002] EWCA Civ 1880; [2003] 1 All E.R. (Comm) 394; *Standard Bank London v Apostolakis (No.2)* [2001] Lloyd's Rep. Bank. 240; *Hillside (New Media) Ltd v Baasland* [2010] EWHC 3336 (Comm); [2010] 2 C.L.C. 986 at [43]. Contrast the different and more broadly worded provision contained in the Judgments Regulation recast Art.17(1)(c) (previously the Judgments Regulation Art.15(1)(c)). And see below, para.26-055.

Contracts governed by the Rome I Regulation: the new preconditions and exclusions

Replace footnote 405 with:

26-052   ⁴⁰⁵ Directive 90/314 on package travel, package holidays and package tours [1990] O.J. L158/59. A new Package Travel Directive (2015/2302/EU) entered into force on 31 December 2015 and is implemented by the Package Travel and Linked Travel Arrangements Regulation 2018 (SI 2018/634) which came into force on 1 July 2018.

Application to contract concluded "online": the Rome Convention

Replace footnote 428 with:

26-057   ⁴²⁸ cf. Directive on electronic commerce, above, para.26-055, Recital (19) and Art.11(1); Electronic Commerce (EC Directive) Regulations 2002 reg.11(2)(a); *Menashe Business Mercantile Ltd v William Hill Organization Ltd* [2002] EWCA Civ 1702; [2003] 1 W.L.R. 1462.

Habitual residence of consumers

Replace footnote 450 with:

26-061   ⁴⁵⁰ See *Hack v Hack* (1976) Fam. Law 177; *Re J (A Minor)(Abduction)* [1990] 2 A.C. 562; Dicey, Morris and Collins, *The Conflict of Laws*, 15th edn, para.6-136; Cheshire, North and Fawcett, *Private International Law*, p.182.

(c)   Applicable Law in Absence of Choice

The general presumption

Replace footnote 461 with:

26-064   ⁴⁶¹ For general discussions, see Dicey, Morris and Collins, *The Conflict of Laws*, 14th edn, paras 32-108 to 32-128, 33-107 to 33-134; Cheshire, North and Fawcett, *Private International Law*, pp.724–727; Kaye, *The New Private International Law of Contract of the European Community*, Ch.9; Plender and Wilderspin, *The European Private International Law of Obligations*, 4th edn, paras 7-004 to 7-027; *Schultsz in Contract Conflicts*, pp.185, 187; Diamond, (1986) 216 *Recueil des Cours*, iv, 233, 273–

276; Lasok and Stone, *Conflict of Laws in the European Community*, pp.361–364; Morse, (1982) 2 Ybk. Eur. L. 107, 126–131; Lipstein, (1981) 3 Northwestern Journal Int'l L. & Bus. 402; Jessurun d'Oliveira, (1977) 25 Am. J. Comp. L. 303.

Characteristic performance

Replace paragraph with:

The concept of the "characteristic performance" of a contract was novel in the **26-065** law of the Member States of the Community and is probably Swiss in origin.[462] It is based on the notion that when the general concept of contract is broken down into types of contract, (e.g. sale, insurance, etc), the performance of one of the parties will be revealed as the performance which characterises or typifies the relevant contract.[463] The notion of characteristic performance has been much criticised,[464] but equally extravagant praise has been heaped upon it.[465] This is not the place to discuss the various arguments for or against the concept, but rather the place to determine how a concept which, for better or worse, has become part of English law applies in relation to a contract of sale. The *Giuliano-Lagarde Report* in analysing the characteristic performance of reciprocal or bilateral contracts in which each party has to perform obligations points out that the performance of:

> "... one of the parties in a modern economy usually takes the form of the payment of money. This is not, of course, the characteristic performance of the contract. It is the performance for which payment is due, i.e. depending on the type of contract, the delivery of goods, the granting of the right to make use of an item of property, the provision of a service, transport, insurance, banking operations, security, etc., which usually constitutes the centre of gravity and the socio-economic function of the contractual transaction."[466]

Thus put, it is tolerably clear that characteristic performance of a contract is a somewhat abstract notion in the sense that it is not the payment of money but the performance for which such payment is due. In the particular context of sale,[467] the passage means that the characteristic performance in a contract of sale is that of the seller since he provides the performance for which the buyer is required to pay the price. This view has been accepted in English decisions.[468] Such a conclusion seems to follow irrespective of the kind of sale (c.i.f., f.o.b., etc.) and irrespective of the fact that the buyer may be under obligations additional to the obligation to pay the price and further irrespective of the fact that the seller may be under obligations additional to that of delivery of the goods (in whatever form, depending on the type of sale involved, such "delivery" must take place).[469] But if the "price" of the contract is not money but some other sort of transfer of value, the court will have to consider which arm of the exchange is more characteristic of the contract as a whole.[470]

---

[462] See Lipstein, (1981) 3 Northwestern Journal Int'l L. & Bus. 402. For present Swiss law see Swiss Private International Law Act 1987 (text in Karrer and Arnold, *Switzerland's Private International Law Act 1987* (1989)) Art.117. Switzerland, it should be noted, is also a party to the Hague Convention on the Law Applicable to International Sale of Goods 1955.

[463] See Lipstein, (1981) 3 Northwestern Journal Int'l L. & Bus. 402, 404.

[464] See Lasok and Stone *Conflict of Laws in the European Community*, Morse, (1982) 2 Ybk. Eur. L. 107, 126–131 andJessurun d'Oliveira, (1977) 25 Am. J. Comp. L. 303. According to the latter, at 326, the concept is "a reflection of the prejudices of Helvetian hotel-keepers and cuckoo-clock makers, prejudices that will not be shared in countries that export tourists and import cuckoo-clocks...".

[465] See, e.g. the *Giuliano-Lagarde Report*, p.20 (concept "defines connecting factor of the contract from the inside, and not from the outside by elements unrelated to the substance of the obligation such as the nationality of the parties or the place where the contract was concluded" and "refers to the function which the legal relationship involved fulfils in the social life of any country. The concept of characteristic

performance essentially links the contract to the social and economic environment of which it will form part").

[466] Giuliano-Lagarde Report, p.20. As to unilateral contracts, see *Waldwiese Stiftung v Lewis* [2004] EWHC 2589 (gift); *Opthalmic Innovations International (United Kingdom) Ltd v Opthalmic Innovations International Inc* [2004] EWHC 2948 (Ch); [2005] I.L. Pr. 109 (indemnification agreement); *Ark Therapeutics Plc v True North Capital Ltd* [2005] EWHC 1585 (Comm); [2006] 1 All E.R. (Comm) 138 (letter of intent); Maher, (2002) Jur. Rev. 317. In the case of an option agreement to buy promissory notes embodying distressed state debt, the characteristic performance, whether the option agreement was regarded as unilateral or bilateral in character, was held to be that of the bank selling the debt (by analogy with a contract of sale): *Standard Bank Plc v Agrinvest International Inc* [2007] EWHC 2595 (Comm) at [4].

[467] See Fawcett, Harris and Bridge, *International Sale of Goods in the Conflict of Laws*, para.13-115; Plender and Widerspin, *The European Private International Law of Obligations*, 4th edn, para.7-059; Dicey, Morris and Collins, *The Conflict of Laws*, 14th edn, paras 32-116 to 32-117; North, (1990) 220 *Recueil des Cours*, I, 13, 186; Feltham, [1991] J.B.L. 413; Lipstein, (1981) 3 Northwestern Journal Int'l L. & Bus. 402, 404.

[468] See *WH Martin Ltd v Feldbinder Spezialfahrzeugwerke GmbH* unreported, 8 April 1998 CA; *Print Concept GmbH v GEW (EC) Ltd* [2001] EWCA Civ 352; [2002] C.L.C. 352; *ISS Machinery Services Ltd v Aeolian Shipping SA* [2001] EWCA Civ 1162; [2001] 2 Lloyd's Rep. 641; *Iran Continental Shelf Oil Co v IRI International Oil Corp* [2002] EWCA Civ 1162; [2004] 2 C.L.C. 696; *Lupofresh Ltd v Sapporo Breweries Ltd* [2013] EWCA Civ 948; [2014] 1 All E.R. (Comm) 484. For Scotland, see *William Grant & Sons International Ltd v Marie Brizard Espana SA* 1998 S.C. 536; *Ferguson Shipbuilders Ltd v Voith Hydro GmbH & Co KG* 2000 S.L.T. 229. See also *Albon v Naza Motor Trading Sdn Bhd* [2007] EWHC 9 (Ch); [2007] 1 W.L.R. 2489 at [29]–[30]. See also the decision of the Dutch Supreme Court to the same effect in *Société Nouvelle des Papeteries de l'Aa v BV Machinefabriek BOA*, 1992 N.J. 750, discussed by Struycken, [1996] L.M.C.L.Q. 18; and Plender and Widerspin, *The European Private International Law of Obligations*, 4th edn, para.7-024; and to the same effect *Baros AG (Switzerland) v Embrica Maritim Hotelschiffe GmbH (Germany)* unreported, 17 October 2008 (see further De Haan, (2013) 15 E.J.L.R. 38). The characteristic performance of a contract of guarantee is the performance of the guarantor: *Giuliano-Lagarde Report*, pp.20-21; *Emeraldian Ltd Partnership v Wellmix Shipping Ltd* [2010] EWHC 1411 (Comm); [2011] 1 Lloyd's Rep. 301; [2010] 1 C.L.C. 993; *British Arab Commercial Bank Plc v Bank of Communications* [2011] EWH C 281 (Comm); [2011] 1 Lloyd's Rep. 664; *Alliance Bank JSC v Aquanta Corp* [2012] EWCA Civ 1588. The donor of a gift is the characteristic performer: see *Gorjat v Gorjat* [2010] EWHC 1537 (Ch). On characteristic performance and agency, see also *Lawlor v Sandvik Mining & Construction Mobile Crushers & Screens Ltd* [2013] EWCA Civ 365; [2013] 2 Lloyd's Rep. 98 and *Kent v Paterson-Brown* [2018] EWHC 2008 (Ch) but cf *Golden Ocean Group Ltd v Salgaocar Mining Industries Pty Ltd* [2012] EWCA Civ 265; [2012] 1 W.L.R. 3674 where the Court of Appeal held that it was not possible to identify the characteristic performance in respect of an agent's warranty of authority.See also, in respect of banking contracts, *Deutsche Bank (Suisse) SA v Khan* [2013] EWHC 482. On the characteristic performance of a share option agreement, see *Pathfinder Minerals Plc v Veloso* [2012] EWHC 2856 (Comm) at [46].

[469] See *Iran Continental Shelf Oil Co v IRI International Corp* [2002] EWCA Civ 1024; [2004] 2 C.L.C. 696. This seems to be the effect of the Swiss case law: see reference at para.26-065, above. See also Swiss Private International Law Act 1987 Art.117(3)(a) (in contracts to pass title, characteristic performance is that of transferor). Switzerland is a party to the Hague Sales Convention 1955 (above, para.26-065), but this places main emphasis on the seller's law also. Although see para.26-072, below in relation to distribution agreements. The supplier of bunkers in the type of sui generis supply contract identified by the Supreme Court in *PST Energy 7 Shipping LLC v OW Bunkers Malta Ltd (The Res Cogitans)* [2016] UKSC 23; [2016] 2 W.L.R. 119, will be the characteristic performer for the same reasons.

[470] *Cecil v Bayat* [2010] EWHC 641 (Comm) at [86]–[90].

Central administration and the Rome Convention

Replace footnote 484 with:

26-068 [484] See above, para.26-067.

(d) The Rome I Regulation—presumptions

Sale of goods

Replace footnote 515 with:

26-070 [515] *PST Energy Shipping LLC v OW Bunker Malta Ltd (The Res Cogitans)* [2015] EWCA Civ 1058 at

[33]; [2016] 2 W.L.R. 1072. For a critical review of this decision see L Gullifer [2017] L.Q.R 244. See also D. Saidov [2019] J.B.L. 1.

Mixed contracts

Replace footnote 519 with:

[519] In *Corman-Collins SA v La Maison du Whisky SA* (C-9/12) the CJEU held that an exclusive distribu- **26-071**
tion agreement was a contract for the supply of services under the Brussels Regulation Art.5(1)(b) on
the basis that the characteristic service was that provided by the distributor in increasing the distribution of the product. A similar conclusion was reached by the CJEU in *Saey Home & Garden NV/SA v
Lusavouga-Maquinas e Acessorios Industriasis SA* (C-64/17).

Displacing the presumptions: the Rome Convention

Replace "n.528" with:
above **26-073**

Displacing the presumptions: particular examples

Replace the second paragraph with:

Where in the case of an f.o.b. sale, the seller's place of business and the place **26-076**
of delivery of the goods are situated in the same country,[556] it is unlikely that any
question as to the displacement of the presumption will arise. This is also likely to
be the case in such circumstances in f.a.s., f.o.r. and f.o.t. contracts. It is also submitted that this result is likely to ensue even if the place of contracting and buyer's
place of business is in another country under the law of which the contract is valid
although the contract is invalid under the law of the seller's place of business and
the place of delivery.[557] A presumption in *favorem negotii*[558] cannot, it is submitted, be resorted to under Art.4. Such a presumption is a presumption as to the
governing law which the parties intended to choose. It is not a presumption which
can operate where, ex hypothesi, there is no choice of law.[559]

[556] cf. *Benaim & Co v Debono* [1924] A.C. 514; above, para.26-011.

[557] cf. *NV Handel Maatschappij J Smits & Co v English Exporters (London) Ltd* [1955] 2 Lloyd's Rep.
317.

[558] Above, paras 26-010, 26-031.

[559] cf. *Sayers v International Drilling Co NV* [1976] 1 W.L.R. 1113, above, para.26-010. See to this effect *Monterosso Shipping v International Transport Workers Federation* [1982] I.C.R. 675 per May L.J.
at 685.

Replace footnote 563 with:

[563] cf. *Gill and Duffus Landauer Ltd v London Export Corp GmbH* [1982] 2 Lloyd's Rep. 627;. This is
probably so if the contract is a "multi-port" f.o.b. contract giving the seller the right to choose a port of
shipment out of a number of ports in different countries: cf. above, para.26-011; para.26-012. The position may be different in relation to other contracts where it might be easier to rebut the presumption in
a case where the place of performance differs from the place of business of the characteristic performer:
see *Bank of Baroda v Vysya Bank Ltd* [1994] 2 Lloyd's Rep. 87 (letter of credit) discussed below,
para.26-087; Dicey, Morris and Collins, *The Conflict of Laws*, 15th edn, para.33-016.

Successive contracts of sale relating to the same goods

Replace paragraph with:

Since, unless displaced by Art.4(3), Art.4(1)(a) of the Regulation points towards **26-078**
the law of the seller's place of business as the governing law, it is the likely result
that a variety of applicable laws may be relevant in the case of successive contracts
of sale of the same goods. To ensure[573] uniformity as to the governing law in relation to such "string" contracts,[574] it will be necessary, as far as possible, to insert

appropriate choice of law clauses or suitably worded arbitration clauses into each contract or for the parties to the successive sales to deal on the same, or at least consistent, standard forms.[575]

[573] Recital (20) of the Regulation provides that in deciding whether to displace the presumption, "account should be taken, inter alia, of whether the contract in question has a very close relationship with another contract or contracts". This does not state that the close connection must be with a contract between the same parties. The CJEU in *Haeger & Schmidt GmbH v MMA IARD* (C-305/13) at [49] referred to "the presence of a close connection between the contract in question with another contract or contracts which are, as the case may be, part of the same chain of contracts."

[574] Above, para.26-010.

[575] Above, para.26-010. For the position in relation to related contracts generally see para.26-074, above. The CJEU in *Refcomp SpA v Axa Corporate Solutions Assurance SA* (C-543/10) held that: at [37] in a chain of contracts transferring ownership, the relationship of succession between the initial buyer and the sub-buyer is not regarded as the transfer of a single contract or the transfer of all the rights and obligations for which it provides. In such a case, the contractual obligations of the parties may vary from contract to contract, so that the contractual rights which the sub-buyer can enforce against his immediate seller will not necessarily be the same as those which the manufacturer will have accepted in his relationship with the first buyer. Thus, a jurisdiction agreement agreed between the manufacturer and initial buyer could not be relied on against a sub-buyer. Applied by the French Cour de Cassation in *X v Platinum Contracts Ltd* [2015] I. L. Pr. 40.

4. CONTRACTS ANCILLARY TO CONTRACT OF SALE

Replace title footnote 624 with:

Contracts of agency[624]

26-084 [624] See Dicey, Morris and Collins, *The Conflict of Laws*, 15th edn, paras 33R-407 to 33-459; *Bowstead and Reynolds on Agency*, 21st edn, Ch.12. See also Rabel, *Conflict of Laws: A Comparative Study*, 2nd edn, Vol.3 pp.125-186, 200-203; Verhagen, *Agency in Private International Law* (1995); Rigaux in Lipstein (ed), *International Encyclopedia of Comparative Law*, Vol.III Ch.29; Breslauer, (1938) 50 Jur. Rev. 282; Reese and Flesch, (1960) 60 Col. L. Rev. 764.

Replace the second paragraph with:

As far as the relationship between principal and agent is concerned, under the Rome Convention, in the absence of a choice of law in the contract,[633] the applicable law is determined by initial reference to the presumption in Art.4(2),[634] subject to the possibility of rebuttal under Art.4(5).[635] The characteristic performance in an agency contract is normally that of the agent,[636] so that, presumptively, the applicable law will be the law of the agent's habitual residence or central administration, as the case may be, unless (as is likely to be the case) the contract is made in the course of the agent's trade or profession in which case that law will be that of the agent's principal place of business unless performance by the agent is to be effected through a place of business other than his principal place of business, in which case it will be the law of the country in which the other place of business is situated which will, presumptively, constitute the applicable law. As regards the relationship between agent and third party, to the extent that the relationship arises out of a contract, the applicable law will be that chosen by the parties, if any, failing which the relevant presumption in Art.4[637] will initially apply and will be subject to displacement under Art.4(5).[638] What will be the characteristic performance of this contract if Art.4(2) is applicable will depend on the type of contract which has been concluded between agent and third party.

[633] *Marubeni Hong Kong and South China Ltd v Mongolian Government* [2002] 2 All E.R. (Comm) 873. See also on the application of the Rome Convention Art.3 in an agency context *Lawlor v Sandvik Mining & Construction Mobile Crushers & Screens Ltd* [2013] EWCA Civ 365; [2013] 2 Lloyd's Rep. 98. Note the potential applicability of Council Directive 86/653 on the co-ordination of the laws of the Member States relating to self-employed commercial agents [1986] O.J. L382/17, implemented in the

UK by the Commercial Agents (Council Directive) Regulations 1993 (SI 1993/3053, as amended by SI 1993/3173 and SI 1998/2868 and in Northern Ireland SI 1993/483(N.I.)). See *Lonsdale v Howard & Hallam Ltd* [2007] UKHL 32; [2008] 1 Lloyd's Rep. 78 for a decision on the interpretation on the Directive and the 1993 Regulations. In *Ingmar GB Ltd v Eaton Leonard Technologies Inc* (C-381/98) [2000] E.C.R. I-9305, the European Court of Justice held that Arts 17 and 18 of the Directive (implemented in regs 17 and 18 of the Regulations), which guarantee certain rights to commercial agents after termination of the agency contract, must be applied, as mandatory rules, where the commercial agent carries out his activity in a Member State even though the principal is established in a non-Member State and a clause in the contract stipulates that it is to be governed by the law of that non-Member State: see Plender and Wilderspin, *The European Private International Law of Obligations*, 4th edn, paras 12-062 to 12-063; Dicey, Morris and Collins, *The Conflict of Laws*, 15th edn, paras 33-420 to 33-429; *Bowstead and Reynolds on Agency*, 21st edn, paras 11-006 to 11-011; Verhagen, (2002) 51 I.C.L.Q. 135. See also on the application of the Directive: *Rossetti Marketing Ltd v Diamond Sofa Company Ltd* [2012] EWCA Civ 1021; [2013] 1 All E.R. (Comm) 308; *United Antwerp Maritime Agencies (Unamar) NV v Navigation Maritime Bulgare* (C-184/12); and *Fern Computer Consultancy Ltd v Integraph Cadworth & Analysis Solutions Inc* [2014] EWHC 2908 (Ch).

[634] Above, paras 26-062 to 26-075.

[635] Above, paras 26-076 to 26-079.

[636] *Bank of Baroda v Vysya Bank Ltd* [1994] 2 Lloyd's Rep. 87; *PT Pan Indonesia Bank Ltd TBK v Marconi Communications International Ltd* [2005] EWCA Civ 422; [2005] 2 All E.R. (Comm) 325; *Albon v Naza Motor Trading Sdn Bhd* [2007] EWHC 9 (Ch); [2007] 1 W.L.R. 2489 at [29]-[30]; *Sharab v HRH Prince Al-Waleed bin Talal bin Abdal-Aziz Al-Saud* [2008] EWHC 1893 (Ch) at [74]–[76]; *Kent v Paterson-Brown* [2018] EWHC 2008 (Ch); Plender, *The European Contracts Convention*, 4th edn, para.7-059; Dicey, Morris and Collins, *The Conflict of Laws*, 14th edn, paras 33-410 to 33-412. cf. *Print Concept GmbH v GEW (EC) Ltd* [2001] EWCA Civ 352; [2001] E.C.C. 36 (characteristic performance of distributorship agreement intended to be fulfilled by individual contracts of sale and purchase is that of the vendor). In *Hillside (New Media) Ltd v Baasland* [2010] EWHC 3336 (Comm); [2010] 2 C.L.C. 986 at [40], *Hillside* was assumed to be the characteristic performer for the purposes of the Rome Convention even though in some cases it was acting as principal and in others as agent for disclosed or undisclosed principals,

[637] Above, paras 26-063 to 26-073, 26-082; and the Rome I Regulation Art.4(3).

[638] Above, paras 26-073 to 26-076.

Contracts of insurance

Replace footnote 651 with:

[651] See para.26-085, above.   **26-086**

Banking contracts

Replace footnote 711 with:

[711] Fentiman, *International Commercial Litigation*, 2nd edn, para.5.97. The Supreme Court in *Taurus*   **26-087**
Petroleum Ltd v State Oil Marketing Co of the Ministry of Oil, Iraq [2017] UKSC 64; [2018] A.C. 690 applied English law to the obligations of the issuing bank in relation to both the beneficiary and the nominated bank. England was the place of the branch of the issuing bank rather than the nominated bank. However, there was no detailed analysis of the Rome I Regulation in this context. For a critical analysis of this decision see R. Gwynne [2018] L.M.C.L.Q.450.

5.   FORMATION AND VALIDITY OF THE CONTRACT OF SALE

Replace title footnote 725 with:

Acts required to conclude the contract[725]

[725] See generally Fawcett, Harris and Bridge, *International Sale of Goods in the Conflict of Laws* (2005),   **26-090**
Ch.13; Plender and Wilderspin, *The European Private International Law of Obligations*, 4th edn, paras 14-060 to 14-070; Dicey, Morris and Collins, *The Conflict of Laws*, 15th edn, paras 32-108 to 32-120; Cheshire, North and Fawcett, *Private International Law*, 15th edn, pp.755-758; Kaye, *The New Private International Law of Contract of the European Community* (1993), Ch.13; Lagarde in North (ed), *Contract Conflicts* (1982), pp.49-51; Jaffey, (1975) 24 I.C.L.Q. 603; Libling, (1979) 42 M.L.R. 169; Thomson, (1980) 43 M.L.R. 650.

Replace footnote 744 with:

26-091 ⁷⁴⁴ e.g. Cheshire and North, *Private International Law*, 11th edn, p.756. It is possible that this view rests on a confusion between the distinct concepts of "the putative proper law" and the "objective proper law".

Third parties and agency

Replace footnote 751 with:

26-092 ⁷⁵¹ This is the more likely result under English law, even where the existence or the name of the principal is not disclosed to the other party: see *Bowstead & Reynolds on Agency*, 21st edn, Art.76 paras 8-068 et seq.

Replace footnote 763 with:

26-093 ⁷⁶³ *Laemthong International Lines Co v Artis (No.3)* [2005] EWHC 1595 (Comm). See also *Secure Capital SA v Credit Suisse AG* [2017] EWCA Civ 1486 at [45] (identification of the parties entitled to sue on a contract, in this case immobilised securities represented by Notes, is governed by the proper law of the contract).

Replace title footnote 764 with:

Elements vitiating consent⁷⁶⁴

26-094 ⁷⁶⁴ See generally Dicey, Morris and Collins, *The Conflict of Laws*, 15th edn, paras 32-118 to 32-120; Cheshire, North and Fawcett, *Private International Law*, pp.756-758; Jaffey, (1975) 24 I.C.L.Q. 603; Libling, (1979) 42 M.L.R. 169; Thomson, (1980) 43 M.L.R. 650.

Replace footnote 766 with:

⁷⁶⁶ *Dimskal Shipping SA v International Transport Workers Federation* [1992] 2 A.C. 152; cf. *Kaufman v Gerson* [1904] 1 K.B. 591. In *Ukraine v Law Debenture Trust Corp Plc* [2018] EWCA Civ 2026 the Court of Appeal applied public policy to disapply the act of state doctrine in order to assess an allegation that a contract governed by English law had been entered into as a result of duress by the state of Russia.

Replace title footnote 773 with:

Capacity of natural persons⁷⁷³

26-095 ⁷⁷³ See generally Dicey, Morris and Collins, *The Conflict of Laws*, 15th edn, paras 32R-168 to 32-180; Cheshire, North and Fawcett, *Private International Law*, pp.761-764; Blaikie, [1984] S.L.T. 161.

Corporate capacity

Replace footnote 781 with:

26-096 ⁷⁸¹ *Risdon Iron and Locomotive Works Ltd v Furness* [1906] 1 K.B. 49; *Carl Zeiss Stiftung v Rayner and Keeler Ltd (No.2)* [1967] 1 A.C. 853. In *Standard Chartered Bank v Ceylon Petroleum Corp* [2012] EWCA Civ 1049 at [24], it was common ground that the capacity to contract of a public corporation created by an Act of Parliament in Sri Lanka was determined by Sri Lankan law. In *Ukraine v Law Debenture Trust Corp Plc* [2018] EWCA Civ 2026; [2019] 2 W.L.R. 655 the Court of Appeal held that the capacity of a foreign state to contract flows from its recognition and personality as a state and was not analogous to the capacity of either a natural person or a foreign company. Fentiman, *International Commercial Litigation*, 2nd edn, para.3.27 argues that the contractual capacity of corporations is not one of status but concerns whether a corporation may be sued, a question which in English law is governed by the law of its domicile, meaning the law in force where it is incorporated. In *Canary Wharf v European Medicines Authority* [2019] EWHC 335 (Ch); 183 Con. L.R. 167 questions of capacity of the EMA were governed by EU law as the law of its place of incorporation.

Replace title footnote 792 with:

Formalities⁷⁹²

26-097 ⁷⁹² See generally Plender and Wilderspin, *The European Private International Law of Obligations*, 4th edn, paras 14-071 to 14-076; Dicey, Morris and Collins, *The Conflict of Laws*, 15th edn, paras 32R-127 to 32-139; Cheshire, North and Fawcett, *Private International Law*, pp.758-761.

Replace title of paragraph 26-100 and footnote 817 with:

Essential validity[817]

[817] See generally Dicey, Morris and Collins, *The Conflict of Laws*, 15th edn, paras 32-121 to 32-125; Cheshire, North and Fawcett, *Private International Law*, pp.755-758.

26-100

Unfair Contract Terms Act

Replace footnote 833 with:

[833] For commentary on s.27, see Fawcett, Harris and Bridge, *International Sale of Goods in the Conflict of Laws*, paras 13-301 to 13-320; Plender and Wilderspin, *The European Private International Law of Obligations*, 4th edn, paras 9-065 to 9-067; Dicey, Morris and Collins, *The Conflict of Laws*, 15th edn, paras 1-058, 1-063 to 1-064, 33-0158 to 33-160, 33-024 to 33-026; Cheshire, North and Fawcett, *Private International Law*, p.747; Thompson, *Unfair Contract Terms Act 1977* (1978), Ch.8; Mann, (1977) 26 I.C.L.Q. 903; (1978) 27 I.C.L.Q. 661. For proposals to reform ss.26 and 27, see Law Commission, *Unfair Terms in Contracts, Law Com. No.292* (2005), paras 7.1-7.64 and Draft Bill cl.18-20. The Law Commission originally proposed reforms to ss.26 and 27: see Law Commission, *Unfair Terms in Contracts, Law Com. No.292* (2005), paras 7.1-7.64 and Draft Bill cl.18-20. These proposals have not been implemented, however, following the European Commission's proposal for a draft directive on consumer rights which would, among other things, harmonise the law on unfair contract terms: Law Commission, *Annual Report 2008-2009* (Law Com. No.316), para.A.38. A Directive on Consumer Rights (2011/83/EC) came into force on June 13, 2014. It replaced Directive 97/7/EC on the protection of consumers in respect of distance contracts and Directive 85/877/EEC on the protection of consumers in respect of contracts negotiated away from business premises. However, Directive 199/44/EC on certain aspects of sale of consumer goods, and Directive 93/13/EEC on unfair terms in consumer contracts remain in force.

26-102

Choice of law by the parties: a foreign law

Replace footnote 855 with:

[855] Regulation Recital (12) suggests that a jurisdiction clause is a material factor in deciding if there is an implied choice of law; though it stops short of saying that it would suffice on its own to demonstrate such a choice. cf. Cheshire, North and Fawcett, *Private International Law*, p.720.

26-107

Replace footnote 863 with:

[863] See Cheshire, North and Fawcett, *Private International Law* p.747, referring to UCTA as an example of a statute of limited overriding effect which overrides freedom of choice but not applicable law in the absence of choice. See also Fentiman, *International Commercial Litigation*, 2nd edn, para.4.17, referring to UCTA as an inalienable rather than an indefeasible overriding rule.

26-108

Replace title of paragraph 26-114 and footnote 874 with:

Consumer Protection (Distance Selling) Regulations 2000[874]

[874] The Directive on Consumer Rights (2011/83/EC), which came into force on 13 June 2014, replaces Directive 97/7/EC on the protection of consumers in respect of distance contracts and is implemented by the Consumer Contracts (Information, Cancellation and Additional Charges) Regulations 2013. The 2013 Regulations do not contain an anti-avoidance provision.

26-114

Replace title footnote 899 with:

Legality[899]

[899] See generally Dicey, Morris and Collins, *The Conflict of Laws*, 15th edn, paras 32-094 to 32-103, 32-121 to 32-125; Cheshire, North and Fawcett, *Private International Law*, pp.769–772; Jaffey, (1974) 23 I.C.L.Q. 1; Wyatt, (1974) 37 M.L.R. 399.

26-118

Replace footnote 901 with:

[901] Rome I Regulation Art.10(1); Rome Convention Art.8(1) and see confirming this general principle *Dana Gas PJSC v Dan Gas Sukuk Ltd* [2017] EWHC 2921 (Comm) and [2018] EWHC 278 (Comm) . See Lagarde in *Contract Conflicts*, p.49; Lasok and Stone, *Conflict of Laws in the European Community*, p.368; Plender and Wilderspin, *The European Private International Law of Obligations*, 4th edn,

para.14–060. This is of course, subject to the foreign law complying with public policy under Art.21 of the Regulation (Art.16 of the Convention).

Replace footnote 913 with:

[913] The principle does not apply if the act is committed outside the foreign country and is only illegal under its law by virtue of the extra-territorial operation thereof: *British Nylon Spinners Ltd v Imperial Chemical Industries Ltd* [1953] Ch. 19; *Sharif v Azad* [1967] 1 Q.B. 605 at 617. See also *Dana Gas PJSC v Dan Gas Sukuk Ltd* [2017] EWHC 2921 (Comm) and [2018] EWHC 278 (Comm).

Replace the third paragraph with:

26-119   Illegality under any other foreign law—for example, the law of one party's nationality or, in respect of a company, the law of its place of incorporation,[938a] or place of business or residence,[939] or, it is submitted, of the place of contracting[940]— did not per se affect the contract's enforceability in England at common law, nor because of the UK's reservation to the Rome Convention Art.7(1)[941] was there apparently any place for the argument that illegality under these laws had any effect, as such, on a contract which fell within the provisions of the Convention. The same is true under the Rome I Regulation.[942]

[938a] *Canary Wharf v European Medicines Authority* [2019] EWHC 335 (Ch); 183 Con. L.R. 167.

[939] *Trinidad Shipping Co v Alston* [1920] A.C. 888; *Kleinwort Sons & Co v Ungarische Baumvolle Industrie AG* [1939] 2 K.B. 678; *Toprak Mahsulleri Ofisi v Finagrain Compagnie Commerciale Agricole et Financière SA* [1979] 2 Lloyd's Rep. 98.

[940] Contra *The Torni* [1932] P. 78; and a dictum in *Re Missouri Steamship Co Ltd* (1889) 42 Ch. D. 321 at 336; but see the comments on these in *Vita Food Products Inc v Unus Shipping Co Ltd* [1939] A.C. 277 at 297–300.

[941] Contracts (Applicable Law) Act 1990 s.2(2) and Sch.1 Art.22. Note, however, Art.9(6) which applies to contracts the subject matter of which is a right in, or right to use, immovable property.

[942] Unless, of course, one of these laws happens to coincide with the lex loci solutionis; in which case, the Rome I Regulation Art.9(3) might be applied.

Exchange control

Replace footnote 943 with:

26-120   [943] Dicey, Morris and Collins, *The Conflict of Laws*, 15th edn, paras 37-062 to 37-077; Proctor (ed), *Mann on the Legal Aspect of Money*, 7th edn (2012). See also Black, *Foreign Currency Claims in the Conflict of Laws* (2010).

6. PROPERTY

(a) General Issues

Renvoi

Replace the second paragraph with:

26-123   Goods in transit. The lex situs principle is subject to an important limitation: it does not apply when at the relevant time the goods are "in transit".[973] The phrase "in transit" in this particular context within the conflict of laws has not been authoritatively defined, though it seems clear that the "transit" in question has a different point of commencement, and a different endpoint,[974] from the "transit" during which the English remedy of stoppage in transit[975] can be invoked by a seller. It is submitted that, for the purpose of conflict of laws, goods are "in transit" when, while being carried from one country, X, to another, Z, they are for a time not situated in any country at all (being, for example, in a ship on the high seas[976]), or are only casually and fortuitously in an intermediate country, Y (being, for example, on a train which on its way from X to Z passes through Y), or are pursuing an uninterrupted journey from their point of departure in X to the border of X, or from the border of Z to their destination in Z.[977] In such circumstances, the lex situs principle is inapplicable; even if the goods can be said to have a legal situs at all, the fortuitous nature of such situs and the fact that it may not be known to the relevant parties make the principle inappropriate. If, however, the journey is interrupted to the extent that the goods come to rest in any country for a reasonable period of time,[978] the lex situs principle will be applicable, even though the interruption was not intended or foreseen by any of the relevant parties.[979] Similarly, if the relevant journey begins and ends within a single country, it is submitted that the goods should never be considered "in transit" but should be subject throughout to the lex situs principle on the basis that they have a situs in that country.

[973] See Fawcett, Harris and Bridge, *International Sale of Goods in the Conflict of Laws*, paras 18-55, 18-59; Carruthers, *The Transfer of Property in the Conflict of Laws*, paras 3-31 to 3-35.

[974] Thus, e.g. in *Inglis v Usherwood* (1801) 1 East 515, the goods were not treated as "in transit", and (on one view at least) were subjected to the lex situs, even though according to the relevant position of English domestic law regarding stoppage in transit (Sale of Goods Act 1979 s.45(1)), transit would have commenced but for the fact that the carrying ship had been chartered by the buyer.

[975] As to the scope of this remedy, see generally Ch.15, above.

[976] It is surely unsatisfactory in such a case that the goods should be subject to the law of the ship's flag as a form of lex situs, yet see Cheshire, North and Fawcett, *Private International Law*, pp.1275–1276. See also *Blue Sky One Ltd v Mahan Air* [2010] EWHC 631 (Comm) at [154] noting an exception in favour of the place where an aircraft is registered which applies to an aircraft in flight over the high seas or a *territoriun nullius*.

[977] cf. the definition of "transit", in the conflicts sense, in Hellendall, (1939) 17 Can. Bar Rev. 7 and 105, 25 et seq.

[978] Wolff, *Private International Law*, 2nd edn (1950), para.494.

[979] *Cammell v Sewell* (1860) 5 H. & N. 728, discussed below, para.26-130; Dicey, Morris and Collins, *The Conflict of Laws*, 15th edn, paras 24-017 to 24-018; Cheshire, North and Fawcett, *Private International Law*, pp.1275–1276.

The proper law of the transfer

Replace footnote 981 with:

[981] Below, para.26-138. It has at times been suggested (e.g. in the 7th edn of Cheshire, *Private International Law*, pp.409–411; Schmitthoff, *English Conflict of Laws*, 3rd edn (1954), p.198) that the proper law of the transfer should have the wider function of determining all proprietary questions as between the parties to a transfer, whilst the lex situs should only operate when third parties are involved. But this view cannot now be supported; it is inconsistent with the leading authorities on the scope of the lex situs and has been abandoned by its leading exponent: Cheshire, North and Fawcett, *Private International Law*, 15th edn, pp.1266–1267. In any event, in cases of sale, it is usually in situations involving third parties that property questions are important: see above, paras 5-003 to 5-004.

26-124

(c) The Passing of Title: The General Rules

(i) Goods not in Transit: No Documents Issued

Passing of property between seller and buyer

Replace footnote 1024 with:

[1024] *Luttges & Co v Ormiston and Glass Ltd* (1926) 6 Reports of the Decisions of the Mixed Arbitral Tribunals 564, 569; and see *Hardwick Game Farm v Suffolk Agricultural Poultry Producers Assoc* [1966] 1 W.L.R. 287 at 330; sub nom. *Henry Kendall & Sons v William Lillico & Sons Ltd* [1969] 2 A.C. 31 at 101; *Glencore International AG v Metro Trading International Inc* [2001] 1 Lloyd's Rep. 284 at 292–295, specifically rejecting the applicability of the law applicable to the contract where the issue of title arises as between buyer and seller and holding that the lex situs applies in such situations in the same

26-132

way as it does when third parties are involved; *District of Columbia v Upjohn Co* 185 F. 2d 992 (1950); *Rayn v McCalley* 228 S.W. 2d 61 (1950); Dicey, Morris and Collins, *The Conflict of Laws*, 15th edn, para.33-027; Cheshire, North and Fawcett, *Private International Law*, pp.1267–1273; Wolff, *Private International Law*, para.498; Rabel, *The Conflict of Laws*, Vol.3, pp.84–85; Morris, (1945) 22 B.Y.B.I.L. 232, 235–237; Hellendall, (1939) 17 Can. Bar Rev. 7 and 105, 8 et seq. Contrast Bridge in Bridge and Stevens (eds), *Cross-Border Security and Insolvency* (2001), Ch.7 pp.126–138; Fawcett, Harris and Bridge, *International Sale of Goods in the Conflict of Laws*, paras 18-51 to 18-54; Carruthers, *The Transfer of Property in the Conflict of Laws* (2005), paras 3-61 to 3-67, 4-22.

(iii) Goods in Transit: No Documents Issued

The proper law of the transfer

Replace footnote 1050 with:

26-138 [1050] Cheshire, North and Fawcett, *Private International Law*, pp.1275-1276, restricting its application to the case of a single transfer occurring while the goods are on board.

(d) Retention of Title

Generally

Replace the first paragraph with:

26-141   In an international sale contract a seller may attempt to retain his title in the goods until the occurrence of a future event, e.g. payment of the price in full. Clauses which purport to do this (*Romalpa* clauses[1060]) may take a variety of forms but the basic function of such clauses is to provide the seller with security in the event of the price not being paid or in the event of the buyer's receivership or insolvency. The complex problems of private international law which may be generated by such clauses have never been directly considered by the English courts[1061] and are treated somewhat cursorily in a handful of Irish[1062] and Scottish[1063] decisions. Accordingly, therefore, any conclusions[1064] on the law relating to the issue must be tentative.[1065] In approaching the question, it is, at the outset, appropriate to bear in mind that the basic problem in these situations stems from a commingling of issues of a proprietary and contractual nature and of the additional considerations of priority in insolvency law which become involved in the paradigm *Romalpa* case, i.e. when the buyer is potentially or actually insolvent.

[1060] See above, paras 5-133 to 5-172.

[1061] Canadian cases deal with the issue of passing of title where goods have been the subject of a prior security transaction, such as a conditional sale or chattel mortgage, and the position has become complicated by one or more changes of situs since the prior transaction and by the presence of provisions for registration of security transactions in one or more of the relevant leges situs: for discussion of some of these cases see Dicey, Morris and Collins, *The Conflict of Laws*, 15th edn, paras 24-021 to 24-042; Falconbridge, *The Conflict of Laws*, pp.452 et seq.; Goode and Ziegel, *Hire-Purchase and Conditional Sale* (1967), pp.209 et seq.; Morris, (1945) 22 B.Y.B.I.L. 232; Davies, (1964) 13 I.C.L.Q. 53; Ziegel, (1967) 45 Can. Bar Rev. 284. These authorities may be of some assistance in determining whether title has passed by virtue of a sale-on by the buyer under the original contract, but they by no means address the further problems to which Romalpa clauses may give rise. *Glencore International AG v Metro Trading International Inc* [2001] 1 Lloyd's Rep. 284 sheds some light on the latter question but the case did not appear to be concerned with a Romalpa clause. In the US, the matter is governed almost exclusively by the UCC: see Scoles, Hay, Borchers and Symeonides, *Conflict of Laws*, 4th edn (2004), pp.1081 et seq.; Mooney in Bridge and Stevens (eds), *Cross-Border Security and Insolvency* (2001), Ch.10. For retention of title in cases falling within the EU Regulation on insolvency proceedings (Regulation 1346/2000 [2000] O.J. L160/1), see below, paras 26-150 to 26-152. The Insolvency Regulation is to be replaced by Regulation 2015/848 [2015] O.J. L141/19 on insolvency proceedings (recast). The Insolvency Regulation recast applies to insolvency proceedings commencing on or after June 26, 2017. For retention of title in relation to Directive 2000/35 on combating late payment in commercial transactions [2000] O.J. 2000 L200/35, see below, para.26-153.

[1062] *Re Interview Ltd* [1975] I.R. 382; *Kruppstahl AG v Quittmann Products Ltd* [1982] I.L.R.M. 551. See Binchy, *Irish Conflicts of Law* (1988), pp.496–499.

[1063] *Emerald Stainless Steel Ltd v South Side Distribution Ltd* 1983 S.L.T. 162; *Deutz Engines Ltd v Terex Ltd* 1984 S.L.T. 273; *Hammer and Sohne v HWT Realisations Ltd* 1985 S.L.T. (Sh. Ct.) 21; *Zahnrad Fabrik Passau GmbH v Terex Ltd* 1986 S.L.T. 84. These cases held that a retention of title clause was an attempt to create a non-possessory security interest which was void under Scots law. However, in *Armour v Thyssen Edelstahlwerke AG* [1991] 2 A.C. 339, the House of Lords held that the clause did not, as a matter of Scots law, have that effect and expressly overruled the first 2 cases cited above, it being implicit also that the remaining cases are no longer authoritative on that point. However, because the House of Lords does not even refer to the conflict of laws' issues since the courts below (1989 S.L.T. 183, see also 1986 S.L.T. 94) had held that German law, the law governing the contract, had not been relevantly pleaded and proved, that decision does not, in principle, affect the issues of conflict of laws discussed in the earlier cases and in the courts below in *Armour v Thyssen*. Accordingly, use is made of these decisions in what follows. For discussion of Scots law see Anton, *Private International Law*, 2nd edn (1990), pp.618–620; Stewart, 1985 S.L.T. 149; Sellar, 1985 S.L.T. 313; Patrick, 1986 S.L.T. 265, 277; North, (1990) 220 *Recueil des Cours*, 1, 3, 267–271.

[1064] See generally Fawcett, Harris and Bridge, *International Sale of Goods in the Conflict of Laws* paras 18-93 to 18-125; Dicey, Morris and Collins, *The Conflict of Laws*, 15th edn, paras 33-029 to 33-031; Cheshire, North and Fawcett, *Private International Law*, pp.1272–1273; Anton, *Private International Law*; North, (1990) 220 *Recueil des Cours* 267–271; Binchy, *Irish Conflicts of Law* (1998); Morse, [1993] J.B.L. 168; For comparative studies see Verheuil in Voskuil and Wade (eds), *Hague-Zagreb Essays on the Law of International Trade* (1985), Vol.5 pp.54 et seq.; Schilling, (1985) 34 I.C.L.Q. 87; Kreuzer (1995) Rev. Crit. d.i.p. 465. For discussion of German conflict of laws rules, see Drobnig in Bridge and Stevens (eds), *Cross-Border Security and Insolvency* (2001), Ch.8. For discussion of French conflict of laws rules, see Kessedjian in Bridge and Stevens (eds), *Cross-Border Security and Insolvency* (2001), Ch.9. For a survey of retention of title provisions in the domestic law of European jurisdictions see Pennington, (1978) 27 I.C.L.Q. 277.

[1065] Potentially relevant foreign law is often not pleaded (see *Aluminium Industrie Vaasen BV v Romalpa Aluminium Ltd* [1976] 1 W.L.R. 676, above, para.26-003) or, correctly or incorrectly, is thought not to be different from English law (*Pfeiffer Weinkellerie Weinenkauf GmbH v Arbuthnot Factors Ltd* [1988] 1 W.L.R. 150).

Retention of title

Replace footnote 1068 with:

[1068] In the Irish cases cited in para.26-151, above, the goods seem to have been situated in Germany   **26-142** (which was also the country of the proper law) at the time of the original contract. In *Hammer and Sohne v HWT Realisations Ltd* 1985 S.L.T. (Sh. Ct.) 21, the relevant lex situs was said to be Scotland, the place of delivery of the goods. The security created by the German retention of title clause was, as a nonpossessory security, held to be opposed to a fundamental principle of Scots law and therefore ineffective (though see now *Armour v Thyssen Edelstahlwerke AG* [1991] 2 A.C. 339). But it would appear that the jewels were in Germany at the time of the contract and the case could just as easily have been decided on the ground that although a valid security had been created by German law as the lex situs at the time of the contract, it would not be recognised in Scotland on the grounds of public policy, a concept which is also referred to in the judgment: see 1985 S.L.T. 21 at 23. cf. Anton, *Private International Law*, p.620.

Claims by original seller against sub-purchaser

Replace the first paragraph with:

Romalpa clauses sometimes attempt to enable the seller to maintain a direct ac-   **26-149** tion against sub-purchasers for the sub-sale price of the goods by stipulating that where the goods are sold by the buyer to sub-purchasers before payment has been received by the seller, any claim against sub-purchasers for the purchase price of the goods under the sub-sale is to vest in or to be transferred to the seller.[1105] The validity and effect of such a provision would seem to involve those principles of private international law relating to the assignment of debts. Although it was not possible to state the English common law[1106] on this topic with confidence, it is suggested that whether the buyer could assign to the seller the debt which was owed to him by the sub-purchaser was a matter governed by the law applicable to the subsale, that being the law which created the debt. If that law regarded the debt as capable of assignment it was then for the law governing the assignment (in this case the original contract of sale) to determine whether, as between the buyer (assignor) and seller (assignee), the debt had been validly assigned.[1107] The same principle was enshrined in cases which fell within the Rome Convention, Art.12 of which drew a distinction between the assignability of a right (governed by the law applicable to the right to which the assignment relates,[1108] in this context, again, the law applicable to the sub-sale) and the mutual obligations arising between assignor and assignee (governed by the law applicable to the contract between them,[1109] in this context, again, the law applicable to the original contract of sale). These provisions have, in turn, been substantially re-enacted in the Rome I Regulation Art.14.[1110]

[1105] Above, para.5-158. Such a provision may, however, give rise to a charge: see, above, para.5-158.

[1106] See Moshinsky, (1992) 109 L.Q.R. 591. See further Rogerson, [1990] C.L.J. 441; Struycken, [1998] L.M.C.L.Q. 345; Fentiman, *International Commercial Litigation*, 2nd edn, para.5.198.

[1107] See Dicey, Morris and Collins, *The Conflict of Laws*, 15th edn, para.24-051 to 24-054; Cheshire, North and Fawcett, *Private International Law*, Ch.32. Application of the lex situs of the debt was rejected in *Raiffeisen Zentralbank Osterreich AG v Five Star General Trading LLC* [2001] Q.B. 825.

[1108] Rome Convention Art.12(2). On the scope of Art.12, see *Raiffeisen Zentralbank Osterreich AG v Five Star General Trading LLC* [2001] Q.B. 825; Stevens and Struycken, (2002) 118 L.Q.R. 15. See also Struycken, [1998] L.M.C.L.Q. 345; Stevens in Bridge and Stevens (eds), *Cross-Border Security and Insolvency* (2001), pp.213–216; Cheshire, North and Fawcett, *Private International Law*, pp.1285–1291.

[1109] Rome Convention Art.12(1).

[1110] See also Recital (38). See further Plender and Wilderspin, *The European Private International Law of Obligations*, 4th edn, paras 13-019 to 13-044; Bridge, (2009) 125 L.Q.R. 671; Verhagen and van Dongen (2010) 6 J. Priv. Int. L. 1; Hartley, (2011) 60 I.C.L.Q. 29; Møllmann, [2011] L.M.C.L.Q. 262; Fentiman, *International Commercial Litigation*, 2nd edn, paras 5.172 to 5.211.

Replace the second paragraph with:
Should the buyer also effect an assignment of the proceeds of sale to a person other than the seller, a question of priority as between competing assignments may arise if each assignment is valid by its governing law. At common law, the better view was that priority was governed by the law which creates the debt (the law applicable to the sub-sale).[1111] The same position probably obtained under the Rome Convention Art.12, since the question of priorities relates to "the conditions under which the assignment can be invoked against the debtor".[1112] The matter is not free from doubt,[1112a] however, since it is apparently envisaged that the Rome I Regulation Art.14, which is in substantially the same terms as Art.12 of the Convention, does not apply to such questions. A review clause in Art.27(2) of the Regulation requires that:

> "By 17 June 2010, the Commission shall submit to the European Parliament, the Council and the European Economic and Social Committee a report on the question of the effectiveness of an assignment or subrogation of a claim against third parties and the priority of the assigned or subrogated claim over a right of another person. The report shall be accompanied, if appropriate, by a proposal to amend this Regulation and an assessment of the impact of the provisions to be introduced."[1113]

On March 12, 2018, the Commission issed a proposal on the law applicable to third party effects of assignments of claims.[1113a] Under that proposal, third party effects of assignments, including priority as between competing assignments, are to be governed by the law of the habitual resudence of the assignor.[1114]

¹¹¹¹ Dicey, Morris and Collins, *The Conflict of Laws*, 15th edn, para.24-054; Cheshire, North and Fawcett, *Private International Law*, pp.1288–1289; *Stevens in Cross-Border Security and Insolvency*, pp.214–215; R. Goode [2015] L.M.C.L.Q. 289.

¹¹¹² Rome Convention Art.12(2). In *Raiffeisen Zentralbank Osterreich AG v Five Star General Trading LLC* [2001] Q.B. 825 it was held that whether notice of the assignment must be given to the debtor is a matter for the law applicable to the debt pursuant to Art.12(2). While the case does not deal with the issue of priorities, it is submitted that the general tenor of the decision supports application of Art.12(2) to priorities as well. And see Dicey, Morris, and Collins, *The Conflict of Laws*, 14th edn, para.24-062; Cheshire, North and Fawcett, *Private International Law*, pp.1290–1291; Stevens in *Cross-Border Security and Insolvency*, pp.214–215. Contrast Bridge in Bridge and Stevens (eds), *Cross-Border Security and Insolvency* (2001), pp.140–143.

^{1112a} On 23 August 2018, a German court requested a preliminary ruling from the CJEU on whether Art.14 is applicable to the third-party effects of multiple assignments of claims (*BGL BNP Paribas SA v TeamBank AG* (C-548/18)).

¹¹¹³ For discussion, see Bridge, (2009) 125 L.Q.R. 671; Verhagen and van Dongen, (2010) 6 J. Priv. Int. L. 1; R Goode [2015] L.M.C.L.Q. 289. See also *Guidance on the Law Applicable to Contractual Obligations (Rome I)* (February 2010), p.9 at *http://www.webarchive.nationalarchives.gov.uk* [Accessed 29 July 2017].

Pursuant to the Rome I Regulation Art.27(1), the European Commission was to submit a report on the effects of assignment and subrogation on third parties. It commissioned the British Institute of International and Comparative Law to produce this study, entitled a "Study on the Question of Effectiveness of an Assignment or Subrogation of a Claim Against Third Parties and the Priority of the Assigned or Subrogated Claim over a Right of Another Person." It is available at *http://ec.europa.eu/justice/civil/files/report_assignment_en.pdf* [Accessed 29 July 2017]. On subrogation, see also Third Parties (Rights Against Insurers) Act 2010 s.18. See also R. Goode [2015] L.M.C.L.Q. 289, 305.

^{1113a} COM (2018) 96 final.

¹¹¹⁴ It may be that different principles should apply to assignment of multiple debts as is common in factoring and securitisation arrangements: Rogerson, *Collier's Conflict of Laws* 4th edn, pp.396–405; Fentiman, [2010] L. & F.M.R. 405; [2010] Indiana Jo. Global Legal Studies 245 and R. Goode [2015] L.M.C.L.Q. 289. However, in its proposal on the law applicable to the third party effects of assignment of claims (COM (2018) 96 final) the Commission advocates the appplication of the law of the habitual residence of the assignor in all cases, including the assignment of multiple and future claims.

Council Regulation on insolvency proceedings

Replace the first paragraph with:

This Regulation¹¹¹⁵ purports to establish¹¹¹⁶ uniform rules of jurisdiction, choice of law and recognition of judgments in relation to insolvency proceedings which fall within its remit.¹¹¹⁷ Only a very brief outline of the Regulation is provided here.¹¹¹⁸ Very broadly, the Regulation permits the opening of "main" insolvency proceedings in the Member State in which a debtor's centre of main interests is situated¹¹¹⁹ and proceedings can only be opened in another Member State if the debtor has an establishment in that state.¹¹²⁰ The latter proceedings are "secondary"¹¹²¹ or "territorial"¹¹²² proceedings and their effects are limited to assets of the debtor which are situated in that Member State.¹¹²³ The general choice of law rule applicable under the Regulation is that a court having jurisdiction shall apply the lex fori.¹¹²⁴ However, certain specific issues are subject to special and different choice of law rules and one such special issue is reservation of title.¹¹²⁵ Where, therefore, the issue of retention of title arises in the course of insolvency proceedings subject to the Regulation, this special rule will be applied and brief consideration is here given to its content.¹¹²⁶

26-150

¹¹¹⁵ Council Regulation 1346/2000 on insolvency proceedings [2000] O.J. L160/1. The Regulation entered into force on 31 May 2002. For implementation in the UK, see SI 2002/1240. For discussion, see Fletcher, *Insolvency in Private International Law*, 2nd edn (2005), with supplement (2007), Ch.7; Virgos and Garcimartin, *The European Insolvency Regulation: Law and Practice* (2004); Dicey, Morris and Collins, *The Conflict of Laws*, 15th edn, paras 30-R-148 to 30-192; Moss, Fletcher and Isaacs (eds), *The EC Regulation on Insolvency Proceedings*, 2nd edn (2009). Regulation 1346/2000 has been

replaced by Regulation 2015/848 on insolvency proceedings (recast) which applies to insolvency proceedings commenced on or after June 26, 2017.

1116 Certain amendments to the Regulation were introduced upon the accession of new Member States to the EU on 1 May 2004: [2003] O.J. L236/711. Further amendments are contained in: Council Regulation 603/2005 [2005] O.J. L100/1; Council Regulation 694 [2006] O.J. L121/1; Council Regulation 1791/2006 [2006] O.J. L363/1; Council Regulation 681/2007 [2007] O.J. L159/1; Council Regulation 788/2008 [2008] O.J. L213/1.

1117 See Art.1 of the Regulation.

1118 See also the UNCITRAL Model Law on Cross-Border Insolvency, implemented in Great Britain (i.e. England and Scotland; separate regulations having been enacted in Northern Ireland) by the Cross-Border Insolvency Regulations 2006 (SI 2006/1030) (as provided for by the Insolvency Act 2000 s.14(1)) and the Solvency 2 Regulations 2015 (SI 2015/575). For detailed discussion of the UNCITRAL Model Law, as implemented in Great Britain, see Dicey, Morris and Collins, *The Conflict of Laws*, 15th edn, paras 30R-352 to 30-433. As r.203 of Dicey, Morris and Collins, 15th edn notes, the Model Law, as implemented in Great Britain, applies where: "(1) assistance is sought in Great Britain by a foreign court or a foreign representative in connection with a foreign proceeding; or (2) assistance is sought in a foreign State in connection with a proceeding under British insolvency law; or (3) a foreign proceeding and a proceeding under British insolvency law in respect of the same debtor are taking place concurrently; or (4) creditors or other interested persons in a foreign State have an interest in requesting the commencement of, or participating in, a proceeding under British insolvency law". See, in particular, Ch.V of the Model Law, as implemented in Great Britain, which concerns concurrent proceedings (discussed in r.207 of Dicey, Morris and Collins, *The Conflict of Laws*, 15th edn).

1119 Regulation 1346/2000 Art.3(1).

1120 Regulation 1346/2000 Art.3(2).

1121 Regulation 1346/2000 Arts 3(3), 27.

1122 Regulation 1346/2000 Art.3(2), (4).

1123 Regulation 1346/2000 Art.3(2).

1124 Regulation 1346/2000 Art.4.

1125 Regulation 1346/2000 Art.7. See also Art.5, concerned with third parties rights in rem.

1126 For more detail, see Fletcher, *Insolvency in Private International Law*, paras 7-104 to 7-107; Fawcett, Harris and Bridge, *International Sale of Goods in the Conflict of Laws*, paras 18-122 to 18-125.

Replace the fourth paragraph with:

26-152   Council Regulation 1346/2000 has been replaced by Regulation 2015/848 on insolvency proceedings (recast).[1132] The Insolvency Regulation recast applies to insolvency proceedings commencing on or after June 26, 2017. The rules relating to the opening of "main" insolvency proceedings remain the same and the general choice of law rule applying the lex fori also remains. Articles 10(1) and 10 (2) are the same as Regulation 1346/2000 Art.7(1) and Art.7(2).

1132 Regulation 2015/848 [2015] O.J. L141/19 on insolvency proceedings (recast).

7. RISK

Risk governed by the applicable law of the contract

Replace footnote 1139 with:

26-154   1139 In the legal systems of the world one finds rules prescribing at least four different times at which, prima facie, the risk should pass: (a) when the contract is concluded (e.g. the Swiss Code of Obligations para.185); (b) when property passes (e.g. the French Civil Code para.1196; English law, discussed above, Ch.6); (c) when the seller has done everything required of him by the contract (e.g. the Uniform Commercial Code paras 2-503, 2-509); and (d) when the goods are received by the buyer (e.g. the German Civil Code para.446). In international sales, such as c.i.f. and f.o.b., these rules are commonly displaced by the contrary intention of the parties: see above, paras 19-111, 20-095.

Connection with passing of property

Replace footnote 1146 with:

[1146] This approach could have been taken in *Kursell v Timber Operators and Contractors Ltd* [1927] **26-155**
K.B. 299, and it is consistent with the decision therein. See also *Glencore International AG v Metro Trading International Inc* [2001] 1 Lloyd's Rep. 284 at 297–298. cf. Fawcett, Harris and Bridge, *International Sale of Goods in the Conflict of Laws*, paras 13-198 to 13-200 and M. Bridge [2019] L.M.C.L.Q. 57, 73–74. On s.20A, see preceding note.

8. PERFORMANCE OF THE CONTRACT OF SALE

Replace title footnote 1147:

General principles[1147]

[1147] See Fawcett, Harris and Bridge, *International Sale of Goods in the Conflict of Laws* (2005), paras **26-156**
13-159 to 13-185; Dicey, Morris and Collins, *The Conflict of Laws*, 15th edn, paras 32-146 to 32-152; Cheshire, North and Fawcett, *Private International Law*, pp.765–766; Plender and Wilderspin, *The European Private International Law of Obligations*, 4th edn, paras 14-026 to 14-032.

Replace footnote 1155 with:

[1155] *East West Corp v DKBS 1912 A/S* [2002] EWHC (Comm); [2002] 2 Lloyd's Rep. 182; affirmed without argument on the point [2003] EWCA Civ 83; [2003] Q.B. 1309; *Import Export Metro Ltd v Compania Sud Americana De Vapores SA* [2003] EWHC 11 (Comm); [2003] 1 Lloyd's Rep. 405. Thus, if waiver of any particular obligation is alleged, its validity and effect is a matter for the applicable law, whereas if a contract governed by, say, English law, provides for delivery of goods in Paris during "usual business hours", French law will determine what hours those are. See, generally, Dicey, Morris and Collins, *The Conflict of Laws*, 15th edn, para.32-151; Cheshire, North and Fawcett, *Private International Law*, pp.765–766. cf. Fawcett, Harris and Bridge, *International Sale of Goods in the Conflict of Laws*, para.13-163.Plender and Wilderspin, *The European Private International Law of Obligations*, 4th edn, para.14-027. According to the *Giuliano-Lagarde Report*, p.33, "manner of performance" includes rules governing public holidays, the manner in which goods are to be examined and the steps to be taken if they are refused.

9. DISCHARGE OF OBLIGATIONS UNDER A CONTRACT OF SALE

Discharge by virtue of frustration or other similar principles

Replace footnote 1293 with:

[1293] Fawcett, Harris and Bridge, *International Sale of Goods in the Conflict of Laws* (2005), Ch.19; **26-176**
Dicey, Morris and Collins, *The Conflict of Laws*, 14th edn, Ch.34, esp. paras 34-020 to 34-028; Cheshire, North and Fawcett, *Private International Law*, 15th edn, pp.778–779; Panagopoulos, *Restitution in Private International Law* (2000); Rose (ed), *Restitution and the Conflict of Laws* (1995), Chs 3, 4 and 5; Dickinson [1996] L.M.C.L.Q. 566; cf. *Fibrosa Spolka Akcyjna v Fairbairn Lawson Combe Barbour Ltd* [1943] A.C. 52; *Arab Bank Ltd v Barclays Bank (Dominion, Colonial and Overseas)* [1953] 2 Q.B. 527 at 572; *Etler v Kertesz* (1960) 26 D.L.R. (2d) 209.

10. REMEDIES OF THE SELLER

(a) Remedies Affecting the Goods

Issues of principle

Replace footnote 1307 with:

[1307] This is recommended (with reservations) by Rabel, *The Conflict of Laws*, 2nd edn, Vol.4 pp.64– **26-178**
66; Falconbridge, (1937) 15 Can. Bar Rev. 215 237–238; Hellendall, (1939) 17 Can. Bar Rev. 7 and 105, 106–109. Characterisation generally is dealt with in Dicey, Morris and Collins, *The Conflict of Laws*, 15th edn, paras 2-001 to 2-047; Cheshire, North and Fawcett, *Private International Law*, 15th edn, Ch.3.

(i)   Lien and Withholding of Delivery

Third parties claiming rights against the goods

Replace footnote 1325 with:

26-182   ¹³²⁵ The third party must of course have taken a valid assignment of the seller's contractual rights. The validity of such assignment should be determined in general by the law applicable to the assignment itself, not the law governing the contract of sale which merely operates to determine whether the right is assignable: Rome I Regulation Art.14; Rome Convention Art.12; Dicey, Morris and Collins, *The Conflict of Laws*, 15th edn, paras 24-051 to 24-063; Cheshire, North and Fawcett, *Private International Law*, pp.1285–1291.

(b)   Personal Remedies of the Seller

Remedies against the buyer

Replace footnote 1352 with:

26-190   ¹³⁵² *Livesley v Clemens Horst Co* [1925] 1 D.L.R. 159 at 160–161; *Drew Brown Ltd v The "Orient Trader"* (1972) 34 D.L.R. (3d) 339; and see Dicey, Morris and Collins, *The Conflict of Laws*, 15th edn, paras 32-153 to 31-155; Cheshire, North and Fawcett, *Private International Law*, pp.766–768. See also commenting on whether the provisions differ from the position at common law *OJSC TNK-BP Holding v Lazurenko* [2012] EWHC 2781 (Ch) at [20].

Currency of judgment

Replace footnote 1389 with:

26-194   ¹³⁸⁹ See *Miliangos v George Frank (Textiles) Ltd (No.1)* [1976] A.C. 443; *Schorsch Meier GmbH v Hennin* [1975] Q.B. 416; *The Halcyon the Great* [1975] 1 W.L.R. 515; *Virani Ltd v Manuel Revert Y Cia SA* [2003] EWCA Civ 1651; [2004] 2 Lloyd's Rep. 14; *Carnegie v Giessen* [2005] EWCA Civ 191; [2005] 1 C.L.C. 259 (charging order may be expressed in foreign currency); *Commerzbank A/G v Large*, 1977 S.L.T. 219. See also *Law Com. No.124* (1983); *Law Commission Working Paper No.80* (1981). For academic commentary, see Black, *Foreign Currency Claims in the Conflict of Laws* (2010), Ch.2; Dicey, Morris and Collins, *The Conflict of Laws*, 15th edn, paras 37-082 to 37-096; Cheshire, North and Fawcett, *Private International Law*, pp.97–104; Lipstein, [1975] C.L.J. 215; Bowles and Phillips, (1976) 39 M.L.R. 196; Mann, (1976) 92 L.Q.R. 165; Libling, (1977) 93 L.Q.R. 212; Marshall, [1977] J.B.L. 225; Isaacs, [1977] L.M.C.L.Q. 356; Morris, *Law and Contemporary Problems* (1977) Vol.41 No.2 p.44; Becker, (1977) 25 Amer. J. Comp. Law 303; Powles, [1979] L.M.C.L.Q. 485; Maher, (1995) 44 I.C.L.Q. 72; Stern, [1995] L.M.C.L.Q. 494. As to procedure, see CPR Pt 16 Practice Direction para.9; CPR Pt 40 Practice Direction 40B para.10.

11.   REMEDIES OF THE BUYER

Rejection of the goods and rescission of the contract

Replace footnote 1414 with:

26-196   ¹⁴¹⁴ While some legal systems (e.g. the English—see above, para.12-057) require notice of defects to be given "within a reasonable time", others insist on notice "quickly as possible" (e.g. the French Civil Code para.1220) or within a specified period (e.g. the Italian Civil Code para.1495, which generally stipulates eight days).

Damages

Replace footnote 1422 with:

26-199   ¹⁴²² Mutatis mutandis, the point made in para.26-196, above, applies here also.

Other remedies against the seller

Replace footnote 1429 with:

[1429] Dicey, Morris and Collins, *The Conflict of Laws*, 15th edn, para.32-155; Cheshire, North and **26-201**
Fawcett, *Private International Law*, pp.767–768; Lasok and Stone, *Conflict of Laws in the European Community* (1987), p.370.

Remedies against the carrier

Replace paragraph with:

The buyer's contractual remedies[1431] against the carrier, like those of the seller,[1432] **26-202**
depend primarily[1433] upon the law applicable to the contract of carriage. This law
will determine generally the nature and extent of any liability of the carrier if the
goods are lost, or misdelivered,[1434] or delivered in a damaged condition,[1435] or
delivered late due to a deviation from the contractual voyage. However, the buyer
must in such a case establish that he is a person entitled to sue upon the contract of
carriage, and this may raise problems if the contract was made in the first instance
with the seller.[1436] It is clear that the question whether the seller's rights under such
contract are assignable at all and the extent of the rights assigned is a matter for the
law applicable to the contract itself.[1437] On the other hand, the question whether such
an assignment[1438] has been validly effected should be referred to the law applicable to the assignment itself.[1439] If the buyer claims contractual rights against
the carrier, not on the basis of an assignment, but on the ground that between
himself and the carrier a new implied contract has arisen (e.g. on tender of documents and receipt of the goods[1440]), this new contract has its own governing law,
which is not necessarily that of the original contract of carriage.[1441]

[1431] As to alternative remedies in tort, see *The Stensby* [1947] 2 All E.R. 786.

[1432] Above, para.26-190.

[1433] Conventions such as CMR and COTIF may be applicable (above, paras 21-048 et seq) and in cases
of carriage by sea the Hague or Hague-Visby Rules may apply even though they do not form part of
the governing law: see above, para.26-083.

[1434] See however para.26-195, above, as to the law determining what constitutes a misdelivery.

[1435] See, e.g. *Vincentelli & Co v John Rowlett & Co* (1911) 16 Com. Cas. 310 at 321–322.

[1436] cf. *The Tilly Russ* (C-71/83) [1985] Q.B. 931; *Reunion Européene v Spliethoff's Bevrachtingskantoor
BV* (C-51/97) [1998] E.C.R. I-6511; *Coreck Maritime GmbH v Handelsveem BV* (C-387/98) [2000]
E.C.R. I-9337; see also *Nisshin Shipping Co Ltd v Cleaves & Co Ltd* [2003] EWHC 2602 (Comm);
[2004] 1 Lloyd's Rep. 38. See Takahashi, [2001] L.M.C.L.Q. 107; Fawcett, Harris and Bridge,
International Sale of Goods in the Conflict of Laws, Ch.14. The converse situation may also arise in the
case of "through" carriage: i.e. the carrier being sued may not be the one with whom the original contract
was made. In *Anspach & Co Ltd v CNR* [1950] 3 D.L.R. 26, the question whether such a carrier could
be made liable on the original contract was referred to the law applicable to that contract. cf. CMR Ch.6;
COTIF Art.55.

[1437] Rome I Regulation Art.14(2); Rome Convention Art.12(2), *Moore v Harris* (1876) 1 App. Cas. 318;
The Torni [1932] P. 78; *The Njegos* [1936] P. 90; *Anspach & Co Ltd v CNR* [1950] 3 D.L.R. 26; *Trendtex
Trading Corp v Credit Suisse* [1980] Q.B. 629; affirmed on other grounds [1982] A.C. 679; *Campbell
Connelly & Co Ltd v Noble* [1963] 1 W.L.R. 255; Dicey, Morris and Collins, *The Conflict of Laws*, 15th
edn, paras 24R-050 to 24-063; Cheshire, North and Fawcett, *Private International Law*, pp.1288–
1290. cf. Takahashi, [2001] L.M.C.L.Q. 107, 115.

[1438] See above, paras 3-042 to 3-043.

[1439] Rome I Regulation Art.14(1); Rome Convention Art.12(1). cf. CMR Art.13; COTIF Arts 28, 54. cf.
Takahashi, [2001] L.M.C.L.Q. 107, 115.

[1440] As in the English common law (above, para.18-138).

[1441] See *The Torni* [1932] P. 27 at 42 (affirmed [1932] P. 78); *The St Joseph* [1933] P. 119; *Illyssia
Compania Naviera SA v Ahmed Abdul-Qawi Bamaodah (The Elli 2)* [1985] 1 Lloyd's Rep. 107.

12. PROCEDURE

Procedure governed by the lex fori

Replace footnote 1442 with:

26-203 ¹⁴⁴² See generally Dicey, Morris and Collins, *The Conflict of Laws*, 15th edn, Ch.7; Cheshire, North and Fawcett, *Private International Law*, 15th edn, Ch.6; Garnett, *Substance and Procedure in Private International Law* (2012).

Limitation of actions

Replace footnote 1148 with:

26-204 ¹¹⁴⁸ The Act was based on the recommendations of the *Law Commission: Law Com. No.114* (1982). For comment see Dicey, Morris and Collins, *The Conflict of Laws*, 15th edn, paras 7-058 to 7-060; Cheshire, North and Fawcett, *Private International Law*, pp.78–79; Carter, (1985) 101 L.Q.R. 68; Stone, [1985] L.M.C.L.Q. 497.

Burden of proof and presumptions

After "French Civil Code Art.1147" add:

26-205 (now Art. 1231.1)

13. FUTURE DEVELOPMENTS

The Proposed Common European Sales Law and choice of law rules

To the end of the paragraph, add:

26-207 On 31 October 2017, the Commission published an amended proposal (COM (2017) 637) which would repeal the Consumer Sales Directive 1999 and create a set of rules common to all consumer sales, both on-line and off-line and including face to face sales.

INDEX